INDIAN ECONOMY

Developmental Perspectives

through

Questions & Answers

About the Author

A V Balakrishnan, a former civil servant, holds a Master's Degree in Economics from Loyola College, Madras (presently Chennai). He was a member of the Indian Economic Association and has been a keen observer of developments in the Indian economy over the past years. He has published papers on various aspects of applied economics.

INDIAN ECONOMY

Developmental Perspectives

through

Questions & Answers

A V Balakrishnan

Title : Indian Economy through Questions & Answers

Language : English

Author's Name : A V Balakrishnan

Typeset & Published by :

Career Launcher Infrastructure (P) Ltd.

A-45, Mohan Cooperative Industrial Area, Near Mohan Estate Metro Station, New Delhi - 110044

Marketed by :

G.K. Publications (P) Ltd.

Plot No. 9A, Sector-27A, Mathura Road, Faridabad, Haryana-121003

ISBN : **978-93-90820-56-6**

Printer's Details: Printed in India, New Delhi.

For product information :

Visit ***www.gkpublications.com*** or email to ***gkp@gkpublications.com***

Preface

"Economics is the study of mankind in the ordinary business of life", said Alfred Marshall, the doyen among economists. The subject deals with every facet one's everyday life such as commodities, prices, markets, inflation, labour, employment, productivity, banking, taxation and trade among others.

From time immemorial, nations have been trying to achieve maximum social and economic progress to give their citizens a life of ease and comfort. But owing to diverse factors such as population, resource endowments, educational levels, health standards and social milieu and mores, countries are at different stages of development. Apart from these, political factors too profoundly impact the pace of progress. That the progress has been uneven within nations, and between nations, is well known and widely studied and documented. The widening inequalities and uneven progress, even as economic growth takes place, are a matter of concern tackling which should be the foremost priority for economists and policy planners.

This book studies various facets of Indian economy, on the basis of these factors, in the contemporary context and attempts to take a perspective view of what lies ahead in the future. It is set in Question– Answer format with spotlight on developmental aspects pertaining to Indian economy. Though the book is written to meet the needs of those appearing for Civil Services and other examinations, it will also be of interest to readers interested in trends in Indian economy.

The Introductory note on "**Evolution of Economic Thought**" gives a broad overview of the development of Economics from ancient times to modern days and the application of the theories in various socio-economic situations. The **Glossary** given at the end will help readers to understand technical terms used in Economics.

Further, the global economy is facing grave challenges compounded by an unprecedented global health crisis caused by the pandemic, Covid-19 which has not spared any country from its impact. That its adverse effects have been felt the most by the weaker and most vulnerable sections makes it even more devastating and distressing. It may take quite a while for economies to bounce back.

While writing this, I gratefully remember two inspirational teachers in the Economics faculty in Loyola College, Madras (now Chennai) during my graduate and PG studies– Professors A. Seshan and V. Ganapathy – the former, a votary of the Classical school, and the latter representing

Keynesian economics, though the dichotomy was more imaginary than real. Both were ardent advocates of their credo on the subject and had a large following of admirers among the students. The inter-collegiate lectures conducted by Prof. Ganapathy in 1950s-60s on Keynesian economics, which was then in vogue, Business cycles and Fiscal policy, used to draw large crowds from city colleges and the lecture halls would overflow with avid listeners.

This book is a sequel to the earlier publication, "Economic Development in India". Statistical data presented here have been sourced from various government and non-government sources and international publications. These include erstwhile Planning Commission's *Five-Year Plan documents*, Reserve Bank of India's *Handbook of Statistics on Indian Economy*, Ministry of Finance's *Economic Surveys*, *Census of India reports* and statistical data put out by NITI Aayog and concerned ministries of the Government of India. International sources from which data has been drawn include UNDP's *Human Development Reports*, UN Population Division and The World Bank. The data provided in these publications is gratefully acknowledged. For providing access to many of these sources, thanks are due to authorities at libraries of Mumbai University, the Institute for Social and Economic Change (ISEC) at Bengaluru and the National Library in Singapore.

The writing of this book has been a labour of love. A major part of the writing, typesetting and editing was done under severe constraints due to Covid-19 pandemic. This could not have been accomplished but for the diligent guidance, wholehearted support and cooperation extended, in particular, by Prakash Kannath of CL Educate, the publishers of the book, and the team under him. I am profoundly grateful to all of them for their painstaking efforts and also the Management of CL Educate who made this publication possible. Thanks are also due to the Press which has undertaken the printing with alacrity.

As always, Ravikumar Mullapudi was there to help with formatting the initial draft of the work and the Tables on computer. I am much indebted to him for sparing valuable time that rightfully belonged to him.

The trigger for setting me on the path of writing the earlier book came from Uday Balakrishnan who has been on the faculty of the Centre for Contemporary Studies, Indian Institute of Science, Bengaluru. His intellectual forays into domains as diverse as history, ancient cartography, labour economics and geopolitical issues have been a source of inspiration to me. And for this I am in debt to him.

Finally, thanks are due to my family, in particular Sharada, Abhinav, Zoya and Ira, for their warmth and affection and providing unstinted support and encouragement which kept me going all through the writing of this book.

The views expressed in the book are entirely the author's and are not to be attributed to the Publishers or those who have rendered help.

While every effort has been made to check the correctness of statistical and other information contained in the book, I may be excused for any inadvertent errors which may have crept in. Any corrections pointed out by readers will be welcome.

Bengaluru

A.V. Balakrishnan

April 2021

Dedicated to Legion of Youth
In whose hands
The Future of India lies

Atmanirbhar Bharat and **Production Linked Incentive (PLI)** schemes are welcome initiatives to make India more self-reliant and put India on a higher growth trajectory. But it should not make India look inward and retract from global economy. Instead, they should serve as launching pads to integrate India even more to the global economy and make India an integral part of global supply chains.

CONTENTS

KEY HIGHLIGHTS OF UNION BUDGET 2021-22

The key highlights of the Union Budget 2021-22 presented in a digital format are as follows:

Six pillars of the Union Budget 2021-22:

1. Health and Wellbeing
2. Physical & Financial Capital, and Infrastructure
3. Inclusive Development for Aspirational India
4. Reinvigorating Human Capital
5. Innovation and R&D
6. Minimum Government and Maximum Governance

1. Health and Wellbeing

- Rs. 2,23,846 crore outlay for *Health and Wellbeing* in BE 2021-22 as against Rs. 94,452 crore in BE 2020-21 – an increase of 137%
- Focus on strengthening three areas: Preventive, Curative, and Wellbeing
- Rs. 35,000 crore for COVID-19 vaccine in BE 2021-22
- The Made-in-India Pneumococcal Vaccine to be rolled out across the country, from present 5 states – to avert 50,000 child deaths annually
- Rs. 64,180 crore outlay over 6 years for PM AatmaNirbhar Swasth Bharat Yojana – a new centrally sponsored scheme to be launched, in addition to NHM
- Main interventions under PM AatmaNirbhar Swasth Bharat Yojana:
  - o *National Institution for One Health*
  - o *17,788 rural and 11,024 urban Health and Wellness Centers*
  - o *4 regional National Institutes for Virology*

- *15 Health Emergency Operation Centers and 2 mobile hospitals*
- *Integrated public health labs in all districts and 3382 block public health units in 11 states*
- *Critical care hospital blocks in 602 districts and 12 central institutions*
- *Strengthening of the National Centre for Disease Control (NCDC), its 5 regional branches and 20 metropolitan health surveillance units*
- *Expansion of the Integrated Health Information Portal to all States/UTs to connect all public health labs*
- *17 new Public Health Units and strengthening of 33 existing Public Health Units*
- *Regional Research Platform for WHO South-East Asia Region*
- *9 Bio-Safety Level III laboratories*

- Mission Poshan 2.0 to be launched:
  - *To strengthen nutritional content, delivery, outreach, and outcome*
  - *Merging the Supplementary Nutrition Programme and the Poshan Abhiyan*
  - *Intensified strategy to be adopted to improve nutritional outcomes across 112 Aspirational Districts*
- Rs. 2,87,000 crore over 5 years for Jal Jeevan Mission (Urban) - to be launched with an aim to provide:
  - *2.86 crore household tap connections*
  - *Universal water supply in all 4,378 Urban Local Bodies*
  - *Liquid waste management in 500 AMRUT cities*
- Rs. 1,41,678 crore over 5 years for Urban Swachh Bharat Mission 2.0
- Main interventions under Swachh Bharat Mission (Urban) 2.0:
  - *Complete faecal sludge management and waste water treatment*
  - *Source segregation of garbage*
  - *Reduction in single-use plastic*
  - *Reduction in air pollution by effectively managing waste from construction-and-demolition activities*
  - *Bio-remediation of all legacy dump sites*
- Rs. 2,217 crore to tackle air pollution, for 42 urban centers with a million-plus population

- Voluntary vehicle scrapping policy to phase out old and unfit vehicles
- Fitness tests in automated fitness centres:
  - o *After 20 years in case of personal vehicles*
  - o *After 15 years in case of commercial vehicles*

2. Physical and Financial Capital and Infrastructure

- Rs. 1.97 lakh crore in next 5 years for Production Linked Incentive (PLI) schemes in 13 Sectors
- To create and nurture manufacturing global champions for an AatmaNirbhar Bharat
- To help manufacturing companies become an integral part of global supply chains, possess core competence and cutting-edge technology
- To bring scale and size in key sectors
- To provide jobs to the youth
- Mega Investment Textiles Parks (MITRA) scheme
  - o *7 Textile Parks to be established over 3 years*
- Textile industry to become globally competitive, attract large investments and boost employment generation & exports
- National Infrastructure Pipeline (NIP) expanded to 7,400 projects:
  - o Around 217 projects worth Rs. 1.10 lakh crore completed
- Measures in three thrust areas to increase funding for NIP:
  - o *Creation of institutional structures*
  - o *Big thrust on monetizing assets*
  - o *Enhancing the share of capital expenditure*
- **Creation of institutional structures: Infrastructure Financing**
  - o *Rs. 20,000 crore to set up and capitalise a Development Financial Institution(DFI) – to act as a provider, enabler and catalyst for infrastructure financing*
  - o *Rs. 5 lakh crore lending portfolio to be created under the proposed DFI in 3 years*
  - o *Debt Financing by Foreign Portfolio Investors to be enabled by amending InvITs' and REITs' legislations*
- Big thrust on monetizing assets with a National Monetization Pipeline to be launched
- Important asset monetization measures:
- *5 operational toll roads worth Rs. 5,000 crore being transferred to the NHAIInvIT*

- *Transmission assets worth Rs. 7,000 crore to be transferred to the PGCILInvIT*
- *Dedicated Freight Corridor assets to be monetized by Railways, for operations and maintenance, after commissioning*
- *Next lot of Airports to be monetized for operations and management concession*
- *Other core infrastructure assets to be rolled out under the Asset Monetization Programme:*
    - o *Oil and Gas Pipelines of GAIL, IOCL and HPCL*
    - o *AAI Airports in Tier II and III cities*
    - o *Other Railway Infrastructure Assets*
    - o *Warehousing Assets of CPSEs such as Central Warehousing Corporation and NAFED*
    - o *Sports Stadiums*
- Sharp Increase in Capital Budget
    - o *Rs. 5.54 lakh crore capital expenditure in BE 2021-22 – sharp increase of 34.5% over Rs. 4.12 lakh crore allocated in BE 2020-21 :*
- Over Rs. 2 lakh crore to States and Autonomous Bodies for their Capital Expenditure.
- Over Rs. 44,000 crore for the Department of Economic Affairs to provide for projects/ programmes/departments exhibiting good progress on Capital Expenditure
- Rs. 1,18,101 lakh crore, highest ever outlay, for Ministry of Road Transport and Highways – of which Rs. 1,08,230 crore is for capital
- Under the Rs. 5.35 lakh crore Bharatmala Pariyojana, more than 13,000 km length of roads worth Rs. 3.3 lakh crore awarded for construction:
    - o *3,800 km have already been constructed*
    - o *Another 8,500 km to be awarded for construction by March 2022*
    - o *Additional 11,000 km of national highway corridors to be completed by March 2022*
- Economic corridors being planned
    - o *Rs. 1.03 lakh crore outlay for 3,500 km of NHs in Tamil Nadu*
    - o *Rs. 65,000 crore investment for 1,100 km of NHs in Kerala*
    - o *Rs. 25,000 crore for 675 km of NHs in West Bengal*
    - o *Over Rs. 34,000 crore to be allocated for 1300 km of NHs to be undertaken in next 3 years in Assam, in addition to Rs. 19,000 crore works of NHs currently in progress in the State*
- Flagship Corridors/Expressways

- *Delhi-Mumbai Expressway – Remaining 260 km to be awarded before 31.3.2021*
- *Bengaluru-Chennai Expressway – 278 km to be initiated in the current FY; construction to begin in 2021-22*
- *Kanpur-Lucknow Expressway – 63 km expressway providing an alternate route to NH 27 to be initiated in 2021-22*
- *Delhi-Dehradun economic corridor – 210 km to be initiated in the current FY; construction to begin in 2021-22*
- *Raipur-Vishakhapatnam – 464 km passing through Chhattisgarh, Odisha and North Andhra Pradesh, to be awarded in the current year; construction to start in 2021-22*
- *Chennai-Salem corridor – 277 km expressway to be awarded and construction to start in 2021-22*
- *Amritsar-Jamnagar – Construction to commence in 2021-22*
- *Delhi-Katra – Construction will commence in 2021-22*

- Advanced Traffic management system in all new 4 and 6-lane highways
  - *Speed radars*
  - *Variable message signboards*
  - *GPS enabled recovery vans will be installed*
- Rs. 1,10,055 crore for Railways of which Rs. 1,07,100 crore is for capital expenditure
- National Rail Plan for India (2030): to create a 'future ready' Railway system by 2030
- 100% electrification of Broad-Gauge routes to be completed by December, 2023
- Broad Gauge Route Kilometers (RKM) electrification to reach 46,000 RKM, i.e. 72% by end of 2021
- Western Dedicated Freight Corridor (DFC) and Eastern DFC to be commissioned by June 2022, to bring down the logistic costs – enabling Make in India strategy
- Additional initiatives proposed:
  - *The Sonnagar-Gomoh Section (263.7 km) of Eastern DFC to be taken up in PPP mode in 2021-22*

  Future dedicated freight corridor projects

- *East Coast corridor from Kharagpur to Vijayawada*
- *East-West Corridor from Bhusaval to Kharagpur to Dankuni*
- *North-South corridor from Itarsi to Vijayawada*

- Measures for passenger convenience and safety:
  - o *Aesthetically designed Vista Dome LHB coach on tourist routes for better travel*
  - o *High density network and highly utilized network routes to have an indigenously developed automatic train protection system, eliminating train collision due to human error*
- Raising the share of public transport in urban areas by expansion of metro rail network and augmentation of city bus service
- Rs. 18,000 crore for a new scheme, to augment public bus transport:
  - o *Innovative PPP models to run more than 20,000 buses*
  - o *To boost automobile sector, provide fillip to economic growth, create employment opportunities for our youth*
- A total of 702 km of conventional metro is operational and another 1,016 km of metro and RRTS is under construction in 27 cities
- 'MetroLite' and 'MetroNeo' technologies to provide metro rail systems at much lesser cost with similar experience in Tier-2 cities and peripheral areas of Tier-1 cities.
- Central counterpart funding to:

  a. Kochi Metro Railway Phase-II of 11.5 km at a cost of Rs. 1957.05 crore

  b. Chennai Metro Railway Phase –II of 118.9 km at a cost of Rs. 63,246 crore

  c. Bengaluru Metro Railway Project Phase 2A and 2B of 58.19 km at a cost of Rs. 14,788 crore

  d. Nagpur Metro Rail Project Phase-II and Nashik Metro at a cost of Rs. 5,976 crore and Rs. 2,092 crore respectively.
- 139 Giga Watts of installed capacity and 1.41 lakh circuit km of transmission lines added, and additional 2.8 crore households connected in past 6 years
- Consumers to have alternatives to choose the Distribution Company for enhancing competitiveness
- Rs. 3,05,984 crore over 5 years for a revamped, reforms-based and result-linked new power distribution sector scheme
- A comprehensive National Hydrogen Energy Mission 2021-22 to be launched
- Rs. 2,000 crore worth 7 projects to be offered in PPP-mode in FY21-22 for operation of major ports

- Indian shipping companies to get Rs. 1624 crore worth subsidy support over 5 years in global tenders of Ministries and CPSEs
- To double the recycling capacity of around 4.5 Million Light Displacement Tonne (LDT) by 2024; to generate an additional 1.5 lakh jobs
- Extension of Ujjwala Scheme to cover 1 crore more beneficiaries
- To add 100 more districts to the City Gas Distribution network in next 3 years
- A new gas pipeline project in J&K
- An independent Gas Transport System Operator to be set up for facilitation and coordination of booking of common carrier capacity in all-natural gas pipelines on a non-discriminatory open access basis
- A single Securities Markets Code to be evolved
- Support for development of a world class Fin-Tech hub at the GIFT-IFSC
- A new permanent institutional framework to help in development of Bond market by purchasing investment grade debt securities both in stressed and normal times
- Setting up a system of Regulated Gold Exchanges: SEBI to be notified as a regulator and Warehousing Development and Regulatory Authority to be strengthened
- To develop an investor charter as a right of all financial investors
- Capital infusion of Rs. 1,000 crore to Solar Energy Corporation of India and Rs. 1,500 crore to Indian Renewable Energy Development Agency
- To increase the permissible FDI limit from 49% to 74% and allow foreign ownership and control with safeguards
- Asset Reconstruction Company Limited and Asset Management Company to be set up
- Rs. 20,000 crore in 2021-22 to further consolidate the financial capacity of PSBs
- Amendments to the DICGC Act, 1961, to help depositors get an easy and time-bound access to their deposits to the extent of the deposit insurance cover
- Minimum loan size eligible for debt recovery under the Securitisation and Reconstruction of Financial Assets and Enforcement of Security Interest (SARFAESI) Act, 2002 proposed to be reduced from Rs. 50 lakh to Rs. 20 lakh for NBFCs with minimum asset size of Rs. 100 crore
- To decriminalize the Limited Liability Partnership (LLP) Act, 2008

- Easing Compliance requirement of Small companies by revising their definition under Companies Act, 2013 by increasing their thresholds for Paid up capital from "not exceeding Rs. 50 Lakh" to "not exceeding Rs. 2 Crore" and turnover from "not exceeding Rs. 2 Crore" to "not exceeding Rs. 20 Cr".
- Promoting start-ups and innovators by incentivizing the incorporation of One Person Companies (OPCs):
  - o *Allowing their growth without any restrictions on paid up capital and turnover*
  - o *Allowing their conversion into any other type of company at any time,*
  - o *Reducing the residency limit for an Indian citizen to set up an OPC from 182 days to 120 days and*
  - o *Allowing Non Resident Indians (NRIs) to incorporate OPCs in India.*
- To ensure faster resolution of cases by:
  - o *Strengthening NCLT framework*
  - o *Implementation of e-Courts system*
  - o *Introduction of alternate methods of debt resolution and special framework for MSMEs*
- *Launch of data analytics, artificial intelligence, machine learning driven MCA21 Version 3.0 in 2021-22*
- Rs. 1,75,000 crore estimated receipts from disinvestment in BE 2020-21
- Strategic disinvestment of BPCL, Air India, Shipping Corporation of India, Container Corporation of India, IDBI Bank, BEML, Pawan Hans, Neelachal Ispat Nigam limited etc. to be completed in 2021-22.
- Other than IDBI Bank, two Public Sector Banks and one General Insurance company to be privatized
- IPO of LIC in 2021-22
- New policy for Strategic Disinvestment approved; CPSEs except in four strategic areas to be privatized
- NITI Aayog to work out on the next list of CPSEs to be taken up for strategic disinvestment
- Incentivizing States for disinvestment of their Public Sector Companies, using central funds
- Special Purpose Vehicle in the form of a company to monetize idle land

- Introducing a revised mechanism for ensuring timely closure of sick or loss making CPSEs
- Treasury Single Account (TSA) System for Autonomous Bodies to be extended for universal application
- Separate Administrative Structure to streamline the 'Ease of Doing Business' for Cooperatives

3. Inclusive Development for Aspirational India

- Ensured MSP at minimum 1.5 times the cost of production across all commodities.
- SWAMITVA Scheme to be extended to all States/UTs, 1.80 lakh property-owners in 1,241 villages have already been provided cards
- Agricultural credit target enhanced to Rs. 16.5 lakh crore in FY22 - animal husbandry, dairy, and fisheries to be the focus areas
- Rural Infrastructure Development Fund to be enhanced to Rs. 40,000 crore from Rs. 30,000 crore
- To double the Micro Irrigation Fund to Rs. 10,000 crore
- 'Operation Green Scheme' to be extended to 22 perishable products, to boost value addition in agriculture and allied products
- Around 1.68 crore farmers registered and Rs. 1.14 lakh crore of trade value carried out through e-NAMs; 1,000 more mandis to be integrated with e-NAM to bring transparency and competitiveness.
- APMCs to get access to the Agriculture Infrastructure Funds for augmenting infrastructure facilities
- Investments to develop modern fishing harbours and fish landing centres – both marine and inland
- 5 major fishing harbours – Kochi, Chennai, Visakhapatnam, Paradip, and Petuaghat to be developed as hubs of economic activity
- Multipurpose Seaweed Park in Tamil Nadu to promote seaweed cultivation
- One Nation One Ration Card scheme for beneficiaries to claim rations anywhere in the country - migrant workers to benefit the most
  - Scheme implementation so far covered 86% of beneficiaries across 32 States and UTs
  - Remaining 4 states to be integrated in next few months

- Portal to collect information on unorganized labour force, migrant workers especially, to help formulate schemes for them
- Implementation of 4 labour codes underway
  - *Social security benefits for gig and platform workers too*
  - *minimum wages and coverage under the Employees State Insurance Corporation applicable for all categories of workers*
  - *Women workers allowed in all categories, including night-shifts with adequate protection*
  - *Compliance burden on employers reduced with single registration and licensing, and online returns*
- Under *Stand Up India Scheme* for SCs, STs and women,
  - *Margin money requirement reduced to 15%*
  - *To also include loans for allied agricultural activities*
- **Rs. 15,700 crore** budget allocation to MSME Sector, more than double of this year's BE

4. Reinvigorating Human Capital

- 15,000 schools to be strengthened by implementing all NEP components. Shall act as exemplar schools in their regions for mentoring others
- 100 new Sainik Schools to be set up in partnership with NGOs/private schools/states
- Legislation to be introduced to setup Higher Education Commission of India as an umbrella body with 4 separate vehicles for standard-setting, accreditation, regulation, and funding
- Creation of formal umbrella structure to cover all Govt. colleges, universities, research institutions in a city for greater synergy.
  - *Glue grant to implement the same across 9 cities*
- Central University to come up in Leh for accessibility of higher education in Ladakh
- 750 Eklavya model residential schools in tribal areas:
  - *Unit cost of each school to be increased to Rs. 38 crore*
  - *For hilly and difficult areas, to Rs. 48 crore*
  - *Focus on creation of robust infrastructure facilities for tribal students*
- Revamped Post Matric Scholarship Scheme for welfare of SCs

- *Rs. 35,219 crore enhanced Central Assistance for 6 years till 2025-2026*
- *4 crore SC students to benefit*

- Proposed amendment to Apprenticeship Act to enhance opportunities for youth
- Rs. 3000 crore for realignment of existing National Apprenticeship Training Scheme (NATS) towards post-education apprenticeship, training of graduates and diploma holders in Engineering
- Initiatives for partnership with other countries in skilling to be taken forward, similar to partnership:
    - *With UAE to benchmark skill qualifications, assessment, certification, and deployment of certified workforce*
    - *With Japan for a collaborative Training Inter Training Programme (TITP) to transfer of skills, technique and knowledge*

5. Innovation and R&D

- Modalities of National Research Foundation announced in July 2019 –
    - *Rs. 50,000 crore outlay over 5 years*
    - *To strengthen overall research ecosystem with focus on national-priority thrust areas*
- Rs. 1,500 crore for proposed scheme to promote digital modes of payment
- National Language Translation Mission (NTLM) to make governance-and-policy related knowledge available in major Indian languages
- PSLV-CS51 to be launched by New Space India Limited (NSIL) carrying Brazil's Amazonia Satellite and some Indian satellites
- As part of the Gaganyaan mission activities:
    - *4 Indian astronauts being trained on Generic Space Flight aspects, in Russia*
    - *First unmanned launch is slated for December 2021*
- Rs. 4,000 crore over five years for Deep Ocean Mission survey exploration and conservation of deep sea biodiversity

6. Minimum Government, Maximum Governance

- Measures being undertaken to bring reforms in Tribunals to ensure speedy justice
- National Commission for Allied Healthcare Professionals already introduced to ensure transparent and efficient regulation of the 56 allied healthcare professions
- The National Nursing and Midwifery Commission Bill introduced for the same in nursing profession

- Proposed Conciliation Mechanism with mandate for quick resolution of contractual disputes with CPSEs
- Rs. 3,768 crore allocated for first digital census in the history of India
- Rs. 300 crore grant to the Government of Goa for the diamond jubilee celebrations of the state's liberation from Portuguese
- Rs. 1,000 crore for the welfare of Tea workers especially women and their children in Assam and West Bengal through a special scheme
- RE (Revised Estimates) for Expenditure is Rs. 34.50 lakh crore as against original BE (Budgeted Estimate) expenditure of Rs. 30.42 lakh crore
    - o *Quality of expenditure has been maintained as Capital Expenditure estimated as per RE is Rs. 4.39 lakh crore in 2020-2021 as against Rs. 4.12 lakh crore in BE 2020-21*
- Estimates of Rs. 34.83 lakh crore BE for expenditure in 2021-2022 including Rs. 5.5 lakh crore as capital expenditure, an increase of 34.5% to give required push to economy
- The fiscal deficit in BE 2021-2022 is estimated to be 6.8% of GDP. The fiscal deficit in RE 2020-21 is pegged at 9.5% of GDP - funded through Government borrowings, multilateral borrowings, Small Saving Funds and short term borrowings
    - o *Gross borrowing from the market for the next year to be around 12 lakh crore.*
    - o *Plan to continue on the path of fiscal consolidation, achieving a fiscal deficit level below 4.5% of GDP by 2025-2026 with a fairly steady decline over the period*
    - o *It will be achieved by increasing the buoyancy of tax revenue through improved compliance, and secondly, by increased receipts from monetisation of assets, including Public Sector Enterprises and land*
    - o *Amendment to FRBM Act proposed to achieve targeted Fiscal Deficit levels*
- The Contingency Fund of India is to be augmented from Rs. 500 crore to Rs. 30,000 crore through Finance Bill
- Net borrowing for the states allowed at 4% of GSDP for the year 2021-2022 as per recommendation of 15th FC
    - o *Part of this earmarked for incremental capital expenditure*
    - o *Additional borrowing ceiling of 0.5% of GSDP will be provided subject to conditions*
- States expected to reach a fiscal deficit of 3% of GSDP by 2023-24, as recommended by the 15th Finance Commission

- The final report of the Fifteenth Finance Commission covering 2021-26 was submitted to the President, retaining vertical shares of states at 41%
- Funds to UTs of Jammu and Kashmir and Ladakh would be provided by Centre
- On the Commission's recommendation, Rs. 1,18,452 crore have been provided as Revenue Deficit Grant to 17 states in 2021-22, as against Rs. 74,340 crore to 14 states in 2020-21
- Corporate tax rate slashed to make it among the lowest in the world
- Burden of taxation on small taxpayers eased by increasing rebates
- Return filers almost doubled to 6.48 crore in 2020 from 3.31 crore in 2014
- Faceless Assessment and Faceless Appeal introduced
- Exemption from filing tax returns for senior citizens over 75 years of age and having only pension and interest income; tax to be deducted by paying bank
- Time limit for re-opening cases reduced to 3 years from 6 years
- Serious tax evasion cases, with evidence of concealment of income of Rs. 50 lakh or more in a year, to be re-opened only up to 10 years, with approval of the Principal Chief Commissioner
- Dispute Resolution Committee to be set up for taxpayers with taxable income up to Rs. 50 lakh and disputed income up to Rs. 10 lakh
- National Faceless Income Tax Appellate Tribunal Centre to be established
- Over 1 lakh taxpayers opted to settle tax disputes of over Rs. 85,000 crore through Vivad Se Vishwas Scheme until 30th January 2021
- Rules to be notified for removing hardships faced by NRIs regarding their foreign retirement accounts
- Limit of turnover for tax audit increased to Rs. 10 crore from Rs. 5 crore for entities carrying out 95% transactions digitally
- Dividend payment to REIT/ InvIT exempt from TDS
- Advance tax liability on dividend income only after declaration/ payment of dividend
- Deduction of tax on dividend income at lower treaty rate for Foreign Portfolio Investors
- Infrastructure Debt Funds made eligible to raise funds by issuing Zero Coupon Bonds
- Relaxation of some conditions relating to prohibition on private funding, restriction on commercial activities, and direct investment

- Additional deduction of interest, up to Rs. 1.5 lakh, for loan taken to buy an affordable house extended for loans taken till March 2022
- Tax holiday for Affordable Housing projects extended till March 2022
- Tax exemption allowed for notified Affordable Rental Housing Projects
- Tax holiday for capital gains from incomes of aircraft leasing companies
- Tax exemptions for aircraft lease rentals paid to foreign lessors
- Tax incentive for relocating foreign funds in the IFSC
- Tax exemption to investment division of foreign banks located in IFSC
- Details of capital gains from listed securities, dividend income, interest from banks, etc. to be pre-filled in returns
- Exemption limit of annual receipt revised from ₹1 crore to ₹ 5 crore for small charitable trusts running schools and hospitals
- Late deposit of employee's contribution by the employer not to be allowed as deduction to the employer
- Eligibility for tax holiday claim for start-ups extended by one more year
- Capital gains exemption for investment in start-ups extended till 31st March, 2022
- Measures taken on GST till date:
- *Nil return through SMS*
- *Quarterly return and monthly payment for small taxpayers*
- *Electronic invoice system*
- *Validated input tax statement*
- *Pre-filled editable GST return*
- *Staggering of returns filing*
- *Enhancement of capacity of GSTN system*
- *Use of deep analytics and AI to identify tax evaders*
- Custom Duty Rationalization had the following objectives
- *Promoting domestic manufacturing and helping India get onto global value chain and export better*
- *80 outdated exemptions already eliminated*
- *Revised, distortion-free customs duty structure to be put in place from 1st October 2021 by reviewing more than 400 old exemptions*

- *New customs duty exemptions to have validity up to the 31st March following two years from its issue date*
- Renewable Energy:
  - o *Phased manufacturing plan for solar cells and solar panels to be notified*
  - o *Duty on solar invertors raised from 5% to 20%, and on solar lanterns from 5% to 15% to encourage domestic production*
- **MSME Products:**
  - o Duty on steel screws and plastic builder wares increased to 15%.
  - o Prawn feed to attract customs duty of 15% from earlier rate of 5%
  - o Exemption on import of duty-free items rationalized to incentivize exporters of garments, leather, and handicraft items
  - o Exemption on imports of certain kind of leathers withdrawn
  - o Customs duty on finished synthetic gem stones raised to encourage domestic processing
- **Agriculture Products:**
  - o Customs duty on cotton increased from nil to 10% and on raw silk and silk yarn from 10% to 15%.
  - o Withdrawal of end-use based concession on denatured ethyl alcohol
  - o Agriculture Infrastructure and Development Cess (AIDC) on a small number of items

Achievements and Milestones during the COVID-19 pandemic

- Pradhan Mantri Garib Kalyan Yojana (PMGKY):
  - o Valued at Rs. 2.76 lakh crore
  - o Free food grain to 80 crore people
  - o Free cooking gas for 8 crore families
  - o Direct cash to over 40 crore farmers, women, elderly, the poor and the needy
- AatmaNirbhar Bharat package (ANB 1.0):
  - o Estimated at Rs. 23 lakh crore – more than 10% of GDP
- PMGKY, three ANB packages (ANB 1.0, 2.0, and 3.0), and announcements made later were like 5 mini-budgets in themselves
- Rs. 27.1 lakh crore worth of financial impact of all three ANB packages including RBI's measures – amounting to more than 13% of GDP

- Structural reforms:
  - o One Nation One Ration Card
  - o Agriculture and Labour Reforms
  - o Redefinition of MSMEs
  - o Commercialisation of the Mineral Sector
  - o Privatisation of Public Sector Undertakings
  - o Production Linked Incentive Schemes
- Status of India's fight against COVID-19:
  - o 2 Made-in-India vaccines – medically safeguarding citizens of India and those of 100-plus countries against COVID-19
  - o Lowest death rate per million and the lowest active cases
- AatmaNirbhar Bharat – an expression of 130 crore Indians who have full confidence in their capabilities and skills
  - o Nation First
  - o Doubling Farmer's Income
  - o Strong Infrastructure
  - o Healthy India
  - o Good Governance
  - o Opportunities for Youth
  - o Education for All
  - o Women Empowerment
  - o Inclusive Development

  Source: PIB, Ministry of Finance

ECONOMIC SURVEY 2020-21

Union Minister for Finance and Corporate Affairs, Smt. Nirmala Sitharaman presented the Economic Survey 2020-21 in the Parliament on January 29, 2021.

KEY HIGHLIGHTS

Strategy during Covid Crisis was Saving Lives and Livelihoods

- India focused on saving lives and livelihoods by its willingness to take short-term pain for long-term gain, at the onset of the COVID-19 pandemic.
- Response stemmed from the humane principle thathuman lives lost cannot be brought back.
- It is expected that GDP growth will recover from the temporary shock caused by the pandemic.
- An early, intense lockdown provided a win-win strategy to save lives, and preserve livelihoods via economic recovery in the medium to long-term.
- Initial measures of lockdown, social distancing, travel advisories, practicing hand wash, wearing masks reduced the spread of the disease.
- Country also acquired self-reliance in essential medicines, hand sanitizers, protective equipment including masks, PPE Kits, ventilators, COVID-19 testing and treatment facilities.
- India's strategy flattened the curve, pushed the peak to September, 2020.
- After the September peak, India has been unique in experiencing declining daily cases despite increasing mobility.

- World's largest COVID-19 vaccination drive commenced on 16th January, 2021 using two indigenously manufactured vaccines which will effectively tackle and end the pandemic.
- V-shaped recovery, as seen in 7.5% decline in GDP in Q2 and recovery across all key economic indicators vis-à-vis the 23.9% GDP contraction in Q1.

Structural Reforms during the Covid Crisis

- India was the only country to announce structural reforms to expand supply in the medium-long term and avoid long-term damage to productive capacities.
- Calibrated demand side policies to ensure that the accelerator is slowly pushed down only when the brakes on economic activities are being removed.
- A public investment programme centered around the National Infrastructure Pipeline to accelerate the demand push and further the recovery.

State of the Economy in 2020-21: A Macro View

- COVID-19 pandemic ensued global economic downturn, the most severe one since the Global Financial Crisis of 2007-08.
- The lockdowns and social distancing norms brought the already slowing global economy virtually to a standstill.
- Global economic output estimated to fall by 3.5% in 2020 (according to IMF January 2021 estimates).
- Governments and Central Banks across the globe deployed various policy tools to support their economies such as lowering policy rates, quantitative easing measures, etc.
- India adopted a four-pillar strategy of containment, fiscal, financial, and long-term structural reforms:
  - ➢ *Calibrated fiscal and monetary support was provided, cushioning the vulnerable sections during the lockdown and boosting consumption and investment while unlocking.*
  - ➢ *A favourable monetary policy ensured abundant liquidity and immediate relief to debtors while unclogging monetary policy transmission.*
- As per the advance estimates by NSO, India's GDP is estimated to decline by 7.7% in FY21, followed by a robust sequential growth of 23.9% in the second half of FY21 over the first half of FY21.

- India's real GDP to record a 11.0% growth in FY2021-22 and nominal GDP to grow by 15.4% – the highest since independence:
  - Rebound to be led by low base and continued normalization in economic activities as the rollout of COVID-19 vaccines gathers traction.
- Government consumption and net exports cushioned the growth from diving further down, whereas investment and private consumption pulled it down.
- The recovery in second half of FY2020-21 is expected to be powered by government consumption, estimated to grow at 17% year-on-year.
- Exports expected to decline by 5.8% and imports by 11.3% in the second half of FY21.
- India expected to have a Current Account Surplus of 2% of GDP in FY21, a historic high after 17 years.
- On supply side, Gross Value Added (GVA) growth pegged at – 7.2% in FY21 as against 3.9% in FY20:
  - *Agriculture set to cushion the shock of the COVID-19 pandemic on the Indian economy in FY21 with a growth of 3.4%.*
  - *Industry and services estimated to contract by 9.6% and 8.8% respectively during FY21.*
- Agriculture remained the silver lining while contact-based services, manufacturing and construction were hit hardest, and are recovering steadily.
- India remained a preferred investment destination in FY 2020-21 with FDI pouring in amidst global asset shifts towards equities and prospects of quicker recovery in emerging economies:
  - *Net FPI inflows recorded an all-time monthly high of US$ 9.8 billion in November 2020, as investors' risk appetite returned.*
  - *India was the only country among emerging markets to receive equity FII inflows in 2020.*
- Buoyant SENSEX and NIFTY resulted in India's market-cap to GDP ratio crossing 100% for the first time since October 2010.
- Softening of Consumer Price Index (CPI) inflation recently reflects easing of supply side constraints that affected food inflation.

- Reignited inter- and intra-state movement and record-high monthly GST collections have marked the unlocking of industrial and commercial activity.
- The external sector provided an effective cushion to growth with India recording a Current Account Surplus of 3.1% of GDP in the first half of FY21.
    - ➢ *Strong services exports and weak demand leading to a sharper contraction in imports (merchandise imports contracted by 39.7%) than exports (merchandise exports contracted by 21.2%).*
    - ➢ Forex reserves increased to a level so as to cover 18 months' worth of imports in December 2020.
    - ➢ *External debt as a ratio to GDP increased to 21.6% at end-September 2020 from 20.6% at end-March 2020.*
    - ➢ *Ratio of forex reserves to total and short-term debt improved because of the sizable accretion in reserves.*
- V-shaped recovery is underway, as demonstrated by a sustained resurgence in high frequency indicators such as power demand, e-way bills, GST collection, steel consumption, etc.
- India became the fastest country to roll-out 10 lakh vaccines in 6 days and also emerged as a leading supplier of the vaccine to neighbouring countries and Brazil.
- Economy's homecoming to normalcy brought closer by the initiation of a mega vaccination drive
    - ➢ Hopes of a robust recovery in services sector, consumption, and investment have been rekindled.

Growth and Debt Sustainability in the Indian Context

- Growth leads to debt sustainability in the Indian context but not necessarily vice-versa.
- Debt sustainability depends on the 'Interest Rate Growth Rate Differential' (IRGD), i.e., the difference between the interest rate and the growth rate.
- Growth causes debt to become sustainable in countries with higher growth rates; such clarity about the causal direction is not witnessed in countries with lower growth rates.
- Fiscal multipliers are disproportionately higher during economic crises than during economic booms.

- Active fiscal policy can ensure that the full benefit of reforms is reaped by limiting potential damage to productive capacity.
- Fiscal policy that provides an impetus to growth will lead to lower debt-to-GDP ratio.
- Given India's growth potential, debt sustainability is unlikely to be a problem even in the worst scenarios.

India's Sovereign Credit Rating and its Economic Fundamentals

- The fifth largest economy in the world has never been rated as the lowest rung of the investment grade (BBB-/Baa3) in sovereign credit ratings.
  - Reflecting the economic size and thereby the ability to repay debt, the fifth largest economy has been predominantly rated AAA.
- India's sovereign credit ratings do not reflect its fundamentals:
  - *India's willingness to pay is unquestionably demonstrated through its zero sovereign default history.*
  - *India's ability to pay can be gauged by low foreign currency denominated debt and forex reserves.*

Inequality and Growth: Conflict or Convergence?

- The relationship between inequality and socio-economic outcomes vis-à-vis economic growth and socio-economic outcomes, is different in India from that in advanced economies.
- Both inequality and per-capita income (growth) have similar relationships with socio-economic indicators in India, unlike in advanced economies.
- Economic growth has a greater impact on poverty alleviation than inequality.
- India must continue to focus on economic growth to lift the poor out of poverty.
- Expanding the overall pie - redistribution in a developing economy is feasible only if the size of the economic pie grows.

Healthcare takes Centre Stage

- COVID-19 pandemic emphasized the importance of healthcare sector and its inter-linkages with other sectors showcased how a health crisis transformed into an economic and social crisis.
- India's health infrastructure must be agile so as to respond to pandemics.

- National Health Mission (NHM) played a critical role in mitigating inequity as the access of the poorest to pre-natal/post-natal care and institutional deliveries increased significantly.
- Emphasis on NHM in conjunction with Ayushman Bharat should continue.
- An increase in public healthcare spending from 1% to 2.5-3% of GDP can decrease the out-of-pocket expenditure from 65% to 35% of overall healthcare spending.
- A regulator for the healthcare sector must be considered given the market failures stemming from information asymmetry.
- Telemedicine needs to be harnessed to the fullest by investing in internet connectivity and health infrastructure.

Healthcare Initiatives

- Pradhan Mantri Jan Arogya Yojana (PM-JAY) – the ambitious program launched by Government of India in 2018 to provide healthcare access to the most vulnerable sections demonstrates strong positive effects on healthcare outcomes in a short time.
- PM-JAY is being used significantly for high frequency, low cost care such as dialysis and continued during the Covid pandemic and the lockdown.
- The proportion of households that had health insurance increased in Bihar, Assam and Sikkim from 2015-16 to 2019-20 by 89% while it decreased by 12% over the same period in West Bengal.
- Significant improvements seen in several health outcomes in States that implemented PM-JAY versus those that did not.

Access to Bare Necessities

- Access to the 'bare necessities' has improved across all States in the country in 2018 as compared to 2012.
- It is highest in States such as Kerala, Punjab, Haryana and Gujarat while lowest in Odisha, Jharkhand, West Bengal and Tripura.
- Improvement in each of the five dimensions viz., access to water, housing, sanitation, micro-environment and other facilities.
- Inter-State disparities declined across rural and urban areas as the laggard States have gained relatively more between 2012 and 2018.
- Improved disproportionately more for the poorest households when compared to the richest households across rural and urban areas.

- Improved access to the 'bare necessities' has led to improvements in health indicators such as infant mortality and under-5 mortality rate and also correlates with future improvements in education indicators.
- Thrust should be given to reduce variation in the access to bare necessities across States, between rural and urban and between income groups.
- The schemes such as Jal Jeevan Mission, SBM-G, PMAY-G, etc. may design appropriate strategy to reduce these gaps.
- A Bare Necessities Index (BNI) based on the large annual household survey data can be constructed using suitable indicators and methodology at district level for all/targeted districts to assess the progress on access to bare necessities.

Simplifying the Process of Reforms

- India over-regulates the economy resulting in regulations being ineffective even with relatively good compliance with process.
- The root cause of the problem of over-regulation is an approach that attempts to account for every possible outcome.
- Increase in complexity of regulations, intended to reduce discretion, results in even more non-transparent discretion.
- The solution is to simplify regulations and invest in greater supervision which, by definition, implies greater discretion.
- Discretion, however, needs to be balanced with transparency, systems of ex-ante accountability and ex-post resolution mechanisms.
- The above intellectual framework has already informed reforms ranging from labour codes to removal of onerous regulations on the BPO sector.

Regulatory Forbearance (forbearance means the quality of being patient and sympathetic) **is an emergency medicine, should not be the norm**

- During the Global Financial Crisis, regulatory forbearance helped borrowerstide over temporary hardship.
- Forbearance continued long after the economic recovery, resulting in unintended consequences for the economy.

- Forbearance represents emergency medicine that should be discontinued at the first opportunity when the economy exhibits recovery, not a staple diet that gets continued for years.
- An Asset Quality Review exercise must be conducted immediately after the forbearance is withdrawn.
- The legal infrastructure for the recovery of loans needs to be strengthened de facto.

Innovation Needs Thrust, Especially from the Private Sector

- India entered the top-50 innovating countries for the first time in 2020 since the inception of the Global Innovation Index in 2007, ranking first in Central and South Asia, and third amongst lower middle-income group economies.
- India's gross domestic expenditure on R&D (GERD) is lowest amongst top ten economies.
- India's aspiration must be to compete on innovation with the top ten economies.
- The government sector contributes a disproportionately large share in total GERD at three times the average of top ten economies.
- The business sector's contribution to GERD, total R&D personnel and researchers is amongst the lowest when compared to top ten economies.
- This situation has prevailed despite higher tax incentives for innovation and access to equity capital.
- India's business sector needs to significantly ramp up investments in R&D.
- Indian resident's share in total patents filed in the country must rise from the current 36% which is much below the average of 62% in top ten economies.
- For achieving higher improvement in innovation output, India must focus on improving its performance on institutions and business sophistication innovation inputs.

Fiscal Developments

- India adopted a calibrated approach, best suited for a resilient recovery of its economy from COVID-19 pandemic impact, in contrast with a front-loaded large stimulus package adopted by many countries.

- Expenditure policy in 2020-21 initially aimed at supporting the vulnerable sections but was re-oriented to boost overall demand and capital spending, once the lockdown was unwound.
- Monthly GST collections have crossed the ₹1 lakh crore mark consecutively for the last 3 months, reaching its highest levels in December 2020 ever since the introduction of GST.
- Reforms in tax administration have begun a process of transparency and accountability and have incentivized tax compliance by enhancing honest tax-payers' experience.
- Central Government has also taken consistent steps to impart support to the States in the challenging times of the pandemic.

External Sector

- COVID-19 pandemic led to a sharp decline in global trade, lower commodity prices and tighter external financing conditions with implications for current account balances and currencies of different countries.
- India's forex reserves at an all-time high of US$ 586.1 billion as on January 08, 2021, covering about 18 months' worth of imports.
- India is experiencing a Current Account Surplus along with robust capital inflows leading to a Balance of Payments (BoP) surplus since Q4 of FY2019-20.
- Balance on the capital account is buttressed by robust FDI and FPI inflows:
- *Net FDI inflows of US$ 27.5 billion during April-October,2020: 14.8% higher as compared to first seven months of FY2019-20.*
- *Net FPI inflows of US$ 28.5 billion during April-December, 2020 as against US$ 12.3 billion in corresponding period of last year.*
- India to end with an Annual Current Account Surplus after a period of 17 years.
- India's merchandise trade deficit was lower at US$ 57.5 billion in April-December, 2020 as compared to US$ 125.9 billion in the corresponding period last year.
- In April-December, 2020, merchandise exports contracted by 15.7% to US$ 200.8 billion from US$ 238.3 billion in April-December, 2019.
- *Petroleum, Oil and Lubricants (POL) exports have contributed negatively to export performance during the period under review.*
- *Non-POL exports turned positive and helped in improving export performance in Q3 of 2020-21.*

- *Within Non-POL exports, agriculture & allied products, drugs &* pharmaceuticals *and ores & minerals recorded expansion.*
- Trade balance with China and the US improved as imports slowed.
- At end-September 2020, India's external debt placed at US$ 556.2 billion –a decrease of US$ 2.0 billion (0.4%) as compared to end-March 2020.
- RBI's interventions in forex markets ensured financial stability and orderly conditions, controlling the volatility and one-sided appreciation of the Rupee.
- Initiatives undertaken to promote exports:
  - o *Production Linked Incentive (PLI) Scheme.*
  - *o Remission of Duties and Taxes on Exported Products (RoDTE).*
  - *o Improvement in logistics infrastructure and digital initiatives.*

Money Management and Financial Intermediation

- Accommodative monetary policy during 2020 resulted in repo rate cut by 115 basis points (bps) since March 2020.(One basis point = to 0.01%; 115 bps = 1.15%).
- Systemic liquidity in FY2020-21 has remained in surplus so far. RBI undertook various conventional and unconventional measures like:
  - o *Open Market Operations.*
  - *o Long Term Repo Operations.*
  - *o Targeted Long Term Repo Operations.*
- Gross Non-Performing Assets ratio of Scheduled Commercial Banks decreased from 8.21% at end-March, 2020 to 7.49% at end-September, 2020.
- NIFTY-50 and BSE SENSEX reached record high closing of 14,644.7 and 49,792.12 respectively on January 20, 2021.
- The recovery rate for the Scheduled Commercial Banks through Insolvency and Bankruptcy Code (IBC) (since its inception) has been over 45%.

Prices and Inflation

- Headline Consumer Price Index (CPI) inflationaveraged 6.6% during April-December, 2020 and stood at 4.6% in December, 2020, mainly driven by rise in food inflation (from 6.7% in 2019-20 to 9.1% during April-December, 2020, owing to build up in vegetable prices).

- CPI headline and its sub-groups witnessed inflation during April-October 2020, driven by substantial increase in price momentum – due to the initial disruptions caused by COVID-19 lockdown.
- Rural-urban difference in CPI inflation saw a decline in 2020.
- During April-December, 2019 as well as April-December, 2020-21, the major driver of CPI-C inflation was the food and beverages group:
- *CPI-C (CPI-Combined) inflation increased in most of the states in the current year.*
- *Regional variation persists.*
- *Inflation ranged from 3.2% to 11% across States/UTs during June-December 2020 compared to (–) 0.3% to 7.6% during the same period last year.*
- Food inflation driving overall CPI-C inflation due to the relatively more weight of food items in the index.
- Steps taken to stabilize prices of food items:
    - o *Banning of export of onions.*
    - o *Imposition of stock limit on onions.*
    - o *Easing of restriction on imports of pulses.*

Gold Prices

- Sharp spike as investors turned to gold as a safe haven investment amid COVID-19 induced economic uncertainties.
- Compared to other assets, gold had considerably higher returns during FY2020-21.

Consistency in import policy warrants attention

- Increased dependence on imports of edible oils poses risk of fluctuations in import prices.
- Imports impacting production and prices of domestic edible oil market, coupled with frequent changes in import policy of pulses and edible oils, add to confusion among farmers/producers and delay imports.

Sustainable Development and Climate Change

- India has taken several proactive steps to mainstream the Sustainable Development Goals (SDGs) into the policies, schemes and programmes.
- Voluntary National Review (VNR) presented to the United Nations High-Level Political Forum (HLPF) on Sustainable Development.

- Localisation of SDGs is crucial to any strategy aimed at achieving the goals under the 2030 Agenda.
    - *Several States/UTs have created institutional structures for implementation of SDGs and also nodal mechanisms within every department and at the district levels for better coordination and convergence.*
- Sustainable development remains core to the development strategy despite the unprecedented COVID-19 pandemic crisis.
- Eight National Missions under National Action Plan on Climate Change (NAPCC) focussed on the objectives of adaptation, mitigation and preparedness on climate risks.
- India's Nationally Determined Contributions (NDC) states that finance is a critical enabler of climate change action.
- The financing considerations will, therefore, remain critical especially as the country steps up the targets substantially.
- International Solar Alliance (ISA) launched two new initiatives – 'World Solar Bank' and 'One Sun One World One Grid Initiative' – poised to bring about solar energy revolution globally.

Agriculture and Food Management

- India's Agricultural (and Allied Activities) sector has shown its resilience amid the adversities of COVID-19 induced lockdowns with a growth of 3.4% at constant prices during 2020-21 (first advance estimate).
- The share of Agriculture and Allied Sectors in Gross Value Added (GVA) of the country at current prices is 17.8% for the year 2019-20 (CSO-Provisional Estimates of National Income, 29th May, 2020).
- Total foodgrain production in the country in the year 2019-20 (as per Fourth Advance Estimates), is 11.44 million tonnes more than during 2018-19.
- The actual agricultural credit flow was Rs 13,92,469.81 crore against the target of Rs 13,50,000 crore in 2019-20. The target for 2020-21 was Rs 15,00,000 crore and a sum of Rs 9,73,517.80 crore was disbursed till 30th November, 2020.

- 1.5 crore dairy farmers of milk cooperatives and milk producer companies were targeted to provide Kisan Credit Cards (KCC) as part of Prime Minister's Aatmanirbhar Bharat Package after the budget announcement of February 2020.
- As of mid-January 2021, a total of 44,673 Kisan Credit Cards (KCCs) have been issued to fishers and fish farmers and an additional 4.04 lakh applications from fishers and fish farmers are with the banks at various stages of issuance.
- The Pradhan Mantri Fasal Bima Yojana (PMFBY) covers over 5.5 crore farmer applications year on year.
    - *Claims worth* Rs *90,000 crore paid, as on 12th January, 2021.*
    - *Speedy claim settlement directly into the farmer accounts throughAadhar linkage.*
    - *70 lakh farmers benefitted and claims worth* Rs *8741.30* crore *were transferred during COVID-19 lock down period.*
- *An amount of* Rs *18000 crore has been deposited directly in the bank accounts of 9 crore farmer familiesin the country in December, 2020 in the 7th installment of financial benefit under the PM-KISAN scheme.*
- Fish production reached an all-time high of 14.16 million metric tons during 2019-20:
    - *GVA by the Fisheries sector to the national economy stood at* Rs *2,12,915* crore *constituting 1.24% of the total national GVA and 7.28 % of the agricultural GVA.*
- Food Processing Industries (FPI) sector has been growing at an Average Annual Growth Rate (AAGR) of around 9.99 % as compared to around 3.12 % in Agriculture and 8.25 % in Manufacturing, at 2011-12 prices, during the last 5 years ending 2018-19.
- Pradhan Mantri Garib Kalyan Anna Yojana:
    - *80.96 crore beneficiaries were provided foodgrains above NFSA mandated requirement free of cost till November, 2020.*
    - *Over 200 LMT of foodgrains were provided amounting to a fiscal outgo of over ₹ 75000* crore.
- Aatmanirbhar Bharat Package: 5 kg per person per month for four months (May to August) to approximately 8 crores migrants (excluded under NFSA or state ration card) entailing subsidy of Rs 3109 crore approximately.

Industry and Infrastructure

- A strong V-shaped recovery of economic activity further confirmed by Index of Industrial Production (IIP) data.
- The IIP & eight-core index further inched up to pre-COVID levels.
- The broad-based recovery in the IIP resulted in a growth of (–) 1.9 % in Nov-2020 as compared to a growth of 2.1 % in Nov-2019 and a nadir of (–) 57.3 % in Apr-2020.
- Further improvement and firming up in industrial activities are foreseen with the Government enhancing capital expenditure, the vaccination drive and the resolute push forward on long pending reform measures.
- Aatmanirbhar Bharat Abhiyan with a stimulus package worth 15 % of India's GDP announced.
- India's rank in the Ease of Doing Business (EoDB) Index for 2019 has moved upwards to the 63rd position in 2020 from 77th in 2018 as per the Doing Business Report (DBR):
    - *India has improved its position in 7 out of 10 indicators.*
    - *Acknowledges India as one of the top 10 improvers, the third time in a row, with an improvement of 67 ranks in three years.*
    - *It is also the highest jump by any large country since 2011.*
- FDI equity inflows were US$49.98 billion in FY20 as compared to US$44.37 billion during FY19:
    - *It is US$30.0 billion for FY21 (up to September-2020).*
    - *The bulk of FDI equity flow is in the non-manufacturing sector.*
    - *Within the manufacturing sector, industries like automobile, telecommunication, metallurgical, non-conventional energy, chemical (other than fertilizers), food processing, petroleum & natural gas got the bulk of FDI.*
- Government has announced a Production-Linked Incentive (PLI) Scheme in the 10 key sectors under the aegis of Aatmanirbhar Bharat for enhancing India's manufacturing capabilities and exports:
    - *To be implemented by the concerned ministries with an overall expenditure estimated at* Rs *1.46 lakh* crore *and with sector specific financial limits.*

Services Sector

- India's services sector contracted by nearly 16% during H1: FY2020-21, during the COVID-19 pandemic mandated lockdown, owing to its contact-intensive nature.
- Key indicators such as Services Purchasing Managers' Index (PMI), rail freight traffic, and port traffic, are all displaying a V-shaped recovery after a sharp decline during the lockdown.
- Despite the disruptions being witnessed globally, FDI inflows into India's services sector grew robustly by 34% Year-on-Year (Y-o-Y) during April-September 2020 to reach US$ 23.6 billion.
- The services sector accounts for over 54 % of India's GVA and nearly four-fifths of total FDI inflow into India.
- The sector's share in GVA exceeds 50% in 15 out of 33 States and UTs, and is particularly more pronounced (greater than 85%) in Delhi and Chandigarh.
- Services sector accounts for 48% of total exports, outperforming goods exports in the recent years.
- The shipping turnaround time at ports has almost halved from 4.67 days in 2010-11 to 2.62 days in 2019-20.
- The Indian start-up ecosystem has been progressing well amidst the COVID-19 pandemic, being home to 38 unicorns – adding a record number of 12 start-ups to the unicorn list last year.
- India's space sector has grown exponentially in the past six decades:
  - o *Spent about US$ 1.8 billion on space programmes in 2019-20.*
  - o *Space ecosystem is undergoing several policy reforms to engage private players and attract innovation and investment.*

Social Infrastructure, Employment and Human Development

- The combined (Centre and States) social sector expenditure as % of GDP has increased in 2020-21 compared to last year.
- India's rank in HDI 2019 was recorded at 131, out of a total 189 countries:

- o *India⊠ GNI per capita (2017 PPP $) has increased from US$ 6,427 in 2018 to US$ 6,681 in 2019.*
- o *Life expectancy at birth improved from 69.4 years in 2018 to 69.7 years in 2019.*

- The access to data network, electronic devices such as computer, laptop, smart phone etc. gained importance due to online learning and remote working during the pandemic.
- Major proportion of workforce engaged as regular wage/salaried in the urban sector during the period of January 2019-March 2020 (quarterly survey of Periodic Labour Force Survey (PLFS).
- Government's incentive to boost employment through Aatmanirbhar Bharat Rozgar Yojana and rationalization and simplification of existing labour codes into 4 codes.
- Low level of female Labour Force Participation Rate (LFPR) in India:
  - o *Females spending disproportionately more time on unpaid domestic and care giving services to household members as compared to their male counterparts (Time Use Survey, 2019).*
  - o *Need to promote non-discriminatory practices at the workplace like pay and career progression, improve work incentives, including other medical and social security benefits for female workers.*
- Under Pradhan Mantri Garib Kalyan Package (PMGKP) announced in March, 2020, cash transfers of upto[1] 1000 to existing old aged, widowed and disabled beneficiaries under the National Social Assistance Programme (NSAP).
- An amount of Rs 500 each was transferred for three months digitally into bank accounts of the women beneficiaries under PM Jan Dhan Yojana (PMJDY), totalling about Rs 20.64 crore.
- Free distribution of gas cylinders to about 8 crore families for three months.
- Limit of collateral free lending increased from Rs 10 lakh to Rs 20 lakh for 63 lakh women SHGs which would support 6.85 crore households.
- Wages under Mahatma Gandhi National Rural Employment Guaranteed Act (MNREGA) increased by Rs.20 from Rs 182 to Rs 202 w.e.f. 1st April, 2020.

Note: The term FY21 used in this note denotes Financial Year 2020-2021.

Introduction
Evolution of Economic Thought

Economics: Its Origin and Ancient Thought – Medieval era – Mercantilism - The Age of Reason and Enlightenment - Physiocrats - Classical economics - Economic Systems: Feudalism- Capitalism - Socialism- Cooperation- Communism and Marx - Neo-Classical school - Keynesian economics -Welfare economics - Mathematical school and Quantitative studies - Post-Keynesian economics- Economics, a Dismal science?

State of the Economy in 2020-21: A Macro View

Alfred Marshall (1842-1924), who carried forward the ideas of the economists of the Classical school defined Economics as: "Political Economy or Economics is a study of mankind in the ordinary business of life; it examines that part of individual and social action which is most closely connected with the attainment and with the use of the material requisites of well-being." (Marshall: *Principles of Economics*, 1890).

It will be seen from the writings and theories propounded by economists from the early days, and particularly from the 18th century, beginning with Adam Smith, that their original thinking, ideas and contributions on how the economic system worked have paved the way, in large measure, for many of the modern concepts and economic theories. It only goes to prove the prescience they had of how economic activity and economies would evolve even in the face of many transformational changes in human progress that was to take place.

Life and Economic activity

While life on earth began in many forms millions of years ago, *homo sapiens*, human species with the ability to think and speak emerged only about 100,000 years ago. But it was around 15,000 years ago that the climate began to change with the last phase of Ice age coming to an end and Earth became habitable with vegetation and wildlife spreading into desolate areas. Human communities began to take shape and within a few thousand years, small villages of farmers made their appearance in parts of China, the Near East and Mexico. Gathering food by hunting animals gave way to farming, and gradually economic activity began to be more organized.

Apart from farming, man learnt the art of pottery making and making tools and implements with stone and bone. Methods of cooking underwent change and houses with clay and stone came to be built for protection from nature and animals.

Ancient Economic thought

The genesis of economic ideas is to be found in household management even in ancient times with families having to fend for necessities of life – food, clothing and shelter. Once agriculture was started, followed by other activities like pottery making, working with tools to make other items, the need for exchange of items between people – barter trade – arose and community activities gained momentum.

But though material civilization evolved, it took a long while for economic ideas and thought to emerge even in a rudimentary manner. Scattered economic ideas are to be found, among others, in the Bible and other religious scriptures, codes of law and moral exhortations in various ancient texts. These works laid stress on ethical and moral precepts and cautioned against greed, acquiring wealth by unethical means and amassing excessive wealth. They urged the use of wealth for the welfare of the poor and needy, notions which are analogous to modern concepts of equality, justice and welfare of society at large.

- **Economics:** The very term 'economics' is derived from the ancient Greek word *oikonomia*, the word *oikos* meaning house or household and *nomos* custom or law. The work *Oeconomicus* by Xenophon (430-335 BC), the Greek historian, consists of a dialogue of Socrates (469-399 BC), the Greek philosopher, which dwells with wealth, agriculture and household management.
    - Plato (428-347 BC), who authored *The Republic*, looked down upon the pursuit of wealth and extolled those engaged in agriculture. He recognized the importance of production and advocated division of labour, a concept which was later developed by Adam Smith. Plato observed: "All things are produced more plentifully and easily, and of a better quality, when one man does one thing which is natural to him and does it at the right time, and leaves other things". He deprecated excessive craving for luxuries and seeking gain for its own sake.
    - Aristotle (384-322 BC), Plato's pupil, who viewed economic issues from a political viewpoint, divided economy into two parts: the household economy and the wealth generating economy. His works, *The Nicomachean Ethics* and *The Politics*, recognized

the function of money as a medium of exchange and measure of value. Aristotle regarded acquiring property as part of managing household but disapproved unnatural modes of amassing wealth like earning interest out of money. In ***Ethics***, Aristotle while dwelling on economics and ethics had observed: "wealth is evidently not the good we are seeking; for it is merely useful and for the sake of something else". It signifies that the question of "means and ends", an important aspect in Economics, had received attention even in those early days.

- Kautilya, a minister under Chandragupta Maurya of the Mauryan dynasty, who authored in the 4th century BC, the comprehensive work on statecraft, *Arthashastra* (translated as Science of Wealth or Economics), has given vivid description of the administrative procedures, the duties of kings, ministers and government officials. He has also dwelt on State finances, public expenditures under various heads such as administration, defence, storage of granaries, etc., raising resources through taxation and ensuring welfare of the state and people.
- Confucius (551-479 BC), the Chinese philosopher, believed that while the pursuit of wealth was human nature, the conduct of people seeking wealth should be restrained by the idea of fairness and justice. In his work *Analects*, he advocated three principles for managing a just and equitable society: administering wealth properly, formulating rules to ensure ethical practices and preventing wrongdoing. As he lived in an era when farming was the dominant part of the economy and the vast majority of the labour force was engaged in farming, Confucius accorded primacy to agriculture and considered it to be the primary source of wealth. He emphasized that farming must be in harmony with the laws of nature, adhere to proper cropping cycles, and minimize corvee time, which means a day of unpaid work to be done by a vassal, a system adopted by feudal lords to exact work with little or no payment.

Medieval era

To understand the course and further development of economic thought, one must understand the changes that took place in the social structure and how economic relationships adjusted to these changes. The Medieval era spanned from the end of the 5th century to the 11th century known as the Dark Ages and from the 12th century to the 15th century when much economic and commercial progress took place. The latter phase and subsequent period also witnessed the Renaissance in Europe, (roughly between the 14th and 16th centuries) when art, architecture and literature flourished.

- **Feudal system:** In the Medieval era, following the disintegration of the Roman empire, feudal order came to be established in Europe. The relationship between the landed aristocracy and the vassals or serfs who laboured on the farms was feudal. Under this system, the tillers became dependent on the nobles or feudal lords who provided them with protection from marauders. As population increased, agricultural activity expanded in villages, and small towns came up where handicraft manufactures were produced. This necessitated trading between villages and towns.

- **Trade and Commerce:** Barter trade between communities had existed from time immemorial when agricultural produce and handicraft items were exchanged. In due course, the traders and merchants became more organized and formed "guilds", like trade associations of modern times. These guilds set standards of skill, sale and purchase prices of products and wage rates.

❖ **St. Thomas Aquinas and Nicholas Oresme**

Medieval-age thinkers like St. Thomas Aquinas (1225-1274) and Nicholas Oresme (1320-1382) also developed certain economic concepts.

- Aquinas who was educated in a Monastery and the University of Naples and whose scholarship was recognized by the Pope wrote on a variety of themes such as pricing of products, division of labour, usury and functions of State. He laid great stress on fairness and justice in dealings and economic transactions. He stressed that price of products should be just and related to their quality and not charged with the motive of making excessive profit. As with Church authorities, he disapproved the practice of charging interest on borrowers of money. These ideas may be based on the Biblical dictum: "Love of money is the root of all evil." Aquinas held the view that no individual should be allowed to issue currency and that the power would vest with the State.

- Oresme, who was a Bishop in France, observed the need for money as a medium of exchange as barter system caused difficulties to people (in finding two persons who both needed the very items offered for exchange which may not always be the case). He put forward the idea that if two kinds of coins, say, of gold and silver, are put into circulation, their relative face values should conform to the values of their bullion (metallic) content. Otherwise, if they are of the same denomination but different intrinsic values, the money with higher intrinsic value (called *good money*) will be hoarded for melting and eventually driven out of circulation by the money with lesser intrinsic value (called *bad money*). This phenomenon that "bad money drives out good money" later came to be known as Gresham's law in Economics, after Sir Thomas Gresham (1518 -1579), an English banker and founder of Royal Exchange, who put forward the concept in a more refined way. Oresme attached much importance to promoting trade and protecting traders from oppression by the rulers.

Mercantilism

Exploratory voyages by Europeans opened up vast opportunities for international trade. With Columbus and Amerigo Vespucci reaching the New World (the Americas) and Vasco de Gama discovering the route to the East towards the end of 15th century, the scope for long distance trade and commerce across continents expanded significantly.

The above developments saw the emergence of a body of economic thought, between the mid-16th and late 18th centuries, known as 'mercantilism' focussed on the relationship between a nation's balance of trade and its wealth. Mercantilists argued for achieving favourable balance of trade, i.e., exports exceeding imports and amassing wealth in the form of gold and silver. Thomas Mun (1571-1641), who joined the East India Company in 1615, wrote two works titled *A Discourse on Trade from England unto the East Indies* (1621) and a more major work *England's Treasure by Foreign Trade* (published posthumously in 1664). Mun argued: "The ordinary means therefore to increase our wealth and treasure is by foreign trade, wherein we must ever observe this rule: to sell more to strangers yearly than we consume of theirs in value." He further said, this would help to bring money into the country even if in the process some gold and silver have to be spent in foreign lands.

Other prominent advocates of mercantilist policies were William Petty (1623-1687), Charles Davenant (1656-1714) and John Locke (1632-1704) in England; Jean Colbert (1619-1683), Richard Cantillon (1680-1734) in France; Ludwig Seckendorff (1626-1692) and Johann Becher (1625-1685) in Germany.

- **Role of the State:** Mercantilism was rooted in the idea of "protection" to ensure favourable balance of trade. Mercantilists advocated regulation and intervention by the State in every sphere to promote general well-being. It was the very antithesis of *laissez faire* policy that governments should not intervene in economic affairs. The policy of mercantilism was prevalent in England, France, Germany and Spain.

  The growth of urban population, increase in manufactures and trade over long distances led to the emergence of nation-state as a centre of power. This gave impetus to mercantilist tradition with the State playing an overarching role. The colonial imperialism with European powers colonising countries in America, Asia and Africa also necessitated the state taking on greater responsibility as no private body would have had the resources to carry on exploration, set up colonies and govern them. With the onset of Industrial Revolution and expansion of industries, protective tariffs became a necessity to nurture the infant industries. As is the case with modern times, the state also had to play an active role in improving infrastructure facilities to cater to the growing population and demands of industry and trade, which private agencies would have been unable to undertake.

The mercantilist system came under attack from Adam Smith who pioneered classical economic theory. Smith, who favoured competition and free markets, advocated *laissez faire* policy of minimum government interference. But mercantilism served the purpose during its time and helped European powers to consolidate their hold over colonies and gain supremacy. It can also be said that some of the ideas propounded by mercantilists such as capital accumulation, expansion of money supply and lower interest rates to support economic expansion have found their way to modern economic theory including Keynesian economics. But with the advent of Physiocrats and Adam Smith, the economic discourse took a different path.

- **The Age of Reason and Enlightenment**

If the ancient and medieval doctrines were dominated by other worldliness, the discourse turned to more mundane matters, material gains and improving human life. In the 17th-18th centuries, Europe was in intellectual ferment stirred by the writings of Hugo Grotius (1583-1645), a Dutch legal luminary, Thomas Hobbes (1588-1679) and John Locke (1632-1704), English philosophers, Voltaire (1694-1778) and Jean-Jacques Rousseau (1712-1778), French thinkers and philosophers.

This was the Age of Reason and Enlightenment which was sweeping England, France and the United States. Science and inventions, accompanied by the Industrial Revolution, opened up limitless possibilities of improving life. The expansion of long distance travel and trade gave further impetus to bring about transformational changes.

Physiocrats

The 18th century gave rise to another school of thought in France known as 'Physiocracy'. The term was coined by Dupont de Nemours (1739-1817) and signified the "rule of Nature". Physiocrats, as the proponents were known, advocated governance according to 'natural order', gave primacy to agriculture and held that 'soil' alone was the source of all wealth.

François Quesnay (1694-1774), Marquis de Mirabeau (1715-89), Anne Turgot (1727-81) and Pierre de Nemours (1739-1817) were the main proponents of this school. They influenced some thinkers in the U.S. and England as well.

The Physiocrats were notable for various reasons. They were bitterly opposed to the mercantilist policies of trade restrictions and state interference in all sphères. They laid stress on minimum regulatory control and maximum economic freedom. The coinage of the term "*laissez faire*" (in French, let go or let (them) do) which was to gain much currency in years to come is attributed to them.

A major contribution of Quesnay, who was foremost among them, was the formulation of ***Tableau Economique*** (Economic Table) in 1758 which assessed the wealth of a nation and its circulation on a macro-economic basis. This is considered to be the direct forerunner of circular flow and input-output studies of later times. Over the centuries, Quesnay's *Economic Table* has inspired many scholars including Karl Marx in his studies of capitalism.

A major flaw in their thinking was that Physiocrats considered land and agriculture to be the only source of all wealth, and that industry, manufacturing and trade were "sterile". They came in for severe criticism for this myopic and lop-sided view. Referring to the Physiocrats, Adam Smith observed, "The capital error of this system, however, seems to lie in its representing the class of artificers, manufacturers and merchants, as altogether barren and unproductive." And Smith went on to argue at length in *The Wealth of Nations* to show how flawed and far from reality their views were. This group did not survive for long.

❖ Classical Economics

The Classical school, which laid the foundations of what was called "Political Economy" and still later "Economics", was spearheaded and dominated by three men, viz., Adam Smith (1723-1790), David Ricardo (1772-1823) and James Mill (1773-1836). Among others who made major contributions were Thomas Robert Malthus (1776-1834) and Jeremy Bentham (1748-1832).

❖ Adam Smith (1723-1790)

Adam Smith's seminal work on political economy,***An Inquiry into the Nature and Causes of the Wealth of Nations***. published in 1776, laid the foundation for modern economic ideas upon which later economists built the superstructure. The work dealt with a wide spectrum of themes such as factors leading to the creation and accumulation of wealth, labour and role of different occupations, division of labour and its benefits, rent and wages and role of markets, trade and free competition. It must be remembered that Smith published the work around the time the Industrial Revolution was unfolding in England and much of what he wrote had a prescience about changes in industry and economy that was to follow in decades to come. His major contributions are discussed below.

- **Division of labour:** For instance, the concept of division of labour led to specialisation, assembly line of factory operation, and increased productivity which became an integral part ofthe modern factory system. However, Smith had also observed the limitations of division of labour in as much as it was limited by the extent of the market, transport and exchange facilities available, density of population and capital available. Its benefits depend on how wide the market is and the extent of demand, and how large is the scale of production. The larger the production facility, the greater is the scope for gains from division of labour.

- **On source of wealth:** Smith opposed the views of physiocrats that agriculture alone was the source of all wealth and stressed the importance of not only agriculture but also industry, manufacturing and trade which form the three sectors and are the pillars of a modern economy, viz., the Primary, Secondary and Tertiary sectors. Smith also opposed the mercantilist doctrine that a nation's wealth is derived from favourable balance of trade – excess of exports over imports. Instead, Smith argued that wealth is derived from production deploying resources (raw materials) and labour.
- **Labour and Wages:** Smith spoke of productive and unproductive labour, and higher wages resulting from economic expansion. While accepting the subsistence theory of wages, Smith pointed out that there would be inequalities in wages and profit "arising from the nature of the employments themselves" and identified the reasons for this. Wages varied with the conditions of work, say in a factory or a colliery which is relatively more arduous, skills of workers, with more skilled jobs fetching higher wages, and cost of apprenticeship and training. These ideas are of much relevance even today when due to rapid technological advancements, the skills of workers get outdated soon requiring reskilling them and governments and industry are undertaking massive skill development programmes. Smith observed that wages of those employed in manufacturing would be higher than those in countryside occupations, which holds good as much today as it did in the 18th century. Wages also depended on the competition for jobs and labour available, a function of demand and supply of labour.
- **Pricing:** The fundamental role which Smith assigned to markets led him to examine how markets would operate and how prices of commodities would be determined. The real or natural value of any product would be dependent on the quantum of labour used, time required to make it, training or education which was required for making the worker skilful for the job, etc. Besides, effective demand for the product, i.e., desire for an article backed by the ability (purchasing power) to buy it and supply available, would be determining factors. Demand exceeding supply would help the producer to hike the price and increase his profits.

- **Trade:** A major contribution of Adam Smith was his advocacy of international trade and its benefits. The rationale for trade between nations has found resonance in Smith's '*The Wealth of Nations*'where he says. "What is prudence in the conduct of every private family, can scarce be folly in that of a great kingdom. If a foreign country can supply us with a commodity cheaper than we ourselves can make it, better buy it of them with some part of the produce of our own industry, employed in a way in which we have some advantage. It is as foolish for a nation as for an individual to make what can be bought cheaper." This is the very concept underlying the '**Theory of Comparative Advantage**' in international trade which was refined and developed later by other economists. In today's globalised world, nations are ever more dependent on one another and, in this respect, trade between nations, the significance of which Smith had highlighted, has assumed much importance.
- **Laissez faire policy:** Smith argued that economic system required minimum of government intervention, and favoured laissez faire policy and free competition in the marketplace. On this, he was opposed to mercantilists and was more in line with the views of physiocrats.
- **Self-interest and Invisible hand:** Adam Smith, the philosopher, recognized that man is motivated by '*self-interest*' and that while man constantly needs the help f his brethren, it is vain for him to expect others to be benevolent to him. Smith says, "It is not from the benevolence of the butcher, the brewer, or the baker, that we expect our dinner, but from their regard to their own interest". But, in the same breath, Smith says that every individual is guided by an *invisible hand* and thus while pursuing his own interest, he frequently promotes the good of the society.

Many liberal economists have interpreted this to mean that according to Smith, individual decisions taking place in the market inevitably leads to the greatest good of the society. In other words, the *invisible hand* which is always at work will reconcile and harmonise private and public interests and result in maximum gains for the society. However, Emma Rothschild, an authority on Adam Smith, says that Smith himself did not attach much importance to the idea of 'invisible hand', a term which Smith used only once in *The Wealth of Nations*, though the idea that individuals' actions have unintended consequences, which may sometimes promote the public good, is a recurring theme in the book.

David Ricardo (1772-1823)

After Smith, Ricardo was the most celebrated among the classical economists. He had little formal education but by the age of 14, he started working in the money market where, in course of time, he made enough fortune to retire when he was just 42 years of age.

While his initial works on money and banking did not fetch him much recognition, his book ***The Principles of Political Economy and Taxation*** published in 1817 was to dominate classical economics for years to come. This work primarily dealt with distribution of produce of industry between the factors of production – land, labour and capital. Other major contributions related to agriculture and the law of diminishing returns and theory of wages.

- **Theory of Rent and the Law of Diminishing Returns:** As population increased and demand for food rises, more and more land has to be brought under cultivation. Assuming that the more fertile lands are cultivated initially, and less fertile lands at later stages, the yield from the lands will progressively keep declining (law of diminishing returns). The output, of say wheat, will come down with each addition of capital (inputs) and labour, and this process will continue, considering the costs involved, until it is no longer profitable to bring any additional plots of land under cultivation. The least fertile land would be cultivated only if its yield would just cover the costs. It would yield just that and nothing more. The higher yields from the more fertile lands, as compared to the yield from the least productive plot (called "marginal land"), would accrue as "rent". This extra return to landowners accruing by virtue of mere ownership of land (a scarce resource), which Ricardo identified as rent, was termed ***unearned income***.

  Though Ricardo developed the concept of rent in more detail and precise terms, the originator of the idea was Dr. James Anderson, a contemporary of Adam Smith, and an agricultural economist, who wrote that rent was a premium for the privilege to cultivate fertile land.

  The "marginal" concept which Ricardo introduced later came to be applied to theories of consumption (utility), production (output), prices and value.

- **The Wage-Fund theory:** The classical economists, Malthus and Ricardo, developed the theory termed the ***Iron law of wages***. The supply of labour was related to the subsistence level of wages required by the workers to maintain a reasonable standard of living. If the wage rate rose above the subsistence level, population would increase and if it fell below it, it would decline. The level of wages would be determined by the capital available which, in turn, depended on savings. The demand for labour was determined by the size of the wage-fund and the level of savings. In a society with increasing capital and rising investment, demand for labour would increase and wages would be higher than the minimum subsistence level. Ricardo was of the view that wages should be left to free and fair competition in the labour market.

- **Distributive justice:** Ricardo, who has made a major contribution to the theory of distribution, had held that the interests of capitalists, landlords, and labour invariably come into conflict. The produce of the earth, which is the result of the contribution of land, labour, machinery, and capital, is divided among three groups of people, viz., landowners, the labour class, and owners of machinery or capital. But the proportion in which the produce is shared between them as rent, wages, and profits would be different at different stages of the society, as it is dependent on many variable factors like fertility of the soil, population, skill and productivity of labour, and capital accumulation. Ricardo's writings placed him in the mould of a socialist and his views came to be known as Ricardian socialism.

- **International trade theory:** Ricardo took from Col. Robert Torrens (1780–1864) the idea of territorial division of labour and systematized the "theory of comparative advantage" on which international trade is based. By using a simple numerical example of two countries and two goods, Ricardo showed that the total output of goods could be more if both the countries specialized in the production of the one good in which it had comparative advantage. Differences in the relative costs of production of goods arise because countries are differently endowed with resources needed for production – raw materials, climate, size and skills of labour, stock of capital, etc. It would be unwise for any country to produce something which some other country can provide cheaper. Such specialization and trading (exchange) of goods will also lead to an increase in the real incomes of the countries concerned.
    - Later, Eli Heckscher (1879–1952) and Bertil Ohlin (1899–1979) of the Stockholm School of Economics further developed this theory with a mathematical model of international trade known as Heckscher–Ohlin model (H–O model). They showed that the relative endowments of the factors of production (land, labour, and capital) will determine a country's comparative advantage. As the profitability of goods is dependent on input costs, countries will have comparative advantage in producing those goods for which the required factors of production are locally available in relative abundance.
    - Notwithstanding the advantages of free trade outlined above, countries resort to restricting trade even in modern times, as mercantilists did, with protective tariffs to achieve a favourable balance of trade or to protect and nurture infant industries from foreign competition. But classical economists disapproved of such restrictions and Ricardo was an even more ardent votary of *laissez faire* than Adam Smith. The push towards liberal trade regime in the 20th century led to the creation of international organisations like General Agreement on Tariffs and Trade (GATT) in 1948 and later its successor, the World Trade Organisation (WTO) to promote liberal international trade.

Malthus (1766-1834) and Population Thesis

Thomas Robert Malthus (1766-1834) was ten years old when Adam Smith published '*The Wealth of Nations*'. In his early years, Malthus' thinking was influenced by many distressing trends in England with the onset of the Industrial Revolution. The changes it brought about were not very beneficial to workers and there were recurring spells of crises and economic depressions. The new industrial regime led to large scale unemployment as machines displaced handicraftsmen and artisans. The market too did not expand adequately to absorb the increasing output, which machines made possible, or the supply of labour and it seemed that England was overpopulated.

Malthus was ordained as a Minister in the Church of England and held charge of a small parish before becoming a Professor of History and Political Economy. He was troubled by the events unfolding around and was in search of some rational solutions to the oppressive problems afflicting the society. Malthus is remembered for his work on population. His ***Essay on the Principle of Population as it Affects the Future Improvement of Society***, which led to heated debates, was published anonymously in 1798. In 1803, he brought out a much larger edition of it under his own name. He presaged that population grew in geometrical progression while the natural resources to support population grew in arithmetic progression. His thesis held that population, if unchecked, would go on doubling every twenty-five years.

A moot question that arises with burgeoning population and longer life expectancy was, would not higher survival rates result in increasing pressure on the requirements of food and, in the event of inadequate supplies of food, would not hunger and malnutrition continue to haunt humanity? These questions that troubled Malthus to no end and led him to enunciate his pessimistic views on unchecked population growth which came to be known as 'Malthusian crisis' and also dubbed as Malthusian pessimism. To contain population growth, Malthus advocated late marriage, self-restraint and couples to have no more children than they could support. If these measures fail, real incomes will fall so low that some 'positive' natural checks will come into play and the population growth will be arrested by famine, starvation and disease, high incidence of mortality, and shorter adult lifespan.

- **Other Economists on Population:** Though the name of Malthus is synonymous with problems posed by population growth, he was not the first to recognize the issue. Francois Quesnay (1694-1774), the French economist of the Physiocratic school, Adam Smith (1723-1790), Richard Cantillon (circa 1680-1734), an Irish-French economist and Marquis de Condorcet (1743-1794), the French philosopher-mathematician, all of whom preceded Malthus, had dwelt on population issues in their writings. William Godwin (1756–1836), an English political philosopher, well known for his work, '*An Enquiry Concerning the Principles of Political Justice and its Influence on General Virtue* *and Happiness*', had written an essay titled '*Of Avarice and Profusion*' which is considered to have prompted Malthus to write his famous '***Essay on the Principle of Population***'.

- Cantillon identified three variables which determined the size of population and its growth, viz., natural resources, technology, and culture. Cantillon's population theory was more comprehensive than that of Malthus in as much as Cantillon recognized a much wider spectrum of factors which affect population growth, including the tendency for population growth to fall to zero as a society becomes more industrialized and developed.
- **Population trends:** Malthus' predictions have not entirely come true though, in contemporary times, in the least developed and many developing countries, the growth of population in relation to resources and economic growth remains a concern. In contrast, the advanced and industrialized European countries and Japan are faced with the problem of declining and ageing population. China which adopted a coercive and controversial One-child policy since 1980 to check population growth had to face criticism and rescind it in 2016, after implementing it for thirty-five years. Not only that, China's age-wise population structure has become rather skewed due to this policy.
- **Demographic transition in India:** A consequence of the demographic transition is that the age-structure of population of India would undergo a major shift, from young to old ages. By the middle of the century, the share of the young, of 0-14 years, would fall to nearly half of the level of 2001 and that of the old age group, of 60 years (or 65 years) and above, would more than double. Clearly, India's population would be ageing. The share of the working age group, of 15-59 years, would keep rising reaching a peak of 65 percent before beginning to decline.

Economic systems

Economic system denotes the way and mode in which a society manages economic activities. It involves wide range of institutions and social customs and practices relating to economic activity. Different systems have evolved over the millennia depending on the evolution and changes in human activities and the way in which they came to be managed. Four distinct systems have thus evolved, viz., feudalism, capitalism, socialism and communism. They have been dynamic and have had varying shades based on the economic, social and cultural progress of society and due to the need to cater to the changed circumstances. These systems and how they evolved are discussed below.

Pre-historic and Pre-Feudal era

In the primeval period when human civilization was just beginning to take shape, the economic order was virtually static. The primitive society sustained itself by hunting and gathering food, adapting to changing seasons and climate and migrating to find new ways of living. Later, as activities such as farming and making tools and implements began to take shape, a tribal economic order emerged. The Hebrew economic thought as found in the Old Testament indicates that a tribal economy prevailed. In the biblical times, land was the main form of property. Wealth was assessed in terms of land, serfs or slaves and animals that one possessed. Inheritance conventions governed the passage of property to successive generations. While agriculture was the primary occupation, trade and commerce were also in vogue.

The beginnings of economic institutions are often traced back to the Hebrew and Jewish times. The society discussed in the Old Testament mentioned some of the characteristics of modern capitalism and private property. The Hebrews belong to the ancient civilizations of the world and their period dates back to 2500 BC to 150 BC. Division of labour, market, exchange, money in the form of bullion, etc., existed in those times. These practices and institutions got further formalized by the Greeks whose economic ideas found expression in the writings of Plato (428-347 BC), Xenophon (430-335 BC) and Aristotle (384-322BC), among others.

Even in ancient India, a feudal system prevailed. The large landholders and village headmen, whose position was hereditary, wielded much power and exercised control over landless agricultural labourers and small peasants.

Feudalism

With agriculture being the main occupation, a feudal system had been taking shape even from early times. *Feudalism* and *feudal system* are terms coined long after the period from when the system existed. But it came to be associated with the social, economic, and political conditions in western Europe during the Middle Ages which covers the period between the 5th and 12th centuries. The system existed in Europe in different forms.

It was a dominant social system in which the nobility held lands from the Crown in exchange for military service, and vassals were in turn tenants of the nobles. The peasants (serfs) were obliged to live on their lord's land and give him homage, labour, and a share of the produce, in exchange for military protection. The manorial system that prevailed in Rome was one in which workers were compensated with protection while living on large estates was feudal.

A system of '**fiefdom**' under which the landowner (lord) gave a 'fief' (a feudal estate), along with military and legal protection, to a vassal – holder of land under feudal tenure – in return for a payment of some kind survived in England until they were abolished by Parliament in 1645. The system also had prevailed in France until it was abolished by the National Assembly between 1789 (the year of French Revolution) and 1793.

- **Decline of Feudalism:** Feudalism was suited for a society in which only local markets existed and in which money transactions were relatively rare. The rise of commerce deepened the markets and made money trades increasingly common, but feudalism was slow to respond to these changes. While the vestiges of feudalism remained, western Europe was turning toward a market economy by the fifteenth century. Manufactured goods were becoming increasingly important, and so was trade. The growth of city populations and making of goods for sale opened new vistas for trade and this led to the emergence of nation-state as a centre of power. The trade network spread through northern Europe and eventually linked with the Mediterranean trade network which involved trade between Italian city states and the Arab world.

On the agricultural front, Europe's food production in good years was sufficient to feed its population, but any crop failure led to famine. Crop failures occurred repeatedly during this time. In France alone there were recurring and widespread famines during the 14th century. Almost all of the arable land had been exploited. The large population meant that there was ample labour to work the land, leaving the landlords prosperous and the peasants poor.

Wars were also frequent, as incipient nation-states battled over borders. Another major blow were the bubonic and pneumonic plagues that ravaged Eurasia during the fourteenth centuries.

Feudalism had ceased to be an effective institution by the fifteenth century, though its imprint was visible in western Europe even in the 18th century. In England the land enclosures of the 17th-18th centuries were implemented to replace an inefficient allocation of agricultural land, a relic of feudalism, with a more efficient one. The distribution of income at the end of the sixteenth century was also a reflection of feudalism, with the economic elite being the owners of the major estates while the labouring class was poor. All these factors led to the decline and eventual end of feudalism.

Capitalism

Capitalism is an economic and social system characterized by free competitive market with private and corporate ownership of the means of production and distribution with the objective to earn profits and reinvest it. It is a free market or free enterprise economy, in which resource allocation is determined by the price system and income is distributed largely through the operation of markets.

Historically speaking, there were shades of capitalism in the early days too. Those who owned landed property were the early capitalists who earned the fruits of labour in the form of rent. Besides, there were moneylenders who financed agriculture and supported village economy and merchants who invested capital and engaged in trade and commerce.

Mercantilism

Mercantilism, which was a dominant force in the 17th-18th centuries in Europe and emphasized the role of foreign trade in enhancing the wealth of a nation, is considered by some to have marked the beginning of capitalism. The merchant traders asserted that their trading activities strengthened the interest of the sovereign power. But mercantilism was only partially a market-coordinated system as it involved regulation and control by the government which granted exclusive monopoly trading rights to groups such as the East India Company. Though mercantilist system relied on regulated and not free market economy, by promoting foreign trade, it did play a part in the growth of what may be called "commercial capitalism".

The economic society that Adam Smith described in *The Wealth of Nations* (1776) is much closer to modern capitalist society, although Smith has not used the word capitalism in the book. The role of government had gradually declined, its functions being confined to defence, protection of society and construction and maintenance of public works and realms like promoting education. But the role of commerce had increased and accumulation of capital was recognized as the driving force of the economy. The process of colonisation and expanding trade and commerce gave fillip to the growth of capitalism. In Smith's view, the market mechanism, tempered by competition and guided by natural forces, would direct production towards those goods and services which consumers desired, and had the means to buy, and which yielded profits for the producers and this would lead to maximum good of the society.

Pre-industrial era

To realize the impact of Industrial Revolution on human civilization, one must look at the long period preceding it. As economist John Maynard Keynes had observed in his 1930 essay on the ***Economic Possibilities for Our Grandchildren***: "From the earliest times from which we have record, that, say, two thousand years before Christ, down to the beginning of the eighteenth century, there was really no great change in the standard of living of the average man living in the civilized centres of the earth." He attributed this to the absence of technological inventions. And for thousands of years, the world did not witness any sustained economic growth, barring modest development of agriculture and primitive industries followed by gradual increase in population. Until the mid-1700s, the world was considerably poor and there was hardly any difference in the living standards of people in the western countries and Asia and Africa. Health conditions were poor everywhere, people were subjected to famines and epidemics and life expectancy was low. The onset of Industrial Revolution changed all that.

- **Industrial Revolution:** The Industrial Revolution which swept Europe and, in particular England, from the mid-18th century accentuated the growth of capitalism. Modern factory system had taken roots with rapid technological advances. Britain was then a dominant imperial power and British capitalism was in full play during the 18th and 19th centuries. The Industrial Revolution brought about marked changes in the methods of production, working conditions in factories and the scale of employment. Even as it opened up new opportunities both for the factory owners, the business class and the workers, a wide gulf began to emerge between them and in their living conditions.

- **Plight of Working class:** Men, women and children who tended machinery laboured hard in factories for 10 to 12 hours. The pathetic condition of mill labour, described in unsparing detail by inspectors who served under England's first Factory Act of 1802, was one of the factors that aroused indignation in Karl Marx and led him to do a critical study of capitalism.

  The plight of factory workers and their life and harsh working conditions, so vividly portrayed by Charles Dickens – in his novels such as *Hard Times and Oliver Twist* – and Charlie Chaplin – in films like *Modern Times* – both of whom had seen and experienced miserable conditions of dreary factory life in their childhood is etched in the memory of generations of people.

➢ **Downside of Capitalism**

Advocates as well as critics of capitalism agree that it contributed significantly to economic growth. The modernisation that followed Industrial Revolution did bring about improvements in life expectancy, material comforts and the overall standard of living. However, capitalist system was not an unalloyed blessing. It had a negative side that caused social and political upheaval in decades to come.

Work conditions

In western Europe, the economic changes produced massive social consequences during the first half of the 19th century. The work pattern was redefined, duration of work remained long, the autonomy enjoyed by wage labourers declined and they had to work under strict regimen. Changes in family life, shifts in modes of livelihood and methods of work, had substantial impact on family members. Older people gained new roles, particularly in working-class families, where they helped out as baby-sitters for grandchildren. Women's economic power in the family decreased. Many groups of men argued vigorously that women's role was to attend to family concerns. By the 1830s and '40s, one result was the inception of laws that regulated women's hours of work. Though this was a humanitarian move to protect women's family roles, it also reduced economic opportunities for women.

Inequalities

The rewards of increased efficiency from Industrial Revolution were distributed unequally. The financial condition of workers was in stark contrast to the growing affluence of entrepreneurs. The capitalists who owned the new factories and mills moved from rickety houses to big mansions.

While production and per capita output increased and real wages went up, the vast masses of people could not reap the benefits of the growing wealth.

Socialism

Socialism, as a political credo, has its roots in the widening gulf between the wealthy and the working class which got accentuated with the onset the Industrial Revolution. But, as already stated, its intellectual underpinnings lay in the ancient religious teachings and writings of philosophers in the pre-Christian era.The clamour for equality also found expression in Christian teachings and ancient Greece. Later, the Age of Enlightenment and the French Revolution brought to the fore egalitarian views.

Socialism advocates public ownership or control of means of production and property as against private ownership under the capitalism. Socialists contend that capitalism leads to unfair concentrations of wealth and power in the hands of few who gain undue powers from free-market competition. Those privileged few then use their wealth and power to reinforce their dominance in society.

As socialists viewed it, society as a whole should own, or at least control, property for the benefit of all its members. So also the *entire produce* belongs to the society as a whole and everyone who contributes to the production is entitled to a share in it. Real freedom and true equality require social control of the resources which will lead to prosperity in society.

Early Socialist thinking

The emerging trends in the 19th century – the plight of the common people – gave impetus to socialist ideas and thinking. As already stated, the socialist ideals were nothing new as such ideas are to be found in the teachings of early religious preceptors and philosophers.

- **French utopians:** The French Utopians like François Babeuf (1760-1797), Saint Simon (1760-1825), Charles Fourier (1772-1837), Louis Blanc (1811-1882) and Pierre Proudhon (1809-1865) all put forth socialist views though they held different shades of opinion.

  Babeuf held that "nature has given to every man an equal right in the enjoyment of all goods." He advocated eventual nationalisation of all private property by abolishing inheritance. Saint Simon, a Parisian who fought in the American Revolution and supported revolutionaries in France stressed "equality of opportunity". He envisioned a regime of public ownership of industry and each receiving an income corresponding to his services.

  Louis Blanc urged workers themselves to bring about labour reforms and that the State should take the lead in creating a new society. Blanc propounded the well-known socialist idea, "From each according to his ability, to each according to his needs." Proudhon, a believer in equality, opposed private ownership of business.

Prominent among English socialist thinkers were Jeremy Bentham (1748-1832), Robert Owen (1771-1858) and the social reformist couple, Sidney Webb (1859-1947) and Beatrice Webb (1858-1943).

- **Bentham and Utilitarianism:** Bentham, a social philosopher, is best known for his concept of "utilitarianism" which advocates" the greatest good to the greatest number". Every institution is to be judged by its utility and the good it does to individuals. Money is the basis and measure of pleasure and pain felt by individuals. Excessive wealth did not enhance happiness and pleasure proportionally and hence if the excess wealth is distributed among the poor, it would result in larger sum of happiness of society as a whole. The idea was akin to Ricardian socialism which aims at distributive justice.
- **Owen and Cooperative Movement:** Robert Owen, who himself ran a mill employing some 2,000 persons, was an idealist entrepreneur who was far ahead of his time. He was moved by the pitiable state of his workers and their families who lived in utter penury. He reduced work hours, increased the wages of his workers, provided them housing and free education to children, avoided employing children under ten. Children above ten years were imparted training during work. He opened a company store to provide food and clothing at economical rates, promoted recreational activities and covered workers through insurance funds. Owen's lasting contribution was laying the foundations for what was to become "Cooperative movement". The consumers' cooperative enterprise started in a small way in Rochdale, England owes much to Owen who devoted his life to developing co-operation, as a practical system to solve many problems. His initiatives on workers' welfare also paved the way for labour and trade union movements to take shape.
- **The Webbs and Trade Unionism:** Sidney and Beatrice Webb, the English couple who imbibed socialist ideas, had profound influence on British political thought in the first half of the 20th century. They defended the rights of the working class and provided a blueprint for welfare state in Britain. This was the forerunner of Beveridge Report of 1942 which created the framework for universal social security system and served as the basis for the welfare state in post-World War II Britain under the Labour Government.
    - Sidney Webb was a prominent member of the **Fabian Society**, founded in 1884, which counted among its members, George Bernard Shaw (1856-1950) and Annie Besant (1847-1933). The principal aim of the society was furtherance of the goal of

socialism through education of the public along socialist lines. The Fabians advocated evolutionary socialism rather than revolutionary methods in bringing about change. The Society later transformed as **Labour Party** in Britain which has played active role in furthering socialist ideas in British politics.

- The Webbs, Sidney and Beatrice, were both intellectuals who wrote extensively and their work extended into areas of historical and social research, educational and political reform, and journalism. Their collaborative effort resulted in publication of a major work, ***The History of Trade Unionism*** (1894) in two volumes, and *Industrial Democracy* (1897). **London School of Economics** (LSE) was the brainchild of Sidney and Beatrice Webb who established it along with Graham Wallas (1858-1932), a political scientist, and writer George Bernard Shaw who were all members of the Fabian Society. *LSE, which became a premier academic institution, was founded with the objective of "study and investigation of the concrete facts of industrial life and the actual working of economic and political relations as they exist or have existed, in the United Kingdom and in foreign countries".*
- Many of these early socialists who held egalitarian views were harbingers of Marxism and benign socialism of later years.

Karl Marx and Communism

Socialist ideas and thinking got a boost and were reinforced with the arrival of Karl Marx (1818-1883) on the scene. The second half of 18th century was a period of turbulence when Europe was in ferment. Many thinkers were assailed by exploitative streaks in society. Industries faced many crises such as long work hours, low wages, harsh working conditions and displacement of labour with induction of machines – all depressing effects brought about by the Industrial Revolution.

Marx fiercely disagreed with the views of other socialists like Pierre Proudhon and found a collaborator in **Friedrich Engels** (1820-1895) in founding Communist movement. A secret international organization, League of the Just, serving the cause of exploited labour enlisted Marx and Engels to draft their proclamation which led to the publication of the famous "***Communist Manifesto***" in 1848. While Marx published the first volume of ***Das Kapital*** in 1867, its second and third volumes were published by Engels in 1885 and 1895 respectively after Marx's death.

In its aim to replace private property and profit-based economy with public ownership and societal control of the major means of production – the natural resources, mills, factories, etc. – Communism was akin to socialism but in a more radical form. Marx himself tended to use the terms *communism* and *socialism* interchangeably.

Marx's economics

- **Class struggle:** Marx firmly held the view that there was class struggle between capitalists and workers which would end with the latter taking over the means of production. His clarion call was: "The proletarians have nothing to lose but their chains….Workers of all countries unite!"
- **Exploitation of labour:** Marx who overturned much of the views of classical economists spoke of various forms of exploitation. The society consists of two classes – the bourgeoisie and the proletariat or the working class – and the capitalist system of production was exploitative of labour. *The value of* a good *produced by* the *labour is greater than the actual price paid for the labour* as *wages* which are equivalent to just the workers' means of subsistence. *The difference between the two (surplus value) is confiscated by the* capitalist (*bourgeois*).
- **Impact of technology:** Besides, technological advancement reduces demand for labour which, as a consequence, is rendered surplus.
- **Periodic crises:** The capitalist system driven by profit motive is susceptible to periodic crises caused by over-production, unemployment and fall in demand due to lack of purchasing power of the labouring class. These will lead to recession in the economy.

Assessment of Marxism

While Marxian ideas and notions may have held good in the 18th and 19thcenturies, they have been largely disproved by the developments in later periods. Technological advancements have not only improved the methods of production and the overall output but has also led to improvements in the skill levels and working conditions of the labour class itself. With the formation of trade unions and labour reforms, the bargaining power of labour and wages and social security benefits like provident fund, healthcare, housing, etc. have significantly improved.

International bodies like the International Labour Organization (ILO) and the World Health Organization (WHO) have played notable role in ameliorating the condition of the working class.

Even countries which had embraced communism in its rigid form have undergone major transformation. The Soviet Union which held together under a communist regime for nearly seven decades disbanded into separate states and restructured their economic and political policy. China, which is a Communist state with one-party rule, effected major economic reforms in late 1970's and introduced market reforms with Chinese characteristics.

This is not to deny the existence of any exploitation of labour which may occur or persist due to other factors. But it has been seen that an enlightened and caring industrial system is beneficial not only to the industry and society at large, but to the workers themselves. And due credit has to be given to both industry bodies and workers' organizations for working in a co-operative spirit and their efforts to ameliorate the conditions of workers in regard to wages, housing, health, and education benefits to the workers and their families. This is exemplified by modern concepts such as tripartism in solving labour issues and managements adopting 'corporate social responsibility' (CSR) policies to contribute to the welfare of society at large.

➢ Neo-Classical School

Many far-reaching changes had taken place since the contributions made by classical economists. Industrial Revolution had brought about transformational changes in the factory system and production methods. Advances in the physical sciences had led to many inventions and discoveries which changed many facets of life. Standards of living were steadily rising. All these called for a re-evaluation of classical theories and it gave rise to new generation of economists who attempted to restate theories in the light of the changed conditions. As Alfred Marshall, a doyen among the economists in the Classical tradition observed, "**Economic conditions are constantly changing and each generation looks at its own problems in its own way.**" Among those who contributed to the restatement of Classical tradition, the most prominent were John Stuart Mill and Alfred Marshall.

John Stuart Mill (1806-1873)

The oldest son of James Mill (1773-1836), one of the Classicists, John Stuart Mill was exposed to the writings of Smith and Ricardo in his very early years by the father. John, who studied law, joined the East India Company in a minor post at the age of 17 where he served for 35 years and rose to a senior position.

Mill's major work, ***The Principles of Political Economy with Some of Their Applications to Social Philosophy*** was published in 1848, the same year the ***Communist Manifesto*** by Marx and Engels came out. It was a comprehensive review of the economic theory at the time and became an influential work among students till the end of the century. This pioneering study was a consummate review of the works of Classical theorists – Smith, Ricardo and Malthus.

Like Marx, Mill was also profoundly influenced by the works of utopian socialists (see earlier section on Socialism) and critics of capitalism. Jeremy Bentham's utilitarian philosophy also influenced his thinking. Though Mill was beset by the turmoil of the times, unlike Marx, he did not see the break-up of the capitalist system. Yet he felt the need to restate the classical notions and chart a new path for human progress.

Mill's work cited above is celebrated for its liberal and generous spirit and lucid prose and literary merit. It was an instant success, was widely read and ran into several editions. With each successive edition, Mill turned out to be more of a socialist in his outlook. It was divided into five books and dealt with Production, Distribution, Exchange, Influence of the Progress of Society and Influence of the Government. Some of his major ideas are outlined here.

- **Production:** The basic factors of production are labour and natural resources. Natural resources included soil, minerals, climate, water, etc. Labour included not only physical labour but mental and other attributes too such as dexterity and skill of workers, specialisation, cooperative spirit, trustworthiness and the scale of production. Mill attributed productive efficiency to all these factors which are akin to factors recognized as contributing to "productivity" in modern parlance. Mill added that man acquires immeasurably powerful command over natural forces, "a command which, great as it is already, is without doubt destined to become indefinitely greater." It was a prophetic vision, indeed, as subsequent human progress has shown.
- **Capital:** Mill distinguished capital from money and stated capital is accumulation of goods that is employed in further production. He also distinguished between fixed and circulating capital, the fixed capital being that part used in production and are more of a permanent nature such as buildings, machinery, etc. Whereas circulating capital, once used, gets consumed and used up and is no longer available for production, such as consumables, wages paid to workers, etc. These are concepts which were later refined and have become part of modern economic theory.
- **Wages:** As per the classical theory known as the iron law of wages and the wages-fund theory, wages depended on the supply of, and demand for, labour. The natural price of labour was that price necessary for workers to subsist whereas market price of labour depended on supply and demand factors. Wages rose if labour was scarce and it fell when supply of labour was abundant. Also, real wages cannot be far above the minimum level necessary for survival, i.e., for subsistence, except for a temporary period. For, if it rose much above the subsistence level, it would lead to larger supply of workers and inevitable decrease in the wage levels. Mill stressed on the duty of the State to improve the lot of workers and provide jobs to all.
- **Free trade:** Mill was a staunch supporter of free trade and held that protectionism – levying import and export duties – would deprive nations of the benefit of comparative advantage of specialising in the production of goods for which they are best suited. It would render the labour and capital less efficient in production.

A major thrust in Mill's revision of classical tradition was that distribution of wealth was not governed by an unalterable natural law but could be decided by the will of man. Distribution of wealth "depends on the laws and customs of society. The rules by which it is determined are what the opinions and feelings of the ruling portion of the community make them, and are very different in different ages and countries." He disapproves of mere material progress being the ultimate goal.While people may aspire to realize their ambitions, people vying with one another for more wealth is undesirable.

Mill was favourably disposed towards socialist thinkers and their views but disagreed with their attack on competition. He held that the absence of competition would lead to monopoly and advancement of privileged groups. Mill was neither a utopian nor a follower of Marxism. His blend of liberty and egalitarianism was in the best tradition of democratic socialism which Britain and some of the European nations began to adopt in course of time.

Alfred Marshall (1842-1924)

Alfred Marshall (1842-1924), the doyen of neo-Classical school, made signal contributions to Economic theory. Though graduated in Mathematics, after joining Cambridge University as Lecturer in Moral science in 1868, Marshall pursued study of economics. In 1885, he became Professor of Political Economy at Cambridge in which post he continued till 1908.

Marshall said that "each generation looks at its own problems in its own way", and this made him look at classical theories and restate them in the light of the changed times. He was deeply assailed by prevailing poverty and said, "The study of the causes of poverty is the study of the causes of degradation of a large part of mankind". Large sections of people in England suffered from lack of bare necessities. He devoted much attention to finding solutions to the social problems he saw around. He viewed economic science as a means for the betterment of mankind.

While Marshall published works on foreign trade, industry, money and commerce, his *magnum opus* was "***Principles of Economics***" brought out in 1890 which ran into as many as eight editions and served as a premier work of reference for generations of students. Marshall, who deemed Economics to be a "**study of mankind in the ordinary business of life**", dwelt with mundane topics of relevance to the real world such as supply and demand, consumption and utility of commodities, effects of income and price on demand, among other things. Many of his concepts centred around the "consumer" and his position in the market. He employed his skills in mathematics in developing many of the concepts in microeconomics which does studies at the level of individual consumers or groups of consumers or firms. That he restated and redefined the theories developed by predecessors with greater incisiveness and precision was his major accomplishment which explains his claim to eminence.

Law of diminishing returns

Ricardo and Malthus had spoken of the "law of diminishing returns" in the context of land and returns from agriculture – that as more and more land of less fertility is brought into cultivation, the returns keep diminishing and the least fertile land (at the margin) would be farmed only if it pays for the costs involved. Marshall agreed with this and said that even if improved methods of cultivation helped to increase output, it would only be a temporary phenomenon and that "a continual increase in the application of capital and labour to land must ultimately result in the diminution of the extra produce which can be obtained by a given extra amount of labour and capital". This finding in the field of agriculture has stood the test of time and is true to this day.

Theories of Consumption

- **Utility:** Building upon the work of his predecessors, Marshall made significant contributions in the domain of consumption which may now appear clichés and commonplace. He showed the relationship between the demand for a commodity and its utility for, or welfare of, the consumer. The basis for this is the concept of diminishing marginal utility, earlier propounded by William Stanley Jevons (1835-1882) and later by Hermann Gossen (1810-1858), that the more of a commodity a consumer has, the less will be the extra utility or benefit he/she will have from additional purchases of it. Consumers will not buy a commodity until this extra benefit falls to zero but will stop buying more when the money to pay for it is worth more to them than the gain (or, utility) from additional purchases.
- **Utility concept and its Limitations:** A major deficiency of the utility concept is that it is neither quantifiable nor measurable. Further it defies making inter-personal comparisons of utility or satisfaction enjoyed by consumers. The assertion that the more of a commodity one has, one derives less and less satisfaction with additional units of it is almost self-evident and seems like a truism. But it is not possible to say how much less satisfaction one has with more of a commodity or how much in comparison with another person in a similar situation. One person's pleasure or happiness cannot be compared with that of another. The varied reactions of people even in comparable conditions make such comparisons difficult. Economists like Kenneth Arrow and Amartya Sen have examined these issues in depth in the context of Social Choice theory and Welfare economics.
- **Utilitarianism and Welfare:** The concept of utilitarianism, despite its limitations, has come to have relevance in welfare economics. Advocates of utilitarianism like Bentham, Marshall, Edgeworth and Pigou held that the sum total of individual welfares could form the basis of choosing what is socially good and in the choice of public policy. They identified individual welfare with utility and utility with individual happiness. But later theorists of "new welfare economics" relied only on utilities but dispensed with the issue of inter-personal comparison. This again poses problems in forming judgements

on what is socially good. However, utility alone cannot be the basis of welfare as many other aspects such as freedom of choice and capabilities enjoyed by people also have bearing on well-being. (For more on this, see section on **Welfare economics** later in this Note.)

The limitation to measurability of utility has been overcome to some extent by the Indifference Curve theory and Revealed Preference approach developed later. (On this, see under **Mathematical school** section later in this Note.)

Marshall developed the concepts of **supply and demand** of which Adam Smith had spoken in ***The Wealth of Nations*** in the context of fixing market price of a commodity. Smith wrote: "The market price of every particular commodity is regulated by the proportion between the quantity which is actually brought to the market, and the demand of those who are willing to pay the natural price of the commodity, or the whole value of the rent, labour, and profit, which must be paid in order to bring it thither." Smith went on to stress the aspect of "effectual demand", that is, desire to buy backed by purchasing power, in other words, the ability of a consumer to buy, to which later economists, including Keynes, would draw particular attention when they spoke of "effective demand".

Marshall dealt with concepts of supply and demand and showed how a fall in price will increase the demand for a commodity. A schedule could be drawn up showing how much would be demanded of a commodity at different price levels. If this is presented graphically, it would show a downward sloping demand curve signifying that more quantity would be purchased as the price goes down and vice versa. Similarly, on the supply side, more supply would be forthcoming at higher prices and with a supply schedule, a corresponding supply curve can be prepared which will be an upward sloping curve signifying higher output and supply as the price goes up. The point at which the two curves intersect will determine the price of the commodity which would be the equilibrium point. This concept put forth by Marshall a century ago remains valid to this day as conventional wisdom.

Marshall recognized that this over-simplified theory does not take into account the impact complementary and competitive goods may have, and the scope for substitution which could take place. From this, he developed the concepts of "**elasticity of demand**" and "**consumer's surplus**".

- **Elasticity of demand:** Marshall coined the expression "elasticity" which refers to changes in a variable due to small changes in a related variable. Elasticity of demand relates to variations in demand in response to changes in price. **Price elasticity** of demand stands for proportionate change in the demand for a commodity to changes in the price for it.

Essential commodities are inelastic with not much change in demand due to changes in their price while luxuries would be highly elastic being very sensitive to price. **Income elasticity** of demand represents the proportionate change in the quantity demanded of a commodity to proportionate change in the income of the consumer with price remaining constant. **Cross-price elasticity** of demand is the proportionate change in the quantity demanded of one commodity divided by the proportionate change in the price of another commodity. Where the two are substitutes, say butter and margarine, the elasticity is positive. If the price of one increases, the demand for the other will go up which is called "**substitution effect**". It shows the rate at which consumers switch spending to, or away from, one commodity when its relative price changes. The substitution effect is always negative as consumers switch from items the prices of which increase.

Exceptions to the theory of demand outlined above are certain luxury items which are status symbols like expensive jewellery like diamond, fancy automobiles or art works of great masters which would be in demand even if their prices go up.

- **Consumer's surplus:** This concept which Marshall expounded refers to the amount by which a consumer values a product over and above what he pays for it. To put it differently, it is the price which the consumer is prepared to pay for a product rather than go without it, which is its real value to him, and the price he actually pays for it. The price a consumer pays for a product is equal to the utility of the last unit of the total quantity purchased while all the earlier units were worth more. These extra utilities over the price paid can be added up and it constitutes the consumer's surplus.

Marginal concept

The "marginal" concept was dominant in much of the classical theories. The concept of **marginalism** can be applied in the context of many of the economic activities such as production, sale, purchase, wages and pricing. How much an entrepreneur would pay for each of the factors of production – land (rent), raw materials (cost), labour (wages) or capital (interest) – depend on their relative marginal productivity. The last unit of each, which he deems it worth paying for, determines its price. A manufacturer would use machinery in place of labour if the marginal value of the product he could get by employing machinery was greater than that of the labour. Conversely, cheap labour entailing low wage costs would deter using machinery by making it more expensive to buy a machine than to engage labour.

- **Marginal product** is the output created by employing one additional unit of a factor of production. The marginal product rises when a factor is employed in small quantities but eventually it will fall as the amount of factor employed increases. Marginal product is measured in physical units of output produced and is called marginal physical product. Marginal cost is the increase in total cost incurred by a firm by increasing output by one extra unit. Firms will keep producing as long as marginal costs and returns are positive subject to availability of demand for the product.

- **Marginal cost** is the increase in total cost incurred by a firm by increasing output by one extra unit. Firms will keep producing as long as marginal costs and returns are positive subject to availability of demand for the product. Marginal cost pricing means setting the price of an item equal to the cost of producing one extra unit of output.
- **Marginal productivity** of capital or labour is the value of output that would be created by employing one extra unit of capital or labour.

Relevance of Concepts

Though the concepts discussed above, enunciated by economists from classical times, and which have evolved over time, may appear to be just pedantic and theoretical, they are of practical value and even applied in modern business practices and industry in different forms. The concepts of marginal cost, marginal product and marginal revenue are helpful in cost-benefit analysis while undertaking projects. They are also of relevance to industries and services sectors in optimisation of their operations and related costs. Industry practices like productivity drives, quality control, work efficiency, Total Quality Management (TQM) and least cost methods incorporate some of the underlying aspects of the above concepts. The internationally recognized ISO Standards concept is about the most efficient way of performing an activity. It could be about manufacturing a product, managing a process, delivering a service or supplying materials (logistics) – the standards cover a wide range of activities. These concepts form part of Business Studies, Cost Accounting, Corporate Management, etc.

National dividend

Marshall extended his analysis of markets and consumers and spoke of "national dividend" and thus laid the path for developing the concept which we now call national income. Dealing with the question of distribution, which had been examined at length by Ricardo, Marshall explained national dividend as follows: "The labour and capital of the country acting on its natural resources, produce annually a certain net aggregate of commodities – material and immaterial, including services of all kinds. The limiting word ***net*** is needed to provide for the using up of raw and half-finished commodities, and for the wearing out and depreciation of plant which is involved in production. All such waste must, of course, be deducted from the ***gross*** produce before the true or net income can be found. And net income due on account of foreign investments must be added in. This is the true net annual income or revenue of the country, or the national dividend."

Marshall, however, was not the first to put forward the concept of National dividend or what later came to be known as National income. William Petty (1623–1687), the English politician and economist, prepared the first estimates of national income in England in the seventeenth century. Later, towards the end of the 17th century, Gregory King (1648–1712) made more systematic estimates for income, saving, and expense of England for the year 1688. In the late 17th - early 18th century, the French economist Pierre de Boisguillebert (1646–1714) developed crude estimates of income and consumption in France which was followed by more precise estimates by Sébastien Le Prestre de Vauban (1633–1707), a military engineer and advisor to the king, in 1707.

In India, Dadabhai Naoroji pioneered national income studies when he calculated per capita income in Bombay Presidency for the years 1867-70.

Other Reformers: Wicksell and Veblen

While there were many economists who contributed to economic theory during this period, two prominent economists, whose lives spanned the 19th-20th centuries, stand out. They were John Gustav Knut Wicksell, a Swedish economist, and Thorstein Veblen, an American economist. Both made some path-breaking contributions with their thinking and writings.

- **Knut Wicksell, a pre-Keynesian**

  Wicksell (1851-1926) started his life as a social reformer. Trained in mathematics, he would later turn to economics like Marshall and later Keynes. Though a scholar in the classical utilitarian tradition, he differed with the views of those who advocated capitalist theories.

  Wicksell spoke of the possibility of changes in economy, rather than a static world where things would work themselves out for the best. With aggregate demand and supply not in balance, a repudiation of Say's law (on this see under Classical economics: Shortcomings, Marx and Keynes in this Note), there would be cycles of rising and falling prices and in explaining this, he drew attention to the circular flow of national income. In what can be said as a precursor of Keynesian analysis, Wicksell viewed national income as the sum total of the individual incomes in an economy which constitutes the economy's total purchasing power or aggregate demand. That portion of this total which is not spent on consumption would be the total savings. If these savings are put into use for productive purposes like infrastructure building, construction of houses, setting up factories, etc., it constitutes investment. If savings exceed investment, then flow of money is interrupted and there will be shortfall in demand resulting in fall in prices. And the converse will happen if investment exceeds savings. This was to form the core of Keynesian analysis following the Great Depression of the 1930s.

Another significant contribution of Wicksell relates to the market structure. He pointed out that between the extremes of monopoly and perfect competition, there could be many situations of firms competing with one another, the kind of monopolistic and imperfect competition which would be further developed more cogently later by Joan Robinson and Edward Chamberlain. (For more on this, see in the next section).

➤ **Thorstein Veblen**

Thorstein Veblen (1857-1929), the American economist, was a rebel, non-conformist and heretic for his times, who broke away from the mainstream to tread a new path. To know of his thinking and rebellious nature, one has to trace his background. Son of an immigrant from Norway, Veblen was brought up on a farm and did higher studies in philosophy, his main interest, at John Hopkins and Yale where he wrote a doctoral thesis on Immanuel Kant's philosophy. Later, he studied economics at Cornell and joined the faculty at the University of Chicago and Stanford. At these institutions, his eccentric views and conduct brought him into conflict with the faculty and soon after his academic journey virtually ended. Then he took up odd assignments in the government, as editor and finally a stint at the New School for Social Research in New York.

Maybe due to his background in philosophy and his concern for the common man, Veblen decried hedonism, extravagance and ostentation. A critic of the classical tradition, Veblen viewed contemporary economic ideas with scepticism and out of sync with the ground realities.

Veblen favoured industries using technology as it improves efficiency in making products that people need. In his ***The Theory of Business Enterprise*** (1904), he pointed out the conflict in the business world between professionals and technocrats who are highly productive, (whom he called "captains of industry"), on the one hand,, and the business class on the other, who are primarily motivated by profit considerations. One makes the goods while the other is after money. In ***The Instinct of Workmanship*** (1914), he lauded the skills of artisans and ordinary workers who took pride in their work.

But the acme of Veblen's accomplishments is to be found in his work, ***The Theory of the Leisure Class*** (1899) in which he criticized aristocracy engaged in big business and rolling in wealth. He attacked Western capitalism for its unseemly pursuit in the accumulation of wealth. He compared their tendencies and avarice for wealth with the characteristics of barbarian societies. He deprecated lavish lifestyle and "conspicuous waste" and "**conspicuous consumption**", the other terms he coined to convey his firm convictions. The latter term has found its way into modern economic lexicon, and is disparagingly used to describe vulgar display of wealth in the context of the wide chasm that exists between the lives of the 'haves' and the 'have-nots'.

➢ **Imperfect and Monopolistic Competition**

By the early part of the 20th century, economists began to challenge the notion of perfect competition advocated by the Classicists including Marshall. Perfectly competitive industry is one in which there are a large number of firms – both buyers and sellers – which are too small to make any impact on market price individually, and can enter or exit the industry without incurring high costs. And all the firms have maximization of profit as their aim. But economists pointed out there are other features also in the industrial structure like monopoly (single producer), oligopoly (with few large firms) and other forms of competition in the market. A general theory of imperfect competition had been suggested by Piero Sraffa (1898-1983), an Italian economist who joined Cambridge and was a contemporary of Keynes. In his paper "***The Laws of Returns under Competitive Conditions***" (1926) in ***Economic Journal***, Sraffa pointed out the flaws in Marshall's theory of the firm which, according to him, did not reflect the real state of a capitalist society. His views prompted other economists to develop theories of production in conditions other than perfect competition.

These ideas were further brought to the fore and prominence by two economists, Joan Robinson (1903-1983) of Cambridge in her celebrated work, ***The Economics of Imperfect Competition*** (1933) and by Edward H. Chamberlin (1899-1967), of the University of Michigan and later Harvard, in his work ***The Theory of Monopolistic Competition*** (1933). It was no longer the case that no producer could influence or control the price. In the extreme case of monopoly, a single producer could set the price in a way to maximize his profits. In between this and a perfect competition, there exist a range of possibilities. Robinson and Chamberlin argued that there could be monopolistic and imperfect markets which are dominated by a few large firms – a case of oligopoly – in which each produce products which are similar but not perfect substitutes. The products have slight differentiation and consumers prefer the product of one firm to that of its competitors, even if its price slightly goes up, exhibiting a degree of loyalty to the brand. In this regard, the firm has some degree of power over the market and price-setting.

Chamberlin extended it further and showed that under monopolistic competition, a producer could advertise the unique features of a product and brand, its superior qualities and establish a limited monopoly. Major industries like automobiles, steel, oil, chemicals, etc. are examples of such market structure. Though oligopoly and monopolistic competition with few firms dominating the market have their pitfalls and the risk of concentration of economic power, they have come to be accepted in the modern corporate world.

Schumpeter defended monopoly due to the potential for innovations that a monopolist entrepreneur could bring to the enterprise which was free from the threat of competition and imitation. The few large firms constituting oligopoly, though socially iniquitous, held the potential of innovation and product improvement with the sizeable financial resources they command.

- **Anti-trust Laws:** However, legislations like the antitrust laws in the US and Competition Commission in India (or formerly, the Monopolies and Restrictive Trade Practices (MRTP) Act) are put in place to check the unfettered freedom that monopolistic firms may command and their tendency to keep out competitors. In the IT sector, global behemoths like Google and Microsoft wield such powers and have been questioned by the US government and the Commission for European Union on their anti-competitive practices.

  In this context, it is worth mentioning that the Chairman of the 15th Finance Commission, N.K. Singh, has cautioned that with privatisation of public sector undertakings (PSUs) set in motion in India, the disinvestment and sale should not distort the principles of competition. Addressing the National Conference on Economics of Competition Law, he called for strengthening the Competition Act to evolve the role of the Competition Commission of India (CCI) as an overarching regulator. The process of privatisation and disinvestment would free valuable financial resources, creating fiscal space for the government for its priority capital expenditure – both physical and social infrastructure. It should generate healthy competition to ensure that the stressed assets in the public sector do not pass into the hands of a few companies. Considering the wide range and scale of PSUs involved, it will require a co-ordinated approach between the Ministry of Finance, the CCI and entities like the RBI and SBI, as the CCI alone would not be able to undertake and ensure it.

Classical economics: Shortcomings

The classical tradition in economics, with all its accomplishments, was found to be inadequate to answer the challenges brought about by changing conditions. The classical system placed implicit faith in a perfectly competitive regime where the market forces – of supply and demand – guided by an "invisible hand" ensured condition of equilibrium: Savings and investment would be equal and there would be full employment and any disequilibrium or underemployment would correct itself, an untenable position as later events like the Great Depression showed. The classical thesis was supported by the famous Say's law, propounded by Jean Baptiste Say (1767-1832), a French economist, which stated that "supply creates its own demand". There would be no over-production or glut and production ensured enough purchasing power in the hands of people to buy up all that is produced.

The above contentions were repudiated by Karl Marx and later by J M Keynes. Commenting on Say's law, Marx wrote in *Das Capital*: "Nothing can be more absurd than the dogma that every sale is a purchase, and every purchase a sale, therefore, the circulation of commodities necessarily implies equilibrium of sales and purchase."

Economic depressions

A series of depressions, or business cycles as they came to be called, had occurred in Europe and the US in the 19th century. Danish state bankruptcy of 1813, post-Napoleonic depression in England in 1815, panic of 1819, 1837, 1857, 1873 and 1893 in the US following bank failures were some of them and their impact lasted for some years. More depressions occurred in England and in 1893 in Australia.

During the years intervening between the two World Wars of 1914-18 and 1939-45, Britain and European countries faced perilous conditions and instability. Much of Britain's overseas investments were sold to pay for war supplies. Most of these countries were battered by sharp fall in prices in 1920-21. Exports declined and there was persistent unemployment.

- **The Gold Standard:** In 1925, under Winston Churchill, then the Chancellor of the Exchequer, England returned to the gold standard at the pre-war gold value of the pound. This action by Churchill was sharply criticized by Keynes. When a country was on gold standard, the Central bank was obliged to give gold in exchange for any of its currency presented to it. A balance of payments surplus results in inflow of gold into Central Bank's reserves. The UK in 1817, and later many developed and developing countries, were on gold standard. Though the system was suspended during World War I, later many countries returned to it. But with the onset of the Great Depression, gold standard was given up worldwide by 1933.

- **The Great Depression:** But the Great Depression which jolted the US economy from 1929 was lethal and threw the world economy into turmoil for several years. It led to rapid decline in national and international economic activity. The stock market faced a 'Great Crash' in 1929 which caused widespread ruin as there were no safety nets in those times. Thousands of local banks failed and lakhs of businesses followed suit. There were sharp declines in output, prices and investments. Between 1930 and 1938, unemployment rates were high – in in the US (26%), Germany (22%), UK (15%) and France (10%). GDP and wholesale prices fell sharply and world trade declined between 1929 and 1933.

The classical theories, which assumed that an economy would return to full employment conditions and equilibrium on its own through a self-correcting process, offered no remedies to counter the devastating phenomenon. The deep crisis dealt a fatal blow to the complacency of the prevailing economic thought and there was imperative need for a radically different approach. Herbert Hoover, US President (1929-1933), who reposed faith in the classical reasoning, failed to respond to the crisis adequately. And it took the next President, Franklin D. Roosevelt (1933-1945) to initiate decisive steps including the New Deal. (See on this later below).

And then came Keynes

John Maynard Keynes, like Marshall, was trained in mathematics, and graduated with a first in Mathematics at Cambridge in 1905. Later he studied Economics under Marshall and Pigou. After a period in Civil Service when he had a brief stint in India Office, he took up lectureship in Economics at Cambridge. From 1912 till 1945, he edited the prestigious ***Economic Journal*** of the Royal Economic Society. While he wrote prodigiously on contemporary economic problems caused by the wars and the depression, his path-breaking work was the 1936 classic ***The General Theory of Employment, Interest and Money*** which opened up new vistas of analysis of the working of an economy and took Economics in a totally new direction.

- **Classicists vs Keynes:** The prescription by the classical economists in the face of the crisis was to persuade labour unions to accept wage cut. The implication was that if labour became cheap, employers would find it profitable to hire more and thereby reduce unemployment. Keynes contended that while this approach may hold good for a particular industry, an across-the-board cut in wages would lower consumption, income and aggregate demand. The reduced effective demand would only exacerbate unemployment.
- **Consumption and Savings:** Another aspect is that as output, employment and income increase, consumption from additions to income decreases – as Keynes puts it, "marginal propensity to consume" (MPC) declines and savings increase. (MPC is the proportion

of small increase in income that would be spent rather than saved). It is also not assured, as the classical economists would have us believe, that by lowering interest rates, the increased savings would all be invested as individuals may hold back the savings for various precautionary reasons – what Keynes called "liquidity preference" factor. Thus, if the income saved is not spent, the effect is again to reduce demand for goods and services, i.e., the effective aggregate demand and, in turn, reduce output and employment.

- **State intervention:** The view that while government budget is to be balanced in good times, it would have to be unbalanced in times of distress and depression gained currency. The excess of expenditure over revenue would help to boost and sustain demand and employment. This was to be one of the main planks of Keynesian prescription to tide over the crisis. However, Keynes was not the first to suggest such a policy. Sweden, which too faced the impact of the crisis, had taken steps to minimize the hardships caused to the people and to uplift the economy by setting up farmer and consumer cooperatives and support to agricultural prices. And Sweden developed a well-knit social security system. Behind these measures were a band of young economists and scholars such as Gunnar Myrdal, Bertil Ohlin and Erik Lundberg among others. These developments had its echo in Britain and the US.
- **The New Deal:** Following the great depression, **through** most of the 1930s, the US Federal administration ran substantial deficit. Though public expenditure went up, the initial steps were aimed at attempts to push up prices of farm and industrial products.

And in 1933, the US, under President Franklin Roosevelt, started the New Deal programme with projects to provide work and financial assistance to large number of people who had lost their jobs. The government resorted to borrowing and spending for public purposes to boost investment and employment. Spending was directed towards providing direct relief, public works and public employment through various government agencies. Though the federal revenues fell far short of expenditures and deficit rose to 4.2 per cent of the Gross National Product (GNP), these harsh measures were justifiable in the prevailing circumstances. As early as 1933, Keynes had urged President Roosevelt on these lines but the final intellectual thrust came in 1936 with the publication of ***The General Theory.*** As if a sort of premonition, in 1935 Keynes wrote to George Bernard Shaw, the well-known litterateur and a Fabian socialist, in response to a letter from the latter: "To understand my state of mind, however, you have to know that I believe myself to be writing a book on economic theory which will highly revolutionise – not, I suppose, at once but in the course of the next ten years – the way the world thinks about economic problems." Prophetic words, indeed, because it had a cataclysmic impact on economic science for the next three generations for it to be called "Keynesian Revolution".

The Impact of Keynes

In the impact it had on economic thinking and practice, ***The General Theory*** can be placed on the same pedestal as Adam Smith's ***The Wealth of Nations*** and Karl Marx's ***Capital***. With Keynesian economics came a whole new branch of study called "macroeconomics" which looked at an economy in its entirety and as whole universe, in contrast to studying it in parts as what was termed "microeconomics".

Keynes viewed the system and its components such as income, consumption, savings and investment in aggregate. Aggregate demand plays an important role in determining the level of real output. The level of investment is not determined by the rate of interest, and investment need not necessarily equal savings as Classical economics assumed and Say's Law, which held ground for a century, had contended. The resulting disequilibrium could lead to high level of unemployment which is to be set right by boosting aggregate demand primarily through fiscal policy measures by the government.

In brief, Keynes' theory centres round four variables – income, consumption, savings and investment. Income is disposed of by way of consumption or savings. And savings would be utilized for investment. Keynes put these components in mathematical form as follows:

$Y = C + I$, where Y is the aggregate income, C the amount spent on consumption and I is the amount (capital) invested. Further,

$S = Y - C$, i.e., savings (S) is aggregate income (Y) minus the amount spent on consumption.

From the above, it follows that $S = I$ or savings equals investment. But in reality, the two may not always equal because they are influenced by diverse factors. Savings depend on income and by what Keynes called propensity to consume or save (liquidity preference). Whereas investment depends on dynamic factors like population growth, demand, technological progress, etc. If more (or less) money is withheld from consumption than is being utilized for investment, it would cause downward or upward swings in the flow of aggregate income resulting in depression or boom in the economy. Unlike classical economists, Keynes argued that an economy does not necessarily find its equilibrium at full employment and there could be shortfall in demand and underemployment and recession which calls for government spending to sustain demand and revive the economy.

With Keynes' incisive analysis of an economy's structure and working, many new concepts became part of the economics lexicon. These include terms like:

- **Marginal propensity to consume** which is the proportion of small increase in income that would be spent rather than saved.

- **Marginal efficiency of capital** is the internal rate of return. It refers to the rate of return over cost expected from the production of an additional or marginal unit.
- **Aggregate demand** is the sum of all expenditures within an economy which constitutes gross domestic product (GDP). It includes consumers' expenditure on goods and services, government spending, investment, exports of goods and services less expenditure on imports. After Keynes introduced the concept, economists have studied how far the level of aggregate demand affects total level of output and growth.
- **Liquidity preference** is the desire to hold money (liquid cash) rather than other forms of wealth like stocks, bonds, etc.
- **Multiplier** is the extent to which national income increases due to increase in expenditure. Public spending or government expenditure generates income in the hands of people in the form of wages, salaries, payments to suppliers. They, in turn, spend it generating further incomes and so on. At each stage, a proportion of income will be spent and a proportion saved depending on marginal propensity to consume and save. This works in a cyclical pattern.
- **Pump priming** is the injection of small amounts of government spending or stimulants, into an economy under depression with the aim of boosting business confidence and reviving private investment on a substantial scale. This policy was adopted following the Great Depression of the 1930s and financial crisis of 2007-08.

The General Theory was a highly technical and intractable work even for serious students of the subject and quite of a few commentaries came to be published to explain its terse content and make it more intelligible. Prominent among them were ***A Guide to Keynes*** by Alvin Hansen, ***The Economics of John Maynard Keynes*** by Dudley Dillard, ***The New Economics*** edited by Seymour Harris and ***The Keynesian Revolution*** by Lawrence Klein. These works introduced the complex concepts in Keynesian theory to readers in a more comprehensible manner.

- **Marx and Keynes**

In some respects, there is semblance between the propositions put forth by Karl Marx and Keynes. As already pointed out earlier, both rejected the validity of Say's law – which classical theorists swore by – and which presupposed assured and unfailing demand for all that is produced and the impossibility of over-production in the system.

- **Business cycles:** Keynes did not challenge Marx's assertion that the capitalist system was susceptible and vulnerable to crises such as unemployment and economic instability. Keynes not only admitted that there could be shortfall in demand and supplies remaining unsold, thereby affecting further production and causing unemployment but showed how the classical theories had no answer to remedy them. Marx also had spoken of under-consumption which forms an essential ingredient in Keynes' analysis in the form of decline in aggregate demand being one of the causes of economic depressions. But in Marxian analysis, neither under-consumption nor over-production are the only causes for recurrence of business cycles. According to Marx, the balance between the various stages of production and exchange and realization of value is an accident under the crude unstable conditions of capitalist system which contains a number of insoluble contradictions.

Marx has analysed the process of circulation of capital in his work, ***Capital*** and argued that the unity between the cycles of production and consumption could be disrupted due to seasonal factors resulting in idle men, materials and money at some stages of production. According to Marx, if equilibrium and stability in the economy is to be maintained, the produce of consumption and capital goods industries should be purchased by different sections of the population who share the total income. Consumption by the masses is constrained by poverty and limited purchasing power and inequitable distribution of income. In Keynesian analysis, the factors behind crises would be low propensity to consume, unequal distribution of income and high degree of propensity to save (liquidity preference).

- **Future of Capitalism:** But where Marx differs from Keynes and other theorists is in regard to the prospects for, and future of, capitalism and the role of class struggle. Marx contended that capitalism is a transitional stage in the evolution of economic order. Economic system has moved from feudalism to capitalism and would eventually move to socialism. He visualized the working class being subjected to exploitation and increasing misery with long hours of work, low wages and other working conditions. In the end, capitalism would falter and collapse due to its own internal contradictions. However, these doomsday Marxian predictions have been largely disproved by the developments in later periods.

  The formation of trade unions and advancements in technology has not only improved the methods of production, productivity and the overall output, but also the working conditions of the labour class itself. And industry bodies, workers' organizations and governments working together in a co-operative spirit of "tripartism" has helped to ameliorate the conditions of workers in regard to wages, housing, health, and education benefits to the workers and their families.

Welfare economics

Though the subject of "welfare" came into more prominence in Economics with the writings of economists of the 19th century like Marshall, Pareto and Pigou, it has its roots in the concepts of "utility' and "utilitarianism" which figured in the works of Classical economists. Later, "welfare economics" developed as a distinct branch of study with wider connotations such as standard of living, quality of life, capabilities and functionings, access to public goods, removal of inequalities, poverty alleviation and social justice. To put it differently, it is that branch of Economics which seeks to promote and evaluate economic policies on the basis of their impact on the well-being of the community.

The term 'welfare' means well-being, happiness and prosperity. It also stands for satisfactory state and health of a person or community. A 'welfare state' means a social system whereby the state assumes primary responsibility for the well-being of its citizens, by means of government-run health and social security systems. The Scandinavian countries of Norway, Sweden and Denmark are held up as prime examples of ideal welfare states.

♦ **Measurement and Comparison issues:** Earlier theorists viewed 'welfare' as the sum total of "utilities", satisfactions and benefits accruing to all individuals in the economy. Later, economists pointed out problems in measuring utilities and satisfactions of individuals, and difficulties in interpersonal comparisons of satisfactions derived by different persons or the state of well-being of two or more individuals.

  To overcome this limitation, an economic policy is judged from the test: "Which market structures and arrangements of economic resources across individuals and productive processes will maximize the sum total utility received by all individuals or will maximize the total of consumer and producer surplus across all markets?" Welfare economics seeks the economic state that will create the highest overall level of social satisfaction among its members.

♦ **Utility and Utilitarianism**

  The concept of utility and utilitarianism was a dominant theme in the works of early theorists of the 18th century. These concepts, which lie at the root of welfare economics, have been the subject of much debate and given to varied interpretations. In essence, "utility" in economic sense means "the pleasure or satisfaction derived by a person from consuming goods or services". Achieving it is the ultimate goal of all economic activities, but its scope goes beyond mere acquisition and use of material goods.

  - **Jeremy Bentham (1748-1832):** who was one of the main proponents of utilitarianism described it as that which augments or diminishes the happiness of a person. It is a complex concept as there can be no precise measure of utility and interpersonal comparisons of utility also poses problems. It is also "subjective" because what makes some people happy, say a film or a work of art or an item of food, may appeal to someone and make the person happy while the same may not generate happiness for another person.

Utilitarianism is a concept which stands for maximisation of the sum of utility, defined in terms of pleasure and pain, in the community as a whole. It applies to a government which aims at ensuring "the greatest happiness of the greatest number" as Bentham put it. It strives to maximise the welfare of people. This concept was further advocated by later scholars in welfare economics like John Stuart Mill, Alfred Marshall, Francis Edgeworth and A C Pigou.

- **Pareto Efficiency:** Vilfredo Pareto (1848–1923), an Italian engineer-economist, is famously known for the postulate known as 'Pareto optimal' which indicates the state of an economy in which no one can be made better off without someone being made worse off. In a state of Pareto efficiency, social welfare is maximized when no resources can be reallocated to make one individual better off without making at least one individual worse off.

  However, in a society with gross inequalities and concentration of wealth, promoting economic and social welfare, as modern states are attempting, necessarily requires redistribution of wealth, incomes, and resources from one group to another in varying degrees and proportions. Such redistribution may be carried out through fiscal measures – taxation – or through outright legislation as was the case with land reforms in India after independence, when ownership of land, in whole or in part, was transferred from the owners to the tenants. Such redistribution does make some groups worse off while trying to make some others better off.

Modern approach to Welfare

The concept of welfare has come to acquire a much wider dimension than what it encompassed till 1950s. It is no longer viewed through the narrow prism of monetary terms or wealth. Till some decades back, development was assessed based mainly on growth in gross domestic product (GDP) and per capita income (PCI). But it was seen that even though GDP and PCI showed impressive growth, they were not getting distributed in a fair and equitable manner. Development experience in many countries has shown that even with increase in incomes, large sections of people were left behind in the process and many of them continued to be trapped in poverty and acute deprivation.

- **Human development:** This led many economists and international development agencies to redraw the parameters to judge development based on various other social and economic indicators and assess improvement in the 'quality of life' on a much broader plane. These parameters included literacy and schooling levels, life expectancy, birth and death rates, extent of poverty and deprivation prevailing, access to safe drinking water and sanitation, gender equality, per capita income, etc. in the country. Based on these, the Human Development Index (HDI) is calculated. International bodies like the UNDP ranks countries according to HDI in three groups – High, Medium and Low Human Development. Such a comprehensive approach takes into account not only individual welfare but welfare of a community as a whole and helps in formulating better policy initiatives to ameliorate the living conditions of people.

  The Human Development Reports being brought out by the UNDP since 1990 has created greater awareness among all countries, especially the developing nations, to focus on improvements in the "quality of life" of the people.

- **Early study:**One of the earliest approaches to assessing development and welfare of the people was made by Sten Johansson of Sweden who conducted Swedish Level of Living Survey in 1968. This survey covered aspects such as health and access to health care, diet and nutrition, employment and working conditions, education and skills, housing and family and social integration. This survey was followed by similar surveys in other Nordic countries.

  It must be stated that leading modern welfare economists like Gunnar Myrdal, Kenneth Arrow, Amartya Sen, Martha Nussbaum, Jean Drèze, among others, have done commendable work in the domain of welfare economics. International bodies like The World Bank, UNDP, UNICEF, etc. have also contributed considerable amount of research and literature on development and welfare economics and have done much practical work in advancing the cause of welfare and reduction of poverty and inequality in collaboration with member-countries in the United Nations system.

All these efforts have pushed the frontiers of Welfare Economics to new heights and brought about perceptible improvements in the lives of disadvantaged and vulnerable sections, especially in The Third World. According to the World Bank, the global extreme poverty rate fell to 9.2 percent in 2017 which is equivalent to 689 million people living on less than $1.90 a day. But still, at higher poverty lines, 24.1 percent of the world lived on less than $3.20 a day and 43.6 percent on less than $5.50 a day in 2017 which points to the dire need for more welfare measures.

Welfare and Happiness

As stated earlier, in mainstream development and welfare economics, '*output of goods and services*' and '*per capita income*' were for long considered as the measures of progress. Later, many other parameters were added to it, and the broader concept of '***quality of life***' was developed to arrive at a more meaningful measure of progress. Still later, the element of '***happiness***' has been added to reckon a nation's progress in a still more realistic manner. Goodness and happiness have been considered as guides to human well-being and advantages enjoyed by people.

- **Bhutan's Happiness Index:** A landlocked country, spread over 46,500 square kilometres, Bhutan was a self-contained rural economy with sustainable relationship with nature. The process of modern development in Bhutan started in 1961 when it opened up to the rest of the world by ending the era of isolation.

  Since 1972, Bhutan has adopted the concept of **'Gross National Happiness'** (GNH) which implies that sustainable development should take a holistic approach towards notions of progress and give equal importance to non-economic aspects of well-being. GNH has influenced Bhutan's economic and social policy and it uses it as a measurement tool to create policy incentives for the government, NGOs and businesses of Bhutan to increase GNH.

- **GNH concept:** The GNH Index includes both traditional areas of socio-economic concern such as living standards, health and education and less traditional aspects of culture and psychological well-being.

  It is a single number index developed from 33 indicators under nine domains based on a multi-dimensional methodology known as Alkire-Foster method.

- **Alkire-Foster method**: The Alkire-Foster (AF) method involves counting the different types of deprivation that individuals experience at the same time, such as a lack of education or employment, or poor health or living standards. These deprivation profiles are analysed to identify who is poor, and then used to construct a multidimensional index of poverty (MPI). To identify the poor, the AF method counts the overlapping or simultaneous deprivations that a person or household experiences in different indicators of poverty. The indicators may be equally weighted or take different weights.

- **Bhutan's GNH concept:** The concept of GNH rests on four pillars:
  - Good governance;
  - Sustainable socio-economic development;
  - Cultural preservation; and

- Environmental conservation.

The 33 indicators are statistically reliable, are normatively important, and are easily understood by large audiences. Within each domain, two to four indicators are selected. Within each domain, the objective indicators are given higher weights while the subjective and self-reported indicators are assigned far lighter weights.

♦ **Bhutan's progress:** Bhutan has since been making significant progress as will be seen from the following facts:

- By 2000, over 90% of the population had access to primary health care and gross primary enrolment reached 72%.
- Life expectancy at birth which was 66 years in 2000 has gone up to 70.6 by 2017.
- As per UNDP's Human Development Report, 2018, Bhutan, with a population of only 0.8 million in 2017, Total Fertility Rate (TFR) has come down from 2.6 in 2005-10 to a healthy rate of 2.0 during 2015-20 period.
- As for literacy, during 2006-16 periods, literacy rate of females in Bhutan was 84.5 per cent and that of males was 90.4 per cent.
- Further, 95 per cent of children of primary school-age and 84 per cent of children of secondary school-age were undergoing education during 2012-17 period.

UN on GNH

The GNH approach has received international recognition. In 2011, the United Nations unanimously adopted a General Assembly resolution, introduced by Bhutan with support from 68 member states, calling for a "holistic approach to development" aimed at promoting sustainable happiness and wellbeing. This was followed in April 2012 by a UN High-Level Meeting on "**Happiness and Wellbeing: Defining a New Economic Paradigm**" designed to bring world leaders, experts and civil society and spiritual leaders together to develop a new economic paradigm based on sustainability and wellbeing.

Mathematical School and Quantitative studies

Many of the economic theories have also been analysed and studied with the aid of mathematical tools by many economists. Besides, many statistical methods have wide application in economic studies and policy making. Mathematical Economics and Econometrics are now distinct branches of study and are applied to solving practical problems in competitive strategies in business and government, economic planning, transportation, international trade, industrial production, marketing, etc. Professor Samuelson, who was with MIT, pioneered in studying problems in these areas using mathematical tools. Some of the areas in which these tools and methods are used are discussed below.

Inter-sectoral Studies

The interdependence of the various sectors of a country's economy has been studied by many economists. One of the earliest attempts in this area was by Richard Cantillon (1680-1734), an Irish banker who studied the economic process and circulation of wealth.

Cantillon was followed by François Quesnay (1694-1774), the Physiocrat, to whom reference was already made earlier. Quesnay's *Tableau Economique* (Economic Table) and *Maximes* (1758), a commentary on it, identified three classes of society and showed how transactions flowed between them. The three classes were landowners, farmers and others. Only the agriculturist class created any surplus product (value) while the others merely produced what they consumed. This was the first attempt at constructing an **input-output model** of the economy at a macro level. Further progress in this field of study had to await the development of matrix algebra and still later computerisation.

Similar was the study by Karl Marx (1818-1883) who, inspired by the work of Cantillon and Quesnay, analysed the class structure of societies and the way in which economies produced goods and services. The class structure of a capitalist state was such that there is division between capitalists and the labouring class. The value of labourers to the capitalists in the production process is greater than what the capitalists pay labourers for their services. This is what Marx calls 'surplus value' which only the labourers provide and which the capitalists appropriate. The desire to maximise profits and wealth induce capitalists to invest in labour-saving machinery and thus the share of plant and machinery in investment rises in relation to wages.

Input-Output Table

Quesnay's *Tableau* later led to a major contribution by Wassily Leontief (1906-1999), an economist at Harvard, who developed the Input-Output table. The inter-relationships between different sectors of a modern economy were complex and had to be studied with a theoretical structure which would serve as a basis for policy making. Leontief made this possible with his input-output analysis. The economy is viewed as an integrated system involving flows and transfers between different sectors. Each sector absorbs output from other sectors and its production, in turn, is used up by other sectors for further processing or ends up in final consumption. These flows are depicted in a rectangular table as an input-output matrix. Leontief's work, which won for him the 1973 Nobel Prize for Economics, has wide application and use in national income accounting, the Goods and Services tax (GST) system and inter-industry studies.

Income distribution and Inequality

This is an area where mathematical-cum-statistical tools have been used. Max Lorenz (1880-

1962), an American economist, devised a graphical representation of variables like incomes, employment and population called Lorenz curve to study the extent of inequality.

- **Lorenz curve:** The data of cumulative percentages of population in a frequency distribution are plotted in a graph against cumulative percentages of incomes or employment. A straight line rising at an angle of 45^0 on the graph indicates perfect equality, say, 10% of the population have 10% share of the income or 10% of the firms employ 10% of the labour force and so on. But if 10% of the population have 60% share of the total income and 90% of the population have a share of only 40%, it is an unequal and skewed distribution. In such cases, the graph will show a curvature below the 45^0 straight line and the degree of curvature will be greater the greater the inequality.
- **Gini coefficient:** A related concept is Gini coefficient developed by Corrado Gini (1884-1965), an Italian statistician to study the degree of inequality in income levels. If in a frequency distribution, the Lorenz curve coincides with the 45^0 straight line, the Gini coefficient and G, G = 0 implying perfect equality. And at the maximum value of G =1, it will be complete inequality.

Index numbers: Index number is a statistical device which is widely used for measuring the changes in the value of variables such as prices of commodities, cost of living, volume of production in different sectors in an economy, etc. It measures changes in the magnitude of a group of related variables. Index numbers are expressed in terms of percentages between different periods/years. The value of the base period is given the index number 100 and the index numbers of other periods will be in proportion with it. If for a selected period the index number is 200, it means that the value is double that of the base period/year. Thus, it helps to gauge how far the value of variables has changed over time.

Statistical surveys

Statistical surveys play a vital role in economic policy making. Such surveys are conducted in a number of fields such as consumer expenditure, household expenditure, income levels, family budgets, industrial and agricultural production, etc. It is also used in the fields of banking, insurance, trade, transport, market surveys on products, etc.

There are well-defined methods of collecting data, preparing questionnaire, selecting target groups and sampling techniques. The analysis of such data provides vital inputs for formulating policies. The decennial Census conducted in India is one of the largest such exercises and it captures voluminous data through door-to-door collection on a wide range of parameters.

Econometrics

This is a field in which mathematical models are created to study relationships between economic variables, test the validity of the hypotheses derived and assess the strength of different independent variables. For instance, how the quantity demanded of a good is related to or dependent on income and price – demand may be related positively on income and negatively on price. Econometrics uses the statistical concepts of correlation and regression between the variables. The relationship is studied over a period of time (time series analysis) or between different subjects (cross section analysis).

- Ragnar Frisch (1895-1973), a Norwegian economist, was a pioneer in this field of testing of hypotheses in economics. He coined the term '*Econometrics*' and founded the Econometrics Society to promote studies in the domain.
- Another dominant figure was Jan Tinbergen (1903-1994), a Dutch economist, who formulated important ideas on economic planning and policy in Netherlands. Frisch and Tinbergen were jointly awarded the first Nobel Prize in Economics in 1969 for "having developed and applied dynamic models for the analysis of economic processes".

Other contributions: Other notable contributions in the field of mathematical economics were those by Cournot, Edgeworth and Walras as outlined below.

- **Antoine Cournot** (1801-1877), a Professor of Mathematics and Mechanics in France, set in mathematical form the theory of firm and using calculus showed how a monopolist would maximize profit when the output is at the level at which marginal cost is equal to marginal revenue. He also showed how monopoly would lead to duopoly (two sellers) and oligopoly (many sellers). His work did not receive much recognition until Marshall developed the theories later.
- **Francis Edgeworth** (1845-1926), a Professor of Political Economy in Oxford, published papers on The Pure Theory of Monopoly and The Theory of Distribution. He served on a Committee to do a study on Index Numbers and made significant contributions in the development of statistical techniques.
- **Léon Walras** (1834-1910), who occupied the Chair of Economics at the University of Laussane, did much original work on the utility theory and developed a mathematical model of an economic system in which all consumers maximized utility and all firms were perfectly competitive. Such an economy will be in unique and stable equilibrium.

Economic Forecasting

Another important area in econometrics is economic forecasting. Such forecasting is done in respect of a wide range of activities pertaining to an economy – likely levels of production, price trends, employment and trends in national income, GDP, etc. Corporates rely on it for making business decisions. Governments undertaking planning create various scenarios for allocation of resources for different sectors and assess likely impact and outcome of growth. It also helps formulating taxation policies. Forecasting is widely used in meteorology and predicting weather patterns.

- **RBI and Price forecasts:** For instance, the introduction of new Consumer Price Indexes (CPIs) in India in 2011, viz, All India CPI-Combined, CPI-Rural and CPI-Urban helped to provide a nationwide retail price index that captures the inflation faced by households, i.e., cost of living inflation. The new CPIs have a comprehensive coverage across regions as well as commodity groups including services. Since October 2013, the Reserve Bank of India has started providing indicative projections of inflation in terms of the broader CPI-Combined. To make price forecasting more robust, the RBI conducts 'Inflation Expectations Survey of Households' (IESH) with wide coverage and methodological improvements, including in sampling design. The survey elicits qualitative and quantitative responses from households regarding their expectations on changes in price levels and inflation three months ahead as well as a year ahead. These surveys provide useful inputs for formulating monetary policy stance of the Reserve Bank.

  With the advent of computers, the task of forecasting has become more sophisticated than it used to be when done manually. Computers can analyze far more numerous factors and variables at a time, and at a much faster speed, and study and assess their likely interactions and possible outcomes which has made the task of forecasting easier.

  Economic forecasting, however, by its very nature, is not infallible. The interrelationships between the variables such as government expenditure, consumer demand, interest rates, market forces, etc. are dynamic and keep changing and are often unpredictable. Statistical analysis of them based on their behaviour in the past and past observations may not hold good in changing circumstances. Notwithstanding the limitations, forecasting serves as a useful and handy tool for businesses and governments to draw up plans and policies for the future.

Indifference curve

Francis Edgeworth (1845-1926) was one of the first to give an account of 'Indifference Curves' relating to consumer's choice in his work, *Mathematical Psychics : An Essay on the Application of Mathematics to the Moral Sciences*. An indifference curve on a graph shows combinations of two goods that give the consumer equal satisfaction and utility. Each point on an indifference curve indicates that a consumer is indifferent between any combination of the two goods and all points on the curve give him the same satisfaction. As income increases, the individual can afford more commodities and can have more choice and hence will shift to a higher indifference curve. A consumer's prefrences over all bundles of commodities can be shown by a family of (multiple) indifference curves which is called 'indifference map'.

Revealed preference

As the classical theory of consumer behaviour based on utility was criticized as it was difficult to quantify utility in precise terms, Paul Samuelson (1915-2009), the American economist at MIT, came up with the theory of 'Revealed preference' which asserts that the best way to measure consumer preferences is by observing their purchasing behaviour. The theory assumes that consumers are rational and have considered a set of choices before making a decision to purchase what is best for them. The preferred option could change based on price, income and budget constraints. This theory, which has been further refined by other economists, is found to be a useful method for analyzing consumer behaviour and choice empirically.

Linear programming

Linear programming is a mathematical technique to optimise operations or activities and achieve the best outcomes. As resources and time are scarce and finite, optimising them is critical. Linear programming is used for obtaining the most optimal solution for a problem, such as maximising profit or minimising cost within the given constraints. It is widely used in mathematics, business, economic studies, and for solving engineering problems. Industries that use linear programming models include transportation, energy, telecommunications, and manufacturing.

The technique could be applied to manufacturing, to calculate how to deploy labour and machinery so as to minimize the cost of operations. In industry, it is used to decide the optimum mix of inputs which will give maximum output at least material cost. It could be applied in high-level business operations, to decide which products to sell and in what quantity in order to maximize profit. In the case of projects, it helps to make strategies to make project team to work efficiently for ensuring on-time delivery. It could also be applied in logistics to decide how to utilize resources to get a job done in the least amount of time.

It is useful in modeling diverse types of options in planning, scheduling and routing in transportation to find the shortest route between two points. Or using this method, a delivery agent could assess different routes for going to different destinations and then come up with the shortest route.

Applications of linear programming were first seriously attempted in the late 1930s by the Soviet mathematician Leonid Kantorovich in manufacturing schedules and by the American economist Wassily Leontief in economic studies but their work was ignored for long. Later, during World War II, linear programming was used extensively to deal with transportation, scheduling, and allocation of resources subject to certain restrictions such as costs and availability.

- **Quantitative studies**

A major accomplishment during the early part of the 20th century was the development and application of statistical methods and tools to study economic trends at macro level. It would take forward the ideas initiated as far back as the 18th century by François Quesnay (already referred to earlier) who worked out the ***Tableau Economique***. Prominent among those who worked in this area were Wesley Mitchell, Simon Kuznets and Wassily Leontief. **(On Wassily Leontief, see under Input-Output Table in the section on Mathematical School).**

Wesley Mitchell (1874-1948)

Mitchell, who served in the Universities of California and Columbia, was one of those who emphasized the use of statistics as a tool for the study of economic trends and measurement of changes in factors like output and prices. He broke new ground in showing how inflation and deflation impacted differently on different kinds of price and income levels. His major work was a statistical study, ***Business Cycles*** (1913) in which he showed business cycle as a continually occurring phenomenon divided into phases and showed the history and pattern of cycles which occurred in the US with available figures.

Mitchell and NBER: Mitchell went on to head the **National Bureau of Economic Research (NBER)** in the US from its inception in 1920 where he built a large collaborative team of experts who worked on two main areas – estimation of National income and analysis of Business cycles. The former measures the total annual product of the economy over long time series showing its sector-wise origins and distribution while the latter analyses the fluctuations in economic activity with their causes and effects on the economy. Together they present a total picture of the behaviour of the economy.

NBER under him published two pioneering works – ***Business Cycles: The Problem and its Setting*** (1927) and ***Measuring Business Cycles*** (1946), a voluminous technical study on the methods of measurement adopted in the research. In their study, a cycle is shown as a complex phenomenon in which all series do not go up or down at the same time. Every month some activities attain the "***peaks***" while others decline to their "***troughs***" and thus expansion and contraction run simultaneously. By analysing the differences in the timings and amplitudes of fluctuations in the interrelated parts of the economic system, one can see how the pressures during the expansionary phase bring on recessions and the uneven contractions in various parts pave the way for revivals.

Simon Kuznets (1901-1985)

Kuznets, who was born in Russia, went to the US in 1922 and studied Economics at Columbia University. After serving in NBER, he moved to the Universities of Pennsylvania, John Hopkins and finally Harvard where he remained till 1971. An influential exponent of Keynesian system, Kuznets made significant contributions in developing applied econometrics by compiling macroeconomic statistics. His forte was the study of the relationship between distribution of income and the growth in per capita income. A proposition he put forth in a paper "***Economic Growth and Income Inequality***" suggested that inequality in income distribution would increase during the early rapid phase of economic growth and would later reduce thus forming an inverted U-shaped curve which came to be known as **Kuznets curve**. However, this finding has not been conclusively established when later studies were done with more extensive data. Inequality has continued to rise even in later stages of growth in advanced and even emerging economies.

- **Post-Keynesian economics**

  The validity of Keynesian theories, which held good during the 1930s and 1940s during the period of depression and the World War II, came to be questioned by economists in later years. There appeared many prominent economists in the post-Keynesian era who made notable contributions to theory in the changed circumstances of the times. **While many were adherents to Keynes, there were many critics of his ideas too.**

  Three renowned economists of modern era are Joseph Schumpeter, Paul Samuelson and Milton Friedman who have made notable contributions to economic thought and theory.

Joseph A. Schumpeter (1883-1950)

Schumpeter who briefly served as Minister of Finance in Austrian Republic after World War I, taught in various universities in Europe before moving to the US where in 1932 he joined Harvard and served there till his demise in 1950. He has many publications to his credit, the more important ones being the trilogy:***Theory of Economic Development*** (1912), ***Business Cycles: A theoretical, historical and statistical analysis of the capitalist process*** (1939) and ***Capitalism, Socialism and Democracy*** (1942). His final publication, a massive tome, ***History of Economic Analysis***, which was unfinished, was edited by his wife and published posthumously in 1954.

Schumpeter was essentially an economic historian and social reformer. Though an intellectual giant and regarded as one of the greatest economists of the 20th century, commonly bracketed with such giants as Keynes, Friedrich von Hayek and Milton Friedman, Schumpeter's work failed to gain the recognition it deserved.

- **On Creative destruction:** He is best known for his theory of "creative destruction – the idea that the capitalist system progresses by constantly revolutionising its economic structure. In his work on the theory of development, Schumpeter extols the power of the entrepreneur as a force for social change. He assigns central role to the entrepreneur who, aided by bank credit, would undertake innovation, develop new product or a new process of production. This would lead to a new equilibrium which would be inevitably disrupted by the next innovator and further change in the production process. This process sets in motion a wave of change each time rendering the old plant and method of production obsolete and replacing them with something superior. Thus, continual progress would happen under capitalism sending gales of "creative destruction" through the economic system.

Schumpeter defines innovation as the setting up of a new production function, to denote the application of new ideas to the production process. For him, the "perennial gale of creative destruction," whereby new products and processes displace old ones, is far more important than price competition among existing firms and products.

This idea of "The Process of Creative Destruction" is further elaborated in Schumpeter's work, *Capitalism, Socialism and Democracy* wherein he says: "The opening up of new markets, foreign or domestic, and the organizational development from the craft shop and factory to such concerns as U.S. Steel illustrate the same process of industrial mutation – if I may use that biological term – that incessantly revolutionizes the economic structure from within, incessantly destroying the old one, incessantly creating a new one. This process of Creative Destruction is the essential fact about capitalism. It is what capitalism consists in and what every capitalist concern has got to live in."

- **On Monopoly:** Schumpeter also spoke in support of monopoly on the ground that a monopolist, who is free from competition, would have more incentive for innovations in his enterprise thus aiding the growth process. In his view, the competitive world, lacking in creativity and motivation to innovate, is sterile. Though this view did not find acceptance, a similar view with variations was to be found in the works of Edward Chamberlain and Joan Robinson as discussed earlier. While Schumpeter did not talk of "animal spirits" in economy, of which Keynes spoke, he envisioned a dynamic society that was constantly being pulled away from a state of equilibrium by the relentless efforts of daring innovators whose remarkable successes would trigger an outburst of fresh investment activity.

- **On business cycles:** His work on ***Business Cycles*** was outstanding as economic and business history but judged by his aim of explaining complex cyclical patterns, the book was not a success and the poor reception it got disappointed him bitterly. Its publication in 1939 was overshadowed by Keynes' ***The General Theory*** which appeared three years earlier and created a virtual revolution. Had Schumpeter's work come out prior to Keynes', it would have gained from the enormous interest everyone had in business cycles which was in play with full force from early 1930's. Instead, it appeared just at the outbreak of World War II which aggravated economic problems to which Keynes' work offered solutions, but Schumpeter's could not be readily adapted.

Simon Kuznets, one of the pioneer theorists on macroeconomics, business cycles and national income, praised Schumpeter for having written a "monumental treatise" that raised all the right questions. But Kuznets observes that Schumpeter's work was more of a "journey through the realm of business cycles and capitalist evolution," disclosing "numerous hypotheses, diverse historical facts, and statistical experiments." Cycles are quantitative phenomena and required tight quantitative analysis but instead of robust numbers, Schumpeter had presented "an intellectual diary".

Paul A. Samuelson (1915-2009)

Samuelson was educated at the University of Chicago and Harvard where he took his Ph.D. in 1941. In 1947, he was appointed to the Chair of Economics at MIT (Massachusetts Institute of Technology). He also served as an economic adviser to the US government. His two early works, *Foundations of Economic Analysis* (1947)and an introductory textbook, *Economics* (1948), are considered as classic works and soon became very popular among the academic community.

Samuelson has contributed to many areas of economic theory through impactful mathematical techniques which he employed essentially as puzzle-solving devices. The wide areas he covered include the dynamics and stability of economic systems, theory of capital and public expenditure, welfare economics, the analysis of public goods, enunciation of the theory of "revealed preference" in consumption analysis and incorporation of the theory of international trade into general economic equilibrium theory.

- **On international trade:** Based on the Heckscher-Ohlin (H-O) model of international trade, Samuelson showed how the increase in the price of a commodity can raise the income of a factor of production used most intensively in producing it – for instance, a labour-intensive product or a capital-intensive product. This led to him formulating the factor price equalisation theorem" according to which free trade in commodities narrows the differences in commodity prices between countries and the incomes (prices) of factors of production (capital, labour, etc.) are also brought in line. Free trade enables and incentivise free movement of factors of production.
- **Multiplier-Acceleration interaction:** In macroeconomics, he was the first to show the interaction between "multiplier" and "accelerator" principles. The multiplier effect refers to how an increase in initial investment would result in multiple times increase in economic activity. Thus expenditure, say by the government, will lead to increase in

incomes of households and firms who, in turn, will save part of that income and spend the rest which will generate more incomes and so on. The increase in government expenditure would raise incomes, demand and output, through the multiplier which in turn, through the accelerator, would lead to increase in investment and incomes. This process of interaction would happen in a cyclical pattern boosting economic growth. This interaction and consequent spurt in economic activities plays an important role in business cycle and economic growth theories.

Milton Friedman (1912-2006)

Milton Friedman is one of the most influential economists of the post-Keynesian era. Starting with the National Bureau of Economic Research in 1937 and later with US Treasury during World War II, Milton joined the University of Chicago in 1946 where he served as Professor till 1977. Finally, he was with Hoover Institution at Stanford University till his demise in 2006.

Friedman was a staunch votary of the Classical competitive and free market economy and defender of Marshallian tradition. He was fiercely opposed to Keynesian approach of focusing on aggregate demand and state intervention to support the economy, policies which stood in good stead during the Depression and post-World War II period. Friedman's ideas attracted other free market thinkers and they came to be called the Chicago School. They favoured downsizing government, deregulation in most areas of the economy, liberalizing rules for businesses, slashing corporate taxes and increased money supply to ensure growth. On the lines of Adam Smith, he urged for maximum freedom for individuals and markets to function.

Friedman's major contribution was to develop the "quantity theory of money" enunciated by Irving Fisher (1867-1947) in 1911. Fisher had given the equation $MV = PT$ where P stands for general price level, M for average quantity of money available for transactions during a particular period of time, V for its velocity of circulation and T for transactions. Friedman extended the equation to include other variables such as rate of interest and wealth and made statistical tests to measure the factors determining the demand for money.

Friedman was primarily a monetarist and argued for monetary policy and control of money supply to keep prices in check. According to Friedman, money supply is to be increased in a limited way to meet the needs of trade for transactions – the T in Fisher's equation – so that prices remain stable. But Friedman's theory also did not fully explain what caused the movements in prices, whether it was the changes in money supply or the volume of trade and transactions. Also, in the modern economy, "money" is a complex entity with not only hard currency and bank deposits but items like credit cards, bank credit, etc. which also add to purchasing power and circulation of money.

Friedman's view that it was not desirable to control the economy using "stabilization policy" has found acceptance. Stabilization policy involves government action at reducing fluctuations in national income by taking steps to expand demand to tackle unemployment and reduce demand when there is threat of inflation. Such a policy was in vogue after the Second World War in most of the western economies.

- **Assessment of Friedman's policies:** Friedman's contention that markets are efficient and be left free while the State which is riddled with inefficiency and corruption is to play a minimal role has come in for criticism. Such a policy was followed in the US during the regime of both Ronald Reagan and George W. Bush. From 1980, the US economy did grow but not fast enough. Not only that, the increase in income and wealth were distributed inequitably accentuating inequalities. There was hardly any "trickle-down" effect as a result of which while those in the top income brackets kept benefiting, the lower income groups suffered. Large swathes of American population were left behind in the process deepening the inequalities. It showed in stark manner the need for the government to play an active role, balance the needs of different sections, provide the required stimulus to activate the economy and ensure adequate levels of employment and income to all sections.

Economics, a Dismal Science?

The notion that Economics was called a "dismal science" by Thomas Carlyle (1795-1881), Scottish historian and essayist, has been a subject of debate. Carlyle was an avowed proponent of power as the main organizing force of society, and was strongly opposed to classical liberalism, particularly the legacies of Adam Smith and John Stuart Mill.

The popular belief is that Carlyle started using the phrase "dismal science" in response to the "dismal" views of 19th-century scholar and economist, Thomas Malthus, who predicted that unchecked growth in population in comparison to the growth in food supply would result in mass starvation and deaths. In 1839, Carlyle did write that Malthus' views on population and preventive check to stem its growth were dreary and dismal, without hope for this world.

But Carlyle used the phrase "dismal science" in 1849 while discussing the labour situation in the West Indies where the white planters were complaining that they were unable to obtain enough labour at the prevailing wages and conditions of work to carry on their business. Carlyle contended that the Negroes would have to be servants of the Whites who are born wiser than them. And compulsion, rather than market forces, should regulate the supply of labour on plantations in the West Indies. He argued that "laws of servitude" should take precedence over the "laws of supply and demand" which he deprecated.

Carlyle also used the term "dismal science" in a derogatory manner later referring to the political scene which, according to him, had certain unwelcome features like universal suffrage, ballot boxes, etc. which he disapproved of.

It was his contemporary John Stuart Mill, the economist and a liberal and progressive thinker, who strongly contested Carlyle's despicable attitude. Mill pointed out that the "law of the strongest", which Carlyle upheld and advocated was "the law against which the great teachers of mankind have in all ages protested". Mill added that history teaches us that human improvement comes not from the tyranny of the strongest but from the struggle against such tyranny.

And it did not take long for the system of slavery to be put an end to. In 1863, Abraham Lincoln issued the historic "Emancipation Proclamation" in the US declaring slavery to be unlawful. And it dealt a severe blow to regressive ideas held by persons like Carlyle.

Economic science

Economic science has come a long way over the last two centuries since Adam Smith published his path-breaking work in 1776. It has responded to changes in the society and evolving situations like rapid industrial and economic progress. It deals with a wide range of themes of concern to common people such as production and distribution, income and wealth, banking, taxation and trade to mention a few. The subject has been nourished and embellished by many progressive ideas like welfare economics and development studies which have opened new vistas for further study and research. Yet, the discipline faces many challenges as the world grapples with problems like unemployment, poverty and inequality not only within nations but between nations. It is further complicated by issues like globalisation, protectionism, geopolitical crises and threats posed by factors like climate change and environmental degradation.

A V Balakrishnan

April 2021, Bengaluru

NATIONAL INCOME AND RELATED CONCEPTS

> Human development is measured in this Report not by the yardstick of income alone but by a more comprehensive index – called the human development index (HDI) – reflecting life expectancy, literacy and command over the resources to enjoy a decent standard of living.
>
> – UNDP in 1990 *Human Development Report.*

Topics Covered

- *National income*
- *GDP, GNP, NNP, GVA*
- *GDP Deflator*
- *Current and Constant price*
- *Estimating national income*
- *Method of Estimating National Income in India*
- *Rationale for Changing Base Year*
- *Recent debate on the National Accounts of 2015 and quality of data*
- *Parallel economy*
- *Limitations of national income.*

1. Explain the concepts of National Income and GDP. Also, differentiate between nominal and real GDP.

Ans. **National income** is one of the important measures of the economic performance of a country, notwithstanding some of its deficiencies and limitations. Supplementing national income figures with data relating to its sectoral composition gives a comprehensive view of the structure of an economy and structural changes in the economy over a period of time. The usefulness of national income estimates critically depends upon the reliability of the sources, and quality, of the data and the method of collection. (See recent 'Debate on the Estimation of National Accounts' in a later section here).

➢ **Gross Domestic Product (GDP):** Gross Domestic Product is the sum total of the value of final goods and services created within the geographical boundary of a country in a given period, say, a year. To put it differently, GDP measures the aggregate production of final goods and services taking place within the domestic economy during a given period.

- GDP includes incomes earned by foreigners within the domestic economy but excludes incomes earned by the citizens in a foreign country.
- GDP growth rate is one of the important barometers of the performance of a country.

Nominal and Real GDP:Nominal GDP is GDP evaluated at current market prices while Real GDP is GDP evaluated at constant prices. (See Question 2 below further on this).

2. Differentiate between Current versus Constant Prices.

Ans. GDP can be measured at prices prevailing during the year for which it is assessed i.e., at **current** prices, or when calculated over a number of years, at **constant** prices of one particular **base year** in the past.

- Current prices are influenced by changes in prices and inflation whereas constant prices discount the effect of price changes occurring after the base year.
- When national income is estimated over a period using current prices, it would not give a proper measure of the real increase in production of the country or the growth of the economy. Computing national income at constant prices of one particular **base year** provides a more realistic measure of the growth of the economy.

3. What do understand by the term GDP Deflator?

Ans. The ratio of nominal GDP to real GDP indicates how the prices have moved from the base year to the current year. While calculating the nominal and real GDP of the current year, the volume of production is the same. Hence if these measures differ, it is only due to the difference in the price level between the base year and the current year. The ratio of nominal GDP to real GDP is called GDP Deflator and is noted as : Nominal GDP /Real GDP.

The above ratio multiplied by 100 will give GDP deflator in percentage terms.

4. What is Gross National Product? How is it different from GDP?

Ans. **Gross National Product (GNP):** Gross National Product = GDP + Factor income earned abroad by the domestic factors of production minus Factor income earned by the factors of production of the rest of the world in the domestic economy (NFIA).

- In other words, GNP = GDP + Net factor income from abroad (NFIA).
- **Net factor Income from Abroad (NFIA):** Net factor Income from abroad is Factor income earned by domestic factors of production employed abroad minus Factor income earned by factors of production of other countries employed in the domestic economy.

➢ **GDP and GNP** include depreciation on fixed assets whereas Net Domestic Product (NDP) and Net National Product (NNP) exclude it. In other words, NDP = GDP minus Depreciation and NNP = GNP minus Depreciation.

  - **Depreciation refers to the** wear and tear or depletion of fixed capital (or fixed assets).
  - **Difference between GDP and GNP :** GDP includes incomes earned by the citizens and foreigners within the domestic territory of a country but excludes incomes earned by the citizens in a foreign country. Whereas in GNP, the aggregate income made by the citizens of the country within the domestic economy and in foreign economies is included while the income earned by foreigners in the domestic economy is excluded.

5. Define National Product and National Income.

Ans. The **national product** measures all goods and services arising out of economic activity during a given period while **national income** is the sum of those incomes which are derived directly from the current production of goods and services called "factor incomes". In other words, national income is the money value of income paid by the producing units to factors of production such as labour and capital.

- An important feature of the measure is that it takes into account only the value added at each stage of processing and excludes "intermediate" products thus avoiding duplication.
- National income does not include other forms of income such as old age pensions, education grants, unemployment benefits, gifts, etc., which are not payments for services rendered in the course of production. They are paid out of factor incomes and being payments for which no goods or services are received in return, they are termed as **transfer payments.**

6. What is the meaning of the term Value added ? Define Gross Value Added.

Ans. Value added is the net contribution made by firms in an economy. It is the value of the production of the firm minus the value of intermediate goods (like raw materials or other inputs) used by the firm in production. In this method of calculating the aggregate value of goods and services, there will be no double counting of items used in production.

- **Gross value added (GVA)** will include depreciation or consumption of fixed capital, i.e., wear and tear of machinery, etc. whereas **Net value added (NVA)** will exclude depreciation.

7. Briefly describe the methods of Estimating National Income.

Ans. There are three methods by which National income is estimated, namely, the Product method, Income method and Expenditure method.

➢ Although national income can be measured in any one of the three alternative approaches but if a complete analysis of the economy is the objective, then it should be measured by all the three different approaches.

(a) **Product or Value Added Method :** The product approach GDP measures the sum of value added of all goods and services produced within the country's territory (sum of output minus intermediate goods). If investment made to replace fixed assets which have depreciated is added, we get **Gross Value Added**.

To measure national income at the point of production, the method generally followed is to divide the whole economy into a given set of economic activities and to estimate the total value of output and the corresponding value of inputs of raw materials and services used for production and then arrive at the value added of each sector. In the case of services, value added is measured in terms of the total amount of money paid in return for the services received minus the cost of inputs like expenditure on transport, advertisement, and other miscellaneous services.

To avoid distortions in the estimation of GDP due to price level changes, GDP at constant prices or real GDP is computed.

(b) **Income Method** : The income (value added) generated through the production activity is distributed between the factors of production. This method measures the total income earned by the factors of production, that is, land (rent), labour (wages and salaries) and capital (interest and profits) within the domestic boundaries of a country and net income from abroad. However, transfer payments such as education grants, unemployment benefits, gifts, etc. are not included.

(c) **Expenditure Method :** This measures the total expenditure incurred by all entities on goods and services within the domestic boundaries of a country. GDP (as per Expenditure method) = C + I + G + (X-IM) where C is Consumption expenditure, I : Investment expenditure, G : Government spending and (X-IM) is exports minus imports, that is, net exports.

- ➢ **Equivalence of the three methods :** The national income by definition is the same whether measured at the point of production or at the point of income generation or at the point of final utilisation (expenditure). In other words, the total of net output, income flows and final expenditure will be identical. The significance of each arises from the fact that they reflect total operations of the economy at the levels of three basic economic functions, namely, production, distribution and disposition (utilisation).

8. Briefly examine the concept of Base Year in an economy. What is the rationale for changing the base year ?

Ans. For examining the performance of the economy in real terms, estimates of the macroeconomic aggregates like Gross Domestic Product (GDP), National Income, consumption expenditure of Government and individuals, capital formation, etc. are prepared at the prices of selected year known as '**base year**'. As mentioned earlier, the estimates at the prevailing prices of the current year are termed as "at **current prices**", while those prepared at base year prices are termed as "at **constant prices**". The comparison of the estimates at constant prices, which means 'in **real terms**', over the years gives the measure of real growth.

- ➢ **Rationale for Changing Base Year :** With the gradual improvement in the availability of basic data over the years, a comprehensive review of methodology for national accounts statistics has constantly been undertaken by the CSO with a view to updating the data base and shifting the base year to a more recent year.
  - This exercise is in line with the best global practices to capture key information more accurately. A base year is carefully chosen because of the critical impact it has on data.
  - It is also done to take into account the structural changes which have been taking place in the economy and to depict a true picture of the economy through macro aggregates like Gross Domestic Product (GDP), National Income, consumption expenditure, capital formation, etc.

9. The 'black money' generated in India results in a 'parallel economy' causing much disruption to the economy. What are the factors behind generation of black money and outline the measures taken to solve the problem?

Ans. The unaccounted black money virtually works as a parallel, underground and shadow economy in India, disrupting the mainstream economy and negating, to a great extent, the policies aimed at social and economic development.

- Unaccounted money is also misused by terrorists, drug cartels and anti-social elements posing serious threat to the security of the country. Illegal activities like smuggling and counterfeiting of currency notes compounds the problems.

- There is no precise estimate of black money circulating in India and stashed abroad by Indians. Studies carried out between 2011 and 2014, at the Government's instance, by three leading institutions in India came up with widely varying estimates. According to a report tabled by the Standing Committee on Finance in the Lok Sabha in June 2019, the estimates of unaccounted wealth stashed abroad by Indians, as estimated by these institutes, ranged from US$ 216.48 billion to US$ 490 billion between 1980 and 2010.

➢ **Factors behind 'black money' generation**

- India has a high amount of cash in the economy when compared to most other countries of the same level and much of this cash is in high-value denominations. When ₹ 500 and ₹ 1,000 notes were demonetised in 2016, they constituted about 86 per cent of all currency in circulation. Such a large percentage of cash and transactions done in cash enables generation of unaccounted wealth.
- Funding of political parties during elections or even at other times, not done in transparent manner, with source of funds not declared generates black money.
- As per the studies by the three institutes referred to above, the sectors which account for bulk of the unaccounted income and wealth are real estate, bullion, mining, tobacco, gutkha, film and education besides in assets held in gold, jewellery, etc. These are convenient means of hiding unaccounted money and illicit wealth by transactions being carried on undetected and/or by under declaration of their actual value.
- Misdeclarations in imports and exports helps in stashing wealth offshore in countries which are tax havens or which have secretive banking systems.
- Part of the undisclosed wealth abroad is routed back to India through illegal means, variously known as 'round-tripping', 'money laundering', hawala, etc., and is invested in various companies and sectors in India without being detected.
- Evading payment of taxes by under declaring incomes and through loopholes in tax system results in unaccounted wealth.

➢ **Measures to combat unaccounted wealth and curb parallel economy**

Based on suggestions put forth by various committees and enlightened citizens to curb the menace of black money and undisclosed wealth, the government has been taking various measures. These include:

- Transparency in funding political parties for election purposes or otherwise; though an 'electoral bonds' scheme has been introduced for this purpose, this is still not a fool-proof solution and needs further tightening as being demanded by the Election Commission and some political parties;
- Transparency in all works, contractual or otherwise, awarded by any governmental or public bodies using state funds;

- The 'Real Estate Regulation Act' (RERA) passed is effective in promoting transparency and curbing black money transactions in the real estate sector and protecting the interests of the customers providing much relief to those acquiring properties;
- Strictly enforcement of Know Your Customer (KYC) norm, mandating the mention of PAN number for all transactions above a certain threshold, inter-linking of Aadhaar, bank accounts, PAN, property registration, and Income Tax returns which can detect any illicit transactions;
- The 'Fugitive and Economic Offenders Act' has proved to be effective in deterring economic offenders who commit frauds and seek shelter abroad. Now India is receiving information in such cases from 146 countries, including Switzerland which has been the epicentre for stashing illicit and unaccounted wealth by Indians for long. India has since concluded agreements with 80 countries for automatic exchange of information and is now receiving information about those who have stashed black money abroad;
- The 'Direct Benefit Transfer' (DBT) scheme under which funds from more than 400 schemes are being directly credited into the accounts of beneficiaries has helped to eliminate middlemen and leakages of funds. During the 2014-18 period, as much as ₹7.30 lakh crore have been transferred through DBT. So far, not only has DBT prevented ₹1.41 lakh crore from being siphoned off, it has also enabled deletion of names of about 8 crore ineligible beneficiaries in various schemes. The government propose to further expand DBT. This measure being implemented at Central and State levels will go a long way in curbing unaccounted money;
- Encouraging and enforcing 'Cashless transactions' above a certain threshold and in the Real Estate sector and for transactions in jewellery where undisclosed wealth could be invested without being detected and converted as legitimate funds;
- Tightening tax collection system to plug loopholes which result in tax evasion;
- Voluntary declaration of undeclared wealth under amnesty schemes introduced periodically though this has had only limited success compared to the extent of black money in the economy;
- In a drive against black money, during the 2016-18 period, registration of 3.5 lakh suspicious companies has been revoked and 4.25 lakh company directors have been disqualified from functioning.
- Though the 'demonetisation' scheme executed in 2016 did not achieve its desired objectives fully, it has helped to formalise the economy to some extent and, along with other corrective measures being taken, it has raised awareness among people of the risks of stashing illicit wealth and punitive measures that may follow from it.

10. The concept of National Income, though an important measure of economic activity, has its limitations. Identify and explain briefly the limitations.

Ans. National income (also called 'Social Accounting') is an important measure of economic activity in a country. But it suffers from the following limitations.

- **Errors in measurement:** Data has to be collected with great care and accuracy at all stages and sources of collection. Errors in collection and estimation could lead to wrong conclusions being drawn and policies drawn up based on them could be misplaced. This problem will be more acute in countries where the statistical systems have not been developed and perfected to the required extent.
- **Unpaid activities :** National accounts measure only paid activities and exclude unpaid activities and the work performed by housewives, domestic help, etc. If over a period of years there is a rise in such activities, then this will not be reckoned in the estimates. Then the figures will underestimate the level of GNP and they will not be comparable over different years.
- **Impact of price changes :** The extent of price changes and inflation can be calculated fairly accurately over a short period, such as one year, but it is much more difficult to do so over a long period.
- **New products and Services :** As new products and services appear and existing ones may become obsolete, national accounts may not show the true picture unless its composition is constantly updated to reflect the changes.

  For instance, with the '**Internet economy**' getting entwined with the 'traditional economy', contribution of the former needs to be properly reckoned. India's digital economy generates about $ 200 billion in value which is 8 per cent of India's GVA in 2017–18 from IT and business processes, e-commerce, electronics manufacturing, digital payments, direct subsidy transfers (DBT), etc.

  So too, the '**gig economy**' is a new evolving sector whose contribution needs to be properly assessed. It involves short-term contracts or freelance work, project-based workers and temporary or part-time hires as opposed to permanent job.
- **Parallel economy :** The existence of 'parallel, underground' economy and the black money which circulates in it in large measure, goes unaccounted in the official estimates. It impacts the assessment of national income and can distort policies drawn up by the government.
- **Economic growth and Externalities :** Economic growth and national income assessments ignores externalities like misuse and exploitation of natural resources, environmental degradation, pollution, etc. which cause harm to society in the long run.

- **National Income and Welfare :** Apart from the aspects mentioned above, there are limitations of national income as a welfare indicator. Increase in national income and GDP is, by itself, no indication of increase in people's welfare and there is no direct correlation between them. This is especially so where there is a high degree of inequality in income distribution, and when the majority of people do not benefit from the increased economic output.

> So far, the economic distance (between nations) has been usually measured by the conventional yardstick of per capita income – this handy expression, in easily remembered numerals, of a country's economic well-being. Economists and statisticians have now produced such estimates for nearly every country. Politicians and planners have seized upon this mystic entity. They have used it as an infallible indicator for diagnosing ills, prescribing remedies, and for measuring progress. But the wider the use of these estimates, the more subject they have become to critical evaluation.
>
> – Surendra J. Patel (1923-2006), economist with UN & UNCTAD, *Economic Distance between Nations: Its Origin, Measurement and Outlook*, 1964, Economic Journal, London.

ECONOMIC GROWTH AND HUMAN DEVELOPMENT

An affluent society, that is also both compassionate and rational, would, no doubt, secure to all who needed it the minimum income essential for decency and comfort........... To secure to each family a minimum income, as a normal function of the society, would help ensure that the misfortunes of parents, deserved or otherwise, were not visited on their children. It would help ensure that poverty was not self-perpetuating.

— John Kenneth Galbraith *(1908-2006), economist in The Affluent Society (1958).*

Topics Covered

- *Underdevelopment*
- *Colonialism and its impact on development*
- *Economic Growth and Human development*
- *Sustainable development and SDGs*
- *India's challenges in SDG implementation on economic and social fronts*
- *India's water resources and looming crisis*
- *Gender issues in development*
- *Gender budgeting.*

1. What are the characteristics of underdeveloped countries? Explain briefly the characteristics.

Ans. In development studies, nations are generally placed in three categories. Underdeveloped countries are referred to as 'Third World' nations to distinguish them from the advanced countries with high incomes (the First World) and other middle-income nations which have attained medium development. Most of the underdeveloped countries are in Asia, Africa and Latin America.

The following are the characteristics of an underdeveloped country with high levels of poverty.

1. **Lack of or inadequate resources and/or their misallocation:** The nation may have inadequate natural resources required for development in relation to its population. Or, even having such resources, it may not be having the capability to exploit them for want of technical knowhow, skilled labour or capital. Another factor could be that the resources are not allocated judiciously with major part of it appropriated by a small section of the population leaving the bulk of the population deprived of their benefits.

2. **Overpopulation:** A concomitant factor may be that the nation is overpopulated with limited land area and resources. The case of India is one such example with ever increasing, and high density of, population which neutralises the fruits of development. Such countries have to take effective measures like family planning to control population. China is another country with high population which adopted steps to check population growth though it has been criticised later for adopting a coercive 'One-child per family' policy for nearly three decades.

4. **Predominance of agriculture and lack of industrial development:** Agriculture is the predominant sector employing bulk of the population, with little or inadequate development of industrial and the services sectors. There is a limit to which the increasing population can be sustained by the agricultural sector. All the advanced countries have achieved economic success and prosperity by the growth of manufacturing following the Industrial Revolution in the 18th to 20th centuries. The expansion of factories helped to shift surplus labour from agriculture to industry and still later to the services sector which offered more productive occupations.

   India which has about 50 per cent of her population engaged in agriculture is facing the challenge of under-employment and disguised unemployment in the sector. India is finding it a difficult to expand the manufacturing sector though the services sector has shown healthy growth. In contrast, China which effected market economy reforms in 1980s has been able to become a manufacturing powerhouse and shift the surplus labour in the rural sector to industries and thereby lift millions out of poverty.

5. **Poor infrastructure:** Facilities such as roads, rail, ports, power supply, telecom, etc. are not adequately developed which are essential to support all other sectors. It may be due to lack of technical knowhow or capital or even poor governance.

6. **Shortage of capital:** Capital required for investment to utilize the natural resources available in the country, set up industries and develop infrastructure will be lacking. To overcome this, many of the under- developed countries have been supported with financial aid in the form of grants and loans by international aid agencies like The World Bank, the IMF, Asian Development Bank, etc. and also by bilateral aid from advanced economies.

7. **Low levels of literacy, education and health:** Social factors such as low levels of literacy, education and poor health of the people hold back development process. Infrastructure for education – schools, colleges, technical institutions – and

public health – hospitals and medical personnel – will be lacking. Poor health, sanitation, lack of safe drinking water will result in high rates of infant and under-5 mortality rates with infants dying before the ages of 1 and 5 years. It will also mean low life expectancy with people not having long life as prevalent in advanced countries.

8. **High level of unemployment:** For lack of development and job opportunities, there will high degree of unemployment. The problem will be accentuated by shortage of skilled labour and mismatch between jobs and skilled personnel available.

9. **Poor governance and Corruption:** Many underdeveloped countries suffer from poor governance and even corruption in administration which retards development. As a result, people and businesses are deprived of efficient public services.

10. **Low per capita income:** As a cumulative outcome of all the above-mentioned deficiencies, these countries have low level of national income and low per capita income.

2. Did colonialism retard the development of various countries which were under colonial rule and cause them to remain backward and poor? Justify your answer.

Ans. Many countries in Asia, Africa and Latin America were colonised by European powers – mainly Britain, France, Portugal and Spain – during the 17th and 18th centuries and their colonial rule spanned over two hundred years. It was only by the middle of the 20th century that most of the colonial nations could gain independence and that too after prolonged struggle.

It is pertinent to note that this was also the period when these western colonising powers forged ahead industrially, following the Industrial Revolution, leaving the colonised nations in the lurch.

Exploration and Exploitation: What began as exploratory voyages by the European powers to the East and the New World ended up in their conquering and subjugating the native rulers, setting up trading outposts and establishing total political and administrative control.

Their primary aim was to exploit the rich natural resources which the colonies had and utilize them to feed the rapidly expanding industries in Europe. The colonies became convenient source of raw materials for the factories in Europe and also served as markets for dumping the finished, manufactured products from those countries. Thus, the colonies ideally served the economic interests of European powers.

The colonial powers followed a deliberate policy of not promoting industrial development of the colonies as that as that would have pitted their industries at home in direct competition with industries in the colonies which had the advantage of not only a wealth of natural resources but cheaper labour.

The trade policy was also discriminatory and skewed against the colonies by protecting the industries in Europe from competition and encouraging imports into colonies without any tariff barriers.

Impact on development: The above policies had far-reaching and deleterious impact on the colonies. Not only that their economic development was retarded but even in the social sphere of education and health, they suffered neglect. The policy of repression followed through administrative and military means over the colonies to keep them under subjugation held back their progress, the effects of which are still visible even decades after these nations gained independence.

➤ **Post- colonial and Independence era**

It was only after these colonies emerged independent from the middle of the 20th century that they could embark on the path of economic and social progress.

Conclusion: Plethora of problems: Even as the western nations forged ahead and became prosperous over two centuries, the colonial nations languished under their exploitative rule. And by the time these countries gained independence, they had inherited a host of problems – overpopulation, stagnant agriculture, hardly any industrial development, and little progress in the critical areas of education and health. They were saddled with poor health and sanitation conditions, high mortality rates, low life expectancy, low literacy and educational standards, unskilled labour, etc. which continue to pose enormous challenges in their progress.

Under the weight of this historical burden, sizeable sections of the population in these countries were pushed to appalling levels of poverty. Even after six to seven decades, most of these underdeveloped and developing nations are struggling to lift millions out of poverty.

The big divide: There is a wide chasm now between the developed and the least developed countries (LDCs), also referred to as the North-South divide with the former – the developed nations – situated in the northern hemisphere and the latter in the southern hemisphere.

Though the advanced nations and international aid agencies are helping the LDCs in their efforts at socio-economic development, there is also friction on various international issues like global trading system, market access and tariff barriers, subsidies in agriculture, action on climate change, etc. in which the interests of the advanced nations and that of the underdeveloped countries come into conflict.

3. British colonial rule resulted in India's social and economic backwardness. Do you agree with this statement? Give reasoning for your answer citing specific instances.

Ans. Before the advent of the Europeans, though the primary occupation in India was agriculture, she had excellent capabilities and skills in manufacturing. By the end of the 17th century, India was the world's main producer of cotton textiles and had a substantial export trade to Britain as also to other European countries.

The Industrial Revolution, following a series of inventions which took place in the West, particularly in Britain, between 1740 and 1860 brought about a major transformation in industrial production, especially in the textile industry. The new factory system revolutionized the industrial methods and led to much higher productivity and lower costs of production. England's shipping opened up new markets and an unlimited supply of her manufactures found their way to India.

Competition from Britain: India, with her traditional manufacturing methods, could not withstand the intense competition from Britain. The native manufactures, handicrafts, and cottage industries, which had flourished gradually declined and were allowed to die. This threw lakhs of workers out of their occupation and impoverished them.

While hitherto, India exported many of these products to the West, the trend was drastically reversed. India became the exporter of raw materials to feed the factories in Britain and importer of finished goods.

Infrastructure development: Though the British promptly introduced railways, telegraphy and telephone and these did benefit India, these were done with a view to serve the interests of the colonial power. Railways helped various raw materials to be carried faster to the Indian ports from where they were shipped to Britain to feed the home industries. Telegraph and telephone enabled much faster exchange of communications and this enabled the British administration to keep a tight grip over the native population, in putting down any unrest or rebellion against their rule and it helped to prolong the colonial rule.

Deindustrialisation: Due to the policy of promoting the industries in Britain, there was a deliberate and affirmative policy adopted to discourage industrial development of India. Barring a few cotton textile and jute mills, there was virtually no industry despite the wealth of minerals India had.

Though Britain possessed the know-how of steel manufacture, no step was taken to build an iron and steel plant in India. The Bengal Iron Works, set up in 1870, could not withstand the competition from imported steel and the plant did not survive.

Whatever little industrialization that took place in India during the period was due to the initiative and enterprise of Indians. The Iron and Steel plant pioneered by Jamshedji Tata, opened in 1907 at Jamshedpur, and the few cotton and jute mills in the country were prime examples of this.

The British also deliberately neglected imparting technical education and managerial training to Indians. The managerial positions in the mercantile, finance and shipping sectors were controlled by British citizens thus keeping a firm control over them.

Absence of capital goods sector: Prior to independence, there were virtually no capital goods industries and the industries that came up were in the consumer goods sector. As a result, when India embarked on industrialisation after independence, she had to meet 90 per cent of the requirements of machinery through imports which placed a heavy burden on the limited foreign exchange reserves she had.

Drain on India's finances: The British also managed India's finances in such a way that led to transfer of wealth and income from India to Britain causing a heavy drain on the economy.

Skewed sectoral and employment pattern: The relative share of the three sectors, viz., Agriculture (the primary sector), Industry (the secondary sector) and Services (the tertiary sector) is an indicator of the progress of an economy.The more developed a nation is, the lesser will be the share of agricultural sector and greater the share of industry and services sectors, both in GDP and employment, i.e., the occupational pattern.

At the time of independence, the share of agriculture in India's national income was 49 per cent, that of industry and mining only 17 per cent and of services and construction sector 34 per cent. As for employment, agriculture accounted for 71.8 per cent of the total workforce, industry for 9.5 per cent, and services for 18.7 per cent.

Conclusion: A dismal picture: At independence, there was widespread and appalling poverty, low life expectancy, and abysmally low level of literacy. Literacy percentage was a mere 17 per cent, male literacy was 25 per cent and female literacy just 8 per cent.

Agriculture which was the preponderant occupation was in dire straits with heavy pressure of population on land, low yields, and high level of indebtedness of farmers. Due to decades of exploitation by the colonial administration, there was virtually no industrial development barring a few industries in steel and textile sectors. There was acute shortage of skilled manpower and a high rate of unemployment.

This state of the economy is to be attributed to the deliberate policy of Britain keeping India suppressed for two centuries not only in regard to economic development but even in the social sectors of education and health.

In short, India's condition at independence presented a dismal picture. Due to this historical burden and legacy, even after seven decades India is struggling to lift millions out of poverty. **(For more on this, see Question 6 in Chapter 14)**

4. Economic growth is not an end in itself but a means to achieve human development which should result in better 'quality of life' for all people. Do you agree with this statement? Justify your answer elaborating on what 'quality of life' means in development studies. (For more on this, see Question 6 in Chapter 14)

Ans. ➢ **Growth vis-à-vis Development:** Development economists draw a distinction between 'economic growth' and 'development' and to the fact that growth and development are not one and the same thing. Economic growth is not an end in itself but only a 'means' to an 'end', that is achieving human development and improving the standard of living and the 'quality of life' of the people.

The focus on economic growth began after many of the colonized nations gained independence in the 1950's and set out on the path of development. These nations were beset with major problems such as gross inequalities, appalling and persisting poverty, and lack of access for large sections of their population to quality educational and health facilities.

➢ **Focus on Human development and Quality of life:** Till about two decades back, economic development was assessed based mainly on growth in Gross Domestic Product (GDP) and per capita income (PCI). But this approach was found to be deficient because even though GDP and PCI may show impressive growth, they may not get distributed in a fair and equitable manner.

- Development experience in many countries has shown that even with increase in incomes, large sections of people were left behind in the process and many of them continued to be trapped in poverty and acute deprivation. Unless the increase in the national or per capita income or savings and investment translate into positive outcomes by improving the 'quality of life' of the people, it does not amount to development in the real sense. Some countries may score high on economic parameters like per capita income but may not necessarily be high on social parameters cited above.

➢ **UNDP on Human development:** These issues began to receive world's focussed attention after the UN Development Programme (UNDP) began in 1990 to highlight them through its annual Human Development Reports (HDRs), covering a wide range of socio-economic parameters and measuring the progress attained by member countries.

- **Quality of life:** The term 'quality of life' covers a broad range of socio-economic parameters such as literacy and educational levels, reduction in infant and maternal mortality, improved health conditions and life expectancy, level of poverty and deprivation, gender equality, empowerment of women, etc.
- The UNDP collects data on attainments on selected parameters such as literacy, schooling, life expectancy and per capita income of each country and calculates the Human Development Index (HDI) and ranks countries according to HDI in three groups – High, Medium, and Low Human Development. Besides, UNDP also assesses other aspects like level of poverty and deprivation, reduction in infant and maternal mortality, gender equality, empowerment of women, etc. to gauge the progress of countries.

- This is a holistic approach to development process and it has helped to sensitize governments, aid agencies, NGOs, etc. on the criticality of issues like inequality, poverty, illiteracy, malnourishment, lack of sanitation and poor healthcare, etc. which even now afflicts large sections of population the world over.

5. Briefly outline the efforts of the United Nations to give a thrust to human development through the 'Millennium Development Goals' (MDGs) and 'Sustainable Development Goals' (SDGs).

Ans. In 2000 and in 2016, the United Nations (UN) launched major initiatives at the global level to give a thrust to the development process and adopted two paths to be followed by the member countries, viz.,

- **Millennium Development Goals (MDGs)** started in 2000 to be achieved by 2015; and
- **Sustainable Development Goals (SDGs)** begun in 2016 to be achieved by 2030.

➢ The 'Millennium Development Goals consisted of eight goals to be achieved by 2015 with the active participation of member countries. The goals and the progress achieved, as assessed by the UN, was as follows:

- **Eradicate extreme poverty and hunger**: the number of people living in extreme poverty declined by more than half.
- The proportion of **undernourished people** in the developing regions fell by almost half.
- The **primary school enrolment** rate in the developing regions reached 91 percent, and many more girls were in school compared to 15 years ago.
- The **under-five mortality** rate declined by more than half, and **maternal mortality** came down by 45 percent worldwide.
- Remarkable gains have also been made in the **fight against HIV/AIDS, malaria and tuberculosis.**
- The target of halving the proportion of people who lack access to **improved sources of water** was also met.
- These were achieved by the concerted efforts of national governments, the international community, civil society and the private sector which generated hope and more opportunities for people around the world.

➢ The Agenda for 'Sustainable Development Goals' was started in 2016 with 17 focussed objectives to be achieved by 2030. All countries would work to achieve the goals taking into account their national realities, capacities and levels of development and respecting national policies and priorities. This Agenda is to be implemented for the full benefit of all, for today's generation as well as for future generations.

The goals set are as follows:

1. **End poverty** in all its forms everywhere currently measured as people living on less than \$1.25 a day and ensure that all men and women, in particular the poor and the vulnerable, have equal rights to economic resources.
2. **End hunger**, achieve food security and improved nutrition for all especially the poor, the vulnerable and infants, end malnutrition. and promote sustainable agriculture.
3. **Ensure healthy lives** and promote well-being of all; reduce the global maternal mortality ratio to less than 70 per 100,000 live births, reduce neo-natal mortality to at least 12 per 1,000 live births and under-5 mortality to at least 25 per 1,000 live births.
4. Ensure quality education and promote lifelong learning opportunities for all; that all girls and boys complete free, quality primary and secondary education leading to relevant and effective learning outcomes; increase the supply of qualified teachers.
5. Achieve gender equality, end violence against, and exploitation of, women and girls in the public and private spheres; ensure women's full and effective participation and provide equal opportunities for leadership and decision-making in political and economic spheres and public life.
6. Ensure availability and sustainable management of water and sanitation for all; provide safe drinking water; ensure sanitation and hygiene for all, especially women and girls, to end open defecation.
7. Ensure access to affordable, reliable, sustainable and modern energy for all; increase substantially the share of renewable energy.
8. Promote sustained, inclusive and sustainable economic growth, full and productive employment and decent work for all; achieve higher levels of productivity through diversification, technology upgradation, skilling and innovation; promote small and medium enterprises; ensure sustained growth of per capita income.
9. Build quality, sustainable and resilient infrastructure, promote inclusive and sustainable industrialization.
10. Reduce inequality within and among countries; progressively achieve and sustain income growth of the bottom 40 per cent of the population at a rate higher than the national average.
11. Make cities and human settlements inclusive, safe, resilient and sustainable; provide safe, affordable and sustainable transport systems; ensure safety on roads.

12. Ensure sustainable consumption and production patterns and efficient use of natural resources; halve per capita global food waste at consumer end; reduce food losses along production and supply chains, including post-harvest losses.
13. Take urgent action to combat climate change and its impacts: integrate climate change measures into national policies, planning and education and create greater awareness; implement the commitments under the United Nations Framework Convention on Climate Change; developed countries to mobilize collectively $100 billion annually by 2020 to meet the needs of developing countries for effective mitigation of environmental pollution and combat climate change.
14. Conserve and sustainably use the oceans, seas and marine resources for sustainable development; prevent and reduce marine pollution of all kinds, in particular from land-based activities, including marine debris and nutrient pollution; regulate and end overfishing.
15. Protect, restore and promote sustainable use of terrestrial ecosystems, sustainably manage forests, combat desertification, and halt and reverse land degradation and halt biodiversity loss; conserve forests, halt deforestation, restore degraded forests and increase afforestation; combat desertification, restore degraded land and soil, including land affected by desertification, drought and floods.
16. Promote peaceful and inclusive societies for sustainable development, provide access to justice for all and build effective, accountable and inclusive institutions at all levels; to reduce all forms of violence and related deaths; end abuse, exploitation, trafficking and torture of children; promote the rule of law and ensure equal access to justice for all; reduce illicit financial and arms flows; combat all forms of organized crime.
17. Strengthen the means of implementation and revitalize the global partnership for sustainable development; strengthen domestic resource mobilization; developed countries to fulfil their development assistance commitments; enhance North-South, South-South and regional and international cooperation on access to science, technology and innovation; work on capacity-building in developing countries to support national plans to implement all the sustainable development goals.

6. Discuss the challenges India faces on the economic front in achieving the targets under the United Nations' Agenda for Sustainable Development Goals (SDGs).

Ans. India has played an important role in the UN forum in shaping the Sustainable Development Goals (SDGs). Many of the country's national development goals are rooted in the SDGs and India is effectively committed to achieving the SDG targets.

India would perform reasonably well on the economic front in view of some of the ambitious schemes implemented in diverse sectors. But India faces two critical issues on the economic front in realizing SDG targets viz., eradicating poverty significantly and providing employment to millions of youth who are joining the labour force month after month. India's progress on the economic front and the challenges it faces are discussed below.

➢ **Infrastructure:**Infrastructure, consisting of transport and communications, which are vital for economic development has been a weak spot in India for long. Since the last two decades, India has made major strides in improving state roads and national highways, railways, ports, and inland waterways. Highways have been built to international standards with many amenities. Improvements are also being effected in transportation like mass rapid transport with Metros and city and town buses which will promote the use of public transport and help in reducing pollution. Telecommunication sector has been liberalised and upgraded resulting in rapid expansion of mobile telephony and broadband connectivity.

- **Rural roads:** The PM Gram Sadak Yojana (PMGSY), a major programme begun in 2000, for linking villages to nearby towns with all-weather roads has helped to energise villages with more economic activity. Upto March 2014, a total of 3.99 lakh kms of roads, including upgradation,was constructed providing connectivity to 97,838 eligible habitations. 1.53 lakh kms of roads was built under this programme between 2014 and June 2019.

  Benefits: Apart from building a durable asset and improving road connectivity in the villages, the scheme has resulted in the following beneficent changes:

- Better employment opportunities for the rural households as villagers had better access to nearby urban centres, besides working on road construction;
- Enabled women to step out of the house to take care of their farms because of better roads;
- More women taking up farm jobs enabled men to shift from farm to non-farm jobs;
- Impact on education as children in middle and high schools continued their schooling.

➢ **Power and LPG facility:** India is making concerted efforts to increase power generation to meet the needs of rapidly growing population and increasing economic activity. Here the challenge is to enhance the share of renewable energy like Solar and Wind and reduce dependence on Thermal power to meet the targets under the Paris Climate accord.

- **Ujjwala Yojana, a Unique scheme:** Out of more than 24 crore households in the country, about 10 crore households have been dependent on firewood, coal and dung cakes, which are harmful for health, for cooking and were deprived of LPG, a much cleaner fuel. The 'Pradhan Mantri Ujjwala Yojana' (PMUY), launched in 2016, was a major initiative to provide **LPG connection** to BPL families with financial support from the government.

- The LPG facility carried a subsidy element for all which caused heavy financial burden to the government. In a unique gesture, the Prime Minister gave a call to the well-to-do sections to voluntarily give up the subsidy so that the money saved could be used to 'light a flame in poor households'. Within a year, over one crore consumers gave up the subsidy which helped the State to save a substantial amount. Under the scheme, nearly 7.26 crore PMUY connections have been provided, a step empowering women in poor households.

➢ **Financial sector:** The following far-reaching schemes were launched since 2014 with a view to uplift and empower the poor and vulnerable sections:

- **Jan Dhan Yojana (JDY)** initiated into promote financial inclusion and extend banking facility to unbanked millions. By May 2019, there were 35.75 crore beneficiaries under JDY with deposits of ₹ 98,320 crore.
- **PM Mudra Yojana (PMMY) was** launched in 2015 to extend credit to small and micro-borrowers for Self-employment and income-generating activity and lift them out of poverty. Between 2015 and 2019, the loans disbursed under the scheme amounted to ₹ 12,50,494 crore. MUDRA refinances loan given by commercial banks, rural banks, cooperative banks and micro finance institutions.

➢ **Digitisation scheme:** This helps to improve governance in general at all levels and reach the beneficiaries of government schemes directly through Direct Benefit Transfers (DBT) thereby eliminating middlemen and scope for corruption. The Digital India programme connecting 2.5 lakh Gram Panchayats is going on apace. This will help to improve government services in the villages and empower people. By training millions of villagers in the use and operation of computers and other devices, it will enhance their skills and help to bridge the Digital divide in society.

119,122 Gram Panchayats have been connected by Optical Fiber and 3,89,000 Common Service Centres (CSCs) set up byJune 2019. CSC consists of Village Level Entrepreneurs who provide Digital Services to the people with the help of Internet and Technology. This project will give major boost to rural economy and rejuvenate it.

➢ **Agriculture:** The Green Revolution which spanned from the late 1960s till the early 1990s in two phases increased farm production to unprecedented levels and ushered in an era of prosperity for the rural sector as well as for the economy as a whole. But thereafter agricultural production decelerated and the farm sector has been under considerable stress due to stagnant output, unremunerative prices, rising input costs, credit crunch, droughts and crop losses, leading even to suicides of farmer. This is despite many supportive measures the state has been taking to alleviate the problems.

- Going ahead, more steps need to be taken as stated below to invigorate the sector:
- Expand irrigation facilities and ensure water conservation;
- Eliminate middlemen and ensure direct marketing of farm produce;
- Improve the terms of trade in favour of farm sector to ensure remunerative prices.
- Counter recurring climate changes by guiding farmers to go in for crops suited for likely weather pattern so as to avoid crop losses.
- Reduce post-harvest wastages by better storage and transport arrangements;
- Promote agro-based industries to improve incomes of rural families.

➢ **Poverty and Unemployment:** While the above measures have helped India to register impressive growth, still large sections – an estimated 22 per cent of the population – are still mired in poverty. Also, the 'quality of life' of not only those below the 'poverty line' but also of those who have been lifted out of poverty continues to be far from ideal. Their living conditions and access to public services like education, health, housing, sanitation and safe drinking water,etc. leave much to be desired despite the many anti-poverty measures implemented. With about one million youth joining the labour force every month, providing jobs for them has become a daunting task. As a result, unemployment levels remain unacceptably high.

- **Rural employment:** The Mahatma Gandhi National Rural Employment Guaranteed Scheme (MNREGS) started in 2005 has helped to provide employment and additional income to rural families while creating durable assets of value to the villages.

  India still has a long way to go to achieve the various targets under the SDG. Reviving the farm sector, boosting manufacturing, providing jobs and fulfilling the commitments under the Climate Change accord would be the main challenges India faces in the coming decade.

7. Elucidate the challenges India faces in the Social sector in achieving the targets under the United Nations' Agenda for Sustainable Development Goals (SDGs).

Ans. On the Social sector front – education, health, housing and sanitation – India faces enormous challenges and the country has a long way to go in achieving the targets set under the UN Sustainable Development Goals (SDGs) by 2030.These aspects are discussed below.

Though India has invested considerable amounts in Five-Year Plans in these areas over the last seven decades, there have not been commensurate results. These problems have been accentuated by the ever-increasing population which neutralises the improvements.

As a result, in the Human Development Index released by the UNDP, India ranks quite low – in the 2018 report, with HDI value of 0.640, India's rank in 2017 was 130 out of a total of 189 nations and was placed among nations in the category of Medium Human Development.

➢ **Education:** India has made much progress quantitatively by opening more schools and colleges and bringing down school drop-outs over the years. Yet, according to latest 2011 Census data, 84 million children do not go to school while 78 lakh children are forced to earn a livelihood even as they attend school.

  Children with disabilities: According to a UNESCO report, 72 per cent of children with disabilities (CWDs) between the age group of 0-5 years never got early education and just 61 per cent of such children between the ages of 5 and 19 attended any educational institution. There are fewer girls with disabilities in schools than boys with disabilities in school. The drop-out of such children increases as the level of school gets higher from primary to higher levels. Significant gaps, therefore, remain even though successive government schemes and programs have brought large numbers of children with disabilities into schools.

  - **Quality of education:** Besides, the quality of education imparted at the primary and secondary levels and facilities provided, particularly in government run schools, is below par and compares adversely with that in private schools accessed by the upper classes of society. Educational surveys have established these findings and the government has to make concerted efforts to improve these deficiencies.
  - **Literacy:** Even in regard to literacy, India, as per 2011 census, had attained total literacy percentage of only 74.04 with male literacy rate 82.14 and female rate 65.46. Hopefully, better results may be seen in 2021 census.

➢ **Health:** The situation in the health sector is even more disturbing. India's public health facilities which are accessed by the lower sections are woefully inadequate and inefficient. Problems like dearth of doctors (India's doctor-patient ratio is 0.79 as against 1:1000 prescribed by WHO) and para medics, shortage of beds and medicines and overcrowding are endemic in government run hospitals. These problems are even more pronounced in the health centres in rural areas. India's expenditure on health, as a percentage of GDP, has been stagnant at 1.3 per cent which is far below that in other emerging economies like Thailand and Brazil which devote more funds for public health. India plans to increase its public health spending to 2.5 per cent of GDP by 2025.

  Shocking instances of deaths of children, on a large scale, in government hospitals in some states point to the above mentioned deficiencies. Though in regard to other indicators like infant and maternal mortality rates and life expectancy, India has made steady progress over the years, more concerted action is required to fulfil the SDG targets.

- **Food and Nutrition:** Food and nutrition are two factors which vitally influence the health of the community. Both these have been weak links in India's development efforts. While India produces enough foodgrains needed and even keep large quantities as 'buffer stock', a sizeable section of the population at the bottom rungs suffer from lack of food and, even more so, nutrition. This is despite India running one of the largest Public Distribution System (PDS) for supplying essential food items at subsidised rates and even free to the very vulnerable sections. The PDS is beset with many deficiencies and corruption with diversion of PDS items to black market by the retail outlets. Both the Union and State governments are trying to improve the PDS system.

  These shortcomings are reflected in the health indicators of the population – high levels of under-5 child mortality, stunted growth and even deaths of children, maternal mortality and morbidity, etc. Inefficient operation of ICDS (Integrated Child Development Scheme), an otherwise ideal scheme to take care of children and lactating mothers with nutritious food, has adversely impacted on women and children. On the positive side, the government and some of the NGOs are providing midday meals to children in schools and nutritious diet to children in Anganwadis on a substantial scale. The immunisation programmes run on a mass scale for children have also been quite successful.

- **Housing:** This, along with sanitation and hygiene, is a critical factor which impinge of the state of health of the population and the quality of life. India has been executing massive housing programme for the poor and vulnerable sections in rural and urban areas. Under the erstwhile Indira Awas Yojana (IAY), since 1985 about 28.5 million houses were built in rural areas. And as of June 2019, a total of 1.53 crore houses have been built since 2014 in rural and urban areas under the PM Awas Yojana (PMAY).

  Providing homes in urban areas poses a greater challenge than in rural areas because of the higher density of population and limited land area available in urban areas – cities and towns – where overcrowding and slums are a common feature. Steady increase in urban population due to migration from rural areas aggravates the problem. The percentage of urban population has gone up from 17.97 in 1961 to 23.38 in 1981 and 31.16 in 2011 and is bound to increase further.

- **Sanitation and Hygiene:** These two issues have received more focussed attention in the last two decades than in earlier years. The Total Sanitation Campaign (TSC) started in 1999 aimed at accelerating sanitation coverage and make villages Open-Defecation-Free (ODF). But by 2011, only 28,000 panchayats could be made ODF. From 2014, under the Swachh Bharat scheme, a concerted campaign to provide a toilet in all households in rural and urban areas was pursued. With this, 10.15 crore toilets were constructed following a concerted campaign and 5,62,400 villages have been declared Open-Defecation-Free (ODF) by 2019. The problem in this context is ensuring availability of water and changing the mindset of people to use the toilet. The campaign also strives to keep surroundings in towns and villages hygienic, clean and green. A major challenge in this is disposal of waste and its scientific disposal.

➢ **Water Resources and Conservation:** India is facing a major, looming crisis in regard to water resource. A NITI Aayog report released in 2018 has painted a grim picture of the state of drinking water resources. The situation has been building up over the years due to the following factors:

- Rampant, unchecked exploitation of ground water resources;
- Increasing urbanisation, construction activity and loss of trees and green cover;
- Lack of proper systems for harvesting rainwater resulting in its overflow into the seas;
- Loss of lakes, ponds and tanks due to construction or other activities;
- Deforestation and felling of trees; and,
- Environmental degradation, erratic monsoon and climate changes resulting in frequent droughts and floods.
- **Jal Shakti Ministry:** Realizing the gravity of the situation, the Union government has formed a separate Jal Shakti (Water Power) Ministry in May 2019 to focus on water management and take remedial measures.The important tasks for the new Ministry are:
- Promote rain water harvesting and water conservation;
- Take up inter-linking of rivers under the National Perspective Plan (NPP);
- Implement scheme to provide piped water facility to all households.

➢ **Demographic challenge:** India's population has grown at a rapid pace in the last seven decades from 361 million in 1951 to 685.2 million in 1981 and 1210.6 million in 2011. India is also tipped to overtake China in the next few years to become the most populous country in the world.

As stated earlier, this rise in population has neutralised much of the fruits of development. Its impact is felt in manifold ways as discussed in foregoing sections – food and nutrition, health, mortality rates, education, unemployment and persisting poverty.

Though India now enjoys a 'demographic dividend' with 62.5 per cent of population in 2011 in 15-59 young, working age-group, this advantage places stress on the economy in finding jobs for this large segment, as the country is already experiencing.

- **Positive sign on India's demographics:** A positive sign is that India's population is slowing according to estimates put out by the U N Population Division in World Population Prospects (2019 Revision). India's fertility rate has been falling faster than predicted earlier. India's TFR (Total Fertility Rate) which was 2.4 in 2012 was down to 2.3 by 2013. TFR of 2.1 is the "Replacement rate" which means if every woman had 2.1 children on an average the population would remain the same.

  A significant fact is that the poorest states with the highest fertility rates are moving the fastest at reducing fertility. The TFR of 23 Indian States and UTs, including all in the south, is now below replacement level. Only Bihar and Meghalaya still had TFR above 3 children as of 2016.

  As a result, the year by when India's population would overtake China's also keeps changing. This healthy trend in India's population would greatly help in overcoming the various challenges the country faces on other multiple fronts.

8. Water resources and water management is a major issue confronting India. Identify the reasons for this and outline the steps the government is taking to overcome the problem.

Ans. India accounts for a meagre 2.4 percent of the world surface area, has about 4 per cent of world's freshwater resources while it supports a whopping 17.8 percent of the world population.With each passing year, scarcity of water is becoming a major, looming crisis for India.

Looming water crisis: Many parts of urban and rural India are reeling under severe water crisis. The *Composite Water Management Index*, a report of NITI Aayog released in June 2018, has highlighted the critical nature and extent of the problem. The following facts will reveal the gravity of the situation.

- About 75 per cent of households do not have drinking water at home; and 84 per cent of rural households do not have piped water.
- Close to half the country, about 600 million people, face severe water scarcity year after year.
- Water levels in India's major reservoirs have fallen to 21 per cent of the average of the last decade.
- India sorely depends on ground water for drinking water purposes and irrigation. But as much as 54 per cent of the country's groundwater is getting depleted faster than it being replenished.
- 70 per cent of India's water is contaminated and the country is ranked 120 among 122 countries in the 'Water Quality Index'.

- 21 major cities, including Delhi, Bangalore and Hyderabad, are expected to soon reach zero groundwater levels, affecting access for 100 million people.

➢ **Factors behind the crisis**

India's water crisis arises from a mix of economic, geographic, and political factors. The major reasons for the water crisis are:

- Pressure of ever increasing population;
- Over-use of water in farming, especially where water and electricity for irrigation are subsidised. While agriculture is crucial to India, the power subsidies extended to the sector and Minimum Support Prices (MSPs) given to a range of crops may be resulting in indiscriminate and inefficient use of water causing the steep decline of ground water levels;
- India uses almost twice the amount of water to grow crops as compared to China and United States;
- The country is heavily dependent on a few major river systems, like the Ganges, the Indus, Brahmaputra, Godavari, Krishna, etc. for its water for agriculture, irrigation and drinking purposes. The level of groundwater utilisation is relatively high in their river basins;
- Rice and sugar which are produced in surplus and exported by India are both water-guzzling crops and may be adding to the water crunch;
- Migration of people from rural areas to urban centres, increasing urbanisation and overcrowding in cities and towns exacerbating demand for water;
- Haphazard land use, unchecked building construction activity on a large-scale resulting in loss of trees and green cover;
- Construction over lake areas and wetlands leading to extinction of lakes, ponds, etc.;
- Indiscriminate exploitation of ground water, which is the most important source of water in the country, and lack of effective water conservation methods is resulting in water tables dipping in most parts of the country;
- Contamination and pollution of rivers, lakes and streams due to a variety of factors is a major problem which adversely affects the supply of safe drinking water. Discharge of effluents by industries into rivers, overuse of fertilizers and pesticides in farming and abuse of rivers by public all cause pollution. These have to be checked effectively and brought under control by various regulatory authorities.
- India critically depends on monsoon rains to replenish most of the country's water sources – underground aquifers, lakes, rivers and reservoirs. But monsoon is becoming increasingly erratic and unpredictable due to global warming and environmental degradation;

- Droughts are becoming more frequent, creating acute problems as about 55 per cent of agriculture is rainfed. Interstate disputes over water and rivers aggravate the problem.

➤ **Remedial measures initiated and proposed by the Government**

There are several strategies to be adopted to attain sustainable development of water resources in India. The government has initiated several measures as detailed below:

- **Separate Jal Shakti Ministry:** Realizing the gravity of the situation, the Union government has formed a separate **Jal Shakti Ministry** in May 2019 to deal with all matters relating to water in an integrated manner. The ambit of this Ministry will encompass all aspects relating to augmenting and conserving water and ensuring its equitable distribution.
- **Jal Shakti Abhiyan:** Beginning with the pre-monsoon season in 2019, the government has launched this programme, an intensive water conservation campaign built on citizen participation to create a mass people's movement to accelerate water conservation across the country.
- **Rain Water Harvesting and Conservation of water:** The **National Water Policy** formulated in 2012 advocates rainwater harvesting and conservation of water. It also enjoins preservation of river and river bodies to be undertaken in a scientific manner with community participation.

  Need for mass awareness campaigns: This is to be effectively enforced by all States and UTs with the cooperation and active involvement of the community, the Corporate sector, industry and trade associations, NGOs, Gram Panchayats, etc. in a comprehensive manner in urban and rural areas. To achieve this, mass awareness campaigns will be organized as done in the case of Swachh Bharat and Sanitation campaigns.

  Special teams to monitor: While Central teams comprising senior-level officers have been deployed in various Districts to monitor time-bound implementation of conservation schemes in rural areas, the Urban Affairs Ministry has also planned to undertake campaign and activities for water conservation, recycle and reuse of grey (wastewater) in urban areas. Urban Local Bodies (ULBs) in States will carry out this task.
- **Piped water to all households:** One important target for the new Ministry is to provide piped water facility to all households, now lacking it, in urban and rural areas.
- **Role of villages and PM's appeal:** Concerned about the water crisis in rural areas and recognizing the crucial role of villages, the Prime Minister has written

a personal letter to 'Gram Pradhans' (Village heads) requesting them to conserve rainwater during the monsoon season.

The PM has made a special appeal to the Pradhans that they should convene a meeting of the Gram Sabha (Village assembly) wherein his message should be read out and discussion held in the village on how to conserve water and make adequate arrangements to save every drop of rainwater. The PM has further suggested to take up construction of check dams and ponds where proper harvesting of rainwater can be done.

- **Prevention of encroachment:** Encroachment and diversion of water bodies and drainage channels not be allowed and wherever, it has taken place, it should be restored to the extent feasible and maintained properly.
- **Promotion of water-efficient nutri-cereal crops:** The government is now promoting cultivation of water-efficient and climate-resilient summer sown crops like millets – *bajra,* hybrid *jowar* and *ragi – which consume less water, unlike water guzzling paddy, and also have high nutritional value. Leading agricultural scientists like Dr. M.S. Swaminathan have been advocating the promotion of these nutri-cereals for production and consumption. The Minimum Support Price (MSP) for these cereals is getting bigger hike than paddy. This may spur farmers to switch over to these crops and optimise the use of water in cultivation. Some of the States have started supplying these cereals in PDS along with rice and wheat.*
- **Inter-linking of rivers:** A major step required to attain permanent self-sufficiency and meet the entire demands of country for water is the inter-linking of rivers and inter-basin transfer of water from surplus rivers to deficit and drought prone regions/basins.

  Under the **National Perspective Plan (NPP)** prepared by the erstwhile Ministry of Water Resources, National Water Development Agency (NWDA) has already identified 14 links under Himalayan Rivers Component and 16 links under Peninsular Rivers Component for inter basin transfer of water based on field surveys, investigation and detailed studies.

  Out of these, Feasibility Reports of 14 links under Peninsular Component and 2 links (Indian portion) under Himalayan Component have been prepared. Draft Feasibility Reports of 7 link projects (Indian portion) of Himalayan Component have also been completed.
- **Desalination plants:** NITI Aayog is working on a plan to tap India's vast coastline of 7,800 kms and its marine waters by desalinating sea water and supplying through a network of pipelines. These plants could be energy-efficient by using

solar or ocean energy for the project. The cost analysis of the scheme needs to be worked out.

There are already some seawater desalination plants operational near Chennai coast, including one linked to Kalpakkam nuclear power plant, and the experience gained from them could help in working out the scheme.

9. Gender inequality and gender bias are major impediments in India's socio-economic development. Do you agree? Mention some specific instances of gender inequality and bias against women in India and the steps taken by the government to ameliorate the condition of women.

Ans. Gender bias and gender inequality are important aspects in the context of social and economic development. Gender bias adversely impacts women and girls in manifold ways which leads to inequality in society, as observed particularly in the less developed countries. Equal opportunities to women in jobs and in the workplace and pay parity will boost economic growth for everyone to share. India's national income will rise significantly if women were to enjoy parity with men in all spheres – education, health, labour force, etc.

The Constitution and Gender Equality

Gender equality is recognized as part of fundamental rights enshrined in the Constitution of India. The Constitution, in its Preamble and various Articles, guarantees equal status and opportunity to men and women, and equal protection of the laws. It also enjoins that there shall be no discrimination on the basis of gender in any manner. The Directive Principles of State Policy in the Constitution further reinforces these aspects to protect women's rights for equality.

Gender inequality and discrimination

While the Constitution guarantees gender equality, it is well known and widely documented that women and girls in India have been subjected to gender bias. Gender equality and bias against women manifests in different forms as detailed below. There are various reasons for this unacceptable situation.

- **Social mores:** Traditionally, India has been, by and large, a patriarchal society in which men dominate in decision-making and running a family. This places women in a subjugated position and they are at a disadvantage in many respects. This situation can be improved, to a great extent, with the spread of education and attitudinal changes in society over a period of time and with women themselves asserting their rights.

- **Literacy and Education:** Literacy and education of females are two of the critical factors that help to reduce gender inequality, bridge the gap between the two sexes and empower women. But in respect of both, though there have been exceptions, women, in general, have traditionally lagged behind men in India.

  This is evident with girls' enrolment in schools lagging behind boys. Due to the burden of attending domestic chores, girls are often unable to attend school or continue studies beyond a point. Factors like distance to school and lack of safety in commuting, or lack of facilities like separate toilet for girls, force them not to attend school or discontinue studies midstream, particularly in rural and far-flung areas. Or, due to economic factors, girls are sent to work to earn a living and supplement family income thus depriving them the opportunity to continue studies.

- **Family life:** For reason of having to look after family and rear children, women have to stay at home and forgo opportunities to work and earn. Even those who are able to join the labour force are forced to give up jobs when they have children and they find it difficult to get back to work at a later stage. This handicap adversely affects their economic independence and their role and position in the family.

- **Sex ratios and Missing Women**: While sex ratio is in favour of female in western and advanced countries – Europe, US, etc. – it is quite skewed against females in most of the Third World, including India. While some states like Karnataka, Andhra Pradesh, Madhya Pradesh and Maharashtra have shown signs of improvement in the sex ratio, many other states, including the economically progressive states like Haryana, Gujarat and Punjab, have low sex ratio which is a cause for concern. While overall India has for decades seen decrease in sex ratio, there has been slight increase during the last two decades – from 927 in 1991 to 933 in 2001 and to 940 in 2011. The main cause for the decline in sex ratio in India is lack of literacy and education and an overtly biased attitude towards women.

- **Child sex ratio:** Child sex ratio is lower than overall sex ratio in many of the States which is not an encouraging sign as it may indicate higher female infant mortality or sex selective abortion and female foeticide following pre-natal sex determination tests. This is indicative of a serious demographic and social problem due to entrenched social mores with bias against females.

  The low and falling child sex ratio in the country is a matter of grave policy concern, not only because it violates the human rights of unborn and infant girls but because it deprives the country of the potential economic and social contribution of these 'missing women'. Imbalance in the number of males relative to female youth has also implications for marriages and could be a factor causing social disharmony.

- **Intra-family bias:** Even in domestic affairs, there is intra-family bias against women such as in handling finances, sharing domestic chores, decision-making and even in sharing of food. There is bias in favour of the males in many families.
- **Equality in pay:** The Constitution has laid down the principle of "equal pay for equal work" for both men and women. But often in many sectors, women are paid less than men for comparable work. Besides, the State has to make provision for ensuring just and humane conditions of work and maternity relief for women.
- **Violence and crime:** Worse still is the fate of women and girls who are subjected to domestic violence and who suffer different types of abuses at home and outside like kidnapping, rape, etc. resulting even in deaths. Besides, there are cases of harassment of women for dowry and assault with intent to outrage their modesty. Though punishable under law, many such cases go unreported for fear of social stigma and women suffer in silence. There has been dramatic increase in violence against women in India in the past decades which has been well reported in domestic and international media.

Remedial measures taken by the government

The State and the civil society, including Women's groups, have taken several steps to improve the condition of women and girls. These include:

- **Education:** Improving literacy among women and ensuring that every girl child undergo school education has been actively pursued since independence. Incentives like exemption from paying fees, free grants for uniforms, books, etc., cycles for girls attending school are provided. Midday meals provided in schools induce children to be in school. Separate toilet for girls is also being provided.
- **Health and nutrition:** Expectant women, lactating mothers and infants are provided special nutritional care under the ICDS programme. Special care is taken to reduce infant and maternal mortality rates though India has still a long way to go to bring down their incidence. Child immunisation programmes have also been successfully implemented in India.
- **Maternity benefits:** India has made some progress in regard to granting maternity leave and related benefits and providing facilities like creche at work places for child care, etc. though much more needs to be done in this direction.
- **Sex ratios:** To prevent sex selection and female foeticide and improve child sex ratios, pre-natal sex determination tests are banned. More stringent measures are required in this regard as still violations take place. This also may improve further with women getting more educated.
- **Empowering women:** Empowerment of women to be agents of socio-economic change and development has been a prime objective under India's development

plans. To empower women, the State has taken many steps. Starting women's Self Help Groups (SHGs), extending them financial support through bank loans and encouraging them to undertake income-generating activities have gone a long way to empower women, especially in rural areas, and instill in them a sense of dignity, independence and self-confidence.

To give them greater voice in public life, efforts are on to increase their representation in electoral politics and in administration at national, state and local (municipal and village) levels. Under the Panchayati Raj system, women have been given important role in the Gram Sabhas. But still there is need to increase representation of women in the Parliament and State Assemblies on which the male dominated political parties are dragging their feet.

- **Violence and crime:** While there are various laws to protect women against child marriage, dowry harassment and physical violence and abuse, their enforcement is lax due to apathy on the part of the Police and the Courts. On the positive side, Women's Police stations and Family courts to hear dowry and other family disputes have been set up but these are found to be inadequate considering the magnitude of tasks and cases involved. Unless radical reform of the police machinery and judiciary, which are saddled with millions of cases languishing in courts, take place, their manpower and infrastructure is increased substantially and laws are enforced with rigour, not much improvement can be expected on this front. Several Commissions have studied the working of both these institutions and recommended reforms but their implementation has been slow and tardy.
- **Women's Commissions:** Women's Commissions have been set up at both the Central and State levels to look into various issues concerning women and redress their grievances. They pay special attention to gross violations against women and make public functionaries and State institutions accountable in such cases.
- **Gender budgeting:** To pay greater attention to the implementation of women-specific programmes, since 2005-06, the Ministry of Finance has been issuing a note on 'Gender Budgeting' which is incorporated in the Budget Document and focusses on 'Women Specific Schemes' having 100 per cent allocation for women and another on 'Pro Women Schemes' which have at least 30 per cent of the allocation for women.

  Gender Budgeting Cells were also set up by the Union Government to serve as focal points for coordinating gender budgeting initiatives within their Ministries and across Departments.

  Impact of Gender Budgeting: Specific programmes and targets designed to improve the welfare of, and empower, women and girl children help to bring about transformational changes in their lives.

10. Explain the concept of, and rationale for, Gender Budgeting. How has this been implemented in India and in what way it has helped in improving the schemes focussed on women?

Ans. Gender Budgeting is an effective tool for achieving gender mainstreaming and to ensure that benefits of development schemes reach women as much as it does in the case of men. It is a strategy to achieve equality between women and men by focusing on how public resources are collected and spent and helps to ensure that fiscal policies and administrative procedures are structured to address gender inequality.

The concept of gender budgeting does not imply a separate budget for either women nor increase in overall public expenditure but prioritising programmes within specific sectors to meet the special needs of women.

➢ **Rationale for Gender Budgeting**

Based on the recognition that national budgets benefit women and men differentially, and may even reinforce patriarchal social norms and biases, India formally adopted Gender Responsive Budgeting (GRB) in 2005-06.

The rationale for it is that macroeconomic policies or a gender-neutral budget may not solve the problem of gender inequality. Gender inequality hampers socio-economic progress, it inhibits women from playing their rightful role, not only in respect of themselves but for the family as a whole, and realizing their full potential. By targeting public spending towards sectors and programmes which will make a direct impact on women and children, gender equity can be ensured to a greater extent. Gender Responsive Budget (GRB) does not merely involve earmarking of funds for women; it is an exercise that scrutinises the budget through a gender lens.

As observed in Economic Survey, 2017-18, "Over the last 10-15 years, India's performance improved on 14 out of 17 indicators of women's agency, attitudes, and outcomes. ……... However, on several other indicators, notably employment, use of reversible contraception, and son preference, India has some distance to traverse because development has not proved to be an antidote. Within India, there is significant heterogeneity, with the North-Eastern states (a model for the rest of the country) consistently out-performing others and not because they are richer; hinterland states are lagging behind but the surprise is that some southern states do less well than their development levels would suggest.……The government's Beti Bachao, Beti Padhao and Sukanya Samridhi Yojana schemes, and mandatory maternity leave rules are all steps in the right direction." (Economic Survey, 2017-18, Chapter 07).

➢ **Evolution of Gender Budgeting in India**

The genesis of the idea of **gender budgeting** in India can be traced back to the early Five Year Plans. Gender mainstreaming and development has been a priority goal in the country's development efforts since the starting of the first Five Year Plan.

While the First to Fifth Five Year Plans treated development of women as a subject of 'welfare', there was a paradigm shift from 'women's welfare' to 'women's development' during the Sixth Plan (1980-85). Sixth Plan also had special thrust for women in three core sectors viz., health, education and employment. The Seventh Plan (1985-90), continued the developmental approach. The major objective was of raising economic and social status of women and bringing them into the mainstream of national development. Subsequent plans also had special programmes for women to complement the efforts of the general development programmes.

Gender Budgeting, as a specific system and tool, began to take shape in India after its special reference in the Union Budget in 2001. Expenditure on women was elicited from the Union Budgets in the succeeding three years and the broad results were studied by the Dept. of Women and Child Development.

Since 2005-06, the Ministry of Finance has been issuing a note on Gender Budgeting which is incorporated in the Expenditure Budget Document. It comprises two parts:

- **Part A** reflects **Women Specific Schemes**, i.e. those which have 100 per cent allocation for women.
- **Part B** reflects **Pro Women Schemes**, i.e. those where at least 30 per cent of the allocation is for women.

In 2010, it was decided to adopt 'Gender Responsive Budget' with sub-targets covering women and SC/ST beneficiaries under various developmental schemes and schemes for the benefit of North Eastern Region. After 2013, Ministries and Departments at the Centre began reporting on Gender issues and reviewing the achievements on Gender Budgeting in their programmes.

Gender Budgeting Cells were set up by the Union Government to serve as focal points for coordinating gender budgeting initiatives within their Ministries and across Departments. States were also asked to set up Gender Budget Cells on the lines of cells and State Planning Departments were instructed to include gender budgeting as a part of their annual plans.

➢ Impact and Benefits of Gender Budgeting

Specific programmes and targets designed to improve the welfare of, and empower, women and girl children can bring about transformational changes in their lives. Some of the areas and instances where gender budgeting and schemes targeted at women and girls have helped to bring about beneficial changes in their lives are mentioned below.

- Incidence and severity of poverty is greater among women than among men. Empirical evidence has shown that promoting and funding women's Self-help groups (SHGs) to undertake income-generating activities help to augment family incomes. India has a large network of women's SHGs, particularly in rural areas, and with financial support provided to them, it has helped to enhance the freedom, self-confidence and self-esteem of women and has had a beneficial impact on the family as a whole.

- Programmes like Integrated Child Development Scheme (ICDS) and nutritional schemes targeting pregnant women and lactating mothers, midday meals in schools and nutrition for pre-school children in Anganwadis have helped to improve their health and also helped to create greater awareness among women and children about health and nutrition.
- Outlays on augmenting supply of safe drinking water, especially in rural areas, benefits women more than men by reducing the time required to fetch water for which they have to trudge long distances to rivers and ponds. Such outlays will be equally beneficial to women of low income households in urban areas who do not have water supply at home and have to depend on common pipe connection provided in streets which, apart from the time consumed, causes much inconvenience to them. The government propose now to provide piped water to all households lacking the facility.
- The "Beti Bachao, Beti Padhao" scheme to incentivise and promote education of girl children and retaining them in schools has helped girls and will benefit the whole family in the long run. An educated girl will have greater awareness about the value of hygiene, health, nutrition, etc. which will have salutary effect when she grows up, assumes motherhood and bring up a family. As the saying goes, educating a boy helps one person whereas educating a girl helps an entire family. The drawbacks of lack of literacy and education among large sections of women in India and how it has held back the country's progress have been only too starkly visible.
- The 'Ujjwala' scheme implemented to extend supply of cooking gas to rural households has gone a long way to help rural women who had to depend on firewood for cooking, which they have to fetch from distant places from their homes, or other fuel which are harmful to health.
- Since 2014, over 10 crore toilets have been provided in households lacking the facility which has helped those families and, in particular, women and girls in their daily lives. It will also vastly improve the health and hygiene of the beneficiaries.
- As with toilets, rural electrification is another scheme which has brought about transformational change in the lives of rural families. Apart from improving the quality of life, it has ensured more security within the villages as well as enabled more mobility and comfort, especially for women, and less drudgery in performing household chores. Availability of electricity during night helps students by facilitating extended hours of study.

Conclusion

As pointed out earlier, while much has been done to ameliorate the condition of women and girls, India has still has a long way to go in regard to security and safety of women and girls as evident from recurring instances of kidnap, rape, dowry harassment, domestic violence, etc. These can be achieved only with the spread of education and attitudinal changes in society towards women.

Civil society experts point out that while many schemes have seen improvement in allocation, which is commendable, some others like the one for the protection of domestic violence victims has not seen allocation. It is also crucial that equal attention is given to the design of all schemes and their timely and effective execution.

India's Union budgets report figures of actual spends with a lag of a year, disaggregated by ministries and schemes, but similar data is not provided for the Gender Budget. Efforts need to be made to firmly institutionalise Gender Responsive Budget (GRB) within the government at the national and sub-national levels. There is also need to strengthen capacity to apply a gender analysis to implementation, monitoring and evaluation – including expenditure tracking and benefit incidence.

> If we are to deal adequately with processes of economic growth, ...in which the very technological, demographic, and social frameworks are also changing .... it is inevitable that we venture into fields beyond those recognized in recent decades as the province of economics proper. .....it is imperative that we become more familiar with .... population growth patterns, the nature and forces in technological change, the factors that determine the characteristics and trends in political institutions, and generally patterns of behaviour of human beings......Effective work in this field necessarily calls for a shift from market economics to political and social economy.
>
> – Simon Kuznets (1901-1985): *Economic Growth and Income Inequality*, Presidential address to the American Economic Association, December 29, 1954.

INEQUALITY AND POVERTY

> So long as all the increased wealth which modern progress brings, goes but to build great fortunes, to increase luxury, and make sharper the contest between the House of Have and the House of Want, progress is not real and cannot be permanent.
>
> \- Henry George (1839-1897), American economist, *Progress and Poverty* (1879).

Topics Covered

- *Manifestation of inequality and poverty*
- *Absolute, relative and extreme poverty*
- *Poverty trap*
- *Methods of measuring poverty in India*
- *Sen's poverty index*
- *Role of the World Bank and other international agencies in poverty eradication*
- *Economic growth and poverty: the Amartya Sen and Jagdish Bhagwati debate*
- *Paradox of India's growth and persisting poverty*
- *Poverty eradication programmes in India*
- *Universal Basic Income – Colonial rule and its impact on India*
- *Paradox of India's growth and poverty*
- *Importance of social and political consciousness of the people and good governance in development.*

1. What are the manifestations of inequality and poverty?

Ans. Poverty and inequality are interrelated and they act upon one another like cause and effect. Since everyone in a group or society cannot be equally well off, some are bound to be poorer or richer than others, and it is the question of degree of inequality or poverty that matters. There is inequality and poverty even in developed countries but not so widespread, severe, or abject as in developing and least developed nations.

There are inequalities between the poor and the rich, women and men, rural and urban areas and populations, developed and underdeveloped regions and different ethnic groups. Such inequalities are not isolated but are interrelated and overlapping. Inequalities and poverty do not always move in the same direction. They may increase or decrease together or move in opposite direction.

Amartya Sen observes that "one can argue that inequality is fundamentally a different issue from poverty. To try to analyse poverty 'as an issue of inequality', or the other way round, would do little justice to either. Inequality and poverty are not, of course, unrelated. But neither concept subsumes the other." (in *Poverty and Famines*).

In studies of inequality and poverty, while factors like income and consumption expenditure are widely used, non-income dimensions like education, health and access to other basic facilities like housing, water, sanitation, etc. have also increasingly come under focus.

➢ **Poverty and inequality manifests in different forms as mentioned below:**

- Misallocation of productive resources due to wrong prioritisation in economic policies. It may also be due to some sections having greater access to the resources while other are deprived of them. Concentration in ownership of land and other assets are examples.
- Lack of income which causes poverty and deprivations in diverse forms – lack of necessities such as food and nutrition, and basic facilities like proper housing, safe drinking water and sanitation.
- Illiteracy and lack of access to educational facilities lead to lack of opportunities for advancement in life and freedom of choice. Children of disadvantaged parents are deprived of these facilities compared to those in families with higher incomes and such divergences perpetuate inequality and poverty.

  The states of UP, Bihar, Orissa and Madhya Pradesh are examples which grossly lack proper public services like education and health compared to many other states and these factors hold them back in progress and remain relatively poor.
- Unsafe environment and social discrimination and exclusion leading to lack of security. These impact women more due to gender bias skewed against them and have implications for overall development.
- Lack of proper health facilities and health care leads to children being ill-fed and malnourished, women and lactating mothers being weak and under-nourished. This will be reflected in other social indicators such as morbidity, high infant and maternal mortality, and high birth and death rates in the population which are indications of poverty and poor living standards.
- Advances in technology has been a key driver of growth but it has led to widening inequality as these advances call for skilled labour. While the highly skilled have benefited from such growth and rising incomes, those lacking the skills have been left behind leading to widening inequalities.

- Unemployment is another major factor resulting in inequality and poverty. Recent experience has shown that despite economic growth, there is joblessness and rising unemployment.
- Spatial factors also cause inequalities due to socio-economic conditions, say, between regions or between rural and urban areas.

  Regional disparities: In India, the eastern region of Orissa and Bihar, despite being well endowed with rich minerals, is relatively underdeveloped and with higher levels of poverty. These states lag behind other states in in the provision of "merit goods" like education and public health which adversely impact the population and result in backwardness.

  Rural-urban divergences: People in urban areas suffer from handicaps like having to live in over-crowded slums amidst squalor compared to their rural counterparts and are more exposed to adverse environmental factors like pollution causing health hazards.Whereas in rural India, where agriculture is the mainstay of the people, vagaries of monsoon, large tracts of unirrigated land, drought, crop losses, rising debts, etc. cause acute distress to farming community and their families. They may also be handicapped by the lack of amenities like proper schools and hospitals and these lead to different outcomes in the quality of their lives.
- Lack of political and social rights: Lack of equal rights to participate in decision-making and in civil, social and cultural spheres and even in labour markets. These factors accentuate inequality and poverty with vested interests playing a dominant role and appropriating the rights and abusing their position. This is clearly visible in India's political and social system which is male-dominated with women relegated to play a secondary role.

➢ **Multi-dimensional approach:** In view of the above factors, contemporary development policies place stress on a "multidimensional human rights" approach which recognize the nature of poverty, view poverty in terms of a range of interrelated and mutually reinforcing deprivations. It also draws attention to the stigma, discrimination, insecurity and social exclusion associated with poverty. The widening of people's choices and the level of freedom and well-being they achieve are at the core of this approach to human development.

International agencies like the World Bank, UNDP, UNICEF, etc. have been urging governments to adopt policies aligned to the above approach.

2. Distinguish between 'Absolute poverty', 'Relative poverty' and 'Extreme poverty"? What is meant by 'Poverty trap'? Mention some schemes India has adopted to eradicate poverty.

Ans. There are different degrees and levels of poverty. As economists like Amartya Sen have pointed out, even among those below the 'Poverty line', there are persons facing different levels of poverty and deprivation. Some may be just below or close to the poverty line while some may be far down below it. This aspect has to be borne in mind while drawing up policies to alleviate poverty and lift them out of poverty.Thus a distinction is drawn between Absolute poverty, Relative poverty and Extreme poverty.

It is also to be borne in mind that the poverty line in advanced countries which have higher costs for food, housing, education, etc. may be at a higher level than in underdeveloped countries. And within a country also, poverty line for urban areas and rural areas will be different due to differences in cost of living.

➢ **Absolute Poverty**

Absolute poverty is a condition characterized by severe deprivation of basic human needs, including food, shelter, good health. It depends not only on income but also on access to public and social services. Those in this state do not have enough means required for bare subsistence.

In other words, absolute poverty indicates the lack of biological necessities such as food, water, clothing, housing, and sanitation facilities. This concept is directly related to the minimum level of consumption. Absolute poverty is more prevalent in the poorer and developing (what are also called 'Third World') countries, where more people are living below a certain threshold of income required for accessing bare necessities.

➢ **Relative Poverty**

Relative poverty is a condition in which people have enough money or income to meet the basic needs required to survive but are still relatively poor when compared to others. It is not based merely on a basic amount necessary for survival but takes into account the 'standard or quality of life' a person enjoys. Thus, a person may live in an affluent neighbourhood and have everything needed for survival but does not have the comforts or luxuries which others may have.

Absolute poverty refers to a set condition, which is the same in every country, and does not change over a period of time. Relative poverty, on the other hand, refers to conditions which are subjective to the society, in which the person lives, and, therefore, vary between regions and countries, and may change over a period of time. For example, countries which are more urbanised and advanced will have higher costs for food, housing, education, energy, and transportation, etc. and so the poverty line will be higher in those countries, compared to that in poorer countries. Again as pointed out earlier, within a country, the urban areas will have more facilities than rural areas and this will be reflected in the standard and costs of living and in the relative poverty level.

Relative poverty is based on the socio-cultural environment around, not on a basic amount necessary for people to subsist. Relative poverty changes more often and adjusts to the changes in society – say, food and housing becoming more expensive in certain areas or over a period of time.

In basic terms, absolute poverty is having a lack of basic resources while relative poverty is more to do with income inequality. People in relative poverty do have an income, but it is lower than the set income level. They are seen as poor because they do not have the capabilities to meet certain standard set by, or prevailing in, the community.

- **Extreme poverty**

  The World Bank is the main source for global information on extreme poverty and it sets the International Poverty Line (IPL). The poverty line has been revised from time to time and since 2015, a person having an income less than $1.90 per day, based on 2011 PPP conversion rates, is considered to be in extreme poverty. (PPP or Purchasing Power Parity conversion rate takes into account differences in prices levels across countries as well as inflation).

  People living in extreme poverty suffer from marginalization, malnutrition, vulnerability to diseases and various other deprivations. It is important to note that the International Poverty Line fixed is extremely low and those living below this low threshold are considered to be in 'extreme poverty'. Focusing on extreme poverty is important precisely because it captures those utmost in need of attention and support. However, it is also important to note that the living conditions of those just above the International Poverty Line can still be characterized by poverty and hardship. The World Bank also reports poverty headcount ratios using a higher line at $3.10 per day on 2011 PPP prices.

  Extreme poverty was prevalent even in today's advanced countries until fairly recently. In fact, in most of these countries, sizeable sections of the population lived in extreme deprivation only a few generations ago. But socio-economic progress took place at a fast pace following the Industrial Revolution and scientific advancement helped to wipe out poverty. It points to the fact that sustained economic progress in the less developed countries of today could definitely bring down, and eventually end, extreme poverty.

  Poverty may also be transient or chronic, transient poverty being short-term, temporary or seasonal poverty, while chronic poverty refers to long-term or structural poverty.

- The 1997 *Human Development Report* of UNDP identifies three perspectives on poverty as stated below:

  Income perspective: A person is poor if, and only if, her income level is below the defined poverty line which is defined in terms of having enough income or a specified amount of food. Many countries have adopted income poverty lines to monitor progress in reducing poverty incidence.

  Basic needs perspective: Poverty is deprivation of material requirements for minimally acceptable fulfilment of human needs, including food. This concept of deprivation is not just the lack of private income but includes the need for basic health and education and essential services that have to be provided by the community to prevent people from falling into poverty. It also recognizes the need for employment and participation.

Capability perspective: Poverty represents the absence of some basic capabilities to function – a person lacking the opportunity to achieve some minimally acceptable levels of functioning which can vary from being well nourished, being adequately clothed and sheltered and avoiding preventable morbidity, to social achievements such as partaking in the life of the community.

The capability approach reconciles the notion of absolute and relative poverty, since relative deprivation in incomes and commodities can lead to an absolute deprivation in minimum capabilities.

➤ **Poverty trap**

Economists use the term 'poverty trap' to denote a situation in which individuals are stuck in deprivation over long periods of time, and there is nothing they can do by themselves to escape their situation. Simply stated, it means that poverty perpetuates poverty in a vicious cycle, so households that start poor continue to remain poor and are unable to break out of it. This is true of those who remain extremely poor and are farthest below from the poverty line.

Insufficient nutrition, which again is due to lack of income, and consequent extreme poverty, can be the cause of poverty trap, both of an individual and a household. Low intake of food and malnutrition impairs the capacity to work; poor nutrition then becomes both the cause and consequence of poor incomes.

Poverty traps can also occur at a collective, 'macro' level. For example, low-income countries might lack the requisite growth fundamentals – technology, education, infrastructure, etc. – that are necessary for the high saving rates which lead to productivity gains and rising national incomes. Such low-income countries have to resort to 'big push' macro policies like expansion of microfinance or public investments which will have permanent positive effects and trigger a virtuous cycle of more savings, more investment, and economic growth to break out of the poverty trap. Governments could also launch programs to reduce poverty through short-term interventions that have lasting effects. While this is not an easy task, there is evidence to suggest that in different countries, multifaceted programs offering short and medium-term support to households have produced lasting progress for the very poor. They produce significant impact on consumption, food security, productive and household assets, financial inclusion, income generation, physical and mental health and women's empowerment.

Poverty eradication schemes in India: India's policy interventions like rural livelihood missions, support to farmers, employment guarantee scheme in rural areas, support to women's self-help groups (SHGs) and others for income-generating activities, the extensive public distribution system (PDS) and provision of houses, water, sanitation facilities and cooking gas for the poor and vulnerable sections are prime examples of affirmative action to eradicate absolute and extreme poverty.

3. Explain Sen's poverty index and the Capability approach to gauging poverty and how they differ from other conventional approaches to studies on poverty?

Ans. The conventional approach to identify the poor and measure poverty is to count the number of people who are below a certain level of income defined as **'poverty line'**. This is called 'head count' method and the index of poverty is the proportion of the total population that happens to fall below the specified poverty line income–called the **'head count ratio'**. This index is widely used and is the mainstay of poverty data on which anti-poverty programmes are based.

Another measure is **'poverty gap'** which is the aggregate shortfall of income of all the poor from the specified poverty line. This can be expressed as the percentage shortfall of the average income of the poor from the poverty line which is the **'income-gap ratio'**.

Poverty gap index also has limitations as focusing only on income gap diverts the attention from qualitative aspects such as capabilities, skills and personal resources that could eradicate poverty in a sustainable way. A better measure would focus on capabilities and consumption side of households in poverty.

Prof. Amartya Sen, who has made signal contribution to the study of poverty issues, has pointed out certain inadequacies of this approach. The head count ratio, which only takes note of the number of people below the poverty line, does not indicate the shortfall in income of those who fall below the poverty line. It does not take into account the relative severity or intensity of poverty among those below the poverty line. Referring to this method, Sen observes: "It matters not at all whether someone is just below the line or very far from it, in acute misery or hunger."

The method suggested by Sen measures not only the proportion of poor people, but looks into the depth of their poverty, inequality among them and the distribution of welfare among the poor. This measure allows one to decompose poverty into three components and asks:

- Are there more poor?
- Are some of the poor poorer?
- Is there higher inequality among the poor?

The headcount index does not indicate how poor the poor are, and hence does not change if people below the poverty line become poorer.

The easiest way to reduce the headcount index, i.e., number of those below the poverty line is to target benefits to people who are just below the poverty line, because they are the ones who will cost the least to be lifted above the poverty threshold. But by most normative standards, people just below the poverty line are the least deserving among the poor but lifting those further below will require more concerted efforts involving more expenditure. Those who are far below the poverty line deserve priority in targeted poverty alleviation measures. This approach has important policy implications.

The Capability Approach

Amartya Sen has proposed the 'capability approach' as an alternative to monetary measures of poverty. This approach focuses on what people effectively do and are their functioning. It assesses the capacity of people to freely choose and achieve these functioning, that is, their capability, rather than on the commodities bought or consumed.

There is broad consensus that functions such as the ability to read and write and being well nourished, healthy, and free from violence and oppression are vital for human development. Focusing on individual achievements in these areas provides a good basis to begin assessing poverty from a non-monetary perspective. Education, health, and security also expand the choices people can make and the range of things they can do and be (that is, their capabilities). But these alone are also not sufficient. Social and political institutions often impede self-realization. Basic personal and political freedoms are equally essential.

The human development index (HDI) and the Multidimensional Poverty Index (MPI) are applications of the capability approach to assessing progress in societies. Both indexes focus on achievements in education, longevity/health, and living standards (through income and assets). This expanded, "multidimensional" criteria view poverty as a much broader, more entrenched problem, underlining the importance of investing more in human capital.

Sen's vision of capabilities and functioning spawned a vast amount of writings on multidimensional poverty and this has been used by the World Bank, UNDP, etc. while assessing poverty.

4. **Elucidate the different methods employed to measure poverty in India? Bring out the deficiencies in these methods.**

Ans. Need for measuring Poverty

There is need for a measure of poverty to evaluate how the economy is performing in terms of providing a certain minimum standard of living to all its citizens. Measurement of poverty has important policy implications. Income and consumption expenditure are two significant parameters for gauging poverty and fixing poverty line in an economy. According to this, the income required by an individual or a household for consumption expenditure to maintain a desirable minimum level of living is assessed. It may include food and non-food items and will take into account minimum calorie requirements to ensure healthy living. India has been adopting income and consumption expenditure (related to calorie intake) criteria for fixing the poverty line.

➢ **Early Attempts at Estimation of Poverty**

Dadabhai Naoroji pioneered the process of poverty estimation in pre-independent India when he made some estimations of per capita income (PCI). Post-independence, several Indian economists have carried out studies of poverty levels in India and arrived at some estimation.

- **Minimum Wages Act:** Soon after independence, India passed the Minimum Wages Act, 1948 which laid down that minimum wages must be paid to skilled and unskilled labour that would be sufficient not only for the bare sustenance of life, but for the preservation of the efficiency of the worker and be adequate for some measure of education, medical requirements, and amenities. Thus, India was conscious, even in the early days, of the need to protect the interests of the working classes.

➢ **Identification of Poverty Line:**

- **Working Group:** A Working Group of eminent economists and social scientists including Prof. D.R. Gadgil, Dr. P.S. Lokanathan, Dr. V.K.R.V. Rao and others, based on the recommendations of a Nutrition Advisory Committee of the Indian Council of Medical Research (ICMR) on balanced diet, proposed a minimum standard of living and recommended as follows:
  (i) The national minimum for each household of 5 persons (4 adult consumption units) should be not less than ₹ 100 per month at 1960–61 prices or ₹ 20 per capita. For urban areas, this figure was to be raised to ₹ 125 per month per household or ₹ 25 per capita to cover the higher prices of the physical volume of commodities on which the national minimum is calculated.
  (ii) This national minimum excludes expenditure on health and education, both of which are expected to be provided by the State according to the Constitution and in the light of its other commitments.
  (iii) An element of subsidy in urban housing will have to be included after taking ₹ 10 per month, or 10 per cent as the rent element payable from the proposed national minimum of ₹ 100 per month.
- **Task Force proposal: A** 1979 Task Force of the Perspective Planning Division prepared a report on 'Projections of Minimum Needs and Effective Consumption Demand'. The methodology as formulated by the Task Force has since then been used by the Planning Commission in estimating the incidence of poverty. The Task Force identified the poverty line as the per capita expenditure at which the average daily per capita calorie intake was 2,435 in rural areas and 2,095 calories in urban areas. Based on the consumption pattern prevalent in 1973–74, the group recommended monthly per capita expenditure of ₹ 49.09 for daily intake of 2,400 calories in rural areas and monthly per capita expenditure of ₹ 56.64 for daily intake of 2,100 calories in urban areas.
- **Lakdawala Committee:** An Expert Group on 'Estimation of Proportion and Number of Poor' was constituted in September 1989 under the Chairmanship of Prof. D.T. Lakdawala which submitted its report in 1993.The Group recommended as follows:

- The Poverty Line recommended by the Task Force on projection of minimum needs and effective consumption demand, namely a monthly per capita total expenditure of ₹ 49.09 (rural) and ₹ 56.64 (urban) rounded off to ₹ 49 and ₹ 57 at all India level at 1973–74 prices be adopted as the base line.
- This was anchored in the recommended per capita daily intake of 2,400 calories in rural areas and 2,100 calories in urban areas with reference to the consumption pattern as obtained in 1973–74. The Group recommended that these norms may be adopted uniformly for all States.

Population below poverty line: It was observed that he percentage of population below poverty line had steadily come down from 54.9 per cent to 38.9 per cent between 1973-74 and 1987-88. However, the number of poor, in absolute terms, showed increase, apparently due to the growing population. The increase in urban poor would also have been due to migration from rural to urban areas.

Expert Groups under Prof. Tendulkar and Dr. C. Rangarajan

The official estimates of poverty released by the Planning Commission was severely criticized on the ground that the poverty lines (threshold) fixed were unrealistic and thus the poverty ratios were much understated. Hence the government set up an expert group headed by Professor Suresh Tendulkar in 2005 to examine the issue and suggest a new poverty line and estimate.

Tendulkar Group pegged the daily per capita expenditure at ₹27 for rural and ₹ 40 for urban poor, which turned out to average monthly per capita expenditure ₹ 816 in rural India and ₹ 1,000 in urban areas.

The poverty lines defined by the Tendulkar Group also faced criticism as it did not reflect the changing times and aspirations of the people. The high rate of increase in per capita income and consumption in the first decade of this century and the consequential changes in the structure of the economy as well as in people's perspectives on poverty warranted a fresh look at the poverty line and its composition. This was the backdrop to the setting up of the Expert Group under Dr. C. Rangarajan) in 2012.

The Rangarajan Group raised the threshold of daily per capita expenditure to ₹ 32 for rural and ₹ 47 for urban poor from the level set by the Tendulkar Group. This worked out to monthly per capita consumption expenditure of ₹ 972 in rural areas and ₹ 1,407 in urban areas in 2011–12. For a family of five, this translates into a monthly consumption expenditure of ₹4,860 in rural areas and ₹ 7,035 in urban areas.

Compared to the poverty lines based on the methodology of the Tendulkar Group, the poverty lines estimated by Rangarajan Group are 19 per cent and 41 per cent higher in rural and urban areas, respectively.

➢ **Methodology used by the Expert Groups**

- The Tendulkar Group used all-India urban poverty line basket as the reference to derive state-level rural and urban poverty. This was a departure from the earlier practice of using two separate poverty line baskets for rural and urban areas. The Rangarajan Group reverted to the practice of having separate all-India rural and urban poverty basket lines and deriving state level rural and urban estimates from these.
- The Tendulkar Group had decided not to anchor the poverty line to the then available official calorie norms used in all poverty estimations since 1979 as it found a poor correlation between food consumed and nutrition outcomes.

  On a review of subsequent research, the Rangarajan Group was of the view that deriving the food component of the poverty line basket would be appropriate considering the full range of policies and programmes for child-nutrition support and on public provisioning of a range of public goods and services for the amelioration of the environmental diseases facing the population.

  Estimates of consumption expenditure seen in the National Accounts Statistics (NAS) and as inferred from the sample surveys of the National Sample Survey Organisation (NSSO) show a large and growing variance. The Rangarajan Group preferred NSSO's estimates and decided not to use the NAS estimates. This is in line with the approach adopted by Expert Groups under Lakdawala) and Tendulkar.

  The capture of spatial and temporal variation in prices in estimating the State-level and rural-urban poverty levels has undergone substantial refinement since 1979. The Rangarajan Group agreed with the methodology adopted by the Tendulkar Group on this.

➢ **Decline in poverty:** The poverty ratio declined from 39.6 per cent in 2009-10 to 30.9 per cent in 2011-12 in rural India and from 35.1 per cent to 26.4 per cent in urban India. And the all-India poverty ratio fell from 38.2 per cent to 29.5 per cent. Totally, 91.6 million individuals were lifted out of poverty during this period.

According to UN's 2019 Multi-dimensional Poverty Index, the number of poor in India declined by 271 million from 641 million in 2005/2006 to 370 million in 2015/2016, i.e., in a period of 10 years. With this, the headcount in percentage terms came down from 55.1 per cent to 27.9 per cent. The global Multi-dimensional Index (MPI) is based on multiple deprivations divided into three categories – health, education and standard of living – each with 33.3 weightage. As the criteria and methodology adopted in India's national surveys and the MPI differ, the MPI findings could differ from the findings in national surveys.

- **Deficiencies in the Income-cum-Nutrition approach to assess poverty**

  Some of the deficiencies in the approach to assess poverty based on calorie consumption and nutritional requirements are:

  - Poverty line derived from personal consumption patterns and levels does not take into account inter-personal differences of consumption behaviour. The consumption pattern varies from family to family and with age composition of its members. Assessing the minimum needs of children and various consumption behaviours of families is a complex process.
  - It does not cover other social needs such as basic education, health, nutrition, drinking water, sanitation, environmental standards, etc. in adequate measure.
  - The poverty line based on consumption and nutritional requirements would not reflect factors like dependence on debt, use of common property resources, and informal social security.
  - The head-count ratio based on the poverty line does not capture the severity of poverty and differences among groups below the poverty line, i.e., between those just below the poverty line and those further down who will be far worse off.
  - While adopting a common commodity basket can be justified, ignoring differences in price levels between states and between urban and rural areas and price fluctuations over time is not in order, since the income required to meet consumption expenditure is a function of the price levels.
  - The present method does not capture changes in consumption patterns over time. In the household consumption basket, demand has shifted to non-cereals whose prices have risen faster than that of cereals. This may distort the assessment of household expenditure which is used to arrive at the poverty line threshold.
  - The Multi-dimensional Poverty Index (MPI) adopted by the UN is a more comprehensive measure that tracks deprivations – health, education and standard of living – to measure poverty.

5. Describe the functions of the World Bank and the role it plays in alleviating global poverty. How far the Bank has helped and aided India in its fight against poverty?

Ans. The World Bank has evolved from the International Bank for Reconstruction and Development (IBRD) which was founded in 1944, along with the International Monetary Fund (IMF), at the UN Conference held in Bretton Woods in USA.

The World Bank is affiliated to the UN, has 189 member countries and has offices in 130 locations worldwide. It is designed to finance projects that enhance the economic development of member states. The bank is the largest source of financial assistance to developing countries.

Together with the IMF and the World Trade Organization (WTO), it plays a central role in overseeing economic policy and reforming public institutions in developing countries and defining the global macroeconomic agenda.

➢ **World Bank's mandate and role**

The primary mandate of the World Bank Group is to eradicate poverty worldwide. It has set two goals for the world to achieve by 2030:.

- To end extreme poverty by reducing the percentage of people living on less than US $1.90 a day to no more than 3 per cent; and
- Promote shared prosperity by fostering the income growth of the bottom 40 per cent of the population in every country.
- It provides technical assistance and policy advice and supervises – on behalf of international creditors – the implementation of free-market reforms.
- Beginning in the mid-1950s, it played a major role in financing investments in infrastructural projects in developing countries, including roads, hydroelectric dams, water and sewage facilities, maritime ports, and airports.

➢ **Operations of the World Bank Group**

- The World Bank is a vital source of financial and technical assistance to developing countries around the world.
- It works in a unique way partnering with member countries to reduce poverty and support development.
- The Bank provides low-interest loans, zero to low-interest credits, and grants to developing countries.
- The aid supports investments in diverse areas such as education, health, public administration, infrastructure, financial and private sector development, agriculture, and environmental and natural resource management.
- Some of the projects are co-financed with governments, other multilateral institutions, commercial banks, export credit agencies, and private sector investors.

➢ **Organization**

The World Bank Group consists of five institutions:

- **International Bank for Reconstruction and Development (IBRD):** The IBRD provides loans at market rates of interest to middle-income developing countries and creditworthy low-income countries.
- **International Development Association (IDA):** The IDA, founded in 1960, provides interest-free long-term loans, technical assistance, and policy advice to low-income developing countries in areas such as health, education, and rural development. Since its founding, the IDA has provided more than US$ 360 billion for investments in 113 countries.

- **International Finance Corporation (IFC):** The IFC operates in partnership with private investors, provides loans and loan guarantees and equity financing to business undertakings in developing countries.
- **Multilateral Investment Guarantee Agency (MIGA):** MIGA provides loan guarantees and insurance to foreign investors against loss caused by non-commercial risks in developing countries.
- **International Centre for the Settlement of Investment Disputes (ICSID):** The ICSID which operates independently of the IBRD is responsible for the settlement by conciliation or arbitration of investment disputes between foreign investors and their host developing countries.

The World Bank and Global Poverty

With concerted and relentless efforts of the World Bank, other international agencies like the UNICEF, WHO and UNDP and the member countries over seven decades, the world's poverty headcount ratio, measured at $1.90 per capita a day (in 2011 PPP level), has come down from 42.1 per cent in 1981 to 9.9 per cent in 2015. The Bank has extended loans totalling US$ 938.9 billion to member countries during the period 1945 to 2015.

➢ The World Bank and India

India's relationship with the World Bank dates back to its founding days having been was one of the 17 countries which met USA in 1944 to prepare the agenda for the Bretton Woods conference. And India was one of the 44 countries which signed the final Agreement that established the Bank.

Aid to India

The World Bank has been lending funds to India for rural and urban development projects related to transport, water and irrigation, health, power and agriculture.

India has been the largest recipient of loans from the World Bank. Total loans from the Bank from 1945 to 2015 amounted to US$ 102.13 billion with IBRD extending US$ 52.73 billion and IDA US$ 49.39 billion.

Focus on Poverty

In extending aid to India, apart from economic development in general, the special focus has been on eradicating poverty. According to World Bank, India's headcount poverty ratio which was 61.6 per cent in 1977 declined to 45.9 per cent in in 1993 and 21.2 per cent in 2011.

And as per the UN's 2019 Multi-dimensional Poverty Index, which is a much broader measure of human development and is based on multiple deprivations– health, education and standard of living – India's poverty headcount ratio has come down from 55.1 per cent in 2005/2006 to 27.9 per cent in 2015/2016.

New World Bank – India Partnership Framework

The World Bank's new Country Partnership Framework (CPF) for India approved in 2018 aims to support India's transition to a higher middle-income country by addressing some of its key development priorities – resource efficient and inclusive growth, job creation and building its human capital.

The India CPF represents the largest country program of the World Bank Group, reflecting the strong collaboration between India and the Group's institutions: IBRD, IFC and MIGA. The Group expects to deliver US$25-30 billion during this CPF period, ending in 2022. There will be increased focus on programmatic support to states.

6. Compare and contrast the views expressed by the Indian economists, Amartya Sen and Jagdish Bhagwati, in eradicating poverty and the role development and economic growth is to play in the process?

Ans. Economists hold divergent views on how far economic growth by itself would help in reducing inequalities in society and lessening and eradicating poverty. There has been engaging debate on this issue between two eminent Indian economists, Jagdish Bhagwati and Amartya Sen.

There is an inherent relationship, or call it conflict or contradiction, between economic growth and equality. While growth can pull people at the bottom of the pyramid out of poverty, it is also bound to lead to widening inequality in varying degrees depending on endogenous and exogenous factors. This inherent conflict is at the root of the differing views between these two economists.

➢ **Bhagwati's view**

According to Bhagwati, economic growth is essential to root out poverty. In their work '*Why Growth Matters: How Economic Growth in India Reduced Poverty and the Lessons for Other Developing Countries*', Bhagwati and Arvind Panagariya hold up growth as the panacea for all of India's ills.

Bhagwati argues that growth while may raise inequality initially, sustained growth will eventually raise enough resources for the state to redistribute and mitigate the effects of the initial inequality.India had too few rich and too many poor. Redistribution, in effect, taking money from the rich and distributing it among the poor, would have increased their well-being only marginally. Growth had to come first, then "redistribution" from the enhanced revenues.

Bhagwati argued that it is the reforms of 1991 that have made even the lowest social classes greatly more prosperous today. Hence, those reforms must be strengthened.

Whereas Sen and Jean Drèze prescribe state-led redistributive efforts as the solution to India's problems in their work '*An Uncertain Glory: India and its Contradictions*', Bhagwati argues that by providing the intellectual foundations for populist excesses and fiscal profligacy that stoke inflation, Sen is actually hurting the life chances of the poor. By arguing for redistribution to precede growth, Sen is putting the cart before the horse.

➢ **Sen's contention**

While Sen believes that India should invest more in its social infrastructure to boost the productivity of its people and thereby raise growth, Bhagwati argues that only a focus on growth can yield enough resources for investing in social sector schemes.

Investing in health and education to improve human capabilities is central to Sen's scheme of things. Sen contends that without such investments, inequality will widen and the growth process itself will falter.

According to Sen, both growth and welfare programs are needed, and not one at the cost of the other. Subsidies that don't aid the poor must go. In a developing country like India burdened with poverty, malnutrition, ill-health, etc., focussing obsessively on growth, without making a direct assault on poverty, is not a rational approach.

A Syncretic view

Commenting on the debate between these two eminent economists, some experts have pointed out that inclusive growth aimed at job creation and measures to lessen inequalities resulting from development would be a balanced approach. There is consensus among economists that while growth is essential, whether the process of growth benefits, or even enriches, some sections leaving out the masses is as crucial as the rate of growth itself.

For growth results from the contributions of the four basic factors of production – land, labour, capital, and organization – and these are possessed by different sections which may keep changing with time and progress. The resultant fruits of growth get distributed in varying degrees according to the interplay of the control of these factors.

To root out poverty and lessen inequality, growth is essential, for without growth, the cake to be distributed will not grow. But as with growth inequality may rise, and not all would benefit from it in equal or proportionate or fair measure, some safety nets to protect those left behind in the growth process becomes inevitable. In a sense, both Bhagwati and Sen are saying much the same and striving for the same end, except that there may be slight difference in emphasis.

Welfare schemes needed but not sufficient

It is seen that welfare schemes, rather than just growth, have helped to pull people out of poverty in India. Yet some question whether redistributive welfare schemes work best in alleviating poverty. According to them, the faster rise in farm wages in the past few years, compared to earlier years, was primarily due to the 'pull' effect of growth.

The agricultural sector as well as the overall economy grew much faster in the second half of the decade 2000-10 than in the first. The higher growth and consequent increases in construction wages had a greater role in driving up farm wages in recent years than MNREGS, the government-sponsored right to employment scheme operational in rural areas.

It is also pertinent to note that merely lifting those below a 'poverty line' is not the ultimate solution. For even though they may be lifted above the poverty line, it can by no means be said that the living conditions, or the 'quality of life', of those brought above the poverty threshold can be considered substantially improved in regard to housing, education, health, sanitation, etc. Apart from being rid of the lack of food and some very basic necessities, their daily existence continue to be far from satisfactory, much less what can be considered ideal. Unless they are able to access and avail such basic facilities on a level reasonably comparable to other sections that are above them, the growth process will not have achieved its full objective.

In the Indian context, it is patently evident that despite lifting the poor above the poverty line, they are not getting good educational and public health facilities. There is need to do much more in these areas as also in spheres like housing, sanitation and drinking water, etc.

Demographics and Environment

Also, the Bhagwati-Sen debate does not dwell on other critical factors like high population growth, fast depleting natural resources, deforestation, environmental factors and their impact on current and future generations which portend to have serious consequences on development.

7. Describe some of the important poverty alleviation programmes India has implemented. How far they have succeeded in bringing down poverty in the country?

Ans. The high incidence of poverty, both in rural and urban India, has been a matter of grave concern. Successive Five Year Plans had emphasized eradication of poverty as one of the primary goals of development. From time to time, India has drawn up and implemented many poverty alleviation and employment schemes to help the vulnerable sections. Important anti-poverty measures are discussed below.

➢ **Employment programmes**

The bulk of the 'Below Poverty Line' (BPL) population is in rural India – agricultural labour, small and marginal farmers, and casual workers engaged in non-agricultural activities. Small land holdings, low productivity, poor educational base and lack of other vocational skills perpetuate poverty. As lack of productive employment has been a major cause of poverty in rural India, the governments at both State and

Central levels have implemented various employment schemes in rural areas to enable people to cope with transient poverty.

- **Integrated Rural Development Programme (IRDP):** A major programme directly targeted poor families for creation of assets, skill development, and self-employment was the IRDP started in 1980.
- **Swarnajayanti Gram Swarozgar Yojana (SGSY):** This was implemented from April 1999 and had the objective of improving the family incomes of the rural poor. This scheme proved to be more effective as several Self-Help Groups (SHGs), particularly run by women, were formed all over India and it helped these groups to take up income generating activities. Necessary financial aid was extended through bank credits.
- **Sampoorna Gramin Rozgar Yojana (SGRY):** This scheme combined the various wage employment programmes which were in operation like Employment Assurance Scheme (EAS) and Food for Work Programme (FWP) and merged under a new SGRY in 2001. The basic aims of the scheme continued to be generation of wage employment, creation of durable economic infrastructure in rural areas, and provision of food and nutrition security to the poor.
- **National Rural Employment Guarantee Scheme (NREGS):** This was a landmark scheme enacted in 2005 for poverty alleviation by merging all the ongoing employment schemes.Later renamed as Mahatma Gandhi NREG scheme (MNREGS), it aimed at enhancing the livelihood security of the people in rural areas by guaranteeing 100 days of wage employment in a financial year to every rural household whose members volunteer to do unskilled manual work. It also aimed to create durable assets in rural areas.

  The private sector has also been involved in designing special projects for capacity building of the poor for wage employment. The convergence of SGSY and other development programmes with MNREGS strengthened the self-employment initiatives through value addition. Skilling unskilled workers are also an integral part under this scheme for poverty eradication on a sustainable basis.

➢ **Public Distribution System (PDS)**

The PDS for supply of essential food items, operated jointly by the Central and State governments, is the largest such operation in the world. The scheme is in operation since independence.

- Under this, rice, wheat, sugar, kerosene, millets, etc. are distributed through a network of lakhs of Fair Price Shops (FPS) at subsidised rates.
- It provides vital food security for the poor and vulnerable sections in BPL and APL category families. Over 18 crore families are availing PDS facility.
- Over the years, efforts have been made to streamline the PDS and remove malpractices and leakages in it. An important measure has been removing ineligible and bogus card holders from the purview of the scheme.

- **Integrated Child Development Services (ICDS) and Midday Meal scheme:**
  - Integrated Child Development Services (ICDS) in India is the world's largest integrated early childhood programme, with over 40,000 centres nationwide. UNICEF had helped launch the ICDS programme and continued to provide financial and technical assistance along with the World Bank.

    Since its inception in 1975, the programme has matured and expanded, despite difficulties in adapting to the vastly different local circumstances prevalent in the country.

    The programme offers health, nutrition, and hygiene education to mothers, non-formal pre-school education to children aged three to six, supplementary feeding for all children and pregnant and nursing mothers and with links to primary healthcare services such as immunization and vitamin A supplements. These services are delivered in an integrated manner at the anganwadi or childcare centre.
  - The Midday Meal Scheme was introduced as an innovative programme in schools to improve the nutritional status of school-age children. It was pioneered on a limited scale in Tamil Nadu and later extended to cover the whole state. Seeing its beneficial impact, later it was introduced in other states and Central government has also been providing funds for the programme.

    The programme supplies free lunches on working days for children in primary and upper primary classes in government, government aided, and local body schools. The scheme has induced families to send children to schools and helped in bringing down drop-out rates at primary and upper primary levels.
- **Housing Programme**
  - **Indira Awas Yojana (IAY):** Initiated in 1985–86, the IAY is the core programme for providing free housing to BPL families in rural areas, including SC/STs and freed bonded labourers. The IAY helped BPL households to build their houses and upgrade old houses. Since inception, about 252.4 lakh houses were either constructed or upgraded as on March 2012.
  - **Pradhan Mantri Awaas Yojana –Gramin (PMAY-G):** In 2016, the Government re-structured IAY and launched the scheme PMAY-G to provide "Housing for All" by 2022, The scheme aims at providing a pucca house, with basic amenities, to all houseless householders and those households living in kutcha and dilapidated house by 2022. The immediate objective was to cover one crore households living in kutcha house/dilapidated house in three years from 2016-17 to 2018- 19.

The minimum size of the house has been increased to 25 sq.mts (from 20sq.mts), with a hygienic space for cooking. The unit assistance has been increased from ₹ 70,000 to ₹ 1.20 lakh in plain and from ₹ 75,000 to ₹ 1.30 lakh in hilly states, difficult areas. The beneficiary is entitled to 90.95 person day of unskilled labour from MGNREGS. The assistance for construction of toilet shall be leveraged though convergence with SBM-G, MNREGS or any other dedicated the source of funding. Convergence of other Government programmes like piped drinking water, electricity connection, LPG gas connection, etc. is also being attempted.

- **Pradhan Mantri Awas Yojana (Urban):** A similar scheme has been launched to address 'Housing for All' in urban areas also. About 4,331 cities/towns have been included under PMAY (U).

  By June 2019, a total of 1.53 crore houses have been provided under these schemes.

➢ **Prime Minister's Gram Sadak Yojana (PMGSY)**

This is an important rural infrastructure – village road connectivity – programme for linking villages with the nearest town. Over the last decade and a half, the PMGSY has carved out a place for itself as a programme characterized by creation of good quality assets, effective management, and technical proficiency.

- A total of 6.02 lakh Km road length has been constructed under the scheme since inception till April, 2019 (inclusive of PMGSY-I, PMGSY-II and RCPLWEA Scheme).
- This programme has helped to rejuvenate not only agriculture, but all other economic and social activities in rural areas by enabling convenient and efficient transportation of people and goods.

➢ **Panchayati Raj and Rural Rejuvenation**

In Indian polity, the Local governments under the Panchayats in the villages and Municipalities in towns occupy an important place. In a historic development, the 73rd and 74th Amendment Acts of 1992 under the Constitution gave primacy to the local bodies in villages and towns, a major step towards democratic decentralization of administrative authority. The Panchayati Raj Act, came into force on April 24, 1993 and the Nagarpalika Act came into effect on June 1, 1993.

Their governance and activities touch upon the day-to-day lives of the people and their efficient functioning and accountability is of critical importance. In villages, the Gram Sabhas play an important role and people have a greater voice in developmental activities.

- **Reservation for Women:** A significant feature of the Constitution amendments was that as a measure of empowerment of women, it provided for reservation of seats for women. Under the Constitution, not less than one-third of the total number of seats to be filled by direct election in the local bodies – Panchayats and Municipalities – (including the seats reserved for women belonging to the SC/ST) would be reserved for women and such seats are to be allotted by rotation to different constituencies in the local bodies.

- **Steps to alleviate rural distress:** As the farm sector continues to be under stress due to a variety of reasons – deficient rainfall and drought in many parts, rising input costs and unremunerative prices for farm products, etc., the government has been taking various steps to alleviate the distress. These include raising minimum support price for (MSP) of products, providing inputs at subsidised rates and crop insurance scheme in case of crop failures.

  - **Digital India project:** Under the project over 1.19 lakh Gram Panchayats have been connected by optical fiber by June 2019 and 3.6 lakh Common Service Centres (CSCs) have been set up across villages in India. These CSCs employ Village Level Entrepreneurs (VLEs) who deliver a range of services under social welfare schemes, education, healthcare, agriculture, digital literacy and skill development. The CSCs will act as a catalyst for Self-help groups. The turnover of the Centres which stands at ₹ 70,000 crore is targeted to go up to ₹ 3 lakh crore over five years.

    The project not only provides crucial non-farm employment to rural population but helps to bridge the rural-urban digital divide by enhancing digital literacy and ensuring more efficient delivery of public services in villages. It will also help to stem the tide of migration from rural to urban centres.

8. Explain the salient features of Universal Basic Income (UBI) scheme. Discuss the pros and cons of implementing such a scheme in India. (On this, see also Q. 5, Chapter 12)

Ans.

- **Features of Universal Basic Income (UBI)**
  - It implies the State or a public institution granting unconditionally a 'basic guaranteed sum of money' on regular basis to every citizen in a country, including children, irrespective of their economic status or occupation. This will be in addition to any other source of income or earnings of the citizens.
  - It is a social security measure, the primary objective being to combat poverty, assist those who are unemployed and enable every citizen to meet the basic needs and maintain a decent standard of life.

- **Rationale and Case for UBI**
  - **Income Distortions in Subsidy:** A good portion of subsidies doled out by governments, which are primarily meant for the poorer sections, are being enjoyed by the well-to-do and affluent sections of the population who do not

merit such assistance. This is one of the main reasons put forth for introducing a social assistance scheme Such a scheme may be in replacement of all or some of the existing schemes involving subsidies so that the amounts saved could be channelled into the universal scheme.

- **Subsidy distortions in India:** As observed in Economic Survey, 2016-17, "the Indian state's generosity is not restricted to its poorest citizens. In fact, in many cases, the beneficiaries are disproportionately the well-off." Subsidies for food (PDS), fertilizers, railway fares, water and electricity charges, LPG, etc. which are "non-merit" subsidies and meant for specific groups of population are enjoyed by those who do really merit to get them.
  * For instance, electricity subsidy benefits only those households which are electrified and even among them, the richer households who consume more power stand to benefit more. This holds true for petrol, diesel and fertilizer where the affluent sections get the benefits.
  * So also, the LPG subsidy is enjoyed by the relatively better off sections while the poorer sections that may not even use LPG for cooking are deprived of the benefit. Recent surveys have shown that while provision of LPG cylinders to millions of poor households have greatly benefited them, a sizeable proportion of them are not replacing used up cylinders apparently due to inability to meet even the subsidized costs.
  * Controlled rail prices actually provide more benefits for wealthy households than poor households, since the bottom 80 per cent of households constitute only 28.1 per cent of total originating passengers on non-suburban rail routes.
  * The exemptions given in personal income and corporate taxes benefit relatively better-off sections especially those in the higher income brackets.
  * 'Merit' subsidies are those given for education, primary healthcare, nutrition, forestry, ecology, environment, rural development programmes, village and small industries, etc. where the benefits are reaped by the society as a whole. These also do not reach many of the poor and deserving sections.
- **Loss of Jobs and Unemployment:** The scheme will also serve as a prop to those who are seeking jobs but can't get employment. The concept of UBI has got traction as automation with increasingly efficient computer systems, robotics and artificial intelligence is causing loss of jobs in various countries. In India, in the Information Technology (IT) sector which has been one with high potential for job creation, IT companies are embracing automation and artificial intelligence in complex areas of business which is resulting in improved productivity and helps to keep down costs. This is taking a toll on jobs in this sector.

- **Ageing population:**With changing demographic landscape and rising number of aged people, there is need to provide adequate assured income to the aged in societies which do not have proper welfare schemes like 'Old age pension' covering all such persons.
- **Poverty and Gross Inequalities:** Rising inequalities in societies, even as development takes place, is a matter of serious concern. Globalisation and technological advances, while improving overall well-being, also dislocate workers and disrupts industries, and results in greater income and wealth disparity, leaving behind the middle and working classes.

  A study, "*Indian Income Inequality 1922-2014*" by two economists, Thomas Piketty and Lucas Chancel, has highlighted that income inequality in India has increased during the post-1991 liberalization period as compared to the previous three decades. While post-liberalisation incomes have grown substantially, the wealthy have got wealthier at a faster rate widening the inequality.

  Universal Basic Income may simply be the fastest way of reducing poverty. In the Indian context, a relatively low level of assured regular income to every individual could serve as a prop and enhance family's welfare. Unlike the present system of subsidies, UBI may empower families at the bottom rung of the ladder and help them to become more self-reliant and take economic decisions relevant to their lives.
- Those in advanced economies enjoy higher levels of income and standards of living and some of these countries have robust social welfare measures like income support for the poor and the aged to protect them vulnerabilities. Whereas thought India has some measures like income support for farmers, food subsidy schemes for those in lower income ranges and old age pension schemes, these are either inadequate or not administered efficiently. There are exclusions of those who merit them.
- One of the main arguments in favour of a 'Universal' scheme is that it obviates the issue of exclusion of anyone from the scheme.

➢ **Case against UBI**

- A crucial question in regard to a universal scheme in the case of a country like India concerns its fiscal and financial implications.Whether it is affordable and sustainable over a long period considering that a fixed sum will have to be paid to every person – adults and children – on a continuing basis which becomes a permanent commitment on the part of the government. This is all the more relevant when there exists already considerable inequality between different income groups – the low income, middle income and high income groups.

- The withdrawal of existing subsidies will not only pose problems but will be impractical due to its political implications and ramifications. If it results in UBI being in addition to even part of the existing subsidies, it will not only be fiscally unsustainable but is unjustifiable from an economic standpoint.
- Also the sum of basic income fixed may have to be revised periodically if it is to cover inflation since, over a period of time, a constant amount of 'cash transfer' may not buy the same amount of goods.
- Since India already incurs substantial amounts of subsidies towards food, fertilisers, petroleum products besides in sectors like railways, roadways, power tariffs, etc., introducing UBI over and above these will be financially unsustainable. Due to opposition from pressure groups, it may be difficult to roll back existing subsidies under PDS, LPG, electricity, water, etc.
- Once introduced, it will be difficult for the government to wind up a UBI scheme or to discontinue it at a later stage in case of failure.
- A minimum guaranteed income may tend to make people lazy and opt out of the labour market. But some studies by economists of welfare programmes in in some countries have found no systematic evidence that cash transfer programs discourage work.
- Being an 'unearned income', it may lead to conspicuous and wasteful spending by households, especially the male members, on items like alcohol and tobacco.
- Gender factors may influence the control and sharing of UBI within a household, with men exercising control over spending of the assured basic income, especially in the lower rungs of society who need it the most. This does not happen with other in-kind transfer schemes like PDS, LPG, etc.
- Given the extent of financial inclusion of the poor and their access to banking, UBI scheme may face implementation issues and cause stress on the banking system. This can, however, be overcome with schemes like Banking Correspondents in rural and semi-urban areas, opening of Payments Banks, Common Service Centres (CSCs) envisaged under the Digital India project, etc.

Conclusion

In the ultimate analysis, while the UBI scheme has merit, considering the pros and cons, it may not be suitable in the Indian context due to various implications involved as pointed out above. A better course is to promote growth, with more affirmative policies than followed hitherto, weighed heavily to benefit the poor in greater measure. These call for improving facilities for education and public health, sanitation and drinking water meant for the poor. Fiscal policies to achieve these goals will have to be framed and executed in a concerted manner.

Spending on Education and Health

- India's expenditure on education and health are quite low as compared to other emerging countries due to which the poorer sections suffer the most as they don't get proper facilities in both these domains.
- India's expenditure on the health sector has risen from 1.2 per cent of the GDP in 2013-14 to a measly 1.4 per cent in 2017-18. The **National Health Policy, 2017 aims** to increase public funding on health to at least 2.5 per cent of GDP.
- While government spending on education, by both central and state governments, is close to 3 per cent of GDP which, according to the World Bank, is less than the world average of 4.7 per cent of GDP. NITI Aayog has suggested that the spending on education be increased to at least 6 per cent of GDP by 2022.

9. Explain the paradox of India's impressive economic growth but low level of human development and 'quality of life' of sizeable sections of population.

Ans. After two centuries of colonial rule and exploitation, at independence India started on a very low base of development. India also faced many societal challenges. A vast country with diverse cultures and languages, a hierarchical social structure with rigid caste system, and wide disparities in the distribution of wealth and incomes, it was an uphill task that India faced after independence. The government had to accommodate these diversities while formulating policies and evolve an integrated perspective for the country as a whole.

➢ **India's significant progress**

Considering the enormity of challenges India faced, the country has made substantial, even if inadequate, progress. While in 2014 India was the 11th largest economy, it is at sixth position in 2019. And based on Purchasing Power Parity (PPP) terms, India is the third largest economy, next only to USA and China.

➢ **Progress on the socio-economic front**

- According to the World Bank, India's GDP has risen from US$ 37.03 billion in 1960 to US$ 2.726 trillion (or, US$ 2726 billion). And India's per capita income which was US$ 82.19 rose to US$ 2015.6 in 2018.
- Literacy rate which was a mere 17 per cent in 1947 has gone up to 74 per cent as per 2011 census.
- Crude birth and death rates (i.e., number of births and deaths per 1,000 in a given year) which were 41.7 and 22.8 respectively during 1951-60 periods has declined to 20.2 and 6.3 by 2017.

- Infant mortality rate (IMR),i.e., possibility of an infant dying between birth and exactly one year of age, expressed per 1,000 live births, has fallen from 151 in 1965 to33 by 2017.
- Life expectancy at birth which was only 41.3 during 1951-61 periods has risen to 68.8 years in 2017.
- Total fertility rate (TFR), which is a significant measure of the rate at which population will grow, and which ideally should be the Replacement rate of 2.1, was as high as 5.4 in 1970-75 period. It has come down drastically to 2.2 by 2017. This is as a result of India's relentless efforts at population control. As a result, India's population growth is slowing and, on a positive trend, the year by when India's population would overtake China's also may get delayed.
- India has also built a strong industrial and technological base in the public and private sectors and made rapid strides in the Services sector.

➢ **India's poverty and low human development** Despite these positive developments, a substantial section of India's population is still steeped in poverty and are subject to low 'quality of life' and deprivations of many basic necessities of life.

UNDP's Human Development Index (HDI) and UN's Multi-dimensional Poverty Index (MPI) assess progress of countries, standard of living and poverty based, apart from income levels, on a range of socio-economic parameters such as literacy and education, health and nutrition, life expectancy, mortality rates, etc. UN's Sustainable Development Goals (SDGs) mission, which is now under implementation globally, also focusses on these areas to lift people, who suffer these vulnerabilities and deprivations, out of poverty.

Based on UN's 2019 MPI, India's poverty headcount ratio has come down from 55.1 per cent in 2005/2006 but is still 27.9 per cent in 2015/2016. And on UNDP's HDI, India ranks a low 130 in Middle Human Development Group out of a total of 189 nations.

➢ **Factors behind India's poverty and low 'quality of life'**

A number of factors account for the slow and tenuous process in the decline of poverty and for the low quality of life.

- **Colonialism:** As noted earlier, following two centuries of colonial rule, when there was hardly any industrialisation and economic progress was stunted, India started on a very low base of development. India had already inherited a host of problems – burgeoning population, widespread and appalling poverty, acute shortage of food and famines, low life expectancy and abysmally low level of literacy.
- **Population growth:** Even after independence, population grew at a steady pace which neutralised the fruits of development.

- **Agrarian distress:** With nearly 70 per cent of the population residing in villages and about 55 per cent of them engaged in agriculture, there is heavy pressure of population on land and under-employment and disguised unemployment in the farm sector. Land ownership is also skewed with over 60 per cent of ownership farms have size smaller than one hectare. Lack of irrigation, erratic monsoon, droughts, loss of crops and income and debts have caused much distress to many farmers and pushed them into poverty.
- **Literacy and education:** There are still gaps in literacy and education. According to HRD Ministry's *Educational Statistics at a Glance*, while gross enrolment ratio (GER) in Elementary (I–VIII) level was 94.8 in 2014-15, GER was much lower at secondary (IX-X) and senior secondary (XI-XII) levels which was only 78.1 and 54.6.

  Discontinuance of education is often due to economic pressure forcing poor families to send young children to work to supplement family income. In the case of girls, distance from schools in rural areas and lack of safety in commuting, lack of separate toilet, etc. force them to discontinue studies.

  Expenditure on education is quite low as compared to other emerging countries due to which the poorer sections suffer the most as they don't get proper facilities in schools.
- **Public health and nutrition:** As with education, public health facilities in India are also appalling both in rural and urban areas. This also impacts the poorer sections the most as they cannot access private hospitals due to prohibitive costs. Health centres in rural areas, where bulk of the population live, woefully lack both manpower – doctors, nurses, etc. – beside infrastructure and equipments.

  According to experts, in India medicines constitute almost 80 per cent of the total health expenditure in the country and the expense on drugs is the second most common cause of indebtedness in the country. This out-of-pocket expenditure puts proper medical care beyond most of the poor.

  Lack of food and proper healthcare has also been causing malnutrition among women and children. There have even been cases of death of multiple children in hospitals in some states leaving a serious question mark on the efficiency of hospitals and the staff manning them.

  India's expenditure on the health sector has also been very low. It has just risen from 1.2 per cent of the GDP in 2013-14 to 1.4 per cent in 2017-18. The **National Health Policy, 2017 aims** to increase public funding on health to at least 2.5 per cent of GDP. Also, the 'Ayushman Bharat' programme announced recently could improve the situation, if implemented efficiently.

- **Housing:** Millions of people live in ramshackle dwellings both in rural and urban areas. In large cities, sizeable sections live in slums amidst squalor. Due to this, members of the families of these most vulnerable sections, especially children in their formative years, are exposed to unhealthy and unhygienic conditions. The government has been providing home for the poor in both rural and urban areas.

  Most of these people lack safe drinking water and the government is now embarking on a major programme to provide piped water to such households. The massive drive to provide a toilet to all houses lacking it has also been a laudable step. So is the proposed programme to provide piped water supply to households lacking it. These will have a salutary impact on the health of the poor and the vulnerable sections.

- **Unemployment:** Unemployment and lack of income is a major cause of poverty. With about one million youth joining the labour force every month for the next one decade and a half or more, providing jobs for them has become the most challenging task for the government. The unemployment rate is also at an unacceptably high level.

  Informal employment: Quality of jobs created is also an issue. According to the Union Ministry of Labour, more than more than 90 per cent of the workforce is in the informal or unorganized sector which accounts for about 50 per cent of the national product. Those employed in the informal sector lack security of job, social security benefits like medical aid, housing, pension, etc. which those in the formal sector enjoy.

- **Lack of Skilled labour and need for Skill development:** The problem of employment is also compounded by the mismatch between the labour seeking work and skills required for jobs on offer.

  According to industry associations, even a good part of the educated youth coming out of schools, colleges, and technical institutions do not possess the specific skills needed in the industry and for jobs. Recruits need to be trained for the jobs which entails considerable time and costs. Imparting skills to the youth has assumed great importance in view of the rapid advances and disruptive changes in technology in the present-day globalized and competitive world.

  The Government has already embarked on a massive programme of 'Skill Development', especially for jobs involving technical skills, which needs to be scaled up.

➢ **Conclusion:** If the problem of poverty is to be solved meaningfully, not only the poor have to be lifted out of poverty but there should be perceptible improvements in the Social sector – education, public health and nutrition – so that those at the lower rungs also receive quality services in these domains and their quality of life improves substantially, which is envisaged in UN's Sustainable Development Goals which India is pursuing.

10. Social and political consciousness of the people and good governance play an important role in the effective implementation of programmes to eradicate poverty. Do you agree with this view? What explains the fact that some States and Union Territories (UTs) in India have registered more progress than other states and UTs?

Ans. The performance and progress of Indian states and Union Territories (UTs) since independence presents a mixed picture. While some of the states and UTs have forged ahead on the economic parameters – industrial development, employment, State Domestic Product (SDP) and per capita SDP, some others have performed well on social indices like education and health. And some other states have fared poorly on both economic and social indices and remained relatively poorer and more backward as will be seen from the following account.

- **Literacy:** As per 2100 census, on literacy, among the major states, Kerala, HP, Maharashtra and Tamil Nadu all had over 80 per cent rate with Kerala topping with 93.91 per cent. Another 10 states had over 70 per cent while the remaining 6 states had percentage between 60 and 70.

  Among the smaller states and UTs, Lakshadweep and Mizoram had over 90 per cent rate while nine others had over 80 per cent and three had between 70 and 80 per cent.

  By the next census due in 2021, most states would have improved their percentages.

- **Education:** In the education sector, while educational facilities did expand, somewhat gradually in the earlier years but at a much faster pace in the last three decades, the expansion, according to many credible surveys, has been more quantitative than qualitative, which has adversely impacted the poorer sections the most. Inadequacy and frequent absence of teachers, lack of trained teachers, poor buildings, and lack of facilities like libraries, labs, and toilets are endemic to schools catering to the poorer sections, both in the urban and rural areas.

Here again, as with health facilities, the more affluent sections of society are able to access facilities like better equipped schools while the poor have to fall back upon less equipped government schools.

NITI Aayog has proposed to prepare an Education Index, on the lines of Health Index (see below), to rank states and UTs on their performance.

- **Health:** On health, NITI Aayog has been doing a comprehensive study, with the assistance of the World Bank, and preparing a Health Index of States and UTs, covering 23 indicators on key aspects of health sector performance, and ranking the States and UTs. The Health Index scores for 2017-18 has revealed large disparities in overall performance across States and UTs. Among the Larger States, the overall Health Index score of the best-performing State is more than two and half times of the overall score of the least-performing State.

  Rank of States/UTs: Kerala topped the Larger States with an overall score of 74.01, while Uttar Pradesh was the least performing State with an overall score of 28.61. Among the Smaller States, scores varied between 38.51 in Nagaland and 74.97 in Mizoram. Among the UTs, the scores varied between 41.66 in Daman and Diu to 63.62 in Chandigarh. It is found that overall, there is room for improvement in all States. Even among the best-performing States, there is substantial room for improvement. Among the least performing States/UTs, particularly, there is an urgent need to accelerate efforts to narrow the performance gap between States and UTs.

  A deeper malady: Some of the tragic cases of multiple deaths of children which occurred in government hospitals in some states, lack of diagnostic equipments, apathy of medical staff, shortage of beds, etc.point to a deeper malady afflicting public healthcare in the country which impacts adversely most the poor and is a contributory factor to the persistence of poverty.

  Greater awareness: Hopefully, the performance audit being done by NITI Aayog on education, health, and, now additionally, on water conservation will create greater awareness and a competitive spirit among States/UTs and spur them to perform better and improve the situation on the ground.

- **Role of the public:** That a literate, well-educated, politically alert and socially conscious people could exert pressure on the State and its agencies to provide improved delivery of public services is amply proved by the examples of states like Kerala, Maharashtra, West Bengal and many Union Territories which have registered progress on social indicators comparable to some of the developed, middle income countries. Sadly, this has been lacking in a majority of other states which are large and much more populous.

Illiteracy and incapacity of large sections of people to exert any pressure and assert themselves is exploited by the people's representatives as well as an inefficient and tainted bureaucracy. The net result is that much of the precious, heavy public investments made in the infrastructure and social sectors go down the drain, do not give proper returns, or commensurate benefits to people.

A silver lining in this entire dismal picture is that some of the hitherto laggard states have belatedly woken up and are striving to improve services, thanks to some enlightened political and executive leadership. As democracy has matured in India, people even in the urban and rural areas have learnt to assert and overthrow ineffective governments and slothful elected representatives.

- **Governance failures:** There was a steady decline in governance standards in many states, in varying degrees, over the years due to the following factors:
  * Decline in the authority of the Central Government;
  * Rise of regionalism and parochialism;
  * Friction between the Centre and the States leading to conflicting agendas;
  * Lack of transparency and integrity in administration resulting corruption in public services; steps against black money and corruption could cleanse the system to a great extent;
  * Delays and cost overruns in projects resulting in wastage of public funds;
  * Perceptible fall in the delivery standards of developmental and welfare schemes which impacted mostly the poor and the deprived sections of society.

  These deficiencies became more pronounced with each passing decade for which the nation has had to pay a heavy price as evidenced by the persistence of poverty and deprivation amongst a still large segment of the population.

- **Role and Accountability of Elected Representatives:** The elected representatives at all levels – Parliament, State legislatures, town, and village levels must render unblemished services and be made more accountable to deliver on the promises they make to the electorate during elections as they have a critical role to play in the success of these efforts.

  Meeting constituents: It should be mandated by legislation that they meet people in their constituencies in small groups at periodic intervals, say every six months, to listen to the people's grievances and needs, and review the progress of delivery of various socio-economic programmes and on the promises they themselves have made in election manifesto. The concerned government functionaries should also be present at such reviews. Public pressure and exposing ineffective representatives will bring in more accountability.

At present, there is no such mandated, institutional arrangement to make people's representatives accountable directly to the people at the ground level – a weakness in the system fully exploited by many of them to get away with no accountability. Their indirect accountability in Parliament, state legislatures or municipal/town councils has not been effective in this regard.

Panchayati Raj and Gram Sabhas: At least in the villages, under the Panchayati Raj system, the Gram Sabhas function as an open forum and meet at intervals where people in a group can confront their representatives and government functionaries on various issues and development programmes.

- **Technology in administration:** With the introduction of technology, programmes like Digital India and computerization in the government at Central, State, and District levels coupled with schemes like Aadhaar, there will be greater transparency in governance and better services to the public. The Digital India programme under execution, which will connect 250,000 Gram Panchayats electronically, combined with the ubiquitous mobile phones, should help to improve services and bring about a sea change in rural India.
- **Empowerment of women:** Empowering women in diverse ways – better representation in legislative bodies, promotion of women's self-help groups (SHGs) to enable them to improve their economic status, increased participation in labourforce, etc. will ameliorate the condition of not only women but of their family as a whole. States like Kerala, Maharashtra and West Bengal have historically had strong movements for women's empowerment and these have helped to better their social standing. This is a model for other states to follow.
- **Role of NGOs:** Non-governmental organizations and social activists play an important role in raising the voice of the people and protecting their rights. Such efforts have proved effective in areas like environmental protection, rights of tribals and protection of women against violence and abuse.

> No society can be surely be flourishing and happy, of which the far greater part of the members are poor and miserable. It is but equity, besides, that they who feed, clothe and lodge the whole body of the people, should have such a share of the produce of their own labour as to be themselves tolerably well fed, clothed and lodged.
>
> - Adam Smith in 'An Inquiry into the Nature and Causes of the Wealth of Nations (1776).

FINANCE AND BANKING

The art of banking is always to balance the risk of a run with the reward of a profit. The tantalizing factor in the equation is that riskier borrowers pay high interest rates. Ultimate safety – a strongbox full of currency – would avail the banker nothing. Maximum risk - a portfolio of loans to prospective bankrupts at usurious interest rates – would invite disaster. A good banker safely and profitably treads the middle ground.

– *James Grant, Money of the Mind: Borrowing and Lending in America from the Civil War to Michael Milken, (1992).*

Topics Covered

- *Price levels in economy*
- *Price indexes (WPI and CPI)*
- *RBI's revenues and Economic Capital Framework (ECF)*
- *Role and objectives of Monetary Policy*
- *RBI and Monetary Policy*
- *Non-banking finance companies (NBFCs)*
- *Financial inclusion*
- *Problem of Non-performing assets (NPAs)*
- *Insolvency and Bankruptcy Code (IBC)*
- *Sovereign bonds issue.*

1. Price levels play an important part in the state of an economy. In this context, discuss the causes and consequences of inflation and deflation.

Ans. In a free market economy, price levels of commodities are determined by the forces of demand and supply. These depend on disparate decisions made by independent agents in the market. When demand is in excess of supply, prices go up and when supply is in excess, prices go down. These result in inflation in the former case or deflation in the latter case.

In an open economy exposed to global markets, inflation and deflation can be caused by both internal and external factors.

- **Inflation:** Inflation occurs when there is persistent increase in the general level of prices. It devalues the worth of money as one has to pay more money to get the same quantum of goods than before the price increase. Inflation is a recurring but only an intermittent phenomenon.
  - **Factors behind inflation**
    - Inflation may be caused by excess demand in the economy known as '**demand-pull inflation**' or due to increase in the costs of inputs and production called **'cost-push inflation'.**
    - **Easy money policy:** It may be the result of 'easy money policy' of the Central Bank with low interest rates or excessive increase in money supply which drives up demand with too much money chasing too few goods.
    - **Deficit financing:** In the event of 'deficit financing', when the government spending is in excess of revenues resulting in budget deficit and the deficit is covered by borrowing from the central bank or printing additional currency, it results in increase in money supply causing inflation.
    - **Supply-side factors:** Supply-side factors such as fall in the production of foodgrains due to poor monsoon, drought, etc. resulting in shortages in their supply, will push up prices.
    - **Input costs:** Increase in the costs of inputs or increase in labour costs (wages) will also trigger inflation.
    - **Import prices:** Hardening of prices of imported items like oil, minerals, metals, etc. would lead to increase in the prices of domestic products dependent on such imports.
    - **Exchange rate:** Depreciation in the value of the country's currency in relation to foreign currencies would add to costs and cause inflation as imports will become more expensive. (as importers will have to give out more of their currency per unit of foreign currency).

      Also, when a large fraction of a country's trade is denominated in foreign currencies, fluctuations in exchange rate caused by external shocks will have greater impact on prices. If the bulk of the country's imports are invoiced in foreign currency, depreciation in the country's exchange rate will push up prices of its imports leading to inflation,
    - **Disruptions in imports:** A deliberate decision by suppliers to reduce output to raise revenues, or disruption in supplies due to embargo or war, could also cause inflation. One such instance was the embargo on supply of oil to many countries by the oil producing countries (OPEC) during the Arab crisis in 1973. Oil prices also shot up during the conflict between Iran-Iraq, both major oil-producing nations, in 1980's and during Iraq's invasion of Kuwait (1990-91) which led to steep hike in the price of oil and had global impact.

➢ **Deflation:** Deflation signifies sustained reduction in the general price levels and may, though not necessarily, result in reduction in output and employment. (Deflation is not to be confused with 'disinflation'. Disinflation is reduction in (the rate of) inflation or elimination of inflation.)

- **Factors behind deflation**

  * **Aggregate demand:** Fall in aggregate demand will lead to decline in the prices of goods and services.

  * **Tight money policy:** A 'tight money policy' involving increase in interest rates by the Central Bank and higher costs for bank loans would result in fall in investments and demand.

  * **Excess supply:** Excess supply of items in the domestic market leads to steep fall in their prices. And in the case of open economies, external factors would cause fall in prices. For instance, increase in the production and supply of export items like tea, coffee, rubber, etc. at competitive rates in the international markets would adversely impact their exports and thus result in a glut of these items pushing down their prices in the domestic market. Thus price levels may be determined not only by domestic factors but could be influenced by external factors also.

  * **Decline in input costs:** A decline in the costs of inputs used in production (e.g., oil) will lower the production costs. And in a competitive market with multiple producers, if demand remains unchanged, producers will need to lower their prices on goods to induce people to buy to avert excess stocks.

  * **Technology and productivity:** Advances in technology and application of new technologies in production will augment productivity and lower production costs which will bring down the prices of products.

➢ **Consequences:** Both inflation and deflation can have adverse consequences on an economy in different ways.

- **Inflation:** Inflation hurts most the poorest and fixed-income sections of people as the amount of goods they can buy falls. A major consequence of inflation which is of serious concern is its impact on the real earnings of the common man, especially when the price increase is sharper in the case of essential commodities. If the rise in prices is prolonged, it will have a bearing on their standard of living.

  * **The** increase in the prices of intermediate products impact the price of final goods and even services. For instance, increase in the price of oil and petroleum products will increase the costs of production in industries and push up the prices of their products. It will also impact cost of transport which affects industries, suppliers, logistic firms and travelling public.

  * Prolonged spell of inflation could impair growth and macroeconomic stability.

- **Deflation:** Moderate drop of prices of certain products, especially essentials such as food or energy, will have some positive effect on consumer spending. But a general and persisting fall in prices can have severe negative effects on growth and economic stability. It will adversely affect output, employment, incomes and aggregate demand resulting in slowdown in the economy.
- **Business or trade cycles:** A related issue is that economies are subject to upswings and downswings known as 'business cycles' (also called 'trade cycles'). During upswings they go through a phase of expansion of employment, output and incomes, while during downswings, these economic indicators contract. In the upswing phase, it may touch the peak while in the case of downswing; it may touch the trough resulting in recession.

  Recession: A slowdown in economies which, should it persist, may even lead to a recession or depression caused by a variety of factors. They tend to spread to other countries as nations are interlinked and interdependent due to trade and globalisation. This happened during the **Great Depression** of the 1930's which saw major declines in output, prices, investment, employment and international trade and the collapse of financial institutions. The 2007-08 financial crisis which erupted in the US and adversely affected the global economy, is dubbed the **Great Recession,** from which the world is yet to fully recover.

  Such outcomes may be due to cyclical factors or structural problems in the economy resulting in persisting fall in output, prices, incomes and employment which may require radical steps or reforms. Once trapped in a recession, economies may take time to rebound and recover. As the saying goes, 'you can only take the horse to the water but you cannot make it drink, unless it is thirsty'.

2. What are the steps a government should take to counter inflation and deflation?

Ans. In countering inflation and deflation, both the Government and the Central Bank of the country have to take various measures. These include both monetary and fiscal measures.

❖ **Measures to counter Inflation**

➢ **Monetary measures:** The Central Bank and the government can take the following monetary measures to contain inflation.

- **Regulating supply of money:** The Central Bank of a country, in India the Reserve Bank (RBI), has various tools to regulate the supply of money in the economy to counter inflationary trends.These tools include the Bank rate, Open Market Operations (OMO) and Cash Reserve Ratio (CRR).

  * **Bank rate:** By raising the Bank rate, the Central Bank causes commercial banks to raise their lending rates and thus lower demand for credit. Firms do not borrow as much to invest when rates are higher while individuals stop buying durable goods against credit and, instead, turn to save. Lower demand leads to a better match between demand and supply, and will bring down the general price level.

It is, however, to be noted that raising interest rates impacts prices primarily by increase in the cost of bank lending and reining in demand. In cases where inflation is of the 'cost-push' kind and rising costs are leading to price rise, raising interest rate may not help.

Another aspect is that a change in the interest rate, say a lowering of rate by the RBI, is not invariably or fully transmitted by corresponding lowering of the lending rates by the banks. As lowering of interest rate may have a dampening effect on bank deposits, banks may be reluctant to fully implement the cut and thus the purpose of the cut may not be fully achieved.

* **OMO:** Central bank can also regulate the supply of money through a mechanism called 'open market operations'. In India, the RBI conducts OMOs by way of sale/ purchase of government securities to/from the market with an objective to adjust the rupee liquidity conditions in the market. When the RBI feels that there is excess liquidity in the market, it resorts to sale of securities thereby sucking out the rupee liquidity. To contain inflation, RBI may resort to sale of securities to reduce money supply.
* **CRR:** Cash reserve ratio (CRR): Along with OMOs, the RBI can also use CRR (CRR is the fraction of deposits which the commercial banks have to keep with the Central Bank) as an instrument to regulate money supply to control inflation as well as promote growth. If the RBI increases the CRR, the available amount with the banks comes down (and vice versa).

- **Supplies and Price control:** The government can take steps to improve the supplies of essential items like food, fuel, etc. and also regulate their prices. For instance, by procuring and supplying foodgrains through public distribution system (PDS), their prices are controlled.
- **Limits on wages:** The government may impose limits on wages of workers so as to control the disposable income in their hands and thereby contain demand.

➢ **Fiscal measures:** The government can also take various fiscal measures to contain inflation. These include:

- **Reduce public expenditure**: With reduction in public expenditure, the government demand for goods and services will come down and result in decrease in the private income and consumption expenditure.
- **Increase in taxes:** Increase in the rates of personal, corporate and commodity taxes will restrain personal consumption expenditure. However, the increase should be moderate so as not to discourage savings, investment and production which will have adverse effect on the economy.

- **Reduction in import duties:** The government can cushion price rise by reducing import duties and allowing freer import of commodities in short supply. If any of such items were being exported, their export will also be banned.

❖ **Measures to counter Deflation**

The most obvious policy response to combat deflation is to stimulate spending to increase demand so that prices start rising and economy stabilizes. But lowering interest rates to increase borrowing and spending may not always be effective.

- **Easy money policy:** The RBI and commercial banks should adopt a policy which aims at credit expansion to promote business and industry and stimulate economic activity. Bank credit should be made easily available to the public and business concerns. This can be done through changes in Bank rate and cash reserve ratio to be maintained by banks, and open market operations by way of purchase of government securities from the market to increase liquidity in the economy.

  It is, however, to be noted that a change in the interest rate, say a lowering of rate by the RBI, is not invariably or fully transmitted to customers by corresponding lowering of deposit rates and lending rates by the banks. As lowering of interest rate may have a dampening effect on bank deposits, banks may be reluctant to fully implement the cut and thus the purpose of the cut may not be fully achieved.
- **Increase in public expenditure:** Government spending is to be stepped up to spur economic activity, to increase employment, production and incomes. During periods of slowdown and recession, public investment is to be increased as private investment may be sluggish.
- **Lowering taxes:** Tax rates, of both direct and indirect taxes, may be lowered and tax concessions extended to businesses to incentivise and accelerate private investment.

3. Explain the terms price index, Wholesale Price Index (WPI) and Consumer Price Index (CPI). Also explain what is meant by Headline inflation and Core inflation. Bring out the relevance of these concepts in assessing price levels and in formulating monetary policy in the context of Indian economy.

Ans. **Index number:** An index number is a statistical device for measuring changes in the value of a group of related variables. It is a measure of the average change in the variables over two different periods or situations, and conventionally expressed in percentage terms. Of the two periods taken up for comparison, the period with which comparison is made is called the 'base year' and its index number value will be 100. This helps to gauge how far the value of variables has changed over time.

➢ **Price index:** The price index is an indicator of the average price movement over time of a fixed basket of goods and services. It allows comparison of the prices of commodities over different years. The choice of the basket of goods and services is done taking into consideration, whether the changes are to be measured in retail, wholesale or producer prices.

Likewise, quantity index numbers measure the changes in the physical volume of production, employment, etc.

In India, separate series of index numbers are compiled to capture the price movements at retail and wholesale level. The two indicators are the Wholesale Price Index (WPI) and the Consumer Price Index (CPI).

- **Wholesale price index (WPI):** WPI captures prices of bulk transactions of goods in the domestic market. The universe of WPI comprises all possible transactions at first point of bulk sale in the domestic market. WPI is compiled and released on monthly basis by the Office of Economic Adviser, Department of Industrial Policy and Promotion (DIPP), Ministry of Commerce & Industry. The prices for compiling WPI are collected at ex-factory level for manufactured products, at ex-mine level for mineral products and mandi level for agricultural products.

  WPI is an important measure to monitor the dynamic movement of prices at the wholesale level. In a dynamic world, prices keep on changing. WPI is used as a deflator of various nominal macroeconomic variables including Gross Domestic Product (GDP). The WPI-based inflation estimates also serve as an important input in the formulation of trade, fiscal and other economic policies by the Government.

- **Consumer Price Index (CPI):** CPI reflects the average change in prices of goods and services at retail level paid by the consumer. It is a measure that examines the weighted average of prices of a basket of consumer goods and services such as transportation, food, education and medical care. Changes in CPI are used to assess price changes associated with the cost of living.

  The CPI comprised CPI for Industrial Workers (IW), CPI for Agricultural Labourers (AL), CPI for Rural Labourers (RL) for which price data are collected. These capture the heterogeneity of the economic structure and the differences in the consumption basket across different population segments.

  The National Statistical Commission (NSC), headed by Dr. C. Rangarajan, in its Report in 2001 had observed that CPI numbers catering to specific segments of the population can be considered as partial indices only. These indices are not oriented to reflect a true picture of the price behaviour and effect of price fluctuations of various goods and services consumed by the general population in the country over a period of time. The Commission recommended for compilation of CPI for rural and urban areas catering to all segments of the population.

The introduction of new CPIs in 2011, viz, All India CPI-Combined, CPI-Rural and CPI-Urban provided a nationwide retail price index that captures the inflation faced by households, i.e., cost of living inflation. The new CPIs have a comprehensive coverage across regions as well as commodity groups including services. Since October 2013, the Reserve Bank of India has started providing indicative projections of inflation in terms of the broader CPI-Combined.

To make price forecasting more robust, the RBI also conducts 'Inflation Expectations Survey of Households' (IESH) with wide coverage and methodological improvements, including in sampling design. The survey elicits qualitative and quantitative responses from households regarding their expectations on changes in price levels and inflation three months ahead as well as a year ahead.

The Base year for calculating the price indexes is changed and updated periodically.

- **Headline and Core inflation:** Headline inflation is a measure of overall inflation in the economy including commodities such as food and energy prices. Whereas core inflation measure excludes the prices of highly volatile items like food and fuel (energy, gas).

  There has also been debate among experts as to whether the RBI's Monetary Policy Committee (MPC) should focus on headline inflation or core inflation while deciding on the policy and fixing the Bank rate, as sometimes these two measures send different signals.

  Both headline inflation and core inflation seem to be important determinants in formulating monetary policy. Core inflation, which excludes the highly volatile food and fuel components, is often termed as 'underlying trend inflation'. It is critical for guiding the future trend of inflation in the economy. Sometimes the headline retail inflation could be low almost entirely because of falling food prices. But if the volatile food and fuel prices are taken out, inflation levels may present a different picture.

  The trend inflation is an indicator of the future path of overall inflation. Hence, even when food and fuel inflation moderates over time, if there is high inflation in non-food, non-fuel components; it would pose an upward risk to overall future inflation, creating challenges to monetary policy.

4. Why did India switch from Wholesale price index (WPI) to Consumer price index CPI) in assessing price trends and inflation?

Ans. India has, off and on, experienced high inflation, despite spells of below-trend economic growth. As a result, controlling inflation has become a key objective for policymakers. As already seen, the two main indicators of inflation in India are the Wholesale price index (WPI) and the Consumer price index (CPI).

Although in India, the WPI has traditionally been the measure for assessing inflationary pressures, the RBI had conducted a review of its monetary policy framework. The Expert Committee, headed by Urjit Patel, set up in 2013 to 'Revise and Strengthen Monetary Policy Framework' had studied, *inter alia*, the issue of choosing an appropriate metric for gauging inflation. Consumer price index (CPI) was chosen, replacing the Wholesale price index (WPI), as a main measure of inflation and for inflation-targeting as part of monetary policy of the RBI.

It recommended Consumer Price Index (CPI) as a better metric for the following reasons:

- The average Indian household's major chunk of expenses is food related, on food and beverages which is the most important category in the CPI (with 45.86 percent of total weight).
- The Urjit Patel Committee had observed that with "food and fuel inflation constituting 57.1 per cent of the CPI basket .... the Committee is of the view that in the current context, targeting headline CPI would be a critical prerequisite for reducing and then anchoring inflation expectations."
- The analysis of data based on the RBI's urban households' inflation expectations survey shows that expectation of households in both the three-month and one-year advance surveys are significantly influenced by food and fuel inflation factors. Empirical evidence also suggests that changes in food and fuel prices drive inflation expectations. This indicates the need to target headline CPI and not core CPI (which excludes food and fuel) to anchor inflation expectations.
- The true inflation that consumers face is in the retail market. Although price indices that relate to consumer expenditures are at best imperfect, they are still close indicators of the cost of living. Unlike WPI, CPI measures the price changes in a basket of goods and services, such as food, transportation, education and medical care. This is why it is also known as Cost of Living Index.
- The consumer price index represents the cost of a basket of goods and services consumed by a typical household and are, therefore, a better guide.
- WPI measures the price changes in the wholesale market. It measures the prices of a set of commodities charged by manufacturers and wholesalers before the retail stage. But WPI is found insufficient as it does not reflect the price position at retail level to which the consumer is exposed.
- WPI skips the prices of Services segment while calculating inflation. An important consideration for replacing WPI with CPI was to include Services which account for over 50 per cent of India's GDP.
- CPI gives the general idea of retail inflation and prices driven by the consumer demand and supply. Although price indices that relate to consumer expenditures are not perfect, they are still close indicators of the cost of living. It is thus a better indicator of inflation for fixing Bank rate and guiding monetary policy decisions than WPI Inflation.

- CPI is the metric familiar to large segments of the population and often used in both public and private sectors as a reference in the provision of government benefits or in wage contracts and negotiations. The choice of CPI establishes an element of 'trust' as monetary policy is being based on an index that is of greater relevance for households and businesses.
- CPI is used to calculate for both the rural and urban parts of the country so that based on its findings, specific measures can be taken for the benefit of rural and urban segments.
- The CPI is a widely used economic indicator used in most of the countries, to measure the rate of inflation and deflation.

5. How does the Reserve Bank of India (RBI) earn income and have surplus funds? The Government of India is seeking transfer of a greater share of this surplus to the government than usually done by the RBI. Critically analyse the government's demand and RBI's response to it.

Ans. The Reserve Bank of India (RBI) is a 'full service' Central Bank which is mandated to undertake various functions relating to the India's monetary system, the banking sector and foreign exchange management.

➢ **The main functions of the Bank are:-**

- Issue of Bank notes.
- Management of the monetary system; ensuring macroeconomic and price stability in the economy.
- Regulation and supervision of banks and Non-Banking Financial Companies (NBFCs).
- Acting as the lender of last resort.
- Regulation and supervision of the payment and settlement systems.
- Acting as the banker to banks and the Central and State governments.
- Acting as the debt manager of the government; manage the borrowings of the Government of India and of state governments;
- Maintaining and managing the country's foreign exchange reserves.
- Regulation and development of foreign exchange market.
- Developmental functions including the areas of rural credit and financial inclusion.

➢ **Sources of income for RBI**

While carrying out the functions and operations, the RBI earns income and will have surplus funds at its disposal.The RBI's income comes from the following sources:

- It earns interest on its holdings of government bonds and securities and through open market operations (OMO) which it undertakes regularly to manage liquidity.

- Earns interest on overnight lending to banks.
- Receives fees on market borrowing programme of Central and State governments.
- Interest income on investments in foreign currency assets which could be in the form of bonds and treasury bills of other Central banks or top-rated securities; rise in yield/interest rates on foreign currency assets enhances RBI's income.

➢ **Transfer of RBI's reserves to Government**

Under Section 47 of the RBI Act, surplus profits of RBI can be transferred to the Central government after making allocations to its statutory reserve funds and after providing for other requirements of RBI. The RBI maintains part of it as risk capital for absorbing the losses in its various money and forex market operations and to meet any financial contingency due to liquidity crisis or other eventualities.

RBI has been transferring funds out of its surplus income/reserves to the government. Between 2013-14 and 2017-18, out of its income of ₹ 3.3 lakh crore, RBI had transferred ₹ 2.48 lakh crore to the government. In 2018-19, ₹ 68,000 crore was transferred to the government.

The Central government's stand: The Central government has for sometime been suggesting that the RBI should transfer to it a much larger share of its surplus reserves contending that there is no need for the RBI to hold a large reserve amount with it. The transfer of a higher surplus could help the government tide over any potential shortfall in tax revenue and contain fiscal deficit. It would also help to meet requirement of funds for welfare schemes like PM Kisan Samman Nidhi, the ambitious Jal Jeevan Mission, PM Kisan Pension scheme, etc. even as tax collection, especially under the GST, has fallen short of targets.

This has triggered a debate, both within the RBI and among experts, on the justification for the government's demand and on how the largesse would be used.

RBI Panel on Transfer of Reserves: As a sequel to this, Reserve Bank of India set up a panel on Economic Capital Framework (ECF), headed by Bimal Jalan, a former Governor of RBI, to study the issue and recommend guidelines on the transfer of surplus reserves from the Bank to the government.

The Bimal Jalan panel, in its report submitted to the RBI in August 2019, recommended as follows:

- The RBI's surplus, or the contingency risk buffer for meeting monetary and financial risks, may be kept at 4.5 – 5.5 per cent of its balance sheet. The buffer helps RBI to maintain India's monetary and financial stability.
- It will further keep 1 per cent buffer to meet credit and operational risks.
- The RBI will transfer ₹ 1.76 trillion to the government in 2019-20 fiscal. This includes ₹ 1.23 trillion of surpluses for 2018-19, ₹ 52,637 crore of excess provisions identified as per the revised ECF. Thus the government is receiving ₹ 86,000 crore over and above ₹ 90,000 crore budgeted.

- The RBI will pay interim dividend to the government, a practice started in 2016-17, only under exceptional circumstances.
- The RBI's capital framework be reviewed every five years and its accounting year which is now July – June be aligned with the fiscal year April – March.

The Central Board of RBI accepted the recommendations of the panel. These measures will not require RBI to sell assets nor it would shrink the size of its balance sheet. This largesse from the RBI would help the government to reduce off-balance sheet borrowings, meet shortfall in revenue collections or to provide fiscal stimulus to a sagging economy.

6. What are the instruments which the Reserve Bank of India has in executing India's monetary policy?

Ans. Monetary policy refers to the use of monetary instruments under the control of the Central bank (in India, the Reserve Bank of India) to regulate interest rates, money supply and availability of credit with a view to achieving the ultimate objective of economic policy.

The Reserve Bank of India has several direct and indirect instruments that are used for implementing monetary policy. These are:

- **Liquidity Adjustment Facility:** Liquidity adjustment facility (LAF) is an important mechanism by which the RBI manages the liquidity needs of the banking system. It helps banks to adjust their daily liquidity mismatches. LAF has two components, viz., Repos and Reverse Repos to regulate liquidity in the economy. (The term 'liquidity' means availability of adequate and timely cash).
  * **Repo (Repurchase) rate:** When banks need liquidity to meet their daily requirements, they borrow from RBI through repo. The repo rate or the repurchase rate is the rate at which RBI lends money to banks, when banks face shortage of funds. These are short-term, usually overnight borrowings. This is done using government securities. RBI buys government bonds from banks adding to their liquidity and agrees to sell them back to banks at a fixed rate.
  * Repo rate is considered as the policy rate as it is the widely used instrument between banks and RBI. Earlier Bank rate was considered as the benchmark but it has lost its relevance as banks seldom take refinance from RBI at bank rate. Repo rate is used by monetary authorities to control inflation as an increase in it acts as a disincentive for banks to borrow from the central bank. This ultimately reduces the money supply in the economy and thus helps in arresting inflation. On the contrary, when RBI reduces the repo rate, banks get money at a cheaper rate.
  * **Reverse Repo:** Under Reverse Repos, the RBI sells government securities at fixed rate of interest and agrees to buy them back from the banks in future. When banks have excess funds with them, reverse repo allows banks to deposit the surplus funds with RBI and earn interest on them at the same time. This process sucks out excess liquidity in the money market.

- **Marginal Standing Facility (MSF):** This is a facility under which scheduled commercial banks can borrow additional amount of overnight money from the RBI by dipping into their Statutory Liquidity Ratio (SLR) portfolio up to a limit at a penal rate of interest. This provides a safety valve against unanticipated liquidity shocks to the banking system. (on SLR, see later below).
- **Bank Rate:** Bank rate is the rate charged by RBI for lending funds to commercial banks, Bank rates influence lending rates of commercial banks. Higher bank rate will translate to higher lending rates by the banks. In order to curb liquidity, the central bank can resort to raising the bank rate and vice versa.
- **Cash Reserve Ratio (CRR) and Statutory Liquidity Ratio (SLR)** are also used to regulate liquidity.
    * Cash Reserve Ratio is the proportion of the deposits which the commercial banks are required to keep with the RBI. Though not used much, it is a potent tool of monetary policy to adjust liquidity. Narasimham Committee on Banking Reforms (1991) had recommended gradual reduction in CRR to ease liquidity and it was brought down gradually from 15 per cent to 4 per cent by 2013 which has helped to release more funds into the system.
    * Statutory Liquidity Ratio is the fraction of the total demand and time deposits with the commercial banks, which they are required by RBI to invest in specified liquid assets. Changes in these ratios help to increase or decrease the liquidity available in the banking system for lending. According to some, SLR is not a monetary tool and is only a prudential requirement to serve as a cushion for safety of bank deposits.
- **Open Market Operations (OMOs):** Open market operations are conducted by the RBI by way of sale or purchase of government securities (g-secs) to adjust money supply conditions. The central bank sells g-secs to suck out liquidity from the system and buys back g-secs to infuse liquidity into the system. These operations are often conducted on a day-to-day basis in a manner that balances inflation while helping banks to continue to lend.

7. Describe the objectives of monetary policy in India and the procedure laid down for formulating it. Is there any divergence between the views of the Government of India and the Reserve Bank of India (RBI) on these objectives and does this impinge on the autonomy of RBI? Critically analyse.

Ans. Monetary policy is the macroeconomic policy laid down by the Central bank (in India, the RBI) with a view to achieving the ultimate objective of economic policy. It involves management of money supply and interest rate, ensuring availability of credit and maintaining the internal and external value of the national currency.

The Reserve Bank of India (RBI) is vested with this responsibility under the Reserve Bank of India Act, 1934.

- **Objectives of Monetary policy**
  - It is imperative that the objectives of monetary policy are aligned with the larger goals of the country's economic policy so as to realize the full potential of the economy. For this, the government and the Central bank (RBI) have to work in unison even while ensuring the autonomy of the latter.
  - Since the inception of development planning, the primary objective of India's economic policy has been rapid and sustained economic growth and maintaining price stability, while also promoting distributive and social justice.

    The objectives of monetary policy have, of late, come under close scrutiny. The question is should maintaining price stability be the sole objective or should it achieve a combination of growth and price stability? It is recognised that, in the long run, the objective of price stability and growth do not necessarily conflict with each other. Maintaining low and stable rate of inflation is a necessary pre-condition for sustained growth.
  - The policy must also foster monetary and financial stability conducive to the development of an efficient and inclusive financial system.
- **Monetary Policy Framework:** The process of laying down monetary policy in India underwent a major change in February 2015 when the government and RBI signed a Monetary Policy Framework Agreement. In May 2016, the RBI Act, 1934 was amended to provide a statutory basis for the implementation of the flexible inflation-targeting framework. Under the new mandate, the RBI is to:
  - Ensure price stability and contain consumer inflation at 4 per cent, within a band of 6 per cent as the upper limit and 2 per cent as the lower limit.
  - Fix the interest rate based on an assessment of the current and evolving macroeconomic situation.
  - Manage liquidity (money supply) and availability of credit in the financial system.
- **The procedure:** Earlier, a Technical Advisory Committee (TAC) advised the RBI on the monetary policy to be adopted and setting the interest rate. But the recommendations of the Committee were only advisory and not binding, and the Governor of RBI had veto power and final say in fixing the interest rate.

  Monetary Policy Committee: As per the amendment of the RBI Act, the Central Government set up a six-member Monetary Policy Committee (MPC) in September 2016. The MPC consists of the Governor of RBI as Chairperson, the Deputy Governor of RBI in charge of monetary policy, an Executive Director of RBI and three domain experts nominated by the government as Members.

The MPC is to meet at least four times a year and will publish its decisions after each meeting. Each member of the MPC has one vote, and in the event of an equality of votes, the Governor has a second or casting vote. Though the Governor has the power of casting vote in case of divergent views among the members, it takes away the sole discretion which was vested in him under the previous system and this is considered to be a more judicious approach in setting the policy.

This has provided for a statutory and institutionalized framework for formulating monetary policy whose objective is to maintain price stability while keeping in mind the objective of growth. Views of key stakeholders in the economy, and analytical work of the Reserve Bank contribute to the process for arriving at the decision on the policy repo rate.

- **Theoretical basis:** Before looking at the stand of the government and the RBI on monetary policy, it would be useful to know the theoretical underpinnings that guide the formulation of monetary policy. These relate to the relationship between, and the interplay of, factors such as economic growth, price stability, inflation and unemployment which are to be factored in while framing monetary policy.

  - **Growth, inflation and stagflation:** In the 1940s and 1950s, the view in the advanced economies was that development process involved a choice between faster growth and low inflation. But the persistence of high inflation and low, stagnant growth in the 1970s – a phenomenon termed **'stagflation'** – brought about a radical shift in the thinking, and achieving price stability became the primary goal of monetary policy.

    Later experience of developing countries also showed that development through unchecked monetary expansion resulted in inflationary pressures which adversely impacted growth. High level of inflation impairs capital accumulation and productivity and affects growth potential of an economy. The countries which experienced high growth in the 1980s and 1990s, viz., Malaysia, Thailand, Singapore, Korea and Indonesia, had a growth rate of about 8 per cent with reasonable level of inflation.

    Money supply and price levels: While it is conceded that there is a positive relationship between money supply and price levels, price changes are influenced by other internal and external factors, mismatch between aggregate demand and supply due to structural bottlenecks and inflation expectations. The lack of capital in developing countries, coupled with the urge for development, compels government to resort to deficit financing resulting in monetary expansion and inflationary pressures.

    Expansionary monetary policy may produce higher growth and employment in the short run. In the long run, however, such an expansionary monetary policy will lead to higher inflation with deleterious consequences for the economy.

Employment and inflation: There may be trade-off between employment and inflation in the short-run. The Phillips Curve named after William Phillips, the British economist who did empirical studies on the relationship between unemployment and changes in wage rates in the U.K. during the period 1861-1957, found that there was an inverse relationship between inflation and unemployment. A low level of inflation meant a higher level of unemployment and high level of inflation would result in lower level of unemployment. This phenomenon also could, at best, hold good only in the short run. In the 1970's, many of the industrialized countries, viz., the US, Canada, UK, and France, experienced high levels of unemployment and high inflation which disproved the contention.

Social and Economic costs of inflation: It is also pertinent to note that there are social and economic costs associated with inflation. It impacts every section of society though the severity of it may vary widely between sections. It is the poor and the lower income groups who are hurt the most by inflation. It has adverse effect on their 'real' income as they are largely unprotected from price rise. Prolonged spells of inflation also has distributional implications causing widening of inequalities in income and wealth.

On the economic side, it causes distortions in the allocation of resources, uncertainty due to inflation expectations that would impact investments, production and output, lead to build-up of inventories and excess unutilized capacity in industry. On the fiscal front, it will cause fiscal imbalance and fiscal deficit and greater burden on the budget in servicing public debt.

- **The RBI and the Government on Monetary Policy**

From time to time, there has been divergence between the government and the RBI on the objectives of monetary policy. This becomes more pronounced in times of economic slowdown when the government is trying to rev up the economy which is in a sluggish mode. While the government bats for easy money policy with easing of interest rate to ensure greater flow of credit to various sectors, the primary concern of the RBI is to maintain stable price levels. By tradition, the government pushes for rate cuts for short-term growth while the central bank's primary mandate is curbing inflation, and, in the long run, only low inflation and price stability can fuel sustainable economic growth.

In the past few years, there have been rather conflicting views between the RBI and the government on the role of interest rates. While the RBI argued for using it to rein in inflation and maintain stable price levels, the government was of the view that a high interest rate impeded growth and egged on for lowering the rate to foster growth.

Efficacy of monetary policy: In this context, it is to be noted that there are multiple factors which influence price levels and economic growth, and setting the benchmark rate, i.e., the rate fixed by the RBI alone may not produce, or serve as trigger for, the desired impact. There have been occasions when, despite demands and expectations from various quarters, the RBI declined to lower the rate keeping in view the imperative need to maintain price stability.

Besides, the RBI has to take into account various other favourable or adverse factors such as volatility in the international oil and commodity prices, recessionary trends and slump in demand in the domestic and international markets while deciding on monetary policy.

Another aspect is that a change in the interest rate, say a lowering of rate by the RBI, is not invariably or fully transmitted by corresponding lowering of the lending rates by the banks. As lowering of interest rate may have a dampening effect on bank deposits, banks may be reluctant to fully implement the rate cut and thus cutting interest rate may not fully achieve the purpose. Raising interest rates impact prices, primarily by increase in the cost of bank lending, and reining in demand. In cases where inflation is of the 'cost-push' kind and rising costs are leading to price rise, raising interest rate may not help.

Autonomy of Central Bank: The debate on differing perspectives that the RBI and the government may have on the economy and monetary policy to be followed also raises the delicate issue of the autonomy of the Bank. Experts are of the view that the autonomy of Central bank is sacrosanct and is not to be impaired by any governmental pressure on it. There could be purposeful discussions between the top echelons of the RBI and the Finance Ministry on the state of the economy keeping in view the broader objectives of the nation's economic policy. In the ultimate analysis, a fine balance has to be struck between the Bank's independence and the imperatives, needs and goals of the economy in the larger national interest.

8. Discuss the role of Non-banking financial companies (NBFCs) in Indian economy and the problems faced by them. How did it impact the economy and what steps have been taken to resolve them?

Ans. Non-banking finance companies (NBFCs) form an integral part of the Indian financial system. They comprise a heterogeneous group of financial intermediaries and come under the regulatory purview of the Reserve Bank. NBFCs play an important role in nation building and financial inclusion by complementing the banking sector in extending credit to the unbanked segments of society.

NBFCs and Housing Finance Companies (HFCs) together constitute about 25 per cent of combined balance sheet of scheduled commercial banks.

➢ **Categories of NBFCs:** A non-banking financial company (NBFC) is a company registered under the Companies Act, 1956. It is engaged in:

- The business of loans and advances;
- Acquisition of shares/stock/bonds/debentures/securities issued by government or local authority or other securities;

- Leasing, hire-purchase, insurance business, chit business.

  But NBFC does not include institutions whose principal business is that of agriculture activity, industrial activity, sale/purchase/construction of immovable property.

  There are NBFCs which are authorised to accept and hold public deposits, and also non-deposit taking NBFCs which do not accept public deposits but raise debt from market and banks.

  Certain categories of NBFCs which are covered by other regulators are exempted from registering with RBI. These are:

- Venture capital fund, Merchant banking companies and Stock broking companies registered with Securities and Exchange Control Board of India (SEBI);
- Insurance company registered with IRDA;
- Nidhi companies notified under the Companies Act, 1956;
- Chit companies covered under the Chit Funds Act, 1982; and
- Housing finance companies (HFCs) regulated by National Housing Bank.

➢ **Role and Functioning of NBFCs:** NBFCs play a vital role in the following respects:

- Financing micro, small and medium enterprises (MSMEs), which foster entrepreneurship and innovation.
- In the development of infrastructure, transport, housing and real estate sectors.
- As important financial intermediaries, for the retail sector in underserved areas and unbanked sectors.
- Providing financial support to rural segments and for economically weaker sections.
- Serves as growth engines for financial inclusion, employment generation and wealth creation.

NBFCs' understanding of their customers' profile and their credit needs gives them an edge, and this helps them to customise products and services to suit the clients' needs better. This makes them the perfect channel and important financial intermediaries for delivering credit to MSMEs and retail sectors in under-served areas and unbanked sectors. They make a significant contribution to state exchequer.

NBFCs act as a bridge to provide last mile connectivity and fulfil the unmet needs of various sectors. Non-traditional and digital players are now entering this arena to deliver financial services by way of innovative methods involving digital platform.

➢ **Limitations of NBFCs:** While NBFCs are performing functions akin to that of banks, there are some differences:

(i) A NBFC, except those authorised to accept public deposits, cannot accept deposits;

(ii) It is not a part of the payment and settlement system and hence cannot issue cheques to its customers; and

(iii) Deposit insurance facility of Deposit Insurance Corporation is not available for NBFC depositors unlike in case of banks.

➤ **Problems faced by NBFCs**

NBFCs typically borrow money from banks, issue debentures or sell commercial papers (CPs) to mutual funds to raise funds. They undertake lending to MSMEs, retail customers, for infrastructure projects, etc.The RBI has been striving to wean away NBFCs from collecting public deposits in order to protect depositors as these deposits are not covered by insurance unlike deposits in banks.

NBFCs have been relying on raising short-term funds which were then lent as long-term loans. This leads to a situation of asset-liability mismatch. For example, an NBFC raises money by selling 6-month debt papers and lends this fund towards purchase of assets, say, a car, with loan tenure of 5 years. This leads to a situation where the NBFC has to roll over (or renew) the 6-month debt paper or raise fresh loans to repay its borrowing. While this may work in good times, as a matter of course, they run into problems when the times are tough and this cycle is broken.When NBFCs do not have money to lend, it reduces the credit flow to the economy, hits economic growth and causes many borrowers to default on loans.

Defaults and debts in the sector: A major problem arose in the NBFC sector in September 2018 when there were large-scale defaults by some firms of the Infrastructure Leasing & Financial Services (IL&FS) group, an infrastructure lending behemoth which has 169 group companies, including subsidiaries and associate entities. The group incurred huge outstanding debt, estimated to be ₹ 91,000 crore, of which about ₹ 57,000 crore was from bank loans. This, in turn, adversely impacted the lending banks.

Yet another major defaulter was Dewan Housing Finance, a non-banking housing finance company, which had an outstanding loan of close to ₹ 40,000 crore when the liquidity crisis erupted.

These and other crises took a heavy toll on the NBFCs when liquidity started drying up for the sector as banks, mutual funds and other investors turned cautious and stalled funding.

➤ **Impact on the economy**

- The crisis in the NBFC sector arose at a critical juncture in the economy when investment was already tepid, exports were flagging, consumption demand, which is a primary engine driving the economy, had been sluggish, and overall growth was slack.

- Apart from compounding the problem of non-performing assets (NPAs), the reduction and choking of credit flow to employment-generating sectors such as MSMEs, commercial real estate, housing and infrastructure added to economic slowdown.

➢ **Remedial measures**

- The problems which the NBFCs face squarely point to poor governance and lack of due diligence resulting in reckless and risky lending causing bad debts. Following this, the government has strengthened the regulatory and supervisory authority of RBI over NBFCs and HFCs.
- NBFC sector has a web of inter-linkages with the banking sector, capital market and other financial sector entities. The RBI is keeping a close watch on these inter-linkages to ensure financial stability.
- To improve credit flow to, and restore confidence in, the NBFC sector, the 2019-20 Union Budget has proposed the following measures:
  * A scheme under which the government would offer a one-time partial guarantee, for first loss of up to 10 per cent, to state-run banks to buy pooled assets worth ₹ 1 lakh crore of financially sound NBFCs.
  * NBFCs which do public placement of debt have to maintain a Debenture Redemption Reserve (DRR) and also a special reserve as required by RBI. To allow NBFCs to raise funds in public issues, the requirement of creating a DRR will be done away with.
  * To bring more NBFCs on the Trade Receivable Discounting System (TReDS) platform, Factoring Regulation Act, 2011 will be amended and steps taken to allow all NBFCs to directly participate on the TReDS platform. TReDS is an online bill discounting platform that helps cash-starved MSMEs raise funds by selling their trade receivables to corporates. It not only ensures the regular flow of operational funds to MSMEs at attractive interest rates, but also ensures that their working capital limits are not affected.
  * Efficient and conducive regulation of the housing sector is extremely important for our economy. The National Housing Bank (NHB), besides being the refinancer and lender, is also regulator of the housing finance sector. This gives a somewhat conflicting and difficult mandate to NHB. To ease the working of NHB, the regulation authority over the housing finance sector will be shifted from NHB to RBI.
- Besides the above, the government has announced more steps post-budget to ease liquidity in the economy which should help NBFCs, HFCs and MSMEs to revive and perform to their potential.

9. Explain the scheme of Jan Dhan Yojana implemented in India to promote 'Financial inclusion'. Critically analyse its merits and shortcomings and the challenges it faces. Outline steps which can be taken to improve the scheme.

Ans. The scheme of 'financial inclusion' implemented in India is a major progressive step to ensure that socio-economic growth is more inclusive and bring into the fold of banking the poor and vulnerable sections who have hitherto been left out of it. Though the government and the Reserve Bank of India (RBI) had been making concerted efforts over the years to extend banking facilities to the unbanked sections, the scheme got much fillip in 2014 when the government launched the PM Jan Dhan Yojana (PMJDY) scheme as a national mission. It ensures access to financial services, viz., Banking, Savings and Deposit Accounts, Remittance, Credit, Insurance and Pension, in an affordable manner.

➤ **Features of PM JDY scheme**

The benefits under PMJDY scheme include the following:

- The account, which is a Basic SB Deposit Account (BSBDA), can be opened in any bank branch or Business Correspondent (Bank Mitra) outlet. It can be a joint account.
- Interest paid on deposit.
- Accidental insurance cover of ₹ 2 lakh.
- No minimum balance required. However, to get cheque book facility, depositor will have to fulfil minimum balance criteria.
- Offers facility of ATM card or ATM-cum-Debit card.
- Life cover of ₹ 30,000/- payable on death of the beneficiary, subject to fulfilment of the eligibility condition.
- Beneficiaries of Government schemes will get the dues directly credited in these accounts under the Direct Benefit Transfer (DBT) facility thus avoiding intermediaries, leakages and delay. It also provides access to pension and insurance products.
- On satisfactory operation of the account for 6 months, an overdraft facility will be permitted. This facility up to ₹ 10,000 is available in only one account per household, preferably the lady of the household.

➤ **Population covered by banking and JDY scheme**

As per 2011census, there was a total of 25 crore households in India of which only 14.68 crore households (i.e., 58.7 per cent of households) were availing banking services.

And as per a 2018 World Bank report, the share of adults in India with a bank account has more than doubled since 2011 to 80 per cent. With an intensive drive, the number of bank accounts under JDY rose from 14.72 crore in March 2015 to 35.27 crore in March 2019. And the total deposits in these accounts rose from

₹ 15,670 crore to ₹ 96,107 crore during the same period, according to Ministry of Finance data. The average deposit per JDY account also rose from ₹ 1,065 in 2015 to ₹ 2,725 in 2019.

An important factor driving this increase was the JDY policy to boost account ownership among unbanked adults through biometric identification cards. This policy benefited traditionally excluded groups and helped ensure inclusive growth in account ownership. Another notable fact is that between 2014 and 2017, account ownership in India rose by more than 30 percentage points among women as well as among adults in the poorest 40 per cent of households.

➤ **Challenges and Opportunities for the Scheme challenges**

Despite the impressive performance under JDY, the scheme faces both challenges, which can be overcome, and opportunities, which can be seized, with concerted efforts on the part of Central, State and Local governments as discussed below.

- **Unbanked segments:** In view of commendable penetration of banking services and sustained policy of financial inclusion, 80 per cent of Indian adults have a bank account today. It is, indeed, a great achievement. However, India still has 190 million (19 crore) adults without a bank account, making it the world's second largest unbanked population after China, which has 225 million (22.5 crore) adults without a bank account.

- **Financial literacy:** Creating awareness about the benefits of banking and educating those who are new to banking system is an important part of the programme. Ensuring 'financial literacy', especially among the poor and vulnerable sections, is a major challenge. The RBI has issued guidelines for conducting financial literacy camps by Financial Literacy Centres (FLCs) and rural branches of banks.

  In this effort, besides banks, Banking Correspondents (BCs), National Savings Scheme (NSS) agents and the Common Service Centres (CSCs) being set up in villages across India under the Digital India project could play a significant role to bring those left out into banking fold. (See Digital India Project discussed later below).

- **Multiple accounts:** Instances have been found where an individual has opened more than one account in various banks. So the number of accounts may not truly reflect the actual number of persons covered under JDY due to duplication.

- **Inactive, inoperative accounts:** A matter of concern is that half of the accounts are rarely used. According to the World Bank study, "The Global Findex Database 2017: Measuring Financial Inclusion and the Fintech Revolution", 48 per cent of India's bank accounts had no transactions over the one year preceding the study. This figure is the highest in the world and about twice the average of 25 percent for developing economies.

The World Bank report states that "part of the explanation might be India's Jan Dhan Yojana scheme, developed by the government to increase account ownership. Launched in August 2014, the program had brought an additional 310 million Indians into the formal banking system by March 2018, many of whom might not yet have had an opportunity to use their new account". The agenda of financial inclusion includes promoting entrepreneurship that can be nurtured only when bank customers can save, borrow, and remit/receive funds.

Large proportion of accounts being inoperative makes them less cost-effective and unviable for banks who incur overhead expenses for their maintenance.

- **Lack of income, earnings:** In many cases, the reason for accounts being inoperational may be that the account holders do not have regular income or income to the extent to save and deposit in bank account. This problem will be partly overcome by the DBT scheme introduced by the government on a wide scale. (See DBT scheme discussed below).
- **Borrowings and Loans:** According to International Monetary Fund (IMF), despite the impressive outreach and development of banking infrastructure, only 13 per cent of Indian adults borrow through formal channels. Notwithstanding priority sector lending norms which banks follow, hardly 35 per cent of Indian farmers utilise institutional loans. The rest probably depend on alternative sources such as moneylenders, indigenous bankers, commission agents, etc. paying high interest rates.

Opportunities

- **Benefits of DBT:** The Direct Benefit Transfer (DBT) is an ideal platform to widen the scope of financial inclusion. Under DBT, benefits or subsidies and dues from the government to beneficiaries are transferred directly to their bank accounts. The government offers 439 subsidy and other schemes, including for cooking gas, fertilizer subsidy, Ayushman Bharat, MNREGS wage payments, educational scholarships, old age pension, etc. which fall under the ambit of DBT.

Direct payment for all these through bank accounts of ultimate beneficiaries not only saves government funds by preventing duplication of claims by beneficiaries and eliminating middlemen who illegally siphon off funds but also avoids delay and ensures prompt payments.

Saving of funds: Since 2014-15, the government has transferred ₹ 7.23 trillion in subsidies and other payments directly to the bank accounts of beneficiaries bulk of whom belong to poor and vulnerable sections. In 2018-19, as many as many as 59 crore individuals gained from the government's DBT scheme. According to the government, since the DBT scheme was launched in January 2013, it has helped plug subsidy leakages by eliminating intermediaries and middlemen, which, in turn, resulted in a saving of about ₹ 1.41 trillion.

- **Greater financial inclusion of women:** Out of total savings accounts, overall 27 per cent of accounts were held by female in March 2014. And under PMJDY, accounts held by women constituted 53 per cent of the total Jan Dhan accounts as on March 2019. The existence of large network of active Women's Self-help Groups (SHGs), particularly in rural areas, which undertake income-generating activities, has greatly helped in this regard and it is a further step towards empowerment of women.
- **Digital India Project:** Broadband for All – Rural and Urban: This is an ambitious project to cover 250,000 Gram Panchayats under the National Optical Fibre Network (NOFN) and is being executed with Telecom Dept. as the nodal agency. For this, Virtual Network Operators would be leveraged for service delivery and communication infrastructure in new urban developments and buildings would be mandated.

  The project has two sub-components, viz., Common Services Centres (CSCs) and Post Offices as Multi-Service Centres (MSCs) for rolling out Public Internet Access Programme.

  Common Services Centres (CSCs): The CSC in each Gram Panchayat would be made viable and multi-functional end-points for delivery of government and business services. DeitY would be the nodal department to implement the scheme.

  Post Offices as MSCs: A total of 150,000 Post Offices are proposed to be converted into multi service centres. Department of Posts would be the nodal department to implement this scheme. Of these, over 80 per cent post offices are in rural areas. Post Office Savings Bank (POSB) already has 37.4 crore Savings accounts in POSB. The newly launched India Post Payments Bank (IPPB) has permission to link around 17 crore POSB accounts with its own setup.

  Synergy with JDY: As the CSCs and MSCs will function close to the people in rural and urban areas, the Digital India project can be leveraged to extend the reach of Jan Dhan Yojana both to promote financial literacy among people, and increase bank transactions and make JDY accounts more active and viable.

10. The banking sector has been under severe stress due to bad loans and non-performing assets. Discuss the reasons which led to this and the steps taken by the government and the Reserve Bank of India to contain the problem.

Ans. The problem of bad loans and stressed assets in banks, especially the public sector banks (PSBs), continue to haunt the India's banking sector. Instances of frauds occurring in the operations of banks is another major problem causing serious concern.

➢ **Extent of NPAs and frauds**

- According to Reserve Bank data, the gross non-performing assets (GNPAs) of banks rose from 9.3 percent in 2016-17 to 11.2 percent amounting to ₹10.39 trillion in 2017-18. Of this, the share of public sector banks (PSBs) stood at ₹ 8.95 trillion (86.14 per cent).
- In contrast, the GNPA ratio of private sector banks stood at a much lower level of 4.7 percent in 2017-18. Concerted efforts through higher write-offs and better recoveries helped private sector banks to maintain lower GNPA ratio.
- The GNPAs of many banks rose to nearly 10 per cent following asset quality review (AQR) by the RBI. This was also due to due to restructured advances slipping into NPAs and better recognition of advances as NPAs. Due to this, the banks had to set aside large sums to cover bad loans which reflected on their balance sheets.
- Power, infrastructure and steel sectors together account for half of the stressed assets.

Bank frauds: Apart from the problem of NPAs, banks are confronted with recurring frauds. According to RBI, banks have been under-reporting frauds. The time-lag between the date of occurrence of a fraud and the date of its detection is significant. RBI has revealed that 90.6 percent of the frauds reported by banks in 2018-19 occurred between 2000 and 2018.

The reasons cited for delays in recognising frauds include delays in completing forensic audits or inconclusive findings of forensic audits.

A comprehensive checking of legacy stock of non-performing loans across state-run banks during 2018-19 helped unearth frauds perpetrated over several years and is leading to increased number of reported incidents of frauds in recent years.

That frauds of high value of ₹ 50 crore and above constituted about 80 percent of all the frauds during 2017-18 is an added concern. Nearly 93 per cent of the frauds worth ₹ 10 lakh or more occurred in public sector banks while private banks accounted for just 6 per cent.

➢ **Remedial measures**

As part of the revamp of state-run banks (PSBs) and to ring-fence the system, the government has taken various measures.

- To improve governance, the post of Chairman and MD/ CEO of PSBs has been separated and selection process for these positions made more transparent and on basis of merit.
- A Bank Board Bureau (BBB) was set up, consisting of eminent professionals and officials for appointment of whole-time Directors and the Chairman replacing the Appointments Board.

- To de-stress banks' position on loan defaults due to delay of projects, meetings are held between banks and concerned sectors to speed up clearances holding up projects.
- For better risk control and to keep close watch on NPAs, RBI has issued guidelines for 'Early Recognition of Financial Distress and Prompt Steps for Resolution and Fair Recovery'.
- To prevent frauds in banks, the RBI has been reviewing its 'Master Direction on Frauds' and issues guidance to banks. It is also considering additional measures for timely recognition of frauds and enforcement action against violations.
- Auditors of companies overseen by the National Financial Reporting Authority (NFRA) will have to disclose their findings separately as the government looks to address audit-related concerns and step up transparency. The government proposes to notify a new form that will require auditors to file key findings in respect of companies and any adverse comments and observations, among other details. This is prompted by cases including the major scam at IL&FS that revealed severe shortcomings and raised questions over governance standards, management interference and the quality of audits.
- **Insolvency and Bankruptcy Code (IBC):** India did not have an effective bankruptcy code and there was no single law dealing with insolvency and bankruptcy. The framework that existed for insolvency and bankruptcy was inadequate, ineffective and resulted in undue delays in resolution.

  A major initiative was the enactment of Insolvency and Bankruptcy Code (IBC) in 2016 for effective resolution of insolvency and non-performing assets (NPAs). Despite certain teething problems, the IBC mechanism is proving to be a game changer.

  * The new regime protects the interests of lenders and creditors to the company in default.
  * It enables failed businesses to wind up in a time-bound manner and helps entrepreneurs exit business quickly.
  * The code aims at early identification of incipient stress in banks' assets and creates an environment in which maximum value can be realised from troubled assets.
  * The RBI is also now empowered to issue directions to any bank to initiate action for insolvency in respect of a default under the IBC.
  * The IBC represents a paradigm shift in which creditors take control of the assets of the defaulting debtors, in contrast to the earlier system in which assets remained in possession of debtors till resolution or liquidation.

Changes in Insolvency and Bankruptcy Code: As some shortcomings were found in the operation of IBC, the government amended certain provisions in it in 2019 to make it more effective. These include:

* Lenders are to recognise incipient stress in loan accounts, immediately on default, by classifying such assets as special mention accounts.
* Defaults are to be recognized within 30 days. During this review period of 30 days, lenders may decide on the strategy for its resolution, including the nature of the resolution plan (RP) and how the plan will be implemented.
* The amended IBC Bill of 2019 gives the Committee of Creditors of a loan defaulting company explicit authority over the distribution of proceeds in the resolution process, and fixes a firm timeline of 330 days for resolving cases referred to the IBC.
* Reserve Bank's resolution framework on recognising bad loans and the IBC have paved the way for attracting investors into the stressed-assets space and helped speed up resolution. Of this, the corporate sector has seen active interest from most investors.

While the IBC has been a major remedial measure to tackle the problem of NPAs of the banking sector, it faces many challenges in its implementation due to delays in settlement of cases in National Company Law Tribunals (NCLTs). The major problems are excessive workload in NCLTs and inadequacy of manpower to handle them resulting in delays to cases.

11. What are the challenges in the implementation of Insolvency and Bankruptcy Code (IBC) and, in this context, identify the problems faced by National Company Law Tribunals (NCLTs)? What measures should the government take to overcome them?

Ans. The enactment of Insolvency and Bankruptcy Code (IBC) in 2016 has been a major step in resolving the problem of bankruptcy of businesses and the stressed assets of lending agencies. With IBC and the National Company Law Tribunals (NCLTs) set up, it was expected that resolution process for NPAs would take place in a time-bound manner, facilitating the speedy redistribution of assets and businesses. There are also Debt Recovery Tribunals (DRTs) for resolution of insolvency and bankruptcy cases and for recovery of debts due to banks and financial institutions.

Recoveries: As per estimates, the IBC has helped address, directly or indirectly, stressed assets worth approximately ₹ 3 lakh crore since the law came into force in December 2016. The estimated amount includes recoveries made through resolution plan and cases settled before admission by the NCLT.

As regards recovery of unpaid corporate loans, the NCLT could resolve insolvency and bankruptcy proceedings involving more than ₹ 80,000 crore in 2018 and this is expected to go beyond ₹ 1 lakh crore in 2019 with several big-ticket default cases pending.

Limitations: But notwithstanding its benefits, the implementation of IBC process has been beset with problems. There are loopholes resulting in deviations and the statutory time limit of 180-270 days for resolutions is not being adhered to in a number of cases due to the following factors.

- **Excessive workload:** One of the main problems is the huge caseload in NCLTs. The NCLT was constituted under the Companies Act, 2013, and handles corporate disputes of all kinds under its provisions. But when the IBC came into force in 2016, it was also made the adjudicator of corporate insolvency cases and this added to their workload.
- **Legacy issues:** After introduction of IBC, all cases pending under the previous regimes, including the Board of Industrial and Financial Reconstruction (BIFR), the Debt Recovery Tribunal (DRT) and the Sick Industrial Companies Act (SICA), as also the ongoing debt-resolution cases in high courts, came under the new insolvency law and the NCLT. As the newly formed tribunals replaced the Company Law Board (CLB), they had to adjudicate those cases as well. As a result, they started with more than 4,000 CLB cases, 15,000 DRT cases, 700 cases BIFR cases and 5,000-plus high court cases.
- **Adhering to time limits:** A critical issue in IBC process has been adhering to the time limit fixed for settling cases.
    * About 30 per cent of over 800 Corporate Insolvency Resolution Process (CIRP) cases have exceeded the time limit, with an additional 20 per cent having crossed the six-month deadline, some even exceeding 400 days.
    * Each day of delay is estimated to cost lenders crores of rupees in interest losses. It is estimated that pendency in the resolution of the original 12 major insolvency cases have caused loss of ₹ 4,000 crore to banks.
    * To improve India's standing on 'Ease of Doing Business' index and attract global investors to India's economy, the resolution process must be robust and timely, and not prone to inordinate delays and bottlenecks. NCLT and the Supreme Court have to ensure this.

Remedial measures:

- The Ministry of Corporate Affairs has proposed a 'pre-packaged bankruptcy scheme'. This would give a stressed company the option to prepare a financial reorganisation plan with the approval of a minimum of two-thirds of its creditors (and shareholders) before the filing of an insolvency application before the NCLT. Its advantage is that the lenders are already on board, so it can bypass processes and interventions, therefore averting delays and pendency.

- Compared to the task on hand, the NCLT set-up is under-staffed and there is imperative need to strengthen the infrastructure and increase the number of NCLT benches and Members manning them to ensure that there is adequate capacity to cope with the workload of cases. Lack of Judicial and Technical Members on benches is a handicap.
- A meticulous training programme for Resolution Professionals (RPs) and Judges in the NCLT system could help improve and expedite the process of handling cases.

12. In the Union budget for 2019-20, the government of India mooted a proposal to "start raising a part of its gross borrowing programme in external markets in external currencies." While some experts supported the idea, some sounded a note of caution and opposed it. Discuss the pros and cons of raising sovereign funds overseas in external currencies in the context of Indian economy.

Ans. The Union budget for 2019-20 contained a proposal to partially fund its borrowing in foreign markets setting the stage for the country's first ever Sovereign Bond issue in foreign currency.

Sovereign bonds: Sovereign bonds are government securities (G-secs), or debt instruments, issued by the government to manage the fund requirements of the government and to finance fiscal deficit. They can be issued in both domestic and foreign currency.

Overseas sovereign bonds: These are bonds issued by the government abroad to raise funds from foreign investors.

- Just like other bonds, the sovereign bonds also promise to pay the buyer a certain amount of interest for a stipulated number of years and repay the entire face value on maturity.
- They also have a 'rating' associated with them which essentially speak of their credit worthiness.
- The government of India has been issuing sovereign bonds only in local currency in the domestic market. For years, the government has resisted issuing sovereign bonds abroad.

Foreign portfolio investors have evinced interest in Indian government bonds traded locally as the real interest rate on Indian bonds is attractive compared to developed countries. But currency stability is vital for such investors, as they take the currency risk investing in rupee-denominated government bonds.

Pros and Cons of Overseas Sovereign Bonds issue

While the government's view is that issue of sovereign bonds in foreign markets in foreign currency will help to boost private investment in the country, some experts, including some of the former Governors of RBI, have cautioned and spoken against the move. The merits and disadvantages and risks of the proposal are discussed below.

Merits and case in favour of the proposal

- One of the government's arguments is that the quantum of its borrowing within India 'crowds out' the private sector from the financial market. In other words, due to government borrowing in domestic market, there are not enough funds available for the private sector to meet its credit and investment needs adequately. And, if the private sector cannot get enough funds to borrow, then its investment is affected, and that cripples economic growth. Therefore, borrowing overseas allows the government to raise funds in such a way that there is enough domestic credit available for the private sector.
- India's domestic savings rate has fallen in the last few years. The decline has been mostly in household savings, which is the main source of borrowing for the government and corporate sector. In view of this, the government wants to tap the sovereign bond market to partially make up for the fall in domestic savings.
- India's sovereign external debt-to-GDP is at less than 5 per cent which is among the lowest globally. Hence government could resort to borrowing abroad without much concern about over-indebtedness.
- Overseas borrowing programme allows the government to maintain the gradual reduction of fiscal deficit.
- Interest rates in the western countries are low and so funds can be raised abroad quite cheaply, almost at half the domestic rate.
- Raising funds abroad would mean that much less domestic funds would be sought by the government. This, in turn, would reduce yields in the Indian bond market, help banks pass on policy rate cuts to the customers of loans and ease availability of credit to the private sector.
- Sovereign bonds get international status and recognition and it makes it easier for the private sector, too, to access loans from the international market.

The Flip side and case against the proposal

However, the proposal is opposed by some of the experts citing its possible ramifications as explained below.

- The proposal involves risk of exchange rate variations. Debt in foreign currency, say dollars, would have to be returned in dollars only. If Rupee weakens during the tenure of the bond, the government's burden to pay back would increase as more rupees would have to be forked out to pay back the same amount of dollars, euros, yen, etc.
- While dollar or yen interest rate may be lower than rupee interest rates, the lower interest rate on foreign currencies may be offset in the longer run by India having to make higher repayments of principal if the rupee depreciates against the foreign currency. Experience has shown that countries which have gone in for sovereign bond in foreign currency have paid dearly.

- Most of the macroeconomic crises in emerging economies have been caused by issues relating to foreign exchange rate or high indebtedness in foreign currencies. The south-east and East Asian financial crisis of 1997-98 and the economic crisis in late 1970s and early 1980s in Latin American economies due to unsustainable debts in foreign currencies are examples.
- Considering that India is just-above-investment-grade country with rating presently in BBB category, the cost of funds could be higher than the rate of about 2 per cent in the western countries.
- India has a larger fiscal deficit than other emerging economies and it also has a wider current account deficit. The government raises debt to finance these deficits. If it is raised in domestic currency, the interest variation can be managed. But interest rates on foreign currencies are not in our control and they may not remain as low as at present.
- Exchange rate risk involving sharp decline in the value of Rupee, or due to global economic shock, may require to be hedged but doing so would entail much cost.
- Rupee's value is largely influenced by the inflows and outflows of capital. An inward rush of dollars would push up the value of rupee which would adversely affect exports.
- An over-dependence on foreign investment could leave exports less competitive and thus affect economic expansion and growth trajectory. A high level of foreign debt could pose threat to India's economic stability.

Conclusion: Those who favour the proposal contend that foreign-currency denominated sovereign bond issued in modest quantities would have a salutary effect on external rating and pricing of the Indian sovereign credit risk, and it would be a step in the right direction. It would not be too risky to borrow in dollar-denominated bond within limits as there is little risk of sudden outflow of dollars in panic and India's foreign exchange reserves are at a healthy level.

But if it is resorted to in unrestrained manner, it could pose threat to Indian economy.

On balance, India has to exercise caution and due diligence while going in for Sovereign Bonds in foreign currencies.

> It is not by augmenting the capital of the country, but by rendering a greater part of that capital active and productive than would otherwise be so, that the most judicious operations of banking can increase the industry of the country.
>
> - Adam Smith, *An Inquiry into the Nature and Causes of the Wealth of Nations* (1776).

TAXATION AND FISCAL POLICY

When there is an income tax, the just man will pay more and the unjust less on the same amount of income.
-- Plato (427 - 347 B.C.)

Topics Covered

- *Features of sound tax system*
- *Role of fiscal policy in an economy*
- *Fiscal policy and distributive justice*
- *Reforms effected in Indian tax system*
- *Goods and Services Tax (GST): its merits and drawbacks*
- *Fiscal Responsibility and Budget Management (FRBM) Act*
- *Finance Commission and Fiscal federalism*
- *Subsidies in Indian economy*
- *Transfer of resources from the Centre to the States*
- *Concept of Universal basic income*
- *Fiscal deficit and its implications*
- *Taxing income from agriculture.*

1. What are the salient features of a sound taxation policy? How far does the Indian taxation system meet those features?

Features of a Sound Tax System and Tax Policy

While discussing about Indian tax system, it is pertinent to know what constitutes a sound taxation. Economists and public policy makers have pointed out some essential features that go to make a sound tax system.

- **Features of a sound Tax system**
  - **Simplicity** A good tax system should be simple and easily comprehensible to all, especially the assessees who are to comply with the tax rules. A complex tax regime provides room for deviant persons to look for loopholes and evade paying taxes. Proper compliance by all also helps to maximize the tax collections.
  - **Transparency** The features of the tax rules should be widely made known to all and not be shrouded in secrecy. Educating the public on taxes levied is important and people have a right to know how the State utilizes and expend the funds collected, to what uses they are put, and how far it benefits the public and their welfare.

    Often, it is at the lower levels of government, i.e., the municipal corporations and panchayats, which are the closest to the general public and which undertake public works of critical importance to the citizens, such as upkeep of roads, water supply, drainage, electricity, etc., that there is lack of transparency, misallocation and misuse of funds.

    Also, the budgets of these bodies—receipts and expenditures—are not so well publicized as that of Central and State budgets. This points to the imperative need for tax regime and budgets to be transparent and made widely known and publicized.
  - **Equity** While the direct taxes are levied on the affluent and the well-to-do sections of society, the burden of indirect taxes falls on everyone irrespective of income earned. Hence, on considerations of equity, the burden due to indirect taxes should be kept as low as possible.
  - **Moderation** Tax rates should be moderate so as to optimize collections. Exorbitant and extortionist tax rates will induce people to not disclose income and wealth, and stash them away or make stealthy investments to evade paying taxes.

    Undisclosed, illicit funds may be used for anti-social activities like smuggling, drug trafficking, etc. which ultimately harms not only the economy, but society at large.

    Apart from this, the taxes on corporates, firms, etc. should be reasonable as not to discourage entrepreneurship and industry which will hurt the economy. Simply put, as the old adage goes, 'don't kill the goose that lays golden eggs'.

    According to a principle known as 'Laffer curve', tax collection will be maximum at a certain level of tax rates which are neither too low nor too high. Raising tax rates beyond a point may prove counterproductive. But this principle is contested on the ground that there is no simple, direct correlation between tax rates and total tax collection as the latter is influenced by many other factors in the economy such as production and income levels, savings and investment, aggregate demand, labour market conditions, etc.

- **Stability and Predictability:** The tax regime should, as far as possible, be stable and not subjected to frequent changes, including retrospective changes. While occasional change in rates may be called for depending on the state of the economy and developmental needs, the broad regime should remain the same so that it becomes predictable and easy to comply with.
- **Non-adversarial** A good tax regime should not be adversarial towards the tax payers. The tax authorities should not harass assesses but, instead, impress upon tax payers that paying taxes properly and on time is a duty to be complied in overall national interest. A friendly tax regime will be will encourage and induce people to comply.

  Conversely, the tax payers too should view paying taxes as a duty and obligation towards society, as a good part of the collections is used by the State towards the welfare of the less privileged sections of society. The concept of Corporate Social Responsibility (CSR) imposed on the corporates to use a small part of their profits to undertake tasks to promote welfare of the society exemplifies this aspect.
- **Economical** The costs incurred in collection of taxes should be kept to a minimum and redundancy avoided. For it is ultimately the public who bears the burden of not only the taxes but the administrative costs involved.

➢ **Tax system in India:** Indian tax system has undergone many changes and refinements over the years. Tax rates have been gradually brought down and tax system is being made people-friendly and hassle-free.

❖ **Tax rates**

- **Personal income tax:** One of the major criticisms of Indian tax structure was that it levied exorbitant tax rates. It was at its peak of 97.75 per cent in 1973–74, and was gradually brought down to 50 per cent by 1985–86 and still later to 30 per cent in 2005. At its maximum, it averaged 32.05 percent from 2004 until 2018 when it stood at 35.88 per cent. The top 5 per cent tax payers contribute over three-fifths of the total income tax collections.
- **Corporate income tax:** India's corporate income tax payable by companies had been relatively high when compared to the rates in other emerging economies. The government has been trying to bring it down in a phased manner. A lower rate of 25 per cent was applicable to companies having annual turnover up to ₹ 250 crore. In the budget for 2019-20, it was widened to include all companies having annual turnover up to ₹ 400 crore. This would cover 99.3 per cent of the companies while 0.7 per cent of companies remained outside this rate. Later, in September 2019, the government took a major step by reducing the corporate tax rate for new companies in the manufacturing sector to an unprecedented level of 15 per cent. Similarly, for the existing companies, the rate was brought down to just 22 per cent. As a result, India's corporate tax rates are amongst the lowest in the world. This should enable companies to expand their businesses

and make fresh investments. Though these measures entailed loss of substantia revenue in the short run, the expectation was that as the economy expands, i would reap more revenue in the medium and long term.

- **Impact of high taxes:** High tax rates make India less competitive in promotin industry and manufactures and exports. Moderate and more equitable ta structure would make industry more competitive; leave more disposable incom in the hands of individuals for consumption and corporates for investment an expansion. High rates will drive business elsewhere.

❖ **Tax administration:** Another major issue has been the way tax system i administered in India. The refrain of a section of tax payers has been that ta department enforces the regulations with too much rigour which borders o harassment. This is partly attributable to the fact that many tax payers have foun devious ways to evade paying taxes. Unaccounted and black money, stashing awa wealth illegally overseas by some sections compels tax authorities go after such case leading to complaints of harassment. It must also be said that honest tax payers hav had no such grievances which puts spotlight on those who try to game the system.

These issues have been addressed by the government over time by smoothenin procedures, enabling payment of taxes and filing tax returns online and reducin physical interface between the assessee and tax officials, thus reducing scope for an disputes and malpractices. This is an ongoing process and needs to be further refine to make the system more people-friendly.

2. Describe the role of fiscal policy in countering ups and downs in an econom and promoting economic growth. Cite such instances which Indian econom has faced and outline remedial measures taken by the government.

Fiscal Policy: Fiscal policy is a crucial macroeconomic tool governments use to alter th levels of taxation, public debt, levels of economic activity, stabilize output an employment, and redistribute income and wealth. It can be grouped into three function – economic stabilization, allocation, and redistribution.

➢ **Objectives of fiscal policy:** Its main objectives are:
- To maintain stable economic growth;
- Counter the cycles of economic boom and depression;
- Stimulate growth during recession;
- Contain inflationary trends and ensure that the vulnerable sections ar adequately protected with some basic income.

➢ **Role of fiscal policy in an economy:** Before the high levels of unemployment in th 1920's and the Great Depression of the 1930's, maintaining balanced budgets wa considered as the primary aim of fiscal policy. However, following these major crise John Maynard Keynes, the British economist, argued that governments should us taxes and expenditure policies to influence output and income and thereby counte the cyclical trends – the ups and downs – in the economy.

Keynes argued that in a period of recession, public spending would stimulate aggregate demand for goods and services and counter unemployment and deflation. It is argued that the government spending or 'pump-priming', as it is referred to, will stimulate private spending, which in turn would lead to economic expansion. This approach was adopted by Franklin Roosevelt, the US President through his 'New Deal' programme with some effect to overcome the debilitating effects of the 'Great Depression' of 1930's.

➢ **Contra-cyclical operations: Role of Monetary and Fiscal policy**

Monetary policy

In times of inflation or recession, contractionary or expansionary policies are to be pursued. The central bank (RBI in India) acts through monetary policy to counter their effects. It uses its powers over the banking system and tools such as interest rate and open market operations (OMO), involving purchase or sale of securities in the process.

- In the event of inflation, the central bank uses contractionary monetary policy to reduce the money supply in the economy, reduce bank lending, raise interest rates, and contain aggregate demand.
- In case of recession, the central bank resorts to expansionary policy to increase the money supply, increase lending by banks, reduce interest rates, to push up aggregate demand to revive the economy.

Fiscal policy

Fiscal policy is another macroeconomic tool the government has to counter inflation or recession by using government spending and taxation policy. When monetary policy, by itself, fails to produce the desired effects, the government has to step in with fiscal measures to counter the economic and business cycles.

- **Expansionary fiscal policy** increases the level of aggregate demand in the economy, through either increases in government spending or reductions in tax rates. Expansionary policy can do this by:
  (i) increasing consumption by raising disposable income with people through cuts in personal income taxes and indirect taxes on goods and services;
  (ii) increasing investment spending by raising profits through cuts in corporate taxes;
  (iii) Increased public expenditure to create assets and boost employment and incomes;
  (iv) increasing government purchases through increased federal government spending on goods and services; and,
  (v) raising federal grants to state and local governments to increase their expenditures on goods and services.

- **Contractionary fiscal policy** does the reverse: it decreases the level of aggregate demand by containing consumption, decreasing investment and reduces public expenditure, through cuts in government spending and increases in taxes.
- Fiscal measures have certain drawbacks in that it takes long time to implement them and make an impact on the economy. In the case of fiscal stimulus, there is also the problem of reversing it once implemented.

➢ **2007 – 08 Financial crisis and Fiscal stimulus**

In the event of severe or prolonged recession, the government may have to resort to fiscal stimulus by pumping in more money into the economy to boost investment and consumption and revive the economy. This was done by many governments, including India, following the global financial crisis of 2007-08 which led to the 'Great Recession'.

As economic growth decelerated in 2008-09, to counter the negative fallout of the global slowdown on the Indian economy, the Central Government responded by taking the following focused fiscal and monetary measures:

- Cut in indirect taxes to stimulate investment and consumption;
- Increased expenditure on public projects to boost employment and create public assets;
- Increased the limit on investment by foreign institutional investors (FIIs) in rupee denominated corporate bonds issued by the Indian companies;
- Besides, the Reserve Bank of India took a number of accommodative monetary measures to enhance liquidity and facilitate flow of funds from the financial system to meet the needs of productive sectors.

Such expansionary measures do result in increased fiscal deficit. But in times of recessionary conditions, the higher fiscal deficit is an appropriate counter-cyclical policy. It is worth noting that increase in Government expenditure causes aggregate income to rise not only proportionately but by a higher amount due to **multiplier effect.**

➢ **Slowdown since 2017-18:** A similar situation has arisen in Indian economy since 2017-18 when there has been perceptible and steady slowdown in industrial production and potential growth resulting in higher level of unemployment. The government has had to ease liquidity conditions and step up public expenditure substantially, as private investment was sluggish, to spur consumption and employment. The government took the following measures to kick-start the economy:

- Roll back of the enhanced surcharge imposed on foreign portfolio and domestic investors in 2019-20Budget..
- A special window for real estate with easier foreign borrowing norms to facilitate low cost funds for affordable housing.

- The central government to put in half of the ₹ 20,000 crore corpus for last mile funding for housing projects which are neither bankrupt nor have not defaulted on their loan repayment.
- Incentives for exports and overhaul of tax refund schemes that will benefit exporters upto ₹ 50,000 crore a year, and priority sector tag for export credit. This will benefit all products including textiles.
- The Export Credit Guarantee Corporation (ECGC) would expand the scope of Export Credit Insurance Service to offer higher insurance cover to banks lending working capital for exports. This is expected to reduce overall cost of export credit including interest rates, especially to MSMEs.
- Further support given to MSMEs and the automobile sector.
- A major step was taken for amalgamation of various public sector banks which will rationalise their working. The problem of economic slowdown was further accentuated in 2020 due to the severe impact of pandemic Covid-19 and the government took more steps to support the economy and revive it. **(For details on this, see Question 6 in Chapter 13 on page 13.29.)**

Need for structural reforms: It is also contended by experts that the problems in Indian economy are not merely **'cyclical'** in nature but **'structural'** and that it warrants wide structural reforms, especially in regard to removing infrastructure bottlenecks and rigidity in land and labour markets. There is also need to easing business conditions and hastening education reform and skill development that can boost employment, output levels, overall demand and growth rate in the medium and long term.

Fiscal deficit challenge: Some experts have even proposed that given the prolonged slowdown in the economy which shows no signs of receding, there is need for a public expenditure-led booster to revive demand even if it means breaching the fiscal deficit target.

It is a challenging situation as fiscal deficit target has been reduced to 3.3 per cent for 2019-20 from 3.4 per cent proposed earlier. While this signals government's commitment to fiscal consolidation, it will be difficult to achieve if tax revenues fall short of targets. Besides, according to Comptroller & Auditor General (CAG), the actual fiscal deficit figure could be higher if the off-budget borrowings made by entities such as National Highway Authority of India, Power Finance Corporation, etc. is reckoned. If the total public sector borrowings by the Centre, States and PSUs are taken into account, the deficit will be close to 8 to 9 per cent of GDP. Following the critical situation the economy faced in 2020 due to the pandemic Covid-19 and the various counter measures the government had to take, the government has relaxed the medium term fiscal consolidation targets. As per the Union budget for FY 2021-22 presented in Parliament on February 1, 2021, the fiscal deficit for 2020-21 is pegged at 9.5 per cent of GDP. The fiscal deficit in 2021-22 (BE) is estimated to be 6.8 per cent of GDP. It is proposed to continue on the path of fiscal consolidation and reach a fiscal deficit level below 4.5 per cent of GDP by 2025-26 with a fairly steady decline over the period. (vide Para 141 of Union budget for 2021-22.)

3. Critically examine how effective is fiscal policy in reducing inequalities in society and ensuring distributive justice.

In a society with gross inequalities and concentration of wealth, promoting economic and social welfare, as modern states are attempting, necessarily requires redistribution of wealth, incomes, and resources from one group to another. Such redistribution may be effected through fiscal measures – taxation – or through outright legislation as was the case with land reforms when ownership of land was transferred from the owners to the tenants.

The effectiveness of taxation in regard to redistribution of income, property, and wealth, and reducing disparities in society has been a subject of debate. The experience of many other countries has shown that economic growth, more often than not, leads to growing inequalities of income and wealth.

➢ **Inequalities:** Many advanced and developing economies are facing the challenge of rising inequality. And it is seen that wealth is more unequally distributed than income. While fiscal policy has played a more significant role in reducing inequality in the advanced economies – the OECD countries such as USA, Canada, Japan, Australia, New Zealand, and the advanced European Union nations, and the Nordic countries (Norway, Sweden and Denmark) – its role has been much more modest in developing countries where poverty is more pronounced.

  Extent of inequality in India: It is estimated that the richest 10 per cent of Indians own 77.4 per cent of the country's wealth, while the bottom 60 per cent, which forms the majority of the population, owns just 4.7 per cent. And the richest 1 per cent own 51.5 per cent. There is thus a huge gap between the rich and the poor.

➢ **Fiscal policy and Inequalities:** The experience of advanced nations has shown that fiscal policy can make a potent contribution to reducing inequality. Fiscal measures to reduce inequalities and achieve redistributive justice include:

- Levying taxes;
- Extending subsidies on goods and services;
- Income transfers; and,
- Other welfare measures (such as guaranteed employment programmes).

❖ **Taxation:** Direct taxes like personal income tax and corporate tax are important means for reducing inequality and redistributing incomes. It involves levying progressively higher rates of taxes on those with higher earnings and exempting those with lesser incomes. It is, however, to be noted that very exorbitant rates of taxes on high income earners are to be avoided.

  Taxes to be moderate: In India in the 1950s, raising maximum revenue and achieving redistribution became the avowed objectives and the tax structure became one of discretionary nature and with confiscatory rates and distortions.

The resultant disincentives led to a high degree of tax evasion, both in regard to income and wealth, with little possibility of detection and ineffective penal measures. Over time, this spawned a vast underground, parallel economy which had deleterious effects on the economy. The tax system had many loopholes and lacked transparency, so much so, it was difficult to assess the social and economic impact of various concessions built into it.

In the present globalised world, exorbitant tax rates may drive high income earners out of the country looking for tax havens where tax incidence is low. This will again impact the economy adversely. In due course, direct tax rates in India were gradually brought down.

Tax Structure and Equity: One of the cardinal principles of taxation is that it should be equitable in its impact on various sections of society so that the vulnerable groups are not made to bear a heavy burden. While the impact of direct taxes is felt by those in the higher and middle income brackets, the effect of indirect taxes, other than the service tax, will affect everyone across the board as the burden of these is passed on by the manufacturers to consumers of products.

Indirect taxes, now termed Goods and Services taxes (GST), are regressive in their effect as their burden is shared by citizens irrespective of income. Hence care has to be taken to ensure that prices of essential commodities are kept in check. Excessive reliance on indirect taxes to garner more resources escalates the costs of items and feeds inflation.

Inheritance tax and Estate duty: Most developed countries in the world levy an inheritance tax. The basic goal of imposing estate duty is to bring in equality of income among taxpayers. The objective is to tax the rich and distribute it to the poor.

But in India, as the existing rate of income tax for high-income groups is high, further burden of an inheritance tax would not be well received by the financially affluent sections of society. Hence, introduction of inheritance tax, if it happens at all, must be carried out with low rates, high thresholds and adequate exemptions such as in case of inheritance of single property.

- **Subsidies:** Subsidy is a sum of money granted by the state or a public body to help an industry or business keep the price of a commodity or service low. Its primary objective is to lessen the financial burden on persons in lower income brackets. In India subsidies are given to a number of goods and services such as food, fertiliser, petroleum which are the three major items. Besides, electricity, cooking gas, rail and bus fare, education, etc. are also subsidised in varying degrees.

Distortions and leakages in subsidies: There is great deal of distortions in subsidies since many of the subsidised items are availed by those in higher income brackets also. For instance, electricity subsidy benefits all households which are electrified and even among them, the affluent households which consume more power stand to benefit more even if they are charged at a higher slab rate for more consumption. Similar will be the case with railway fares where full costs are not recovered through the fares and the government bears part of the costs.

In the case of Public Distribution System (PDS) for food, while it is better justifiably targeted towards only the lower income groups, there have been heavy leakages due to mismanagement and diversion of stocks to black market. A detailed study made by the erstwhile Planning Commission revealed that for every kilogram of grain delivered to the poor, the government had released 2.4 kg from the Central pool of foodgrains. The PDS system has been gradually improved by State governments by adopting stricter checks and use of technology in its operations.

Besides, subsidy system suffers from another handicap of 'exclusion' in as much as many of the eligible people get excluded from its benefits, while many undeserving persons may enjoy them due to malpractices in administration.

Thus only those subsidies which are well targeted at those who really merit them and are efficiently administered would help in bringing about distributive justice and reducing equality.

❖ **Income transfers and welfare measures:** Various benefits which are transferred in the form of cash/income to the poor and lower sections go a long way in uplifting them from poverty and indigence and is one of the effective means of reducing disparities.

Since the last few years, India has been resorting to Direct Benefit Transfer (DBT) of benefits like pensions, old age pensions, scholarships, various subsidy elements like for cooking gas, MNREGS wage payments, etc. directly to the bank accounts of beneficiaries eliminating any intermediaries. This has not only ensured that the benefits reach the target persons correctly and without delay, but has saved thousands of crores of rupees for the government which were hitherto being siphoned off by unscrupulous elements and was a sheer wastage of precious public funds.

This reform in administration of benefit transfers has been quite effective and is greatly aided by the Aadhaar identification system, crores of bank accounts opened for the poor under the Jan Dhan Yojana and use of technology which helped to weed out duplicate claimants and beneficiaries.

These and other welfare schemes like guaranteed employment under the MNREGS and housing scheme for the poor have gone a long way in redistribution of resources and helping the poor and reducing inequalities and ensuring social justice.

➢ **Conclusion:** However, in the long run, apart from the various fiscal measures, sustained and inclusive economic growth which benefits all, particularly those in the vulnerable sections, will be the best antidote to bridging inequalities and uplifting the poor to better living standards. For this, providing efficient public services like education and health, housing, sanitation, power and water supply, etc. to all is a vital prerequisite.

4. **India's earlier tax structure was found to be regressive. Explain the reasons for this and the measures that the government took to make it less regressive? Suggest further steps to be taken to make the tax regime more equitable.**

➢ **Tax Structure and Equity**

One of the cardinal principles of taxation is that it should be equitable in its impact on various sections of society so that the vulnerable groups are not made to bear a heavy burden.

- **Direct and Indirect taxes**

  Direct taxes are taxes on income, property, capital gains etc. The main direct taxes are corporate income tax, personal income tax and capital gains tax. While indirect taxes are taxes on goods and services, now reformed and recast as Goods and Services Taxes (GST) which has replaced multiple Central and State levies.

- **Impact of Direct and Indirect taxes**

  The direct taxes are levied on the affluent and well-to-do persons in the higher income brackets and its impact is on them. Whereas, the impact of indirect taxes, other than the service tax, is on everyone across the board as the burden of these is passed on by the manufacturers of goods and products to consumers. The indirect taxes by their very nature are regressive in their effect as their burden is shared by citizens irrespective of income.

  Hence while levying indirect taxes, items of conspicuous consumption must be curbed and the burden of taxing such items should be borne by the affluent sections. Care has to be taken to ensure that prices of essential commodities and products used by the common people are kept in check. Excessive reliance on indirect taxes to garner more resources escalates the costs of items, feeds inflation, and is regressive in its impact.

➢ **Indian tax system**

In India, for long the share of indirect taxes outstripped the share of direct taxes in total revenue collections. It is rather ironic that when India was following 'socialistic' policies, indirect taxes, which adversely impacted the common people, should have had a greater share in total tax revenues. This is partly explained by the fact the tax base for direct taxes were rather narrow in the earlier years.

The other reason was that as the economy expanded and production and range of goods increased, with the levy of excise duties and custom duties, the collection and share of indirect taxes was bound to go up. There was thus imperative need to rectify this distortion in the tax system to ensure the principle of equity.

In the early 1990s, the share of indirect taxes in total tax revenues was about 80 per cent and that of direct taxes about 20 per cent, both in the case of Central taxes, and

Central and State taxes combined. But by 2019, in the case of Centre, the share of direct taxes in total tax revenue has risen to 50 per cent and the share of indirect taxes has been steadily brought down. This indicates that the Indian tax system is getting less regressive and more progressive.

- **Low Direct tax base and poor compliance:** As observed in the Union budget for 1992-93, even with a population of over 800 million, hardly about 7 million people paid income and corporate tax. And in 1997-98, only about 12 million people, out of 900 million, were assessed to income tax, and worse still, only about 12,000 assessees were in the tax bracket of income above ₹ 10 lakh.

  According to the Union budget for 2017-18, "India's tax to GDP ratio is very low, and the proportion of direct tax to indirect tax is not optimal from the view point of social justice." The budget put out the following data to indicate that the direct tax collection is not commensurate with the income and consumption pattern of Indian economy.

  * As against estimated 4.2 crore persons engaged in organised sector employment, the number of individuals filing return for salary income was only 1.74 crore.
  * As against 5.6 crore informal sector individual enterprises and firms doing small business in India, the number of returns filed by this category are only 1.81 crore.
  * Of the 5.97 lakh companies which filed tax returns for Assessment Year 2016-17, 2.76 lakh companies showed losses or zero income, 2.85 lakh companies showed profit of less than ₹ 1 crore, over 28,000 companies had profit of ₹ 1 crore to ₹ 10 crore, and only about 7,700 companies had profit of more than ₹ 10 crore.
  * Even in respect of income tax paid by 3.7 crore individuals in 2015-16, 99 lakh persons had income below the Exemption limit of ₹ 2.5 lakh, 1.95 crore persons had income of ₹ 2.5 to ₹ 5 lakh, 24 lakh had income above ₹ 10 lakh and 1.72 lakh above ₹ 50 lakh income.

  The above data is in stark contrast to the expenditure pattern as seen from the number of cars sold and the number of Indians who undertook foreign travel for business or tourism in the preceding five years. This shows that the country is largely a tax non-compliant society.

- **Problems with GST:** While the introduction of Goods and Services Tax (GST) has been a landmark reform in India's indirect tax regime, it has been beset with some problems as mentioned below:

  * While essential items that make up about 50 per cent of the Consumer Price Index (CPI) basket including foodgrains are exempted from GST, there are as many as four rates under GST, viz., 5 per cent, 12 per cent, 18 per cent and 28 per cent. Ideally, GST regime should have few tax slabs, say, one or two with very few items under the exempted category.

* Multiplicity of slabs and rates makes the system less beneficial and more complex in operation. But in a country like India, with a large part of the population in lower and middle income groups and even below the poverty line, a one-slab GST or no exempted items will mean taxing essential commodities which will make them unaffordable to large sections.
* The highest rate of 28 per cent has been kept to cover "sin/demerit" goods, luxury items and those items which create negative "externalities" for the economy.
* There is demand from various quarters to simplify the regime by reducing the number of rates and moving certain items from the higher slabs to lower slabs. The GST Council, consisting of Finance Ministers from the Centre and the States and UTs, has to take a call on this.

- **Factors influencing tax realisation:** The predominance of transactions in cash in the economy makes it possible for people to evade taxes. And when more people evade taxes, the burden falls on those who are honest and tax compliant. Gradually, after tightening checks on expenditure, cash handling, bank deposits, real estate transactions and shell companies, the tax base has widened with more people filing returns and declaring more income.

  In a positive sign, the number of effective tax payer base increased from 6.47 crores in 2014-15 to 8.27 crores in 2016-17.The direct tax collections also increased significantly from ₹ 6.38 lakh crore in 2013-14 to almost ₹ 12 lakh crore in 2018-19. Making the process of direct tax payment easy, moderating tax rates for the middle class and ensuring that the interface with the tax department much simpler and largely faceless has helped to augment tax collection.

  It is also to be noted that tax collections depend on the overall state and performance of the economy. During periods of economic slowdown, when industry, business and the agriculture sector are under-performing, revenue collections are bound to show decline.

5. Discuss briefly the various tax reforms implemented in India post-independence.

Early Tax Reforms

Tax reforms and rationalization of taxes is an ongoing process and evolves over a period of time. While frequent and drastic changes in taxes are to be avoided to ensure a measure of stability and predictability, the tax regime need to be attuned to the changing requirements of the economy and the imperatives of development. The Indian tax system, involving both direct and indirect taxes, has also been reformed from time to time to make it more equitable, moderate and efficient.

➢ Direct tax reform

The Indian tax system, as it evolved in the 1950's, was aligned to a planned economy with the State and the public sector playing a dominant role. Personal income tax rates in India were quite high in earlier times. Raising maximum revenue and achieving redistribution became the avowed objectives and the tax structure became one of discretionary nature and with confiscatory rates and distortions.

Exorbitant rates and tax evasion: The resultant disincentives led to a high degree of tax evasion, both in regard to income and wealth, with little possibility of detection and ineffective penal measures. Over time, this spawned a vast underground, parallel economy which has had deleterious effects on the economy. The tax system had many loopholes and lacked transparency, so much so, it was difficult to assess the social and economic impact of various concessions built into it.

Wanchoo Committee (1971): A Committee was set up in 1971, headed by Justice K.N. Wanchoo, a retired Chief Justice of the Supreme Court of India, to look into various aspects of the tax system including the problem of tax evasion.

As per this Committee, factors like high tax rates, controls, licenses, and ineffective information system were major problems plaguing the direct tax regime. At its peak in 1973-74, the maximum marginal rate of tax (with surcharge) was as high as 97.75 per cent. The Committee recommended significant reduction in marginal tax rates. Following the recommendations of this Committee, marginal tax rates were reduced gradually to 50 per cent by 1985–86.

Chelliah Committee (1991): As part of economic reform measures initiated in 1990-91, a Tax Reforms Committee (TRC) headed by Prof. Raja J. Chelliah, a renowned expert on India's public finance, was set up to make comprehensive study of the tax structure. The TRC laid out a framework and a roadmap for reform of both direct and indirect taxes as part of the structural reform process.

The TRC's recommendations included:

- Simplification and rationalization of the rate structure;
- Reduction in the rates of all major taxes, both direct and indirect, to reasonable levels;
- Rationalize the structure and scope of tax incentives;
- Broadening the tax base;
- Improving the tax administration;
- Promoting fairness in the tax system to check adverse effects on efficiency and neutrality;
- Building a proper information system and computerization of tax returns;
- Revamping, and modernization of administrative and enforcement machinery.

Radical reform: The measures suggested by the Chelliah Committee marked a radical shift and was in keeping with the best fiscal practices such as broadening the base, lowering marginal tax rates, reducing rate differentiation, minimizing exemptions and concessions, simplifying the tax structure, and making the tax administration more effective.

The reforms were to bring about revenue neutrality in the short term and enhance revenue productivity in the medium and long term. The overall thrust of TRC was to increase the relative contribution of direct taxes and reduce the share of trade taxes in the total tax revenue.

Further reforms: Direct taxes were rationalised in the Union budget for 1997-98 when the then existing income tax slabs with rates of 15, 30, and 40 per cent were replaced by new rates of 10, 20, and 30 per cent respectively.

Over time, successive governments have striven to simplify the tax system to make it more friendly to tax payers and easy to comply. It is being further modernised by capturing data relating to assessees digitally so that physical interface between tax authorities and assessees is avoided thus eliminating any room for abuse and disputes.

Towards a more equitable tax regime: To make the tax structure equitable and just, the share of indirect taxes, viz., excise duties, sales tax, etc., in the total tax revenues should be kept low as compared to that of direct taxes, viz., income and corporate taxes. This is because the indirect taxes, by their very nature, are regressive as the burden of these levies is passed on to consumers of goods and is shared by everyone in society irrespective of income. The impact of direct taxes is whereas on the affluent and well-to-do persons in the higher income brackets.

In India, until the early 1990s, the share of indirect taxes in total tax revenues was about 80 per cent and that of direct taxes about 20 per cent, both in the case of Central taxes, and Central and State taxes combined. This was partly because the tax base for direct taxes was rather narrow in the earlier years. Also, as the economy expanded and production and range of goods and imports increased in the decades from 1950 to 1990, involving levy of excise duties, sales tax and custom duties, the collection and share of indirect taxes steadily went up. This distortion in tax structure had to be corrected.

As stated earlier, following the economic reforms of 1990-91, measures were taken in a phased manner to set right the above imbalance between direct and indirect taxes. And by 2018-19, in the case of Centre, the share of direct taxes in total tax revenue had risen to 50 per cent and the share of indirect taxes has been steadily brought down. This indicates that the Indian tax system is getting less regressive and more progressive.

- **Indirect tax reform**

The indirect tax system also had many deficiencies with multiplicity of levies at the Central and State levies which impeded the growth of industry and trade.

L K Jha Committee: Recognizing the need for a major overhaul of the indirect tax system, the Central Government appointed a Committee in 1976 headed by L.K Jha. A major recommendation of the Committee, made in 1978, was to gradually transform the Central Excise into a Value Added Tax (VAT) to be levied at the manufacturing stage.

ModVAT: However, it was only by 1986–87 that, as a step towards the VAT scheme a Modified VAT (ModVAT) could be introduced to minimize the incidence o taxation on inputs. Under the ModVAT scheme, a manufacturer could take credit o excise duty paid on raw materials and components used in manufacture, and paid tax only on "value added" portion thus avoiding duplication of levies at each stage This mitigated the cascading effect of taxes on inputs, made the system more transparent, and helped to reduce costs and prices.

Chelliah Committee (TRC): As already stated, the 1991 Tax Reforms Committee (TRC) had made several recommendations to reform both the direct and the indirec tax structure.

As ModVAT gave rise to many disputes in assessment and to further simplify th system, in the 2000–01 budget, ModVAT was replaced by Central VAT (CenVAT) This also enabled the manufacturer of final product to take credit of duty of excis and service tax paid on any input.

Meanwhile, the government worked on major reform of indirect taxes at State leve by replacing the Sales tax with a unified Value Added Tax (VAT). The eventual goa was to cover the entire production-distribution chain by a national VAT or a Good and Services Tax (GST) encompassing both the Centre and the States. Though mos States had agreed to it in principle, the issue got delayed due to various reasons an protracted discussions in the meetings of State Finance Ministers. Finally, the GS law could be passed and the GST regime became operational from July 1, 2017.

While the introduction of GST is the most radical reform in independent India's ta history and has brought about many improvements, it needs further refinement such as reducing the multiplicity of rates, lowering the rates on many items an simplifying the process of submission of returns by assessees. The GST Council an the government are periodically reviewing these aspects.

6. Mention the salient features of the Goods and Services Tax (GST implemented in India. In what way it is an improvement over the previou indirect tax system? Are there any shortcomings in the GST regime adopte in India?

The adoption of a fully integrated Goods and Services Tax (GST) on national basis wa recommended in 2004 by a Task Force headed by Vijay Kelkar. This landmark legislatio the biggest indirect tax reform since Independence, replaced a slew of central and stat levies with a uniform GST rate to convert the country into a single territory and single market.

After the Central and State governments and Union Territories passed the necessary legislation, the GST regime finally became operational from July 1, 2017.

➢ **Salient Features of GST**

The following are the main features of the pan-India Goods and Services Tax regime:

- GST unites the country into a common, unified market and removes barriers across states.
- GST is a destination-based tax that subsumed various Central indirect taxes like excise duty, countervailing duty and service tax, and the State levies such as value-added tax, octroi and entry tax, entertainment tax and luxury tax.
- It avoids the cascading impact of taxes, brings in efficiency.
- It checks and deters tax evasion and ensures better compliance.
- It expands the tax payer base and thereby increases tax revenues.
- It is estimated that implementation of GST will add up to 2 per cent to the country's gross domestic product (GDP) and ensure revenue buoyancy.
- The final consumer will bear only the GST charged by the last dealer in the supply chain, with set-off benefits and tax credits at all the previous stages thus reducing tax burden.

➢ **The GST regime** consists of:

- Central GST (CGST) collected by the Central Govt.;
- State GST (SGST) collected by the State Govt.;
- Union Territory GST (UTGST) collected by the Union Territories; and
- Integrated GST (IGST) collected by the Central Govt.

For sale within a state, CGST and SGST will be levied. The collection goes equally to the Central and the State government. In the case of inter-state sales, the whole of IGST goes to the Central government.

GST Council and Tax rates: Under the GST Act, the government has set up the all-powerful GST Council (GSTC) which consists of the Union Finance Minister as Chairman, the Union Minister of State of Finance and the Finance Minister of each state as members. The rate at which items are to be taxed and any changes in rates for items is decided by the GST Council.

The constitution of the Council is such that neither the Centre nor the States will be able to take a decision without the other's concurrence – a move that will necessitate consensual approach and promote cooperative federalism. It also gives the States a major say in the way indirect taxes will be administered across the country.

In case voting becomes necessary for a decision, it will require at least a three-fourths vote in favour. The Centre has one-third vote in the Council while States have two-thirds vote.

Essential items of mass consumption like foodgrains are exempted from the levy of GST. There are four rates under GST into which other items are grouped, viz., 5 per cent, 12 per cent, 18 per cent and 28 per cent.

Demerit /sin goods and luxury items are subjected to the highest rate of 28 per cent.

Composition scheme: To give relief to small traders, dealers and manufacturers with lower turnover, they are covered by a Composition scheme under which they pay a fixed low rate of tax. This helps to ensure lesser compliance burden, provide a seamless supply chain, make the scheme more attractive and check tax evasion.

Shift from Originating Point to Destination: As against the previous system where the taxes like Excise and Central sales tax were levied on manufacturing at the factory gate or on inter-state movement of goods, the GST involves taxation at the destination point.

Compensation for revenue loss: This could result in gains for the consuming states and loss for the manufacturing states. Due to this, states with good manufacturing base like Tamil Nadu was opposed to the GST while consuming states like Bihar, West Bengal and Odisha favoured it. But the GST Bill provides for fully compensating the losses sustained by the States for five years.

➢ **Advantages of GST over previous indirect tax regime**

Previous indirect tax regime: The previous indirect tax framework in India suffered from the following shortcomings:

- The various indirect taxes being levied were not necessarily mutually exclusive. When the goods are manufactured and sold, both the central excise duty (CenVAT) and State-Level VAT were levied and they could not be set off against one another as CenVAT was a Central levy while the other was a State levy.
- CenVAT was applicable only at manufacturing level and not at distribution levels. It was a combination of origin-based Central tax and destination-based multi-point system of taxation (State-Level VAT) resulting in cascading effect.

Merits of GST regime:

- Elimination of multiplicity of taxes and their cascading effects;
- Benefits both consumers and industry. As credit of input tax is available against output tax, it reduces the tax burden on producers. Reduction in production cost benefits consumers and makes exports more competitive;
- Rationalization of tax structure and simplification of compliance procedures;
- Harmonization of Central and State tax administrations which would reduce duplication and compliance costs;
- Plugs the loopholes in the earlier regime and ensures better tax compliance as GST creates a continuous trail of transactions at every stage. The electronic mode used in GST greatly aids in this process;

- Widening tax base and eliminating classification disputes; and,
- Automation of compliance procedures to reduce errors and increase efficiency in tax administration.

➢ **Deficiencies of GST:** GST as implemented in India has some drawbacks. These are:

- A GST regime must have few tax slabs – ideally, one rate or two, and with no or very few items in exempted category. India has opted for four slabs, apart from zero tax for a large number of items.
- Multiplicity of slabs and rates, as exists now, makes the system less beneficial and more complex in operation.
- But in a country like India, with a large part of the population in lower and middle income groups, and even below the poverty line, GST with just one rate or no exempted items will mean taxing essential commodities. It will have inflationary impact and make many items unaffordable to large sections of people.
- Higher rates have been kept for luxury and demerit/sin items with a view to disincentivise their consumption.
- Certain critical items like petroleum and alcohol, and the real estate sector have been kept out of the purview of GST due to insistence by the States. These need to be brought under the regime to make it more effective from the economy's point of view.

7. Enumerate the main objectives of the Fiscal Responsibility and Budget Management (FRBM) Act, 2003. A Committee headed by N K Singh had reviewed the FRBM Act. What are the main recommendations of this Committee?

Fiscal policy and monetary policy are two critical planks in the economic policy of any economy. Fiscal discipline, prudent fiscal management and containing fiscal deficit is crucial for sustained economic progress.

With a view to achieving equity in fiscal management and ensuring long-run macro-economic stability, better coordination between fiscal and monetary policy and transparency in fiscal operation of the Government, the Fiscal Responsibility and Budget Management (FRBM) Act, 2003 was passed. The Act also aims at prudential debt management consistent with fiscal sustainability.

➢ **Objectives of the Fiscal Responsibility and Budget Management Act, 2003**: The objectives of the FRBM Act are:

* Limiting Central Government borrowings, debt, and revenue and fiscal deficits;
* Ensuring greater transparency in fiscal operations of the Central Government; and
* Conducting fiscal policy in a medium-term framework.

- **Mandates under the Act:** The Act also enjoins upon the Central government:
  * Not to borrow from the Reserve Bank to India except under exceptional circumstances when there is temporary shortage of cash.
  * To place, in each financial year, in both Houses of Parliament, a Medium-term Fiscal Policy Statement, Fiscal Policy Strategy Statement, and Macro-economic Framework Statement along with the Annual Financial Statement and Demands for Grants.
- **Merits and benefits of the Act:**
  * It has streamlined the Budget presentation process and helped to enforce fiscal discipline.
  * The enactment has demonstrated government's commitment to prudent fiscal and financial policies.
  * The implementation of the Act at the Centre and corresponding Acts at the State level has helped in the consolidation of fiscal balance prior to the global financial crisis of 2008.

➢ **Fiscal deficit challenge**

However, following the passage of the FRBM Act, India faced the challenge of adhering to the fiscal deficit target. (Fiscal deficit is the difference between the government's total expenditure and its total receipts excluding borrowings.) The outbreak of the financial crisis of 2007-08 coincided with the year when the mandated targets of 3 per cent fiscal deficit and elimination of revenue deficit were to be achieved. The Government had to postpone these targets due to fiscal stimulus which had to be injected into the economy to counter the situation arising out of the crisis..

While the revenue deficit was to be wiped out by March 2008, this was not achieved and in the budget for 2013-14, it was mentioned that revenue deficit would be brought down to 1.5 per cent by 2016-17. The target time for bringing down the fiscal deficit to 3 per cent also had to be postponed.

➢ **N K Singh Committee on FRBM Act and Fiscal Policy**

The FRBM Act had been under implementation for over a decade and both the Central and the State Governments had benefited from its implementation. There was a view that instead of "fixed fiscal deficit" targets, it would be better to have a "fiscal deficit range" as the target which would give necessary policy space to the government to deal with dynamic situations, especially in the context of volatile global economic conditions.

Against this background, while remaining committed to fiscal prudence, the Govt. of India set up a committee in 2016, headed by N.K. Singh, a former Secretary in the Finance Ministry, to review the FRBM Act and give recommendations. The Committee included Governor of Reserve Bank of India, Chief Economic Advisor to the Union government and two other experts.

- **Committee's mandate:**
  * To review the working of the FRBM Act and to suggest the way forward keeping in view the broad objective of fiscal consolidation and prudence and the changes required in the context of the uncertainty and volatility in the global economy.
  * To make its assessment and provide its views on the expected impact of it recommendations on the general government deficit and other FRBM parameters.
  * To examine and give recommendations on any other aspect considered relevant in relation to the determination and implementation of the FRBM road map.
- **Committee's recommendations**: After detailed examination of the various aspects of the Act and its working, the Committee recommended as follows:
  * A sustainable debt path must be the primary target and principal macro-economic anchor of the fiscal policy. A debt-to-GDP ratio of 60 per cent should be targeted with a 40 per cent limit for the Centre and 20 per cent limit for the States.
  * Within this framework, it recommended fiscal deficit of 3 per cent of GDP for 3 years from 2017-18 to 2019-20.
  * Fiscal deficit to be brought down to 2.5 per cent of GDP by 2022-23.
  * The Committee also provided for 'escape clauses' for deviations from the stipulated fiscal deficit target up to 0.5 per cent of GDP.
  * For taking recourse to the 'escape clauses', the Committee suggested "far-reaching structural reforms in the economy or unforeseen events such as war, calamities of national proportion, setbacks in agriculture and sharp decline in real output growth with unanticipated fiscal implications" as some of the factors and criteria.
  * The panel recommended enacting a new **Debt and Fiscal Responsibility Act** after repealing the existing FRBM Act.
- **Fiscal Council:** An important recommendation of the Committee was to set up a Fiscal Council which will do fiscal analysis round-the-year and advise the government on any corrective action to be taken. It will also advise on whether conditions appropriate for triggering the 'escape clauses' exist.

  This was considered necessary as the government, which administers the FRBM Act, did not have the benefit of analytical inputs of a robust independent organization like many countries have.

The Committee suggested the following role for the Fiscal Council:

(i) Preparing multi-year fiscal forecasts;

(ii) Recommending changes to the fiscal strategy;

(iii) Improving quality of fiscal data;

(iv) Advising the government if conditions exist to deviate from the fiscal target; and

(v) Advising the government to take corrective action for non-compliance with the Act.

8. Explain the functions and role of Finance Commission in India. What are the main criteria followed, and challenges faced, by the Commission in the transfer of financial resources from the Centre to the States? Are there any contentious issues in the matter and, if so, how the Commission tries to resolve them?

Under Article 280 of the Constitution of India, the President appoints a Finance Commission, once in every five years to look into the financial relations between the Union and the States. The Commission plays a significant role in ensuring transfer of financial resources from the Centre to the States in a just and equitable manner.

The recommendations of the Finance Commission with an explanatory memorandum stating action taken on them are to be laid before each House of Parliament.

Since 1951, there have been fourteen Commissions and the report of the 15th Finance Commission, set up in 2017, is to cover the five-year period 2020-2025.

➢ **Composition of the Commission:** The Finance Commission is headed by a Chairperson and will have four other Members who are selected from among those who are qualified to be Judge of a High Court, or have knowledge of Government finances or accounts, or have had experience in administration and financial expertise, or have special knowledge of Economics..

➢ **Tasks for the Commission:** The Commission will make recommendations on the following aspects:

- The distribution of divisible pool of taxes between the Union and the States and the allocation of shares of individual States;
- The principles that should govern the grants-in-aid of the revenues of the States out of the Consolidated Fund of India and the sums to be paid to each of the states under Article 275 of the Constitution;
- The measures needed to augment the Consolidated Fund of a State to supplement the resources of the rural (Panchayats) and urban (Municipalities) bodies in the State based on the recommendations of the State Finance Commissions (SFCs); and

- Any other matter referred to the Commission by the President in the interest of sound finance.

➢ **Commission's role:** The Commission's recommendations relate to a prospective five-year period and it takes into account the following factors:

- The resources of the Central and State Governments for the five-year period under reference (the recommendations of the 15th Finance Commission will be for the period 2020-21 to 2025-26);
- The levels of tax and non-tax revenues likely to be reached by the Centre and the States;
- The demands on the resources of the Central Government on account of expenditure on civil administration, defence, internal and border security, debt-servicing, and other expenditure and liabilities;
- The resources of the State Governments and the demands on such resources under different heads such as administration, law and order, welfare and development, and the impact of debt levels on resource availability, particularly in States stressed by debt;
- The level of subsidies required, keeping in view the need for sustainable and inclusive growth, and equitable sharing of subsidies between the Central and State Governments;
- Balancing the receipts and expenditure on revenue account of all the States and the Union and generating surpluses for capital investment.

➢ **Challenges faced by Finance Commissions:** Every Commission has had to face challenges in discharging its mandate. This was due to a variety of factors mentioned below:

- **Imbalance in Responsibilities and Taxing powers:** Under the division of administrative and financial powers, there was sharp imbalance between the responsibilities and financial liabilities devolving on the Centre, on the one hand, and the States and local bodies, on the other, and their powers to tax and raise revenues. As the more potential revenue sources, viz., the income and corporate tax, excises, and customs duties, have been with the Centre, there was concentration of revenues in favour of it.

  The assignment of a large share of responsibilities involving expenditure to lower governmental levels, i.e., States, urban and rural bodies, results in fiscal gap which is to be covered by transfer of resources from the Centre to the States.

- **Determining the quantum of devolution:** A major problem for the Commission is to determine the likely fiscal gap during any given period on which will depend the quantum of devolution. There could be no uniform theoretical approach which the Commission could rely upon for proper determination of the fiscal gap. While major part of the fiscal gap is to be covered through devolution of tax revenues, the rest has to be covered by grants-in-aid to states.

- **States' concerns:** States have expressed concerns before Finance Commissions that the Union Government exercises excessive discretion in distributing the resources among them through the transfer mechanism, especially in regard to centrally sponsored schemes (CSS). The States have generally described these transfers as being 'non-formula-based' and 'discretionary'. The 14th Commission recommended the evolution of a new institutional arrangement, consistent with the overarching objective of strengthening co-operative federalism, by expanding the mandate of Inter-State Council.
- **Differences between the Centre and the States:** Often differences crop up between the Centre and the States during the work of the Finance Commission. The Commission has to grapple with divergent views between, and demands from, the Centre and the States and take a balanced view. It is to the credit of successive Commissions that, by and large, they have steered clear of disputes and displayed objectivity in their recommendations.
- **Extent of devolution:** The First Commission, set up in 1951, had recommended that the States get one tenth of total taxes collected centrally. That share has steadily increased. The devolution to States recommended by the 14th Commission, covering the period 2015-20, was 42 per cent of taxes. It is, however, to be noted that after this devolution, the Centre resorted to raising additional revenue from taxes through cesses and surcharges which are not shareable.

➢ **Criteria followed by Commission**

- **Population:** Population of states is one of the important criteria followed in determining devolution of funds. While the past Commissions were asked to go by 1971 population data while deciding the devolution formula, the 15th Commission has been asked to use the 2011 population figures. This is considered to be unfair as between 1971 and 2011, population has declined in four southern states as also in 10 other states which have performed well on population control and who, therefore, stand to lose in tax share. The 14th Commission, which also considered the 2011 population data, gave 17.5 per cent weightage to 1971 data and 10 per cent weightage to 2011 population figures to take into account the demographic change.

  But the direction to 15th Commission to reckon 2011 population data can be justified since current population has more relevance to the expenditure to be incurred by States on public goods. To overcome this anomaly, the Commission could incentivize states that curbed population growth in some form.
- **Performance-based transfer of funds to States:** An important task for the 15th Commission was to examine linking transfer of funds to a range of parameters, such as efforts made by States to deepen GST, how quickly a state moves towards the replacement level of fertility (TFR of 2.1), eliminates power sector losses, improves the ease of doing business, adopts direct benefit transfer (DBT) and

shows progress in sanitation. These parameters clearly reflect the policy preferences of the Union government.

- **Goods and Services Tax (GST):** The task before the 15th Commission was unique as it is the first Finance Commission to do its work under GST, the new indirect tax regime. That its work was affected by the outbreak of Covid-19 added to the uncertainties the Commission faced. The rules of fiscal federalism have been profoundly reset by the introduction of GST. Under this, indirect taxes are fixed by a GST Council, in which both the Centre and all the States are represented, and the revenues from it are shared between the Centre and the States in a pre-determined manner. The powers which the States had to levy indirect taxes have been taken away save in respect of few items. Also, GST being a destination levy, will shift the incidence of taxation from production point to consumption point due to which the distribution of indirect taxes between different states could change significantly. For this, the Centre has agreed to compensate loss in revenue sustained by States for a limited period.
- **Changes in Terms of Reference (TOR):** A controversy erupted with the Centre, while extending the tenure of the 15th Commission, amended the TOR to examine whether "....a separate mechanism for funding of defence and internal security ought to be set up and, if so, how such a mechanism could be operationalized". This is criticized by some as an attempt by the Centre to nudge the Commission to apportion larger share of taxes to it before devolution.

➤ **15th Commission report:** The 15th Finance Commission, headed by N. K. Singh has submitted its Report to the President of India in November 2020. Its recommendations lay down the blueprint for devolution of Centre's tax revenue to States for the five-year period 2020-21 to 2025-26. Its main recommendations are:

- For the year 2020-21, the Commission had recommended that States be given 41 per cent of the divisible tax pool of the Centre. The same will hold good for the full five-year period. The 14th Finance Commission had recommended 42 per cent tax devolution to states including the then J & K state for the period 2015-20.
- The 1 per cent decrease is to provide for the newly formed union territories of Jammu and Kashmir, and Ladakh from the resources of the central government.
- Further, out of all revenues received by the Centre, including the divisible taxes and borrowed funds, a tidy sum will be earmarked each year during the five-year period for a dedicated special fund for modernisation of defence/internal security forces. This will effectively reduce the states' tax receipt from the Centre.
- Efforts to be made to raise the public outlay in the health sector to 2.5 per cent of GDP as envisaged in the National Health Policy, 2017. The Commission has observed that the allocation for the health sector is woefully inadequate as was evidenced by the pandemic Covid-19. It is also deficient due to the skewed geographical spread of the health infrastructure.

- The report is said to address the concerns of southern states on population criteria adopted.

The full report will be available in public domain once it is tabled in Parliament by the Union Government.

➢ **Conclusion:** In conclusion, it can be said that within the limitations, successive Finance Commissions have acted independently and objectively to take a balanced view of the needs of both the Centre and the States.

This is demonstrated by the action of the Ninth Finance Commission which, when faced with an objection by a Chief Minister on the methodology, which the Commission was directed to follow in making an assessment of revenues and expenditure of the states, wrote to all the Chief Ministers assuring them that Article 280 (4) of the Constitution and the Finance Commission Act empower it to adopt any approach or methodology it considers appropriate, and while doing so, it would apply a yardstick "uniform, just and equitable" to both the Union and the States.

Thus, it can be said that the working of Finance Commissions has helped to safeguard and strengthen the fabric of fiscal federalism.

9. Explain the main features of fiscal federalism in India. Examine how far the work of Finance Commissions has helped to promote co-operative federalism between the Centre and the States. Give reasons for your answer.

India's political and financial landscape has undergone vast changes since independence and this has impacted the Centre-State relations in a perceptible manner. From centralized planning to greater decentralisation of power structures and market-oriented economic policies, India has seen dramatic, even if gradual and slow, transformation spanning over seven decades. This trend critically helped to strengthen the federal characteristics of Indian Union giving greater voice to States and local bodies in the polity.

➢ **Planning and Centralisation:** In the initial three decades from 1950 to 1980, centralized economic planning, with pronounced socialist bias, resulted in concentration of powers in the Centre. Planning covered a wide gamut of sectors, and lopsided allocation of financial resources between the Centre and the States negated the principle of true federalism. The Centre had not only exclusive powers over many activities of national and strategic importance but also shared concurrent powers with States over certain other domains while states were left with exclusive powers over the remaining domains.

➢ **Trend towards decentralization:** As time passed, with the rise of many regional parties which came to power in the States and at times even at the Centre, the clamour for more powers for the states arose and this led to greater decentralization. The passage of the 72nd and 73rd Amendments to the Constitution in 1992 vested greater powers in the Panchayats and Municipal bodies strengthening local governance from district level to the villages.

- **Skewed allocation of Resources and Responsibilities:** One of the features of the Indian federal set up has been the skewed division of powers and responsibilities between the Centre and States and financial powers and resources assigned to them. There is sharp imbalance between the powers of the Centre and the States and local bodies to tax and raise revenues, as against the responsibilities and financial liabilities devolving on them.

  While the major sources of revenue have been with the Centre, the States and urban and rural local bodies bear sizeable share of responsibilities in the social sector – education, health, housing, sanitation, etc.– involving expenditure which results in fiscal gap to be covered by transfer of resources from the Centre to the States. It was keeping this in view that the framers of the Constitution provided for the mechanism of Finance Commission for periodic review of overall resource position and its division between the different tiers of administration.

- **Competing claims:** The Finance Commission faces a difficult task in the face of competing claims of the Centre and the States for allocation of more resources to them.

  - **The Centre:** Apart from rising commitments on defence, national security, etc., the increasing integration of India with the global economy requires the Union Government to be empowered to manage global shocks, reassure financial markets and adopt counter-cyclical policies as and when the need arises. Also, global opinion makers and credit rating agencies give over-riding importance to the Union Government's fiscal position in their assessment of the national economy.

  - **The States:** At the same time, the Union government is increasingly aware of the need to provide greater flexibility and funds to the States for implementing socio-economic policies at state level, including large number of Centrally Sponsored Schemes (CSS). The share of state spending on rural and urban development, and on capital expenditure, primarily to fund sanitation and housing, has seen sharp spurt in recent years.

  - **Local bodies:** The local governments, both rural and urban, are constrained not only by the lack of resources, but also by the inadequate administrative infrastructure, as well as the lack of discretion available to them in providing basic services. They contend that they are the most appropriate level of government for the provision of most of the local-level public goods. And they face constraints in raising resources locally and look for higher allocations.

- **Finance Commission and Fiscal Federalism**

  The Finance Commission, as a Constitutional body, plays an impartial and neutral role in following the mandate given to it. As already seen, the Commission has a delicate task with both the Centre and the States demanding higher share in the devolution of funds citing increased commitments on various schemes and more expenditure.

In the changed and fast evolving scenario, impacted by domestic and external factors, the Finance Commission has to look at a wider canvas while giving its recommendations. The balance between the public and private sectors, the government and the public enterprises, and the fiscal and non-fiscal elements have dramatically changed over the years and this has had a significant impact on the Centre-State fiscal relations. Several fundamental issues relating to the economy such as those in the financial and banking sector, fiscal deficit, public debt levels, subsidies, disinvestment, environmental concerns, regulatory policies, etc. have also to be taken into account. In short, the Commission has to take cognisance of the new realities of macro-economic management.

The work and recommendations of the Commission plays a vital role in ensuring just, equitable and healthy financial relations between the Centre and the States. It has helped to promote co-operative federalism, improve the quality of public spending and ensure fiscal and financial stability.

10. Explain the concept of 'Subsidies' and the rationale behind it. Elucidate the merits and drawbacks of the system of subsidies for an economy.

➢ **The concept:** A subsidy is a benefit in the form of cash payment or tax credits or tax exemptions (which are distinct from general tax reductions) extended usually by the government to an individual, business or institution. It is some kind of government support – mostly of a monetary nature – to the citizens or the private sector serving a public purpose or a social cause.

It can also be defined as a direct or indirect payment, economic concession, or privilege granted by a government to private firms, households, or other governmental units in order to promote a public objective.

In other words, a subsidy is given keeping in view overall public interest or to promote asocial good or an economic policy or on grounds of equity.

➢ **Categories of subsidies:** Subsidies are classified as 'merit' and 'non-merit' subsidies depending on their social and economic benefits to wider population and the positive externalities they generate.

Merit subsidies are those provided for sectors such as education, healthcare and family welfare, nutrition, social welfare, agricultural programmes and research, water conservation, irrigation and flood control, ecology and environment, science and technology, village and small industries, rural and urban development and forestry. Non-merit subsidy is directed towards specific groups of population, such as subsidy given for food, fertilizer, cooking gas, kerosene, etc.

Subsidies may also be 'explicit' or 'implicit'. Explicit subsidies are those specifically recorded in the budget and government documents. However, there are also off-budget subsidies or those not declared as such which are implicit subsidies.

Explicit subsidies given by the Central Government include subsidies on food, fertilizers, export promotion, petroleum products, etc. There are implicit subsidies in railway fares and electricity and water tariffs, and also in the form of financial support extended to public sector undertakings and departmental enterprises.

➢ **The rationale and merits of subsidies**

- Subsidies play a distributive role when they are extended to provide a commodity or service at a price lower than the market price to sections of society which cannot afford the higher market prices. In other words, it is a means to keep down the prices of essential commodities so as to make them affordable to the poor and vulnerable groups and ensure minimum level of food and nutrition to them. The food subsidy under India's Public Distribution System (PDS) is one such example.
- The economic rationale of subsidies is provided by the 'positive externalities' they generate. The positive externality is when the social benefit from using up a subsidised commodity or service is greater than the sum of the private benefits to the consumers. Education, healthcare, and research and development are prime examples which generate positive externalities.
- In some cases, the normal market or pricing mechanism does not ensure the true benefits or value of goods and services or produce efficient outcomes in society. Subsidies provide necessary correctives in such cases.
- An efficiently administered and properly targeted subsidy regime will have a significant impact on the equity and efficiency of the fiscal regime.
- Subsidies are also provided to boost production, say, for inputs like fertilizers, irrigation and power to augment agricultural production.
- Subsidies may play an important role in developing countries and in the transformation of centrally-planned economies to market economies. There are subsidies in international trade also. Least-developed and developing countries may give subsidies to promote exports and have import-substitution subsidies, i.e., subsidies designed to avoid imports to help domestic industries.
- Subsidies given to education sector provide externality benefits such as more employment opportunities and occupational mobility, and potentially higher incomes and productivity for current and future generations. Increased spending on education would also provide a stimulus for higher-level research which can add to the long-run trend rate of growth. Other external benefits might include building up a more enlightened and cultured society and ensuring equality of opportunity.

➢ **Drawbacks of subsidies**

- Price subsidies are often regressive in the sense that in many cases the well-to-do and affluent sections benefit more from the subsidy than the poorer households. If one were to plot the distribution of welfare gains against income, the benefits of a regressive price subsidy would increase as one moves up the income distribution curve.

For example, even with higher rates charged for more consumption of electricity, the inbuilt subsidy in electricity tariffs would apply to the relatively better off households also who will gain from it. The same holds true for subsidies in petrol where all vehicle owners enjoy the benefit irrespective of income differences. In fact, its benefit will not accrue to those in the poorer sections who may not even own vehicles.

- The large amounts of subsidy given for various products or sectors can be justified if it served the cause of equity and higher production. However, various field studies of subsidy regimes have shown that subsidies are not properly targeted towards the intended beneficiaries, and there are significant errors of exclusion and inclusion in the list of beneficiaries.
- Subsidies could cause distortions in the utilization of resources and tend to divert resources from more productive to less productive uses thus reducing economic efficiency.
- Subsidies, in some cases, could result in 'negative externalities'. For example, subsidy given for fertilizers may prompt farmers to use excessive doses of fertilizers in farming which may be unhealthy, nay even harmful, from the viewpoint of consumers of those farm produce. Likewise, subsidy provided for irrigation and power to farmers may cause them to use water indiscriminately which will lead to depletion of groundwater resources. Again, subsidies for power plants, such as coal-based thermal units, will cause environmental damage in the long run with serious climate change consequences.
- The government may have to resort to borrowing funds to meet subsidy obligations and liabilities, some of which may not be justified on equity or economic grounds. It not only has implications for the fiscal position of the state but crowds out private investment and capital expenditure for development.
- Lack of transparency, bureaucratic inefficiency and corruption may lead to significant leakages and result in benefits not reaching the beneficiaries. It will mean misallocation of resources and wastage of precious public funds.
- Dominant political groups and other vested interests will try to exercise control over allocation of public funds for their own benefit and narrow interests. It results in proliferation of subsidy payments and grants to placate pressure groups. This could also lead to further distortions and misallocation of scarce resources.

- Once introduced, subsidies tend to continue in perpetuity and it will be difficult to withdraw it even if it is no longer required or justified. Government may face political pressure to continue them, or fear backlash from the beneficiaries and larger voter constituency in case the subsidies are withdrawn.

11. Mention the major subsidies provided in Indian economy and examine their merits and implications for the economy. Are there any shortcomings in these subsidy schemes and, if so, explain the measures taken by the government to remedy them.

As India has large segments of population below the poverty line and even sizeable sections in the lower middle class, providing a safety net through social security measures has been an imperative need and part of policy from the very inception of planning in 1951. In fact, the 'rationing' system for food was in vogue even during the World War II to regulate supplies and contain price levels of food.

Price subsidies have been an important part of the anti-poverty measures. Both the Central and State governments subsidise the price of a wide range of products with the expressed intention of making them affordable for the poor. Rice, wheat, pulses, sugar, LPG, kerosene, fertiliser, etc. are subsidised. Besides, water and electricity tariffs and bus and railway fares carry varying levels of government subsidy.

➢ **Major subsidies and their quantum:** The major subsidies provided in India are for food, fertilisers and petroleum. Of these, the highest amount of subsidy incurred is on food. To put it in perspective, the Revised estimate (RE) for subsidies for 2018-19 was ₹ 1,71,298 crore for food, ₹ 70,075 crore for fertilizer and ₹ 24,833.18 crore for petroleum. The total amount of subsidies for these three items came to ₹ 2,66,206.38 crore which is 1.40 per cent of India's GDP of ₹ 19.01 million crore in 2018-19.

Besides, subsidies of lesser amounts are given to various sectors like public sector undertakings (PSUs) and departmental enterprises, and for items such as select exports and imports from time to time, on interest payments and for Rural Development programmes.

The total amount of subsidies for all the subsidised items put together in the Union Budget (Revised estimate) for 2018-19 was ₹ 2,99,210.61 crore, which works out to 1.57 per cent of GDP. Some of these subsidy amounts are bound to go up despite the efforts made to rationalise their production and pricing.

➢ **Subsidies and distortions:** While there is justification for subsidising essential items for certain income groups, there are distortions, leakages and wastages due to coverage and implementation issues. These aspects and the steps taken by the Centre and States to remedy them are discussed below.

❖ **Food subsidy:** Prima facie, price subsidy for food has helped poor and low-income households to weather inflation and price volatility. The Public

Distribution System (PDS) of India is the largest scheme of its kind in the world. It provides rice, wheat, sugar, pulses, millets and kerosene at subsidised rates to a target population through a network of over 5 lakh Fair Price Shops (FPS).

In 1997, PDS became a targeted scheme instead of a universal intervention. The National Food Security Act passed in 2013 has reinforced the PDS to ensure food security to over two-thirds of India's population.

Coverage: Out of about 25 crore households, over 18 crore families of Below Poverty Line (BPL) and Above Poverty Line (APL) strata are availing the PDS facility.

➢ ***Deficiencies***: Though a laudable programme, it is beset with the following problems:

- **Exclusion** of eligible families and inclusion of ineligible ones in the scheme, duplicate and fake family cards. Thus, many ineligible families have BPL cards while some of the eligible ones are excluded from the facility. Though exclusion errors in PDS targeting have declined, inclusion errors have increased. Inclusion of ineligible beneficiaries means subsidies being wastefully spent.
- **Falsification of records**: Falsification of records of stocks and diversion of stocks to black market by FP shops and siphoning of funds.
- **Storage problems:** Inadequate storage capacity to stock items procured for distribution resulting in foodgrains rotting and resultant wastages.
- **Carrying costs:** Heavy cost incurred in carrying buffer stocks in storage.
- **Leakages:** According to a study by the erstwhile Planning Commission, about 58 per cent of the subsidized foodgrains issued from the Central Pool did not reach the BPL families because of identification errors, non-transparent operation, and unethical practices in implementation. Another study, the '*Performance Evaluation Report of the Planning Commission on Targeted PDS*' (2005), which was a detailed study, found that for every kilogram of grains delivered to the poor, the Government of India released 2.4 kg of grains from the central pool.
- **Increasing reliance on PDS:** Another expectation which has been belied is that with a rise in incomes, households would increasingly buy higher quality grains from the market rather than the PDS shops. But, according to a NITI Aayog study on "*Role of Public Distribution System in Shaping Household and Nutritional Security India*", research findings have found that rather than declining, use of PDS by the poor as well as the non-poor has risen in both urban and rural areas.
- **Distortions due to MSP:** The policy of Minimum Support Price (MSP) given to farmers on procurement of items for PDS may be justified to ensure that farmers get remunerative prices for their produce. But it has the following implications:

  (a) When high MSP is given to farmers for cultivating rice and wheat, the Food Corporation of India has to purchase and store these items incurring higher cost. High MSPs lead to less cultivation of crops which get no MSP support. The resultant supply-demand mismatch raises prices of non-MSP supported crops and makes them more volatile. This contributes to food price inflation that hurts poor households.

(b) Rice, wheat and sugar ae water-guzzling crops as they require large quantities of water in cultivation. High MSPs and price subsidies for water together lead to water-intensive cultivation that causes depletion of groundwater tables, which eventually hurts farmers, especially those without irrigation facility.

- **PDS and Health and Nutrition:**

(a) Heavy reliance on consumption of cereals, subsidized under PDS, leads to skewed dietary habits of households. This has implications for the health of country's population which is facing transition from the dominance of communicable diseases to rise in non-communicable diseases like heart diseases, diabetes and cancer. India has the highest number of people with diabetes in the world.

(b) Consumption patterns in India are shifting rapidly from calorie-rich diet to protein and vitamin-rich one. Main source of protein for Indian masses is pulses. **More cultivation of wheat, rice and sugarcane will be at the cost of pulses, horticulture crops and coarse, but nutritious, grains.** This reduces protein-based items in diet in India as their supply gets reduced and become very expensive and unaffordable.

(c) A NITI Aayog report has observed that although the number of households that purchase cereals from the PDS has grown sharply, the per capita amount of grain purchased from the PDS has risen only slightly. It further states that households also buy grains from the market, making the PDS a relatively small component of the household food basket.

➤ **Reforms in PDS:** Many states have taken steps to reform the PDS. As a result, leakages in the PDS have shown a secular decline. It is noteworthy that those states which are making efforts to expand coverage, lower prices and putting in place reforms in the PDS are precisely the ones which are also showing lesser leakages in the system.

Among some radical measures taken to improve the PDS are:

- Door-step delivery has been started in some states;
- Digitisation of fair price shops (FPS's) has been completed in 28 states;
- Digitisation of ration cards/beneficiary database has been completed in 13 states and is in progress in 17 states;
- Ration/Family Cards are being linked to Aadhaar to prevent fake/duplicate cards; and
- Numbers of states have introduced toll-free helplines for redressal of grievances and SMS alerts.

❖ **Fertilizer subsidy:** The fertilizer subsidies are borne by the Central Government. The need for the fertilizer subsidy arises from the government's fertilizer pricing policy which has the following two objectives:

- Making fertilizer available to farmers at a low and affordable price.
- Ensuring fair returns on the investment to fertilizer industry and attract more investment in the fertilizer industry.

➢ **Reforms:** The government has taken various steps to rationalise the fertiliser subsidy, keep the selling prices of fertilizers static and low, and to check the excessive use of fertilizers, especially urea, which adversely impacts soil health and overall crop yield.

The government has made it mandatory for fertilizer firms to 'Neem coat' at least 75 per cent of their urea production. This has helped to prevent diversion of urea for industrial use and reduce the subsidy outgo.

New pricing scheme for urea was introduced in a phased manner to bring transparency and reduce the cost of production.

- **DBT scheme:** The government has implemented direct benefit transfer (DBT) scheme for fertilizer subsidy payments across India to prevent diversion of fertilizers for commercial use and generate data on the usage of the nutrients to help farmers.

  Under this, 100 per cent payment is made to fertilizer companies on sale of fertilizers to farmers at **subsidized rates**. At the time of sale, details of the buyer, the quantity, Aadhaar number, land records wherever available, and soil health will be captured using a point-of-sale (POS) machine. The subsidy amount will be settled in a few days with the manufacturer.

  This procedure ensures that farmers get the full benefit of subsidy without the intervention of any intermediaries and prevents leakages. It also ends the possibility of subsidy in the fourth (last) quarter spilling over to the next fiscal year.

❖ **Petroleum subsidy:** India is the third largest consumer of oil after the US and China. About 80 per cent of India's crude oil requirements are met by imports which is a heavy drain on her foreign exchange resources.

India's annual oil import bill amounts to about $120 billion (₹ 8 lakh crore) and is the single largest item in the total import bill. Oil accounts for a third of the value of all items imported by India.

- Petroleum subsidy consists of subsidy on LPG (cooking gas) and kerosene, two items vitally needed by households.
- The increase in the petroleum subsidy is mainly due to the government's drive on LPG as a source of cleaner cooking fuel and to promote it among the poorer households. There are two major schemes under this:
- The **Ujjwala Yojana** which seeks to give free LPG connections to poor households. 8.03 crore LPG connections have been released under Ujjwala scheme by 2019.

- The **PAHAL scheme** involves direct cash transfers of LPG subsidy to over 9.75 crore consumers.

Distortions: As Economic Survey 2014-15 has pointed out, fuel subsidies can be regressive as explained below.

LPG: A striking fact is that the poorest 50 percent of households consume only 25 per cent of LPG. Thus the lower-end households gain less from subsidised LPG whereas the households in higher income brackets gain relatively more.

However, the government is eliminating, in a phased manner, the subsidy given to households with income above a threshold. From Jan 2016, subsidy on LPG (cooking gas) was stopped for those tax payers with annual income of more than ₹ 10 lakh.

Also, a sizeable number of people who could afford to give up the LPG subsidy have forgone the benefit voluntarily.

Kerosene: In regard to kerosene, the Economic Survey 2014-15 has observed that the popular perception that poor households are more likely to use kerosene than rich households is only partly correct. A majority (51 percent) of subsidised kerosene is consumed by the non-poor and almost 15 percent of subsidised kerosene is actually consumed by the relatively well-off (the richest 40 percent).

Conclusion: In conclusion, it may be said that wider use of technology, digitisation of records and payments of subsidies, linking them with Aadhaar, spread of banking and the facility of DBT in payments to beneficiaries have gone a long way in ensuring transparency, efficiency and promptness, and in eliminating intermediaries and siphoning off public funds.

The very fact that overall more than ₹ 8,40,000 crore has been paid out to beneficiaries under the DBT facility for various welfare and subsidy schemes between 2014 and 2019 shows the significant impact it has had. This has been greatly facilitated by having 37.11 crore bank accounts under the Jan Dhan Yojana (JDY).

12. Explain the concept of 'Universal Basic Income' and examine if it is better than the present subsidies and income support schemes in India. Compare the relative merits and demerits of these schemes from India's point of view. (On this, see also Q. 8, chapter 3).

The concept of Universal Basic Income (UBI) implies that the State or a public institution grants unconditionally a 'basic guaranteed sum of money' on regular basis to every citizen in a country, including children, irrespective of their economic status or occupation. This will be in addition to any other source of income or earnings of the citizens. It is a social security measure, the primary objective being to combat poverty, assist those who are unemployed and enable every citizen to meet the basic needs and maintain a decent, minimum standard of life.

This idea has been put forth by some Indian and foreign economists and been part of public discourse in India.

- **Subsidies in India**

  In India, there are non-merit subsidies like those for food under the Public Distribution System (PDS), fertilizers, cooking gas, kerosene, etc. which are 'targeted' towards specific groups of population and 'merit' subsidies for education, primary healthcare, nutrition, forestry, ecology, environment, rural development programmes, village and small industries, etc. where the benefits are reaped by the society as a whole.

- **Deficiencies and Distortions in Subsidy System**

  The proponents of UBI scheme point to the gross deficiencies and drawbacks in the present subsidy regimes under which the benefits of subsidy do not reach all the beneficiaries and thus results in wastage of precious public funds defeating the very purpose of the schemes. The deficiencies in the system are mentioned below.

  - Subsidies in PDS and fuel are found to be regressive. A good portion of the subsidies doled out, which are primarily meant for the poorer sections, are being enjoyed by the well-to-do and affluent sections of the population who do not merit such assistance. For example, subsidies for cooking gas and kerosene and in electricity and water tariffs are enjoyed more by the affluent sections that use these facilities relatively more than the poor.
  - Besides distortions, there is considerable amount of leakage in subsidies meant for specific target groups. Items meant for the poor are diverted to black market resulting in misappropriation of public funds.
  - There are errors of exclusion and inclusion in these schemes due to which many eligible families/persons in the target groups get excluded from receiving benefits and those ineligible get included thereby defeating the very purpose of such social assistance schemes.
  - Apart from identification errors, subsidy schemes suffer from non-transparent operation, and unethical practices in implementation. For instance, according to '*Performance Evaluation Report of the Planning Commission on Targeted PDS (2005)*', *which was* a detailed study of the PDS carried out by the erstwhile Planning Commission, about 58 per cent of the subsidized foodgrains issued from the Central Pool did not reach the BPL families. The study further showed that the cost of handling foodgrains by public agencies is also very high. For ₹ 1 worth of income transfer to the poor, the government spends ₹ 3.65, indicating that one rupee of budgetary consumer subsidy is worth only 27 paise to the poor. However, these deficiencies are being gradually rectified by State governments.

- The well-to-do sections that pay income tax enjoy benefits of various tax rebates which are, in effect, revenue forgone by the State. Not only that, the burden of taxes on many goods under the GST is borne equally by the poorer sections as indirect taxes are levied irrespective of incomes.
- Inefficiency in dispensing subsidies results in misallocation of resources which could otherwise have been put to better use. In other words, there are opportunity costs involved in subsidy regime. (Opportunity cost is the value of an item which must be given up to acquire another item).

➤ **Case in favour of UBI scheme**

In view of the drawbacks in subsidy regime, some of the Indian and foreign economists have put forth arguments in favour of replacing it with a Universal Basic Income (UBI) scheme. They point out the following advantages in UBI scheme.

- As the UBI scheme will be universal covering all citizens uniformly without any exception, none will get excluded. The scheme could use the Aadhaar for identity of beneficiaries and with the financial inclusion drives and Digital India programme covering rural areas, roll-out of a UBI scheme can be worked out.
- UBI may just be the fastest way of reducing poverty. In the Indian context, a relatively low level of assured regular income to every individual could serve as a prop and enhance family's welfare. Unlike the present system of subsidies, UBI may empower families at the bottom rung of the ladder and help them to become more self-reliant and take economic decisions relevant to their lives.
- The scheme will also serve as a prop to those who are seeking jobs but can't get employment. The concept of UBI has got traction as automation is causing loss of jobs. In India, in the Information Technology (IT) sector, which has high potential for job creation, IT companies are embracing automation and artificial intelligence in complex areas of business which results in improved productivity and helps to keep down costs. This is taking a toll on jobs in this sector.
- With changing demographic landscape and rising number of aged people, there is need to provide adequate assured income to the aged in societies which do not have proper welfare schemes like 'Old age pension' covering all such persons.
- Rising inequalities in societies, even as development takes place, is a matter of serious concern. Globalisation, while improving overall well-being, also dislocates workers and disrupts industries, and results in greater income and wealth disparity. In such a scenario, providing assured income will be a prop to weather the disruptions.
- The UBI scheme may be in replacement of all or some of the existing schemes involving subsidies so that the amounts saved could be channelled into the universal scheme. The money saved by the abolition of subsidies and welfare schemes like MNREGA, and even tax exemptions enjoyed by tax payers, would

be utilized to fund the UBI scheme. It is estimated that the expenditure incurred on some of the present regressive subsidies compares with the expenditure that may be involved in raising the income of the poorest sections, the very objective of UBI policy.

- An argument put forth by some experts in favour of UBI is that the existing 'non-merit' subsidies cost nearly 6 per cent of GDP, while the revenue forgone on tax exemptions and concessions account for another 5 per cent of GDP. Suitably modifying these subsidies and concessions, the government could find about 1 per cent of GDP required for an unconditional universal income transfer scheme that would directly reduce poverty, bring down administrative cost and plug leakages and errors of inclusion or exclusion.

  This is considered to be feasible as India has already executed an income transfer scheme to all farmer households to provide ₹ 6,000 per annum with a budget provision of ₹ 75,000 crore. The proposed universal scheme will be an extension of such a scheme.

Case against the UBI scheme

There are also many credible arguments against the UBI scheme as enumerated below.

- Though the proponents of the UBI scheme contends that it is fiscally feasible, a crucial question in regard to it in the Indian context is its affordability considering that a fixed sum will have to be paid to every person – adults and children – on a continuing basis which will become a permanent commitment on the part of the government.
- The sum fixed may also have to be revised periodically if it is to cover inflation since, over a period of time, a constant amount of 'cash transfer' may not buy the same amount of goods and services. It will further add to the expenditure involved.
- While such a hand-out will assuredly help the poor and destitute, who are at the very bottom of the pyramid, to lead a better life and be rid of abject poverty and starvation, the better off and affluent sections would not need this prop and extending it to them would be an unjust diversion of public funds. It would also further aggravate the existing inequalities in society.
- To overcome this, the Finance Ministry's *Economic Survey 2016-17* (in chapter 9), which has discussed at length the case for and against UBI, has put forth the following suggestions:
  * Define those non-deserving of UBI based on ownership of key assets such as automobiles, air-conditioners or bank balances exceeding a certain size.
  * Adopt a 'give it up' scheme wherein those who are non-deserving choose to opt out of the programme just as in the case of LPG and give them due recognition for doing so.

* Introduce a system where the list of UBI beneficiaries is publicly displayed; this would "name and shame" the rich who chose to avail of the UBI benefit.
* Self-targeting: Develop a system where beneficiaries regularly verify themselves in order to avail themselves of their UBI – the assumption here is that the rich, whose opportunity cost of time is higher, would not find it worth their while to go through this process and the poor would self-target into the scheme. But the *Economic Survey* observes that such an approach would conflict with the essence of JAM, whose appeal lies in its direct, costless transfer of the state's welfare subsidies to beneficiaries' accounts.

- The UBI scheme would require that every citizen in every family across the country is identified and listed as beneficiary of the scheme. Such a list would require periodic updating to account for births and deaths to keep it error-free. Considering the complexity of such an operation, and the efficiency and capacity of the administrative machinery at state, district and village levels in India, it is doubtful if it can be implemented in a flawless manner and that too on a continuing basis.
- An alternative approach suggested in the *Economic Survey* is "to phase in a UBI for certain vulnerable groups – widows, pregnant mothers, the old and the infirm – first. This would serve as a means for the state to make good of its promise – sometimes mandated by law – to support the most vulnerable. Furthermore, these are easily identifiable groups of individuals".
- It is also argued by some that 'cash transfers', in place of in-kind subsidies, would encourage some individuals to become spendthrifts or take to vices like alcohol, smoking, etc. which would have adverse consequences for the welfare of families. This is a serious moral hazard from the society's welfare viewpoint, an outcome which cannot be wholly ruled out.

➢ **Conclusion:** Considering the various pros and cons of UBI scheme, it would be better to continue with in-kind transfers of essential commodities but make them more efficient and fool-proof by employing technology like digitisation of records, identification through Aadhaar, and direct credit of other subsidy or welfare benefits to beneficiaries through Jan Dhan accounts.

Any scheme patterned on UBI, if implemented, may be confined to the very poor and vulnerable sections using technology and other measures, mentioned above, as is being done in the case of income transfers to farmers. The modalities of such a scheme will have to be worked out in great detail so as to ensure that it is foolproof and the benefits go to the really deserving sections and with minimum leakages or distortions.

13. i) **Explain the term 'fiscal deficit' and its implications for an economy.**

ii) **Maintaining fiscal prudence and containing fiscal deficit is essential to achieve macroeconomic stability. Discuss.**

Fiscal deficit is the difference between government's total expenditure and its total receipts excluding borrowing. Total receipts include revenue receipts and capital receipts which are not borrowings and are not debt - e.g., it includes recovery of loans and proceeds from sale of public sector undertakings. Fiscal deficit arises due to either increase in expenditure or shortfall in revenues.

Fiscal deficit can be financed through borrowing from domestic and foreign sources or by printing money. The borrowing can be either from the central bank of the country, or raising money from capital markets by issuing different instruments like treasury bills and bonds.

➢ **Implications for the economy:** Fiscal deficit and the above methods of covering it has the following implications for an economy.

- By printing new currency. But printing money in excess of what is justified for the growth of 'real' national income will lead to inflationary trends which will be a burden on the people. If deficit financing is maintained at a steady money level, it may not lead to 'spiral inflation' but will lead to price rise. The price rise can be minimised by either reducing the scale of deficit financing or imposing price controls.
- Borrowings from domestic sources consist of market borrowings, small savings of households, state provident funds and term loans from financial institutions. Financing by borrowing can be unsustainable if the interest rate involved exceeds the growth rate of GDP.
- If the borrowings are high and they are utilized for financing activities which give zero or low returns, the burden of interest payments will be unsustainable. The non-productive current expenditures will give rise to higher revenue deficits.
- If debt service payments form a high proportion of both revenues and expenditures, other activities of the government will suffer. Since expenditures on wages and salaries, defence expenditures, pensions, food subsidies, etc. are all committed expenditures, the main casualty will be capital expenditures in social and infrastructural spheres.
- A high fiscal deficit, even if sustainable, will 'crowd out' private investment and adversely affect growth. Such impact on growth of GDP will be more direct and severe if the borrowings lead to unproductive public consumption.
- A continued high level of public borrowing will put pressure on the interest rates. In order to finance government deficit, the central bank (RBI in India) will have to keep the level of reserves high on deposits in commercial banks. This will necessitate banks to have higher margins on their commercial and lending activities thereby subjecting the rest of the economy to high interest rates.

➢ Fiscal policy and macroeconomic stability

The prime objective of macroeconomic policy is to ensure growth and stability in the economy and maximize social welfare. Stability implies low inflation and maintaining stable levels of investment, output and consumption. The policy should be such as to achieve distributional justice to see that fruits of development reaches all and alleviates poverty.

The effect of fiscal policy on economic growth has for long-been a subject of debate in economic theory, empirical research, and economic policymaking. Rising budget deficit has been considered as one of the main constraints on economic growth in developing economies.

Economists are generally agreed that large and persistent fiscal deficits are inimical to good macroeconomic performance. As pointed out earlier, such deficits tend to crowd out private investment and increase inflationary potential. It would also weaken the balance of payments position, make financial sector reforms more difficult and impose a burden of debt on future generations.

➢ The theoretical basis

According to classical economists, fiscal deficit financed by domestic borrowing will result in increased government investment at the cost of private investment. But government spending will lead to increase in aggregate demand and expansion of the economy. As the economy expands, the private sector and businesses will find it profitable to ramp up production to meet the rising consumer demand.

Keynes, the Cambridge economist, advocated deficit spending by the State during the Great Depression of 1930s as a means of overcoming depression. **He argued that in a period of recession, public spending would stimulate aggregate demand for goods and services and counter unemployment and deflation. The government spending or 'pump-priming', as it is referred to, will stimulate private spending, which in turn would lead to economic expansion.** This approach was adopted by Franklin Roosevelt, the US President through his 'New Deal' programme to overcome the debilitating effects of the depression of 1930's.

After the Second World War, many of the newly independent countries, including India, which embarked on economic development and were faced with paucity of financial resources, resorted to deficit financing to meet developmental needs.

➢ Need for fiscal prudence

The dilemma faced in promoting economic growth and welfare is whether this is best achieved by the government itself, on the Keynesian approach of spending more than what it earns, or by restraining its expenditure to make space for private investment and market forces. Profligate spending and slippage in fiscal deficit target will end up in high inflation and retarded growth.

Against this background, adhering to a policy of fiscal prudence and reducing fiscal deficit assumes importance. The government must strive to keep deficit under control so as not to hamper growth. Expenditure ought to be within limits to avoid massive deficits leading to debt financing and the crowding-out effect of private investment. If deficits become unsustainable, it can lead to higher interest liabilities, and the government may well even have to default.

Counter-cyclical measures

In the event of business cycles, with ups and downs affecting the economy, macroeconomic stability will call for a counter-cyclical policy stance, i.e., allow the deficit to go up when growth dips below the desired level, and contain it when growth spikes above the norm.

Most advanced economies and several emerging market economies now target a structural deficit, which serves as an automatic counter-cyclical stabilizer. The structural deficit is the deficit consistent with sustainable public debt under conditions of normal growth. The actual deficit is allowed to exceed or fall below this target when growth is too low or too high.

Maintaining fiscal deficit as targeted is crucial for sustained economic growth. Lower fiscal deficit leads to lower interest rates and higher investment and growth. In exceptional circumstances such as the global financial crisis of 2007-08 which led to the 'Great Recession', fiscal stimulus may be required to counter recessionary trends even breaching deficit target.

14. Critically examine India's record in managing fiscal deficit. It is argued by some experts that rigidly adhering to fiscal deficit target may hurt economic growth and hence the government need not adhere to it strictly but could adopt a flexible approach. Do you agree with this view in the context of Indian economy? Justify your answer.

Since the early years of planning in the 1950s, the Government of India adopted deficit financing as a means to mobilise resources necessary for the five-year plans as the levels of outlays were of such an order which could not be met only by taxation and borrowing from the public or external aid.

Also, in the early phase of planning, the private sector was not in a position to provide the necessary investment for industrialisation. Hence the government had to undertake investment in the public sector to develop core sector of basic and heavy industries. This necessitated resort to deficit financing.

- **Economic growth and Fiscal deficit**

  The decade starting from 1980 was relatively better for the economy. While the annual rate of growth of GDP for the preceding 30 years (1950 to 1980) was only 3.52 per cent, which is cynically referred to as the 'Hindu rate of growth', during the decade 1980-81 to 1989-90, the annual rate of growth was 5.13 per cent.

But there were many ominous signs on the fiscal front which became visible during this period. Prudent fiscal management requires that revenue receipts not only meet revenue expenditures, but also generate surplus to finance the Plan and other capital and development outlays. But all through the 1980's, the government revenues fell short of expenditure. The fiscal imbalance persisted and worsened during the 1980's, and the gross fiscal deficit surged to 8 per cent by the end of the decade.

Another disturbing trend was that almost throughout the 1980s, non-development expenditure increased faster than development outlays which meant that long--term development of the country received less priority.

The persistent fiscal imbalances accentuated inflationary pressures. These and the critical foreign exchange position towards the end of 1980s and the early 1990's forced India to launch radical reform measures. With determined effort at fiscal consolidation, the central government brought down the combined deficit of the Centre and the states by the mid-1990s.

But later, instances such as hikes in salaries of government employees at both the Centre and the states, increase in subsidies, and payments to farmers towards debt relief made the government's task of adhering to fiscal deficit targets challenging.

➢ **The FRBM Act and Fiscal prudence**

An important step towards ensuring fiscal prudence was the enactment of the Fiscal Responsibility and Budget Management Act in 2003 which mandates the Central Government to ensure equity in fiscal management and long term macro-economic stability. The Act streamlined the Budget presentation process and helped to enforce fiscal discipline.

There was a view that instead of fixed fiscal deficit targets, it would be better to have a fiscal deficit 'range' as the target which would give necessary policy space to the government to deal with unforeseen and dynamic situations such as natural calamities or volatile global economic conditions which would have adverse repercussions on the economy.

➢ **Committee on FRBM Act:** Therefore, in 2016, an Expert Committee, headed by N.K. Singh, was set up to review the implementation of the Act. The Committee made the following important recommendations:

- To reach a fiscal deficit target of 3 per cent of GDP over a three-year period between 2017 and 2020, and the same to be further brought down to 2.5 per cent by 2022-23.
- 'Escape clauses' provided for deviations from the stipulated fiscal deficit target up to 0.5 per cent of GDP in certain contingencies such as effecting far-reaching structural reforms in the economy, or in the event of unforeseen events such as war, calamities of national proportion, setbacks in agriculture or sharp decline in real output growth with unanticipated fiscal implications.

- Enacting a new Debt and Fiscal Responsibility Act replacing the existing FRBM Act.
- Set up a Fiscal Council which will do fiscal analysis round the year, advise the government on any corrective action needed and advise if conditions exist to justify triggering the 'escape clauses' for deviating from the fiscal deficit target.
- Make an independent assessment of the Central Government's fiscal performance and compliance with targets under the proposed Debt and Fiscal Responsibility Act.

➢ **Fiscal deficit: The real picture**

A key concern is that the fiscal deficit numbers, put out by the government, do not present the true picture of public finances. Though the deficit has been brought down over the years, the government's off-budget borrowings have increased manifold.

There is a problem with budget data because the central government overstates the receipts and understates the expenditures figures. The government borrows funds using 'off-budget' methods which enable it to finance capital and revenue expenditures while seemingly adhering to deficit targets.

For instance, fertiliser subsidies are cleared through special banking arrangements; irrigation scheme is financed through borrowings by NABARD and power projects through Power Finance Corporation. Further, instead of paying the food subsidy bill during the current year, the central government carries it over to the following year which creates future liabilities and also add to interest payment liabilities.

This leaves the fiscal deficit figures cited in Union budgets questionable. These aspects have been pointed out by the Comptroller and Auditor General (CAG) also.

➢ **Conclusion:** While the need for stimulating growth is paramount, there is a limit to which fiscal deficit may be stretched. The consequences of breaching the deficit target could be severe and it may last over a long period. It will also take longer to bring the debt-GDP ratio to the prescribed limit. The longer also will be the period during which interest payments claim an unduly large portion of revenue receipts.

In view of these considerations, it would be prudent to adhere to the path of fiscal discipline and fiscal deficit targets, save in exceptional situations of economic slowdown or recession requiring stimulus, or to meet other unforeseen contingencies as pointed out by the Committee on FRBM Act. **(See also Question 2 in this chapter for more on this)**

15. India does not tax income from agriculture. Should India levy tax on income from agriculture? Give arguments for and against it.

Presently, all agricultural income is exempted from taxation, the main purpose being to protect farmers. Over the years, the issue has been debated by economists and examined by expert committees. There are arguments both for and against it.

Six states have agricultural tax legislation on the books – Tamil Nadu, Kerala, Assam, Bihar, Odisha and West Bengal – though its implementation varies substantially, from taxes not being levied at all to being levied only upon income from plantations. Some other states such as Uttar Pradesh and Rajasthan have dithered on the issue over the decades, introducing and then rolling it back.

A sensitive issue: This has been a sensitive issue because agriculture contributes nearly 14 per cent to India's GDP, accounts for about 11 per cent of the country's exports, and supports half of our population's livelihood. Besides, agriculture is also the source of raw material for a large number of industries.

The sector is also vulnerable to vagaries of nature, periodic failure of crops and income losses and consequent distress to farming community, resulting even in suicide of farmers.

➢ **Committees on the issue**

- An early attempt on this dates back to 1947 when an expert committee on financial provisions to the Constituent Assembly suggested consulting States on it.
- But it was in 1972 that it received serious attention when a Committee on Taxation of Agricultural Wealth and Income, headed by the noted economist K N Raj, was set up to comprehensively examine the issue. The Raj committee had recommended imposing a progressive 'Agricultural Holdings Tax' on agriculturists, taxing income from livestock, poultry, dairy farming etc., including income from agriculture in respect of assessees paying non-agricultural tax and levying a wealth tax on agricultural property.
- Later a Task Force on Direct and Indirect Taxes, under Dr. Vijay Kelkar, also examined the issue in 2002, and observed that States should be persuaded to pass a resolution authorizing the Centre to pass a tax on agricultural income that would then be assigned to the respective states.
- Bibek Debroy, economist and Chairman of the PM's Economic Council has suggested that agricultural income above a certain threshold may be taxed.

➢ **Arguments for taxing income from agriculture**

- Agricultural income above a certain threshold should be taxed. There are large landholdings which fetch substantial income and equity and justice demands that they should be liable to pay tax.
- There is an anomaly in exempting agricultural income from being taxed, especially where such income is substantial, when income tax is levied on non-agricultural incomes.
- A study of cooperative farms by the erstwhile Planning Commission showed incidence of tax avoidance as mechanized farms with hired labour took advantage of the exemptions provided to cooperative farms. That evasion grew over the decades. In assessment year 2014-15, for instance, nine of the top ten claimants for tax exemption of agricultural income were corporations and the tenth was a state government department.

- The Tax Administration Reform Commission report of 2014 observed that agricultural income of non-agriculturists is being increasingly used as a conduit to avoid tax and for laundering funds, resulting in leakage to the tune of crores in revenue annually.
- According to the 70th round of National Sample Survey, over 86 per cent of agricultural households have land holdings of less than 2 hectares. Low-income farmers would obviously fall outside the ambit of an equitable tax regime. But there is no justification to exempt those who derive substantial income from agricultural sources. It is due to the pressure brought to bear on governments by the political class and the rural elite, many of whom are large landowners, command substantial income and can fetch votes in large chunks in elections and have vested interests that they remain outside the tax net.
- There are two limitations which comes in the way of taxing the agriculture sector., viz., most of the payments and transactions in the sector are in cash or kind, and there is no standard system of account-keeping. These limitations can be overcome by the following means:
  * Have a crop-specific levy on landholdings above a threshold, assessed and implemented at the panchayat level for accuracy and flexibility.
  * Now all forms of cash transactions above ₹ 2 lakh are barred, which will expose all high-value agricultural transactions, thereby limiting the scope for tax evasion.
  * The Income-Tax Act can also be amended to provide for mandatory maintenance of books of accounts as a condition to avail tax exemptions and also subject to satisfactory explanation of any diversion of non-farm income to farm.

  And to incentivise and promote agriculture, the revenue collected could be ploughed back into agriculture for developing the farm sector – for facilities like irrigation, water conservation, soil rejuvenation, etc.
- Where 'contract farming' is being done by farmers, in group or otherwise, and in collaboration with corporates and multi-nationals, appropriate levy could be collected keeping in view cost-income considerations.
- Granting exemptions to small farmers with marginal holdings, or those covered under land ceilings of respective state laws, is justifiable. This will leave out a major part of the rural economy. Still, it is estimated that about eight lakh taxpayers disclosing farm income shall come under the tax net, presuming they don't fall under the 'small farmer' category.

➢ **Arguments against taxing income from agriculture**

- Given the extent of the informality that still exists in the agricultural sector, implementation of an agricultural tax would admittedly not be easy. Evolving crop-specific norms of returns to land poses problems.

- Taxing agriculture pose a problem everywhere and more so in developing countries like India. Records of inputs, yields, costs incurred, etc. are not maintained except in the plantation sector or where contract farming is done. Transactions by farmers are done in cash and not through banking channels making verification and assessment of income difficult.
- Agriculture in India being largely dependent on monsoon which is quite unpredictable, it is highly subject to the vagaries of nature. In years of erratic monsoon or drought, farmers incur heavy losses.
- Apart from the periodic adverse impact of nature, volatility in prices of agricultural commodities, due to both domestic and international factors, farmers incur losses. In fact, the government has to subsidise and support major crops through a policy of 'Minimum Support Price' (MSP). In these circumstances, it becomes unjust to tax farmers.
- Farming has increasingly become unremunerative and unprofitable due to rising costs, declining soil fertility, lack of water and irrigation facility, heavy debts incurred and inability of farmers to repay loans, etc. The country has been witnessing acute distress in large parts of rural areas resulting in even farmer suicides on a substantial scale. In the above scenario, there is not much scope to introduce taxes on agriculture.

➢ **Conclusion**

To sum up, taxing agricultural income in India poses many problems, save in the case of organized plantations and contract farming. Also, the prosperity of the rural population and rural sector is critical for the performance of the industrial and tertiary sectors and it has an overall impact on the performance of the economy. Any taxes, if at all, levied on agriculture has to be done prudently and with caution since, as already pointed out, this sector is vital lifeline of the nation on which a large section of the population is dependent and any adverse impact on it will set off a chain reaction in the economy.

> Any government, like any family, can, for a year, spend a little more than it earns. But you and I know that a continuance of that habit means the poor-house.
>
> \- Franklin D. Roosevelt (1882-1945), 32nd President of USA (1933-1945).

FOREIGN TRADE AND COMMERCE

> Let everyone engage in the business with which he is best acquainted.
>
> \- Sextus Aurelius Propertius (circa 50 B.C.)

Topics Covered

- *Role of international trade: its benefits and disadvantages*
- *Closed economy vs open economy*
- *Tariff and non-tariff barriers*
- *Role of GATT and WTO in world trade*
- *Need for WTO reform*
- *India and Capital account convertibility*
- *Foreign exchange management by RBI*
- *Trends in India's Forex reserves*

(On Free Trade Agreement (FTA), India's free trade agreements, Regional Comprehensive Economic Partnership (RCEP) and Trans-Pacific Partnership (TPP) see Questions 3, 4, 5 and 6 in Chapter 12)

1. Explain the concept of 'comparative advantage' which is the basis of international trade and bring out the advantages of international trade for an economy. Bring out also adverse impact, if any, which international trade could have on an economy.

Ans. Foreign trade plays an important part in the process of development of any economy. Just as no man can live in isolation, no country can either. This is even more so in the present-day context of globalization which has brought about greater integration of nations than ever before. Nations are ever more dependent on one another and, in this respect, trade between nations has assumed much importance.

➢ Rationale of International Trade

The rationale for trade between nations has found resonance in Adam Smith's classical work, "***An Inquiry Into the Nature and Causes of the Wealth of Nations***" (1776) where he says, "What is prudence in the conduct of every private family, can scarce be folly in that of a great kingdom. If a foreign country can supply us with a commodity cheaper than we ourselves can make it, better buy it of them with some part of the produce of our own industry, employed in a way in which we have some advantage. It is as foolish for a nation as for an individual to make what can be bought cheaper." This is the very concept underlying the 'Theory of Comparative Advantage' in international trade which was refined and developed later by other economists.

The idea of 'territorial division of labour', the original description of the concept, finds mention in the1815 work, '***An Essay on the External Corn Trade***' by Col. Robert Torrens (1780–1864). But it was David Ricardo (1772–1823), the English economist, who refined it and provided a theoretical basis for the idea in his 1817 classic titled, '***The Principles of Political Economy and Taxation***'. The idea was further developed by James Mill (1773–1836) in his work, 'Elements of Political Economy' in 1821. Finally, the concept became a central theme of international trade theory.

➢ Concept of Comparative advantage

In simple terms, the theory states that if country A can produce some goods at lower cost than country B, and if country B can produce some other goods at lower cost than country A, and if both countries need these goods, then it would be advantageous for both to produce those goods in the production of which they have comparative advantage and trade the goods between each other. In this way, both the countries stand to gain from trade and exchange of these goods.

However, in assessing the relative advantage, it is not enough to compare only the monetary costs of production or the resource costs (labour needed per unit of output) of production. Instead, one must compare the 'opportunity costs' of producing goods across countries. Opportunity cost is the value of an item which must be given up to acquire another item. The comparative advantage can also be assessed by comparing productivities across industries and countries.

The application of this concept becomes more complex when the study and comparison involves not just two countries and few goods, but involves multiple countries and production and exchange of a wide range of goods.

➢ Heckscher-Ohlin model

Eli Heckscher and Bertil Ohlin of the Stockholm School of Economics further developed Ricardo's theory of comparative advantage, known as Heckscher-Ohlin model (H-O model).

According to it, the relative endowments of the factors of production (land, labour, and capital) will determine a country's comparative advantage. As the profitability of goods is dependent on input costs, countries will have comparative advantage in producing those goods for which the required factors of production are locally available in relative abundance. This is because it will be cheaper to produce goods that require inputs which are available in abundance than to produce goods that require inputs that are locally scarce and dear. For instance, a country having labour and natural resources in abundance but little capital will find it advantageous to specialize in labour-intensive industries as the price of labour and natural resources will be cheap while the cost of capital will be high.

➢ Advantages and Benefits of International Trade

The need for, and benefits from, international trade arises due to relative differences in costs of production in countries. This is because countries are differently endowed with conditions and resources required for production of commodities. Countries are differently endowed with natural resources (raw materials), climate, capital, skill sets of labour force, technology, organisational capabilities, etc. As stated earlier, countries will have advantage in the production of those items which require more of those resources with which it is well endowed. The benefits of international trade are mentioned below.

- **Volume of output:** With countries specializing in the production of goods in which they have comparative advantage, the total output of goods could rise. If an appropriate terms of trade (i.e., amount of one good traded for another) were chosen, then both countries could end up with more of the goods after specialization and free trade than what they would have had in the absence of trade.
- **Specialisation:** It promotes specialisation and division of labour among countries. Nations would specialise in the production of those commodities for which they are more suited given the various endowments they possess. Specialisation helps to maximise output.
- **Skills and productivity:** With division of labour and specialisation, there will be improvement in the skills of labour and resultant higher productivity.
- **Economies of scale:** With more countries requiring the products and with exports, it helps to scale up production, providing economies of scale and keep down production costs.
- **Technology and quality:** Competition between countries helps to improve labour skills, upgrade technology and production methods thereby enhancing quality of products and overall output.
- **Optimising resource use:** It helps to optimise the use of factors of production with countries saving up on those resources which are scarce.

- **Reducing risks:** It reduces risk factors countries may face from financial crises or natural disasters which may impact their production processes. In such circumstances, international trade enables them to source items from other countries.
- **Investment and technology:** International trade and cooperation can bring in foreign investment and better technology to promote those industries in which it has comparative advantage. This will result in increased employment, upgrade of technology and help in the overall growth of the economy.

➤ **Disadvantages of international trade**

International trade also have some disadvantages and adversely affect countries.

- **Impact on home industries:** Competition from other countries could adversely impact the growth or even survival of home industries. This is evidenced by some home industries having to close down in the face of intense competition from large-scale MNCs who have the advantages of better technology, more skilled labour and more capital. Due to competitive pricing and quality issues, home industries may not be able to survive the competition.
- **Trade deficit:** If imports of a country are more than its exports, it will have adverse balance of trade and face foreign exchange issues. If the trade deficit is considerable and prolonged, it can harm the domestic economy. This is the case of trade between China and a large number of countries, including India, where the trade balance is tilted heavily in favour of China. It is also at the root of the US-China trade conflict due to the US having huge trade deficit with China.
- **Dumping:** Countries which are able to produce goods at much lower costs may dump the products on other countries. China's dominance in manufacturing has prevented many other countries from developing their industries and also led to dumping of relatively cheap Chinese goods in other countries.

  Such adverse factors lead to nations following a policy of 'protectionism' as against 'free trade' to protect the native industries against foreign competition. The dominance of industrially advanced nations over the developing and poor nations in trade as well as economic development has led to protest movements in different countries.

2. Explain what is meant by the terms 'closed economy' and 'open economy' and their implications for an economy. Examine India's foreign trade policy over the years and see how far India has been an open economy.

Ans. **Closed and Open economy:** A closed economy is one which has little or no external trade at all whereas an open economy is one which engages in imports and exports, and in which foreign trade forms a significant proportion of its GDP. An open economy allows movement of labour and capital into and out of the country.

A closed economy will have negligible or no trade activity at all with other economies. The rationale in favour of closed economy is to insulate the domestic economy from the cyclical fluctuations in the world economy, or to protect certain industries or sectors from foreign competition. The more a country is open to foreign trade and investment, the more vulnerable it will be to the upswings or slowdowns in the global economy.

- **Closed economy, an anachronism:** In the modern era, there is practically no nation whose economy is totally closed. It is now virtually impossible to remain as a closed economy because of requirements of raw materials, oil or even consumer goods as no nation can have all these and be totally self-sufficient. It will have to depend on other countries for some item or the other. Also, most economies have some item in surplus which it will have to export in order to pay for its essential imports. With globalisation and greater inter-dependence between nations, countries have to engage in foreign trade.

- **Developing countries:** Most economies in their initial stages of development follow relatively closed economy policy as they fear that competition from other countries and multi-national corporations (MNCs) may crush their nascent domestic industries. Such a policy of protection was followed even by the advanced countries like UK, USA, Germany, etc. in their early stages of industrialisation. And it has been adopted, in contemporary times, by many of the developing countries, including India, in the early phase of development. To attain self-reliance, to some extent, and to protect domestic industries from competition was a major objective behind such a closed economy policy.

- **India's foreign trade regime:** In the initial years of planning and development during the 1950s and 1960s, India opted for a policy of self-reliance and self-sufficiency, virtually shutting herself out from the world markets. For nearly three decades from 1950, India traversed on this path of 'import substitution' (IS) and discarding the approach of 'export strategy' (ES) which, in hindsight, proved to be much to her disadvantage.

  One of the reasons for this was that India faced shortage of foreign exchange and had to conserve it for the ambitious policy of industrialisation initiated in the Second Plan (1956-61).The Plan faced serious foreign exchange crisis in 1956-58 when India had also exhausted the Sterling balances accumulated during Second World War. (The foreign exchange asset in the form of Sterling balances of over ₹ 1,700 crore was for purchases made by Britain in India for her requirements for the war).

  Another factor which led India to adopt a restrictive trade regime during the initial phase of development was what the economists called "export pessimism". Surprisingly, many prominent development economists like Raul Prebisch and Ragnar Nurkse were pessimistic about opportunities that foreign trade offered in that period. They had a misconception about the global environment which the under-developed countries faced then and failed to recognise that an export-led growth policy could be an 'engine of growth'. This prompted many of the developing economies, with the exception of some of the East and South-east Asian economies (see 'East Asian Miracle' later below), to adopt inward-looking, import-substitution policies instead of export-promotion strategy.

- **A retrograde policy:** A policy of liberal imports to meet the needs of the Second Plan led to the foreign exchange crisis. This necessitated the imposition of exchange controls which became endemic and developed vested interests. The development strategy of industrialisation based on import substitution, and the system of exchange controls adopted, failed to usher in rapid growth or self-sufficiency. It also did not help in eradication of poverty. Instead, it led to lacklustre growth and a globally uncompetitive industrial structure, perpetually precarious balance of payments and, above all, it engendered corruption in the social and economic fabric of the country.

➢ **East Asian miracle:** In contrast, the East and South-east Asian economies, who were in the same position as India was, in late 1940s and the early '50s, opened up their economies, invited foreign capital and technical know-how, imported new-generation machinery and equipments, and developed a robust industrial base. They also developed strong banking and financial sectors and built modern ports and world class infrastructure. The economies of South Korea, Taiwan, Hong Kong and Singapore adopted 'Export Promotion' strategy, in contrast to India's 'Inward-looking, import substitution policy', and developed manufacturing capacity which they effectively used to cater to the world markets and registered high growth rates. Malaysia and Thailand too made remarkable progress. Between 1965 and 1990, they were growing at 8 to 9 per cent per annum and raised real incomes as fast as the rich countries. It is then no wonder these countries have all been aptly dubbed 'Asian tigers'.

- **China's rise:** From late 1970's, Communist China, under Deng Xiaoping, also began to implement market-oriented reforms which was to lead the country on a path of unprecedented growth in the next three decades, and make China an economic powerhouse by 2015. China maintained 32 years of uninterrupted growth at a 9.9 per cent annual growth rate and an average of 16.3 per cent growth in international trade.
- **India's growth:** In contrast, India's annual (compound) growth rates of national income was 3 per cent in 1951-60, 2.9 per cent in 1961-70, and 2.5 per cent in 1971-80 period which was termed 'Hindu rate of growth' by Prof. Raj Krishna, an eminent economist.

➢ **Reforms: A turning point:** Following a serious economic crisis towards the end of 1980s and the early '90s, India embarked on major reforms in 1991 which was a turning point. Faced with a precipitous balance of payments crisis and high fiscal deficit, India undertook short-term and long-term measures to revive the economy and put it on a stable path.

- **Trade policy:** As part of the reform measures, India opened up the economy, adopted a New Trade policy marking a radical shift from the Import Substitution policy followed in the preceding four decades and took steps to promote exports. Various restrictions on imports and exports were removed.
- **Industrial policy:** Under a New Industrial policy, industrial licensing was abolished, except in respect of industries involving security and strategic factors, social considerations, and hazardous and environmental aspects. Foreign investment was encouraged in high priority industries, requiring large investments and advanced technology.
- **Further reforms:** In due course, India continued to liberalise foreign direct investment (FDI) regime to promote investment, trade and economic growth. These include:
    * Relaxed FDI policy in over a dozen sectors, including defence, railway, medical devices and civil aviation;
    * Hike in FDI ceiling in the defence sector under the automatic route;
    * Increased foreign investment cap in insurance and pension sectors;
    * Higher limit for investment by foreign portfolio investors (FPIs) in central public sector enterprises, other than banks;

  The government also took various measures to improve the 'Ease of Doing Business', both at the level of Central and State governments due to which India's rank has improved significantly in World Bank assessments.

➢ **Conclusion:** From the factors enumerated above, one may conclude that there is evidence that economic growth calls for policies oriented towards integration into the global economy. Nations withdrawing into a shell and unwilling to engage with other nations may get marginalized and lag behind other countries in terms of growth and human development. At the same time, nations have to guard against the impact of adverse global trends like the financial crisis of 2007-08 and free trade pacts – regional and multilateral – which may be inimical to their core interests.

3. What are tariffs and non-tariff measures in international trade? Explain in what way they impact international trade and economies.

Ans. International trade is critically influenced by the tariff policies and various non-tariff measures adopted by countries. These have a vital bearing on the unhindered flow of goods and services between countries. The GATT (General Agreement on Tariffs and Trade) entered into by countries in 1947, and its successor body, the World Trade Organisation (WTO), formed in 1995, have played an important role in regulating these aspects, promoting multilateral trading system and settling trade disputes between countries.

The UNCTAD (UN Conference on Trade and Development), which works to improve the developing countries' trade and investment prospects, also offers support and advice to developing countries in their trade negotiations with the advanced countries.

➢ **Tariff and Non-tariff measures**

- **Tariffs measures:** Tariff measures are restrictions to 'free trade' which affect the distribution, pattern and levels of international trade. (The term 'tariff' signifies customs duty imposed by countries on imports or exports). Tariff measures include import tariffs, import quotas and export subsidies or export incentives.

- **Quantitative Restrictions**: Countries also resort to 'Quantitative Restrictions' (QRs) which are the limits imposed on the quantity of goods that are imported or exported. It includes import quotas and Voluntary Export Restraints (VERs) which are signed by the exporters of foreign countries.

  Quantitative restrictions are imposed to discourage imports and thus, protect domestic industries from competition from cheaper and technologically advanced goods manufactured by other nations. Developing countries with balance of payments problems also imposed quantitative import curbs.

  Though quantitative restrictions have been phased out by WTO in world trade, the GATT and certain WTO Agreements allow them under specific circumstances. For example, in cases of balance of payments problems, national security considerations, or in certain other exceptional cases. Many WTO Member-countries have notified that they maintain quantitative restrictions in one form or the other, including prohibitions or restrictions relating to trade in nuclear materials, narcotic drugs, weapons, and measures to protect the environment. In some cases, these prohibitions or restrictions to trade result from international obligations undertaken outside the WTO framework,

- **Non-tariff measures (NTMs):** Non-tariff measures are those that restrict imports or exports of goods or services of a country through mechanisms other than the imposition of tariffs. In other words, non-tariff barrier is any measure, other than a customs tariff, that acts as a barrier to international trade.

  NTMs can potentially have an economic effect on international trade in goods, changing quantities traded, or prices or both.

➢ **Categories of NTMs:** Broadly speaking, non-tariff measures include import licensing, rules for valuation of goods at customs, pre-shipment inspections, rules of origin ('made in'), and trade prepared investment measures.

Non-tariff measures also include sanitary (relating to health and hygiene) and technical conditions, labour standards and other checks on imports and exports as mentioned below.

(i) **Health and environment:** To ensure safety and protection of health of human, plant and animal life, environment and wildlife. To prevent risks arising from contaminants, toxins or disease-causing organisms in food. For example, sample test on imported oranges, mangoes, etc. to check for the residue level of pesticides.

(ii) **Labour standards:** Consumer groups, social advocates and labour unions have tried to have labour standards included in WTO's mandate and on the multilateral trade agenda. Labour standards may include a wide spectrum of issues such as wages, hours of work, freedom of association and collective bargaining, prevention of child labour and forced labour, benefits like housing, medical care, potable water and sanitary facilities, and worker safety and training.

Some of the above-mentioned issues are those adopted by the ILO (International Labour Organisation). European Union and USA also follow a policy of enforcing certain labour standards while negotiating trade agreements. For instance, they insist on banning child labour in apparel and garment industry in India, Bangladesh, etc. which have sizeable exports to the US and the European Union.

The rationale behind advanced countries insisting on labour standards is that, firstly, disparate labour standards distort terms of trade between countries and inhibits fair competition. Because, low cost unskilled labour constitutes the main comparative advantage of developing countries to the detriment of advanced countries where labour costs are high. Secondly, low labour standards give rise to negative externalities such as long working hours, overcrowding and unsanitary conditions at work, poor nutrition and stress which can lead to ill-health and adverse effect on the quality of life and life expectancy of workers and lead to social tension.

But resort to the above trade restrictions to ameliorate labour conditions may worsen the precarious poverty and employment situation prevailing in the developing countries.

(iii) **Technical standards:** Products and production processes conform to proper standards and technical specifications. For example, the restrictions on toxins in children's toys.

(iv) **Labelling, marking and packaging:** This will ensure requisite information on products is provided to the consumer so that the consumer can chose not to consume a product that was produced in ways he/she considers unacceptable. For example, a consumer may wish to forgo consumption of a product where child labour was used in its production or its production could have been a source of environmental damage.

(v) **Pre-shipment inspection and other formalities:** Live animals need to be cleared at a designated customs office for inspection. Goods must be shipped directly from the country of origin, without stopping at a third country.

(vi) **Trade protective measures:** These are to counteract adverse effects of imports in the market of the importing country. For example, an anti-dumping duty on imports of biodiesel products from another country, to offset in case of harmful dumping of such products by the exporting country. Or, a countervailing duty on imports of semiconductors from another country in case the exporting country is found to have granted subsidies in the production of semiconductors.

(vii) **Quotas and quantity control:** Control measures aimed at limiting the quantity of goods that can be imported.

(viii) **Price control:** Measures to control or affect the prices of imported goods. For instance, a minimum import price is set for fabric and apparel. Imports of some fruits may be allowed, free of duty, during specified months; while in other months seasonal duties may be levied.

(ix) **Export-related measures**: These are measures followed by the exporting country on exported goods. For example, exports of processed sea food products must be inspected for sanitary conditions. Exports of cultural heritage objects – sculptures or precious items like antiques – are prohibited.

➢ **Implications of tariffs and NTMs for international trade**

Tariffs and non-tariff measures impact international trade and economies in a variety of ways.

- International trade increases the number of goods that domestic consumers can choose from, brings down the cost of goods through increased competition, and allows domestic industries to ship their products abroad.
- Trade barriers, in the form of tariffs or non-tariff measures, prevent the flow of goods and services and deprives nations these benefits of trade.
- Protectionism imposes high cost. Tariffs (customs duties and fees) add significantly to the costs of commodities and trading.
- By closing borders or otherwise restricting markets, consumers are made to pay more, firms incur higher costs, and choice gets limited.
- Imports are not the only ones to be taxed. Some countries, mainly the developing and least-developed ones, also levy duty on their exports which will add to their revenues. They set minimum export prices or reduce VAT rebates, which increases export prices, as a means of restricting exports. They may also impose export bans, quotas and licensing requirements which will affect export prospects.
- Trade barriers decrease overall efficiency and productivity within economies. While protecting industries in their infant stages may be justified, prolonged course of protection from competition may result in firms not upgrading their technology and production processes. This causes them to remain less productive, inefficient and less competitive and, with no scope for expansion, they may not be able to reap the economies of scale.
- Protectionist policies through non-tariff measures, and practices like anti-dumping and countervailing measures adopted by industrialised countries have adversely affected the export prospects of developing countries and stalled their progress.

4. Discuss the role played by GATT (General Agreement on Tariffs and Trade) and WTO (World Trade Organization) in promoting world trade and examine the limitations faced by them in furthering their objectives.

Ans. The Great Depression of 1930s and the Second World War (1939 - 45) disrupted global economy, particularly the US, Western Europe and Japan, which were shattered by the ravages of the war. These years also were marked by a high degree of protectionism and tariff barriers which adversely affected international trade.

➢ **General Agreement on Tariffs and Trade (GATT)**

It was against this background that after the war ended, 23 countries met and signed the General Agreement on Tariffs and Trade (GATT) in 1947 which came into effect in 1948. The Agreement provided the rules for much of world trade, brought about reduction in tariffs and led to significant growth in international commerce.

GATT pledged the member countries to:

- the expansion of multilateral trade with minimum barriers to trade;
- reduction in import tariffs and quotas; and
- abolition of preferential trade agreements.

It is an accepted principle under the Most- Favoured-Nation (MFN) clause of the GATT that tariffs should be non-discriminating and any concessions agreed between two or more countries should automatically be extended to all, with an exception made for the developing countries.

➢ **Assessment of GATT**

Though GATT was provisional arrangement with a limited field of action, it made some significant contribution in promoting liberalization of world trade. Between 1947 and 1986, eight Rounds of trade negotiations were held. Continued reductions in tariffs during the period helped spur high rates of growth of world trade during the 1950s and 1960s – around 8 per cent a year on average.

In 1965, a provision was made with focus on the special problems of the developing nations and a committee on trade and development was formed to ensure progress on the elimination of barriers on the trade in products of particular interest to developing countries.

A Ministerial meeting of GATT held in 1982 reaffirmed that determined efforts would be made to resist protectionist measures and taking any steps inconsistent with the objectives of GATT. The eighth round, called the Uruguay Round of negotiations, continued from 1986 to 1993.

The continued momentum of trade liberalization ensured that trade growth consistently out-paced production growth throughout the GATT era. This is a measure of' the increasing ability of countries to trade with each other and to reap the benefits of trade.

The rush of new members during the Uruguay Round demonstrated that the multilateral trading system was recognized as an anchor for development and an instrument of economic and trade reform.

- **The challenges for GATT**

But all was not well. Despite its success, GATT was becoming less relevant and inadequate to meet the needs of the evolving world trade and investment landscape. Its success in reducing tariffs to a low level, combined with a series of economic recessions in the 1970s and early 1980s, drove governments to devise other forms of protection for sectors facing increased foreign competition.

Western Europe and North America sought bilateral market-sharing arrangements with competitors and resorted to a spree of subsidies to maintain their hold on agricultural trade. These changes undermined GATT's credibility and effectiveness.

The world trade scene had become far more complex than the preceding 40 years. Globalization was underway, and trade in services – an area not covered by GATT rules – was gaining in importance and international investment had expanded. The expansion of services trade was also closely linked to increases in world merchandise trade.

For instance, in agriculture, loopholes in the multilateral system were heavily exploited, and efforts at liberalizing agricultural trade met with little success. Even GATT's institutional structure and its dispute settlement system were causing concern.

These factors prompted GATT members to reinforce and extend the multilateral system and the Uruguay Round and the Marrakesh Declaration led to the creation of the WTO.

- **Creation of WTO**

Set up in 1995, the World Trade Organization (WTO) replaced GATT. The primary functions of WTO are:

- Further development and oversight of the multilateral system based on principles laid down under GATT and which WTO continued in the Doha Round of negotiations.
- Ensure that trade flows as smoothly, predictably and freely as possible.
- Serve as a forum for governments to negotiate trade agreements.
- Help producers of goods and services, exporters, and importers protect and manage their businesses.
- Settle disputes and reduce trade tensions. It provides resources and legal status for resolution of trade disputes through independent disputes panels.
- Stimulate economic growth and employment.

➢ **Progress under WTO**

The WTO agreements uphold the principles of binding tariffs, and applying them equally to all trading partners (MFN – Most-Favoured-Nation – principle) which are key to the smooth flow of trade in goods. But it also provides for exceptions in some circumstances. Three of these exceptions are:

- Actions taken against dumping (selling at an unfairly low price).
- Subsidies and special "countervailing" duties to offset the subsidies. (Countervailing duty is an additional import duty imposed on a commodity to offset a reduction of its price due to an export subsidy granted in the country of origin.)
- Emergency measures to limit imports temporarily, designed to "safeguard" domestic industries.

❖ **Consensus and disputes:** Though the WTO is a "member-driven" body and all major decisions are normally taken by "consensus" among all member governments, differences and disputes do arise on certain contentious issues between countries on trade. Two such issues are the 'Special provisions' for developing countries and 'Subsidies'.

❖ **Special provisions for developing countries:** The WTO Agreements also contain special provisions which allow developing countries to enjoy "special and differential treatment" (SDT). This has been a major point of contention in the WTO negotiations. It is contended by the US that China, India and some other countries have been taking unfair advantage of SDT benefits meant for developing countries. It is argued that while China and India may have once been poor countries deserving trade concessions, they are now strong enough to do without them.

But, paradoxically, the US and other rich countries have always enjoyed enforceable SDTs in the agreements on textiles and clothing, and also agriculture. It took 10 years for the agreement on textiles – which allotted export quotas to developing countries – to come to an end in 2005.

The US has sought a review of the "developing country" status at the WTO. There is some merit in the contention and the WTO could consider different levels of "developed status" of countries and provide for varying levels of concessions.

❖ **Subsidies:** Subsidy in WTO parlance is a form of financial contribution by government or a public body which confers a benefit to an enterprise or industry, or income or price support which operates directly or indirectly to increase exports or reduce imports of any product.

Subsidies have potentially distortive effects on trade flows. In WTO, there are two categories of subsidies: Prohibited and Actionable subsidies.

- Prohibited subsidies include "export subsidies" which give an artificial competitive advantage to exporters, and "import substitution subsidies" which are contingent upon the use of domestic products over imported goods.
- The actionable subsidies are subject to challenge in the WTO or to countervailing measures.

❖ **Phasing out subsidies:** WTO's Subsidies and Countervailing Measures (SCM) Agreement provides a period of eight years for least developed and developing countries, with gross per capita of $1,000 per annum at 1990 exchange rate, to phase out export subsidies. But such countries need to stop all export incentives if their per capita Gross National Income (GNI) crosses $1,000 for three consecutive years.

- **India loses a case at WTO:** In 2019, India suffered a setback at the WTO in a dispute against the US that had challenged India's key export subsidy schemes, including the one for special economic zones (SEZs). It was observed that India was giving prohibited subsidies to producers of steel products, pharmaceuticals, chemicals, information technology products, textiles, and apparel and the US challenged India's export programmes at the WTO claiming them to harm American workers.

  The Dispute Settlement panel of WTO ruled that the export subsidy programmes violated provisions of WTO norms for SCM agreement as India's per capita gross national product crossed $1,000 per annum.

  India proposes to appeal the ruling before the organisation's Appellate Body.

❖ **Subsidies in agriculture:** Subsidies in agriculture has been a contentious issue in WTO. The agricultural trade rules in the WTO's 'Agreement on Agriculture' do not bar public procurement and stockholding for food security. However, if food for such programmes is acquired at administered prices and not market prices, then it is deemed to be support to farmers. As per WTO rules negotiated in the Uruguay Round, all such support has to be kept within a limit of 10 per cent of the value of production of the product in question.

The main reason for the objection to farm subsidies and support to farmers in the Developing countries is that the developed nations want greater access for their farm products to markets in developing countries like India, China, Brazil, Vietnam, etc. which could cause great deal of harm to farmers in these countries.

The irony of it all is that while objecting to farm subsidies in developing countries and the subsidized Public Distribution System (PDS) in India, advanced countries like the US and those in Western Europe extend subsidies to their farmers. This is despite the farmers in these countries being far better off than those in developing nations. Not only that the extent of subsidy given in the advanced countries is many times more than what is given in developing countries.

Income transfer scheme: It may be noted that since India's farm subsidy and export subsidy are being increasingly challenged at the WTO for violating multilateral trading rules, the scheme of income support for farmers introduced in India may be more in sync with WTO rules.

And if the direct income transfers to farmers are gradually scaled up, it may ultimately help to do away with the policy of Minimum Support Price (MSP). The MSP policy could pull India into a confrontation at the WTO as higher MSPs will likely make Indian farm subsidies breach the limit laid down by WTO and result in face-off between India and the US and other countries.

5. There is a view that the World Trade Organization (WTO) has fallen short of expectations and keeping in view the changing global scenario and the needs of present times, it needs to be reformed. Comment.

Ans. The World Trade Organization (WTO) was set up in 1995 as a successor to the General Agreement on Tariffs and Trade (GATT) which was formed in 1947 and served the cause of international trade for nearly five decades.

The WTO is based on agreements signed by the majority of the world's trading nations. As of 2019, the WTO has 164 member countries and 23 "Observer "countries.

WTO's functions are:

- Administering multilateral trade rules;
- Serving as a forum for trade negotiations; and
- Providing a mechanism to settle trade disputes.

➢ **Globalization and changes:** During the last three decades, there has been increasing trend towards greater integration of economies and globalisation of trade. This has meant reduction in the barriers to the movement of people, goods, services, capital, etc., between countries and it has brought immense benefits to the world at large.

With the rise of many developing countries and their emergence as economic powers in their own right, the balance of economic power has undergone a perceptible change. While this has helped global economy as a whole to grow, it has also led to friction between them and the advanced countries. This has been particularly visible in the arena of international trade posing challenge to the WTO as will be seen from the following developments:

- While the advanced countries seek greater access for their products to the markets in the developing countries, the latter are cautious and tend to adopt a protectionist approach to safeguard their economic interests.
- The last round of multilateral trade negotiations, the Doha Development Agenda (DDA), started by member-countries in 2001, collapsed in 2008 and was virtually abandoned by 2015.

- The US has been critical of the dispute settlement mechanism of WTO saying that it has been unable to deter China from violating WTO rules and has blocked filling up vacancy in WTO's Appellate Body. The functioning of the body will be in jeopardy if it does not have the required quorum of three members. This would mean there will be no final resolution to disputes between members.
- The intense trade dispute between the US and China on account of adverse trade deficit sustained by the former and even dispute between the US and the European Union (EU) are just two instances. The effects of the US-China trade dispute are felt far beyond these two countries and virtually rattled many economies and global trade. The dispute has hit not only hundreds of billions of dollars' worth of goods they sell to each other but has disrupted the extensive global supply chains that produce the goods. The feud is a sign of headlong collision between the American free market economy and China's state-driven economy.
- With dominant influence in global economy, China has been an aggressor in trade disputes with other major economies. China's predatory policies in trade, heavy-handed state intervention in the industrial sphere, forcible technology transfer from foreign companies and even theft of their intellectual property, in its relentless efforts to become a superpower in high-end manufacturing and latest technologies, have caused much friction in international relations. Besides, China's abuse of the "Special and different treatment" (SDT) provision under the GATT to subsidise export industries and dump oversupplies in other countries has come in for much criticism. In the face of such defiance of WTO's free trade regime, the trade body has been unable to enforce its rules even as China claims it is compliant with WTO regime.
- The US is also not free from blemish as it has pulled out of multilateral trade deals like the Trans-Pacific Partnership (since resurrected by other countries as Comprehensive and Progressive Agreement for Trans-Pacific Partnership – CPTPP) and Paris Climate Change Agreement. It has also unilaterally imposed tariffs on steel and aluminium from other countries, including India, on grounds of "essential security interest" under a GATT clause. Such unilateral actions could undermine the effectiveness of WTO.

➢ **Need for Reforms:** Due to the above-mentioned factors and divergent views among members on various issues, the WTO has come under pressure and the US and many other countries have been clamouring for reforming it. Discussions between member countries have been initiated on this and they have been ongoing. Some of the issues needing solution are:

- **Development status:** An area for reform concerns the problem that there is no agreed definition as to what constitutes a "developed" or "developing" country at the WTO and that members self-designate their status. Members who claim developing country status in WTO benefit from concessions due to so-called 'special and differential treatment' (SDT).

The fact that 10 of the G20 countries – including China, India, and South Korea – claim developing country status at the WTO is a major point of contention. US contends that they are no longer poor countries meriting special treatment. There is some merit in this argument. Brazil's decision to forego its developing country designation is significant, and it could stir debate on setting certain definitive criteria to gauge a country's development status. Different levels of development could be specified, say, based on per capita income, into which countries could be grouped.

- **Monitoring trade policies:** There is a need to improve the ability of the WTO to administer and monitor member states' trade policies. The failure by many countries (including China) to comply with the WTO's notification requirements – for instance, to notify government subsidy programmes – has been a matter of concern for years. But now WTO members are seeking to address the notification issue – with the US, EU and others suggest penalties for non-compliance.
- **Problem of consensus:** Efforts to resurrect the WTO's relevance as a forum for trade liberalization is an area where some positive outcomes are visible. The virtual collapse of the Doha Round in 2008, especially over agricultural subsidies, as a major controversial issue, raised questions about the viability of conducting trade talks involving more than 160 members based on consensus where all members must agree to arrive at a decision. This also hindered members from focusing on updating global trading rules in the light of the changes that have occurred since the WTO was set up in 1995. In particular, the WTO is not currently able to deal with the increased role of state-owned enterprises or digital trade.
- **Trade agreements:** To tackle some of these new trade issues, countries have turned to bilateral or regional free trade agreements – such as the CPTPP and RCEP. A section of WTO members has pursued plurilateral negotiations by focusing on narrower issues. 76 WTO members – including the US, China, Japan and the EU – agreed to start negotiating rules on e-commerce.
- **Role of small, medium nations:** As the role of the US as a leader is on the wane, other WTO members are beginning to take on a more active role and work towards rules-based international trading system. While major trade powers like the EU and Japan assume a bigger role, it is important that the medium-sized and smaller countries play greater role in WTO. For them, safeguarding the WTO is especially vital because the organization serves as the main platform for setting the rules for new trade policy which will impact their economies.
- **WTO's Appellate body:** The US administration under President Trump has voiced concerns about 'judicial overreach' by WTO's Appellate Body, which is a controversial issue and will be difficult to resolve. The US seems inclined to go back to the practice of non-binding dispute settlement prevalent under the GATT.

As stated earlier, the US raising tariffs in the name of national security and blocking the appointments of members to the Appellate Body will impair the working of WTO dispute settlement system and further weaken the organisation. This has to be guarded against.

- **Move for reform:** There is growing momentum among many WTO members to "modernize" the organization, including the Appellate Body though the details and feasibility of reform are unclear. Members aim to draft proposals that would improve the WTO's deliberative and monitoring functions and ability to solve trade concerns without litigation.

  China for WTO reform: In the context of what China deems is an "existential crisis of the WTO", China has also urged for reforms and released a paper putting forth its suggestions. According to China, the reform process should cover the following areas:

  - Increase WTO's relevance in global economic governance and improve its operational efficiency.
  - Make multilateral trading system inclusive, non-discriminatory and open, so as to create a stable and predictable environment for international trade.
  - Eliminate development deficit in the existing WTO rules.
  - Safeguard the development interests of developing Member-countries and enable their integration into economic globalization.
  - Follow the practice of decision-making by consensus.

  In conclusion, it may be stated that the WTO has an important role to play in promoting hassle free international trade and it needs to be reformed to meet the challenges of changing global economic landscape.

6. Explain the concept of capital account convertibility and the pros and cons of an economy adopting it. Examine the reasons as to why India has not adopted it.

Ans. The "balance of payments" in foreign trade of a country consists of '*Current account*' and '*Capital account*'.

- **Current account and Capital account**
  - The '**current account** 'refers to trade in goods (also called merchandise or visible trade) and services plus profits and interest earned from overseas assets, net of those paid abroad. Items which are not visible goods in the current account are called '**invisibles**' and consist of services like financial services such as banking and insurance, tourism, shipping and air transport services. Gifts sent to, or received from, abroad, interests, profit and dividends and private transfer of funds.
  - The '**capital account** 'is made up of cross border transactions in assets such as equity, debt, immovable property or any combination of these. It includes inward and outward flow of money for investment and international loans and grants.

- **Capital account convertibility:** Capital account convertibility implies that a country's currency is freely convertible with foreign currencies. It is the ease with which a country's currency can be converted into gold or another currency through global exchanges.

  In other words, there is no restriction on conversion of the domestic currency into a foreign currency or on conversion of a foreign currency to the domestic currency. The former process enables a resident of the country to acquire foreign assets while the latter enables a non-resident to acquire a domestic asset. It enables unrestricted mobility of capital.

  - **Conditions for Full convertibility**

    Liberalisation of capital account transactions as a policy objective gained prominence in the 1990's. The 1990's saw significant increase in global capital flows, following the triumph of market capitalism and increasing trend towards globalisation, and advocacy of capital account convertibility as a policy goal, particularly for the developing countries, started gaining momentum.

    An economy should fulfill certain conditions before it can adopt full capital account convertibility as given below:

    * Full capital account convertibility calls for sound macroeconomic policy.
    * A country needs a strong and resilient banking and sound financial framework.
    * Economy with competitive financial parameters and environment.
    * Robust prudential regulatory and supervisory policies.
    * Capital flows carry risks, and unless nations have a high level of financial and institutional development, such capital flows could accentuate those risks.
    * Countries showing high productivity growth would be able to attract more capital.

- **Advantages and Pitfalls**

  Capital account convertibility has both advantages and drawbacks for an economy. While the opening up of capital account could make available more capital at lower cost and help to foster growth, it would require certain conditions in the economy such as fiscal consolidation, control of inflation, and a robust financial system.

  Capital flows in general are welcome in developing economies. They all add to the productive capacity of the country and lead to the development of financial markets. Such flows are also viewed as vehicles for the transfer of technology and management skills.

  Benefits of Capital Account Convertibility

  (i) Free global capital outflows result in more efficient allocation of the global pool of savings to the more productive uses.

  (ii) Developing countries benefit from free access to global capital markets, as they get more investible resources which augment domestic savings, reduce marginal cost of capital, and accelerate investment and growth.

(iii) Open capital accounts widen the channels through which countries can finance trade and investment and thus support the multilateral trading systems.

(iv) It will deepen capital markets and will help India to play a more meaningful role in the global economy.

(v) It provides greater scope for investors in both developed and developing countries to invest in diverse portfolios.

(vi) Since capital account convertibility calls for sound macroeconomic policy, it induces the countries concerned to commit themselves to healthy macroeconomic management.

(vii) Currencies of all developed countries are fully capital account convertible; by striving to make their currencies fully convertible, developing countries progress on the path towards development.

➢ **Drawbacks and pitfalls of Capital Account Convertibility**

(i) Capital flows are sensitive to macroeconomic conditions. Any deterioration in fiscal conditions, inflation management, balance of payments, or any other macroeconomic shock may cause a disruption, stoppage or reversal of capital flows.

(ii) Capital flows which result mainly from trade in financial assets are prone to volatilities caused by information asymmetries, herd behaviour, panic reaction, etc.

(iii) An open and unfettered capital account calls for complete abandonment of the exchange rate management and can lead to extreme volatility in the exchange rate and large fluctuations from its equilibrium value.

(iv) It is recognized that capital flows carry risks, and that liberalisation of capital flows before nations reach a certain level of financial and institutional development can accentuate those risks. Under certain circumstances, cross-border capital flows need to be regulated to avoid the worst effects of capital flow surges and sudden cessation.

(v) The practice of capital controls in times of currency and banking crisis is now part of the accepted wisdom. Capital controls are used by the state to protect the economy from potential shocks from unpredictable capital flows. It may be noted that India has been using capital controls to effectively manage the flows.

➢ **India' position: The background**

The decade of the 1990s witnessed a number of financial crises in several countries with risks originating mainly from the capital account of balance of payments. The lessons from the East Asian and other financial crises of 1990s have brought about a marked shift in the approach towards capital account liberalisation, particularly among developing countries. It is now recognised that although global capital flows have a potential for improving efficiency and growth prospects, they could also trigger instability, due to a variety of factors.

❖ **India's approach:** India's approach to capital account convertibility has been one of cautious liberalisation, taking gradual and calibrated steps and treating liberalising capital account as a continuous process rather than a one-off event.

India had set up a Committee in 1997 headed by S.S. Tarapore to examine the issue of on Capital Account Convertibility. The committee's report provided the framework for liberalisation of capital account transactions in India. The Committee recommended a phased implementation of CAC and prescribed the macroeconomic framework for implementing full convertibility.

Reforms implemented

After economic liberalisation process set in motion in 1990s, India took following measures to unshackle India's external sector.

- A significant step was to move to a flexible exchange rate regime to allow the overvalued Rupee to float. However, down the years the exchange rate was sometimes 'managed' in response to prevailing conditions.
- Another important step was to comply with the obligations under Article VIII of the Articles of Agreement of the International Monetary Fund (IMF) that there will not be any unreasonable restriction on current account transactions.
- Finally, India put in place a new statute – the Foreign Exchange Management Act (FEMA), 1999 that recognised and discriminated between current and capital account transactions – the former was unrestricted while the latter was subject to regulations. Capital account transactions have been further progressively liberalised.
- While India has not opted for full capital account convertibility, the government has taken steps to ease access to foreign capital, be it Foreign Direct Investment (FDI) or Foreign Portfolio Investment (FPI) which includes equity and debt. Any foreign individual or firm or any other association of people can invest in any Indian company or set up an Indian company through FDI which essentially means long term engagement with influence on management. There is virtually no restriction on FDI barring certain sectors on account of security or strategic interests, such as the defence sector.
- New instruments have been made available for foreign investors such as rupee-dominated offshore bonds (called 'masala bonds') and alternate investment funds.

Conclusion

Considering that India is still an emerging economy and not matured and fully developed economy, India needs to move towards full capital account convertibility in a calibrated manner. This is especially pertinent as changes in US fiscal and monetary policy will impact on India's capital flows and exchange rates.

Markets are factoring in a regime change in advanced countries, especially US macroeconomic policy, with expectations of changes in interest rates, fiscal stimulus and monetary policies which would impact emerging nations. Yet the fact remains that foreign capital brings in modern technology and management practices and aids in promoting growth and welfare which is at the root of programmes like 'Make in India'.

The pace of further liberalisation would depend on domestic factors, especially further progress in financial sector reforms, fiscal consolidation and the evolving international financial architecture.

7. Elucidate the salient features of the management of foreign exchange reserves by the Reserve Bank of India (RBI) before and after the 1991 liberalisation of the economy.

Ans. The Reserve Bank of India (RBI), as the custodian of the country's foreign exchange reserves, is vested with the responsibility of managing their investment and operates within the overall policy framework agreed upon with the government. The RBI oversees the foreign exchange market in India and supervises and regulates it through the provisions of the Foreign Exchange Management Act, 1999.

➢ **Managing Foreign exchange (forex) reserves**

The foreign exchange reserves include the following items. (See Table 6.1 on page 6.29 in Question 8 in this chapter):

- Foreign currency assets (FCA).
- Special Drawing Rights (SDRs) and
- Gold.

SDRs are held by the Government of India. SDRs refer to an international reserve currency created by the International Monetary Fund (MF) in 1969 that serves as a supplement to the money reserves of member countries. It was created in response to concerns about the limitations of gold and dollars as the sole means of settling international accounts.

➢ **Exchange rate system**

The two main types of exchange rate systems are 'fixed exchange rates' and 'floating exchange rates', each with variants based on the monetary policy of the country.

- Fixed exchange rate implies a rate of exchange of a currency which is fixed (pegged) in relation to a foreign currency or a group of currencies.
- Floating exchange rate is when the rate of exchange of a currency is determined by market forces in relation to foreign currencies.

- **India's Exchange rate system**

India's exchange rate policy has evolved overtime in line with the global situation and as a consequence to domestic developments. Its evolution can be seen in three distinct phases: 1947-1971, 1971-1992 and 1992 to the present.

- **1947-71:** After independence, India followed a "fixed exchange rate" regime under the Bretton Woods System. This system was formed in 1944, following World War II, when representatives from 44 countries met at Bretton Woods in the US to establish an efficient and effective world monetary system. This meet gave birth to the International Monetary Fund (IMF).

  Under the Bretton Woods System, gold was the basis for the U.S. dollar and other currencies were pegged to the U.S. dollar's value. The US was to maintain the price of gold fixed at 35 dollars per ounce and was to exchange dollars for gold at that price without restrictions or limitations. Other nations were required to fix the price of their currencies directly in terms of dollars and indirectly in terms of gold. The exchange rate could fluctuate within plus or minus 1 percent around the agreed par value.

  India was also a part of this system. The Indian Rupee's external par value was fixed in terms of gold with Pound Sterling as the intervention currency.

  The Bretton Woods System effectively came to an end in the early 1970s when the U.S., under President Richard Nixon, announced that US would no longer exchange gold for U.S. currency.

  With the breakdown of the Bretton Woods system, India moved towards the "pegged exchange rate" system. India continued with a variant of fixed-exchange rate regime for two more decades. India's external sector was then dominated by trade and foreign capital flows were limited. The license-permit regime made foreign exchange transactions straightforward as every transaction had to be backed by a license or a permit.

  The Indian Rupee was linked to U.K. Pound Sterling on account of the country's historic links with Britain. This pegging of currency to another country's currency results in a fixed exchange rate system. It maintains stability among the trading partners. However, though a currency peg can minimize fluctuation, at the same time it increases the imbalances between the countries. Therefore, in 1975, Rupee was pegged to a basket of currencies of India's major trading partners. This was done to ensure the stability of Rupee and avoid weaknesses associated with a single currency peg.

- **1971-1992:** During 1990 and 1991, India faced a major Balance of Payments crisis which led the country to near bankruptcy. India was forced to borrow money from the IMF against the country's gold reserves. India resorted to devaluation of the Rupee which meant decrease in the exchange rate. This boosted exports and increased the inflow of foreign currency.

  India ended the pegged exchange rate system and based on the report of a High-level Committee headed by Dr. C. Rangarajan, India moved towards a "market determined exchange rate" system.

- **1992-2018:** A Liberalized Exchange Rate Management System (LERMS) was introduced in March 1992 to boost the foreign exchange earnings and improve the balance of payments. Under this system, Rupee was made partially convertible. As India was going through a period of deficit, it was risky to impose full convertibility of the Rupee.

  In 1994, the Current account under the balance of payments was made fully convertible. While the Rupee became a floating currency and the current account of India was made fully convertible, the Capital account is only partially convertible. This is done to protect the domestic market from foreign competition.

  Though the system adopted is known as "managed float", it is a market determined exchange rate regime mostly based the demand and supply of foreign exchange, with provision for timely intervention by the RBI to stabilise the market.

➢ **Importance of Forex Reserves**

Foreign exchange reserves play an important role in an economy.

- A strong reserve of foreign exchange gives fillip to the Government and the Central bank (RBI) to implement fiscal and monetary policies and manage liquidity and cash flows in the domestic markets.
- This reserve helps to meet any contingency in case of an abrupt interruption in capital flows from external sources, which could occur during an emergency.
- Holding fluid forex provides cushion against such impacts and gives the certainty that there would be sufficient reserve to meet the nation's critical imports.
- This rise in reserve will also strengthen currency, Indian rupee, against the dollar.

➢ **Deployment of Reserves**

In deploying reserves, RBI pays close attention to currency composition, interest rate risks and liquidity needs. All foreign currency assets (FCA) are invested in assets of top quality and a good proportion can be converted into cash at short notice.

One crucial area in the process of investment of the foreign currency assets in the overseas markets relates to the risks involved in the process. The counterparties with whom deals are conducted are subject to a rigorous selection process. While there is no set formula to meet all situations, the Reserve Bank follows the accepted portfolio management principles for risk management. It involves identifying and analysing risks, developing responses and monitoring and containing the risks.

In assessing the returns from deployment, the total return (both interest and capital gains) is taken into consideration.

➢ **Objectives of Foreign exchange reserves management**

The basic parameters of the RBI's policies for managing foreign exchange reserves are safety, liquidity and optimising returns. Within this framework, the Reserve Bank focuses on:

- Maintaining market's confidence in monetary and exchange rate policies.
- Enhancing the Reserve Bank's intervention capacity to stabilise foreign exchange markets.
- Limiting external vulnerability by maintaining foreign currency liquidity to absorb shocks during times of crisis, including national disasters or emergencies.
- Providing confidence to the markets that external obligations can always be met, thus reducing the costs at which foreign exchange resources are available to market participants.
- Adding to the comfort of market participants by demonstrating the backing of domestic currency by external assets.

➢ **Evolution of Foreign exchange management policy**

For a long time after independence, foreign exchange in India was treated as a controlled commodity because of its limited availability. The early stages of foreign exchange management in the country focused on control of foreign exchange by regulating the demand due to limited supply.

The seeds of rigid exchange control were sown in the 1950s. During the Second Five Year Plan (1956-61), the priority of centralised planning was setting up basic and heavy industries which required import of capital equipment. This and three wars in 1962, 1965 and 1971, in a span of a decade, created acute shortage of foreign exchange reserves. This was compounded by the need to import basic food items to meet the acute food shortages which further strained foreign exchange resources.

Against this background, conserving foreign exchange was considered a national priority. The situation eased following the success of Green Revolution in agriculture and with increased inward remittances from Indians working abroad. The exchange control regime saw gradual relaxation and fine-tuning during the 1980s.

➢ The 1991 crisis and External sector reforms

The serious crisis which the economy faced towards the end of 1980s and the early 90s caused a major shift in foreign exchange policy and opening up of the economy itself. As the economic crisis was triggered by an acute balance of payments problem, the external sector went through a complete regime change. The reform of the sector comprised of two elements:

- Changes in the trade sector, and
- Changes in the exchange rate management.

■ Changes in the trade sector

The changes in the trade sector signalled the movement away from an inward-looking approach to the adoption of an open policy of integrating with the rest of the world.

- ♦ Quantitative controls over imports were removed step by step and tariff rates were brought down steadily from the high levels at which they stood till then.
- ♦ Imports of raw materials and capital goods were freely allowed on Open General Licence (OGL) but the foreign exchange required for these had to be obtained from the market.
- ♦ Earlier, to provide incentive for exports, a complex scheme of import replenishment was there under which an exporter was allowed to import certain raw materials and components equal to the actual import content of exports. Besides, a cash support scheme to compensate for taxes not refunded was also in vogue. By eliminating import licensing and introducing partial convertibility of the Rupee, the reforms got rid of these complex incentive schemes.

■ Changes in exchange rate management

In 1991, the foreign exchange reserves had touched rock bottom. It was barely enough to meet the needs of two weeks of imports, and payments towards external debt were in danger of default. A part of the gold held by the RBI had to be used to garner temporary resources from abroad. Devaluation of the Rupee by about 18 per cent in two steps was undertaken in July 1991. These steps helped to stabilize the foreign exchange position.

- ♦ **Committee on Balance of Payments:** As referred to earlier, in 1991 the government appointed a High-level Committee on Balance of Payments, headed by C. Rangarajan, who later was Governor of RBI, to look at the capital account of India's Balance of Payments. Apart from recommendations relating to the management of capital account, the Committee also made key recommendations with respect to exchange rate.

- ♦ **Exchange rate system:** Based on the interim report of this Committee and other inputs, the government and RBI moved to a dual exchange rate system in March 1992. Until that time, the exchange value of the rupee was determined by the RBI every day.

  Under the new system, 40 per cent of foreign currency under current receipts was required to be surrendered to RBI at an official exchange rate, while the rest (60 per cent) was allowed to be sold at the market determined exchange rate. The Committee, in its final report, recommended the adoption of a unified market determined exchange rate system.

  The experience with the dual exchange rate system provided impetus to move to a full-fledged market determined exchange rate system.

- ♦ The foreign exchange surrendered at official exchange rate could be used to meet the foreign exchange requirements of certain essential imports.
- ♦ The benefit of dual exchange rate of 40 per cent-60 per cent, extended to exporters, was made available also to Indians working abroad who were making considerable amount of remittances and thus making valuable contribution to India's foreign exchange earnings.

➢ **Paradigm shift in Exchange rate policy**

The Reserve Bank's approach to foreign exchange reserves management has undergone significant change over the years. Until the balance of payments crisis of 1991, India's approach to forex reserves was essentially aimed at maintaining reserves at appropriate levels to cover imports.

The approach underwent a paradigm shift following the recommendations of the 1991 Rangarajan Committee referred to above. The Committee stressed the need to maintain sufficient reserves to meet all external payment obligations, ensure a reasonable level of confidence in the international community about India's capacity to honour its obligations, and counter the speculative tendencies in the market. After the introduction of the system of market-determined exchange rates in 1993, the objective of smoothening out the volatility in the exchange rates assumed importance.

➢ **Conclusion**

The RBI's function of managing foreign exchange reserves has in recent years grown, both in terms of importance and sophistication, for two main reasons.

- First, the share of foreign currency assets in the balance sheet of the Reserve Bank has substantially increased.
- Second, with the increased volatility in exchange and interest rates in the global market, the task of preserving the value of reserves and obtaining a reasonable return on them has become challenging.

8. Examine the trends in India's foreign exchange reserves and its utilisation by the Reserve Bank of India (RBI).

Ans. India's foreign exchange (forex) reserves have risen steadily especially after the 1991 economic reforms and liberalisation. But there have been occasions when India faced foreign exchange crisis and acute shortage of foreign exchange. Two such episodes can be cited:

➢ **Second Plan period:** At the time of Independence, India had accumulated foreign exchange reserve of over ₹ 1,700 crore in Pound Sterling known as Sterling balances. This foreign exchange asset was on account of purchases made by Britain in India for her requirements for the war. This asset came quite handy after independence to pay for imports and developmental purposes.

But by the time India was implementing the Second Five Year Plan (1956-61), India had exhausted the Sterling balances. The Plan which involved industrialisation on a large scale and required heavy imports of capital equipments and due to shortage of foreign exchange, it led to serious foreign exchange crisis during the years 1956–58 which necessitated the imposition of rigid exchange controls.

➢ **Economic crisis of 1990's:** The decade of the 1990s began on a precipitous note when the economy was on the verge of collapse. The balance of payments was in deep crisis, foreign exchange reserves had touched rock bottom, and payments towards external debt were in danger of default. Despite large external borrowings, there was sharp reduction in foreign exchange reserves. The government had to pledge a part of the gold held by the Reserve Bank of India to mobilise temporary resources from abroad. The Rupee had to be devalued in 1991 and international confidence in our economy had eroded considerably. The situation could be tackled only by India undertaking major structural changes in the economy including on the trade and foreign exchange fronts.

➢ **Trends in Forex reserves:** In between such dire situations, India has been able to improve the foreign exchange reserves position and forge ahead with her ambitious development plans. The dramatic improvement on the food front following the Green Revolution that occurred between 1970 and 1990 and the bold economic reforms post 1991 crisis helped India to salvage the position on the foreign exchange front and build substantial reserves as can be seen from Table 6.1.

It will be seen from the Table that the relative shares of Gold, Foreign currency assets (FCA) and Special Drawing Rights (SDRs) have undergone much change over the years. The share of FCAs has become consistently dominant post-1991 reforms and that of gold has come down. The share of SDRs also is much less.

Foreign currency assets (FCA) consist of capital inflows to the capital markets, foreign direct investment (FDI) and external commercial borrowings (ECBs). External commercial borrowing (ECB) is an instrument used to facilitate access to foreign funds by Indian corporates and PSUs (public sector undertakings).

- **Capital flows - FDI and FPI:** FDI is investment made by a company or individual from abroad for establishing a new business or acquiring the existing business. FPI is an investment made by a company or an individual from abroad in the stock markets or debt markets in India. FDI is relatively more stable while FPI is quite volatile. Nations with a high level of FPI can encounter heightened market volatility and currency turmoil during times of uncertainty.

A major factor behind the significant rise in India's forex reserves has been the spurt in foreign direct investments (FDIs) and foreign portfolio investments (FPIs). Foreign investors have acquired stakes in several Indian companies. The increased interest shown by foreign investors is because of expectation of a turnaround in the economy. Following the reforms agenda, the government and the Reserve Bank have liberalised the provisions relating to such investments.

India's accretion of forex reserves has largely been through its capital account surplus while the current account has mostly been in deficit. Though in the recent past, India had a rare surplus in current account due to fall in the price of oil and sharp fall in imports; this trend is not seen to be sustainable.

Hence, in managing forex reserves, considerations of safety and liquidity should remain critical.

Table 6.1: India's Foreign Exchange Reserves **(Figures are in ₹ crore)**

End of Financial Year	SDRs	Gold	Foreign Currency Assets	Reserve Tranche Position	Total
1	2	3	4	5	6
1970-71	112 (15.2)	183 (24.9)	438 (59.8)	--	733
1980-81	497 (8.9)	226 (4.1)	4822 (86.9)	--	5545
1990-91	200 (1.7)	6828 (59.8)	4388 (38.4)	--	11416
1992-93	55 (0.18)	10549 (34.3)	20140 (65.5)	--	30744
2000-01	11 (0.005)	12711 (6.4)	184482 (93.5)	--	197204
2010-11	20401 (1.5)	102572 (7.5)	1224883 (89.9)	13158	1361013
2014-15	24940 (1.16)	119160 (5.5)	1985460 (92.8)	8080	2137640
2016-17	9380 (0.39)	128830 (5.37)	2244940 (93.6)	15050	2398200
2019-20	10800 (0.3)	230527 (6.4)	3333815 (92.5)	27013	3602155

Note: SDRs stand for Special Drawing Rights of a Member-country with IMF(for more on this, see under Glossary in Appendix) Figures in brackets are percentages to total in column 6. Percentages may not add up to exactly 100 due to rounding off. -- denotes Negligible.

Source: Table 149, Handbook of Statistics on Indian Economy, 2019-20, Reserve Bank of India.

- **Role of Gold**

  While RBI's gold stocks were quite stable with changes only every few years, these stocks have increased more frequently in recent years, suggesting the gold is being used more actively as part of India's overall international reserves. This is a welcome development since gold reserves, now although only a small part (about 6.4%) of India's overall international reserves, can help to progressively diversify India's reserve portfolio.

  Gold can play a stabilising role for India's external position given the uncertain global economic recovery, a prolonged period of near-zero or negative interest rates and loose monetary policies followed by the advanced economies. The search for higher yields by international investors can result in greater volatility of capital flows to emerging market economies like India in the coming years. Diversification of investment is a key strategy and gold is a key factor in this.

  However, RBI's holdings in gold remain conservative even when compared to other emerging economies. While Russia held 23 per cent of its reserves in gold by June 2020, Turkey's gold holdings constituted over 45 per cent of its foreign reserve portfolio, according to data by the World Gold Council.

➢ **Utilisation of Forex reserves**

With the exception of a small proportion of gold, the forex reserves are invested in liquid assets like U.S. treasuries and Euro-denominated bonds of other advanced economies. Most of these economies have seen interest rates fall to near zero, with some securities even trading at negative yields.

According to the RBI data, as much as 64 per cent of the foreign currency reserves are held in securities like Treasury bills of foreign countries, mainly the US, 28 per cent is deposited in foreign central banks and 7.4 per cent is also deposited in commercial banks abroad.

Monetary easing by the U.S. Federal Reserve and other advanced economies has reduced the lure of traditional reserve currencies. With further rounds of quantitative easing by the U.S. Federal Reserve during the current Covid-19 crisis, the attraction of the U.S. dollar as a reserve asset is likely to reduce further and the demand for gold as part of emerging economies' international reserves may continue to rise.

The RBI also uses its forex resources for stabilising the rupee. It sells the dollar when the rupee weakens and buys the dollar when the rupee strengthens. Of late, the RBI has been buying dollars from the market to shore up the forex reserves. When the RBI mops up dollars, it releases an equal amount in rupees. This excess liquidity is sterilised through issue of bonds and securities and LAF operations. (A liquidity adjustment facility (LAF) is a monetary policy tool used in India by RBI. It helps to manage liquidity and provide economic stability by offering banks the opportunity to borrow money through repurchase agreements (repos) or offer loans to the RBI via reverse repo agreements. LAF's helps in managing price trends in the economy by increasing or reducing the money supply.)

➢ **Alternative uses of Forex**

There have been often debates over alternative uses to which forex reserves may be put. One common demand is that India's foreign exchange reserves may be used to finance infrastructure development in the country. Yet another view is that RBI could deploy excess forex reserves for commercial returns which would mean the central bank breaking away from the conventional role and turning partly commercial.

Also, in the last few years, RBI has become a critical part of the Union Budget as the surpluses in its earnings are being transferred to the Centre, and these transfers go up to nearly ₹ one lakh crore which adds to the non-tax revenue of the government.

But experts and purists are opposed to such ideas and put forth the following arguments.

- Even if the foreign fund influx is sizeable, reliance on these floating funds to stimulate the economy would not be advisable. Since these reserves are not created from current account surpluses, they are akin to borrowed funds and don't really belong to us. The potential of these funds to exit at any time should not be underestimated. The 2008 global financial crisis proved the volatility nature of reserves as the country faced significant capital outflows.
- A key objective of forex reserves is for the central bank to manage India's monetary policy, to keep exchange rates stable and in times of crises to defend the rupee. As India gets increasingly plugged into the global economy, it will be difficult to predict how big a war chest it will actually need in a financial crisis.
- Though when investors and ratings agencies compare India to other emerging markets, the external vulnerability is significantly lower because of these reserves, India stands out as quite vulnerable on the fiscal front.
- Further, any such move undermines the RBI's autonomy as the sole arbiter on the use of forex reserves. The quality of governance in any democracy improves with the independence of its institutions. The RBI must be free to manage monetary policy, without undue interference from the executive.

➤ Conclusion

Significant developments in the external sector over the past two decades such as substantial increase in foreign exchange reserves, growth in foreign trade, rationalisation of tariffs, current account convertibility, liberalisation of Indian investments abroad, increased access to external commercial borrowings by Indian corporates and participation of foreign institutional investors in Indian stock market have resulted in a radically changed environment.

Notwithstanding these positive and salutary signals, both the RBI and the government need to keep a watchful eye on India's foreign exchange position.

> What is prudence in the conduct of every private family, can scarce be folly in that of a great kingdom. If a foreign country can supply us with a commodity cheaper than we ourselves can make it, better buy it of them with some part of the produce of our own industry, employed in a way in which we have some advantage. It is as foolish for a nation as for an individual to make what can be bought cheaper.
>
> \- Adam Smith, *An Inquiry into the Nature and Causes of the Wealth of Nations (1776).*

LABOUR AND EMPLOYMENT

Each needs the other: capital cannot do without labour, nor labour without capital.

– Pope Leo XIII (1810-1903), (Pope (1878-1903).

Topics Covered

- *Assessing employment and unemployment*
- *Organised and Unorganised sectors*
- *Formal and informal employment*
- *Challenge of job creation*
- *Labour reforms initiated*
- *Importance of skill development and steps taken*
- *Automation and employment*
- *Automation in Indian context*

1. Mention the agencies responsible for collecting data on employment and unemployment in India. Outline the methods and measures adopted by them and their relative advantages and deficiencies.

As the subject of employment and unemployment has been a matter of much debate in India, it is pertinent to know the agencies which collect data on them and the sources relied upon which reveals the complexities involved in the process of collection and estimation.

It is also to be noted that there has been much change in India's data requirements, as well data collection methods and techniques, since the initial data-gathering systems were instituted decades back due to transformational changes in the economy over the years.

- **Agencies and data sources:** The following are the agencies involved in the collection of employment data and their sources for the data. These sources may be classified into four broad categories: household surveys, enterprise and industry surveys, administrative data and data from government schemes as detailed below.
  - **Household surveys:** Household surveys are the primary method of generating employment and unemployment data. Of the available options, it is the one that covers most comprehensively the entire labour force and thus provides the most valid statistical estimates of employment and unemployment for an entire economy. This is especially true in India, where a large section of the workforce is either self-employed or spread over a vast number of small, unorganized enterprises.

    The following are the employment statistics collected from household surveys, of which two are periodical official surveys while the third is collected during decennial Census from households.

    - Employment-Unemployment Survey conducted by the National Sample Survey Organisation (NSSO);
    - The Annual Labour Force Survey conducted by the Ministry of Labour; and
    - The decennial population census conducted by the Registrar General of India and Census Commissioner.
    - **NSSO Survey:**The Employment-Unemployment Survey (EUS), conducted by the National Sample Survey Organisation (NSSO), is the most comprehensive survey providing labour force statistics in India. The EUS survey is carried out over an entire year to account for seasonal variation in employment.

      This survey measures economic activity for three different reference periods: a year, a week and a day, and gives three different measures of activity status – Usual Status (US), Current Weekly Status (CWS) and Current Daily Status (CDS) as explained below.

      - **Usual Status**: A person is considered unemployed on Usual Status (US) basis, if he or she was not working, but was either seeking or was available for work, for the major part of the reference year. The US unemployment rate is generally regarded as the measure of chronic, open unemployment during the reference year.
      - **Current Weekly Status:** A person is considered unemployed by Current Weekly Status (CWS), if he or she had not worked even for one hour during the week, but was seeking or was available for work. Conversely, a person is considered working (or employed) if he or she, while pursuing any economic activity, had worked for at least one hour on at least one day during the 7 days preceding the date of survey.
      - **Current Daily Status**: The third concept of unemployment is the Current Daily Status (CDS), which is in terms of total person-days of unemployment, and is the aggregate of all the unemployment days of all

persons in the labour force during the reference week. On CDS criterion, a person is considered working for the entire day if he or she had worked for four hours or more during the day. If the person had worked for one hour or more but less than four hours, he/she was considered employed for half-day. This method records every day's, and even half-day's, work of the person over a week.

The person-days unemployment rate is derived as the rate of person-days in unemployment to the person-days in the labourforce. This measure emphasizes the unemployment of those employed on a weekly status.

The usual status definition represents the most liberal definition of employment while the daily status definition is the most conservative one. Accordingly, the unemployment rate is the lowest as per the Usual Status definition, ranging between 2 to 3 per cent and the highest as per the daily status, varying between 5 and 8 per cent. According to the latest NSSO EUS survey, the total workforce in India was 47.36 crore in 2011-12. Of these workers, 23.16 crore were employed in agriculture and 24.2 crore in industry and services.

- **Labour Bureau:** The Labour Bureau of Ministry of Labour has been conducting the Annual Labour Force Survey since 2010. The survey generates employment and unemployment estimates based on the Usual Status definition and the data is collected only for part of the year, instead of being spread over the entire year to reckon seasonal variations which occur. Also, it covers only population aged 15 and above, in contrast to the entire population being covered in the NSSO EUS survey.

- **Census survey:** The Office of the Registrar General & Census Commissioner conducts the Population Census. It uses different concepts and definitions than the two surveys discussed above, collecting data on main, marginal and non-workers in the economy.

  As Census data is collected only once in ten years, the estimates are available after much time lag. So these estimates rarely form the basis of formulation of employment policies.

- **Enterprise surveys**

  - **The Economic Census:** The Economic Census covers the entire universe of non-agricultural establishments regardless of size or sector. As such, it extends to both industrial and services establishments. In principle, the Economic Census could serve as the sample frame for conducting enterprise surveys. However, it has been conducted at low frequencies and at irregular intervals in the past.

    According to the sixth and latest round of the Economic Census, the total workforce employed in all establishments in 2013-14 was 13.1 crore. But as per 2011-12 NSSO household survey, workers employed in industry and services was 24 crore. The difference may be due to the following factors:

- A substantial part of non-agricultural workforce is not captured by the Economic Census.
- It does not cover self-employed workers that are not a part of any establishment and many small establishments may not have been covered.
- The own-account enterprises (OAEs), which do not employ regular workers and enterprises employing less than 10 workers together accounted for almost 79 per cent of India's workforce engaged in industry and services establishments. Nearly 70 per cent of this workforce was employed in enterprises with five or less workers.
- As per the 2013-14 Economic Census, only 2.7 crore workers in India were employed in establishments with 10 or more workers. These establishments represented a miniscule 1.37 per cent of all establishments in India.

♦ **Annual Survey of Industries**: The Annual Survey of Industries (ASI) is the only regular and frequent establishment survey that India conducts currently. It uses the enterprises registered under the Factories Act, 1948 as its sample frame and covers industrial units with 10 or more workers, if using power, and units with 20 or more workers, if not using power. Since as per 2013-14 Economic Census, all establishments in industry and services with 10 or more workers employ only 2.7 crore workers, its coverage is very limited.

Hence, though ASI provides a wide range of employment-related indicators, such as number of employees, man days, product(s) manufactured, capital invested, value of plant and machinery, wages and salaries, PF contribution, workmen welfare expenses, total output, net value added, etc., it has rarely been used to count the total number of workers in the economy.

♦ **Unorganized Sector Surveys of Industries and Services:** Using the Economic Census as the sample frame, the NSSO has occasionally conducted surveys of unorganized industry and services. While surveys of industry exclude establishments covered by ASI, those of services have included establishments of all sizes. It also suffers from infrequent collection and time lag between data collection and dissemination. Like the ASI, these surveys have not been used to evaluate growth in employment.

♦ **Quarterly Employment Survey:** The Labour Bureau conducts the Quarterly Enterprise Surveys (QES) to measure employment in eight broad sectors of industry and services including manufacturing, construction, trade, transport, education, health, hotels and restaurants and business process outsourcing. The survey covers enterprises with more than 10 workers in both urban and rural areas and covers about 81 per cent of establishments with more than 10 employees.

- ♦ **MSME Census:** Data on Micro, Small and Medium Enterprises (MSME) sector is also being collected. It covers manufacturing enterprises with investments in plant and machinery of up to ₹ 10 crore and services enterprises with investments of up to ₹ 5 crore. Data is collected on the number of units, economic activity, output and employment of MSMEs. Its coverage has been expanded to include unregistered and registered small scale industries.

❖ **Government schemes:** Administrative data and government schemes are also potential source for gathering data on job creation. The former includes data from the Employees' Provident Fund Organization (EPFO), the Employees' State Insurance Corporation (ESIC), the National Pension Scheme (NPS) and other similar sources relating to large private organizations.

And government schemes such as the Mahatma Gandhi National Rural Employment Guarantee Act (MGNREGA), Pradhan Mantri Grameen Sadak Yojana (PMGSY), Micro Units Development and Refinance Agency (MUDRA), Integrated Child Development Services (ICDS) programme, Housing for All, Pradhan Mantri Kaushal Vikas Yojana (PMKVY), Deen Dayal Upadhyaya Grameen Kaushalya Yojana (DDUGKY), and various infrastructure projects and livelihood schemes create jobs. These sources have not been properly tapped to estimate job creation. The major limitation in using data from these schemes is that, in some cases, additions to payrolls may not represent new jobs and simply indicate employment shifts. Duplication of data also is to be guarded against.

➢ **Deficiencies and advantages:** As the above account shows, there is a broad spectrum of sources from which India collects data on employment generation in various sectors and to assess the level of unemployment. But as mentioned below, while they have merits, they also suffer from deficiencies which need to be removed to make the data as accurate as possible.

♦ **Deficiencies**

- The major limitation of the NSSO survey is its low frequency and the time lag between data collection and availability of the results. Typically, data collection takes place once every five years. The survey results usually become available with a lag of more than a year. This delay makes the data less relevant as policy inputs.
- Enterprise surveys do not adequately cover the self-employed and farm workers.

- The Enterprise Census fails to capture the entire non-agricultural workforce.
- The Annual Survey of Industries has several gaps such as out-dated sample frame, limited coverage and time lag in collecting data.
- Further, available fields for drawing samples for such surveys often do not cover small, unorganized enterprises and, therefore, leave out workers employed by them.
- Sources in administrative datasets are even more partial in coverage than enterprise surveys. Also, individuals enrolled in them may be those already working but not previously enrolled, so duplication must be guarded against.
- Jobs generated in education and health sectors are particularly important from the viewpoint of job creation and they can provide valuable data. But this source is limited by its highly partial coverage.
- As for Census data, the frequency of data collection, being once every ten years, is very low, so estimates become available after much lag. As a result, these estimates rarely form the basis of media debates or policy formulation on employment.

♦ **Advantages**

- Enterprise surveys have the advantage of capturing more accurately the industry structure of employment, associated wages and other enterprise characteristics.
- Enterprises have a more accurate idea of their industry classification than households, which increases the accuracy of workers' industry classification in these surveys.
- Apart from household and enterprise surveys, administrative datasets created in the course of enrolling workers in pension and medical insurance programs as well as information contained in tax returns can provide data on the employment status of large groups of individuals. In the Indian context, employment statistics from these sources can be useful sources of counting workers engaged in formal employment.

2. Distinguish between the organised and unorganised sectors and outline their role in Indian economy.

Ans. The Indian economy comprises Organised and Unorganised sectors. In India, the unorganized sector enterprises outside government, corporations and cooperatives account for the bulk of total employment.

➢ **Organised sector in India**

In India organised or formal sector refers to licensed organisations, i.e., those who are registered and pay taxes. The Annual Survey of Industries (ASI) regularly compiles detailed information on formal manufacturing.

This sector mainly comprises the following units:

- Manufacturing units registered under the Factories Act, employing 10 or more workers using power, and those employing 20 or more workers without using power.
- All electricity undertakings engaged in generation, transmission and distribution of electricity registered with the Central Electricity Authority (CEA).
- Certain servicing units and activities like water supply, cold storage, repairing of motor vehicles and other consumer durables like watches etc. are covered under the survey.

The organised, formal sector is subject to laws and regulations and the workers have social protection, economic security and have certain incentives which those of the informal sector do not enjoy.

➤ **Unorganised, informal sector**

The term "informal sector" was used by the ILO in 1972 to denote tiny units, engaged in the production of goods and services but whose activities were not protected or regulated by the public authorities. The motivation for these activities is employment and income, and not maximization of profit or return on investment.

The economic activities in the unorganised sector are outside the purview of formal regulation, including labour laws, wage policies, health and safety rules, and accounting for tax purposes.

In India, the units not covered under the Annual Survey of Industries (ASI) are treated as part of unorganized sector in respect of manufacturing activities. Apart from these, the units belonging to the Trade, Hotels and Restaurants and services are treated as unorganized sector, except those in the public and private corporate sector and co-operatives.

According to the National Commission for Enterprises in the Unorganised Sector (NCEUS), the unorganised sector consists of all unincorporated private enterprises owned by individuals or households engaged in the sale and production of goods and services operated on with less than ten workers.

The Commission considers all agricultural activities, excluding plantation sector and other types of organised agriculture, e.g., corporate or co-operative farming, undertaken individually or in partnership, as being in the unorganised sector.

➤ **Role in Indian economy:** The unorganised or informal sector is dominant and plays a pivotal role in the Indian economy. While the informal sector contributes around 50 per cent of the GDP, its dominance on the employment front is such that more than 90 percent of the total workforce is engaged in the informal economy.

A high proportion of socially and economically underprivileged sections of society are concentrated in informal economic activities. Informal sector has in recent years undergone some type of formalization leading to employing people on a regular basis. One would argue that employment opportunities has come up in the lowest economic strata and, as a result, it has had significant impact on poverty reduction. Thus the growth of informal sector, though not an ideal outcome, was a vehicle for bringing about significant reduction in poverty.

At the same time, another trend since the initiation of economic reforms in 1991 has been to employ contract workers and outsource the production. The Annual survey of Industry (ASI) data has also shown that the share of contract workers in total employment in the manufacturing sector has increased between 2000-01 and 2008-09.

- **Linkage between organised and unorganised sectors:** The high levels of growth of the Indian economy during the past two decades were accompanied by increasing informalisation and expansion of the unorganised sector. The growth and profitability of formal industries and businesses was aided partly by employing workers on an informal basis without their being covered under social security system. This growth is facilitated by the emergence of a low cost support system, and industries in the unorganised sector supplying ancillaries and semi-finished products at cheap rates.
- **Need to foster firms with potential for growth:** A crucial aspect of Indian industry is that, for long, policies have fostered small firms that do not grow, instead of encouraging infant firms that have the potential to grow substantially and become competitive in global markets.

  As pointed out in Economic Survey, 2018-19, while "firms with less than 100 workers, despite being more than ten years old, account for more than half of all organized firms in manufacturing by number, their contribution to employment is only 14 per cent and to productivity is a mere 8 per cent".
- **Social security system:** The social security system covers less than 10 per cent of the total workforce, mostly belonging to the organised sector. Attempts have been made to cover the unorganised workforce but in a piece-meal fashion through a plethora of legislations. The existing legislations and occupational benefit schemes such as provident fund, pension, medical care, housing, etc. are in urgent need of overhaul in order to cover the unorganised workforce in the country.
- **Unorganised sector, a world-wide phenomenon**

  The predominance of unorganised sector is not a phenomenon peculiar to India. The unorganised, informal sector contributes significantly to employment generation and national income in developing economies. According to the International Labour Organisation (ILO), "more than 60 per cent of the world's employed population earn their livelihoods in the informal economy. Informality exists in all countries regardless of the level of socio-economic development, although it is more prevalent in developing countries. The 2 billion women and men who make their living in the informal economy are deprived of decent working conditions. Evidence shows that most people enter the informal economy not by choice, but as a consequence of a lack of opportunities in the formal economy and in the absence of other means of livelihood".

- **Transition to formal, organised economy**

  International bodies like the UN, the World Bank and the ILO are trying to help emerging and developing countries to transition from unorganised economy to more formal, organised economy. One of the UN's Sustainable Development Goals (SDGs) is to "promote inclusive and sustainable economic growth, employment and decent work for all". This will help to improve the economies as well as the working conditions of labour.

  The ILO has made formalization of the informal economy one of its strategic outcomes and supports tripartite constituents – the government, employers and employees – in facilitating the transition to the formal economy at the national level. This calls for suitable labour reforms and more measures on "Ease of Doing Business" to boost investment.

3. Distinguish between formal and informal employment. Examine why the Indian economy is dominated by informal employment and identify the measures to be taken for greater formalisation of the economy.

Ans. Predominance of informal employment is one of the distinct features of India's labour market.

There are varying figures on the structure of employment. While the Economic Survey 2018-19 mentions that 93 percent of workers are in the informal economy, the NITI Aayog's "Strategy for New India @75" document, released in 2018, says that India's informal sector employs about 85 percent of all workers. While sources may differ on the precise numbers, the enormity of the informal workforce in India is an accepted fact. These workers account for 50 percent of India's national income.

- **Formal and informal employment**

  Employment could be formal or informal depending on the conditions under which labour is employed. There is informal employment in the organised sector, as also formal employment in the unorganised sector.

  Thus the concept of 'informal employment' is distinct from employment in the informal sector enterprises.

  - **Informal worker/employment:** Unorganized workers consist of those working in the unorganized sector or households (excluding regular workers with social security benefits provided by the employers) and the workers in the formal sector without any employment and social security benefits provided by the employers.
  - **Informal economy:** The informal sector and its workers plus the informal workers in the formal sector constitute the informal economy.

- **Role in Indian economy**

- **Formal employment:** Formal sectors are legalized and the workers have social protection, economic security and certain incentives which those in informal employment do not enjoy. These include fixed hours of working, fixed pay, leave arrangements, maternity leave, housing and medical care, pension, etc.

- **Informal employment and growth**

  The high levels of growth of Indian economy during the past two decades was accompanied by increasing informalisation. Informal employment is outside the purview of formal regulation, including labour laws, wage policies, health and safety rules, and accounting for tax purposes.

  Apart from the predominance of informal employment, it is to be noted that a high proportion of socially and economically underprivileged sections of society are concentrated in the informal economic activities.

  But this does not imply that informalisation necessarily leads to impoverishment and one cannot deny its positive impact on poverty. If income and employment in the sector are on the rise, and factors such as skill development and provision of certain minimum social security measures are extended, it can play a positive role in ameliorating the condition of workers.

  It must be noted that pro-poor growth of a typical developing economy is closely linked to the issue of relative expansion of both the formal and informal sectors. The bulk of the production of goods and services in the developing world takes place in the informal sector.

- **Features of formal and informal employment**

- **Formal employment:** Employees in formal jobs are protected by labour laws and enjoy various benefits not enjoyed by those in informal employment. These include fixed hours of work, provision for leave, security of job, provident fund, pension, medical care, housing, etc.

- **Informal employment:** Unorganised or informal employment refers to those working in the unorganised enterprises or households, and workers in the formal sector without any employment or social security benefits provided by the employers.

  - The wages and employment benefits received by informal workers are much less than those of regular wage workers and the incidence of poverty is much greater among informal workers than the regular wage workers. Hence, informalization of jobs may also lead to widening income inequality.
  - These employees, in general, do not enjoy employment security or protection against arbitrary dismissal, protection against accidents and illness at the work place and social security benefits like maternity and health care, etc.

  There are substantial disadvantages in such informal workers not being under the purview of legal sanctions as they do not get any legal protection and are not covered by social security. These workers are deprived of these benefits which the workers in the formal sector generally enjoy.

Pension scheme: The Centre has introduced a pension scheme for unorganised sector workers called the PM Shram Yogi Maan-Dhan Yojana, 2019 which offers a regular pension after they attain 60 years of age. As on December, 2019, 39.25 lakh subscribers have joined the scheme.

➢ **Measures to formalise the economy**

The task before the governments, both at the Central and State levels, is not only to boost creation of jobs but to ensure that the jobs created are of good quality from the viewpoint of employees. This issue has been highlighted while framing the Twelfth Five Year Plan (2012-17) when the Planning Commission observed as follows:

"A critical issue in assessing employment behaviour of the economy is the growth of employment in the organised sector vis-à-vis the unorganised sector and particularly in terms of formal and informal employments. It is generally opined that unorganised sector employment is of low quality compared to organised sector employment".

It further stated that there was "a decline in the employment in the unorganised sector from 86 per cent in 2004-05 to 84 per cent in 2009-10. This means that the share of organised sector employment has increased to 16 per cent in 2009-10 from 14 per cent in both 1999-2000 and 2004-05. However, the increase in the organised sector employment is mainly in the informal category. The informal employment in the organised sector has increased from 46.4 per cent in 2004-05 to about 57.8 per cent in 2009-10. The informal employment in the unorganised sector remains the same. Nearly 93 per cent of the total workforce in 2009-10 is in informal employment, a rise from 91 per cent in 1999-2000. If agriculture is excluded from the workforce, the share of informal workers in the total non-agricultural workforce drops to 85.6 per cent from 93 per cent, which is still very high as compared to that in Brazil (51 per cent), Mexico (50 per cent), Indonesia (78 per cent), Philippines (72 per cent), and Thailand (49 per cent)". (Twelfth Plan, Vol. 3, Chapter 22, Employment and Skill Development).

The problem was that formal employment in the organised sector has not been increasing. This shows that organised enterprises are increasingly hiring workers on contractual terms due to labour laws and other concerns. Small and medium size enterprises generally belong to the unorganised sector and employ informal workers.

♦ **Recent steps at formalisation:** Since 2014, some measures have been taken to formalise and modernise the economy though they are an ongoing process and yet to yield results to the full extent. The measures taken include:

- Demonetisation to unearth black money and undeclared wealth which has been roiling the economy for decades through a parallel, underground economy. This measure wasn't successful as undeclared wealth was not so much in the form of cash but in assets like real estate, jewellery, etc.

- Promotion of digital payments to reduce the circulation of cash and make India a less-cash economy. But even after abolishing high-value notes in 2016, cash as a proportion of GDP has been rising. While there has been increase in digital payments, it still remains much lower than in major advanced and emerging economies. Around **70 per cent of all payments in value are made through cash in India,** whereas in Sweden, South Korea, Denmark and Canada, the percentage of cashless transactions is as high as 75 to 85 per cent. The mobile phone being ubiquitous and held by almost every adult citizen, with greater internet coverage under the Digital India project covering all Gram Panchayats, and more robust telecom service, the share of digital payments could rise significantly.
- Introduction of Goods and Services Tax is a positive step towards formalisation of the economy though the system is still to fully stabilise. Apart from removing the cascading effect of taxes, it ensures greater transparency and better tax compliance. Further steps like reducing the multiplicity of slabs, simplifying the process of filing returns, prompt issue of input tax credits and refunds, and plugging leakages and evasion through fake invoices would go a long way to streamline the GST regime.
- The passage of Insolvency and Bankruptcy Code (IBC) is another notable step in speedy resolution of insolvencies aimed at minimising the time and cost involved in liquidation process.
- The financial sector has seen measures such as unification and recapitalisation of public sector banks, bringing down the non-performing assets (NPAs) and cleaning up their balance sheets, strengthening the Non-Banking Finance Companies (NBFCs) and ensuring better oversight over their working.
- While the government has taken many steps in regard to "Ease of Doing Business", there are still some areas where India has to show further improvement. These include starting a business, enforcing contracts, registering property, paying taxes and resolving insolvency. By amending the Commercial Courts Act, the government has facilitated the establishment of commercial courts in 250 districts for faster disposal of cases.
- **Digital India project:** It is one of, if not, the world's largest rural connectivity programme which will link 2.5 lakh Gram Panchayats (GPs) covering 6 lakh villages. By December 2019, 1,31,000 GPs have been connected by optical fiber and 3.89 lakh Common Service Centres (CSCs) have been set up.

  These centres will provide the rural public with 50 Central and about 300 State-related services of essential nature. These include a wide range of services such as certificates on income, birth and land records, old age and widow pensions, scholarships, Aadhaar, PAN card and passport services, payments for electricity, water and property dues, employment and recruitment matters, Tele health services for people and animals. There is also a Farmers' Portal to deliver various technical and marketing services in the agriculture sector.

Apart from promoting digital literacy and making people in rural areas tech-savvy, the programme would generate millions of jobs in the rural sector. When fully functional, it would change the very face of rural India.

➤ **Conclusion**

The process of formalisation of the economy faces multi-faceted challenges which calls for action on the following lines:

- Shifting more labour from agriculture sector to non-agriculture jobs with better service conditions.
- Such a transition should be, to the extent possible, within rural areas itself so as to stem the influx of people to urban areas to avoid creating more problems in urban centres.
- The small-scale and medium-sized firms find complying with extant labour laws burdensome and hence they have an incentive to remain small rather than grow. Such enterprises need to be supported to grow in size, so as to make them more viable to engage workers on formal basis and become competitive in global markets.
- The above measures will require suitable reforms in labour laws ensuring the security of workers' rights and taking into confidence both the labour unions and employers.
- There is need for reducing tax and regulatory burdens on people and businesses.
- Disinvestment in, and divestment of non-strategic and loss making public sector units.

Greater role for private sector: Above all, the government is still having too prominent a role, with the State placed at "commanding heights" of the economy, thus denying the private sector of its due place in the scheme of things. The State must recede further, acting more as a facilitator, and making room for a rejuvenated private sector.

4. India is facing a major challenge of creating jobs even as the labour force is growing. Critically analyse the problem and suggest measures to boost creation of jobs. (On this, see also Chapter 10, Q.19, Page 10.75)

Ans. One of the major challenges facing the Indian economy is the creation of adequate number of jobs to absorb the burgeoning labour force. India's working-age population will grow by about 10 million per year during the decade 2021-31 though it will drop to 4.2 million per year during 2031-41. Thus for the next two decades, India will continue to have a growing young population that is also part of the workforce and it will pose a severe challenge on the employment front.

➢ **Problems in job creation:** Some of the problems India has been facing in job creation are mentioned below.

- **Jobless growth:** A worrying trend is that there has been deceleration in creation of jobs in Indian economy since 2011-12. Further, a paradoxical aspect is that even as the economy grows, there isn't much growth in employment indicating it as "jobless growth".

  Growth and Employment: It is because the link between economic growth and jobs is now much weaker and less direct than before, and growth in output does not by itself translate into growth in jobs.

  The **employment elasticity** which measures percentage change in employment due to 1 percentage point change in growth has steadily come down. As was observed by the Planning Commission, the employment elasticity in India during the decade 2000-2010 declined from 0.44 during 1999–2000 to 2004–05 to as low as 0.01 during second half of the decade 2004–05 to 2009–10. Similar trends have been witnessed at the sectoral level, namely agriculture, service and manufacturing sectors. While the employment elasticity in agriculture was only 0.04, it was higher in mining and quarrying (0.52), in construction (1.13) and in real estate and allied sectors (0.66). (Twelfth Five Year Plan, Vol. 3, Chapter 22).

  It means a much higher rate of sustained GDP growth, say 8 or 10 per cent, is required to achieve the same rate of increase in jobs as before. This may be due to a variety of factors like production being more capital-intensive and less labour-intensive, greater degree of automation which replaces labour, labour skills not keeping pace with rapidly changing technology and modes of production, etc.

- **Quality of jobs:** Apart from lack of creation of enough jobs, a problem is that the jobs being created are of low quality and of informal nature which does not provide the workers job security or social security benefits enjoyed by those in formal employment. By not being able to create quality jobs, those at the bottom of the pyramid are not able to move up the escalator thus hindering upward "social mobility" and resulting in widening inequalities.

- **Skills and productivity:** Normally as economies grow creating quality jobs, productivity rises and per capita incomes increase. With greater skills, labour is able to improve their capabilities and is able to earn more which results in inclusive growth.

  But manufacturing has become highly skill-intensive and largely based on high level technology. Hence the importance of improving and upgrading the skills of labour to take up jobs of specialised nature.

- **Coordination between Government, Industry and Educational institutions:** In regard to skilling labourforce, the government and the industry have to work hand in hand and there should be close coordination between industry and technical and educational institutions to ensure that the curriculum followed in education and skills imparted are in sync with latest and evolving technology and which the industry requires.
- **Technology development:** Much will depend on India's ability to either procure advanced technology through technology transfer mode or develop advanced technology at home. India's scientific community and institutions have to play a leading role in this effort.
- **Investment climate:**Providing a competitive environment for corporations to invest and set up industries in India is essential. The slow pace of progress in 'Make-in-India' programme is a pointer to the challenges ahead. Though India has taken various steps on "Ease of Doing Business", there are still some areas like enforcing contracts, exiting loss-making businesses, delay in settling litigation in courts, etc. to which the World Bank, which is ranking countries on these parameters, has drawn the government's attention.
- **Labour laws and Tax regime**: India's labour laws are complex and highly restrictive which deters potential investors. When labour market is highly regulated, industrialists tend to use more of capital and automation which adversely affects job prospects of labour. The labour laws need to be reformed suitably taking care of the interests of both employees and employers.

  On the tax regime, India has lowered corporate taxes substantially which is a right step to boost investment. However, the personal income tax and the indirect tax, GST, need tweaking to boost consumption and create demand without which the industrial and manufacturing sector will not invest and expand leading to creation of jobs.
- **Infrastructure:** Though India has improved her infrastructure – highways, ports, airports, railways – considerably in the last two decades, still the power sector, water supply, telecommunications, etc. are still below par and need upgradation.

➢ **Sectoral shift in employment:** According to ILO/World Bank data, 43.21 per cent of workers in India are employed in agriculture in 2019, 24.89 per cent in industry and 31.90 per cent in services. Though the labour engaged in agriculture has come down from 48.96 per cent in 2011, there is need to shift more of the surplus, underemployed workers from this sector by creating non-farm jobs.

Also, such shift has to be, to the extent possible, within the rural and semi-urban areas itself to prevent migration of people to urban areas in search of jobs and adding to problems in urban areas. Agro and other industries have to be set up in these areas where the surplus labour from agriculture could be gainfully employed.

Sectors with potential for job creation: In short, growth has to be inclusive and with adequate job potential to provide productive and gainful employment to those in both rural and urban areas. The crux lies in India creating jobs on a substantial scale in both the manufacturing and the service sectors. Besides manufacturing, sectors like infrastructure, real estate, tourism and hospitality, etc. are those with maximum potential for generating employment.

Among the social sectors, education and health have great potential to provide jobs as India is still lagging far behind in these sectors compared to many emerging economies.

➢ **Challenges in manufacturing:** All developed countries like UK, US, Germany and Japan scaled the economic ladder and attained prosperity by shifting surplus labour from agriculture to industry during the early stages of industrialisation. The growth and expansion of factories helped them to shift labour from agriculture to more productive occupations.

South-east and East Asian countries, and later China, developed their manufacturing sector on these lines and China became a manufacturing powerhouse in a span of two decades.

But these conditions no longer exist. In the light of various transformational changes taking place in the world of manufacturing, India faces a difficult task in replicating the experience of those countries.

Global competition: It is now more difficult for newcomers to break into world markets due to intense competition and other factors like protectionist tendencies, tariff and non-tariff barriers, and reluctance on the part of advanced nations to part with high technology.

With globalization, competition has become more intense with many emerging countries vying for global markets. India faces competition from other emerging countries like Brazil, Mexico, Viet Nam, Bangladesh, Indonesia, etc. who are also capturing the potential for manufacturing in sectors like light engineering, textile and apparels, leather goods, etc.

India has to overcome these challenges by improving the various factors mentioned above. India is endowed with the advantage of "demographic dividend", with working age population (15-59 years) above 50 per cent. Besides, India offers a huge market which the manufacturing sector could take advantage of.

With wages of labour rising and excess capacity built up in China, India has an opportunity in attracting units exiting China which would help to provide jobs to millions. Already, many automobile manufacturers and players like Apple, Foxconn, Samsung, etc. have set up base in India. India also has strong foundation in the services sector, particularly in the domain of Information technology in which organisations like IBM, Dell, Microsoft, Cisco, and Google have set up offices and R & D units here. India has to build on this base and expand both the industrial and service sectors.

Conclusion: For India's sustained growth, the following course of development is essential.

- The manufacturing sector is to register employment growth with focus on expanding the labour-intensive manufacturing, even as it faces the challenge of automation in some areas.
- The contribution of non-manufacturing sectors, particularly construction and services, which have higher employment elasticity, must steadily increase to provide jobs to new entrants to the labour market and absorb the surplus labour from agriculture.
- Social sectors, like education, health and housing, which not only have high potential for expansion, upgradation and boosting employment but also to uplift the living standards of those at the bottom of the pyramid must receive high priority. In this context, the government's focus on improving sanitation and water supply, which will also have beneficent impact on health, are steps in the right direction.
- Furthermore, agriculture, which is still the dominant sector from employment point of view and for ensuring rural prosperity, has to grow at 4 per cent rate with improvements in productivity and diversification.

5. India needed to reform its labour laws to boost employment for the increasing labour force. Examine the reforms introduced and their implications.

Ans. Economists and industry bodies have for long argued that India's labour laws are stringent and rigid and create perverse incentives in the industrial sector hampering its growth. This is especially so in respect of units with over 100 employees. They acted as incentives for small firms to remain small in size, so they are not subject to these rules. This held back investments, growth of industries, job creation and productivity.

Successive governments have been trying to reform the labour laws to remove these drawbacks. The main objective and challenge in reforming these laws has been to reduce compliance burden, facilitate ease of doing business and generate more formal jobs while protecting workers' rights. The process of enacting these laws, initiated in 2003, has taken 17 years to be completed. It involved extensive discussions with various stakeholders before being finalized, examined and approved by the Parliament.

- **Four codes passed:** The Parliament passed in September 2020 three labour codes. A code on minimum wages was already passed in 2019. A total of 44 extant labour laws have now been subsumed into four codes. The laws merged with these codes include the Factories Act, the Trade Union Act, the Mining Act, the Industrial Disputes Act, the ESI Act, the EPF Act and the Maternity Benefit Act.

The labour ministry is to frame the rules and guidelines under these laws which will clarify many of the new provisions and the laws are expected to be implemented by April 2021.The four codes approved are:

- Industrial Relations Code Bill, 2020.
- Code on Social Security Bill, 2020.
- Occupational Safety, Health and Working Conditions Code Bill, 2020.
- Minimum wages code (passed in 2019).

➢ **Role of States:** As labour is a concurrent subject under the Constitution, the 100-odd State level acts that exist now will need to be rationalized in line with the codes passed by the Union government. Sixteen states have already effected many of the changes which have been newly incorporated under these four labour codes.

➢ **Salient features:** The salient features and implications of these codes are mentioned below.

■ **Industrial Relations Code**

This Code deals with recognition of trade unions, conditions on strikes and lock-outs, standing orders and resolution of industrial disputes. It subsumes the Industrial Disputes Act, 1947, the Trade Unions Act, 1926, and the Industrial Employment (Standing Orders) Act, 1946.

♦ **Standing orders:** Standing orders on matters related to workers' classification, holidays, paydays, and wage rates, termination of employment and grievance redressal mechanisms is mandated for establishments with at least 300 workers, instead of 100 workers. This raises concern that units with less than 300 workers not being covered by such a mandate could make the terms of employment of workers in such units ambiguous and less secure.

♦ **Layoffs and Retrenchment:** The threshold for layoffs and retrenchment has been raised from 100 workers or more to 300 workers. Thus, establishments with less than 300 workers have flexibility in setting terms for hiring and firing. A worker could be dismissed for alleged misconduct or retrenched on economic grounds jeopardizing employee's security.

Experts opine that this would enable industrial establishments with less than 300 workers to introduce arbitrary service conditions for workers. As about 90 per cent of India's workforce work in small-size firms, they may be adversely affected by this provision.

♦ **Striking work:** This code introduces new conditions for resorting to strike.

- Flash strikes will be illegal.
- Earlier, workers could go on strike by giving between two weeks and six weeks of notice. Henceforth, Unions have to give 60 days' strike notice.

    - Further, if proceedings are pending before a labour tribunal or the National Industrial Tribunal, workers cannot go on a strike for 60 days after they are concluded. These conditions apply to all industries.
    - These provisions significantly limit the scope for striking work.
- ♦ **Trade unions:** It lays down new provisions for recognition of unions. Trade unions that have a membership of at least 10 per cent of the workers or 100 workers will be registered. The union with 51 per cent of workers in an establishment will be the sole negotiating union.
- ♦ **Dispute Resolution:**
    - **Works Committee:** Establishments with 100 or more workers will have a Works Committee which will help resolve conflicts between workers and employers.
    - **Conciliation Officer:** The central or state governments may appoint Conciliation Officers to mediate and promote settlement of industrial disputes.
    - **Tribunal:** Industrial Tribunals consisting of a Judicial Member and an Administrative Member may be set up for settling industrial disputes.
    - **Arbitration:** The Code allows for industrial disputes to be referred to arbitration by the employer and workers if both parties agree to do so.

■ Social Security Code

This Code on social security brings together laws relating to Employees' Provident Fund, (EPF), Employees' State Insurance (ESI), Maternity Benefit, Gratuity and other entitlements and the Unorganised Workers' Social Security under a single law.

- ♦ **Social security benefits:** It provides for universal social security for both organised and informal workers as well as gig and platform workers. The government shall formulate and notify, from time to time, suitable welfare schemes, including schemes relating to provident fund, employment injury benefit, housing, skill upgradation of workers and educational schemes for children.
- ♦ **Social Security Fund:** Provision has been made for creation of a Social Security Fund to fund schemes for extending benefits like death and accident insurance, maternity benefit and pension to cover 80 per cent of the county's workforce who do not now come under any kind of social security cover.
- ♦ **Social Security Board:** A National Social Security Board will be set up for formulating suitable schemes for unorganized workers, gig workers and platform workers. It also brings these sections of workers under the ambit of social security schemes that include life and disability insurance, PF, health and maternity benefits and skill upgradation.

- **Gender equality:** To promote gender equality, employment of women has been allowed in all establishments for all types of works and in the night shift, subject to their consent and subject to provisions of safety, holidays, working hours or any other condition being in place. The Codes also ensure their pay parity with their male counterparts.
- **Formalisation of jobs:** All employees will get appointment letter, a step to promote formalisation of workforce. Contractors have to pay wages electronically. They will be issued pan-India licence for five years as against work order-based licensing at present.

■ **Occupational Safety, Health and Working Conditions Code**

This Code brings together all laws relating to health and hazardous working conditions.

- **Safety and health:** The Central Government shall declare, by notification, standards on occupational safety and health for work places relating to factories, mines, dock work, building and other construction work and other establishments.
- **Working environment:** The employer shall ensure cleanliness and hygiene, proper ventilation, temperature and humidity, environment free from dust, noxious gas, fumes and other impurities, cooling in work rooms, potable drinking water and hygienic sanitation facilities.
- **Migrant worker:** The Code defines inter-state migrant workers to be those not only engaged by an establishment through a contractor but also those workers who have come on their own from one state and obtained employment in another state and earning up to ₹ 18,000 a month. They will be duly protected as unorganized workers.
- **Housing for Migrant workers:** To ensure ease of living at affordable rent, the Central Government has announced a scheme of housing for migrant workers, as being done for urban poor. This will be done by converting government funded houses in the cities into Affordable Rental Housing Complexes (ARHC) under PPP mode through concessionaire. State and Central Govt. agencies, industries and other institutions will be incentivized to develop ARH complexes for migrant workers which will help industries to improve productivity.
- **Ration card portability:** It is also proposed to make the Ration (Family) Card portable so that any member of a family included in a card could draw ration anywhere in the country. This will particularly help migrant workers and others who move places due to job requirements or other reasons. The government has developed technology to implement this scheme and by March 2014, 17 States have successfully operationalised "One Nation One Ration Card" system.

➢ **Conclusion:** The new labour laws remove the rigidities which persisted and which was one of the reasons impeding India's industrial growth, especially in the manufacturing sector.

While the reforms should aim at faster development and growth in employment, it must also protect workers' incomes and jobs when they get disrupted when technology and modes of production change. When employers have to change the production processes, they must provide workers opportunities to learn the new skills required and arrange to provide in-house training as off-line training institutions may not be able to respond properly.

Understandably the unions have expressed concern about radical reforms which may hurt their interests. The unions demand fair treatment, decent working conditions and adequate social security to take care of their families when employers retrench them because of economic exigencies.

Role of Tripartism: The reforms need to be implemented taking the workers and their unions into confidence. It has to be executed without disrupting the harmonious relations between the employers and workers. Even the ILO has urged the aspect of protecting the genuine rights of workers in the course of reforms.

A tripartite approach involving the government, the workers and the employers is needed in resolving labour issues smoothly. A via media has to be found and a middle ground struck with all the parties adopting a conciliatory approach.

It must be impressed upon workers' representatives that advancements in technology have not only improved the methods of production and the overall output, but also the working conditions of the labour class itself. It has been seen that an enlightened and caring industrial system is beneficial not only to the industry and society at large, but to the workers themselves.

For such a milieu to prevail, both the industry bodies and workers' organizations have to work in a co-operative spirit and focus efforts to ameliorate the conditions of workers in regard to wages, housing, health and education benefits to the workers and their families. This can be realized by adopting modern concepts such as 'corporate social responsibility' (CSR) devolving upon industries.

6. According to industry bodies, a large proportion of youth entering the labour market are not readily employable and need reskilling. In this context, examine the challenges faced and the steps taken by the government and industry to promote "skill development" and state how far they have succeeded.

Ans. Apart from the problem of creating jobs for the burgeoning young population, India faces the mammoth task of imparting skills to workers seeking jobs to make them "employable" – i.e., suitable for the nature of work and the skills which the jobs demand, as will be evident from the following facts.

According to NSSO Report 2011-12, only 2.2 per cent of the total workforce in India had formal sector skill training till then and 8.6 per cent were reported to have received non-formal vocational training. This is far less than that in South Korea (96%), Japan (80%), Germany (75%), United Kingdom (68%) and the United States (52%). Thus India has a long way to go in skilling vast number of workers.

➢ **India's demographic profile**

- According to 2011 Census data, the proportion of economically active population (15-59 years) has increased from 57.7 to 62.5 per cent during the decade 1991 to 2011.
- Changes in the size of working-age population plays a key role in determining the size of labour force and the pressure for job creation.
- India's demographic dividend is considered to be the biggest social and economic asset, with more than 54 per cent of our population younger than 25 years in age.
- As per the NSSO Periodic Labour Force Survey (PLFS) 2017-18, India's labour force participation rate (LFPR) for the age-group 15-59 years is around 53 per cent (80 per cent for males, 25 per cent for females). [The term 'labour force' denotes the total number of people in a country who are either in work, or unemployed but looking for work. LPFRis defined as the proportion of working-age population (say, in the age group of 15 to 59 or 60) in the economy currently employed or seeking employment.]
- By 2023, 70 million more people will have entered India's workforce. The total workforce will then comprise approximately 404.15 million people.[The term 'work force' refers to the number of persons actually employed and does not include those who are willing, or are offering, to work.]
- India's working-age population will continue to increase up to 2041, rising by 96.5 million during 2021-31 and by 41.5 million during 2031-41. The projected increase in working-age population is 9.7 million per year during 2021-31 and 4.2 million per year during 2031-41.

Demographic dividend phase: As observed in the Economic Survey, 2018-19, "These developments suggest that India has entered the next stage of demographic transition with population growth set to slow markedly in the next two decades along with a significant increase in the share of working-age population (the so-called "demographic dividend" phase)". (Economic Survey, 2018-19, Chapter 7, India's Demography at 2040).

Skilled labour force is essential to meet diversified demands of a growing economy, to tap the benefit of demographic dividend. As per the India Skill Report 2016, the present demographic advantage of India is predicted to last only till 2040.

The above facts have major implications for the required rate of job creation in the economy. Depending on the trajectory of labour force participation during 2021-41, additional jobs will need to be created to keep pace with the projected increase in working-age population.

- **Skill development: Present status**

While the schooling system improves the educational level of the population, it is skill training that equips the youth to enter the labour market and improve their employability. There is, therefore, need for speedy reorganisation of the ecosystem of skill development and fostering entrepreneurship in the country to suit the needs of the industry and ensure decent quality of life to its population.

Between 2014 and 2018, about 2.5 crore individuals have been trained under various skill development programmes of the government. Out of this, more than 50 lakh have been trained under the Skill Development Ministry's flagship scheme – Pradhan Mantri Kaushal Vikas Yojana (PMKVY). The revamped PMKVY scheme has a target of 10 million persons to be trained.

- **National Policy on Skill Development**

Skill Development Policy was framed in 2009 and a National Skill Development Mission was launched in 2010. The policy has been continuously reviewed and modified to meet the changing needs of various sectors and changes in labour market scenarios.

- **National Policy on Skill Development and Entrepreneurship, 2015** aims to empower individuals through improved skills, knowledge, qualifications, to provide access to decent employment and ensure India's competitiveness in the global market. It encompasses a comprehensive skill development programme on the following lines:
- **Industry and private sector collaboration:** Creating avenues for private sector engagement has been a crucial strategic plank.The not-for-profit National Skill Development Corporation (NSDC), set up as a public-private partnership (PPP), helps to stimulate private sector participation in the programme.
- **Skill development models:** There are a variety of skill development models – government-funded programmes that fully or partially subsidize training/ apprenticeships, market-led trainings (where trainees pay for the course), market-led apprenticeships and industry-led On-the-job training.
- **Vocational training:**In its core role, the NSDC provides long-term development finance to organizations to build vocational training initiatives. It works with the Ministry of Skill Development and Entrepreneurship (MSDE) to organise vocational training programmes with government grants, where infrastructure is set up by private providers and training costs are subsidized by the government.
- **Human resource needs:** NSDC, under the Ministry of Skill Development, had studies carried out to assess the Human Resource (HR) requirements between 2013-17 and 2017-22 across 24 high priority sectors. This was done

through extensive interaction with key stakeholders including industry, training providers, trainees, sector skill councils and government departments, and involved more than 1,000 industry experts, 500 job roles and over 1,500 trainees. The human resources needed for these sectors is estimated at 103.4 million. Besides, incremental human resource requirement across States for the period 2013-22 was estimated at 120.33 million.

- **Training needs:** Likewise, sectoral training needs upto 2022 was also assessed to develop a Skill Action Plan. The Incremental Training needs across 34 Sectors (for 2017 to 2022) was estimated at 128.21 million.
- **Entrepreneurship:** The policy also aims to encourage entrepreneurial culture through formal skill education, enhanced support for entrepreneurs in terms of credit and market linkages. It will help to foster social enterprises and improve ease of doing business. There will be special focus on women and socially and geographically marginalised and disadvantaged groups.
- **International mobility:** India is committed to becoming the "skill capital" of the world and has structured efforts on the following lines:
  - The India International Skill Centre (IISC) programme: IISC has a market-driven network to counsel and guide potential emigrants on skills tests, upgrading skills, language and pre-departure orientation.
  - Japan is cooperating with India to implement an on-the-job Technical Intern Training Programme (TITP), which offers three-to-five years of internship opportunities for foreign nationals in Japan.
  - Technical collaborations have been undertaken with countries such as the UK, Australia and the UAE for benchmarking and mutual recognition of standards.
  - Government-to-government and B2B partnerships are being developed for new markets in Western Europe, Canada, Australia and East Asia to increase the mobility of blue and white-collar Indian workers to those countries.
  - With population on the decline in Europe, Canada, Japan, etc., there is scope to find work opportunities for Indians qualified and well trained in diverse sectors.

Challenges faced in Skill development

Skill development programme faces many challenges on account of rapid changes in technology, the massive numbers of persons to be trained, training institutions involved and the widely dispersed locations where the skilling takes place. The challenges, mentioned below, require timely intervention by the government agencies and industry bodies.

- Information asymmetries: Persons aspiring for training may not be aware of government-run skill development programs. Certain surveys have shown that large numbers of youth were not aware of various training facilities being provided. Disseminating information widely in both urban and rural areas is required.
- A person trained for a specific sector or skill may not be able to readily get placement due to lack of such jobs. For this, the government is taking steps under the PMKVY and other programmes to assist trained workers to find placement. This also presupposes that enough jobs in those sectors need to be created to accommodate those trained.
- Dovetailing educational system with industry needs: General, professional and vocational education, both at school and higher levels, need to be overhauled to prepare students to become "employable" on completion of education. This is especially relevant for polytechnics, ITI's and engineering institutions which have to prepare students in emerging and cutting-edge technologies like robotics, artificial intelligence, machine learning, nano technology, etc. for which there will be demand from industries in coming years.
- There should be close coordination between Skill Development agencies and industry to ensure that priority is given for imparting those skills which the industries need.
- Industries or firms may be reluctant to spend on in-house training or upskilling staff since those trained may quit jobs to join other firms seeking better prospects thus benefitting the latter firm and not the firm that incurred the training cost. In such cases, facilities for training through external agencies would be required.
- Low level of female participation in the labour force is a matter of concern. Skilling initiatives need to be complemented by a wider push towards women's empowerment through gender sensitization and creation of economic opportunities for women. Facilities like hostels for women trainees, flexible work models and preparing women for jobs more suited to them such as in "gig economy", electronics and hardware industry, health and education sectors are especially relevant in this context.

The Central and State governments have been proactively pursuing the skill development programmes and these need to be periodically reviewed and suitably adapted to meet changing requirements of various sectors.

7. Automation and new technologies are emerging trends. Analyse the impact they will have on employment and job creation, and their benefits and disadvantages.

Ans. Automation is an emerging trend which will have a perceptible impact on the way industry operates in the years to come. Advances in robotics, artificial intelligence (AI), and machine learning, autonomous transport, cloud computing and Internet of Things (IoTs) are ushering in a new age of automation, as machines match or outperform human performance in a range of work activities, including those which require cognitive capabilities.

Anxiety about the world of work and security for labour is not new, but it is claimed that this time around, the speed and spread of technological change will be unprecedented. Unlike in the wake of the First and Second Industrial Revolutions which occurred during the 18th and the 19th centuries, when the adoption of inventions took place with longer time-lag, the pace at which new technology of the present Fourth Industrial revolution is being adopted in Industry is much faster and this makes the impact of changes on labour more severe.

- **Impact on Employment and Job creation**

  Automation has been a major concern due to its likely impact on labour and jobs. There are, however, divergent views on the impact automation will have on employment. One view is that it would help to improve product quality and living standards while another view is it would result in massive dislocation of jobs. Many jobs and ways of working will become redundant while many other jobs will be created anew.

  The pace and degree at which automation will take place depends on various factors – technical, economic and social. Technical feasibility, the relative cost of technology vis-à-vis labour, supply and demand factors and social acceptance will determine the extent of automation. Also despite automation, humans will be needed to work alongside machines. Labour displaced by automation could find alternate modes of employment as happened with computer revolution.

  - Technological advances are creating ever smarter and more flexible machines that will be deployed on an ever larger scale at the workplace. Significant efforts are underway in Japan and the western world on various modes of automation – robotics, 3D printing, artificial intelligence and advancements in digital technology–that will change the way industry and the corporate world function.
  - Disruptive technologies are creating new industries and business models and making old ones redundant and irrelevant.
  - Production processes, business models, service delivery mechanisms are likely to be reconfigured.

- The impact of automation will be mostly on jobs involving highly structured physical activity in predictable environments, such as manufacturing and retail, data collection, processing, etc. Jobs that are more of a routine and repetitive nature are more susceptible and at threat than others.
- New systems like data analytics, IoTs, cloud computing and social networks are having a huge impact on the way people communicate, handle data, collaborate and work.
- Japanese are ahead of the curve in robotics technology which finds application in domains like assembly line in manufacturing, energy efficiency, climate change, nursing and elder care and boosting productivity in a tight labour market. For instance, researchers have been able to train a robot to imitate natural human actions. It has been found that humans and robots can effectively co-ordinate their actions during high-stakes surgeries. This may ensure more safety during surgeries because unlike their human counterparts, robots do not tire and can carry out endless series of precise movements.
- Automation threatens to impact women more than men as women form a large proportion of the workforce in retail, business processing outsourcing and textiles, clothing and footwear. This is primarily because automation threatens sectors where women form a major part of the workforce.

➢ **Benefits and Disadvantages of Automation**

There are pros and cons of adopting automation in industry and various other domains as discussed below.

♦ **Benefits**

- **Productivity and output:** Higher output and increased productivity have been two of the primary reasons to justify the use of automation. Unlike human labour, machines do not tire out and thus it will lead to higher production rates and increased productivity.
- **Efficiency and optimisation:** With automation, there will be more efficient and optimum use of materials and it will ensure better consistency of product quality.
- **Safety of workers:** Worker safety is an important aspect of automating certain hazardous industrial operations. Automated systems keep workers away from endangered workplace, thus safeguarding them against the hazards of the factory environment.
- **Saving of time:** The time required to process a typical production order through the factory is generally reduced with automation.
- With advances in automation, computerisation and networking, the physical location of the workplace or of the clientele becomes less relevant. This helps to avert transportation and physical movement of people and thus

saves fuel and reduces environmental pollution. And on-line repair of gadgets, machines, etc. has helped firms in saving a great deal time, effort, and costs. In the health field too, measures like telemedicine help in on-line patient treatment thus averting physical movements.

- **Quality of life of workers:** With higher productivity and reduced production lead times, workers engaged to manage the machines could have shorter work-hours, and thus more time for leisure and other personal needs which will eventually ensure better quality of life for them and benefit their family too.
- **Improved ambience:** Automated plants generally help to maintain a better and cleaner ambience and environment. This is especially true of industries manufacturing food and dairy products, electrical and electronic items, firms in the IT and sector, etc. where employees work in much cleaner conditions. Factories like those in the automobile and aircraft sector are also highly amenable to automation resulting in higher productivity.
- **Labour issues:** With reduced labour employed, firms may face relatively less pressure from labour and trade unions as compared to labour-intensive firms. This, of course, presupposes that the welfare of the labour employed is duly taken care of as there have been labour problems even in automated automobile plants, aircraft industry, etc.

♦ **Disadvantages**

- **Loss of jobs:** The main disadvantage associated with automation is displacement of labour. If the emerging disruptive technologies result in less workforce being needed to perform tasks, it would pose yet another challenge on the employment front in the future.
- **Dislocation of labour:** Apart from loss of jobs, those workers may be displaced geographically having to relocate to other places in search of alternate jobs causing emotional stress to them and their families.
- **Capital expenditure:** Automation may entail higher capital expenditure for industries as they have to invest in designing, fabrication, and installation of equipments. It may also result in higher level of maintenance expenses than with manually operated machines. This may be, partly, compensated by the saving of labour employed, wages and other employee benefits, etc.
- **Variable costs:** Apart from fixed costs, employers and businesses must consider the variable and recurring costs of developing and deploying equipments, hardware and software, including their maintenance and the supply and demand from providers and customers vis-à-vis the current labour costs. Manual labour which is relatively less expensive is still readily available around the world and may remain the more economical option.
- **Lower flexibility:** Generally, there would be lower degree of flexibility in terms of the possible products with automation as compared with a manual system in which human labour plays a versatile role. Any changes in the design of products or even the machines would prove costly.

8. In what way automation and new technologies will impact the Indian economy. Outline the steps that India could take to prevent its adverse impact.

Ans. India is burdened by large influx of young population into the labour force and is facing major unemployment crisis. Over and above that, India also face the problem of employability of labour. The emerging technologies are bound to have significant impact on India even as it has to create employment opportunities and remain competitive in global markets.

➢ **Impact on India:** ILO has done studies to assess the extent to which work activities could be automated in various countries using current and new technology. In the case of India, as much as 51.8 per cent of activities is amenable to automation. According to ILO, "Robotic automation is having the greatest impact, replacing low-skilled jobs and simple assembly tasks."

In the case of Japan and Thailand, the percentages of their activities being automated are 55.7 and 54.8 respectively and activities that can be automated across the world works out to over 40 per cent.

- **Employability and Reskilling:** An important aspect of adopting new technologies is the need to reskill employees. A significant observation by the ILO is that over 50 per cent of Indian businesses are looking for very different set of skills among new recruits than they did three years ago. This points to the enormity of the task of skill development involved and that too to be achieved in the shortest possible time.

  What is true about India on employability is also true about other countries. The ILO has observed that a sizeable proportion of businesses in the U.S.A., Brazil and Germany are also looking for quite different skills in new recruits. These businesses are not always able to find candidates with the required skills.

- **Realigning education system:** India's employability crisis is mainly due to the fact that education systems are not well equipped to adapt to changes at the workplace. This calls for radical changes in the curriculum at secondary and higher education levels and in technical institutions. The government and industry bodies have to coordinate with educational bodies and Universities to bring about changes and expose students to cutting-edge technologies like robotics, artificial intelligence, machine learning, nano technology, etc. Some steps have been initiated in this direction and they need to be speeded up.

- **Need for Hi-tech industries:** While India will have to adopt automation in a calibrated manner to remain competitive in global markets, she will have to simultaneously take steps to develop hi-tech industries which could supply products to domestic industries and consumers and also for export. This will minimise the adverse impact of emerging technologies, and provide scope for job creation and upskilling Indian labour. India has the advantage of vast stream of technical and engineering personnel who could be gainfully employed. India has to seize the opportunity provided by MNCs which are withdrawing from China, or planning to do so, and looking for alternative locations.

- **India's strengths:** Already, major MNCs like Apple, Samsung, Foxconn, etc. have set up production or assembly units in India. Besides, major IT firms like Microsoft, IBM, Dell, Cisco, Google, etc. also have major operational and/or R & D units in India. Besides, major automotive firms such as Hyundai, Ford and Toyota are manufacturing automobiles to cater to India's vast domestic market as well as for export. Indian companies are also sources for supply of components for major aircraft manufacturers like Boeing and Airbus. India has to build on these strengths further.

  India's Space sector under ISRO has initiated steps to open up to the private sector which will provide more opportunities to the private industry to participate in this high-tech sector. So also expanding indigenous defence production will offer more opportunities for the private sector to develop and deploy high-tech systems to cater to domestic market and for export. Both these sectors will be amenable to automation.

- **IT sector:** India's experience and resounding success in the Information Technology sector in the last three decades is a pointer to India's capabilities, and this trend has to be replicated in the new sunrise industries. This sector has not only provided job opportunities at home on a substantial scale, it has also provided highly skilled personnel to firms in many other countries.

  Also, while automation has led to job cuts in certain segments of India's IT industry, new jobs are also being created due to economic growth and export prospects. For instance, according to Nasscom, the IT sector added 1.7 lakh jobs in 2016-17.

➢ **Conclusion**

While automation is desirable or even expedient for many of the advanced nations which are faced with the problem of declining and ageing population, it will pose a real threat to most of the developing countries in Asia and Africa where ever increasing population makes creation of jobs a dire necessity.

There is need to create new job opportunities, retrain workers in jobs and widen their technical skills by enhanced investment in human resources, which will complement investment in automation, so that overall economies can be achieved in production processes.

> Labour is prior to, and independent of, capital. Capital is only the fruit of labour and could never have existed if labour had not first existed. Labour is the superior of capital and deserves much the higher consideration.
>
> -Abraham Lincoln (1809-1865), 16th President of USA, in *Message to Congress*, 1861.

AGRICULTURE, FOOD SECURITY AND NUTRITION

The discovery of agriculture was the first big step toward a civilized life.

– **Arthur Keith (1866-1955)**, Scottish anatomist and anthropologist

Topics Covered

- *Agricultural sector at Independence and after*
- *Challenges facing Indian agriculture*
- *Issues in Agricultural marketing*
- *Reforms introduced in agriculture sector*
- *Causes for distress in farming sector and Farmers' loans*
- *Food security and malnutrition*
- *Contract farming and its benefits*
- *Shifting labour from the farm sector to non-farm sectors*
- *Support schemes for agriculture sector and farmers.*

1. What was the state of Indian agriculture after Independence and before the Green Revolution set in? Outline the steps that the government took then to improve the conditions in the agriculture sector.

Ans. At the time of independence, India inherited an inequitable system of land tenure perpetuated over centuries, with highly unequal distribution of agricultural land. Bulk of the cultivable land was held by a relatively small section of the population with the rest forming a large segment of small peasants and landless labour. This led to the following problems in the agricultural sector:

- Land records were not maintained systematically.
- Indeterminable rights over land and insecurity of tenure for tenants.

- It made mortgaging of land to raise funds difficult for the farmer and they had to depend on usurious moneylenders. It placed heavy burden on the peasantry and sporadic riots and peasant uprisings broke out in different parts of the country.
- These deficiencies impacted on the efficiency of agricultural operations and output.

➢ **Land reforms:** One of the first tasks of the government was to implement land reforms and laws were passed by all the State Governments in 1950's. The main features of the land reforms were:

- **Abolition of intermediaries:** Intermediaries like zamindars and jagirdars were abolished. This measure which covered about 40 per cent of the cultivated area, was a significant step. It made about 20 million tenants owners of the land, and placed them in direct relationship with the State.
- **Security of tenure:**As a result of the reforms, tenant-farmers were able to get security of tenure, have their rents reduced, or buy up the land from the landlords at less than the market price. If they did not buy the land, they could continue perpetually as tenants on that land without being evicted and their children too could enjoy that property.
- **Imposition of ceilings:** Ceilings on landholdings were fixed to ensure fair distribution of land. On this, there were two rounds of legislation, in the 1950'sand the 1970's, and State legislatures passed radical laws. But due to pressure exerted by vested interests and exemptions granted in many cases and litigations on compensation, this measure fell short of the objective.
- **Redistribution of surplus land:** As laws on ceilings on land holdings were not enforced strictly, this measure too had only limited impact.
- **Consolidation of landholdings**: Due to division of large holdings by families into smaller holdings in order to circumvent land ceiling laws, and division of holdings within families with each passing generation, lands continued to be subdivided and fragmented.
- **Wasteland and forests:** Sizeable areas of cultivable wasteland and private forests came under the management of government.

Result of land reforms: Thus, in essence, the land reforms were implemented in a half-hearted manner and the objectives were not achieved uniformly all over the country. Absentee ownership of land and insecure tenancy continued to persist in many parts of the country.

The objectives of reform were achieved mainly in Kerala, West Bengal, Maharashtra, Karnataka, Himachal Pradesh, Gujarat, and Assam. Whereas, it did not meet with much success in parts of Bihar and former Andhra state where erstwhile landlords continued to hold on to large holdings.

➢ **Steps to augment output:** Another major objective in the initial years of planning and development was to augment agricultural production, particularly the output of foodgrains to meet the needs of the growing population. Towards this, the government took a series of measures in the First (1951-56), Second (1956-61) and Third (1961-66) Five-Year Plans as mentioned below:

- Increase in area under cultivation: The gross area under cultivation of foodgrains (cereals and pulses) rose from 101.2 million hectares (mn. ha.) in 1950-51 to 115.6 mn. ha. in 1960-61 and 124.91 mn. ha. in 1970-71. Whereas total cropped area rose from 131.89 mn. ha. in 1950-51 to 165.77 mn. ha. in 1970-71.
- Execution of large and small irrigation projects: Total irrigated area increased from 22.56 mn. ha. in 1950-51 to 27.48 mn. ha. in 1960-61 and 38.19 mn. ha. in 1970-71. The irrigated area as percentage of total cropped area rose from 17.11 per cent to 23.04 per cent in 1970-71.
- Other steps included distribution of improved varieties of seeds, supply of fertilisers and manures, use of better ploughs and other agricultural implements, soil conservation, plant protection and dry farming and land reclamation.
- The government also stepped up agricultural research with a view to encourage farmers to adopt scientific agricultural practices.

- **IADP programme:** Another major initiative and strategy to enhance food production was the Intensive Agricultural District Programme (IADP) put into operation in selected districts from the Third Plan beginning in 1961. The farmers responded favourably to this scheme which involved a combination of use of high-yielding varieties of seeds, fertilisers and water supply, backed by adequate institutional credit. They took to the improved farm practices readily and positively, and these initiatives were gradually expanded to cover more parts of the country.
- **Increase in output:** As a result of these sustained steps during the first three Plans, the output of foodgrains increased steadily from 50.83 mn. tonnes in 1950-51 to 82.02 mn. tonnes in 1960-61 and 95.1 mn. tonnes in 1967-68.
- **Challenging period:** Despite all these favourable trends, the years through 1950's and the '60s were very challenging for Indian agriculture. Due to acute shortage of food in some years, India had to depend on food imports from other countries including the U.S. under the PL 480 programme. These imports helped to meet the shortages and prevent the incidence of runaway food-price inflation.

  Two back-to-back droughts in 1965–66 and 1966–67 made matters even more difficult. There was also considerable pressure from the U.S. government on India, during the Presidency of Lyndon B. Johnson, by discouraging dependence on the U.S. for food aid, and goading India to take effective steps to adopt scientific measures to boost food production and strive towards self-sufficiency.

  This further induced India to adopt extensive use of high-yielding varieties of seeds supported by other measures which helped to increase food production dramatically. In fact, it may be said that the seeds for the Green Revolution, which was to occur in the coming years, were sown in the early sixties.

2. Critically examine the problems and challenges faced by Indian agriculture and farmers and steps taken by the government to overcome them. Suggest further measures to be taken to remedy the situation.

Ans. The agriculture sector in India is critical as bulk of the population lives in rural areas and are dependent on it for their livelihood. Any setback to the sector will have adverse effects not only on the rural economy but also the industrial sector as rural India is a vital source of demand for the products of industry.

For the past few years, the agriculture sector and farmers have been facing challenges on multiple fronts. The problems vary based on geographical, agro-climatic, hydrological, and ecological factors in different regions.

Besides climatic factors, farmers face other issues such as declining soil fertility, low productivity, marketing problems and unremunerative prices, loss of income and burden of financial debts which drive many of them and their families to despair and ruin. These issues are discussed below.

- **Climatic factors:**With assured irrigation covering only about 40 per cent of arable land, monsoon is critical for India as the rest of the area depends entirely on rain. India receives 70 per cent of the annual rainfall during the south-west monsoon in June-September period, which is the 'kharif' crop season, and it is crucial for the country's rural economy.

  The timing, pattern, and spread of this monsoon have become increasingly unpredictable and undependable due to 'climate change' factors.

  Adverse monsoon, unseasonal showers, deficit in rainfall, and drier and warmer weather result in crop losses, lower output, and financial distress to farmers. Such events have become more pronounced and recurring in recent years, leading to even unfortunate incidents of farmers committing suicide.

  There is need to diversify crops cultivated and change the cropping pattern in line with climate changes to avert loss of crops and incomes for farmers.

- **Lack of irrigation**: As farmers are largely dependent on rainfall, lack of irrigation is a major constraint in many parts of the country. Out of the gross sown area of 192 million ha, rainfed agriculture contributes to 60 per cent of the gross cropped area and 45 per cent of the total agricultural output.

  Total irrigated area (under all crops) which was 40.2 per cent of total cropped area in 2000-01 rose to 48.6 per cent in 2014-15. Whereas irrigated area for foodgrains which was 43.4 per cent of total cropped area in 2000-01 has risen to 53.1 per cent in 2014-15. It leaves the rest of the cultivated area at the mercy of the monsoon.

  Successive governments have taken up projects to bring more land under irrigation. The latest Pradhanmantri Krishi Sinchai Yojana (PMKSY), launched in 2015, is aimed at irrigating the field of every farmer and improving water use efficiency to provide "Per Drop More Crop."

Under micro-irrigation, around 7 lakh hectares used to be covered per year on an average. Now it has risen to 1.2 million hectares a year. Micro-irrigation saves water, reduces the cost of cultivation and increases productivity.

Measures like reducing dependence on water-guzzling crops and water conservation schemes have to be implemented in a sustained manner.

- **Soil fertility:** There are signs of technology fatigue in agriculture sector in India. Various factors such as intensive farming resulting in nutrient imbalance, greater mining of soil nutrients depleting soil fertility, deficiencies of micro-nutrients, falling ground water levels, and erosion and degradation of soil are leading to overall deterioration of soil fertility and health.

  There is need to optimise the use of fertilizers in farming to retain the health and quality of soil. This, in turn, will lead to around 50 per cent increase in the crops production and also help farmers to enhance their income. Indian Council of Agricultural Research (ICAR) has done studies and developed technologies to address this problem. The government's drive to provide neem coated urea helps to reduce the amount of urea or nitrogen farmers have to use.

  For wider reach, the Ministry of Agriculture & Farmers' Welfare, in association with ICAR, organises "Awareness Programmes" on this for farmers at Block level in villages all over thecountry. This is also being propagated through television programmes meant for farmers, and through awareness campaigns conducted by more than 700 Krishi Vigyan Kendras (KVKs).

- **Low Productivity:** Apart from the size of holding, the productivity levels primarily determine the income of the farmers. Though India has had the Green Revolution and seen dramatic increase in yields and output, the per unit area productivity of our crops is much lower as compared to that of the other major crop producing countries. There is also a wide gap in the yield levels among and within the states in India.

  To raise productivity, the government has been taking steps to improve rural infrastructure such as irrigation, drainage, water and soil conservation, rural roads connectivity and educating farmers through agricultural institutes and extension farming.

  Horticulture crops, and crops like potato and tomato, need cold storage facility. For want of this facility, farmers lose out on such items because when they harvest, the market may be low on prices. The government need to invest in setting up such facilities on a wider scale.

  Agriculture involves crop husbandry, animal husbandry, forestry and fisheries. Apart from growing foodgrains, farmers need to be encouraged and supported to supplement their income through dairy, poultry, horticulture, etc. Horticulture now accounts for 16 per cent of net sown area. The nation's livestock population counts at more than 512 million.

  The income of farmers will go up only if one views the system as a whole and not just at one crop alone. Farmers are to be given suitable orientation on adopting such systems.

- **Unremunerative prices:** Prices which farmers are able to get for their produce play a key role affecting their incomes. For some time past, the rise in prices for agricultural produce has been much lower than general rise in prices. Market prices for several agricultural commodities have been lower than those of minimum support prices (MSP). This has caused the terms of trade to be moving against, and adverse to, agriculture.

  Despite two key government interventions viz., Minimum Support Price (MSP) and procurement by government agencies, farmers are compelled to sell their produce below the support price, either due to exploitation by middlemen or large market players or due to bumper harvest resulting in surplus produce causing them losses.

  To alleviate the problem, the government has introduced income support scheme, "PM Kisan Samman Nidhi", under which ₹ 6,000 per year is given to farmers in three instalments. The amount granted, however, is modest compared to income support under "Rythu Bandhu" scheme of Telangana and the "KALIA" scheme of Odisha.

  The government could enhance the amount by rationalising the subsidies given for inputs to farmers.

- **Labour issues:** Shortages of labour and rise in wages in rural areas have also been posing problems to farmers in different parts of the country. Factors mentioned below have led to shortages of labour to undertake farm jobs and also resulted in farmers having to pay higher wages causing production costs to rise.

  ♦ Shift of rural workers from farm to non-farm jobs;

  ♦ Migration of labour from rural areas to urban centres in search of better employment prospects; and

  ♦ Higher wages given to rural workers under the Mahatma Gandhi Rural Employment Guarantee (MNREG) program.

  Shift of rural workers from farm to non-farm jobs is in itself a positive sign as it reduces the pressure of population on land and reduces under- or disguised unemployment in the farm sector. To tide over this situation, farmers had to resort to labour-saving mechanization. This trend towards mechanization led to significant increase in private investment in agriculture.

  The aforementioned problems have been compounded by rise in the costs of other inputs resulting in rising debts for farmers and farming becoming unprofitable.

- **Limits to technology**: The adoption of improved technological practices, including use of High Yielding Varieties (HYV) seeds helped to transform Indian agriculture in the 1970s and the '80's. The new technology and cultivation of HYV seeds needs intensive use of fertilizers and pesticides with adequate and assured water supply.

  A significant factor limiting the adoption of the new technology is that about 60 per cent of country's cultivated land is rain-fed and lacks irrigation, and a substantial portion of the country is drought prone. In the absence of proper irrigation facilities, the cultivation of HYV seeds involves greater risk of variations in yields, as compared to the traditional varieties of seeds.

- **Need for diversification:** Since 1990s, there has been deceleration in the growth of yields with output not showing dramatic increase as before. But though the output of major crops, rice and wheat, has shown only marginal increase year-on-year, the overall foodgrains output, including output of maize and nutri-cereals, has been showing good increase.

  For instance, the total foodgrains output which stood at 257.13 million (mn.) tonnes (tns.) in 2012-13 rose to 275.11 mn. tns. in 2016-17 and 284.83 mn. tns. in 2017-18. Of this, the share of maize and nutri-cereals which together was 62.3 mn. tns. in 2012-13 has gone up to 75.71 mn. tns. in 2017-18.(Data sourced from Agricultural Statistics, 2018 of Ministry of Agriculture & Farmers Welfare).

  The above data shows that India will have to go in for crop diversification, cropping pattern in tune with climate changes, reduce dependence on water-guzzling crops and ensure efficient water management to remedy the situation as has been stressed by expert bodies.

- **Conclusion:** While the challenges remain, it should be noted, as observed by **Ashok Dalwai Committee on Doubling of Farmers' Income**, set up in 2016, that "India today is not only self-sufficient in respect of demand for food, but is also a net exporter of agri-products occupying seventh position globally. It is one of the top producers of cereals (wheat & rice), pulses, fruits, vegetables, milk, meat and marine fish." Given the necessary guidance, facilities and support, farmers in India are capable of meeting the challenges before them.

3. What are the deficiencies and drawbacks in the agriculture marketing system in India? What steps have been taken to improve the system and state what further measures need to be taken to reform it?

Ans. Agricultural markets are crucial not only to supporting farmers' incomes, they are the lifeline between production and consumption points. They interlink farmers with consumers, agrarian and non-agrarian sectors, villages with towns and cities.

Farmers dispose their surplus produce through village markets, mandis or wholesale markets, agents such as arhatiyas. If they sell through cooperative marketing societies, they may get better price for the produce.

The wholesale agriculture markets have been governed by various state specific Agricultural Produce Marketing Acts which date back to the 1960s. The Acts provided for **Agricultural Produce Market Committees (APMC)** tasked with operating these markets.

While the intention of the Acts was to ensure that farmers were offered fair prices in a transparent manner, it has led to the creation of local monopsonies, with just a single or a few buyers controlling the market. Mandi functionaries often do not allow new entrants in the market further reducing competition. Their combined effects have ensured fragmented and inefficient markets making the farmers the ultimate losers.

- **Drawbacks in the system**

  - **Excessive regulation:** Agriculture markets have been subject to rigorous regulatory regime creating barriers in trading which adversely impacted farmers. These regulations include controls on storage, transport, processing, exports, imports, credit access and market infrastructure development.

    Farmers needed multiple licenses for trading in different APMCs. It resulted in multiple levy of mandi fees at various levels, for entry, registration etc. Once an area was declared a market area and fell under the jurisdiction of a Market Committee, no person or agency was allowed freely to carry on wholesale marketing activities elsewhere.

  - **Role of middlemen:** The agriculture markets are dominated by middlemen and commission agents. Local traders, commission agents and regional processors, who have gained from the regulatory controls, exercise considerable local and regional clout. The state governments have found it difficult to initiate and sustain reforms to open up agricultural markets to competition.

    Public procurement of commodities often results in commercially and politically powerful forces in the local and regional markets forcing procurement through middlemen such as *arhatiyas* or commission agents or agro-processors due to which farmers are unable to get remunerative prices for their produce.

  - **Infrastructural and logistics issues:** Lack of grading and auction facilities, drying yards and cold storage arrangements add to the problems faced by farmers. It is estimated that as much as 40 per cent of all fruits and vegetables are lost annually in India between the grower and the consumer mainly due to lack of proper warehousing facilities, weak transportation system and bad roads. That a sizeable portion of even the rice and wheat stocks procured by the State for Public Distribution System (PDS) and stored in excessive quantities are lost in storage is well known.

  - **Lack of competitive environment:** The stranglehold of intermediaries in rural markets deprives the farmers the option of choosing between multiple market sites and options to sell their produce at most competitive rates. They are also deprived of other benefits of commodity exchange, such as accurate weighing, reduction in marketing costs and timely payments.

Mandi functionaries often do not allow new entrants in the market further reducing competition. Their combined effects have ensured fragmented and inefficient markets. This makes it imperative to open up the current APMC mandi system to competition from multiple channels and points of exchange.

- **Information gaps:** Two key government interventions that affect agriculture markets and commodity prices are the policy of Minimum Support Price (MSP) and procurement by government agencies. The rationale of the MSP is to ensure that farmers are not forced to sell their produce below support price either due to exploitation by large market players or due to bumper harvest. But most farmers are not even aware of the existence of MSPs and there are also considerable variations in this across states.

➢ **Reforms initiated**

A Committee of State Ministers on Agricultural Marketing and Reforms in 2013 has studied the issues involved and remedial measures needed. Further, the Committee on Doubling of Farmers' Income, headed by Ashok Dalwai, set up in 2016, which has made a comprehensive study of the agriculture sector, has also looked into marketing issues.

➢ **e-NAM:** A major reform initiated was setting up the **e-National Agricultural Market (e-NAM)**, launched in 2016, and designed to serve as a pan-India electronic trading portal which networks the existing APMC mandis to create a unified national market for agricultural commodities.

Proposed in the Union Budget 2014-15, NAM networks physical "mandis" which can be accessed online enabling buyers situated even outside the State to participate in trading at the local level. The e-NAM would network 585 APMC mandis across 18 states.

- **Salient features of e-NAM**
  - It will facilitate transparent sale and price discovery in regulated markets, kisan mandis, warehouses and private markets.
  - It will help farmers to get remunerative prices for their produce.
  - Enables liberal licensing of traders/buyers and commission agents by State authorities without any pre-condition of physical presence or possession of shop / premises in the market yard.
  - One license for a trader valid across all markets in the State.
  - Harmonization of quality standards of agricultural produce and provisions of quality testing infrastructure in every market to enable informed bidding by buyers.
  - Single point levy of market fees, i.e., on the first wholesale purchase from the farmer.

- **Challenges in Registration:** One of the major challenges in the system is to get farmers registered on the portal. According to data furnished in Parliament, e-NAM has not reached majority of farmers. By June 2019, out of almost 12 crore cultivators in the country, just over 1.64 crore cultivators and over 1.24 lakhs traders had been registered on e-NAM platform. While trade transactions having total volume of 2.59 crore million tonnes valued at ₹ 71,069 crore, had been recorded on e-NAM platform till June 2019.
- **Role for CSCs:** It shows that there is a long way to go in getting farmers on the portal. One factor may be that most of them are not tech-savvy and also may not have easy access to the portal facility in their villages. To popularise the scheme, the State governments could utilise the **Common Service Centres (CSCs)**, being set up under the Digital India programme which covers 2.5 lakh Gram Panchayats as Facilitation Centres to serve e-NAM scheme and help farmers get registered and also do transactions through these centres.

➢ **Further steps required:** Alongside these, other measures also need to be taken to improve the plight of farmers, reduce the risk of loss of crops and incomes. These are:

- A critical part of the relationship between production and markets is the farmer's capacity to respond to markets by changing production decisions and diversifying cropping systems in line with changing climate patterns.
- Agricultural institutes and scientists will have to work closely with farmers in diversifying production and educating farmers on optimising the use of fertilisers and water.
- Research has shown that cereals like rice and wheat may not be constant source of nutrition. There is need to bring about changes in dietary habits of the population, in consultation with experts in health domain, and promoting items like millets and other nutritious cereals, vegetables, fruits, etc. These will have to be chosen suited to local conditions like climate and nutri-items grown locally.
- Such nutritious cereals will have to be brought into the Public Distribution System to cater to local population.
- These changes are crucial as the *Global Hunger Index Report of 2019* has ranked India a low 102 among 117 countries. Various studies have highlighted persistence of high levels of malnutrition, especially among children and women.
- Warehousing and cold storage infrastructure need to be improved. This could be done enlisting agro-business firms in the private sector.

(For further major reforms initiated in the Agriculture sector in September 2020, see Question 4 below).

4. The Union government initiated major steps in 2020 to reform the agriculture sector. Examine how far these reforms would solve the problems faced by the farmers in India and the challenges faced in their implementation.

Ans. In September 2020, the Union government introduced three bills in Parliament aimed at transformation of agriculture sector in the country and raising farmers' income. They became Acts after approval by both the Houses of Parliament.

- The Farmers' Produce Trade and Commerce (Promotion and Facilitation) Act 2020 (FPTC Act).
- The Farmers (Empowerment and Protection) Agreement on Price Assurance and Farm Services Act 2020 (FAPAFS Act); and
- The Essential Commodities (Amendment) Act 2020 (ECA Act 2020).

➢ **Objectives:** The overall objective of the three Acts is to ensure that there are more buyers for farmers' produce, allow them to trade freely without any license or stock limit, so that increase in competition among them results in better prices for farmers.

Essentially, the FPTC breaks the monopolistic powers of Agriculture Produce Market Committee (APMC) markets, while FAPAFS allows contract farming, and ECA removes stocking limits on traders for a large number of commodities, with some caveats in place.

➢ **The Farmers' Produce Trade and Commerce (FPTC) Act 2020:**

♦ This Act permits intra-state and inter-state trade of farmers' produce beyond the premises of Agriculture Produce Market Committee (APMC) markets. Trade could be conducted in any place of production and collection of farmers' produce such as farm gates, silos, factory premises, warehouses and cold storages. Thus, it provides greater flexibility to farmers and buyers resulting in more competition and realisation of better prices for farmers.

♦ State governments are prohibited from levying any market fee, cess or levy on farmers, traders, and electronic trading platforms for trade of farmers' produce conducted outside APMC areas.

♦ An electronic trading and transaction platform may be set up to facilitate the direct and online buying and selling of produce through electronic devices and internet.

♦ The Standing Committee of Parliament on Agriculture (2018-19) had also observed that availability of a transparent, easily accessible, and efficient marketing platform is a pre-requisite to ensure remunerative prices for farmers.

♦ The Standing Committee also recommended that the Gramin Agricultural Markets scheme (which aims to improve infrastructure and civic facilities in 22,000 GraminHaats across the country) should be made a fully funded central scheme and scaled to ensure presence of a Haat in each panchayat of the country.

➢ **The Farmer Agreement on Price Assurance and Farm Services (FAPAFS) Act 2020**

- This Act creates a framework for "Contract farming" through an agreement between a farmer and a buyer prior to the production or growing of any farm produce.
- The minimum period of an agreement will be one crop season, or one production cycle of livestock.
- The price of farm produce should be mentioned in the agreement. For prices which are subject to variation, a guaranteed price for the produce and a clear reference for any additional amount, above the guaranteed price, must be specified in the agreement.
- For settling disputes, there will be a Conciliation Board as well as a conciliation process. The Board will have a fair and balanced representation of parties to the agreement. If the dispute remains unresolved by the Board after thirty days, parties may approach the Sub-divisional Magistrate for resolution. Parties will have a right to appeal to an Appellate Authority (presided by Collector or Additional Collector) against decision(s) of the Magistrate.

➢ **The Essential Commodities Act (ECA) 2020**

- This Act was passed in 1955 when the country was facing acute shortage of food and hence distribution needed to be regulated. It has lost its relevance in the original form now that the country has adequate food supply and even surplus in cereals, viz., wheat and rice. Hence the amendment.
- The Act now amended allows the central government to regulate the supply of certain food items only under extraordinary circumstances (such as war and famine).
- Limits on stocking on agricultural produce may be imposed only if there is a steep price rise – if there is 100 per cent increase in the retail price of horticultural produce or 50 per cent increase in the retail price of non-perishable agricultural foodstuffs over the price prevailing immediately preceding 12 months, or average retail price of last 5 years, whichever is lower subject to certain other conditions.

➢ **Rationale for Reforms**

♦ **Marketing:** According to experts on agriculture, these reforms have been under consideration for a long time and were long overdue and are far-reaching. The major problem in agriculture was not production but was on the marketing front. The APMC markets function as monopolistic and exploitative entities and charge high rates of commission.

The changes introduced create alternative channels for farmers to sell their produce. Farmers will have the freedom not just in production of commodities but also to directly join hands with processors, exporters or retailers to sell the produce. These measures would unshackle commodities like onion, potatoes, oilseeds, etc. from the clutches of regulation.

- **Contract farming:** This will ensure that farmers have an assured buyer of their produce and are assured in advance of the price which will be paid. Presently, most farmers do not have that option. Often, the produce is sold at prices well below the minimum support price (MSP). Though the government announces MSP for many crops, the actual price which farmers get is lower than the MSP in many instances.
- **Wide disparities in prices:** Data collected on wholesale prices across 122 centres by the Ministry of Consumer Affairs, Food and Public Distribution has shown wide disparity in prices across regions. Prior to these reforms, farmers were required to sell their produce via auctions to licensed traders at the APMC mandis (markets) in the specified geographical jurisdictions.

  Most major states had implemented the APMC Act, Kerala and Bihar being notable exceptions. There were considerable differences in the scope and stringency with which APMC Act was implemented. This resulted in fragmented markets and hampered the emergence of a single national market.
- **Price volatility:** Price volatility of vegetables is much more than that of cereals and pulses, as there is no government procurement of vegetables. In the absence of MSP, vegetables also lack a floor price. Since vegetables are mostly perishable, the lack of efficient storage and distribution networks inhibits long distance trade, and markets for vegetables remain largely localized. With more freedom and choices for marketing and improved cold storage facilities, vegetable growers will have more options to get better returns.
- **Inter-state barriers:** There were inter-state barriers in moving produce which also worked to the disadvantage of farmers. The restrictions on inter-state trade due to the APMC law undermined market power and it adversely affected prices accruing to farmers. Studies have shown that removal of inter-state barriers could significantly increase prices accruing to farmers. The barriers have now been removed. India is now one common market for agri-produce.
- **Stocking:** While the passing of EC Act removing restrictions on stock limits is an important step, the Act provides for "regulating stock limit of any agricultural produce" subject to certain conditions mentioned earlier. The restrictions on stocking discouraged private sector investments in storage facilities as under the earlier Act, stock limits could be imposed on a trader, processor or exporter at will. Due to this there was lack of storage facility. So when farmers bring their produce to the market after harvest, there is a glut and prices tend to fall steeply, while in the lean season prices shoot up hurting the consumers. So both farmers and consumers are adversely affected by the lack of storage facilities.

  But on the conditions laid down in the Act for intervention in the event of price changes (mentioned earlier), experts have reservations. They say, for instance, if the price of a vegetable, say potato which is at ₹ 20/kg rises to ₹ 40/kg, it would be absurd to impose restrictions under the Act (condition of 100 per cent increase in price). Hence, the provisions of the Act have to be applied only under exceptional circumstances when the burden of price rise inflicts unusually heavy burden on the food budget of households. In short, the Act has to be applied with utmost discretion or else, its very purpose would be defeated.

♦ **Farmer Produce Organisations (FPOs):** Another major step the government has taken is to create 10,000 FPOs to transform agri-economy on the lines of successful farmer-owned milk co-operatives and enterprises like Amul. NABARD was tasked with formation of 2,000 FPOs in 2014-15 and by 2020 about 7,000 active FPOs have come into being and they are getting financial support. NABARD has to ensure that they get working capital at reasonable rate of interest.

  To be successful, these FPOs must be based on local community interests, attain scale and be managed by farmers themselves with sufficient autonomy on an entrepreneurial mode, without any political or bureaucratic interference. With large membership of farmers, they must get linked to nearest markets; develop bargaining power to deal with large buyers. They may be guided by some experts or NGOs working in the domain of agriculture who will serve as Consultants.

➢ **Opposition to Reforms**

■ **Vested interests:** There has been strident opposition to, and protests against, these reforms from some States and certain groups of farmers, especially from Punjab and Haryana, whose vested interests would be adversely impacted. However, the dire need for reforms in agricultural marketing which has been a major weak link in the chain of agricultural operations in India and causing problems to farmers has been emphasized by many Committees, experts and even previous governments.

  While preparing the Twelfth Plan (2012-17), the erstwhile Planning Commission had observed: "Reforming the Agricultural Produce Marketing Committee (APMC) Acts should, therefore, have priority as emphasised in the Eleventh Plan and the Mid-term Appraisal. The introduction of the **Model Act in 2003** was directed towards allowing private market yards, **direct buying and selling**, and also to **promote and regulate contract farming** in high-value agriculture with a view to **boost private sector investment** in developing new regularised markets, logistics and warehouse receipt systems, and in infrastructure (such as cold storage facilities)." Twelfth Plan, Vol. II, Chapter 12, Agriculture, P. 23).

  Nearly 85 per cent of farmers in India are small and marginal farmers who hold less than 2 hectares (and of them about 65 per cent hold less than just one hectare). These small farmers are unable to go to mandies which may be located far away while the large farmers are able to go to wholesale markets. The small farmers are in a vulnerable position as they face difficulties in storage and transportation of produce and have little bargaining power which the buyers, who are mostly moneylenders, traders, or commission agents, exploit.

- **Fears unfounded:** The fears that deregulation of APMCs would lead to farmers switching *en masse* to private markets are misplaced. The experience of Bihar, Kerala and Maharashtra do not indicate such a trend. Bihar annulled the APMC Act in 2006 and Kerala never had an APMC Act. Still there have been no private investments in these states. Most big corporate retail firms purchase their food items directly from APMC markets, and not directly from farmers.
- **Revenue loss:** States where state-run procurement is wholly routed through APMC mandies levy high taxes on agricultural trade which inflates Centre's food procurement expenditure. Punjab and Haryana are two such states. Punjab levies an aggregate tax of 8.5 per cent of MSP (price) at which FCI and other agencies buy grains. This levy includes market fee, rural development cess and 'arhtiyas' commission. Both these states collect substantial sums as mandi fees. With the reforms introduced, FCI and other agencies could start procuring grains at market rates bypassing the mandies. These states and middlemen in the trade stand to lose revenue which is why there is vociferous protest from states like Punjab and Haryana.
- **MSP:** One of the main contentions against the reforms is that it does not assure continuance of the policy of minimum support price (MSP) and APMC markets, and it would leave the farmers at the mercy of big companies and corporate entities. Though the government has assured that the MSP regime would continue, it has not assuaged the fears of farmers. Nor are the APMC markets going to be abolished. Only that farmers are given the freedom to sell produce not only in a specific APMC market or location but anywhere and to anyone as per their choice with a view to get the best return.

  Furthermore, a National Sample Survey on key indicators of agricultural households showed that only 19 per cent of households were aware of MSP and 15 per cent of procurement agency. Only 7 per cent of households sell crops to procurement agency and only 10 per cent of total crops are sold at MSP. This indicates that almost 93 per cent of households sell produce in open market and face market imperfections, according to the study.
- **State laws:** Some States who are opposed to the reforms have enacted laws undoing the reforms enunciated in the Central laws. Agriculture is a Concurrent subject under the Constitution, with both the Centre and the States having powers to legislate. It remains to be seen if the laws enacted by the States would come into effect as they require the assent of the President of India. States could possibly circumvent the problem by issuing executive orders.

➢ **Conclusion**

To sum up, these long overdue and far-reaching reforms in the crucial agriculture sector are positive steps in the right direction and have the following implications:

- **More choice and freedom:** The economic rationale of all these bills is to provide greater choice and freedom to farmers to sell their produce and buyers to buy and store, thereby creating competition in agricultural marketing. In effect, they unshackle farmers from archaic restrictions which fettered them and kept them subjugated to intermediaries and middlemen who thrived at the expense of farmers.
- **Benefit of competition:** This competition is expected to help build more efficient value chains in agriculture by reducing marketing costs, enabling better price discovery, improving price realisation for farmers and yet reducing the price paid by consumers.
- **Price and market trends:** In the absence of regulation, market forces may induce buyers to move to regions where prices are low. In that case, farmers in regions that have a relative cost disadvantage might lose out. On the flip side, barrier-free trade and more supply chain investments can increase earnings for farmers.
- **Storage facilities:** It calls for creating more silos and warehouses for storage and cold storage facilities for perishables closer to villages for easy access. India processes less than 10 per cent of its food production and loses about ₹ 900 billion ($12.3 billion) a year due to wastage from inadequate cold storage.
- **Cold storage facilities:** The government has been promoting private investment in storage facilities to reduce wastages and help contain the seasonal price volatility. Private sector has been showing interest in expanding facilities like cold storage chains.

  The Ministry of Food Processing Industries has been having a scheme, since 2008, of building "Cold Chain, Value Addition and Preservation Infrastructure" to provide integrated cold chain and preservation facilities, without any break, from the farm gate to the consumer.

  The integrated cold chain projects are set up by Companies, Corporations, Cooperatives, Self Help Groups (SHGs), Farmer Producer Organizations, NGOs and Central and State PSUs.

  There are 308 approved Cold Chain Projects across India as of October 2020 with total project cost of ₹ 8,358 crore against which ₹ 2,314 crore have been approved as grant-in-aid. Of this grant, ₹ 1,675 crore had been released.
- **Improved transportation:** Further improving transport facilities from villages to nearby towns, on which – village all-weather road connectivity – much work has been already done through PM's Gram Sadak Yojana. There is need to connect remaining villages and hamlets too to nearby towns. Private sector could be enlisted in providing better transport facilities.

5. **Elucidate the problems and causes for distress in India's agriculture sector. In this context, examine the pros and cons of writing off farmers' loans.**

Ans. Though India is self-sufficient in food since the Green Revolution and overall agricultural output has been showing year-on-year increase, the farm sector has, of late, come under severe stress due to a variety of factors as stated below. These factors have led to loss of incomes for farmers and consequently their inability to repay loans and indebtedness.

➢ **Causes for farmers' distress**

- Prices play a key role affecting the incomes of farmers. Due to rise in input costs and unremunerative prices for produce, farmers are not able to cover costs of production.
- Low prices due to surplus production of certain crops. When output increases well beyond the market demand at a price remunerative to producers, market prices decline. In the absence of an effective price support policy, farmers are faced with loss in income, the loss depending on how much the price declines.
- Market prices for several agricultural commodities have been lower than that of minimum support prices (MSP) set by the government. These trends show that the terms of trade are moving against agriculture in the last few years.
- Loss of crops due to erratic weather and unpredictable and extreme climate changes resulting in deficient monsoon, drought or floods causing loss of income to farmers. Though the government has introduced farm insurance scheme, its coverage has been inadequate.
- Low productivity in agriculture and related supply side factors are equally important.
- Declining average size of farm holdings, due to subdivision and fragmentation, makes farming unviable. Due to the rising pressure of population on farming and land assets, average farm size in India is small, at 1.15 hectare, and since 1970-71, there has been a steady declining trend in land holdings. The small and marginal land holdings (less than 2 hectares) account for 72 per cent of land holdings. This predominance of small operational holdings is a major limitation to reaping the benefits of economies of scale. Since small and marginal farmers have little marketable surplus, they are left with low bargaining power and no say over prices.
- Other related issues are unfinished agenda in land reform, lack of irrigation facility and quantity and quality of water available, technology fatigue, access to, and adequacy and timeliness of, institutional credit, and lack of facilities for assured and remunerative marketing.

- **Consequences of distress in farm sector**

The above factors endanger the livelihoods and incomes of small farmers and undermine the viability of the agriculture sector and its potential to solve the problem of the endemic poverty of farmers.

In case of agrarian distress, it has resulted in farmers being unable to repay loans borrowed and, in extreme cases, even to resort to suicide. It has also had a deleterious effect on the overall morale of the farming sector, especially the small and marginal farmers who have no recourse to alternate wherewithal.

However, it has been argued by some observers that the reason for suicides being indebtedness among farmers is overstated. Citing National Crime Records Bureau, it is said that the number of suicides among farmers has been on the decline and that many other factors are behind suicide cases. Whatever it be, in genuine cases of crisis in farm sector due to climatic factors and natural disasters, when farmers face substantial loss of crops and income, there is need to provide them succour – either in the form of loan waiver or income support or through crop insurance schemes.

- **Impact on the economy:** There is close inter-relationship between the agricultural and industrial sectors. The performance of agriculture and the overall prosperity of the rural sector is vital as the rural sector is a major source of demand for goods, particularly fast-moving consumer goods (FMCGs) and consumer durables, manufactured by the industry.

  Thus, any setback to agriculture due to drought, poor rainfall, etc. causing rural distress, adversely impacts the industrial sector and the overall performance of the economy.

  Agriculture is also an important source of raw materials for the agro-based industries such as sugar, textiles, and jute besides tea and coffee, and also contributes significantly to export earnings.

- **Farmers' debt and loan waivers**

There has been much debate over the issue of waiver of farm loans.

- **Arguments in favour of loan waivers**
  - Waiving farm loans is not just an ethical or moral issue but has vital social and economic implications. It is the lifeline for bulk of the rural population who depend on it for their livelihood and survival. Any serious crisis causes much distress to farmers and rural population at large.
  - Despite grant of loan waivers, there has been no evidence of slackening in repayments of farm loan or of repeated demands being made for loan waivers.
  - The banks and RBI have shown greater forbearance towards large loans given to the corporate sector many of which remain unpaid and have become stressed assets as evidenced by the mounting NPAs in the loan books of banks.
  - Agricultural loans by banks are mandatorily insured by the Agriculture Insurance Company of India (AIC) Limited whose liabilities are covered by

the Central government through budgetary support. Hence, even if loans are not waived, there is no loss to banks. In situations of severe and widespread distress to farmers resulting in substantial loan defaults, the Centre will step in and provide funds. The difference is that while loan waivers are borne by the States, defaults are borne by the Centre.

- As farming has become more technology driven and commercial, farmers have to incur higher costs towards inputs which entail greater risks, especially in case of crop failure due to various factors. Where farmers, especially the small and marginal ones, depend on moneylenders for loans, the risks become even greater.
- Despite subsidies on power, fertilizers, etc., input costs have been rising faster than prices realised thus squeezing the meagre income of small farmers and driving them into debt. Over 50 per cent of farming households are estimated to be debt-ridden. In case of crop failure or price shocks, farmers are driven to extreme despair.

♦ **Arguments against farm loan waivers:**

- Loans waived are those given to farmers by public sector banks and cooperative credit societies and when they are written off, the latter have to bear the loss which affects their balance sheets.
- Loan waivers also hurts State finances breaching fiscal deficit threshold of States.
- Waiving loans undermines honest credit culture, impacts credit discipline and may induce borrowers not to repay loans in future.
- When loans are waived, ineligible farmers may get the benefit while deserving farmers may be left out, resulting in possibility of fraud. In 2008, the then UPA government at Centre came out with Agricultural Debt Waiver and Debt Relief Scheme (ADWDRS) under which 3.69 crore small and marginal farmers and 60 lakh other farmers were granted debt relief to the tune of ₹ 52,516 crore. Comptroller and Auditor-General (CAG) had found in several cases that ineligible farmers were given benefit while those deserving were left out, pointing to large-scale possibility of fraud.

➢ **Conclusion:** The moot question is in what form farmers are to be provided succour in case of genuine losses of crops and income which are beyond their control, be it as loan waiver or income support or through crop insurance schemes.

MSP scheme, as an intervention, affects cropping patterns because farmers tend to grow more of those crops for which support is given or whose support price is higher. Income support is better than the MSP scheme as it does not influence the crop cycle. Also, income transfer gives money in the hands of the farmers and they can make crop portfolio choice based on information they have about what to grow and what not to. So one is not influencing that choice by farmers.

6. Critically analyse why despite sufficient food production and surplus buffer stocks of food under the Public Distribution System, there is still widespread hunger and malnutrition and India scores very low on Global Hunger Index. Suggest remedial measures.

Ans. Following the Green Revolution, India has been largely self-sufficient in food and has even surplus stocks which has enabled the country to export food and even donate to some countries in times of need. Though granaries are overflowing and buffer stocks of foodgrains with the Food Corporation are far above the prescribed levels, sizeable sections of the population suffer from hunger and malnutrition.

Freedom from abject poverty, hunger, and under-nutrition is one of the foremost priorities of United Nations' Sustainable Development Goals (SDGs) – Agenda 2030.

- **India and Global Hunger Index:** This is evidenced by India's position on ***Global Hunger Index (GHI) Report 2019*** where it is ranked 102 out of 117 countries. Not only has India slipped in ranking from 95 in 2010, its rank is even lower than that of Bangladesh (88) and Pakistan (94). Countries like Rwanda, Mozambique and Niger, which are otherwise less developed and with slower economic growth than India, also rank above India.

  The GHI is based on four parameters viz., **undernourishment (share of population whose** caloric intake is insufficient), **stunting** (children with low-height-for-age), **wasting** (children with low-weight-for-height), and **under-5 infant mortality** (which reflects inadequate nutrition and unhealthy environment).

  Paradoxically, India's performance on the above indicators have shown improvement over the years (except on child wasting), yet the overall progress has been below par. The methodology and criteria adopted for GHI has also been questioned by some experts because factors like height and weight are not comparable across countries and continents due to widely different genetic and biological factors. Yet, it is a wake-up call for India.

- **The transformation:** On the positive side, India, through the Green Revolution ushered in the 1960s, followed by White, Yellow and Blue Revolutions, registered unprecedented gains in the production of foodgrains ,vegetables and fruits, milk (highest in the world), and fish, turning India into the second largest agrarian economy of the world.

  Significantly, the incidence of poverty and hunger has been considerably reduced, and transformed the nation as India emerged as an exporter of foodgrains and other agricultural products. This dramatic change was largely due to a combination of factors – technologies, enlightened policies, farmers' response and strong political will.

India's initiatives: To be fair, successive governments in India have taken various programmes to improve the health and longevity of the population, especially children and women. These include:

- **Integrated Child Development Services (ICDS):** ICDS, launched in 1975 and supported by UNICEF, is the world's largest integrated early childhood programme to improve the health, nutrition and development of children. It provides health, nutrition and hygiene education to mothers, non-formal pre-school education to children aged 3 to 6 through Anganwadis, supplementary feeding for all children and pregnant and nursing mothers, and monitoring growth. It also offers links to primary healthcare services such as immunization and vitamin A supplements. Studies conducted on the programme have confirmed the positive impact of ICDS.

  A national study conducted in 1992 by the National Institute of Public Cooperation and Child Development confirmed the positive impact of ICDS. Where the programme was operating, there were lower percentages of low-birth-weight babies, lower infant mortality rates, higher immunization coverage, higher utilization rates for health services, and better child nutrition. The percentage of severely malnourished children declined, the positive effects of preschool were evident, and a larger percentage of mothers were getting their children medically examined.

- **Public Distribution System (PDS):** The PDS which supplies essential food items and operated jointly by the Central and State governments, is the largest such operation in the world. It distributes essential food items at highly subsidized rates to about 16 crore families through a network of over 4.5 lakh Fair Price Shops (FPS). For better efficiency, it has introduced Targeted distribution to families under Below Poverty Line (BPL) and Above Poverty Line (APL) categories. Further, another scheme, Antyodaya Anna Yojana (AAY), was started to cater to the poorest among the BPL families by providing them 25 kg. of cereals per family per month at low price.

  PDS needs to be constantly monitored as it has problems like exclusion of eligible beneficiaries and problems like poor quality of items stocked and supplied.

- **Food security: National Food Security Mission:** A 'National Food Security Mission' (NFSM), was launched in October 2007 to increase the production of rice, wheat, and pulses during the Eleventh Plan (2007– 12). In 2013, the government passed the National Food Security Act (NFSA), which was a major intervention to ensure food security in the country.

  It sought to provide assured quantum of foodgrains – 5 kg. per person – to all priority and Antyodaya households, covering 75 per cent of the rural population and 50 per cent of the urban population at subsidized rates of ₹ 3/2/1 per kg. of rice/ wheat/millets. It also provides for free mid-day meal for children aged 6-14 years in government and government-aided schools up to grade VII and free meal for pregnant and lactating women from Anganwadis. This mission has resulted in increased production of cereals and pulses though there have been some fluctuations in output.

- **National Nutrition Mission:** The National Nutrition Mission (NNM), also known as Rashtriya Poshan Mission was launched by the Government of India, commencing from 2017-18, with a three year budget of ₹ 9046.17 crore. The Mission, under the Ministry of Women and Child Development, fixes targets, monitors and guides nutrition-related interventions including schemes which address malnutrition.

  The programme in particular strives to reduce the level of stunting, under-nutrition, anaemia and low birth weight babies and assess the height of children at Anganwadi Centres. Nutrition Resource Centres will involve masses through 'Jan Andolan' for participation on nutrition issues. Social Audits are to be conducted to evaluate the impact of the mission.

- **Food consumption pattern:** The pattern of consumption of food and dietary habits has significant impact on nutrition intake, health and overall welfare of the population. Various studies conducted in India have shown shift in dietary habits of people both in urban and rural areas. There has been shift in consumption away from cereals to high calorie commodities such as meat, milk, fish, etc, in other words, a shift from low value to high value commodities. While the traditional food basket was dominated by cereals, there is higher expenditure on beverages and milk & milk products.

  The trend of decline in the expenditure on cereals, and correspondingly a substantial rise in the expenditure on milk & milk products, fruits & nuts and beverages, has been seen in both urban and rural areas.

- **Need for further changes:** While the above developments augur well, experts have pointed out the need for further changes in the fight against hunger and malnutrition.

  Dr. M.S. Swaminathan, the well-known agricultural scientist and father of the Green Revolution, has urged for moving from the notion of "food security" to "nutritional security" through steps such as getting nutrient-rich minor millets like ragi, and introducing bio-fortified varieties of crops into the food basket. He has pointed to nutritional problems such a protein hunger and hidden hunger caused by the deficiency of micro-nutrients such as iron, zinc, iodine and Vitamin-A. According to him, nutritional security involves both food and non-food factors, such as attention to balanced diet and ensuring clean drinking water, as well as sanitation. He has stressed the need for promoting bio-fortified nutritional gardens having nutrient-rich vegetables and crops.

  The international rice research body, ICRISAT, opines that "pearl millet" is a nutritious dryland cereal, rich in protein, fibre and essential micronutrients like iron, zinc and folate. Nutrition studies have shown its potential to fight iron deficiency, the most widespread micronutrient deficiency and major cause affecting the health and development of a third of the global population. Pearl millet is grown on about 27 million hectares worldwide and is a daily food for more than 90 million people, among the most vulnerable in arid and semi-arid Africa and Asia. It is also an important source of fodder for millions of farms.

Dr. M S Swaminathan has been a strong advocate of nutritious pearl millet, which is now included in the food basket of the public distribution system in some Indian states, including Karnataka.

- **Conclusion:** There is need for a farm-based approach to development and tackling malnutrition. According to experts, biofortification, a process of breeding crops to increase their nutritional value, which is relatively simple and economical, and cultivation of micro-nutrient rich crops would help to mitigate hidden hunger and malnutrition.

  Simultaneously, food items provided under the PDS and other schemes need to be suitably altered, in consultation with health experts, keeping in view local and regional conditions and bring about changes in people's dietary habits through sustained education and informed campaigns.

7. Explain the main features and advantages of Contract farming and its benefits in the Indian context. Are there any shortcomings in the system? Cite some instances of contract farming adopted in India.

Ans. In India, 86 per cent of farmers fall into the small and marginal category and the average farm size is 1.15 hectares. Consolidation of farmlands is not possible under the Indian conditions and so there is no scope for benefiting from efficiency of scale. Hence the need to aggregate the produce of farmers which contract farming enables.

Under the system of 'Contract farming', the farmer enters into contract with a firm to plant the crop on his land, harvest and deliver a quantum of produce, based upon anticipated yield and contracted acreage. The produce is delivered at a pre-agreed price.

Contract farming arrangements of different types have existed in various parts of the country for both subsistence crops and commercial crops like sugarcane, cotton, tea, coffee etc. Even in the case of some fruit crops and fisheries, contract farming arrangements, involving mainly the forward trading of commodities, have been prevalent. In the wake of economic liberalization, the concept of contract farming under which national or multinational companies enter into contracts for marketing of the horticultural produce and also provide technologies and capital to contract farmers has gained importance.

- **Main Features and benefits of Contract Farming:** Contract farming brings with it the following benefits and advantages:
  - Farmers in India mostly lack capital and other resources and are unable to make major investment in land improvement and quality inputs. Contract farming fills this gap by providing the farmers with quality inputs, equipments needed, technical guidance and management skills.

- Bipartite agreements are made between the farmer and the company and the latter contributes directly to the management of the farm through input supply as well as technical guidance and also markets the produce. The inputs and services supplied by firms may include seeds, fertilizers, pesticides, credit, farm machinery, technical advice, extension, etc., or may involve only the supply of hybrid seeds and marketing of produce.
- Selected crops are grown by farmers under a buy back agreement with an agency engaged in trading or processing. The agency or company agrees to purchase a specified quantum of the commodity at agreed prices. It also provides technical support and resources, including planting materials and, if need be, crop supervision.
- The farmer assumes the production-related risks, while the price risk is transferred to the company. The contracting company may also bear the production risk, depending on the stage of crop growth at which the contract is made. If the contract is made at flowering or fruiting stage, the company bears the production risks also.
- The corporate entity undertakes to do collection, transportation, processing and marketing of the produce. The company bears the entire costs of transaction and marketing. A company will have more resources and capabilities than farmers to undertake these operations and this helps the farmers.
- Although the company may deal only with the contracted crop, the arrangement helps to improve the farmer's overall management skill, thereby helping him to raise the yields of both contracted and non-contracted crops, if any.
- From the standpoint of contacting companies or bodies, this system reduces the supply risk and risk of non-availability of raw material, while the farmer benefits by being insulated from price risks.
- Corporates can be involved in providing warehousing and cold storage facilities to minimise and prevent loss and wastage of large quantities of fruits, vegetables and other perishables value of which runs into thousands of crores. The system also helps agro-based and food industry to acquire timely and adequate supply of good quality agricultural produce.
- The system can better respond to changing consumption patterns and the needs of the fast-food sector and supermarkets.
- As stated earlier, agriculture sector is handicapped by the presence of small, fragmented land holdings. Contract farming helps to consolidate their operations and undertake group farming with various benefits for the small farmers.

➢ **Importance of Contract Farming in Indian context**

Contract farming has particular relevance in the Indian context where farmers face many hurdles such as lack of capital, inputs like seeds and fertilisers, lack of technical knowhow, poor infrastructural facilities, transportation arrangements, inadequate dissemination of information to farmers, exploitation by middlemen for disposal of produce at unremunerative prices, etc. Contract farming helps to tackle these issues.

According to Government of India's National Policy for Farmers, 2007, "Symbiotic contracts which confer benefits to both producers and purchasers, would be encouraged for ensuring assured and remunerative marketing opportunities to the farmers. Contract cultivation based on a well-defined code of conduct will be helpful to small producers in getting good quality inputs, fair prices and prompt payment for their produce. A code of conduct for contract farming or a model contract will be developed to meet the commodity-specific requirements. Farmers will not be alienated from their land under any circumstances under contract farming. State governments may set up a monitoring committee involving farmers to encourage a farmer-friendly contract farming system."

In the Union budget for 2017-18, the Finance Minister stated that the government "propose to integrate farmers who grow fruits and vegetables with agro processing units for better price realisation and reduction of post-harvest losses. A model law on contract farming would therefore be prepared and circulated among the States for adoption.".

In 2018, the government released the model law on contract farming which aims at reducing farmers' risks by creating an assured market for their produce at a pre-agreed price, while encouraging investment from agribusiness and food processing industries by enhancing productivity and cost efficiency. It provides for State-level boards to be set-up to promote and facilitate – rather than regulate – contract farming, and sets out a framework for registering and recording agreements. It also provides for a dispute settlement authority. The model law stipulates that the sponsor will not be allowed to build any permanent structure on the farmers' land.

Issues with Contract Farming: Studies of the system of contract farming have highlighted following problems and issues which may arise.

- Either the contracting firms or the farmers breach contracts when market conditions change and provide arbitrage opportunities, i.e., switching to more favourable deals.
- Firms reject the contracted produce citing quality grounds when market prices fall below contracted prices.
- Farmers resort to side-selling in open markets when market prices rise higher than the contract prices.
- Restrictive and regulated agricultural marketing system and presence of middlemen act as disincentives.

- Companies prefer medium and large farmers because of economies of scale and to optimise transaction costs. If firms want farmers to dedicate a certain minimum acreage, say, five to ten acres of land, to the contract crop, with 85 per cent of the farmers being marginal or small operating less than two acres, they will be outside the scope of contract farming. For this, collectivisation of farms of say, 10 to 15 farmers would be needed. It will also help to bring down the operational and transaction costs and the farmers will be better protected.

➢ **Experience in India: Private Sector Involvement:** Recognising the need for, and merits of, such a linkage with the farming/producing community, several corporates involved in agro- commodity trading, processing, exports, etc. have established suitable systems and models that ensure timely and consistent supply of raw material of the desired quality and reasonable cost.

Farm produce covered under contract farming in India include wheat, basmati rice, maize, pulses, spices, fruits and vegetables, soyabean, flowers, cotton, poultry and milk.

The companies which have entered the field of contract farming include Pepsi Foods, Hindustan Unilever, Cargill, Nestle, Rallis India, ITC-International, Mahindra Shubhlabh, Escorts, Himalaya Drugs, United Breweries, Marico, Nijjer Agro Foods, Venkateshwara Hatcheries, Global Green Company, DD International, Appachi Cotton Company, AVT Natural Products and Gherkin Exporters.

Pepsico's success items like Basmati rice, spices (chillies) and oilseeds (groundnut) and vegetable crops like tomato and potato in Punjab and other states, Hindustan Unilever with tomato, Appachi's Integrated Cotton Cultivation in Coimbatore district, Ugar Sugar's experience with barley in Belgaum (Karnataka) are some of the promising ventures in contract farming.

States that provide favourable conditions for contract farming are Andhra Pradesh, Chhattisgarh, Haryana, Karnataka, Madhya Pradesh, Maharashtra, Punjab, Rajasthan, Tamil Nadu, Uttarakhand, and Uttar Pradesh. The success of contract farming in these States owes to availability of land under marginal fields, better irrigation facilities, soil productivity and yield per hectare.

➢ **Conclusion:** To strengthen and revitalise India's agriculture sector, ensure food and nutrition security to a population of over a billion, raw material for its expanding industrial base, surpluses for exports, and a fair and equitable returns to the farming community, contract farming offers a viable alternative farming model. It could at once provide assured and reliable input services to farmers and required farm produce to the contracting firms.

8. While India has been taking various steps to shift labour from the farm sector to non-farm sectors, she needs to do more on this. Discuss the steps taken by the government and problems encountered in achieving this, and suggest measures to overcome them.

Ans. At the time of independence in 1947, India was predominantly an agrarian economy. The share of agriculture in national income was 49 per cent and in employment 71.8 per cent of the total workforce.

Presently, about half of the national income and more than two-thirds of the total employment is generated in rural areas. Apart from producing almost all agricultural output, rural areas contribute about half of the output in the manufacturing and construction sectors and one quarter of the output in the services sector. However, the rural areas suffer from low level of, and wide disparity in labour productivity.

➢ **Workforce in agriculture**

Though between 1950-51 and 1990-91, the share of agriculture and allied activities in GDP had gone down from 55.8 per cent, its share in the total workforce declined only marginally from 72 per cent in 1951 to 64.75 per cent in 1993-94. While the share of agriculture in GDP declined further, more than half of the workforce – 263 million persons out of a labour force of 477.9 million, constituting 53 per cent as per 2011 census – was engaged in it as the principal occupation. And by 2018-19, with its share in GDP only about 15 per cent, agriculture sector still employed about 44 per cent of the workforce.

➢ **Changing structure of Rural economy**

According to a NITI Aayog study on "*Changing Structure of Rural Economy of India: Implications for Employment and Growth*", there have been profound changes in India's rural economy and "contrary to the common perception about predominance of agriculture in rural economy, about two-third of rural income is now generated in non-agricultural activities" which is a positive sign. Rural areas contributed 51.3 per cent of the manufactured output in 2011-12.

Among the non-farm sectors in rural areas, manufacturing and construction experienced healthy growth, while the services sector saw decline, during the 40-year period between 1970-71 and 2011-12. The share of rural sector in total output in manufacturing, construction and services which was 25.8, 43.2 and 32.8 per cent in 1970-71 stood at 51.3, 48.7 and 25.9 respectively in 2011-12.

But the flip side is that according to the study, though "the share of rural areas in output of manufacturing sector doubled and exceeded the manufacturing production in urban areas, ...this sharp increase in the rural share in output did not fetch any increase in rural share in employment in manufacturing sector........ Clearly, manufacturing sector was shifting to rural areas but without commensurate increase in the employment."

➢ **Need for non-farm jobs**

Traditionally, agriculture is the prime sector of rural economy and source of rural employment. The transition in the composition of output and occupation from agriculture to more productive non-farm sectors is an important indicator of economic growth and transformation in rural as well as the entire economy.

There is imperative need to create non-farm jobs in the rural sector for the following reasons:

- To make employment commensurate with output in agriculture and reduce under-employment, an estimated 84 million agricultural workers have to move out of agriculture and join more productive non-farm sectors. This works out to about 70 per cent increase in the non-farm jobs in rural areas.
- Lack of non-farm jobs in rural areas means that more people continue to rely on working in agriculture sector with resultant under-employment and disguised unemployment.
- It results in unplanned migration of rural population to urban areas, in search of jobs and better economic opportunities, putting severe pressure on urban amenities and infrastructure, and accentuates the problems in urban areas.
- The influx of large number of low-wage migrants from rural areas forces them to live in unhygienic and deprived conditions in urban centres. The urban population which was just 17.97 per cent of total population in 1961 rose to 27.81 per cent by 2001 and 31.16 per cent in 2011. It is further bound to go up.
- To check such unplanned migration and to improve socio-economic conditions of vast majority of population in the country, there is a need to strengthen rural economy and create employment opportunities in productive activities in rural areas.
- The improvement in the socio-economic conditions of rural households is essential for reducing the disparity between per capita income in rural and urban areas which has remained persistently high. This requires significantly higher growth with more productive activities in rural economy, as compared to urban India.

➢ **Employment and Quality of life in rural India**

There is much scope to create non-farm jobs in rural areas as discussed below. These initiatives will not only provide jobs in villages and stem rural-urban migration, but also enhance the quality of life in rural areas.

♦ **Services sector:** The areas which have potential to provide non-farm jobs in rural areas are wholesale and retail trade, hotel and restaurants, transport, storage and communication, and financial services and repair of motor vehicles. These sectors have shown remarkable growth in rural areas between 1993-94 and 2004-05.

- **Construction**: This is another sector with high potential. Rural areas are handicapped by poor infrastructure and civic amenities. Also, a large percentage of houses are in need of upgradation. These facts indicate considerable scope for growth of construction sector in rural areas.
- **MSME units:** While manufacturing also offers scope to create jobs in rural areas, it will have to be more of the labour-intensive nature with enterprises in medium, small and micro (MSME) sector which are suited to local conditions and skills available.
- **Skill Development centres:** Lack of skills in rural areas is one major impediment in shifting labour out of agriculture. Setting up skill development centres, suited to local needs, in villages will not only provide jobs but help to develop skills of local population and act as a catalyst to set up small industries and further enhance job opportunities. For instance, under the **PM Gramin Digital Saksharta Abhiyan (PMGDISHA)**, the Ministry of Electronics & IT is implementing the world's largest digital literacy programme under which 1.96 crore people in rural backward areas have been imparted training to become digitally literate. Under this scheme, a total of 6 crore persons will be trained, thus, bridging the digital divide and helping people access benefits of the digital world.
- **Post-harvest activities:** The reasons for workers preferring to move from agriculture to non-agriculture are low wages, stress of manual work and irregular employment. These three problems can be addressed by innovative approaches in production and post-harvest activities. These can be harnessed by developing and promoting new farm models based on knowledge and skill based agriculture and post-harvest on-farm value addition. **PM Kaushal Vikas Yojana(PMKVY)** can play a major role in this by promoting and imparting skills required in modern agriculture, value addition and primary processing. This will diversify farm activities and reduce the manpower required to work on farm and cultivation itself.
- **Digital India scheme:** This is a major rural sector initiative which will cover 2.5 lakh Gram Panchayats and provide a wide array of government services to villagers without having to depend on urban centres. By 2018-19, over 3 lakh km. optical fibre cable has been laid connecting 1.21 lakh Gram Panchayats. Common Services Centres (CSCs) are bringing e-Services to the doorsteps of people in the rural areas in an affordable manner. There are around 3.12 lakh CSCs across the country providing over 350 services ranging across sectors like education, health, agriculture, etc. and have generated employment to 12 lakh persons including 55,000 women.
- **Health and Education:** These two sectors, which are critical from human development viewpoint, and facilities for which are grossly inadequate in rural areas as compared to urban centres, need to be developed and this could provide not only more job opportunities but also go a long way in improving the standard of life in rural areas.

- **Conclusion:** A concerted drive on rural rejuvenation on the above lines could uplift rural economy and reduce pressure of population on agriculture. In this context, it is pertinent to recall the visionary scheme "**PURA**" (Providing Urban amenities in Rural Areas) which was so passionately advocated by Dr. Abdul Kalam, former President of India, to revitalise rural India. Though some initiatives were taken in the Twelfth Five-Year Plan (2012-17), the scheme was not actively pursued and was abandoned.

9. Mention the various forms of support and subsidies provided to the agriculture sector and farmers in India. Examine the relative merits and demerits of these support measures and suggest which of these measures would be the more efficient and preferable. Justify your answer.

Ans. Agriculture, the preponderant sector in India, had all along faced multiple challenges and had to be supported by the government through various measures. The risks in this sector are aggravated by a variety of factors, ranging from erratic weather, uncertainties in yields and prices, recurring natural disasters and crop losses, weak rural infrastructure, imperfect markets and inadequate and sub-optimal financial services. These factors not only endanger the livelihoods and incomes of farmers, especially the small and marginal farmers, but also undermine the very viability of the sector.

According to a sample study of "***All India Rural Financial Inclusion Survey 2016-17***", conducted by NABARD, the all-India average income of an agricultural household was ₹ 8,931 per month (p. m.). The income figure, however, varied widely between the states – from ₹ 6,670 p.m. in Uttar Pradesh to ₹ 23,133 p.m. in Punjab.

The income would be inadequate to meet all the needs of a family, as also to bear the expenses incurred in farming – cost of inputs, wages of labour employed, interest burden on loans availed, transportation and marketing expenses, etc.

The government at Central and State levels have been extending aid to farmers in different forms, viz., Minimum Support Price (MSP) for produce, interest subvention on loans taken or, in extreme cases, even loan waiver, direct income support, subsidies on inputs like seeds, fertilisers, irrigation and power, and crop insurance schemes. Their relative merits and disadvantages are discussed below.

- **Minimum Support Price (MSP)**

  The price support policy for selected agricultural products has been in vogue since the 1960s. To ensure a stable and remunerative price environment, minimum support prices (MSP) for major agricultural products are fixed by the government, each year, after taking into account the recommendations of the Commission for Agricultural Costs and Prices (CACP).

  - The CACP considers factors such as the cost of production, change in input prices, market price trends, demand and supply, and a reasonable margin for farmers. The CACP analyses the cost of production data for various states for different commodities in consultation with the state governments and declares the appropriate prices.

- MSPs are usually announced at the beginning of the sowing season and this helps farmers make informed decisions on the crops they must plant.

♦ **Merits**

* The government uses the MSP as a market intervention tool to incentivise production of specific crops. For instance, pulses are one of the least expensive source of protein for Indian consumers and hence the government could encourage their production by ensuring MSP for them.
* MSP protects farmers from any sharp fall in the market price of a commodity. When prices of major crops fall way below the announced MSPs, as has happened in some years, the farming community come under stress despite good harvest. Factors such as unanticipated increase in domestic production, surge in global production and influx of imports, uncertainty about the market trends, fall in demand for the product and resultant glut, etc. could cause the fall in prices.
* Where MSPs are higher than market prices, the bargaining power of farmers vis-à-vis traders would go up and lead to a larger fraction of the value accruing to farmers relative to traders.

♦ **Disadvantages**

* Because the MSP formula is based on just cost plus pricing, without considerations of the demand side of the commodities and their inter-crop price parity, it is likely to cause major distortions in the functioning of agricultural markets.
* Farmers may find it profitable to allocate more area for a crop due to higher MSP announced for it and may opt to increase its production. But if there is no commensurate demand, market prices for it may fall below the MSP. It will then necessitate large-scale procurement by the government at MSP which would not be economically rational. It may also result in excess buffer stocks and entail storage and carrying costs, spoilage of stocks, etc.
* MSP benefits only farmers who grow those items for which the minimum price is set and not others who grow other crops.
* When market prices are higher than the MSP, large farmers, who have bargaining power relative to traders, are able to secure prices higher than the MSP. In contrast, the small and medium farmers, with less bargaining power, are forced to sell their produce at MSP which is less than the market prices.

Agricultural loans and Debt Relief

- **Agricultural loans** Short-term and long-term loans are advanced to the agriculture sector by institutions such as cooperatives credit societies, commercial banks, regional rural banks, and State Governments. Besides, they may also borrow from money from commission agents, traders or even moneylenders, often at exorbitant interest rates.
  - The farmers borrow loans from these sources to meet farming expenses such as cost of inputs, wages of labour employed, post-harvest operations, etc.
  - As a measure to check distress sale, post-harvest loans are extended to farmers for storage of the produce in accredited warehouses.
- **Debt relief:** In years of severe drought, floods, or crop failure due to other factors, farmers suffer loss of crops causing them much financial loss and hardship and they are then unable to repay loans. In such contingencies, the government provides relief to them through "loan waiver" or "interest subvention" schemes.
  - **Loan waiver:** From time to time, the government has had to waive thousands of crores of farm loans given to farmers, especially the small and marginal farmers.

    Interest subvention scheme: To provide relief on debt to farmers, the government may also extend "interest subvention scheme" under which short-term credit or crop loan is given to farmers at subsidised interest rate.

    The budget provision for interest subvention for short-term credit to farmers in FY 2019-20 was ₹ 17,863.43 crore while in the budget for FY 2020-21 it is ₹ 21,175 crore.

    There are arguments for and against loans and debt relief provided to farmers. These are:
- **Arguments in favour of debt relief**
  - Agriculture is the lifeline for bulk of the rural population who depend on it for their livelihood and survival. They also have the onerous task of providing food to the entire population against many odds such as declining soil fertility, and unforeseen contingencies such as erratic weather leading to crop losses, and volatility in market and international competition which may adversely affect demand for their produce and their income. In such serious crisis situations, the government has to provide relief to farmers.
  - Bulks of India's farmers are those with very small land holdings and without access to irrigation. Cultivation on such lands becomes mostly uneconomic as they do not offer the economies of scale. With barely subsistence income, prevalence of endemic hunger and chronic under-nutrition is high among such families. Hence, there is a strong case to extend support to such families in times of crisis.
  - In contrast, the banks and RBI have, over the years, shown greater forbearance towards large loans given to the corporate sector many of which remain unpaid and have become stressed assets as evidenced by the mounting NPAs in the loan books of banks.
  - Waiving farm loans is not just an ethical or moral issue but has vital social and economic implications.

♦ **Arguments against debt relief**

- As a rule, loan waivers apply only to those who borrow from banks and cooperatives. Surveys done have shown that small farmers account for 82 per cent of all indebted farm households in India and they borrow mostly from private moneylenders or local traders as banks are unwilling to lend without collateral like jewellery, tractors, etc. which the small and marginal farmers may not have. Thus, majority of indebted farmers do not benefit from loan waivers and they benefit more the undeserving borrowers.
- Loans waived are those given to farmers by public sector banks and cooperative credit societies and when they are written off, the latter have to bear the loss which affects their balance sheets. Loan waivers also hurts State finances breaching fiscal deficit threshold of States.
- Waiving loans undermines honest credit culture, impacts credit discipline and may induce borrowers not to repay loans in future.

➢ **Subsidies**

Apart from the expenditure on price support (in the form of MSP discussed earlier) and costs of procuring, storage and distribution of selected crops, India spends significant public resources on agricultural subsidies detailed below.

♦ **Fertilizer subsidies:** The fertilizer subsidies have largely gone to sustain inefficient and high cost fertilizer plants and led to use of massive overuse of nitrogenous fertilizers, resulting in damage to soil health and pollution of local water bodies. Excessive use of urea – urea prices in India are perhaps the lowest in the world – has led to increased acidity in the soils even as they are highly deficient in micro-nutrients like zinc.

Fertilizer subsidies in the Union budget for FY2019-20 was around ₹ 80,000 crore. Besides, there are pending bills of fertilizer industry of over ₹ 30,000 crore. In the budget for FY 2020-21, the government has made a lesser provision of ₹ 71309 crore.

♦ **Power subsidies:** Power subsidies have led to an alarming overuse and depletion of groundwater which is one of India's gravest challenges. Besides, it has severely damaged the financial health of power distribution companies and retarded the growth of industry which is saddled with a high cost crucial input.

There has been a sharp increase in the use of electricity in agriculture sector, especially since the 1980s with consumption rising from 3,465 million units (mu) in 1969 (8 per cent of total consumption) to 173,185 mu in 2016 (17 per cent of total). This is supplied either free or at subsidised rates, and a large part of it is not metered.

States like Punjab have seen depletion of ground water table at an alarming rate and more than 75 percent of blocks in Punjab are overexploited. It is a grave situation, and India has been extremely slow to recognize the magnitude and gravity of the problem. Future generations will pay a very heavy price if the government does not act to address this with utmost urgency.

- **Other subsidies**: These include price support (MSP) and credit subsidies like loan waivers and reduced interest (interest subvention) already mentioned.

➢ **Crop insurance scheme**

Another important step to mitigate the problems faced by farmers following crop losses due to erratic weather, monsoon failure, droughts, etc. is crop insurance. Agricultural Insurance Scheme (NAIS) and later Modified NAIS were in operation but it was replaced by the **Pradhan Mantri Fasal Bima Yojana (PMFBY)**, which was introduced in January 2016.

This scheme helps in decreasing the burden of premiums on farmers who take loans for their cultivation and also safeguards them against the inclement weather. It aims to make the settlement process of the insurance claim, fast and easy so that the farmers do not face any trouble regarding the crop insurance plan.

The scheme has deficiencies such as inadequate awareness about the scheme among farmers and hence low coverage, discrepancies in the data relating to area sown and area insured and delays in release of compensation by states to affected farmers. There is need for greater publicity at village level and proactive action by district authorities to reach out to farmers and educate them on the benefits of insuring.

➢ **Income transfer scheme**

In 2018, the government introduced a Direct Income Support (DIS) scheme, "PM Kisan Samman Nidhi", under which ₹ 6,000 is provided to all farmer families across the country in a year in three equal instalments of ₹ 2000 each.

This amount is, however, modest compared to income support under "RythuBandhu" scheme of Telangana and the "KALIA" scheme of Odisha.

➢ **Conclusion:** According to experts, income support is better than the MSP scheme as it does not influence the crop cycle. Intervention through MSP affects cropping patterns because farmers tend to grow more of those crops for which support is given or whose support price is higher. Also, income transfer gives money in the hands of the farmers and they can make crop portfolio choice based on information they have best about what to grow and what not to. So one is not influencing that choice by farmers.

The government will have to consider raising the amount suitably by scaling down subsidies granted to farmers for Minimum Support Price and for water, power, etc., on which there may be leakages and wastages, without hampering productivity. This will have to be done in a calibrated manner, in consultation with all stakeholders and domain experts.

> Let us not forget that the cultivation of the earth is the most important labour of man. When tillage begins, other arts follow. The farmers, therefore, are the founders of civilization.
>
> – Daniel Webster (1782-1852), American statesman.

INDUSTRY AND SERVICES

> The First Industrial Revolution used water and steam power to mechanize production. The Second used electric power to create mass production. The Third used electronics and information technology to automate production.
> The Fourth Industrial Revolution has the potential to empower individuals and communities, as it creates new opportunities for economic, social, and personal development. But it could also lead to the marginalization of some groups, exacerbate inequality, create new security risks, and undermine human relationships.
>
> -- Klaus Schwab: Engineer & Economist, Founder of World Economic Forum, Davos.

Topics Covered

- *Challenges facing Indian industry*
- *Ease of Doing Business in India*
- *Progress of Make in India programme*
- *India's progress in Services bypassing manufacturing and its implications*
- *Role of MSME sector*
- *Logistics sector and its importance*
- *Role of IT industry*
- *Industrial corridors*
- *Start-ups in India*

1. What are the constraints faced by industries in India? Outline the steps taken by the government to resolve them and suggest further steps to be taken.

Ans. Industries in India face a plethora of problems when compared to industries in other developing and emerging economies like China, Brazil, South Africa, and Indonesia. Limited land availability, a burgeoning population, lack of skilled manpower, migration from rural to urban areas, and overburdened urban centres all pose severe challenges in development. The following are the major problems.

- **Infrastructure**

  One of the major constraints faced by the industrial sector is inadequate and poor quality infrastructure. Interruptions in power supply, transportation bottlenecks, communication problems, delays in transportation by rail and cargo handling at ports are adding to the real costs of manufacture and thus affecting the competitiveness of domestic manufacturers and providers of services. These are also affecting exports adversely.

  Unless the existing infrastructural capabilities – roads, rail, ports, power supply, etc. – are upgraded and strengthened substantially, it would be difficult to achieve high targets of industrial growth. With the opening up of the economy and globalization, the importance of competitiveness and the need for quality of infrastructure cannot be overemphasized.

  Infrastructure programme: In December 2019, the Central government has come up with the ambitious ₹ 103 lakh crore National Infrastructure Pipeline programme consisting of 6,500 projects across various sectors. Much will depend on ensuring availability and allocation of funds, avoiding contractual issues and its speedy and timely implementation.

- **The land issue:** Availability of land for industrialization has been another vexatious issue. There are many legal and administrative impediments in acquiring land for industry due to opposition from the owners of land, much of which lies in the hinterland and agricultural belts. While conversion of cultivable and fertile land for non-agricultural purposes should be guarded against, especially in view of the imperative need to augment food production, a way out has to be found to release non-arable land for industrial purposes.

  Providing jobs and CSR: To procure land needed to set up units, it would be better for the enterprise concerned to negotiate directly with landowners and arrive at suitable compensation to be paid. Under certain circumstances, the industrial unit could offer some jobs to the local and affected persons as an incentive for providing the land. And other benefits like promoting education, improving infrastructure and environment in the area could be extended under Corporate Social Responsibility (CSR) schemes which will act as added incentives to the local population.

  Land records: A related issue is management of land which is the sovereign duty of the government. Maintaining reliable and robust land records, of land titles, transfers, etc., is essential for smooth governance. State governments have started the process of digitising land records to avert disputes and this task needs to be completed if proper utilisation of land for various developmental purposes is to be ensured.

- **Skilled manpower:** Lack of skilled manpower is a major handicap that industries face. Industry and manufacturing has become highly skill-intensive and is largely based on high level technology which requires skilled manpower. Employability of labour has become a major issue with industry associations stating that even students coming out of technical institutions and colleges are not readily employable.

Skill development: The mismatch between labour force and jobs has meant that recruits have to be specially trained for the jobs which entails considerable time and costs. Imparting skills to the youth has assumed great importance in view of the rapid advances and changes in technology in the present-day globalized world. Unless manufacturing industries keep themselves abreast of these changes and have an efficient, skilled workforce, India will not be able to succeed in her ambitious programmes like 'Make in India' or compete with other nations in the international markets.

India has a low percentage of skilled labour and hence the various skill development schemes being implemented need to be expedited. Besides, the academic curricula followed in educational institutions also need to be revamped to keep pace with emerging hi-tech areas like artificial intelligence, robotics, cloud computing, nanotechnology, etc. For more on skill development, see Question 6 in Chapter 7, page 7.21).

- **Low share of industry and manufactures in GDP:** The share of manufactures-- capital and consumer goods-- is recognized as one of the widely accepted indices of development. Manufacturing industry provides the driving force for stimulating rapid economic growth. The growth rate of industry normally surpasses that of the agriculture and the service sectors. It is for this reason that industry is considered the backbone of an economy.

  According to World Bank data, India's share of industry (including construction) and manufacturing in GDP at 26.7% and 15 % respectively in 2018 is very low compared to China's 40.7% and 29%, Malaysia's 38.3% and 22%, South Korea's 35.1% and 27 % and Thailand's 35% and 27 % respectively. From this point of view, special emphasis is to be placed on raising the share of both industry and manufacturing in GDP. India's share in the world export of manufacturers is also low as compared to some of the other countries in Asia.

  India's potential: India already has shown the potential in the manufacture and export of products in the defence, electronics, automobiles, aerospace, pharmaceutical sectors. Major multinational and Indian corporations are successfully operating in India in these fields. These advantages have to be further leveraged, especially in the context of firms moving out of China in recent times.

  Reforms: The government has been taking various measures like reform of the legal and judicial processes, simplifying direct and indirect tax system, easing foreign investment regulations and instituting bankruptcy and insolvency code with seamless exit provisions to give a boost to the industry.

- **Trade barriers and Competition**

  Tariffs and non-tariff barriers imposed by the industrialized countries are much loaded against manufactured imports from developing countries like India, making it more difficult to penetrate those markets. Resort to non-tariff measures like anti-dumping, social safeguards and standards and imposing rigid technical standards have limited the opportunities for developing countries.

In the agriculture sector, the subsidies provided by the developed nations to their farmers (while, at the same time, contesting subsidies given by India to her farmers) make it difficult for India to export agricultural products to those countries.

Further, India is facing stiff competition in the international markets from countries like Brazil, Mexico, Turkey, Viet Nam, Bangladesh, etc. in the export of manufactures like textiles and apparels, leather goods, etc. which are highly labour-intensive and advantageous for India from employment point of view. India has to improve skills, adopt suitable technologies and modernize systems to enhance productivity and become competitive in global markets.

♦ **Conclusion: Industry and Employment:** The occupational structure in India is skewed in favour of the agriculture sector which has high degree of under-employment. There is imperative need to shift surplus labour from agriculture to industry. The government has to act as a facilitator in this process by creating an environment conducive to growth of the manufacturing sector. That a number of MNCs like IBM, Microsoft, Dell, Samsung, Apple, Hyundai, etc. have set up large units in India is a positive sign and the government has to build further on this momentum to create jobs on a substantial scale.

2. What steps have been taken by the government to improve the "Ease of doing Business" in India? Where does India stand in ranking by the World Bank on this and what further measures need to be taken to improve the ranking?

Ans. If the development of industry and services sector is to be speeded up, the process of starting industries and business has to be made smooth and hassle-free. One of the main constraints of industrial development in India has been the labyrinth of complex procedures infamously referred to as 'red tape' hampering growth.

➢ **Reform of Regulations:** Regulatory environment has an important impact on the business development. Low regulatory burden means that entrepreneurs can devote their time on productive activities. It also leads to lower costs as the requirement of engaging regulatory experts is reduced.

Since 2014, India is striving to create conducive working environment by streamlining the regulations and processes and eliminating unnecessary requirements and procedures. A detailed plan of regulatory reforms has been implemented not only in the Central Ministries but also in States, through the active engagements with State Governments.

➢ **World Bank's Ranking**

The World Bank has been reviewing the systems in 190 countries and ranking them in a *Doing Business Report* (DBR). As per DBR 2019, India ranked 77 among 190 countries assessed by the World Bank Team, improving its rank by 23 over its rank of 100 in the DBR 2018. Further, India jumped 14 places to rank 63rd on the World Bank's Ease of Doing Business report of 2020 riding on the Government's 'Make in India' scheme and other reforms attracting foreign investment.

These improvements are as a result of the regulatory reforms launched to make it easier to do business in India. The program represents a great deal of effort to create a more business-friendly environment.

The World Bank Doing Business report is based on surveys only on Delhi and Mumbai.

- **Criteria adopted:** The DBR covers 10 indicators which span the lifecycle of a business.
    - Among the indicators, India has ranked high on Protecting Minority Investors (rank 7), Getting Credit (22), Getting Electricity (24) and Dealing with Construction Permits (52).
    - But on certain other crucial parameters, India ranks low, viz., Trading Across Borders (80), Resolving Insolvency (108), Paying Taxes (121), Starting a Business (137), Enforcing Contracts (163) and Registering Property (166).
    - While the 2019 report acknowledges that India is one of the top 10 improvers, second time in a row, with an improvement of 53 ranks in two years, the highest jump by any large country since 2011, India has a long way to go on other important parameters like Registering Property, Enforcing Contracts, Resolving Insolvency and Starting a Business.

➢ **Action by States:** Though the World Bank survey covers only Mumbai and Delhi, the Department for Promotion of Industry & Internal Trade (DPIIT) has initiated similar reform exercise in all States and UTs since setting up businesses concerns them also. States and UTs are being ranked based on implementation of reforms by them to create conducive business environment by streamlining regulatory structures and creating an investor-friendly business climate.

- **World Bank's role:** The World Bank has also partnered with DPIIT in this reform plan and 18 joint workshops were conducted along with World Bank specialists to help Departments in the States and UTs understand the essence of the reforms better and to give the exercise momentum.
- **Progress in States/UTs:** The assessment of Business Reform Action Plan, 2017-18, released jointly by DPIIT and the World Bank in July 2018, showed the progress achieved by states/UTs States as follows:
    - 9 states had achieved over 95 per cent of targets and were ranked "Top achievers". This included Andhra Pradesh, Telangana, Haryana, Jharkhand, Gujarat, Chhattisgarh, MP, Karnataka and Rajasthan.
    - 6 states had achieved 90-95 per cent of targets and were ranked "Achievers". These were West Bengal, Uttarakhand, UP, Maharashtra, Odisha and Tamil

Nadu.

- Himachal Pradesh, Assam and Bihar had achieved 80-90 per cent of targets and were ranked "Fast movers".
- Remaining 18 states/UTs had achieved less than 80 per cent of targets and were ranked "Aspirers". This included Punjab, Goa, Kerala, J&K, Delhi and other states and all UTs.

♦ **Reform measures by states/UTs:** States and UTs have taken some significant steps to make it hassle-free to set up enterprises and carry on business. These include:

- Designed an **Information Wizard** providing information for all approvals, licenses, registrations timelines, and procedure to establish business/ industrial unit.
- Implemented online **Single Window System**.
- **Construction Permits** to be provided within 45 days: with Building plan to be approved in 30 days, Plinth level inspection to be done in 7 days and final occupancy certificate to be given in 8 days. Some states have mandated even shorter timelines.
- Implemented a **GIS system** to provide details about the land earmarked for industrial use across the State.
- Reduced the number of documents needed for getting **Electricity connection** to just 2.
- Brought all **Compliance inspections** done by Labour, Factories, Boilers Depts. and Pollution Control Boards under Central Inspection Framework.
- Merged the payment of **Court fees and Process fees** into a single transaction with some states even repealing process fees from the Court Fees Act.
- Notified a list of **white category industries** exempted from taking pollution clearances.

➢ **NITI Aayog study and findings:** NITI Aayog has also done a study, "***An Enterprise Survey of Indian States***" in association with IDFC Institute, a Mumbai-based think tank in 2017. It is a survey of manufacturing firms across Indian states and union territories with a view to assess the business regulations and enabling environment across India from the viewpoint of firms. This survey included in-depth interviews with lawyers, chartered accountants, and company secretaries in several states and is, therefore, a comprehensive study.

The Survey which covered over 3,200 manufacturing enterprises, including 141 early stage firms, across 23 manufacturing sectors, have revealed some positive aspects but also areas needing further action and improvement. The crucial findings were as follows:

- The awareness among enterprises about single window systems, instituted by states, is low. Even among experts, only 41 per cent have any knowledge of the existence of these facilities. There is, therefore, a clear need for creating greater awareness.
- On average, only about 20 per cent of start-ups, which are of recent origin, report using single window facilities introduced by state governments for setting up a business.
- Enterprises in high-growth states are significantly less likely to report major or very severe obstacles in land and construction related approvals, environmental approvals and water and sanitation availability as compared to enterprises located in low-growth states.
- Enterprises in high-growth states take less time on average for nearly all aspects of doing business.
- Specific areas where high-growth states do very well are in getting construction permits, labour renewals, and access to electricity and water connections.
- Firms in high-growth states also report 25 per cent less power shortage in a typical month, compared to firms in low-growth states.
- Comparison of young firms with old ones showed that newer and younger firms report a more favourable business environment in that they take less time in obtaining approvals. And they don't find regulatory processes a major obstacle to doing business which is a positive sign.
- Labour-intensive sectors have a special place as they can create proportionately more jobs per unit of capital investment. The survey found that these sectors felt more constrained by labour related regulations. For them, finding skilled workers, hiring contract labour, and terminating employees, is a major obstacle. It points to the centrality of labour law reforms for expansion of labour-intensive sectors and job creation.

➢ **Conclusion:** To sum up, India has made significant strides in creating a more investment-friendly and hassle free environment for businesses and enterprises, both at the central and state levels. This has helped India to improve her rank in the World Bank surveys. But, as pointed out earlier, in some areas like Resolving Insolvency, Tax Payment, Enforcing Contracts and Registering Property, India still has to show much improvement if she is to break into the top 50 rank in all these parameters.

3. Bring out the salient features of the 'Make in India' programme, the steps taken by the government to promote it and the opportunities it offers India. Elucidate the challenges facing the programme and suggest measures to overcome them.

Ans. The 'Make in India' programme was conceived and piloted by the Department of Industrial Policy and Promotion (DIPP) of the Government of India and launched in September 2014. It is part of a wider spectrum of nation-building initiatives and is one of the main planks of the government's plans for re-energising the economy. It aims to give fillip to the industrial and manufacturing sector and transform India into a global design and manufacturing hub.

➢ **Initiative, need of the hour**

This initiative is crucial and has come none too soon, not only from the viewpoint of economic growth and modernising and diversifying the economy, but due to the imperative need to create jobs for the millions of youth who are joining the labour force each year.

The current environment for international trade presents India an unprecedented opportunity to chart a China-like, labour-intensive, export-driven growth and thereby create job opportunities on a large-scale for our burgeoning youth.

By integrating 'Assemble in India for the world' into 'Make in India', India can create an estimated 4 crore well-paid jobs by 2025 and 8 crore jobs by 2030. Exports of network products, which is expected to equal $7 trillion worldwide in 2025, can contribute a quarter of the increase in value-added for the $5 trillion economy by 2025.

Salient features

- The initiative aims at raising the contribution of the manufacturing sector, which is now around 16 per cent to 25 per cent of the GDP.
- The programme is a collaborative effort involving the Central and State governments, industry leaders, chambers and associations and various knowledge partners.
- It seeks to leverage the transformational power of public-private partnership (PPP), including India's global partners, as evidenced by the in-depth interactions between India and various other countries and transnational corporations at the highest levels.

➢ **India's potential**

♦ India, the world's fifth largest economy, is on the cusp of major changes and far-reaching reforms, and is poised to become the third largest economy of the world by 2030.

♦ Endowed with the advantages of being a democratic polity, a young population, who can be skilled, and a huge internal market creating massive demand, the country could well draw on these strengths to forge ahead if proper policies are put in place and implemented with rigour. Having a vast English-speaking, highly qualified technical and engineering work force are added strengths.

- ♦ Indian corporates are targeting global markets with acquisition of foreign business entities. This has helped to place India on the global industrial map and make our companies globally competitive.
- ♦ Several leading automobile and other companies such as Hyundai, Toyota, Honda, Samsung and Apple have established assembly plants in India and some of them have begun to use India as an export base within their production networks. Also, major aircraft manufacturers like Boeing and Airbus are sourcing parts and components from Indian manufacturers.

➢ **Measures taken by the government.** The government has been taking various steps to promote the Make in India programme and reinvigorate the economy. These include

- **Ease of doing business:** Launching a business venture entails many initial steps which could be complex and time-consuming such as land acquisition with proper land titles, registration and raising capital, and getting infrastructural facilities, some of which involve interface with the State or Central government. Both the Central and the State governments have taken a series of measures under the "Ease of Doing Business" to make the procedure hassle-free. India is working with the World Bank on these and India has improved her ranking in the World Bank's survey.
- **Infrastructure improvement:** Having world class infrastructure –roads and highways, rail transport, ports, power and communication facilities – is *sine qua non* for nurturing and supporting a globally competitive industrial and manufacturing sector. China's phenomenal rise in the last few decades was primarily due to the vast and sprawling infrastructural facilities she built and the inexpensive labour she had to offer. The Indian government has taken steps to speed up highway projects, modernise and upgrade railways and airports and expand port facilities.
- **Skill Development:** With rapid advances in technology, training workers to upgrade their skills has assumed importance, especially in the light of the drive to boost the manufacturing sector and India trying to become a manufacturing hub. The constant refrain of industry and their chambers and associations has been that the labour available are mostly unskilled and not suited for the jobs on offer and training them costs both time and money. The government has initiated many training programmes under the PM Kaushal Vikas Yojana.
- The government has enacted a bankruptcy and insolvency law to facilitate smooth exit for enterprises under stress.
- India has liberalised Foreign Direct Investment (FDI) regime and the economy has been moving on a trajectory with greater inflow of foreign capital. Opening up key sectors including railways, aviation, defence and insurance to higher levels of FDI is part of this.

- India has been assiduously trying to bring in transparency in all its dealings, enhance credibility globally and drive investment, foster innovation, develop skills, protect Intellectual Property (IP).

➤ **Challenges facing 'Make in India'**

Historically, all developed countries – UK, US, Germany, Japan or S. Korea – have scaled the economic ladder and attained prosperity driven by the growth of manufacturing. The growth and expansion of factories helped them to shift labour from agriculture to industry which provided more productive occupations and through value-addition contributed to the prosperity of the nation and its people.

♦ **Boosting manufacturing:** India faces a difficult task in replicating the experience of the advanced countries during the Industrial Revolution and of the South-east and East Asian countries which experienced rapid growth in the 1970s and China in later years through industrialization.

♦ **Competition and Protectionism:** It is now more difficult for newcomers to break into world markets due to intense competition and other factors like protectionist tendencies, tariff barriers and reluctance on the part of advanced nations to part with high technology.

With globalization, competition has also become more intense with many emerging countries like Viet Nam, Malaysia, Indonesia, Brazil, Bangladesh etc. vying for global markets.

♦ **Changed scenario:** In the early stages of industrialisation, manufacturing became a powerful engine of economic development due to following factors which no longer exist:

- **Skill requirements:** Manufacturing jobs didn't require much skill. Farmers could become industrial workers in factories with little additional training. Now manufacturing is highly skill-intensive and largely based on high level technology.
- **Technology issues:** It was easier to procure and absorb technology from other countries and generate high productivity jobs.
- **Scope for exports:** Demand for manufactured goods was not constrained by low level of domestic incomes or domestic market. The manufactured goods could be exported to foreign markets.

♦ **Technology and Skill upgradation:** Procuring advanced technology, rapidly upgrading the skills of labour and providing a competitive environment for corporations to invest and set up industries in India.

♦ **Reforming labour laws:** Making labour laws flexible, even while protecting the interests of workers, is found necessary to generate jobs. The government has linked reforming labour laws as part of its 'Ease of doing business' programme to encourage investments. The initiatives taken by the Rajasthan government in this regard are a pointer to this. But the labour unions are resisting changes and hence protracted negotiations are to be held with the unions to convince them that changes are needed for creating jobs and are in the long-term interest of employees and that their interests would be safeguarded. The Government of India has since implemented labour reforms which have been approved by the Parliament. (For details on this, see Question 5 in Chapter 7 on page 7.17).

➤ **Conclusion:** India should reap gains from participation in "global value chains" (GVCs) by promoting strong linkages among domestic industries and engaging in GVCs wherein linkages are globally dispersed.

In the short to medium term, the objective may be large-scale expansion of assembly activities by making use of imported parts and components. But giving a boost to domestic production of parts and components should be the long-term goal. Assembly is highly labour- intensive and can provide jobs on a large scale, while domestic production of parts and components can create high skill jobs.

Shift of Manufacturing from China

A new dimension has since emerged with many large manufacturing enterprises in China planning to pull out of that country following the Covid-19 pandemic and, even otherwise, due to rising wage costs in that country. This offers opportunities for India to draw those firms to India. The Central and State governments are already working on this by trying to make available enough land and power supply on attractive terms.

These should be followed by other steps like easy Single-window approvals and setting up Economic and Export zones with seamless rail connectivity and easy access to ports and further upgrading infrastructure to international standards.

India cannot afford to delay action on these lines as other countries like Viet Nam, Malaysia, Indonesia, Myanmar and Bangladesh are also ideal locations for those enterprises to relocate and are vying to attract them.

4. Contrary to the usual pattern of development, India leapfrogged from agriculture to services bypassing manufacturing. Do you agree with this statement? Justify your answer.

Ans. India's growth pattern has not followed the traditional theory of development which held good for two centuries since the Industrial Revolution. According to this theory and conventional wisdom, nations transition from a traditional agrarian economy to manufacturing and industrial nation and then to wider growth in the services sector. Structural transformation – the movement of workers from low-productivity to high-productivity activities – is an essential ingredient of inclusive growth.

➤ **Path followed by other nations**

The assumption was that there could be explosive growth only in manufacturing which would absorb the growing population and the surplus labour force in agriculture. This was the path tread by the developed nations in the west following the Industrial Revolution and by the East Asian economies when they registered rapid growth between 1960s and 1990s. The growth path of China, which witnessed astounding growth since the 1980s, also conforms to this trend.

As observed by the Commission on Growth and Development, 2008 (The World Bank), among the early industrializing Asian economies, such as South Korea, Taiwan and China, the transfer of workers from agriculture to manufacturing was rapid, leading to very sharp increases in economic growth that was sustained for a prolonged period of time. The pace of structural transformation was slower in the late industrializing Asian countries, which implied that a large proportion of the workforce was still employed in agriculture, even after rapid economic growth in many of these countries.

As observed by the Asian Development Bank, the low-income countries with large shares of employment in agriculture, such as Bangladesh, India, Pakistan and Thailand, have been moving directly from the agricultural sector to the services sector, bypassing industrialisation. There is need to develop industries, besides services, to absorb the surplus labour in agriculture.

Also, the major Asian economies, viz., Japan, the Republic of Korea, Singapore, and Taiwan, and, more recently, Vietnam, moved from the import-substituting phases of their economic development to an export-oriented development strategy, through a strong growth in the labour-intensive segment of the manufacturing sector. But this was not the case with India, where the labour-intensive manufacturing's share in total output has fallen over time.

➢ **India's experience, industry lags behind**

India's growth did not follow the path of many other countries. Though India did embark on industrialisation from the Second Plan (1956-61) and tried to follow it through subsequent plans, India could not become a manufacturing powerhouse. The following factors explain this trend:

- The policy of 'import substitution' and self-sufficiency, and not an export-driven strategy, adopted in the first three decades after independence hampered industrial growth.
- The predominant role assigned to the public sector, relegation of private sector and highly restrictive industrial policies further impaired the process. In consonance with the planning and socialist strategy adopted, the role of private sector was controlled and stifled through investment control, import licensing, and controls on foreign exchange, credit allocation and prices.
- To prevent undue concentration of economic power, additional mechanisms such as Monopoly and Restrictive Trade Practices (MRTP) Act, which imposed severe constraints on expansion by large firms and groups, and the Foreign Exchange Regulation Act (FERA), were put in place which further inhibited industrial growth.

- ♦ Rigid labour laws combined with the constraints on the scale of private enterprises limited India's presence in labour-intensive manufacture, the usual trend in a populous developing country.
- ♦ India did not make efforts to adopt advanced technology and to produce high quality products with a view to promote exports to capture a share of world markets.
- ♦ There are severe hurdles in the acquisition of land for industrial use and for public projects. Given high labour-land ratios in rural areas, land remains a scarce resource as well as a source of livelihood for millions of Indian farmers, and this acts as a constraint on setting up industries.
- ♦ Another distinctive feature of the Indian manufacturing sector has been its dualism – the existence of a relatively small number of firms in the formal sector, which has a largely protected workforce, along with a large number of firms in the informal sector, where workers have little access to social security, employment protection, and other benefits. Labour productivity in the formal sector firms is also higher than that in the informal sector firms.

➢ **Services sector forged ahead**

- All this while, in the first four decades from 1950, the services sector, especially transport, construction and banking segments, kept growing at steady pace to meet the needs of a growing population.
- The onset of computer revolution in the 1980s and the '90s further accentuated the growth of the tertiary sector. India's dominance in Information Technology (IT) and IT-enabled services and its exports led to rapid growth of the services sector, steadily increasing its share in National Income.
- The opening up of the telecom and aviation sectors following the reforms in 1990s saw phenomenal growth in both these sectors.
- Heavy investment in infrastructure – roads, railways and ports – too gave a boost to the services sector.

➢ **Sectoral shares in GDP**

- ♦ While there has been substantial decline in the share of agriculture in total output from 55 per cent in 1955 to 20 per cent in 2008, much of the shift in economic activity occurred toward services and not manufacturing as explained above.
- ♦ Between 1980 and 2002, India's share of services in value added went up from 37 percent to 49 percent, while the share of manufacturing in value added remained broadly unchanged at 16 percent, and the share of agriculture declined.
- ♦ The share of services (tertiary sector) in GDP rose from 36.0 per cent in 1980-81 to 59.6 per cent in 2012-13. Whereas the share of agriculture (primary sector) came down from 38.1 per cent to15.6 per cent and that of industry (secondary sector) declined from 25.9 per cent to 24.8 per cent during the same period. And the share of manufacturing in the secondary sector is a low 15 per cent only.

- In contrast, out of 37.0 per cent share of Industry in China's GDP, the share of Manufacturing was as high as 29.9 per cent in 2013.

➢ Manufacturing and World trade

In view of the above, there is dire need for India to step up the share of manufacturing which is the primary goal of 'Make in India' programme. Investments in physical infrastructure and human resources is crucial for attracting new enterprises in both manufacturing and service sectors to drive growth and job creation. But there is need for a word of caution here.

- While promoting domestic production, India should not revert to the policy of 'import substitution' followed in the initial years of planned development by raising barriers against imports or subsidising our products which will only undermine the gains from international trade.
- International trade enables a country to export products that it produces at the lowest cost and import those that the trading partners produce at the lowest cost which will be more beneficial for both countries. However, limited tariffs on certain products to promote domestic industry and ensure job creation can be justified provided productivity levels and quality of products are not compromised. India is following this policy in regard to electronic industry.
- Sustainability of services-led growth is another aspect to be kept in view. There is rapid growth in global trade in services in contrast to trade in goods. Services account for over 70 per cent of global output. A host of services which can be digitized are transportable, tradable and scalable. Globalization, digital revolution and expanding internet usage has helped to boost the growth of services across countries.
- But some of the countries are unwilling to allow free flow of services and manpower as found by India in negotiations under the Regional Comprehensive Economic Partnership (RCEP) trade agreement. The restrictions placed by the US on offshoring of services by Indian IT companies are also a pointer to this trend. India will have to overcome these challenges.

➢ Conclusion

The US-China trade war is causing major realignments in Global Value Chains (GVCs) and firms operating in China are now looking for alternative locations for their operations. Even before the trade war began, China's image as a low-cost location for final assembly of industrial products was rapidly changing due to labour shortages and increases in wages.

These developments present India an unprecedented opportunity to chart a similar export-oriented strategy, as was pursued by China, and create unparalleled job opportunities for its youth. As no other country can match China in the abundance of its labour, India must seize the opportunity and grab the space being vacated in labour-intensive sectors, even in the face of competition from Vietnam, Thailand, Indonesia, Philippines and Bangladesh.

5. Elucidate the role played by micro, small and medium industries in Indian economy. Examine the constraints faced by this sector and how they can be overcome.

Ans. The role of micro, small and medium enterprises (MSMEs) in the economic and social development of the country is well established. The MSME sector is a nursery of entrepreneurship, often driven by individual creativity and innovation

They have played a very significant role in India's economic progress during the post-independence era. From the very First Five-Year Plan, their importance for generating employment and income and broadening the industrial base has been recognized.

➢ **A diverse sector:** The Micro, Small and Medium Enterprises (MSMEs) covers diverse segments such as khadi, village and small industries, handlooms, power looms, handicrafts, coir industry, and sericulture.

They can be grouped into 'traditional' small industries which relied more on human skill, primitive tools, and manual power, and 'modern' small industries which use mechanical power and higher skills and better tools. Now food processing industry (FPI) is also part of this sector.

➢ **A vital segment, salient features:** As per the NSSO survey 2015-16, there was a total of 6.3 crore MSMEs in India, employing over 111 million persons. It is the second largest employer after agriculture. The sector accounts for 45 per cent of total industrial production, 40 per cent of total exports and contributes 30 per cent of the country's GDP.

- **Promotes entrepreneurship:** The MSMEs have been contributing significantly to the expansion of entrepreneurial endeavours through business innovations. They are widening their domain across sectors of the economy, producing diverse range of products and services to meet demands of domestic as well as global markets.
- **Micro units dominant:** The Micro sector with 630.52 lakh estimated enterprises accounts for more than 99 per cent of the total estimated number of MSMEs. Small sector accounts for only 3.31 lakh units and Medium sector with 0.05 lakh units.
- **Rural and Urban spread:** A notable feature is that the rural and the urban sector have almost equal number of these enterprises, with the rural sector having an even slightly larger number. Out of 633.88 MSMEs, 324.88 lakh (51.25%) are in rural areas and 309 lakh (48.75 per cent) in urban areas.

This is a significant aspect as these enterprises provide non-agricultural occupation to the rural population which also helps to prevent migration of rural populace to urban areas.

- **Promotional measures:** With its significant share in output, employment and exports, the government has been taking several measures to support and strengthen this vital sector.

  To provide more focused attention for its development, the Ministry of MSME and its attached organizations have launched several schemes and programmes to promote the sector. These include:

  - Adequate flow of credit from financial institutions and banks;
  - Support for technology upgradation and modernization;
  - Integrated infrastructural facilities;
  - Modern testing facilities and quality certification;
  - Access to modern management practices;
  - Entrepreneurship development and skill upgradation through appropriate training facilities;
  - Support for product development, design intervention and packaging;
  - Assistance for better access to domestic and export markets;
  - Cluster-wise measures to promote capacity-building and empowerment of the units and their collectives; and
  - Welfare measures for artisans and workers.

- **Industrial corridors and SMEs**

  - The five industrial corridors being developed – Delhi-Mumbai, Amritsar-Kolkata, Mumbai-Chennai, Bengaluru-Mumbai, Chennai-Bengaluru and Vizag-Chennai — will drive the growth of industries, supported by a network of multi-modal transport to demand centres, urban clusters, and international gateways.
  - Small and medium-sized enterprise (SME) development will also be a key priority within the corridor, with emphasis on developing supply chains to integrate SMEs. By clustering producers and suppliers in the same location, their regular interactions will be strengthened and domestic suppliers can observe the business models and practices used by global firms and suppliers.

- **MSMEs: Criteria changed**

  Hitherto, MSMEs were classified under the MSME Development Act, 2006 based on investment in plant and machinery in the case of enterprises engaged in Manufacturing, and investment in equipment for enterprises providing Services.

In May 2020, the government changed the criteria to recognize MSMEs based not only on their investments but also on their turnover. Also, the distinction that existed earlier between manufacturing and services units has been removed.

The revised norms are as follows.

(i) A unit with investment up to ₹ 1 crore and turnover up to ₹ 5 crore will qualify as a Micro enterprise.

(ii) A unit with investment up to ₹ 10 crore and turnover up to ₹ 50 crore will qualify as a Small enterprise.

(iii) A unit with investment up to ₹ 50 crore and turnover up to ₹ 250 crore will be a Medium enterprise.

The revised criteria came into effect from July 1, 2020.

The changes in the definition of MSMEs may result in many enterprises which were earlier classified as Small enterprises being reclassified as Micro, and those classified as Medium enterprises being reclassified as Small. Further, there may be many enterprises which were not hitherto classified as MSMEs, which may now fall under the MSME classification as per the new definition. Such enterprises will also now benefit from the various schemes related to MSMEs mentioned earlier.

➢ **Constraints faced by MSMEs:** *The Economic Survey for 2018-19* has done a detailed study of the MSME sector, its progress over the years and constraints which shackle them. It also makes a comparative study of firms that are small and large, and those that are young and aged (in existence for long). The following are the main findings of this study.

♦ **Small versus Large firms:** Firms that have continued to remain small and not grown are at a disadvantage compared to firms that are large or have grown in size over the years.

- MSMEs that grow over time not only create greater profits for their promoters but also contribute to job creation and productivity in the economy. The policies must, therefore, focus on enabling MSMEs to grow by unshackling them.
- Job creation in India, however, suffers from policies that foster small firms that never grow, because it is the infant firms (those newly set up and young and not old in age) that have the potential to grow and become giants rapidly.
- Even among the small firms, firms with less than 50 employees dominate in number but create the least jobs and remain the most unproductive. Thus, the contribution of small firms to output and employment in the manufacturing sector is insignificant though they constitute nearly 85 per cent of all firms.

- Firms that did not grow and remained small in size, dominates the Indian economy and holds back job creation and productivity.

♦ **Old and large firms:** Old, but large, firms (firms that have more than 100 employees and are more than 10 years old) account for only 10.2 per cent of firms by number, but contribute half of the employment as well as the value added. Thus, firms that are able to grow over time and become large are the biggest contributors to employment and productivity in the economy. In contrast, units that remain small, despite being older, contribute the least to employment and productivity in the economy.

♦ **Impact of SSI Reservation policy:** The Small-Scale Industries (SSI) reservation policy was introduced in 1967 to promote employment growth and income re-distribution. From 1997 to 2007, reservation for small-scale firms in respect of several product categories was eliminated

After the elimination of reservations, large firms – be it new entrants or incumbents – have created more employment than small firms. Among both new entrants and incumbents, the small firms destroyed jobs while the large firms created jobs.

♦ **Priority Sector Lending:** The guidelines under Priority Sector Lending (PSL) may be re-calibrated to direct credit flow to young firms in sectors, with high employment elasticity, which will help to accelerate employment generation. Focus must be on service sectors such as tourism, which has high spill-over effects on other sectors such as hotel & catering, transport, real estate, entertainment, etc. Identifying and promoting tourist spots for development will also help create jobs.

♦ **Adverse impact of labour laws:** India has a plethora of labour laws, regulations and rules, both at the centre and the state levels that govern the employer-employee relationship. These rigid labour laws create perverse incentives for firms to remain small.

  - Each of these legislations exempts smaller firms from complying with these laws.
  - For instance, the Industrial Disputes Act (IDA), 1947 requires companies to get permission from the Government before retrenching employees but this stipulation is applicable only to firms with more than 100 employees. Thus, firms with less than 100 employees are exempt from the need to get permission from the Government before retrenching their employees.

- As complying with such regulations entail transaction costs, naturally a large majority of firms would prefer to remain below the threshold of 100 employees and thus will continue to remain small.
- Deregulating labour law restrictions can create significantly more jobs, as seen by the recent changes in Rajasthan, when compared to the rest of the States. Rajasthan took steps to reform labour laws.

There is, therefore, need to put in place various policies that incentivise firms to grow in size over time, leverage economies of scale, become more productive and competitive and are able to create more jobs.

➢ **Challenges on the Export front:** Some of the challenges faced by this sector in exports are:

♦ Limited information about products and services in demand in various countries.

♦ Working of the foreign markets, and in particular, difficulties in accessing export distribution channels and in connecting with overseas customers.

♦ Lack of awareness on export promotion and assistance programmes offered by the government.

♦ Unfamiliarity with legal and regulatory frameworks of the exporting and importing countries. Lack of awareness on Intellectual Property Rights (IPR) issues and various International Trade Agreements (ITAs).

➢ **Measures to boost Exports:** With MSMEs accounting for 40 per cent of total exports of India, providing adequate support to them is of critical importance.

Besides the schemes and programmes launched by the Ministry of MSME mentioned earlier, the government has announced Nirvik (Niryat Rin Vikas Yojana) scheme to provide enhanced insurance cover and reduce premium for small exporters. The scheme will expand the scope of export credit and it will offer high insurance cover. This will enable reduction in overall cost of export credit, including interest rates speciality to the MSMEs.

To improve marketability overseas, the National Small Industries Corporation (NSIC) extends the following facilities to MSME exporters:

- Helps in material testing and product design;
- Provides information about the changing pattern of fashions / tastes in the international market and about the trends in exports and potential for export;
- Exploring new avenues for their products and help to adopt new business practices;
- To seize market opportunities, NSIC participates in selected International Exhibitions and also facilitates the participation of small enterprises in such exhibitions;

- Acts as an incubator for prospective entrepreneurs and start-ups in small enterprises sector;
- Provides Information Technology support;
- Organises Tech Marts in collaboration with the Asia and Pacific Centre for Transfer of Technology and also helps SSI units in technology transfer from abroad through the Technology Transfer Centre. An Internet portal has been set up for sourcing technologies from international partner institutions.

➢ **Conclusion:** MSMEs are complementary to large industries as ancillary units and this sector contributes significantly in the inclusive industrial development of the country. They are widening their domain across sectors of the economy, producing diverse range of products and services to meet demands of domestic as well as global markets. Considering their potential for generating employment, an eco-system needs to be created in such a way that these enterprises shall be able to integrate in the Global Value Chain (GVC) on their own and attain adequate economies of scale. (For more on MSMEs, see item 13 in Part 2 of Appendix).

6. Examine the role played by the logistics sector in Indian economy. What are the constraints faced by it and what measures have been taken by the government to overcome them? Suggest further steps needed to improve this sector.

Ans. The existence of a robust logistics system that facilitates seamless movement of goods is essential for an economy's development. The logistics industry is the backbone of the economy on which other commercial sectors depend for efficient and cost effective flow of goods.

♦ **Logistics sector in India:** This sector in India has been evolving rapidly due to improved infrastructure, adoption of technology and new types of service providers. The sector is dominated by transportation, which has over 85 per cent share in value terms while warehousing has 15 per cent share.

This sector provides livelihood to 22 million-plus people. The industry is projected to be worth $215 billion by 2020-21, recording a 10 per cent compounded annual growth rate (CGAR) over about $160 billion in 2016-17.

♦ **Infrastructure status:** In 2017, in a major push to developing an integrated logistics framework including industrial parks, cold chains and warehousing facilities, the government granted "Infrastructure status" to the logistics sector, enabling it to access cheaper finances.

This move enables the logistics sector to access infrastructure lending at easier terms with enhanced limits, larger amounts of funds as external commercial borrowings (ECB), longer tenor funds from insurance companies and pension funds and also make it eligible to borrow from the India Infrastructure Financing Co. Ltd (IIFCL).

- **Significant growth:** The rapid growth of the sector has been fuelled by the following factors, including various proactive measures taken by the government.
  - The sector has got fillip from the growth of industry and services sectors, emergence of skilled professionals.
  - Strides in manufacturing, retail, fast-moving consumer goods (FMCG) and e-commerce sectors.
  - Development of logistics-related infrastructure, like dedicated freight corridors, logistics parks, free trade warehousing zones and container freight stations.
  - In 2017, the task of "Integrated development of Logistics sector" was allocated to the Dept. of Commerce with the mandate to draw up an Action Plan to effect policy changes, improve the existing procedures, identify bottlenecks and induct technology in the sector.
  - The 2018-19 budget announced a scheme of "Operation Greens" on the lines of "Operation Flood" to promote Farmer Producers Organizations (FPOs), agri-logistics, processing facilities and professional management. A sum of Rs. 500 crore was allocated for this purpose. Besides, a plan to develop logistics parks and a National Logistics Portal, to be set up by the Dept. of Commerce to serve as a "single window online marketplace" to link all stakeholders, was also announced.
  - Ministry of Road Transport & Highways (MoRTH) had a detailed scientific study conducted about the movement of goods from production to consumption centres across the country and this report provided necessary inputs for the development of the sector.
  - MoRTH also signed MoU with States for setting up of 35 Logistics parks where land will be owned by the States, and connectivity to nearby ports and consumption centres will be provided by MoRTH and Railways.
  - Logistics sector required multi-skilled personnel for which the Dept. of Skill Development & Entrepreneurship has initiated several measures in cooperation with sector Skill Council.
- **Logistics sector and GST**
  - The introduction of GST regime has been of great benefit to the logistics sector. For decades, the transport and logistics sector was designed and structured based on the state taxation system which made it inefficient and cumbersome. With GST, the scenario has undergone much change. The entire transport and

logistics infrastructure has become more competitive not only within India but in global markets also.

- **Drawbacks in the old system:** For this sector, the concern was not so much about the rates of taxation or mode of collection of taxes but speedy movement of goods across the length and breadth of the country traversing thousands of miles.
- The delays and hazards faced by personnel manning containers, trucks and lorries in covering long distances due to the condition of roads and highways, traffic bottlenecks, toll gates, etc. were exacerbated by delays and harassment caused at border check points and octroi posts. Such delays resulted in substantial wastage of time, labour and money and consequent delays in turnaround of vehicles and productivity losses for both manpower and vehicles.
- The inter-state taxation system required companies to set up and maintain warehouses in each state, which made the supply chain longer and inefficient. With such a complex structure and convoluted tax system, the logistics industry spent nearly 50 to 60 percent of its time in tax compliance, interstate check points manoeuvring, scrutiny and tracking of inter-state sales tax.
- Unlike in the earlier regime, the manufacturer or supplier does not require a warehouse in each state, tranship goods at multiple warehouses for supply to the distributors at final destinations. This will lead to consolidation and economies of scale in logistical operations.

♦ **India improves in global ranking:** In the last few years, this sector has witnessed significant development which is reflected in the global rankings. According to the World Bank's 2016 Logistics Performance Index, India moved up to 35th rank in 2016 from 54th rank in 2014 in terms of overall logistics performance. This indicates progress in Customs, Infrastructure, International shipments, Logistics competence, Tracking & tracing, Timeliness of delivery – areas that are benchmarked with other countries.

♦ **Constraints:** Despite various steps taken to improve the logistics sector, it still faces challenges as detailed below.

- **Logistics costs:** Logistics costs in India are high at 13 to14 per cent of GDP compared to 8 to 9 per cent in developed countries. The lead time for export and import is also very high in India. The high logistics cost reduces the competitiveness of Indian goods both in domestic as well as export market.
- **Post-Harvest Losses:** In India, the annual value of harvest and post-harvest losses of major agricultural produce was estimated to be of the order of Rs. 92,651 crore, calculated based on production data of 2012-13 and wholesale

prices of 2014. There is need to set up more cold chains and warehousing facilities to bring down such wastages.

- **Lack of skilled manpower:** Lack of skilled manpower due to inadequate training and proper leadership and support impacts efficiency. The sector needs to specifically build a pool of personnel comprising truck drivers, seafarers, warehousing managers, quality inspection supervisors, among others. There are not enough institutes for soft skills, operational and technical training.
- **Slow adoption of technology:** Awareness about the economic benefits of using digital technology is low. As a result, the logistics ecosystem is fraught with operational inefficiencies and poor asset utilization. There is need for greater collaboration among stakeholders on this.
- **Land issues:** Obstacles in land acquisition and consolidation, and changes in land use continue to be major impediments. This retards development of infrastructural facilities.
- **Unorganized sector:** Due to the unorganized nature of the sector, which is characterized by poor working conditions and low pay scale, it is not a preferred choice among skilled personnel.
- **Performance Standards:** With a diverse customer base, there are diverse consumer expectations. Both individual and corporate customers demand personalized services, flexibility and faster services. There is a need for standardized services, transparency and time-bound compliance to meet requisite performance standards. Logistics service providers need to align their strategy with the targeted customer segments.

♦ **Conclusion:** Integrated development of the logistics sector is essential for improving the overall logistics performance of the country. It will give a boost to performance in both the domestic and export markets. The crucial test for the sector is whether it is able to provide smooth and cost-effective services help its customers reduce their operational costs while maintaining efficiency.

(On this see also Question 4 in Chapter 10 on Multimodal Transport on Page 10.15)

7. What were the factors which helped India to become a major player in the Information Technology (IT) sector at the global level? Assess the strengths of this sector and challenges confronting it.

Ans. Information technology became one of the premier segments of the services sector of Indian economy from the 1990s. It not only helped to generate millions of jobs but was able to garner a sizeable share of global exports and place India on the global map for its tech prowess.

- **India's strength in IT and ITeS sector**

  India's performance in the IT and IT-enabled services has grown from strength to strength over the years. According to a Nasscom, the industry's apex body, the software services and products sector generated US$105 billion revenue over a decade from 2009 to 2019, created 2 million jobs and added 10,000 companies, including start-ups.

  The resilient IT sector generated a whopping US$191 billion in fiscal 2019-20. The IT-BPM (Business Process Management) sector grew 7.7 per cent to $191 billion, including $147billion in exports and hired 205,000 people during fiscal 2019-20.

- **Employment**

  - In addition to being one of the largest job provider and creator in the organized industry segment, this sector also plays a key role in enabling higher levels of indirect employment in other verticals such as transportation, real estate and hospitality, security services, and housekeeping.
  - Total direct employment in the sector which stood at 3.267 million (mn.) in 2013-14 rose to 3.968 mn. In 2017-18.
  - A notable feature is that the IT/ITeS workforce is becoming increasingly diverse in terms of socio-economic, linguistic, multinational and regional backgrounds.
  - Out of total of 3.968 million employees in the sector in 2017-18, women employees constituted 34 per cent which is significant.

- **India's strategic advantages**

  India had several strategic advantages which helped her to secure a premier position in the global IT industry. The following factors helped India to forge ahead in the sector.

  - **Early entrant:** India was an early entrant in this domain and has continued to maintain its first mover advantage and retained its leadership position in the global sourcing arena with a share of 55 per cent.
  - **Skills and Start-ups:** India developed and honed the IT skills and formed many start-ups, which with their technical expertise, innovative, and entrepreneurial capabilities have captured much of the overseas business. These companies steadily grew into large enterprises and earned global fame for their impeccable performance and excellence in service delivery.
  - **Proficiency in English:** India's skilled, English-speaking technical personnel, and relatively low-cost operations, helped to attract much of the outsourced business from abroad.
  - **Technology competence:** India also showed prowess in technology development and innovation as a result of which some of the major MNCs

set up not only their offices in India, but even R&D centres in Bengaluru, Hyderabad, etc.

- **Telecom expansion:** The opening up of the telecom sector, following reforms of 1990s, led to phenomenal expansion of the telecom facilities. The introduction of broadband and rapid growth in mobile services gave fillip to the IT sector. This also coincided with the rapid development of the software industry, IT-based automation in various industries, development of supercomputer technology, etc.
- **Sourcing destination:** India was the leading sourcing destination across the world, accounting for approximately 55 per cent market share of the US$ 185-190 billion global services sourcing business in 2017-18. Indian IT & ITeS companies have set up over 1,000 global delivery centres in about 80 countries across the world.
- **Potential market:** India also remains a high potential market worldwide, offering multiple opportunities. With the world's second largest population, 1189 million mobile subscribers, 494 million Internet users, a US$ 38.5 billion e-Commerce market, India offers a large, burgeoning end-user market which will further propel the IT industry.
- **Digital India scheme:** The Digital India programme launched by the government, which is designed to transform India into a knowledge-based economy and a digitally empowered society, will give further boost to this sector. The National Optical Fibre Network (NOFN) under BharatNet is envisaged as an information super-highway which will provide broadband connectivity and digital access to 2.5 lakh Gram Panchayats. Over 3 lakh km. optical fibre cable has been laid by 2019-20 connecting 1.21 lakh Gram Panchayats.

➤ **Challenges faced by IT sector**

- **Offshoring issue:** The transfer of work and jobs to India and other countries, causing loss of job opportunities to the citizens in the US and Europe has been a major issue. The major threat is from the US which provides sizeable chunk of the outsourced business to Indian IT companies. Consequently, many of the major Indian IT firms have set up offices in the US and Europe to undertake the jobs onshore and, to the extent possible, employing locals.
- **Visa restrictions:** The US has also been placing quantitative restrictions on the number of visas issued to personnel from different countries to be stationed in the US by overseas IT firms, and this has impacted India which has a major share of business in the US. The US has also raised the Visa charges as a restrictive measure, to discourage IT firms from engaging foreign personnel for jobs in the US.

- **Competition:** India is also facing competition from other emerging countries like China, Philippines, Vietnam, countries of the Commonwealth of Independent States (CIS), South Korea, etc. who are also trying to grab the global IT business. Many of those countries which were not proficient in English have taken steps to overcome this deficiency. India would have to plan strategies for retaining competitive advantage in terms of pricing, skills, and efficiency in service delivery.

- **Insourcing:** After nearly two decades of outsourcing back-office operations and software projects to Indian IT firms, some of the transnational companies have been shifting the work – software development, programming, maintenance, etc. – back to their own offices to get the jobs done in-house. This will mean more productive use of their personnel.

- **Global Slowdown:** Amidst the current global economic slowdown, hiring companies are also forced to cut their IT spending. The increasing competition among IT companies will put pressure on prices and margins. This is bound to impact the profit margins of Indian IT companies. Automation and digitisation in IT sector could help to bring down operating costs.

➢ **Outlook for future**

- **Dispersal of IT units:** Until recently, India's IT industry was mostly concentrated in the large Metros, viz., Bengaluru, Hyderabad, Chennai, New Delhi, and Mumbai which are almost saturated.

  As these cities are bursting at the seams, with consequent problems of land availability, overcrowding, transportation bottlenecks, housing shortages, and rising costs both for the employers and employees, the IT companies have been moving towards Tier-II and Tier-III cities and towns which could mitigate some of these problems.

  This is a healthy trend as it will provide greater opportunities to potential job seekers in the smaller towns and help upgrade their skills. It will also give fillip to development of these towns and their hinterland areas supported by the Digital India programme.

- **Digital transformation:** A key trend witnessed now is the prominence of digital technologies and systems. There is continued focus on digital revenues, which is growing at a steady pace. Indian enterprises have spent over US$ 2 billion domestically to accelerate digital transformation.

- **Skills programme:** Investment in digital skills continues to rise with organisations building their capabilities and aligning business models to digital practices.

Nasscom has launched a Future Skills platform that seeks to initially upskill 40 lakh IT employees and prospective job seekers in eight emerging technologies that could drive IT jobs in the future.

These technologies include Artificial Intelligence (AI), virtual reality, robotics, process automation, Internet of Things (IoT), big data analytics, 3D printing, cloud computing. Nasscom has also identified 55 job roles that are going to be in high demand globally.

Nasscom and Ministry of Electronics & IT will work together to enable "skill development and continuous learning" not only for IT employees but also for those in the other sectors.

➢ **Conclusion:** The IT industry remains a key catalyst for the country's overall growth, with increasing focus on the digital transformation of businesses and expansion of digital-driven services to enterprises the world over.

To keep pace with the advances in technology, the industry is embracing disruptive technologies such as artificial intelligence (AI), machine learning (ML), cloud computing and big data analytics leading to substantial increase in digital revenue.

8. India is building a series of Industrial corridors. Mention which are these corridors and examine how they will benefit Indian economy.

Ans. Building a network of Industrial Corridors is a flagship programme of Government of India to significantly enhance India's competitiveness in manufacturing through the creation of world class infrastructure and reduced logistics costs. The project aims to create smart, sustainable industrial cities by leveraging high speed, high capacity connectivity between cities and towns along the corridor and areas around them.

Five corridors: Five industrial corridor projects have been identified, planned and launched by the Government of India. The five corridors and their lengths are:

- Delhi-Mumbai Industrial Corridor (DMIC) – 1504 kms.
- Bengaluru- Mumbai Economic Corridor (BMEC) – 1,000 kms.
- Chennai-Bengaluru Industrial Corridor (CBIC) – 560 kms.
- Vizag-Chennai Industrial Corridor (VCIC) – 800 kms., and
- Amritsar-Kolkata Industrial Corridor (AKIC) – 1,839 kms.

➢ **Facilities proposed:** These corridors will provide for industrial and commercial areas, warehousing and container depots, townships for housing and residential complexes, rental factories, social infrastructure like schools, technical institutions, hospitals etc., management of city utilities, renewable energy development, components for Smart cities like sewage and effluent treatment plants, and scientific waste management facilities.

- **Objectives**
  - These corridors, spread across India, with strategic focus on inclusive development, aims to provide a boost to industrialization and planned urbanization.
  - By creating manufacturing clusters with ancillary industries, it will accelerate the growth of Micro, Small and Medium enterprises (MSMEs) which will provide more employment opportunities.
  - With freight corridors also coming up along the routes, and being well connected by road, rail, air and sea, it will speed up transportation and help to reduce freight and logistic costs.
  - Promoting manufacturing is a key economic driver in each of these projects and they are expected to play a critical role in raising the share of the manufacturing sector in GDP from the current16 per cent to 25 per cent by 2025.
  - It will give a boost to "Make In India" programme.
  - They will lure investment and accentuate industrialisation of India.
  - The corridors will ring-fence fertile agricultural land for industrial use, and thus benefit both sectors.
  - The Smart cities, with state-of-the-art infrastructure, will house the new workforce required to power manufacturing.
- **Implementation:** The projects are in various stages of implementation. The crucial part is land acquisition, ensuring environmental clearance and arranging the finances. Foreign governments and aid agencies have evinced interest and are collaborating in these projects.

  These five projects pass through several states, as mentioned below, and will result in holistic and sustainable development of cities, towns and hinterland areas around them.

  - **Delhi-Mumbai corridor: DMIC** is one of the world's largest infrastructure projects and is expected to fetch $90 billion investment. Six states, viz., Uttar Pradesh, Haryana, Madhya Pradesh, Gujarat, Rajasthan and Maharashtra, have formed Special Purpose Vehicles (SPVs) for the development of DMIC's nodes.

    DMIDC has been registered as a company with 49 per cent equity of the Government of India, 26 per cent equity of the Japan Bank for International Cooperation (JBIC) and the remaining is held by government financial institutions.
  - **Amritsar-Kolkata Industrial Corridor (AKIC)**: This will cover seven states, viz., Punjab, Haryana, Uttar Pradesh, Uttarakhand, Bihar, Jharkhand and West Bengal. It will give a boost to industrial development in the densely populated

states of Northern and Eastern India. This project is structured around the Eastern Dedicated Freight Corridor (EDFC) and the highway system that exists in this route. The AKIC will also leverage the Inland Water System being developed along National Waterway-1 which extends from Allahabad to Haldia.

- **Bengaluru-Mumbai Economic Corridor (BMEC):** This project will facilitate development of a well-planned and resource-efficient industrial base served by world-class, sustainable connectivity infrastructure, bringing significant benefits in terms of innovation, manufacturing, job creation and resource security to Maharashtra and Karnataka..
- **Chennai-Bengaluru Industrial Corridor (CBIC):** This Industrial Corridor will have priority nodes at Tumakuru (Karnataka), Ponneri (Tamil Nadu) and Krishnapatnam (Andhra Pradesh), It will address the infrastructure bottlenecks in the region while benefiting from the inherent strengths and competitiveness of each of the three states.
- **Vizag-Chennai Industrial Corridor (VCIC):** This will be India's first coastal corridor covering about 800 kms and will form the East Coast Economic Corridor (ECEC). The key idea behind it is port-based industrial development along the eastern coastal belt of India, in alignment with the "Sagarmala" initiative, and integration of India's industrial clusters with value chains extending to Southeast Asia and East Asia.

  This project includes policy reforms to support development of a major hub port on the eastern coast of India and a major air cargo hub at Chennai, streamlining of customs procedures and removal of protective measures in road freight markets and the establishment of Free Trade and Warehousing Zones.

  The successful development of ECEC is also critical to India's Act East Policy, which focuses on the integration of the Indian economy with the economies of the Association of the Southeast Asian Nations (ASEAN).

  The Asian Development Bank (ADB) has extended loans and grants for the infrastructural development along the VCIC.

Benefits

Apart from the beneficial aspects mentioned above, such as industrial and manufacturing growth, large-scale employment opportunities and vast improvements in infrastructure, these Industrial Corridors will confer other benefits to the Indian economy.

- With improved transportation and logistical facilities, it would make Indian manufactures competitive and give fillip to exports.
- With China facing challenges on multiple fronts, including rising labour costs and trade disputes with the US, and firms in China looking for alternate locations, India could seize the opportunity. The setting up of industrial

corridors could lure foreign companies to come to India.

- The corridors would have institutionalised set-up with single-window agencies that can cut through inter-state issues and help businesses to be set up seamlessly.
- India imports about $300 billion worth of capital and consumer goods, and if 80 per cent of it is produced in India, it will create massive job opportunities and investment prospects. The corridors will become catalyst in this process.
- India's integration with neighbouring countries and South-east Asia, which these projects will facilitate, has immense political and strategic ramifications in the context of India's growing stature and increasing role in the global arena, especially in the Indo-Pacific region.

➢ **Conclusion**

It is important to note that these economic corridors are a function of much more than mere physical infrastructure and geographical connectivity. While the services sector has driven India's growth in the last two decades, going forward, the manufacturing sector must be the engine of growth and job creation, and play a critical role by participating in global supply chains.

While building physical capital is an important aspect of corridor development, the vision must encompass appropriate policy reforms and critical interventions to reduce the costs of doing business by creating an enabling environment for logistics and other ancillary business services.

9. What are the main features of the 'Startup India' mission launched by the Government of India? Critically examine how successful the programme has been.

Ans. Though the Indian start-up ecosystem has been evolving since over a decade and a half, it was still undeveloped and had not matured. Only a few investors were active and the support system such as incubators and accelerators was limited.

The start-up movement got a fillip when the "Startup India" mission was launched by the government of India in 2016 with the primary objective of tapping in a systemic way the entrepreneurial potential and talent, particularly among the youth who are driven by an idea or an urge to solve a problem. It was intended to catalyse start-up culture and build a strong and inclusive ecosystem for innovation and entrepreneurship in India.

The start-up India programme has rolled out several programs with the objective of supporting entrepreneurs, building up a robust start up ecosystem and transforming India into a country of job creators instead of job seekers. Apart from, or even more than, earning money, start-up innovators are often driven by a sense of compassion and desire to contribute to society.

➢ **Salient features**

- Under the scheme, eligible companies can get recognized by the Department for Promotion of Industry and Internal Trade (DPIIT) as Start-Ups in order to access a host of tax benefits, easier compliance, IPR fast tracking and other benefits.
- An entity shall be considered as Start-up up to a period of ten years from the date of incorporation/registration, with an annual turnover not exceeding ₹ 100 crore for any of the financial years since incorporation/ registration.
- For providing fund support for Start-ups, government created a 'Fund of Funds for Start-ups' (FFS) at Small Industries Development Bank of India (SIDBI) with a corpus of ₹ 10,000 crore to establish incubators and introduce self-certification.
- According to DPIIT, by March 2019, 17,390 start-ups had been recognized under the programme across 499 districts in 29 States and 6 Union Territories.
- As per employment data reported by 15,478 start-ups, 1.77 lakh jobs had been created with average number of 11 employees per start-up.

➢ **Steps taken by the government to nurture Start-up ecosystem**

♦ **Tax Incentives:** The Finance Act, 2016 made a provision for Start-ups (Companies and LLPs) to get income tax exemption for 3 years in a block of 5 years, if they are incorporated between 1st April 2016 and 31st March 2019. To avail these benefits, a Start-up had to get a Certificate of Eligibility from the Inter-Ministerial Board.

♦ **Credit Guarantee Fund for Start-ups**: Since debt funding for Start-ups is perceived as high risk activity, a Credit Guarantee Fund for Star-ups was set up with a budgetary corpus of ₹ 500 crore per year, for four years, to provide credit guarantee cover to banks and lending institutions providing loans to Start-ups.

♦ **Investment Clearance Cell:** To promote entrepreneurship, the Union budget for 2020-21 has proposed to set up Investment Clearance Cell that will provide, through a portal, "end to end" facilitation and support, including pre-investment advisory, information related to land banks, incentive schemes and taxation policies of states and centre, and facilitate clearances at Centre and State level.

♦ **Public Procurement:** A Government-e-Marketplace (GeM) is set up to serve as an online procurement platform for government ministries and departments where MSMEs, recognised start-ups and other private companies can register as sellers and sell their products and services directly to government entities. Further, in public procurement, norms pertaining to prior experience/turnover have been relaxed in the case of MSMEs and Start-ups. Start-up India portal allows registered Start-ups seamless connectivity to GeM Portal.

♦ **Ease of application:** To further the ease of application, Start-ups are not required to submit investor income and net worth details. Keeping confidentiality of investor tax returns and net worth certificate in mind, the investors can directly upload these details on the DPIIT portal.

- **Legal Support and Fast-tracking Patent:** Facilitators have been formed to provide legal guidance and handholding to Start-ups through the entire patent acquisition process, free of cost. A scheme for IPR Protection, which provides for expedited examination of patents filed by Start-ups, is put in place for fast-track filing of Patents, Trademarks and Designs by Start-ups who are also eligible for rebate in patent and trademark filing fees.
- **Self-certification based Compliance regime:** To reduce the regulatory burden on Start-ups thereby allowing them to focus on their core business and keep compliance costs low, the Ministry of Environment and Forests has prepared a list of "white category" industries. Start-ups under this category can self-certify compliance in respect of certain Environment Acts.

  Further, the Ministry of Labour and Employment has issued guidelines to State Governments whereby Start-ups are to be allowed to self-certify compliance in respect of certain Labour laws for a period of 5 years
- **Incubators and Tinkering Labs:** Under Atal Innovation Mission (AIM), NITI Aayog is setting up Atal Incubation Centres (AICs) in both public and private sector, and they are provided requisite funds. Besides, to promote entrepreneurship at the grassroots levels, schools have been selected for establishing Atal Tinkering Labs (ATLs) which are provided with Rs. 12 lakh each.
- **Research Parks:** Research Parks are being set up to propel innovation through incubation and joint R&D efforts between academia and industry. 8 Research Parks are being setup at IITs under Start-up India initiative. Of this, 7 Research Parks have been setup and sanctioned funds. Besides, Bio-incubators, Technology transfer officers and bio-connect officers are being established in research institutes and universities across India.

Opportunities and Challenges facing Start-ups

Opportunities

- **Demographic dividend**: India has a high percentage of youth population which augurs well for the country. With proper education, skilling and healthcare, the youth can lead the economy on a high trajectory. Skilled youth can provide the talent that start-ups need and they can be the driving force behind innovation.
- **Large domestic market:** India, with over a billion people, presents a very large home market for goods or services. Increasing disposable income and growing aspirations of a vast middle class will lead to ever-increasing demand. Start-ups can tap this potential with innovative ideas and products and finding solutions to various problems.
- **Emerging countries' challenges:** India faces a unique set of problems in health, education, infrastructure, sanitation, etc. which are akin to the problems faced by most of the developing and less developed countries in Asia and Africa. And with a large educated and technically qualified workforce, India is ideally placed to develop solutions for problems in these areas which can be replicated in other countries. Indian Start-ups could work on solutions in these domains in conjunction with the academia and industry.

- **IT and Mobile penetration:** Compared to other developing countries, India has an edge in information technology, mobile and internet penetration. These advantages can be leveraged by Start-ups. Given the size of India, the scale of her problems and resource constraints, low-cost, high-impact solutions are required. Technology start-ups could play a crucial role in accomplishing this, because of their potential for scalability and exponential growth.
- **Potential for Start-ups in IT sector:** Nasscom, the apex body of IT industry, expects that the future of the sector lies in 'Digital at Scale' as global digital spending is growing at 20 per cent annually. India's digital revenues have been growing at a healthy pace, demonstrating the base for a solid foundation in digital capabilities built by the sector. The software and services industry has tripled in size in less than a decade. The growth of the B2B start-up sector represents a unique opportunity for India to build innovative digital solutions for India and the world.
- **Hardware start-ups:** To nurture the growing start-up ecosystem in the country, IT industry body Nasscom, has launched TechMarch, an initiative to provide mentorship, investment and partnership opportunities to start-ups. The initiative invites applications from "smart hardware" start-ups. Tech March will provide strong support to the hardware innovators in the country and help them grow in an efficient and proficient way. This initiative will build robust smart hardware space in India which can compete at a global level.

❖ Challenges

- **Starting and funding Start-up:** For operating a start-up, a significant amount of working capital is required. Many start-ups, being self-funded through own savings of founders, or using capital from friends and family, face funds crunch, especially in the initial stages. In many cases, finding the right investor and raising funds is found to be difficult, even when their product has had a positive response from the market.

  However, there has been some positive development as more capital has become available in recent years. Some of the Indian cities have seen high growth rates in venture capital deals. Overall, Indian start-ups have been able to raise sizeable funds in the last few years.
- **Building a team:** Building a cohesive team suited for the vision of the start-up poses a challenge. For many job-seekers, joining a start-up is not an attractive career option, due to the inherent risk that the start-up might not take off. Highly qualified persons prefer to work for large corporations or established companies, which provide better job security. In scouting for talent, start-ups have to compete with reputed firms and also may not be able to offer comparable compensation. Further, when technologies are changing at a fast pace, if the recruits are not adequately skilled, start-ups have to invest in training them which costs both time and money.
- **Regulatory environment:** Though the governments, both at centre and state levels, have been making efforts to ease the burden for businesses in

general and start-ups in particular, the extant regulatory framework in which start-ups operate is still complex and unpredictable. The World Bank Ease of Doing Business index (though it covers only Mumbai and Delhi) still ranks India only 77th out of 190 countries.

Start-ups in India often feel encumbered by bureaucratic processes, which appear to lack predictable standards and norms. They have insufficient possibilities to get information, and there is little certainty about how long processes and approvals would take. In addition, regulations could suddenly change and start-ups get random notices. As a result, start-ups have to face frustrating workarounds, wasting valuable time which impacts their business venture.

- **Failures and closures:** There have been failures among start-ups and many had to be closed down. The challenges faced by Indian start-ups begin with hiring and managing a team, dealing with customers, and developing a marketing strategy. Most of the start-ups in India fail within the initial few years of inception. This results in a cautious mood in the market, with venture capitalists and angel investors taking a step back from further investments and funding. Even with government support in funding and mentoring, not all businesses can survive unless the venture itself takes off and is successful in a highly competitive market. Choosing a right business proposition and translating it into a successful venture is in itself a challenge.

Conclusion

The performance of Indian start-ups presents a mixed picture. While there have been quite a few entities which have done exceptionally well, there have been many cases of failures and they had to be wound up. As the first generation of Indian entrepreneurs have learnt from their mistakes and experiences, more knowledge has become available in the ecosystem. Some of the founders eventually became successful and inspired more to follow their entrepreneurial steps. Moreover, a sense of community among the people in the start-up ecosystem has emerged over time. Overall, the Indian ecosystem has now attained a certain size and maturity, and support has increased significantly in all dimensions.

> The final problem of the productive society is what it produces. This manifests itself in an implacable tendency to provide an opulent supply of some things and a niggardly yield of others..........The schools are old and overcrowded. ... The parks and playgrounds are insufficient... Streets and empty lots are filthy, and the sanitation staff is underequipped. Internal transportation is overcrowded, unhealthful and dirty.
>
> In most of the last thirty years, the discussion of this public poverty was matched by the stories of ever-increasing opulence in privately produced goods.
>
> - John K. Galbraith (1908 - 2006), economist on unchecked consumerism in the US in the first half of the 20th century.
>
> - in The Theory of Social Balance in *The Affluent Society (1958)*.

INFRASTRUCTURE

India faced four major challenges in 1994, and they remain the main challenges a decade later, albeit in somewhat less acute form. First, the reforms needed to be extended. Liberalization had begun, but the key sectors of the Indian economy remained hamstrung by the systems put in place a half century earlier. Second, India needed to invest heavily in basic infrastructure - roads, ports, power, water and sanitation, telecommunications - to reduce production costs and deepen India's integration domestically and with world markets. Third, India needed to invest much more in the health and education of its own people.........Fourth, India needed to figure out how to pay for the infrastructure and social investments, since by 1994 the budget was in a perilous state, with large deficits both at the central (union) government as well as the state levels.

- Jeffrey Sachs, Economist, *The End of Poverty* (2005).

Topics Covered

- *Importance of infrastructure*
- *Development of Highway projects*
- *Deficiencies in India's infrastructure*
- *Multimodal transport system*
- *Waterways and Coastal shipping in Indian economy*
- *Public Private Projects (PPPs) – Issues in Public Private Projects in India*
- *Telecom sector, the opportunities and challenges*
- *Spectrum allocation and pricing*
- *Power sector progress and reforms*
- *Rural electrification and its benefits*
- *Renewable power and Climate change*
- *State of Discoms*
- *Infrastructure and Employment.*

1. Explain the role and importance of infrastructure in economy. Do you think inadequacies and deficiencies in infrastructure hampered India's development? Explain with cogent reasons.

Ans. Infrastructure, which consists of a country's physical facilities such as roads and bridges, railways, ports, airports, power plants, communication facilities, etc., is critical for socio-economic development of a country.

- **Role of infrastructure:** The role and importance of infrastructure cannot be overemphasized. While agriculture, industry and services are important and integral parts of an economy, infrastructure is another important cog in the wheels on which any economy moves. No other sector can develop and contribute to their fullest potential unless infrastructure is well developed. An efficient and well-developed system of transport and communications is vital for the success of plans which lays stress on rapid industrialization.

  A decrepit transport system, malfunctioning electricity grids, outdated and inefficient telecom networks, and above all, a cumbersome red tape will have a crippling effect on productivity and competitiveness of various sectors. Power outages hurt factory productivity. Bad roads, ports and airports stifle the movement of people and goods, and smooth flow of services. Inadequate water and sanitation facilities prevent millions from leading healthy, productive lives.

  Apart from slowing economic growth, poor infrastructure also limits the investment needed to create the jobs that help to lift people out of poverty.

- **India's infrastructure:** One of the major drawbacks and hindrances in India's developmental efforts has been the poor state of her infrastructure. India's roadways – both in cities, towns, and villages as well as the highways – have been notorious for their poor standards and maintenance, though the highways are being built to international standards in the last two decades which is a major step forward. The railways, though one of the largest networks in the world and has expanded and progressed a great deal over the years, still suffers from many infirmities.

  But in order to ensure high and sustainable growth, there has been a substantial step up of investment in infrastructure in the last three decades, mostly on transportation, energy, communication, housing and sanitation and urban infrastructure sector. As a result, there has been substantial and perceptible improvement in highways, ports and airports, telecommunications and power sectors.

- **Infrastructure expansion:** The exponential growth in some of the core sectors in the last three decades can be seen from data below:

Roadways	**1991**	**2019**
National Highways/Expressways	33,650 km	1,32,500 km
State Highways	1,27,311 km	1,56,694 km
Other Roads	21,66,401 km	56,08,477 km
Total	**23,27,362 km**	**58,97,671 km**
Electricity	**1991**	**2020 (Jan.)**
Total Installed Capacity	74,700 MW	3,67,281 MW
Telecom		
No. of Phones	36.01 million (2000)	1197.8 million (2018)
Tele-density (per 100	0.52 (1988)	91.90 (2017)

Investment in Infrastructure

Over the years, there has been massive under-investment in infrastructure sector until when the focus shifted to invest more on infrastructure. The investment was far below the requirements of India's expanding economy. There were many factors behind the shortfall in investment such as inadequate financial resources, issues related to land & forest clearances, long gestation periods in getting returns on investment which kept private investment away, and lack of Public Private Partnership (PPP) especially in power and telecom projects. Stressed balance sheet of private companies and banks due to rising non-performing assets (NPAs) also deterred investment.

Highways: The ambitious Golden Quadrilateral project, launched in 2001, to link the four Metros cities with four/six-lane highways and further extension of these corridors, proved to be the turning point. National Highways (NH) came to be built to international standards which also gave a boost to the logistics sector by faster movement of goods and passenger traffic. It also benefited hinterland areas – towns and villages – along the NH routes.

Rural roads: Equally significant was the PM's Gram Sadak Yojana (PMGSY) started in 2000 to link rural habitations with a certain population with the nearby town through all-weather roads. About 1.67 lakh 'Unconnected Habitations' were eligible for coverage under the programme. This project has helped to revitalise the rural economy.

Telecom: Another major development were the reforms since the 1990s in the Telecom sector which opened it to the private sector leading to exponential growth and increased accessibility of telephone facilities, especially mobile telephony, to the masses. This development coincided with India's rise and dominance in the Information Technology (IT) sector which helped to raise India's standing on the global scene.

Other sectors: In the following years, there was thrust on modernisation of railways, ports and airports giving a boost to these sectors.

Steps taken by Government

- **NIIF:** As proposed in the Union budget for 2015-16, the government set up National Investment and Infrastructure Fund (NIIF) to raise funds and provide long-term capital for infrastructure-related projects. It provides an investment platform for international and Indian investors who are looking for investment opportunities in infrastructure and other high-growth sectors of the country.
- **Aid from ADB:** Asian Development Bank (ADB) made a commitment to invest \$ 100 million into the NIIF's Fund of Funds (FoF). With ADB's investment, the Fund of Funds has secured \$ 700 million in commitments. ADB will join the Government of India and Asian Infrastructure Investment Bank (AIIB) as an investor in the Fund.

- **NIP:** Further, in December 2019, the government announced the launch of National Infrastructure Pipeline (NIP) involving projects with an outlay of ₹ 102 lakh crore (about $1.43 trillion) to be executed over the next five years – till 2025. As reiterated in the Union budget for 2020-21, this proposal envisages more than 6,500 projects across various sectors and are classified as per their size and stage of development. These projects will include housing, safe drinking water, access to clean and affordable energy, healthcare for all, world-class educational institutes, modern railway stations, airports, bus terminals, metro and railway transportation, logistics and warehousing, irrigation projects, etc. A high-level Task Force on NIP has proposed to the government to raise the total outlay to ₹ 111 lakh crore.
    - **NIP – sector-wise outlay:** Broadly, the sector-wise break-up of outlay under the NIP is 24% for Energy, 18% for Roads, 17% for Urban schemes, 12% for Railways and balance for other schemes. Of the total outlay, Centre is to bear 39%, States 40% and private sector 21%.
    - **NIP implementation:** Out of the NIP projects, ₹ 44 lakh core worth of projects are under implementation, ₹ 33 lakh crore are under planning stage and ₹ 22 lakh crore are being developed. Thus, considerable work is already in progress and they are being closely monitored.
    - **Reassessing NIP:** In the light of the situation following Covid-19 pandemic which has disrupted global economy, the government will have to reassess the timeline and financial resources for implementation of NIP. Further, the government has to work on easing tariffs, non-tariff barriers and customs regulations, minimise trade policy uncertainty and improve supply of energy, logistics and port facilities if India is to take advantage of companies exiting China and attract them for India to become part of global supply chain.

Outlook for Future

To achieve high and sustainable growth, there has to be substantial step up of investment in infrastructure mostly on transportation, energy, communication, housing and sanitation and urban infrastructure sector. The investment proposed under NIP in infrastructure sector will go a long way in creating both direct and indirect jobs. There is a strong co-relation between investments in infrastructure and economic growth, with roads accounting for about 3.1 percent of gross value added.

According to *Global Infrastructure Outlook*, a global study of 56 countries under G-20 Initiative, India needs to invest $4.5 trillion in infrastructure across 7 sectors, viz., Transport – Roads, Rail, Ports and Airports— Energy, Telecom and Water up to 2040. Against this, current trends indicate only an investment of $3.9 trillion leaving an investment gap of $526 billion. The additional resources will have to be found from both domestic and external sources.

2. Elucidate the steps taken to develop and modernise India's national highways. What are the problems faced in executing highway projects and what steps have been taken by the government to overcome them.

Ans. Carrying more than 65 percent of the road traffic, India's national and state highways are critical lifelines of the economy. The National Highways (NHs) network of 1.32 lakh kilometres (km.), is just 2.2 per cent of the country's total road network of 58.97 lakh km. while they carry 40 percent of total traffic. Due to inadequate expansion to cater to the traffic, they are quite overstretched.

➢ **Golden Quadrilateral**

For long, the NHs in India were not adequately developed and were far below par when compared to international standards. It was against this background that in 1999 the 'Golden Quadrilateral' project was launched to build high-class roadways between the four Metros, passing through many other cities and towns *en route*, and comparable to international standards.

Having total length of 5,846 km. and with four and six-lane highways, this was a transformational step which was to change the very landscape of Indian economy, enabling faster and more efficient transportation of both passenger and freight traffic. Besides, 7300 km. long North-South, East-West corridors linking Srinagar-Kanyakumari and Silchar-Porbandar with four and six-lane highways was also taken up. National Highways Authority of India (NHAI) has been executing these projects.

➢ **Bharatmala Pariyojana**

This project envisages construction and upgradation of National Highways of 34,800 km. length over five years from 2017-18 to 2021-22 at an estimated outlay of ₹ 5.35 lakh crore. The programme focuses on optimizing efficiency of freight and passenger movement across the country by bridging critical infrastructure gaps. Multi-modal integration is also built into this program. It involves:

- Development of Economic Corridors, Inter Corridors and Feeder Routes.
- Border and International Connectivity roads.
- Coastal and Port Connectivity roads and Greenfield expressways.
- Roads connecting backward and tribal areas.
- Places of religious and tourist interest, and
- Trade routes with neighbouring countries.

The project will take longer than the target date. According to the 2018-19 Annual Report of the Ministry of Road Transport and Highways (MoRTH), projects with aggregate length of approximately 6400 km. have already been awarded under Bharatmala Pariyojana (including residual NHDP works), while work on preparation of Detailed Project Reports for about 25,000 km. was under progress.

➢ **Setu Bharatam**

This project aims to ensure safe and smooth flow of traffic by replacing Level Crossings on National Highways by 174 road-over or road-under bridges. Out of this, 91 works have been sanctioned with an estimated cost of ₹ 7,104 crore of which by 2018-19, 59 works were in various stages of execution.

➢ **Constraints and problems encountered in project execution**

Many of the highway projects had got stalled due to the following factors:

- Issues associated with land acquisition.
- Shifting of electric poles, transformers, drainage and sewerage lines.
- Obtaining environment and forest clearances.
- Approval for road-over or road-under bridges.
- Poor progress of some contract works due to cash flow constraints, and
- Law and order problems in some cases.

➢ **Project models**

Highway projects involve heavy outlays and have long gestation periods to fetch returns on investment. Not many private investors are in a position to invest huge sums in these projects. Over time, the NHAI has adopted different models for execution of the projects as discussed below.

- **Build-Operate-Transfer (BOT)** model: Under this, private agencies build, operate and maintain the road for a specified period of time before transferring the asset back to the government. In this, the government's capital commitment is minimal.

  The private developer arranges all the finances for the project, while collecting toll revenue or annuity fee from the Government, as agreed. The annuity fee arrangement is known as BOT-Annuity scheme under which the toll revenue risk is taken by the government, while the private player is paid a pre-fixed annuity for construction and maintenance of roads.

- **EPC model:** Under the Engineering, Procurement and Construction, or EPC, projects, the government meets the entire project cost. This method is followed when both private developers and banks find it difficult to finance the projects under the BOT or HAM model.

- **Hybrid Annuity model (HAM):** Under this, the government bears and pays upfront or, in tranches linked to milestones achieved, 40 percent of the project cost and the balance 60 per cent is arranged by the road developer. In some cases, the developer may invest only about 20-25 per cent of his share while the remaining amount is raised as debt.

As the term itself suggests, HAM is a hybrid – a mix of the EPC and BOT models. Under the EPC model, NHAI pays private agency to execute the work. The private agency has no role in the road's ownership, toll collection or maintenance which is taken care of by the government.

- **Toll-Operate-Transfer (TOT) model:** Under this scheme adopted by NHAI for roads, the right to collect user-fee or toll on selected national highway stretches, built through public funding, is auctioned and assigned to a concessionaire for a period of 15 or 30 years against an upfront payment of a lump-sum amount to the government. The winning bidder (concessionaire), who is licensed to collect toll, is also responsible for the operation and maintenance of the roads during the tenure. At the end of this period, a fresh auction would be held for a further long tenure.

  In 2016, the government had authorized NHAI to monetize 75 public-funded national highways with a road length of around 4,500 km that can together fetch around ₹ 1 trillion. The first TOT auction of highways, covering 698 km in Gujarat and Andhra Pradesh, fetched ₹ 9,681 crore in 2018, the winner being a joint venture between an Indian entity and an Australian firm.

  The TOT model helps NHAI raise capital upfront to fund road projects based on the EPC and HAM schemes. The investor who gets to manage the asset is able to take a long-term perspective and will seek to manage it profitably and responsibly.

➤ **Problems**

- ♦ Many of the highway projects got bogged down in the past resulting in time and cost overruns.
- ♦ Due to challenges and risks involved in financing, delays in land acquisition and environment clearances and lower than estimated revenues, the private sector has not shown interest in BOT projects and works have stalled in the last few years.
- ♦ In HAM projects, developers went in for aggressive bidding with the bids being below the reserve price.They found their profit margins squeezed, were stuck with unviable projects and unable to complete the projects, they virtually abandoned them. The loans extended by banks to the projects turned bad and added to banks' non-performing assets (NPAs).
- ♦ NHAI has found it difficult to award projects through the BOT and less-taxing HAM modes. And where it has to execute projects though the EPC route, it has to bear all the expenses. Experts are of the opinion that the NHAI's debt situation is a cause for concern. It is expected to touch ₹ 1.8 lakh crore by the end of the fiscal year 2019-20. The payment outgo on account of interest is expected to be about ₹ 25,000 crore annually in the next two decades.

- Land acquisition costs have also risen considerably after fair-price laws were introduced in 2013, and this alone accounts for more than 30 percent of NHAI's project costs.
- The Comptroller & Auditor General (CAG) has also red-flagged the burgeoning costs of highway projects and observed that NHAI's borrowings are also government borrowings and should be accounted as such. Experts have expressed concern over NHAI's debt situation.

➢ **Remedial measures**

The government has taken the following measures to overcome the problems:

- **Monetizing assets:** As mentioned earlier, the NHAI has started the process of monetizing toll-based operational road assets under the TOT model. Proceeds from TOT auctions will free up valuable taxpayer capital that can then be recycled for much-needed new infrastructure projects.
- **Investment Trusts:** The government has also approved NHAI to monetize publicly funded highway projects through infrastructure investment trust (InvIT) route. The InvIT will be a Trust set up by NHAI and it may hold assets either directly or through a Special Purpose Vehicle (SPV) or a holding company. InvIT is a relatively untapped funding source enabling investors to invest in infrastructure assets. It provides a ready platform for monetizing road projects.
- **Augmenting investments:** The above steps will help to bring in new investments to the highways sector. This process can also be adopted in other infrastructure areas such as railways, ports, airports, etc.

3. Critically examine the limitations and deficiencies of transport infrastructure, namely, roads, railways, ports and aviation in India and the steps taken by the government to improve and upgrade them.

Ans. Adequate development of infrastructure is a pre-requisite for higher economic growth. Due to inadequate investment in infrastructure development, India had for long suffered from a huge infrastructure deficit. According to data compiled by McKinsey & Company, the average infrastructure investment in India during the period 1992-2010 constituted 4.7 per cent of the Gross Domestic Product (GDP) as against 7.3 per cent in countries like China, Indonesia and Vietnam.

India's low rank: As per the World Economic Forum (WEF) *Global Competitiveness Report 2014*, India ranked 85 among 144 countries in terms of the quality of infrastructure and 'inadequate supply of infrastructure' being listed as the most difficult factor in the ease of doing business. According to the report, India's infrastructure rankings vary from 84 in quality of roads to 111 in quality of electricity supply.

The status of various critical infrastructural facilities and steps taken by the government to improve and upgrade them are discussed below.

➢ Roadways

Roadways is the dominant mode of transport in India accounting for the largest share in both passenger and freight traffic, with 85 percent of the former and 65 percent of the latter. Compared to railways, roads have the advantage of greater accessibility to interior parts, hilly and difficult terrains.

However, though the country's road network has expanded exponentially from 3.99 lakh kilometres (km.) in 1950-51 to 59.64 lakh km. in 2018, the standard of construction, quality and upkeep of roads, in towns, villages and highways, had been poor when compared to international standards.

Two major, game-changing developments took place in the road sector towards the end of 1990's and the early part of 2000's.

- **National Highways:** Firstly, the decision taken in 1999 to launch a 'Golden Quadrilateral' project to develop National Highways (NHs) comparable to international standards, linking the four major Metros, and passing through many other cities and towns.

- **Rural roads:** Secondly, the decision in December 2000 to launch the PM's Gram Sadak Yojana (PMGSY) to link rural habitations with a certain population with the nearby town through all-weather roads. About 1.67 lakh 'Unconnected Habitations' were eligible for coverage under the programme. And it involved construction of about 3.71 lakh km. of roads for New Connectivity and 3.68 lakh km. under upgradation of existing roads. Against this, by 2016, 4.90 km of rural roads connecting 1,21,241 habitations has been completed. With improved roads and better connectivity, it has greatly helped to rejuvenate the rural economy.

  Increasing the coverage and quality of roads and highways has enhanced connectivity, aided speedier movement of passenger and freight traffic and helped to augment internal and external trade.

- **Limitations of Roadways**

  - **Capacity of existing highways:**

    - The present NH network of 1.22 lakh km. forms just 2.2 per cent of the country's total road network of 58.97 lakh km. and carry 40 per cent of India's total road traffic. Hence there is much more ground to be covered in expanding the highway network.
    - Of the total NH network, highways with 4-lane and higher standards forms only 22.6 per cent while 51 per cent is of 2-lane standard.
    - National and state highways are overstrained, carrying more than 65 per cent of the road traffic.

■ **Safety aspects:**

- Safety on roads is of major concern in India with daily incidence of nearly 400 road-related deaths. In 2013, India's accident death rate of 18.9 for every 100,000 people was higher than in other South Asian countries such as Bangladesh (11.6), Mauritius (12.2) and Sri Lanka (13.7).
- Part of the fatalities is because of the poor quality and maintenance of roads.
- Thus, much more needs to be done to improve and expand roadways and ensure greater safety of users.

■ **Environmental concerns:**

- Vehicular traffic in cities and highways is a source of pollution and pose risk of health hazards. The solution to this lies in promoting mass public transport and a switch to electric vehicles. The government has initiated steps in this direction by providing Metro rail system in larger cities and initiating steps to promote Electric Vehicles (EVs) on roads which is still only at a nascent stage and needs to be expedited.

➢ Railways

India has the fourth largest railway network under a single management. The railways have expanded exponentially since 1950s. Running track kms. (which refers to all running tracks on routes) have gone up from 59,315 kms. in 1950-51 to 95,981 kms. in 2018-19 and number of originating passengers from 1, 284 million to 8,439 million during the same period.

■ **Electrification:** Electrification of railway tracks has received priority as it helps to reduce dependence on imported petroleum which is also a source of environmental pollution. It has helped to conserve foreign exchange, enhance country's energy security and make railways more eco-friendly.

By 2018-19, 61.62 per cent of running track kms. have been electrified. Railways plan to electrify all broad gauge (BG) routes by 2021-22.

Presently, about 65 per cent of freight and 54 per cent of passenger traffic is hauled by electric traction.

♦ **Limitations:** But despite this impressive expansion, railways suffer from the following limitations and deficiencies:

- **Loss in freight share:** Despite its extensive reach and the substantial growth in freight load, the modal share of railways in the transportation of freight has declined from 86.2 per cent in 1950-51 to 33 per cent in 2015 losing out the share to roadways. This is despite railways being more suited for transporting bulk freight.

- **Cross subsidisation of fares:** The decline in share of freight carried is partly due to a shortfall in carrying capacity and lack of price competitiveness. Railways are perforce using profits from its freight business to provide for losses in the passenger segment, and also to manage its overall financial situation. Such cross-subsidisation results in high freight tariffs adversely impacting the competitiveness of railways vis-vis other modes, especially roadways, in carrying freight. **According to the World Bank, such cross-subsidisation of fares makes rail freight costs in India one of the highest globally.**
- **Over-utilization of capacity:** The golden quadrilateral (connecting four major metros) and its diagonal routes make up only 15 per cent of the total route of the railways but it transports 52 per cent of passenger traffic and 58 per cent of total freight load. This points to the high saturation and over-utilized capacity on popular routes.

➢ **Ports and Shipping**

With a coastline spanning about 7,500 km, forming one of the biggest peninsulas in the world, and 14,500 km of potentially navigable waterways, shipping and ports play an important role in Indian economy. India has 12 major ports and 205 non-major ports and about 95 per cent of India's external trade by volume and 68 per cent by value are handled by ports. Despite being the most cost-effective and efficient mode, water transport accounted for only 6 per cent of freight transport in India in 2016-17.

Globally, maritime nations such as China, South Korea, Japan and the United States of America have effectively used their coastline for "port-led development".

■ **Limitations:** Indian ports and shipping have suffered from various limitations mentioned below.

♦ **Draught levels:** Most Indian ports lack the capability to handle mainline container vessels (also called "mother ships"), and they require dredging to increase draft depth. Presently, the Dredging Corporation of India (DCI) and a limited set of private vendors undertake dredging, limiting competition. The dredging operations at ports have to be opened up to attract international players.

♦ **Trans-shipment facility:** As international trade is carried on with economically viable large container vessels, Indian ports, with shallow draft, are unable to berth them and this constrains them from becoming a hub. Most of India's container traffic is being transhipped through Colombo, Singapore, Dubai and Salalah (Oman) which have better facilities. This leads to increased costs and delays due to routing and additional handling of shipment at foreign ports.

- While India's seaborne trade has been growing exponentially over the years, there is a sharp decline in the share of Indian ships in the carriage of India's overseas trade from about 40 per cent in the late 1980s to 7.9 per cent in 2018-19.
- **Connectivity to ports:** Weak connectivity of Indian ports to hinterland areas which are main production centres leads to higher costs and delays, adversely impacting both India's industries and export prospects.
- **Charges by the shipping lines:** The business practices of shipping lines play a key role in the competitiveness of marine transport. The high rate and multiplicity of charges imposed by shipping lines in India has been a deterrent.
- **Skewed modal mix:** As noted earlier, apart from sea route, India has vast inland waterways which have not been exploited despite being more cost-effective and efficient mode, and roads and rail have bulk of the share in carriage of freight and passenger traffic. Coastal shipping and inland waterways form just 6 percent of the total modal mix in India, compared to around 10 to 20 percent in other emerging countries.
- **Shipbuilding industry:** Though India has some shipyards, an economy of India's size and stature requires a more vibrant and robust shipbuilding and maintenance industry for economic as well as strategic and security reasons. From a geo-political angle, India is strategically situated in the Indian Ocean which has assumed importance due to the increased focus of major powers on Indo-Pacific region and they look upon India to play a major role to counterbalance China's expansionist policy. At present, Indian shipbuilding industry has less than 1 per cent of global share.

  Besides, shipbuilding is a manufacturing activity endowed with the potential of nearly 65 per cent value addition coming from other technology and ancillary industries such as steel, electronics, engineering and electrical equipment, and services like port infrastructure and trade. It can thus give boost to programmes like "Make in India" and substantially add to direct and indirect employment.

■ **Solutions and steps taken:** The port sector needs to be strengthened by upgrading facilities if it is to compete with foreign ports and shipping services. The government has initiated various steps in this direction.

- **Dredging and Draft depths:** To enable major ports to handle larger vessels, an action plan to increase the draft depth of ports is under implementation. Most major ports have already achieved a draft of 14 metres or more, except Kolkata Port, where deeper draft has not been feasible because of the riverine nature of the port. The outer harbour in Visakhapatnam has very deep draft of more than 18 metres. Some major ports are striving to achieve deeper drafts up to18 metres. Work is in progress to create a draft of more than 18 metres in Mormugao and Kamarajar Port (Chennai).

- **Trans-shipment Ports:** Most of the major ships carrying cargo between East Asia and Africa, and between Europe and East Asia, pass directly through or close to Indian territorial waters. Hence there is an advantage in having a trans-shipment port in India to garner more freight traffic and avoid dependence on other foreign ports.

  India tried to develop Kochi port as a container trans-shipment hub but it has not taken off for various reasons including need for frequent dredging and tariff-related issues. Now Vizhinjam port at Thiruvananthapuram is being developed as a trans-shipment port. Located only 10 nautical miles from the major international sea route, Vizhinjam is a natural, deep-water harbour with a depth of more than 20 metres within a nautical mile from coast and can ideally become a major trans-shipment port. It can handle the cargo of not only India but Bangladesh, Nepal and Bhutan now being handled at Colombo. It will save Indian companies millions of dollars in transport costs, as well as ease concerns over the growing strategic clout of rival China which has made huge investments in Sri Lankan ports at Colombo and Hambantotain India's neighbourhood.

  However, India's port tariffs need to be made competitive as they are high compared with Sri Lanka and Singapore, the two popular ports that handle bulk of Indian trans-shipment cargo.

- **Ease of Doing Business:** To facilitate 'Ease of Doing Business' (EoDB), Shipping Ministry has taken steps to reduce dwell time and transaction costs in the Major Ports. These include simplification of procedures, installation of Container Scanners, E-delivery orders, enhanced RFID security and seamless movement of traffic across port gates. Logistic data bank service for enabling track and trace movement of EXIM containers has also been implemented under the Delhi Mumbai Industrial Corridor (DMIC) at all Major Ports.

- **Sagarmala programme**: A major initiative to revamp the port and shipping sector is the Sagarmala Programme approved by the government in 2015. Its main objectives are:
  - To modernise and improve connectivity to ports.
  - Enhance the role of 'coastal shipping' for carrying bulk materials like coal, iron ore, cement and steel.
  - Stimulate port-linked industrialization.
  - Create an IT-enabled multi-modal logistics system to reduce logistics costs and time and boost exports.

- **Improved Port Connectivity:** Improving road-rail connectivity to ports is crucial for better performance of ports. A total of 89 road connectivity projects have been identified under the Sagarmala programme. The Indian Port Rail Corporation Limited (IPRCL) has taken up 29 projects of which 12 projects have been completed and 17 projects are in progress. Besides, 54 rail connectivity projects are being taken up by Ministry of Railways.
- **The Merchant Shipping Bill:** The Merchant Shipping Bill, 2016, pending to be passed by the Parliament, will bring in further reforms in the shipping sector to promote ease of doing business and develop Indian coastal shipping. The Bill will replace the Merchant Shipping Act, 1958, and repeal the Coasting Vessels Act, 1838.

➢ **Aviation:** The civil aviation sector in India has been expanding at rapid pace in the last two decades even as the economy was on a high growth trajectory. India has an extensive aviation infrastructure. India is considered the third largest domestic civil aviation market in the world and is expected to become the third largest air passenger market by 2024.

- **Significant growth:** Air travel in India has been showing robust growth over the years, a sign of vibrant economic growth. According to DGCA data, India's domestic air passengers on Indian carriers doubled from 60.8 million in 2011-12 to 123.3 million in 2017-18 while international air passengers on Indian carriers increased from 14.3 million to 23.8 million during the same period.

  And domestic freight carried by air has nearly doubled from 3.6 lakh tonnes in 2011-12 to 6.9 lakh tonnes in 2017-18 while international air freight showed modest increase from 3.6 lakh tonnes to 3.7 lakh tonnes during the same period.
- **RCS-UDAN scheme:** A major initiative of the government has been to expand the reach of air travel facility to Tier-I & II towns through Regional Connectivity Scheme-UdeDesh Ka AamNagrik (RCS-UDAN) scheme. This facility would spur growth in the hinterland areas which has great potential and has helped in generating economic activity and employment opportunities. By 2020, 252 routes and 45 airports have been operationalised under this flagship scheme.

  The UDAN scheme will have a great role to play in the coming years as it can boost industrial growth away from the major cities which have reached a stage of saturation and are bursting at the seams creating many intractable urban problems. Developing the airports in the smaller towns will help them to serve as industrial magnets, stem rural-urban migration and have a multiplier effect on India's vast rural economy.

➢ **Conclusion:** Further developing the transport infrastructure, along with the power and telecom sectors, at a fast pace is imperative if India is to take advantage of attracting industries from abroad which are planning to relocate from China, and become a manufacturing powerhouse. This should be aligned with other measures such as easing customs procedures, tariff and tax regime, reforming land and labour markets to improve 'Ease of Doing Business' in India.

4. Explain the concept of 'Multimodal transport'. Mention the various modes of transport in India and modal imbalances in their utilisation. Outline the measures taken by the government to correct the imbalances and state how these measures would benefit the economy.

Ans. 'Multimodality' in the transport sector or 'multimodal transport' refers to the use of different modes of transport on a same journey. It applies to transport of both freight and passengers.

➢ **The concept:** Multimodality draws on the strengths the different modes of conveyance offer when utilized in combination rather than in isolation.

For instance, roads can have easy access to villages, remote and inaccessible areas, hilly and desert terrains which railways may not be able to reach. Goods originating from such areas would be trans-shipped to rail or waterways, as may be available *en route*, for transport to distant destinations for which they are better suited than roadways.

This system is ideally suited for transport of bulk goods in containers which can be easily transhipped from one mode to another using fork-lifts, cranes, etc.

➢ **Multiple modes:** India has various modes of transport, viz., roads, rail, waterways and airways. The advantage of multimodal transport lies in the fact that each of the modes has certain advantages and drawbacks and utilizing them in combination, rather than in isolation will give optimum outcomes. The relative advantages and drawbacks of different modes are discussed below.

- **Roadways:** Unlike all other modes, roadways have high level of penetration into populated areas, remote and difficult terrains, easy accessibility and adaptability to individual needs. It can act as a feeder service to railway, shipping and air traffic. But it is beset with problems like high density of traffic, overcrowding and congestion and high incidence of accidents and fatalities. It also entails dependence on fossil fuels causing high levels of greenhouse gas (GHG) emissions and pollution which adversely impacts the environment and health of the population.
- **Railways**: Railway is better suited and more cost-efficient than roadways for haulage of bulk materials over long distances. It is a more energy efficient mode and with electrification of rail routes, there will be less dependence on fossil fuels and less scope for environmental pollution.

But railway networks have become congested and over-stretched with over 60 percent routes utilized more than 100 per cent. Railways' financial position is also tight as passenger fares are subsidised with little scope to raise them. With increase in fares, railways may also lose traffic to other modes of travel. Though railways generate most of its revenue from freight, the freight rates are already higher than in other modes of transport.

Decline in rail traffic and falling revenue generation tells upon fresh investments in expansion and renewal of network.

- **Coastal shipping and Waterways:** India's long coastline spanning about 7,500 kms, with twelve major ports and 205 non-major ports, and a large number of rivers, canals, and backwaters for inland water transport (IWT) makes water transport an ideal mode. Out of total navigable length of 14,500 kms, about 5,200 kms of rivers and 4,000 kms of canals can be used by mechanized crafts. Waterways is also being used for cruises and movement of cargo between India and Bangladesh.

  Despite being the most cost-effective and efficient mode, it accounts for just 6 per cent of freight transport. Inland Water Transport (IWT) carries less than 2 per cent of organized freight traffic and negligible passenger traffic.

- **Aviation:** India's aviation sector is expanding fast and supports about 1.3 million direct and indirect jobs. About 3.3 million tonnes of air cargo was handled in 2017-18. According to IATA, India is poised to be among the top 10 air freight markets.

➢ **Case for Multimodal system**

- **Importance of Logistics sector:** As of 2016, the logistics sector in India employed more than 22 million people and serves all sectors of the economy. Between 2011-12 and 2015-16, the logistics sector's value has grown at a compound annual growth rate (CAGR) of 7.8 per cent. Underdeveloped infrastructure, poor connectivity between different modes of transport and an unfavourable modal mix add to logistics costs.

- **Logistics costs in India:** The logistics costs in India are relatively high and are estimated to be 14 per cent of the country's GDP as against 9 per cent of GDP in the United States, 11 per cent in Japan, 12 per cent in Korea and 14.9 per cent in China. A 10 per cent decrease in indirect logistics cost has the potential to increase exports by 5 to 8 per cent.

  Logistics has four key components that account for the major part of the sector: transport, warehousing, freight forwarding and value-added logistics. Each of these falls under different segments of regulatory oversight, which adds complexity to the system. The presence of multiple agencies often leads to duplication of processes adding to cost and time involved.

- **Multimodal transport in India:** Multimodal transport signifies 'point to point' or a 'hub-and-spoke' model of moving freight using different modes of transport. It may involve combination of roadways, railways, coastal shipping, inland waterways or aviation to form an effective transportation grid. For a large and diverse country like India with varied terrains and geographical conditions and transportation poses a challenge, multimodal transport can be an effective solution.

  In the 1960s, Railways played a crucial role in promoting multimodal transport in India when it introduced containerized freight transport. In 1993, the Multimodal Transport Act was passed by the Parliament to establish a standardized regime for the multimodal transport operators (MTOs) under which the Director General of Shipping was identified as the competent authority. This paved the way for MTOs to register themselves and start operations and provided a boost to the inland movement of traffic under a single authority.

- **Modal imbalance:** Roads with 54 per cent is the dominant mode of transporting cargo in India, followed by rail with 33 per cent. Due to competition from roadways, the modal share of railways in freight transport declined steeply from 86.2 per cent in 1950-51 to 33 per cent in 2015. As stated earlier, transportation of cargo through waterways – shipping and inland water – accounts for a minuscule share of 6 per cent though it is the most cost-effective and efficient mode. Such imbalances in transport impacts the efficiency and cost benefit of the system.

  - **Correcting the imbalance:** The government has been taking various steps to promote multimodal transport which will also result in more balanced development of all regions and augment employment opportunities in hinterland areas helping to stem rural-urban migration

    - **Private freight terminals:** A liberalized Private Freight Terminals (PFT) policy has facilitated development of a network of freight terminals with private investment (on PPP mode). This policy aims to provide efficient and cost-effective logistics services with warehousing solution to end users. As of 2018, 58 Private Freight Terminals (PFT) have been commissioned and are functioning.

    - **Dedicated Freight Corridors (DFCs):** To resolve the increasing need for decongestion of roads, accident reduction and ensuring energy security, the Government launched the construction of 'Dedicated Freight Corridors' (DFCs), planned to be 'freight-only' railway lines. These corridors and feeder routes to them will make it cheaper, faster, and more reliable to move goods between industrial heartlands in the North and ports on the Western and Eastern coasts.

      Western DFC: The 1,502 km Western DFC from Dadri (Uttar Pradesh) to Jawaharlal Nehru Port (Navi Mumbai) passes through Haryana, Rajasthan, Gujarat and Maharashtra.

Eastern DFC: 1,840 km Eastern DFC from Ludhiana to Dankuni near Kolkata traverses Punjab, Haryana, Uttar Pradesh, Bihar, Jharkhand and West Bengal.

These lines along congested transport corridors will give much relief to the Golden Quadrilateral that connects the four major metros and two diagonal routes (Delhi – Chennai and Mumbai – Howrah). It will also ramp up the average speed of freight, which had reduced considerably to 20 kmph.

- **Sagarmala Project:** The Sagarmala programme, approved in 2015, focuses on modernizing and developing ports, enhancing port connectivity, supporting coastal communities and stimulating port-linked industrialization. It aims to reduce the logistics costs for foreign and domestic trade, leading to an overall cost savings of about ₹ 40,000 crore annually by 2025. It also aims to double the share of water transportation in the modal mix.
- **Improved Rail-Road and Port Connectivity:** A total of 89 road connectivity projects have been identified under the Sagarmala programme to improve road-rail connectivity to ports. The Indian Port Rail Corporation Limited (IPRCL) has taken up 29 projects of which 12 projects have been completed and 17 projects are in progress. Besides, 54 rail connectivity projects are being taken up by Ministry of Railways.
- **RoadRailer:** India has also developed and tested a RoadRailer, a bi-modal transportation unit, which runs as a semi-trailer on road and as a wagon on rail. Goods are loaded on to a RoadRailer unit and it travels by road and is then directly coupled with railway wagons at a rail terminal. The unit, with wheels attached as in a normal truck, will be moved by rail and then decoupled from the wagon at the receiving end, and attached to a truck to be moved on to the final destination by road.

  This will help to divert cargo traffic from road to rail, to a great extent, and to offer seamless door-to-door goods transportation.

  The system has been in operation in the US since the mid-1980s and has a long-proven track record. There are over 7,000 RoadRailer units in operation with 14 terminal locations across Eastern US and Canada.
- **Inland Water Transport (IWT):** Inland Waterways Authority of India (IWAI), set up in 1986, is focused on developing the technically and economically viable National Waterways to create IWT network across the country to supplement the congested road and rail networks.

  National Waterways: Three waterways have been already developed with fairway, navigational aids, jetties and terminals with mechanized equipment handling facilities for loading and unloading of cargo. These waterways are operational and vessels are plying on them. These include Allahabad to Haldia (NW-1) on Ganga, Dhubri to Sadiya (NW-2) on Brahmaputra and a West Coast Canal (NW-3) in Kerala. According to Ministry of Shipping, there are 13 operational National Waterways as of 2020.

Waterways traffic: The traffic on National Waterways during 2018-19 was 72.31 million tonnes, an increase of 32 per cent over 2017-18.

- **Logistics Parks:** As part of an integrated approach for the country's transportation, the government has decided to set up 35 multi-modal logistics parks at an investment of ₹ 50,000 crore development of economic corridors. The scheme envisages participation of states and the private sector for setting up special vehicles for implementation. 15 logistics parks are to be constructed over five years, and 20 more over the next 10 years. These parks will act as hubs for freight movement enabling freight aggregation and distribution with modern mechanized warehousing space.

  To give fillip to the idea, the government hosted a multi-modal summit – India Integrated Transport and Logistics Summit – in May 2017 which had wide participation of concerned stakeholders.

➢ **Conclusion**: Multimodal transport is an evolving solution in India with different modes of transport in their various stages of evolution. For its robust growth, more private investment in logistics infrastructure must be encouraged along with easier regulations which can attract foreign companies with expertise in the field.

(On this, see also Question 6 in Chapter 9 on Logistics sector on Page 9.20)

5. Discuss the role which inland waterways and coastal shipping can play in Indian economy. Critically examine the steps have been taken by the government to develop them and suggest further measures to be taken.

Ans. Both coastal shipping and inland waterways are essential infrastructure for socio-economic development of the country and can be effectively utilized for carrying bulk materials and passenger traffic. As these waterways are environment-friendly modes of transport and will bring down the logistics cost in India significantly, they deserve better regulation and development across the country.

➢ **India' s potential for Waterways transport**

- India, bound by sea on three sides with a long coastline spanning about 7,500 km, can be a significant maritime nation, with a dominant role for shipping in the promotion of trade. Around 90 per cent of India's external trade by volume and 70 per cent by value are handled by ports. There are twelve major ports and 205 non-major ports operate on India's coast.

- Besides, India has a large network of inland water bodies in the form of rivers, canals and backwaters and out of their total navigable length of 14,500 km, about 5,200 km of the river and 4,000 km of canals can be used by mechanized crafts.

❖ **Coastal shipping: Advantages**

- Coastal Shipping is a fuel efficient and environmentally friendly mode to reduce road and rail congestion.
- Its ability to move large volumes in a short period gives coastal shipping a distinct comparative advantage over other modes of transport. Despite the inherent advantages, however, Coastal Shipping is still in its infancy in India.
- Promoting coastal shipping and inland waterway transport (IWT) would supplant trucks and trains for cargo transport, alleviate pressure on the country's roads and rails.
- It would save billions of dollars in lower logistics costs, boost efficiency, make the economy more competitive and spur growth.
- Reduced dependence on road and diversion of freight to waterways will cut down carbon emissions and air pollution and help improve the environment with its beneficial impact on the health of the community at large.

❖ **Hurdles to, and limitations of, Coastal shipping**

Various factors, as mentioned below, have worked against India's coastal shipping industry from developing in the past.

- Coast to coast shipments by sea have to go round the southern tip of the peninsula while companies prefer the direct route by roads and rail.
- Also like many other developing economies, India has for long focused on building up its road infrastructure which ensured cross-country mobility, both for freight and passengers. This has provided greater links between various towns and cities and also direct access to interior parts and hinterland regions where many industries are located.
- Though coastal ships can carry heavier loads than trucks and are better suited for transport of bulk materials, road transport facilitates carriage of goods between originating and destination points and thus averts the need for trans-shipments of cargo midway.
- India's regulatory environment has also stood in the way of developing coastal shipping. Cabotage laws have restricted domestic transport on foreign-flagged vessels. (Cabotage is a term of maritime law and refers to exclusive rights of a nation for allowing transit of a vessel along its coast for trade from one port to another within the territorial limits of that nation. The terms coastal trade or coastal trading is more used now instead of cabotage.).

- **Steps to promote Coastal shipping:** To promote coastal shipping, the government has taken the following measures:
  - **Sagarmala Project:** The Sagarmala programme, approved in 2015, focuses on modernizing and developing ports, improving port connectivity, supporting coastal communities and stimulating port-linked industrialization. It aims to reduce the logistics costs for domestic and foreign trade, leading to an overall cost savings of about ₹ 40,000 crore annually by 2025. It also aims to double the share of water transportation in the modal mix.
  - **Improved Port Connectivity:** A total of 89 road connectivity projects were identified under the Sagarmala programme to improve road-rail connectivity to ports. The Indian Port Rail Corporation Limited (IPRCL) has taken up 29 projects of which 12 projects have been completed and 17 projects are in progress. Besides, 54 rail connectivity projects are being taken up by Ministry of Railways.
  - **Dedicated Freight Corridors (DFCs):** The 1,502 km Western DFC from Dadri (Uttar Pradesh) to Jawaharlal Nehru Port (Navi Mumbai) and the 1,840 km Eastern DFC from Ludhiana to Dankuni near Kolkata will vastly improve connectivity between rail and ports and ensure more reliable movement of goods between industrial heartlands in the North and ports on the Western and Eastern coasts.
  - The stipulation of cabotage has been relaxed under Merchant Shipping (MS) Act, 1958, for coastal movement of EXIM/EMPTY containers, agriculture, horticulture, fisheries, animal husbandry commodities and fertilizers.
  - The requirement of licensing for chartering vessels under section MS Act, 1958 has been exempted for the above-mentioned items.
  - According to Ministry of Shipping, in May 2018, the government finally relaxed the Cabotage laws enabling the foreign-flagged vessels to carry coastal cargo in India. The international trade world has acknowledged it as an encouraging move in a direction to increase coastal shipping in India. The Government cited that reform shall dramatically increase the attractiveness of Indian ports as direct ports of call for ocean carriers. With the change, foreign carriers can transport laden export-import containers for trans-shipment and empty containers for repositioning between Indian ports without any specific permission or license.

❖ **Further steps needed:** More steps need to be taken to give fillip to coastal shipping.

- **Impact on Indian vessels:** While the move to relax Cabotage rules would help the Indian coastal shipping industry, it is argued that it would benefit more foreign-flag vessels and would adversely impact domestic port trusts and drive Indian ship owners to losses.

To remedy the situation, the government could remove taxes on marine fuels. It would benefit the economy since against the revenue loss of around ₹ 56 crore annually, the surge in cargo handling operations on export and import will fetch direct and indirect revenue of over ₹ 700 crore.

- **Potential to augment freight:** Another major concern has been the availability of cargo of critical mass. At present, coastal cargo in India consists mainly of petrol, oil lubricants, iron ore and coal and fertilizers which are primarily for the use of PSUs (Public Sector Undertakings). But there is much potential for transporting more cargo by coastal ships by inducing modal shift from road/rail to coastal marine highways.

  There is potential for transporting steel, cement, automobiles, engineering goods, foodgrains and minerals like manganese, bauxite, silica and limestone by linking ports on southern, eastern and western coasts through coastal shipping.

- **Cost benefit:** Apart from reducing the congestion on the road and rail network, coastal shipping and inland navigation will be very cost effective. It is estimated that the cost per tonne per kilometre of moving cargo through the coastal or inland navigation route can be 60 to 80 per cent cheaper than moving the cargo through rail or road.

  The above measures will cut down the logistics cost substantially to make industry and trade more competitive.

❖ **Inland Water Transport (IWT)**

Inland Water Transport (IWT) carries less than 2 per cent of India's organized freight traffic and negligible passenger traffic. Compared to other large countries like the United States, China, and the European Union, freight transportation by waterways is highly under-utilized in India. The total cargo moved (in tonne-kilometres) by the inland waterway is very less of the total inland traffic in India, compared to the 21 per cent in the United States.

Transportation by waterways is receiving greater attention in recent times in view of its potential to bring down the logistics costs in India and other advantages.

- **Inland Waterways Authority of India:** The Inland Waterways Authority of India (IWAI) came into existence in 1986 for development and regulation of inland waterways for shipping and navigation. The Authority undertakes projects for development and maintenance of IWT infrastructure on national waterways.

IWAI has been focussing on developing technically and economically viable 'National Waterways' under the National Waterways Act, 2016 to create IWT network across the country to supplement the congested road and rail networks.

♦ **National Waterways (NW)**

- Three National Waterways have been already developed – Allahabad to Haldia (NW-1) on Ganga, Dhubri to Sadiya (NW-2) on Brahmaputra and a West Coast Canal (NW-3) in Kerala. They are equipped with fairway, navigational aids, jetties and terminals with mechanized equipment handling facilities for loading and unloading of cargo. They are operational and vessels are plying on them.
- Multimodal terminals have been provided at Varanasi and Sahibganj which will have rail and road connectivity. Such a terminal is also being provided at Haldia Dock complex.
- Jal Marg Vikas Project (JMVP) for augmenting navigation capacity on NW-1 (Haldia-Varanasi stretch) is taken up with the technical assistance and financial support of the World Bank at an estimated cost of ₹ 5,300 crore.
- Development works in Vijayawada – Muktyala stretch of river Krishna (Part of NW-4) have also commenced.
- Goa has 255 kms of navigable inland waterways and a better part of them is being used by the mining and export industry for transportation of iron ore to the port of Mormugao and Panaji from the loading points in the hinterlands. Their optimum use will provide quick and economical transportation facilities for both passengers and cargo.
- According to Ministry of Shipping, there are 13 operational National Waterways as of 2020.

♦ **Waterways traffic:**

■ The annual freight volumes carried on inland waterways using National Waterways (NW-1, NW-2, and NW-3) and Goa Waterways was 21.91 MMT in 2016-17.

■ The traffic on National Waterways during 2018-19 was 72.31 million tonnes, an increase of 32 per cent over 2017-18.

♦ **Steps to strengthen IWT**

■ Inland waterways should be further integrated to multimodal/ intermodal connectivity to improve logistics.

- Inland terminals with proper road and/or rail connectivity for seamless transfer of goods from one mode to the other would make the supply chain more efficient.
- Enhance linkages between national waterways and state waterways and feeder canals.
- Projects under Sagarmala programme, especially those aimed at improving port connectivity, setting up coastal economic zones (CEZs) and establishing new ports to be expedited.
- The new Merchant Shipping Bill to replace the Merchant Shipping Act, 1958, needs to be enacted early to promote the ease of doing business, ensure transparency and effective delivery of services.

6. Explain the concept and salient features of Public Private Partnership (PPP) bringing out its advantages, risks involved and the precautions to be taken in its implementation in an economy.

Ans. Public Private Partnerships (PPPs) are long term contracts between a government entity and a private enterprise that may cover financing, construction, operation, and maintenance of a project or activity under a single firm or a consortium of firms. The World Bank defines PPP as a "long-term contract between a private party and a government entity, for providing a public asset or service, in which the private party bears significant risk and management responsibility, and remuneration is linked to performance".

➢ **Genesis and Rationale for PPPs**

- The concept of PPP had its origin and application in the 1980s when there was rising evidence of inefficient public spending, poorly managed state-owned enterprises, and widespread fiscal and debt crises which called for a new model of economic development led by market liberalization and involvement of the private sector.
- PPPs as an innovative financing instrument for infrastructure and development, have the potential to generate both public and private return. This template is being increasingly implemented by countries across the globe.
- Developing countries had to make massive investments in infrastructure and social sectors to promote socio-economic development but the capacity and resources of governments were limited.
- Faced with challenges, governments developed strategies to attract private-sector involvement through PPPs, to meet the growing resource gap.
- In addition to financing, private-sector partners could provide managerial and technical expertise which helped to increase efficiency in the form of better designs and innovative construction techniques.

- The PPP regime has been used in diverse sectors. These include roads, energy, water supply, communications, health, and education. In India, it has been widely used in the construction, operation and maintenance of national highways.
- PPPs can help leverage private investment through risk-sharing between the public and private sectors.

Salient Features of PPP regime

- It is a contractual arrangement between a government or statutory body and a private sector entity.
- It is generally for the provision of public assets or public services through investments and/or management to be undertaken by the private sector entity.
- PPPs aim to harness the potential of private sector for efficient execution of projects and may also include delivery of quality services to the users post execution.
- The agreement will be for a specified period of time. While some PPP contracts may have short tenure, most PPP projects are of long terms of 20 to 30 years or even longer.
- Private sector entity receives cash flows for their investments or management of the PPP either through a performance-linked fee payment from the government body and/or through user charges from the consumers of the service provided.
- Outcomes of the PPP are normally pre-defined and provisions for incentives and penalty are made in the arrangement to ensure that the private partner is benchmarked for quality of service delivery.
- The manner in which any risk involved in the scheme or project is to be borne between the private investor and the public entity is well defined in the agreement.

Types/Models of PPP

Some of the commonly adopted forms of PPPs are:

- Design-build-operate-transfer (DBOT).
- Build-operate-transfer (BOT).
- Build-lease-transfer (BLT).

The models where ownership of the underlying asset remains with the public entity during the contract period and the project is transferred back to the public entity after the termination of contract are the preferred models of PPP.

- Further, the BOT model may be of the User-fee based or Annuity-based variant.

The User-Fee based BOT model is adopted in medium to large scale PPPs in the energy and transport sector – roads, ports and airports. While there are different versions in this approach, the PPP model preferred has been competitively bid concessions where costs are recovered mainly through user charges or, in some cases, partly through Viability Gap Funding (VGF) from the government.

Under the Annuity based BOT model, in sectors/projects where sizeable cost recovery is not possible through user charges, such as in infrastructure projects involving heavy investments or schemes in health and education sectors, the government may adopt "annuity model" which requires payment to the private partner a guarantee amount, either upfront or in tranches based on progress of the work.

➢ **Advantages and benefits of PPPs**

- ♦ It helps to build better-quality infrastructure, both physical like roads, rail, ports, etc. and in the social sector like improving schools and hospitals which are necessary conditions for spurring economic growth.
- ♦ PPP helps to augment "public utilities" like electricity, gas, water supply, etc. which require heavy capital expenditure, specialised capital equipment, organisation and expertise which the government alone may not be able to provide due to resource and other constraints. Here the private sector could partner with the State and implement such schemes which would benefit society at large.
- ♦ Its benefits eventually, and to a large extent in the short-term, reach the poor by expanding wage employment and livelihood opportunities.
- ♦ Also, with economies of scale which well-designed PPP's could achieve in providing public services, low-income households, which generally spend more on basic goods and services, would have access to affordable services.
- ♦ Through PPPs, the infrastructure growth link becomes stronger, especially when partnership arrangements emphasize the quality of infrastructure services, better maintenance, and delivering projects on time and within budget.
- ♦ Investments and improvements through PPP would free up more public resources and enable the State to divert resources into other public services like defence and security, and public needs which are more pressing, such as pro-poor interventions (conditional cash transfers, old age pension, etc. for example) and for expenditures in times of national disasters (like droughts, floods, etc.). It offers real advantages by helping governments close gaps in resources and spur economic growth, especially when faced with fiscal constraints.

➢ **Assessing Risk in Public–Private Partnerships**

PPPs also come with considerable risks and challenges. A noticeable trend since the 1980s has been instances of delays in execution and disputes between contract parties in PPPs as seen in such projects in Asia, including India, Africa, Latin America and the Caribbean. Problems encountered in PPP projects are outlined below.

- ■ Delays and cancellations due to various reasons have bogged down PPP projects and are a big concern in developing economies, where countries are grappling with stringent fiscal constraints.

- Delays and cancellations in infrastructure projects impose large efficiency losses, discourage private investment, and disrupt the provision of infrastructure and public services.
- Friction between contract parties in PPPs have caused contracts to run into difficulties or even being terminated midway leading to problems in reviving them.
- Where PPP projects have been abandoned without being completed, because either the private or public sector partner was unable to fulfil contract obligations, have led to time and cost overruns. The resulting cost escalation further adds to financial constraints of the State.
- There are different aspects of risks in PPPs including general risk to the economy, specific fiscal risk, and institutional risk concerning banks and financial agencies funding the projects. But the risk involved in government guarantee is the biggest because it has bearing on the balance sheet on the government.
- Fiscal and monetary risks have also political implications since the government may get entangled if issues in PPP remain unresolved for long. While there are instruments that can be used to insure and mitigate risks, and which could be leveraged but they come with a cost to the PPP.

➢ **Mitigating risks in PPP**

There are many considerations to be kept in view and care taken while finalizing PPP agreements to avoid disputes later. These are mentioned below.

- Due diligence must be exercised by both the Public and Private partners while entering into the relationship in a project or scheme. The viability of the project, costs involved and returns anticipated must be weighed properly to avert unrealistic expectations and eventual failure to meet targets.
- Caution should be taken in fixing the partnership because when PPPs are structured poorly, government and/or the private entity would face challenges. Hence governments should choose the PPP path, only if they have the discipline and commitment to do it in a sustainable manner that mitigates risk taking into consideration the duration, costs and other aspects of the project.
- PPPs are very context and project specific and it is important to understand the development process of a country, on a case by case basis, to better evaluate the risks they may be posing. For instance, in the case of infrastructure projects like highways or railway lines, they run into bottlenecks due to delays in land acquisition or labour issues. If these are foreseen before the start of the project, it would smoothen the process of execution and ensure timely completion.

- In cases where PPPs are finalised by bidding process among private partners, there may be a tendency to underquote and make unrealistic bids, even below the reserve or floor rate fixed, to win the contract. It could eventually lead to inability of the partner to fulfil the contract leading to disputes, delays, litigation, arbitration, etc. Hence the financial and technical bids should be carefully assessed to ensure the feasibility of completing the project.
- The credit worthiness and the past experience of the partner agency in executing projects of comparable magnitude need careful assessment while finalising the PPP arrangement.
- The allocation of monetary or other risks involved in the project, to be borne by the Public and Private partner should be clearly delineated in the contractual agreement so as to avoid disputes or legal issues later.

7. Public Private Partnership (PPP) in implementing projects and schemes have advantages and risks also. In the light of this, critically examine what has been India's experience with PPPs citing specific instances. Outline steps that can be taken to improve the system of PPP.

Ans. ➢ **Introduction**

As with all developing economies, infrastructure has played an important role in the socio-economic development of India. In the last decade and a half, Public Private Partnership (PPP) has played a key role in developing infrastructure. It has helped to provide vital facilities like highways of international standards, expanded railways, power and telecom sectors, ports, airports, etc. Apart from giving boost to the economy, along with agriculture and industry, infrastructure has provided employment to millions and helped to pull them out of poverty.

➢ **Role of PPP in India**

Since infrastructure development requires huge upfront investments, it became increasingly clear that the Government alone could not have undertaken the task and, therefore, embarked on a policy of promoting PPP as a means of augmenting investment in this crucial sector.

■ **Increasing role**

- Besides supplementing the public resources, PPP provides opportunity to tap the private sector for technical expertise and efficiencies in the provision of public assets and services.
- While measures were taken since the mid-1990s to induct private participation in different infrastructure sectors, the PPPs gained momentum during the Tenth (2002-07) and Eleventh (2007-12) Plan periods as more ambitious projects came to be launched.

- To improve the level and quality of economic and social infrastructure services across the country, the government came out with a Draft **National PPP Policy** in 2011.
- Since then, several initiatives were taken to systemise PPP regime. These included:
  - Setting up a robust institutional structure for appraising and approving PPP projects.
  - Increasing the availability of finance by creating dedicated institutions and providing viability gap funding.
  - Developing standardised documents such as model concession agreement across infrastructure sectors.

PPP scheme in India

India has seen considerable growth in PPPs and emerged as one of the leading PPP markets in the world, due to several policy and institutional initiatives taken by the central as well as many state governments.

A PPP Cell which was set up in 2006 in DEA, Ministry of Finance, which is responsible for policy matters on PPPs, clearance of projects by PPP Appraisal Committee Scheme, Financial Support to PPPs in Infrastructure, preparing Model Concession Agreements and Capacity Building.

According to the data provided by PPP Cell, Infrastructure Division, Dept. of Economic Affairs (DEA), Govt. of India, between 2011 and 2019, a total of 1824 projects involving ₹ 24.96 lakh crore have been awarded under PPP regime in India.

Assessment of PPP scheme in India

Problems and Challenges

The experience of the PPP projects in the infrastructure sector in India has been a mixed bag with successes and failures.

- **Uneven implementation:** While the PPP mode has contributed a lot to India's infrastructure development, implementation of PPP projects has been uneven across sectors and States. While PPP has taken off in sectors like roads, ports and electricity generation, it is yet to take off in sectors like railways and "social" sectors. Further, the geographical spread of PPPs has also not been uniform, and states like Madhya Pradesh, Andhra Pradesh and Maharashtra are much ahead of others in implementing PPPs.
- **Bureaucratic delays and hurdles:** Delays in decision-making both at the initial stages and for finalizing the project details and award of the work is a major issue. This may be due to problems of co-ordination between various ministries and between the Central and State governments concerned.

Fragmented decision making due to the involvement of multiple public agencies, tendering process being lengthy and split in two or three phases, from planning to final operation, cause problems in the implementation of PPP projects. Such delays deter investors and make them hesitant to invest in PPP projects in India.

- **Clearance delays and unrealistic assumptions:** Various other factors like delays in land acquisition for the project and environment impact assessment and contentious conditions in tenders also cause problems. Such delays lead to cost escalation and time overrun which upset the calculations on which the successful bidder would have made the offer. This later leads to disputes with the private partner, and if it is unresolved could even result in the private partner abandoning the project.

  DMRC-Reliance Infra project: A case in point is the Delhi Metro (DMRC)-Reliance Infrastructure-led Airport Express Line project which was a showpiece railway PPP project. Even before its commissioning in 2011, the project was impacted by failed safety clearances and technical glitches and a tussle arose between DMRC and the private partner.

  Another issue was inflated traffic projection made in the beginning. While the private partner expected daily footfall to exceed 40,000, the actual footfall was much less and by the time DMRC took over the line, the daily ridership was even less. This skewed the projections of financial viability for the operator. As a result, DMRC had to take over the operations of the Express line in public interest. And, the private partner slapped a penalty on DMRC, which led to arbitration and protracted legal battle in courts between the two entities.

- **Aggressive bidding and stalled projects:** In many highway projects, there were instances of aggressive bidding as the pre-qualification criteria made a large number of applicants eligible to bid – a practice that is contrary to well-established international norms. Such aggressive or unsustainable bids led to project failures.

  The stalling of projects adversely impacts public sector banks and other financiers who have lent funds and it results in non-performing assets (NPAs) and impairs their balance sheets. This, in turn, constrains future private investments. In 2014-15, 80 projects were stalled in the electricity sector and 54 of these 80 were PPP projects. Reviving these projects posed problems.

- **Lack of transparency and integrity:** This is an issue which may arise on the part of both the public and private partner. PPP projects are capital-intensive running into thousands of crores of rupees and complete transparency on both sides is of paramount importance. There will be competing bidders and with an urge to win the bid, there is scope for resorting to irregularities and miscalculations in assessing the project cost, likely rate of return, in preparing and processing the tender and finally in the award. Integrity is also vital because, in the absence of it, the bidders will tend to inflate the project cost, due to hidden costs of underhand payments, resulting in hike in expenditure and eventually even rendering the project unviable.

For instance, in Metro projects, private players look for a return of around 12-15 per cent, while metro project may yield an investment return of not more than 3 to 4 percent. These are also long-haul projects and will take long to break-even. If the returns can only be augmented by steep hike in fares, it will be problematic for various reasons. Such issues must be clearly weighed and reflected at the tender processing stage so as to avoid dispute and litigation later.

- **Dispute resolution:** Infrastructure projects are fraught with risks of disputes that will cause inordinate delays due to slow resolution processes. Arbitration awards are almost invariably appealed against, resulting in long drawn out disputes that may take 3 to 10 years to be settled.

  The number of disputes in the PPP projects has shown a significant increase from 56 cases involving ₹ 803 crore in 2013 to 116 cases worth ₹ 11,580 crore in 2015. Absence of a clear and fast dispute resolution mechanism increases the cost of projects and dampen investors' sentiments.

- **Political factors:** A risk that private partners carry when they execute the PPP projects is uncertainty due to political factors. If, with a change in the government, a project comes up for review and is cancelled after it has been finalised and even the work has commenced, it results in losses for the private partner, as they would have invested substantial amounts of money, time, manpower and effort in undertaking the project.

  Amaravati capital project in AP: This is an instance where the project was approved with the Singapore government partnering Andhra Pradesh government, and the World Bank was providing financial aid. The previous government which had planned it had acquired tens of thousands of acres of agricultural lands from farmers, giving them compensation and also agreed to return part of land in the new capital. When the project had made quite some progress in planning and initial works, a new government which took office reviewed the project and decided to annul it. Such cancellations do cast a shadow on the credibility of PPP regime in India, especially where foreign entities are partnering and institutions like the World Bank were funding it. It impacts the credibility of government and could discourage potential foreign investors showing interest in future projects.

- **Remedial measures to improve PPP regime**

The government has been taking measures to strengthen and revitalise PPP regime and had appointed a Committee headed by Dr. Vijay Kelkar, a former Finance Secretary and expert on economic matters, to make a study. The Committee, in its report in 2015, has made several recommendations in this regard. NITI Aayog has also looked into various aspects of the working of PPP and made suggestions.

The steps to be taken to improve and strengthen PPP are outlined below.

- **Focus on service delivery:** PPPs have the potential to deliver infrastructure projects better and faster. Currently, PPP contracts focus more on fiscal benefits whereas the focus should be on service delivery for citizens. PPPs should not become a tool for the government to evade its responsibility of service delivery to citizens.
- **Role for Private sector:** The PPP model requires the involvement of a private partner to leverage financing and improve operational efficiencies. Therefore, State-owned enterprises or Public sector undertakings should not be allowed to bid for PPP projects.
- **Viability of projects:** The PPP model should be adopted only after checking its viability for a project, in terms of costs and risks. PPP structures should not be adopted for very small projects, since the benefits are not commensurate with the costs.
- **Risk allocation and management:** Inequitable and unsustainable allocation of risk between the partners has been a major factor leading to failure of PPPs. PPP contracts should ensure optimal risk allocation across all stakeholders by ensuring that it is allocated to the entity that is best suited to manage the risk. A generic risk monitoring and evaluation framework should be developed covering all aspects of a project's lifecycle.
- **Strengthening policy and governance:** Kelkar Committee has recommended that the Ministry of Finance develop a national PPP policy document to be endorsed by Parliament. It has further suggested to examine the feasibility of formulating a PPP law.
- There is need for sector-specific approach to PPP models adopted as needs and conditions of different sectors – roads, power, rail, ports, aviation and social sectors – vary. There should be better monitoring of performance of PPPs.

8. Discuss the salient features of the telecommunications sector in India and its growth since independence.

Ans. Telecom, a vital sector

The telecom sector plays a critical role in an economy and serves as a powerful mode of development and poverty reduction through empowerment of masses due to its wide reach and networks driven by ever improving technology.

It facilitates instant communication, provides ideal links for population in remote and inaccessible places and averts the need for travel thus reducing scope for pollution and impact on environment.

Its importance has increased manifold with the advent of Computer and Internet facilities and Cellular wireless (mobile) telephony.

It is one of the key elements of the Sustainable Development Goals (SDGs) of the United Nations agenda to be accomplished by all countries by 2030.

Telecom sector in India

For over four decades since independence, the telecom sector in India was a monopoly under the Telephone Department. Over time, this resulted in various shortcomings and constraints as mentioned below:

- The lack of finances and resources hampered its expansion and growth.
- Due to lack of development, the demand for telephones far outstripped supply and there was a huge waiting list for phone connections.
- Despite the best efforts of the department to upgrade the systems, the quality and standard of service was below par.
- Issues such as frequent disruptions in the lines, delays in getting through long-distance calls, etc. led to complaints and dissatisfaction among public.

As a result, there was pressing demand to open up the sector to private operators and liberalize it with a view to allow competition and improve the services.

Growth and Salient features of Telecom sector in India

The pace of growth over the years and the salient features of the sector are discussed below.

- ♦ **Second largest:** Indian telecom network is the second largest in the world after China, in terms of the number of telephone connections. It is also one of the fastest growing in terms of telecom subscribers.
- ♦ **Impact of liberalisation:** After liberalisation and opening up telecom to the private sector in 1990's, the total number of telephone subscribers has grown at a Compound Annual Growth Rate (CAGR) of 35 percent. The comparable rates in the 1980s and 1990s were 9 percent and 22 percent respectively.

- **Exponential growth:** As will be seen from Table 10.2, the growth has been exponential, especially in the case of mobile cellular phones after 2000. The growth, both in absolute numbers and Tele-density (i.e., the number of phones per 100 people), has been driven mainly by mobile subscribers. The share of wireless telephones in total telephones is over 98 per cent.

Table 10.2: Growth of Telecom Sector in India

	Year	**1960**	**1980**	**1990**	**2000**	**2018**	
1	Fixed phones (Million):	0.33	2.14	5.07	32.4	21.9	
2	Fixed phones (per 100 people)	0.074	0.31	0.58	3.07	1.62	
	Year	**1995**	**2000**	**2010**	**2015**	**2017**	
3	Mobile cellular subscribers (Million)	0.07	3.58	752.2	1,001	1,169	
4	Mobile cellular subscribers (per 100 people)	0.008	0.34	60.94	76.41	87.32	
	Year	**2001**	**2005**	**2010**	**2015**	**2018**	
5	Fixed Broadband subscribers (Million)	0.05	1.35	10.99	16.94	18.17	
6	Fixed Broadband subscribers (per 100 people)	0.005	0.117	0.89	1.29	1.34	
7	Individuals using Internet (Percentage of population)	0.66	2.39	7.5	17	34.45 (2017)	
	Year	**1997**	**2000**	**2005**	**2010**	**2015**	**2019**
8	Tele-density (No. of phones Per 100 people)						
	Rural:	0.3	0.7	1.74	24.31	49.82	57.5
	Urban:	4.8	8.3	28.2	119.45	152.57	159.66
	Total:	1.6	2.9	9.08	52.74	81.85	90.10

Source: Dept. of Telecom, India, International Telecommunications Union (ITU) and World Bank data.

- **Growth in Mobile phones:** The growth in the widespread usage of mobile phones has been driven by affordable tariffs, wider availability, roll-out of Mobile Number Portability (MNP), expanding 3G and 4G coverage, evolving consumption patterns, supportive policy and regulatory environment.
- **Low tariffs:** India has one of the lowest mobile tariffs in the world. Prepaid mobile rates have declined more than Postpaid tariffs.

- **Rural-Urban tele-density:** Tele-density shows wide variation between rural and urban areas. The gap is significantly greater after 2000 though it is getting somewhat reduced lately.
- **Internet penetration:** Though the percentage of population using Internet (Internet subscribers) in India has steadily increased, this percentage in 2017 was only 34 whereas the percentage in US was 87, UK 94, China 54 and Brazil 67. The overall percentage for the world was 49.7. The percentage in India has gone up to 50 by 2020.
- **Broadband connections:** The number of Broadband connections steadily rose from 20 lakh in 2006 to 661 million in 2019.
- **India leads in data consumption:** India's leap towards wireless broadband has been a driving force for rapidly rising data consumption making India the global leader in data consumption. The average monthly consumption per subscriber increased 146 times from 62 MB in 2014 to 9.06 GB in 2019. This has created opportunities for the government to reach out to weaker and marginalized groups and accelerate social progress by providing various services.
- **Dominance of private sector:** The private sector having a share of over 88 per cent dominates the telecom sector. Telephone connections provided by the private sector in 2019 stood at over 1040 million while that provided by the public sector stood at 133 million.
- **Universal Service Obligation:** As telecom growth in rural areas lagged behind and to give impetus to the rural telephony, the government established in 2002 a "'Universal Service Obligation Fund (USOF)". It provides subsidy support to various services such as mobile services, broadband connectivity and creation of infrastructure like optical fibre cable (OFC) in rural and remote areas. The Fund raises 'universal levy' out of a percentage of the revenue earned by the telecom operators under various licenses.

9. Critically examine the role played by telecom sector post-independence and the impact it has had on Indian economy. Outline the major steps taken by the government in developing this sector.

Ans. ➢ **Telecommunications, a game-changer**

The telecommunications sector plays a pivotal role in the economy providing support to all other sectors through the facility of instant communication. This helps not only to avert the need for physical movement and travel but, saves time and energy and in reducing environmental pollution.

Telecom, especially with the advent of wireless (cellular mobile) phones has become a powerful tool in aiding communication in remote and far-flung areas, more so in times of disasters and emergencies. People in rural areas which have less transport and other facilities get connected to urban centres to fulfil their essential needs. It enables medical consultations over long distances through the facility of telemedicine, videoconferencing between large groups which have all had a transformative change in the way people work and business is conducted in an economy.

♦ **Role of Telecom sector**

Since India's independence in 1947 and until it was liberalised in mid-1990s, telecom sector, which was a monopoly under the government's Dept. of Telecommunications, witnessed growth only in fits and starts. Though the number of phone connections rose from less than a lakh in 1951, when the population was 360 million, to 5.07 million when the population was 680 million in 1981, it was far below the needs of India's growing economy.

As a result, by 1980's demand far outstripped supply and there was a huge waiting list for phones. Besides, the systems were not adequately upgraded to cope with the ever-growing traffic due to lack of financial resources with the government, and there was dissatisfaction about the quality of service.

♦ **Initial steps at Liberalisation**

- **C-DoT set up:** In 1984, on the initiative of Sam Pitroda, a telecom innovator and entrepreneur, the government created the Centre for Development of Telematics (C-DoT) to develop indigenous technologies and private manufacturing of telecom equipments. Its immediate goals were to build small rural exchanges and develop a small rugged switch that would work in India's tropical heat. This initiative helped to expand phone facilities in rural areas and improve tele-density levels in the vast, under-serviced rural parts of the country.

  C-DoT also provided some relief for problem of scarcity of telephone equipment as the decade of 1980's drew to a close. With these moves, India's telecommunications and computing sectors reduced the dependency on imported equipment.

- **PCOs - Rise and Decline:** Another important initiative which Pitroda took was to establish, in the early 1990s, a vast network of Public Call Offices (PCOs) across the length and breadth of the country. The rationale behind this was to provide easy access to basic phone services to those who did not have a telephone – for making Local, STD and ISD calls. In expanding the network, Pitroda stressed on the aspect of "accessibility" of phone rather than "density" so that everyone could have unfettered access to this essential facility.

  The franchise for running the PCOs was granted to weaker sections of the society, namely, the unemployed, physically handicapped, war widows, etc. These ubiquitous booths that linked virtually every corner of the country provided employment to millions of people.

But with the advent and spread of mobile phones since 1995, the need for PCOs declined drastically as almost everyone, including those at the very bottom of the pyramid, had a mobile in hand. The number of PCOs which rose from 1.97 lakh in 1994 to a peak of over 6 million in 2008 began to decline from 2009. By 2015, there were just 5.6 lakh PCO booths.

▶ **Mobile telephone**

India was rather late in introducing mobile phone facility. Advanced countries like USA and UK introduced it in mid-1980s. While even China and Malaysia had made a beginning by 1986-87, India lagged behind and introduced it only in 1995. By 2000, China had 85 million mobile subscribers while India had just 3.5 million. However, thereafter India did catch up and in 2010 while China had 859 million mobile connections, India had 752 million subscribers and in 2017, India had 1.17 billion mobile connections against China's 1.4 billion connections.

♦ **Thrust on Telecom reforms**

The 1990s saw the launch of a series of far-reaching reforms in the telecom sector. The National Telecom Policies (NTPs) of 1994, 1999 and later of 2012 brought about significant changes.

■ **National Telecom Policy, 1994:** The **NTP-1994** had the following objectives:

- Provide telephone on demand.
- Ensure world class services at reasonable prices.
- Universal availability of basic telecom service in all villages.
- Make India a major manufacturing/export-based hub for telecom equipment.
- As it was recognized that funds required would not be available out of Government sources, private enterprise was allowed to enter the sector to bring in the much needed investments. Thus, a major step was taken to open up basic telecom services and Value-added services such as mobile services, to private sector.

■ **TRAI:** Another major step was the setting up of Telecom Regulatory Authority of India (TRAI) in 1997. It was recognized that an independent regulatory framework was needed to separate government's regulatory role from its service-providing functions. This was in line with the best global practices. TRAI's mandate included the following:

- Regulating telecom services, including fixation and revision of tariffs.
- Determining Quality of Service (QoS) standards, and
- Fixing the terms and conditions for inter-connectivity between service providers.

■ **National Telecom Policy, 1999:** As the objectives of 1994 policy were not fully achieved and to cope with the changes that had taken place in the telecom and allied sectors, the government came out with NTP-1999 which was more ambitious and had the following objectives:

- Ensuring affordable and effective communication facilities for citizens.
- Improving Telecom development in remote, hilly and tribal areas.
- Creation of modern and efficient telecom infrastructure with the convergence of telecom, IT, media, and electronics.
- Making the Telecom sector more competitive by providing equal opportunities and level playing field for all entities.
- Strengthening of R & D efforts.
- Provide impetus to build world class manufacturing capabilities.

■ **Universal Service Obligation (USOF):** It was recognized that the cost of providing telecom services in rural and remote areas was higher and these areas do not generate commensurate revenue due to lower population density, low income and lack of commercial activity. Thus, commercial considerations would not justify provision of telecom facilities in backward and rural areas. Hence most countries of the world have put in place special policies and arranged special funds to provide universal telecom service in such areas.

NTP-1999 provided that the resources for meeting the Universal Service Obligation (USO) would be raised through a "Universal Access Levy (UAL)" which would be a percentage of the revenue earned by the operators under various licenses.

The Universal Service Obligation Fund (USOF) was introduced in India and it was approved by the Parliament in December 2003.

♦ **Assessment of NTPs:** As a result of this liberalisation undertaken with NTPs 1994 and 1999, India took further strides in the expansion of telecom services. It, however, shows mixed results in the case of Fixed phone lines and Mobile services. (See Table 10.3).

While the fixed phone lines rose from 11.9 million (mn) in 1995 to 32.4 mn. lines in 2000, its growth between 2000 and 2010 was rather muted as only 2.7 million connections were added in this decade. This was because of the explosive growth of mobile services which had taken off after 2000 and mobile service became very affordable and offered more convenience in usage. It offered wider services like messaging and internet facility apart from making voice calls.

By 2010, "a mobile in every hand" became a catchy slogan and even almost everyone at the "bottom of the pyramid" came to have a mobile which helped them in their daily chores and to connect to near and dear ones.

Table 10.3: Growth of Telecom Sector in India

	Year	**1960**	**1990**	**1995**	**2000**	**2010**	**2018**
1	Fixed phones (Million):	0.33	5.07	11.9	32.4	35.1	21.9
2	Fixed phones (per 100 people)	0.074	0.58	1.2	3.1	2.8	1.6
	Year	**1995**	**2000**	**2010**	**2015**	**2017**	**2018**
3	Mobile cellular subscribers (Million)	0.07	3.6	752.2	1,001	1,169	1,176
4	Mobile cellular subscribers (per 100 people)	0.01	0.34	60.9	76.4	87.3	86.9

Source: International Telecommunications Union (ITU) and World Bank Data.

Not only that fixed line service did not show much expansion, it has even declined considerably between 2010 and 2018. Whereas mobile services expanded exponentially both in absolute numbers and in tele-density, i.e., the number of phones per 100 people.

- **NTP 2012:** Keeping in view the modern technological advancements in the telecom sector such as 5G, Internet of Things (IoT), Machine to Machine (M2M) interface, etc., need was felt to introduce a 'customer focused' and 'application driven' policy for the Indian telecom sector.

  Hence the government came out with National Telecom Policy-2012 (NTP-2012) to maximize public good by providing affordable and reliable and broadband services across the entire country. Its main thrust was to reap the multiplier effect and transformational impact of these services to advance the national development agenda while enhancing equity and inclusiveness.

- **NTP 2018:** As India was moving towards greater 'digitisation' in diverse sectors, the NTP-2012 was re-christened as National Digital Communications Policy-2018 (NDCP-2018) and launched in 2018 after detailed consultations with all stakeholders.

  The key objectives of the policy, to be achieved by 2022, are:

- Providing Broadband for all.
- Creating 4 Million additional jobs in the Digital Communications sector.
- Enhancing the contribution of the Digital Communications sector to 8% of India's GDP from ~ 6% in 2017.
- Propelling India to the top 50 Nations in the ICT Development Index of ITU from 134 in 2017.
- Enhancing India's contribution to Global Value Chains and ensuring Digital Sovereignty.

For accomplishing these objectives by year 2022, the NDCP-2018 envisages three Missions viz., Connect, Propel and Secure India.

■ National Broadband Mission

To give fillip to the process of digitisation, the National Broadband Mission (NBM) was launched in December 2019 with the following objectives:

- Fast track growth of digital communications infrastructure by laying 30 lakhs route km of Optical Fibre Cable (OFC) and increase in tower density.
- Facilitate universal and equitable access to broadband services for people across the country, especially in rural and remote areas.
- Bridge the digital divide with Broadband access to all villages by 2022 and by providing affordable and universal access to the facility. The ambitious "**BharatNetDigital India**" project under implementation will go a long way in achieving this.
- Significantly improve the quality of services for mobile and internet.
- Investment of US$100 billion (₹ 7 lakh crore) from stakeholders, including ₹ 70,000 crore from Universal Service Obligation Fund (USOF).

➢ Conclusion

The various positive developments in the Telecom sector augur well for India despite many challenges the sector faces.

The policy initiatives taken in this sector should give a greater push to the Digital India programme which will not only bridge the digital divide but go a long way in rejuvenating rural India. It goes without saying that, going forward, rural India and semi-urban areas will have to play a greater role as "growth engines" if Indian economy is to gain more traction as urban centres are bursting at the seams and are largely overburdened with intractable problems.

10. Despite its impressive growth in the last two decades and the opportunities it provides, the Telecom sector in India faces many challenges and stress which are impeding its progress. Identify the challenges and the steps the government has taken to overcome them.

Ans. Telcom industry, which plays a critical role in the country's socio-economic development, has registered sustained and impressive growth especially after the liberalisation era of 1990s when it was thrown open to the private sector and with the advent of mobile phones. This sector makes significant contribution to the economy in both direct and indirect ways through fixed-line telephony, mobile phones and wireless Internet.

➢ **Contribution to the economy**

- Direct contribution includes capital investment, production of goods and services, generation of employment and international trade, among others.
- Indirect ways include an increase in business efficiency, enhanced speed and quality of information flows, better access to markets and diffusion of innovation.
- Its role in linking rural, remote and inaccessible areas with the rest of the country gives considerable boost to economic activity. For a vast country like India with about 70 per cent of population living in rural and far-flung areas, this is of crucial importance.
- The role it plays in the education and health sectors through on-line education and spread of knowledge through fixed-line telephony, mobile phones, wireline and wireless Internet, telemedicine, etc. makes significant impact on the society.

➢ **Employment generation:** The sector generates employment in diverse ways: jobs for engineers, infrastructure and cyber security experts, application developers, sales executives, in manufacturing of phone equipments, service and repair technicians, call centre executives among others. In addition, it creates employment in various dependent and allied sectors such as e-commerce, online content industry, etc. In 2015, the mobile industry in India provided direct and indirect employment to 4 million people.

➢ **Impressive growth**

♦ India is currently the world's second-largest telecommunications market with a subscriber base of 1.18 billion (1,180 million) in 2019 of which 1.15 billion are wireless telephone connections.

♦ Thus, the share of wireless telephones in total telephones is 97 per cent.

♦ The overall tele-density (i.e., the number of phones per 100 people) in the country is 88.81%, urban tele-density being 156.82% and rural tele-density 56.71%.

- ♦ The mobile industry has witnessed exponential growth over the last few years driven by affordable tariffs, wider availability, roll out of Mobile Number Portability (MNP), expanding 3G and 4G coverage, evolving consumption patterns and supportive policy and regulatory environment.
- ♦ India is also the world's second largest market in terms of total internet users. The number of internet subscribers in the country has reached 687 million by September 2019.
- ♦ In 2018, the wider mobile ecosystem supports a total of 4 million direct and indirect jobs. This is expected to increase substantially with more manufacturing to come up in the sector.

➢ **Opportunities and Challenges**

But despite the rapid growth over the last few years, the telecom sector is beset with many challenges and constraints as detailed below.

▸ **Internet and Broadband facility**

■ **Opportunities**

- India's leap towards wireless broadband can be the driving force of the economy due to rapidly rising data consumption and deployment of requisite technologies by service providers.
- India has one of the lowest telephone tariffs and data prices in the world.
- This has helped the government to reach out to weaker and marginalized sections and to promote social progress by providing services that were previously not feasible.
- **BharatNet, the Digital India programme,** is being rolled out to digitally connect 2.5 lakh Gram Panchayats (GPs) and with Common Service Centres (CSCs) to provide efficiently a wide range of government services and welfare benefits in villages. This project will provide last mile connectivity to all GPs through Wi-Fi or other suitable broadband technology. It will go a long way in not only improving rural economies and provide employment to lakhs of people, but also spread digital literacy among rural populace.

■ **Constraints**

- **Low internet penetration:** The percentage of population using Internet in India was only 34.45 in 2017 as against 87.3 % in USA, 94.6% in UK, 80.1% in Malaysia, 54.3% in China and 52.9% in Thailand. India has to step up further to increase the percentage by skilling and spread of digital literacy. It has gone up to 50% by 2020.
- When Digital India is completed providing greater Internet and Broadband access in villages, and with mobile technology becoming the critical means of accessing a broad range of public services and empowering the masses, India could improve its position on internet penetration.

- Some of the major reasons behind low Internet penetration in India are lack of accessibility, lack of information and literacy, inconsistent power supply, and high price and maintenance cost of personal computers (PCs). Mobile Internet access could have a substantial impact on Internet users in the country.
- Digital literacy needs special focus at the school/college levels. The National Digital Literacy Mission should focus on introducing digital literacy at the primary level in all schools. Under the Pradhan Mantri Gramin Digital Saksharta Abhiyan (PMGDISHA), by 2019, 1.5 crore persons in rural India have been trained in computer operations. But as the target is to train 6 crore persons, with at least one person in 40 per cent of rural households to be trained, there is still a long way to cover.

▸ **Spectrum issues**

♦ **Sale and Auctions:** Spectrum is sold in auctions and the telecom firms take various factors into consideration while making the bids which influence the final outcome of the auction. These include factors such as the company's vision, network's potential, pricing, the number of participants and level of competition in the auction, availability of finances, etc. The government's promotional and marketing efforts will also be a factor. Due to these, there is no guarantee that all the spectrum put to auction will be sold. This has been the experience in some of the spectrum auctions in India which hampers the expansion of the sector.

♦ **Availability:** Availability of adequate Spectrum and its pricing have been critical factors affecting the expansion and efficiency of telecom services. On this, often there are conflicting views between the service providers, on the one hand, and the Dept. of Telecom and the regulator, TRAI, on the other.

While the governmental bodies say that enough spectrum is available, telecom companies cite lack of adequate spectrum for factors like call drops, interruptions in speech during calls, delay in calls getting connected, etc. It is also a paradox that while it is said that spectrum is scarce in India, the spectrum put on sale goes abegging in some auctions.

♦ **Pricing:** Sometimes, the telecom companies find the reserve prices fixed by the government too high and they find it unaffordable. Where sufficient spectrum is not available for an auction, then it will become a stress auction for all the competing participants. This would distort the entire purpose and the process of auction and could lead to irrational bidding with exorbitant prices quoted which leads to unviable consequences for the operators.

- **Financial state of the sector**

As already stated, the industry has contributed immensely to the country's overall growth and has been the backbone of the nation's economy. Factors such as India's large population, steady economic growth, intense competition in the sector, low tariffs, infrastructure sharing and the introduction of enabling regulatory reforms, all have helped the telecom industry in India grow at a rapid pace.

- **Revenue:** In the decade from 2006 - 2016, the sector's revenues increased from ₹ 873.12 billion to ₹ 2,453.51 billion, at a CAGR of more than 10 percent.
- **Capital investment:** Capital investment in gross fixed assets has risen continuously since 2001. During the period from 2001-2016, it increased by more than seven times, from ₹ 1,031 billion to ₹ 7,605 billion.
- **Financial stress and AGR:** But the industry is reeling under a daunting debt burden of about ₹ 4 lakh crore and is in dire financial straits. The problem is compounded by the dispute regarding Adjusted Gross Revenue (AGR) dues under which telecom companies together are asked to pay a huge sum of ₹ 1.47 lakh crore to the Department of Telecom (DoT). Of this, ₹ 92,000 crore is towards licence fee and ₹ 55,100 crore as spectrum usage charges.

  The genesis of the issue is that in 1999 the government gave an option to telecom licensees to migrate from "fixed license fee" regime to the "revenue sharing fee" model. Under the latter, mobile telephone operators were required to share a percentage of their AGR with the government as annual license fee and spectrum usage charges.

  The dispute between DoT and the mobile operators was mainly on what constitutes AGR. The DoT argued that AGR includes all revenues from both telecom and non-telecom services. Whereas the companies claimed that AGR should comprise just the revenue accrued from core (telecom) services and not revenue from dividend, interest or profit on sale of any investment or fixed assets. The matter went to courts and eventually the Supreme Court upheld the contention of DoT. This has added to the financial woes of telecom companies. Following this the companies have made part payments and sought time to pay the balance over a long-term settlement.

- **Manufacturing**

A major challenge for India is to become a manufacturing hub for mobile devices and telecom equipment. While government policies relating to electronics and handset manufacturing domestically have paid rich dividends, there is need to give greater thrust to them.

- **Progress:** The production of mobile phones in the country has gone up significantly from around ₹ 18,900 crore (US$ 3 billion) in 2014-15 to ₹ 1,70,000 crore (US$ 24 Billion) in 2018-19 and the domestic demand is almost completely being met out of domestic production.

♦ **PLI scheme:** The government has come up with a productivity-linked incentive (PLI) scheme for manufacture of electronics and mobile devices as detailed below.

- **Objective:** It aims to boost domestic manufacturing and attract large investments in production of mobile phones and specified electronic components including assembly, testing, marking units.
- **Incentives:** The scheme will extend provide an incentive of 4% to 6% on incremental sales of goods manufactured in India to eligible companies, for a period of five years from the base year.
- **Scope:** The scheme is expected to benefit 5 to 6 major global companies and few leading domestic firms, in the field of mobile manufacturing and select electronics components thereby making India a major electronics manufacturing base.
- **Financial Implications:** The total cost of the scheme is estimated to be ₹ 41,000 crore.
- **Benefits:** The scheme has the potential to generate 2 lakhs direct and 6 lakhs indirect jobs over five-year period.
- **Scheme for telecom equipments:** A similar PLI scheme is proposed to promote manufacture of specified telecom products by international companies in India. These products could include access network equipment and associated systems for next generation 5G and core equipment, switches, routers, optic fibre cables and digital microwave radios, among others.
- **Suitable ecosystem:** For the above schemes to fully succeed, India will have to create suitable "ease of doing business" climate with predictable tax policies and legal framework which are not often tweaked or changed creating uncertainties. Besides, infrastructure support like land, power, water, transport facilities need to be extended to the companies as India is facing stiff competition from Vietnam, Thailand, Malaysia, etc. Already some states have extended such facilities and some major manufacturing companies have evinced interest in setting up units in India which augurs well.

(For more details on issues relating to Spectrum, see Question 11)

11. India's spectrum allocations policy has been beset with problems and inconsistencies which have hampered the progress of the telecom sector. Critically examine this statement and suggest remedial measures.

Ans. Communication airwaves, also known as radio frequency spectrum, are a critical resource for mobile communication. While spectrum is not depletable, technology effects can limit the extent to which it can be beneficially utilized at a point in time. Governments license the use of spectrum to regulate its application and maximise social benefit. Advances in mobile technology have led to its innovative applications in education, healthcare, transportation, and commerce, among others.

- **Spectrum management:** With the exponential demand for mobile phones and Internet, radio spectrum has become a scarce commodity in many countries including India. The advancement in new technologies and proliferation of wireless communications has made spectrum management and allocation a critical task.

  Since the introduction of the first generation network in 1980s, India has introduced 3G and 4G systems and is now on the verge of launching the highly advanced 5G network which will make communications manifold faster and efficient.

  - **Spectrum allocations:** Initially spectrum was being allocated through an administrative process. As this system was rigid, entailed delays and lacked transparency, in 2010 India adopted the system of auction which is more transparent, eliminates subjectivity in the allocation process and helps to discover market price. It also allows spectrum to be placed in the hands of operators who are able to use it best.
  - **License fee regime:** The license fee framework also underwent changes over the years.

    Cellular service licensees were initially required to pay a fixed annual license fee, based on the amount agreed during the bidding process. This proved to be unsustainable due to the significant losses incurred by the service providers. Hence, in 1999, they were permitted to migrate to a regime under which they would pay license fee based on revenue share.
  - **Spectrum auctions:** A study the spectrum auctions held in India since 2010 shows a mixed picture.
    - **2010 auction:** In 2010, for the first time, spectrum was sold through an online auction to ensure optimum use of spectrum, prevent hoarding, stimulate competition and promote the roll out of 3G and broadband services. It also helped the government to raise better revenue.
    - **2012 and 2013:** Though it was expected that future auctions would also be smooth and successful, the auction held in 2012 did not have the same degree of success. Of the two bands put on sale, only a small portion of one band was sold, while the other band was completely unsold. When this unsold spectrum and an additional spectrum were put on auction in 2013, the response was lukewarm due to prevailing market conditions.
    - **2014:** The 2014 auction saw active bidding but still the total spectrum sold was less than 60 per cent of what was on offer. The cost of spectrum acquisition was felt to be quite steep. Also, the spectrum prices for certain bands in the metros was much higher than international averages.
    - **2015:** In 2015, in the biggest auction held till then by volume of spectrum, the government auctioned spectrum across four bands. For operators whose

licenses were expiring after 20 years, spectrum was essential for continuity of business. Besides, operators spent on procuring new spectrum to provide high speed 3G coverage.

- **2016:** In 2016, while the government offered for sale even more spectrum in a number of bands, the outcome was uneven. The steep reserve prices in certain bands dissuaded operators from bidding and hence spectrum in those bands were completely unsold.

♦ **Revenue realised:** The 2010 auction fetched ₹ 1.06 lakh crore, 2015 auction ₹ 1.09 lakh crore and 2014 and 2016 auctions over ₹ 65,000 crore. The other auctions fetched only lesser amounts.

♦ **Spectrum pricing:** Pricing of spectrum sold in auctions has been a major issue between the service providers, on the following grounds.

- **Reserve price:** Telecom companies fault the government for fixing the base reserve price for different spectrum bands unreasonably high. High reserve prices and/or unrealistic pre-determined spectrum value have resulted in poor response from potential bidders and led to valuable spectrum being left unsold and unused.
- **5G spectrum:**The base price of 5G spectrum in 3400 to 3800 megahertz (MHz) band is highest in India. The base price per MHz for spectrum in this band is $65 million (mn.) in India as compared to $26 mn. in Italy, $18 mn. in South Korea, $10 million in the UK and $5 mn. in Australia. Though various industry bodies and Broadband India Forum (BIF) have taken up the issue of exorbitant spectrum price with the government, their plea has not been acceded to.
- **Financial woes:** There is also the prospect of demand for 5G spectrum being low as the sector is highly concentrated with very few service providers, and the major players like Airtel and Vodafone are virtually crippled by debt and financial woes arising out of Supreme Court orders to pay huge amount to the government on account of Adjusted Gross Revenue arrears.
- **Task Force:** A task force appointed by the Finance Ministry had underlined what the operators had stated – that the 5G spectrum price suggested by the Dept. of Telecom (DoT) is too high.

♦ **Impact of high prices:** The high prices might also undermine the country's National Digital Communications Policy (NDCP) goals, making the provision of inclusive and affordable high-speed 5G services to all sections of the population, notably users in rural areas, uneconomic.

♦ **Impact on investments:** The undue financial burden due to high spectrum prices will also have impact on the capacity of service providers to make investments in infrastructure required to ensure quality service to customers, meet demand in highly populated urban areas and expand networks to provide coverage to people in rural areas.

- **Timing of auctions:** The timing of auction of spectrum also plays a major role. The opportunity cost of unused spectrum is enormous and far outweighs any short-term gains in auction revenue by postponing the auction process. For instance, the sale of 5G spectrum bands has been put off repeatedly which delayed its roll-out with consequences for the efficiency of not only the telecom sector but a host of other entities in the industrial and services sectors who would benefit from this vastly upgraded technology. It is to be noted that quite a few other countries have already gone ahead and started roll-out of 5G service.
- **5G for rural areas:** A positive development in regard to providing 5G services in rural areas is that Telecom Standards Development Society, India (TSDSI), a national body responsible for the development of Indian telecom standards, has successfully introduced an indigenously developed 5G candidate standard. The TSDSI 5G technology will deliver, mobile internet and next-generation IoT services.

  It is a key enabler for 5G based rural broadband usage scenario in India and similarly placed geographies. This enhancement will ensure that nearly all of India's villages can be covered from towers located at gram panchayats, whereas nearly a third of such villages would be out of coverage otherwise.

  Expert groups at International Telecommunication Union (ITU) meetings which evaluated the TSDSI technology have ratified that the technology meets ITU requirements.

  Adoption of TSDSI's 5G standard in India by the government will enable India to leap-frog in the 5G space, with key innovations introduced by Indian entities accepted as part of global wireless standards for the first time. The nation stands to gain enormously both in achieving the required 5G penetration in rural and urban areas as well as in nurturing the nascent Indian R&D ecosystem to make global impact.

  This innovation suited for rural coverage and connectivity will find its rightful place in the 5G eco-system that will be deployed in India and in other countries similarly placed.

- **Conclusion:** At this juncture, there is a need to review the effectiveness of India's spectrum allocation strategy and the basis on which reserve prices are fixed, which are out-of-line with international norms, and result in non-discovery of proper market prices.

  The success of an auction is determined not only by the ability to sell a large proportion of spectrum up for auction, but also by the market/clearing price being significantly above the reserve price.

  Reserve prices should be set at levels that are high enough to keep non-serious bidders at bay, but low enough to achieve vibrant price discovery.

  There is obviously much to be done to improve the effectiveness of spectrum auctions and balance the socio-economic benefits over revenue maximization.

12. Assess the performance and state of the power sector in India. Outline the shortcomings and challenges it faces and the steps and reforms the government has taken to overcome them.

Ans. India is the third largest producer and also third largest consumer of electricity in the world and is also the fastest growing energy market in the world. The country's investment in the energy sector grew at a rate of 12 per cent in 2018, which, according to the International Energy Agency (IEA), is the highest growth rate compared to any other country.

The power sector in India has made steady progress since independence but it has not been adequate enough to meet the demands of the economy. The achievements and shortfalls of the sector can be summed up as follows:

➢ **Achievements:**

- **Installed capacity:** The all-India installed capacity of electricity supply (Utilities and Non-utilities) rose from 2,300 megawatts (MW) in 1950-51 to 33,400 MW in 1980-81 and to 3,70,348 MW (370 GW) in 2019-20.
- **Electricity generation:**The electricity generation from conventional sources increased from 420.6 Billion Units (BU) in 1997-98 to 1,376 BU in 2018-19.
- **Per capita electricity consumption:** The per capita consumption of electricity has also risen steadily over the years from 17.9 kW/h in 1950-51 to 132.3 kW/h in 1980-81 and 1,181 kWh as of 2018-19.
- **Renewable energy:** In a significant thrust, generation of power from renewable sources increased from 3.4 billion units (BU) in 2003-04 to 126.8 BU in 2018-19.
- **Rural electrification:** An ambitious scheme of providing electricity in India's vast rural hinterland has been in operation since 1969 with Rural Electrification Corporation (REC), a public sector enterprise (which has been renamed REC Limited in 2018), tasked with its implementation. The scheme has made significant progress and covered all villages with electricity. But it faces the onerous task of ensuring that every household in rural areas gets electric connection with 24-hour supply and that too reliable service with no power outages or power cuts.
- **Access to electricity:** More than 115 million people have gained access to electricity since 2013, increasing the share of population with access to electricity from about 80 percent in 2013 to 86 percent in 2017.
- **Energy efficiency:** India has taken important steps to improve energy efficiency. Under the Unnat Jyoti by Affordable LEDs for All (UJALA) scheme, launched in 2015, 240 million energy efficient LED bulbs and 1 million energy efficient fans have been distributed to consumers as of July 2017.

- **Shortcomings**
  - **Shortage in energy:** While the gap between the requirement and availability of energy has been brought down from 34,175 million units (MU) in 1997-98, i.e., the beginning of the Ninth Five-Year Plan, to 7,070 MU in 2018-19, there is still shortage to be made good.

    Power shortage adversely impacts the productivity of all sectors, particularly industries and services.
  - **Per capita electricity consumption:** India's per capita (P.C.) electricity consumption lags behind the global average as well as that of the advanced countries.

    The global per capita consumption of electricity was 3,130 kWh in 2014, according to the World Bank, when India's consumption that year stood at 805 kWh. The difference is even more stark when compared with the per capita consumption figures for that year of USA (12,997 kWh), South Korea (10,497 kWh) and other industrialised nations. Even Malaysia (4,652 kWh), China (3,927 kWh) and Brazil (2,620 kWh) had much higher figures.
  - **Over-dependence on thermal power:** Even by 2019-20, 62 per cent of India's installed capacity is based on thermal power. With such heavy dependence on coal-based power generation India will miss the emission norms that were to be met by 2022.
- **Challenges faced by the Power sector**
  - **Growing demand:** Despite impressive progress, India still faces an enormous task to meet the growing demand for electricity. Because of India's growing population, rapid urbanization, and economy that is expected to grow at an average rate of almost 7 percent per year, the electricity demand in India is projected to increase almost three-fold between 2018 and 2040 according to International Energy Agency (IEA).
  - **Electricity to households:** India has to further expand the access of households to electricity and improve the quality of electricity services. As of 2017, about 178 million people were still living off grid. Although the power deficit has been substantially reduced over the last few years, the reliability of electricity is still low compared with the international standards. The *2018 Global Competitiveness Report* ranks India 80th among 137 economies on the reliability of its electricity supply. **(For more on this, see Questions13 and 14 in this chapter).**
  - **Dependence on coal:** Expert studies have pointed out that India's continued dependence on coal-based thermal plants for generating power would mean that the country would find it difficult to meet targets set for reduction of carbon emission in line with commitments made under the 2015 Paris Climate Agreement. Already, despite having the world's fourth largest coal reserves, India imports millions of tonnes of coal. The government has announced that the country will stop importing thermal coal from 2023-24.

Yet, as part of India's strategy to revive and boost economic activity, the government has opened up coal blocks for commercial mining and set in place a new auction process for awarding coal and lignite blocks on revenue-sharing basis.

To reduce the harmful effects of coal, Coal India, the major public entity extracting coal, is tasked to generate 5 GW of solar power by 2023-24 and to diversify into coal gasification with a target of 50 million tonnes by 2030 to achieve a sustainable energy mix for the country.

India has to phase out thermal power plants older than 25 years and this whole process would require around ₹ 50,000 crore and could take years to achieve. **(For more on this, see Question 15 in this chapter).**

- **Transmission & Distribution (T & D):** Transmission system plays an important role in the efficient delivery of power to the ultimate consumer. The transmission network in India has expanded over the years and although power curtailment caused by transmission constraints has gradually declined, a significant amount of electricity is still lost to congestion in the electric network.

  Various factors affect T & D losses, including managerial efficiency, condition of the distribution network, size of the workforce, lack of adoption of modern technology, and density of the population served.

  Poor infrastructure, faulty metering, and outdated equipment all contribute to high network losses. One major factor responsible for electricity losses is pilferage and theft of electricity in the network.

  Although these losses have gradually declined since 2001, they remained as high as 22 percent in 2016, among the highest in the world.

- **Financial woes of Discoms:** The monetary losses incurred by distribution utilities can be attributed to T & D losses (including pilferage), low and under-priced tariffs, and collection losses. They find that distribution losses were the largest contributor to the total losses of distribution companies in 2003–11. Tariffs that were prescribed below the full cost of operation were another important contributor.

  Moreover, although many states have unbundled and corporatized their utilities, state governments continue to interfere in utility operations, undermining the principle of commercial operation. They also add to the difficulties of utilities by pressuring them to keep tariffs low and to buy expensive power to cover short-term deficits during elections.

  These problems erode the functional independence of the unbundled entities, making it difficult to hold them accountable for their performance. Meanwhile, repeated bailouts from the government create budget constraints, further weakening incentives for improving the efficacy of the system. **(For more on this, see Question 18 in this chapter).**

➢ **Remedial steps taken**

The government initiated various measures to reform and revamp the functioning of the power sector as detailed below.

♦ **Central Electricity Act, 2003:** A new Central Electricity Act was passed in 2003 replacing the old legislation of 1948. It was a major step towards reforming the power sector with the following objectives:

- Promoting competition to ensure healthy development of the sector.
- Protection of the interests of consumers.
- Consolidating the laws relating to generation, transmission, distribution, trading, and use of electricity.
- Taking measures to promote the development of electrical industry.
- Ensuring supply of electricity to all areas.
- Rationalization of electricity tariffs and adopting transparent policies regarding subsidies.
- Promotion of efficient and environment friendly policies.

The Act also provided a regulatory framework for the sector and prescribed the functions of the Central Electricity Authority (CEA) and the Central Electricity Regulatory Commission (CERC). Setting up of State Electricity Regulatory Commission (SERC) in states was made mandatory.

♦ **Improvements in Distribution Network**

Various steps were initiated during the Seventh Plan (1985–90) and thereafter to incentivise reforms in the distribution system and bring down T&D losses. These included:

- Theft of energy was made a cognizable offence under the Indian Electricity Act with stringent punishment of offenders.
- An incentive scheme was introduced in 1989 for the reduction of T&D losses.
- Upgradation and revamping of distribution systems in urban and rural areas was undertaken with financial support of Power Finance Corporation (PFC) and Rural Electrification Corporation (REC).
- Accelerated Power Development and Reforms Programme (APDRP) was launched in March 2003 with provision for investment financing and incentive for improved performance.
- Use of technological and managerial tools such as smart metering and GIS mapping for real time monitoring was to be put in place.
- Accountability was enforced at each distribution transformer with target set for the State Governments to bring down Technical &Commercial losses.

- IT-enabled accounting and auditing was introduced to improve collection efficiency.
- Metering of distribution feeders/transformers and consumers in urban areas., and
- Fixing roof top solar panels was promoted to rationalise power consumption.

♦ **Expansion of Transmission System**

One of the main reasons for power shortages was the lack of transmission capacity to evacuate power and distribute it. For instance, power shortages in South India was due to southern grid not being connected to other grids in the country. By commissioning new lines, electricity transmission to southern states increased by 71 per cent in 2014 - 15.

The large increases in production and consumption of electricity needed to be supported by a significant expansion and strengthening of the transmission network.

Public investment in transmission expansion was supplemented by private investment starting with the Eleventh Plan (2007-12). The power transmission sector which was the preserve of the state-owned Power Grid Corporation was opened up to the private sector.

A model policy framework for public–private partnership (PPP) and standardized documentation was prepared for use by the States.

The strengthening of transmission lines in the Western Region saw many private firms/consortia joining the fray.

♦ **Creation of National Grid**

The power system in the country is demarcated into five regions. During 2013-14, the power network was integrated into one grid as South India's grid was linked with the national grid making it "One Nation, One Grid" in a single synchronous mode.

13. Describe the main features of India's Rural Electrification programme. Examine the challenges it faces and assess the progress it has made.

Ans. Access to reliable electricity is a prerequisite for sustainable social and economic development. Low access and poor quality of electricity supply would have an adverse effect on the quality of life of people and the operation and growth of various sectors in the economy.

With India having about six lakh villages, and nearly 70 per cent of the population living in rural areas, the government realized the imperative need for providing electricity in villages in the early years of planning.

- **Rural Electrification Corporation**

  Rural Electrification Corporation (REC), a public sector enterprise under the Ministry of Power, was set up in 1969, with the objective of financing and promoting rural electrification projects all over the country in a planned and speedy manner. REC provides financial assistance to State Electricity Boards, State Government Departments, and Rural Electric Cooperatives for rural electrification projects sponsored by them.

- **Sustained efforts at Rural electrification**

  From 1970s, various programmes have been launched to give thrust to electrification of both villages and rural households. These include:

  - **MNP:** Rural electrification as a component under Minimum Needs Programme (MNP) in the Fifth Five Year Plan (1974-79).
  - **Kutir Jyoti Scheme:** This was started in 1988-89 to provide single-point light connections to rural households below poverty line (BPL) with higher weightage given to States having larger population of poor and low electrification levels. The scheme was later merged with RGGVY (see below).
  - **PMGY:** As part of Pradhan Mantri Gramodaya Yojana (PMGY) in 2001-02, rural electrification was executed by State Electricity Boards and Public Utilities. The scheme was discontinued from 2005-06.
  - **AREP:** Accelerated Rural Electrification Programme (AREP) introduced in 2003-04 with financial assistance given for electrification of unelectrified villages, tribal villages and hamlets and 'dalit bastis'.
  - **AE:** Accelerated Electrification of One Lakh villages and One crore households started in 2004-05 by merging the AREP interest subsidy scheme and Kutir Jyoti programme. This scheme was later merged with RGGVY.
  - **Rajiv Gandhi Grameen Vidyutikaran Yojana (RGGVY):** Launched in 2005 with REC as the nodal agency for the programme, it aimed to provide access to electricity to all rural households over a period of four years. Under this, 648 projects were sanctioned during the Tenth (2002-07) and the Eleventh Five Year Plan covering1.12 lakh unelectrified villages, intensive electrification of 3.8 lakh partially electrified villages and release of free electricity connection to 2.76 crore BPL households in the country.

- **Lacuna and Challenges**

  Providing electricity facility to all villages and electric connection to rural households was a mammoth task due to the sheer numbers involved. The number of villages is about 6 lakhs and the number of rural households stood at about 17.96 crore in 2017. Before assessing the progress made so far, it would be useful to look at the challenges faced in its implementation.

- **Electricity for agriculture:** Initially, the thrust of rural electrification programmes was for "irrigation" as power was required by farmers to operate pumpsets. The objective was to enhance agricultural produce. By March 1985, the end of the Sixth Plan (1980–85), out of 12 million pumpsets, 5.7 million had been energized. With rural electrification, the number of pumpsets energised increased to about 18 million in January 2012.

  The has led to less reliance on conventional irrigation sources such as tanks and canals and to substantial increase in the extraction of ground water and increased consumption of electricity.

  A Task Force on Micro-irrigation (TFMI), appointed by the Ministry of Finance in 2004 has also underlined the fact that switching to drip irrigation can save enormous amount of electricity, if adopted extensively.

  The government is now promoting farming through micro irrigation for optimum utilization of water under the PM Krishi Sinchayee Yojana (PMKSY) with the concept of "per drop more crop".

- **Criteria of "Electrified village"**

  Earlier, a narrow criterion was followed in determining if a village was electrified. The government considered "a village as 'electrified' if electricity is used for any purpose within the revenue boundary of that village".

  As per this norm 85 per cent of villages in the country was considered as electrified by March1996 and as many as 13 States had achieved 100 per cent village electrification. But in these electrified villages, power connection may not be available on demand and households and hamlets adjoining the villages may not have got the facility.

  Then the Government notified a change in the definition of "village electrification" as follows: "A village will be deemed to be electrified if electricity is used in the inhabited locality, within the revenue boundary of the village for any purpose whatsoever".

  Still later, the criteria was amplified and a village was considered electrified if at least 10 per cent of households in the village had electricity and the facility was provided to public buildings such as schools, health centres, dispensaries, community centres and village councils.

  Even this was found wanting by a Standing Committee on Energy in 2013 which observed that according to the above criteria, a village would be deemed electrified even if up to 90 per cent of households in it did not have the basic electricity connection. This gave a momentum to the scheme and there have been concerted efforts on the part of the Centre and the States to ensure 100 per cent coverage of households in villages with electricity.

➢ **Significant progress**

The number of villages which had electricity facility in 1950-51 was just 3,061 which formed only 0.5 per cent of total number of villages. The number increased to 21,750 by 1960-61 which formed 3.8 per cent of villages in the country.

Since its formation, the REC has made significant progress in ensuring that villages are provided the facility of electricity following various schemes launched by the government as explained above. The progress in electrification of villages from 1950-51 till 2017 (for selected years) is shown in Table 10.4 below. By 2018, India achieved the target of 100 per cent village electrification.

Table 10.4: Progress of Rural Electrification

Year	Total No. of Villages	Total No. of Villages electrified	Percentage of Villages electrified
1950-51	6,12,250	3,061	0.5
1980-81	5,76,374	2, 72,625	47.3
2012-13	5,97,464	5,61,613	93.9
2016-17	5,97,464	5,97,464	100.0

Source: Central Electricity Authority and Energy Statistics, National Statistical Office (NSO), Ministry of Statistics and Programme Implementation, Govt. of India.

➢ **Household electrification: Saubhagya scheme**

■ **Progress up to 2017:** As mentioned earlier, action had been initiated to extend electrification to all rural households in a big way with the RGGVY scheme of 2005. By April 2017, out of a total of about 17.96 crore rural households, 13.36 crore households had been electrified. India's household electrification rate rose from 67 percent in 2005 to 86 percent in 2017. To give further fillip, the Pradhan Mantri Sahaj Bijli Har Ghar Yojana (Saubhagya Yojana) was launched in October 2017 with the following objectives:

- ♦ To achieve universal household electrification by providing electricity connections to all remaining households in rural and urban areas.
- ♦ About 4 crore poor households were to be provided with electricity connection free of charge.
- ♦ Non-poor households will have to pay ten instalments of ₹ 50 each, along with the bill each month, totalling ₹ 500.
- ♦ The scheme was estimated to cost of ₹ 16,320 crore.
- ♦ Financial assistance was given to the DISCOMs/Power departments from the Union government.
- ♦ As a means of sourcing funds for the scheme, instead of subsidizing the under-recovery for kerosene by oil companies, the same money could be progressively re-allocated for Saubhagya.

- ♦ A positive aspect was that most villages were by now connected to the grid, and locations far from the grid were slated for generation of mostly renewable power.

- **Progress since October 2017:** Under the Saubhagya scheme, about 2.63 crore rural households have been electrified since October 2017. With this the total number of households electrified works out to 15.99 crore. That leaves another 1.97 crore households still to be electrified.

- **Challenges ahead:** Thus by 2020, about 89 per cent of rural households have been provided electric connection. But providing connection to the remaining, especially remote, households in the surrounding areas can be expensive and pose a challenge.

  Some people may also forgo accessing electricity by choice because of the monthly bills that come with it, especially if power supply is not reliable and blackouts are frequent. The ability of some households to pay the charges could be a hindrance.

  A major challenge will be to provide quality service, ideally 24x7 supply to all households.

  Mandating the provision of a meter is a welcome step to ensure that consumers pay notified tariffs even if the tariff is low and subsidized. This creates the mindset and culture of paying and instils the habit of economising in usage and consumption of power.

14. Examine how India's rural electrification scheme has benefited rural population and what further improvements are called for in the scheme.

Ans. Supply of electricity is vital for agriculture, industry, and all other activities and it is a key catalyst for economic development and raising the living standards of people. With India having about six lakh villages, and nearly 70 per cent of the population living in rural areas, providing electricity in rural areas and to all rural households has been a priority in India's Plans.

Rural electrification scheme has brought about a perceptible change in the living conditions of the rural households. These benefits include:

- **Energy benefit:** It has altered the household energy mix by replacing traditional kerosene-based lighting with electric light which is healthier and less polluting. This has helped rural households to depend less on kerosene, save on energy expenses as families would no longer be subject to problem of excessive price of kerosene.
- **Economic outcomes:** Household survey data suggest that economic outcomes are better for households with access to electricity and for households with a better quality of electricity.

  Households having grid-connection and households with more hours of electricity supply consume less kerosene. They also have higher incomes and expenditures and a lower poverty rate.

- **Women:** For women and girls, electrification helps free up time traditionally spent on collecting fuel, and less drudgery in performing household chores. It allows them to spend more time on other productive activities. Gaining access to the grid has a positive effect on women's hours of employment. Access to electricity also increases women's empowerment, measured by their decision-making ability, security, mobility, financial autonomy, and social participation.
- **Education:** Among the long-term benefits of electricity is its potential to improve households' education outcomes. Availability of electricity during night helps students by facilitating extended hours of study.
- **Agriculture:** Electrification helps to energize pumpsets used in agriculture.
- **Rural economy:** It also helps village and cottage industries, shopkeepers, and other entrepreneurial activities in villages giving boost to economic activity.
- **Security:** It enhances overall security and law and order within the villages besides improving the quality of life.
- **Digital India project:** The availability of electricity in rural areas will help to achieve better outcomes, such as more convenience of working at night, where the Digital India (BharatNet) programme is rolled out. 2.5 lakh Gram Panchayat villages are being covered under this project.

➢ **Further action:** Rural electrification needs to be strengthened by ensuring that power supply is available in villages for 24 hours, every day of the week, and that power outages are kept to a minimum so that villagers get steady, uninterrupted supply as in towns and cities.

This can be achieved to a great extent when solar energy system reaches villages on which action is already under way. Having rooftop solar panels in houses and other buildings like panchayat and village offices, banks, schools, marketplaces, shops, etc. in villages can ensure better and assured power supply.

15. Mention the relative share of Hydel, Thermal and Nuclear power in India's overall power production. Discuss the steps India is taking towards fulfilling the commitments given at International Climate Change conferences and state how it will impact the relative shares of different sources of power.

Ans. India is the third largest consumer of energy in the world behind China and the USA. India meets its energy needs from a variety of sources – hydro-electric, thermal power which include fossil fuels such as coal, lignite, crude oil and natural gas – and nuclear power which are called 'conventional' sources and are exhaustible in nature. Besides, India is steadily increasing reliance on renewable sources like solar, wind and tidal (ocean) power and biomass which are inexhaustible and known as 'non-conventional' sources of energy.

➤ **Relative shares:** For long, thermal power has been having a dominant share in India's electricity matrix as can been from Table 1 below. Its share has risen over the years while the share of hydel power has declined. Thermal power meets over 70 per cent of India's electricity needs while the share of nuclear energy is very low. The share of various renewable sources is given in Table 2.

Table 10.5: Sources of Installed Capacity of Electricity in India (In Thousand MW)

Year	Utilities				Total	Non- Utilities	Grand Total
	Hydel	Thermal	Nuclear	RES*			
1	2	5	4	5	6	7	8
1950-51	0.6	1.3	Nil	Nil	1.9	0.6	2.5
	(31.6)	(68.4)			(100)		
1960-61	1.9	2.8	Nil	Nil	4.7	1	5.67
	(40.4)	(59.6)			(100)		
1980-81	11.8	17.6	0.9	Nil	30.3	3.1	33.4
	(38.9)	(58.1)	(3.0)		(100)		
2000-01	25.1	73.6	2.8	Nil	101.5	16.2	117.7
	(24.7)	(72.5)	(2.8)		(100)		
2009-10	36.9	102.4	4.5	15.5	159.3	31.5	190.8
	(23.2)	(64.3)	(2.8)	(9.7)	(100)		
2015-16	42.8	210.6	5.8	42.8	302	48.3	350.3
	(14.2)	(69.7)	(1.9)	(14.2)	(100)		
2019-20	42.3	143.7	6.8	4.0	196.8	173.6	370.4
	(21.5)	(73.0)	(3.5)	(2.0)	(100)		

Source: India, Statistical Year Book, Ministry of Statistics & Programme Implementation, Economic Survey 2014 – 15, Ministry of Finance & Ministry of Power, Annual Reports, Data for 2019 – 20 is as on 30 – 04 – 2020 from Central Electricity Authority: http://www.cea.nic.in/reports/monthly/executivesummary/2020

* **RES:** Renewal Energy Resources

Note: Figures in brackets denote percentage of different sources of Power (Cols 2 to 5) to Total of Utilities only (Col 6)

➢ The Paris Climate Agreement

At the Paris Climate Conference in 2015, 195 nations reached a historic agreement to reduce greenhouse gas emissions blamed for global warming and cut dependence on fossil fuels by shifting to clean energy sources.

It was agreed to cut emissions in a bid to limit the rise in global average temperatures to below 2° C above pre-Industrial era.

♦ India & Climate Change target

India is the world's third largest carbon emitter after China and the US, although India's per capita emission is much lower than that of many countries. India has set very ambitious targets for reducing dependence on fossil fuels for generation of electricity and for promoting renewable energy.

Under the 2015 Paris Climate Agreement, India has committed to install around 40 per cent of its power generation capacity based on non-fossil fuel (renewable) resources by 2030. This will help India to pursue a development path with low carbon emission.

♦ India's drive for Renewable energy

India has set an ambitious target of having 175 GW of clean energy capacity by 2022, including 100 GW solar and 60 GW of wind energy.

As will be seen from Table 2, the installed capacity of renewables has reached 87.3 Gigawatt (or 87,270 megawatt) by April 2020 constituting 23.6 per cent of the total installed capacity of 370.4 GW. This includes 34.8 GW of solar power and 37.7 GW of wind power.

Besides, 42 solar power parks with an aggregate capacity of around 23.40 GW have been approved by the government so far towards achieving the 100 GW target and their execution is in progress. Most of the grid connected RE projects in the country are being implemented by private sector developers selected through transparent bidding process.

Table 10.6: Installed Capacity of Renewable Energy sources

Break-up of Renewables as on 30 – 04 – 2020 (Both Utilities &Private) (In Thousand MW)					
Small Hydro Power/Cogen.	Wind Power Energy	Bio-Power BM Power	Waste to Energy	Solar Power	Total Capacity
4.7	37.7	9.9	0.1	34.8	87.3

Source: Ministry of New and Renewable Energy, Govt. of India, Annual Report, 2019-20, p. 10

- **Problem of Thermal power**

  Coal-based thermal plants are central to India's energy needs and will remain the dominant source of power for the next couple of decades. But these thermal plants are major sources of greenhouse gas emissions (GHG) causing environmental pollution with adverse consequences for public health.

  A major challenge India faces in living up to commitments made on Climate change is in regard to thermal power plants. Many of the state utilities have old and inefficient thermal plants which are to be closed or retrofitted to comply with emission standards. Presently, 70 per cent of total installed capacity consists of thermal power and this has to be brought down considerably. About 170 such plants have been already closed.

  NTPC: National Thermal Power Corporation (NTPC) is the largest thermal power generating company in the country. It has total installed capacity of 62.9 GW, of which 45.4 GW is coal based. NTPC is now adopting environmentally sustainable power generation.

  In a positive development, NTPC is adding renewable energy in its portfolio and, by 2032, it plans to have a 32GW (32000 MW) capacity through renewable sources which will be nearly 25 per cent of its overall power generation capacity.

- **Need for Clean Coal Technology**

  Adoption of clean coal technologies such as ultra-super critical thermal power technology could help reduce emissions. Experts are of the view that such technologies are available and techno-economically feasible to bring down emissions.

  There are advanced technologies with low-to-zero emissions through carbon capture, utilization, and storage (CCUS) which could help to develop environment-friendly coal energy systems.

  India and the US are collaborating on research on transformational power generation based on supercritical CO_2 power cycles, advanced coal technologies and hydrogen production, including the CCUS. Since India needs to rely on coal for power production due to the large reserves of coal India has and increasing power requirements, having thermal plants based on these efficient technologies is imperative.

➢ **Conclusion:** As India pursues its ambitious renewable energy targets and seeks to transform its energy sector, India needs to integrate renewable energy and other new technologies into the grid and modernize the power distribution system. India could also deploy "distributed energy technologies" in which electrical generation and storage is performed by small-scale units locally and which are connected to a larger power grid at the distribution level. Further India has to promote rooftop solar extensively and promote electric vehicles and battery storage systems.

With these measures, India's power generation matrix will be transformed and will become more environment friendly and help to reduce pollution to a significant extent.

(See also Question number 16 below for more on this)

16. Discuss the potential for renewable sources of power such as Solar, Wind, Tidal and Biomass in India's power sector and the steps being taken by the government to promote them. How far, do you think, it can make India's power generation environment friendly?

Ans. As the world is facing the devastating impact of global warming and climate change, largely caused by developmental activities, the role of renewable energy has assumed much importance. Renewable energy, also known as non-conventional energy, consist of solar energy, wind energy, tidal power, and biogas.

Unlike the traditional and conventional energy, except hydropower, they are inexhaustible sources. They are also much cleaner than the conventional energy based on fossil fuels such as coal, lignite, natural gas and petroleum.

➤ **India's commitment on Renewables**

- India has committed to reduce greenhouse gas (GHG) emissions intensity by 33-35 per cent below 2005 levels and achieve 40 per cent of installed electric capacity from non-fossil sources by 2030.
- India has set ambitious target to install 175 gigawatts (GW) of renewable power (RE) capacity by 2022.The installed RE capacity in April 2020 was 87.3 GW which formed only 23.6 per cent of total installed capacity. As against this, the share of coal-based thermal power was around 70 per cent.
- More RE projects are under various stages of implementation. The government has estimated an investment of about ₹ 4 lakh crore during 2019-22 period to meet the country's 175 GW renewable energy target by 2022.
- Most of the grid connected RE projects are being implemented by private sector developers selected through transparent bidding process.

➤ **Potential and Capacity installed**

- **Solar power:** Based upon availability of land and solar radiation, the potential solar power in the country has been assessed to be around 750 GW. Against this, solar power of 34.8 GW capacity has been installed till April 2020. In addition, 22.8 GW are in pipeline and works for around 28.5 GW are due to be issued.
- **Wind energy:** It is estimated that India has gross wind power potential of 302.25 GW at 100 meter above ground level. Most of this potential exists in seven windy States. The installed capacity of grid-interactive wind power in the country in April 2020 is 37.50 GW.
- **Biomass:** India is promoting Biomass Power and Bagasse Co-generation Programme with the aim to recover energy from biomass including bagasse, agricultural residues such as shells, husks, de-oiled cakes and wood from dedicated energy plantations for power generation. The potential for power generation from agricultural and agro-industrial residues is estimated at about 18,000 MW. Over 500 biomass power and cogeneration projects with aggregate capacity of 9186.50 MW have been installed in the country up to December 2019.

- **Small hydro power**: The small hydro power projects have capacity up to 25MW and the estimated potential from this source is 21 GW. They have the potential to meet power requirements of remote and isolated areas in a decentralized manner besides providing employment opportunity to local people. By April 2020, projects with capacity of 4.7 GW has been implemented.

➢ **Promotion of Renewables**

- India is endowed with abundant natural and renewable resources of energy viz., sun, wind, and biomass.
- India holds 5th Global position for overall installed renewable energy capacity, 4th position for wind power and 5th position for solar power.
- In the infrastructure sector, renewable energy projects are giving good returns and hence have been attracting significant foreign capital. This is supported by robust government policy.
- The initiative of NTPC, the major state-run thermal producing undertaking, to take up RE projects will be an added boost. NTPC is adding significant capacities of RE and by 2032, the company plans to have a minimum of 32,000 MW (32 GW) capacity through RE sources constituting nearly 25 per cent of its overall power generation capacity.
- The cost of solar power has been steadily coming down and, if sustained, it will provide electricity cheaper. The per unit cost of solar power had come down to as low as ₹ 2.36. But some experts are of the view that the true cost of renewable energy has to be higher if it is to be sustained over the long term.
- The reduction of cost of power for industries will help in promoting local manufacturing and make exports competitive.
- Under the Solar Park Scheme, the target was to develop at least 50 solar parks with aggregate installed capacity of 40,000 MW of solar power by 2021-22. As of December 2019, 39 solar parks of aggregate capacity 22,879 MW (22.8 GW) have been approved and these solar parks are at different stage of development.

➢ **Challenges**

While India is making concerted efforts to promote renewable energy and meet the targets set, there are some challenges in the way. These can be overcome by suitable policy changes even if it takes some time to fructify. These challenges are:

- **Supply of equipments:** China has been a major supplier of equipments for solar power. India is trying to reduce imports from China and encourage domestic manufacturing by levying customs duty on cells, modules and inverters. But as the local manufacturing capacity is able to meet only part of the demand and ramping up production will take time, India will have to source them from other countries and prices will go up which could impact power tariffs.

- **Land Scarcity:** Land is a scarce resource in India and per capita land available is very low. Having dedicated land area near substations for exclusive installation of solar cells have to compete with other demands for land.
- **Solar parks:**The scheme for development of Solar Parks and Ultra Mega Solar Power projects and grid connected Solar Power plants face problems of land acquisition and right of way and challenges in evacuating the power generated in these parks.
- **Energy Storage:** Off-grid PV systems typically use batteries for storing energy, and the use of batteries could increase the size, cost and complexity of the system.
- **Lead-acid batteries:** Where grid connections are not possible or reliable, as may be the case in rural areas, lead-acid batteries are used for storage in rooftop solar installations. They pose risks of health and environmental problems from contamination, if recycling of these batteries is not adequately regulated and done properly.

➤ **International Solar Alliance (ISA)**

Apart from the initiatives to promote generation of solar power in India, India has also taken steps for its adoption across countries as part of efforts to combat climate change. Towards this, the International Solar Alliance (ISA) was jointly launched in 2015 at the UN Climate Change conference (COP 21) in Paris by PM Narendra Modi and French President Francois Hollande. The goal of ISA is to install 1,000 GW of solar energy by 2030 and mobilise US$ 1,000 billion to achieve the target.

- ♦ Global drive: India has called upon sunshine-abundant nations to join the International Solar Alliance in larger numbers to hasten the global energy transition from fossil fuels.
- ♦ Objective: The purpose of ISA is not just reducing the global carbon footprint but to help the 121 member countries, mostly developing economies, with solar power solutions, and provide modern energy access to everybody. It is pertinent to note in this context that women and girls are more likely to be put in harm's way when extreme weather events in developing countries displace millions of people every year.
- ♦ Since its founding, 83 nations located between the Tropic of Cancer and Tropic of Capricorn have joined the alliance in just four years. ISA has launched five programmes to boost different sectors where solar technologies can be applied.
- ♦ The goal of the ISA is to facilitate affordable access for member countries to funding for solar projects. To this end, the World Bank and the Agence Francaise de Development(AFD) have launched, in partnership with the ISA, the Solar Risk Mitigation Initiative (SRMI) at Climate Change Conference (COP24) in 2018.

- This move by India also has geopolitical implications. As an emerging power on the global arena, it helps India to collaborate with many developing countries in the Asia-Pacific, Africa and Latin America regions. Once India starts manufacturing solar equipments and scales it up, she can also supply them and technical support to those countries and collaborate with projects there.

➢ **Conclusion:** On the one hand, India will have to continue to rely on coal-based thermal power considering India's rising energy needs and abundant coal reserves she has. But India can adopt clean-coal technology in power generation, so that its ill-effects can be largely contained.

At the same time, India has to pursue vigorously sourcing power from renewable sources. Considering the measures so far taken by the government and if this momentum is maintained, India will be on course to achieve an affordable, secure, inclusive and environmentally friendly energy ecosystem.

17. The world is turning more and more to renewable sources of energy, especially solar and wind energy. Identify the advantages and limitations of Solar and Wind energy.

Ans. Introduction

Currently many countries are dependent on fossil fuels which are highly polluting. Most countries have to import them which exposes them to an element of uncertainty in supplies and volatility in international market and price conditions.

Reducing carbon dioxide (CO_2) emissions is at the heart of the world's accelerating shift from climate-damaging fossil fuels towards clean, renewable forms of energy. In addition to fulfilling the 2015 Paris Agreement on Climate Change, renewables are crucial to reduce air pollution, improve health and well-being, and provide affordable energy access worldwide. Solar and Wind energy form an important part of this key environmental and energy solution.

Both these major energy sources among the renewables, have both advantages and limitations. These are discussed below.

■ **Solar energy:** Solar energy is the conversion of sunlight into usable energy forms. Solar photovoltaics (PV), solar thermal electricity and solar heating and cooling are well established solar technologies.

➢ **Advantages of Solar Energy**

1. **Renewable Energy Source:** The most important advantage of solar energy is that it is a truly renewable source which can be harnessed in all parts of the world and is available every day. The world will not run out of solar energy, unlike some of the other energy sources. Solar energy will be accessible as long

the sun is there and, according to scientists, sunlight will be available for at least 5 billion years when the sun is estimated to become non-existent.

Rooftop solar installations are ideal for eco-conscious home and other building owners.

2. **Reduces Electricity Bills:** If part of the energy needed in a home or any premises is met by electricity generated by solar system, the energy bills will be reduced. The extent of saving on the bill will depend on the size of the solar system and the usage for lighting or heating.

   An added advantage is that if more electricity is produced with solar system than is needed, one could supply the surplus to the grid, where solar panel is connected to the grid, and receive payments.

3. **Diverse Applications:** Solar energy can be used for diverse purposes. It can generate electricity, produce heat, distil water in regions with limited clean water supply and to power satellites in space. Solar energy can also be integrated into the materials used for buildings. A company has unveiled a transparent solar panel that can be mounted on balcony railings or high-rise windows without obstructing the view.

4. **Low Maintenance Costs:** Solar energy systems generally don't require a lot of maintenance. The cables need maintenance to ensure that the solar power system runs at maximum efficiency. As there are no moving parts, there is no wear and tear.It is only to be kept relatively clean, so cleaning them a couple of times per year will do. Most reliable solar panel manufacturers offer 20-25 years' warranty. There are specialised servicing companies for maintenance.

   The inverter is usually the only part that needs to be changed after 5-10 years because it is continuously working to convert solar energy into electricity and heat. So, after meeting the initial cost of the solar system, there will be very little spending on maintenance and repair work.

5. **Technology Development:** Solar power technology is constantly advancing and there will be further improvements in the coming years. According to experts, innovations in quantum physics and nanotechnology can potentially increase the effectiveness of solar panels and double, or even triple, the electrical potential of the solar power systems.

➢ **Disadvantages of Solar Energy**

1. **Cost:** The initial cost of purchasing a solar system is fairly high. This includes paying for solar panels, inverter, batteries, wiring, and for the installation. Nevertheless, solar technologies are constantly developing, so it can be assumed that prices will go down in the future.

2. **Weather Dependent:** Solar panels are dependent on sunlight to effectively gather solar energy. Although solar energy can be collected during cloudy and rainy days, the efficiency of the solar system drops. Therefore, a few cloudy, rainy days can have a noticeable effect on the energy system.

   Besides, solar energy cannot be collected during the night. If power is required for water heating to work at night or during wintertime, thermodynamic panels can be an alternative.

3. **Solar Energy Storage Is Expensive:** Solar energy has to be used right away, or it can be stored in large batteries. These batteries, used in off-the-grid solar systems, can be charged during the day so that the energy is used at night. While this is a good solution for having solar energy all day long, but it is also quite expensive.

   In most cases, it is better to just use solar energy during the day and take energy from the grid during the night where the system is connected to the grid. Since energy demand is usually higher during the day most of it can be met with solar energy.

4. **Occupies a Lot of Space:** The more electricity you want to produce, the more solar panels you will need, as you want to collect as much sunlight as possible. Solar panels require a lot of space and some roofs are not big enough to fit the number of solar panels that one would like to have. An alternative is to install some of the panels in a yard but they need to have access to sunlight.

   Where there isn't enough space for all the panels required, fewer panels may be installed to meet part of the energy needs.

5. **Associated with Pollution:** Although pollution related to solar energy systems is far less compared to other sources of energy, solar energy can still cause some pollution. Transportation and installation of solar systems have been associated with the emission of greenhouse gases (GHG).

   If lead-acid batteries are used for storage in rooftop solar installations which are off-grid, they pose risks of health and environmental problems from contamination, if recycling of these batteries is not carried out properly.

   Also, some toxic materials and hazardous products are used during the manufacturing process of solar photovoltaic systems which can indirectly affect the environment. Still, solar energy pollutes far less than other alternative energy sources.

- **Wind energy**

  Different modes of electricity generation have been a subject of debate amongst experts. Wind energy is one of the frontrunners of the technological breakthroughs that points to more efficient mode of energy production.

  To obtain wind power, the kinetic energy of wind is used to create mechanical power. A generator converts this power into electricity which can be used for the benefit of mankind.

➢ Advantages of Wind Energy

The advantages of wind energy are more apparent than the disadvantages. The main advantages are:

1. **An unlimited source:** Wind is an abundant, inexhaustible, and affordable source, which makes it a viable and large-scale alternative to fossil fuels. Wind is a natural occurrence and harvesting the kinetic energy of wind does not affect currents or wind cycles in any way.
2. **Clean and eco-friendly:** Harnessing power from the wind is one of the cleanest and most sustainable ways to generate electricity as it produces no toxic pollution or global warming emissions. Unlike other types of power plants, it emits no air pollutants or greenhouse gases. The wind turbines harmlessly generate electricity from wind passing by them. Thus, it is far more eco-friendly than the burning of fossil fuels for electricity.
3. **Economical:** While constructing turbines and wind facilities is very expensive, once they have been set up, the cost of maintaining turbines and generating wind power is very nominal. The cost of electricity for onshore wind is already competitive compared to all fossil fuel generation sources and is set to decline further as installed costs and performance continue to improve.

   Increasing economies of scale, more competitive supply chains and technological improvements will further reduce costs of wind power. Globally, the total installation cost of onshore wind projects is expected to decline in the next three decades.
4. **Land use:** Wind turbines placed in flat areas use more land than those located in hilly areas. However, wind turbines do not occupy all of this land. The turbines themselves and the surrounding infrastructure (including roads and transmission lines) occupy a small portion of the total area of a wind facility. The remainder of the land can be used for a variety of other productive purposes, including livestock grazing, agriculture, highways, and hiking trails. Wind facilities can also be sited on brownfields (abandoned or underused industrial land) or other commercial and industrial locations, which significantly reduces concerns about land use.
5. **Ease of location:** An advantage of wind power is the ability to place turbines wherever necessary. After experts conduct survey and find areas that have adequate wind, the turbines would be placed in desired areas. These areas are usually unpopulated such as in the case of offshore wind turbines.
6. **High potential:** In fact, offshore winds tend to blow harder and more uniformly than on land, providing the potential for increased electricity generation and smoother, steadier operation than land-based wind power systems.

According to the International Renewable Energy Agency (IRENA), "floating foundations are potentially a "game-changing" technology to effectively exploit abundant wind potential in deeper waters and thus could lead the way for rapid future growth in the offshore wind power market."

For offshore wind, Asia would take the lead in the coming decades with more than 60% of global installations by 2050, followed by Europe (22%) and North America (16%).

The ongoing innovations and technology upgradations towards larger capacity turbines would help improve yields for the same location.

➤ **Disadvantages of Wind Energy**

While at a glance, the future of wind energy seems promising, there are also some downsides to it that must be considered. Despite its vast potential, there are a variety of environmental impacts associated with wind power generation that should be recognized and mitigated.

1. **Initial cost:** While maintaining turbines and generating wind power is cheap, the initial costs of constructing turbines and setting up wind facilities are very expensive.
2. **Offshore facilities:** Offshore wind energy produces more energy than onshore wind energy, but it costs much more to establish. But offshore wind facilities require larger amounts of space because the turbines and blades are bigger than their land-based counterparts. Depending on their location, such offshore installations may compete with a variety of other ocean activities, such as fishing, recreational activities, sand and gravel extraction, oil and gas extraction, navigation, and aquaculture.
3. **Remoteness of location:** Although locating wind turbines in desolate areas, far away from populated areas may be an advantage, it will increase the costs on maintenance of turbines. Offshore wind turbines require boat facilities and will be more difficult to attend.
4. **Wildlife and Habitat:** Wind turbines may be dangerous to flying creatures. The impact of wind turbines on wildlife, most notably on birds and bats, has been widely studied. Recent research has found evidence of bird and bat deaths from collisions with wind turbines and due to changes in air pressure caused by the spinning turbines, as well as from habitat disruption though these impacts are relatively low and do not pose a threat to species populations.

   Offshore wind turbines can have similar impacts on marine birds, but as with onshore wind turbines, the bird deaths associated with offshore wind are minimal. Wind farms located offshore will also impact fish and other marine wildlife. Some studies suggest that turbines may actually increase fish populations by acting as artificial reefs.

5. **Public health and community**

   Sound and visual impact are the two main public health and community concerns associated with operating wind turbines. Most of the sound generated by wind turbines is caused by the movement of turbine blades through the air and there is also mechanical sound generated by the turbine itself. Overall sound levels depend on turbine design and wind speed.

   Some people living close to wind facilities have complained about sound and vibration issues, but industry and government-sponsored studies in Canada and Australia have found that these issues do not adversely impact public health. However, it is important for wind turbine developers to take these community concerns seriously by following "good neighbour" best practices for siting turbines and initiating open dialogue with affected community members. Further with technological advances, minimizing blade surface imperfections and using sound-absorbent materials, wind turbine noise can be reduced.

6. **Safety at Sea:** In the darkness/at night it may be difficult for incoming boats to see offshore wind turbines thus leading to possible collisions. This needs to be guarded against.

7. **Wind energy potential:** Recent research suggest that increasing global average surface temperatures may reduce the amount of wind energy available for electricity production. Global air circulation is influenced by many aspects of the global climate, including differences in atmospheric temperatures between the equator and the North and South Poles. It has been observed that across North America, average wind speeds have decreased slightly over the past 40 years.

8. **Need for improvements:** New technology is needed to further lower costs, increase reliability and production, expand the resource area, develop better infrastructure for tapping wind power.

Wind-Solar Hybrid Policy: The Ministry of New and Renewable Energy has issued National Wind-Solar Hybrid Policy in May 2018. The main objective of the policy is to provide a framework for promotion of large grid connected wind-solar PV hybrid system for optimal and efficient utilization of wind and solar resources, transmission infrastructure and land. The wind - solar PV hybrid systems will help in reducing the variability in renewable power generation and achieving better grid stability.

A scheme for setting up of 2500 MW Inter State Transmission System (ISTS) connected wind-solar hybrid projects was sanctioned on 25.05.2018. The Solar Energy Corporation of India (SECI) was nodal agency for implementation of the scheme.

➢ **Conclusion: Socio-economic benefits:** If accompanied by sound and holistic policies, wind and solar energy sectors can bring major socio-economic benefits. The employment potential with scope for expanding manufacturing, work of installation and operations and continuing R & D for improving technology will be major spin-offs from promoting renewable energy apart from salutary impact on global warming and climate change.

As stated at the outset, unleashing the huge potential of renewable energy in the coming decades will be crucial to achieving the goals set under the UN Climate Change Accord of 2015.

18. Elucidate the problems faced by State Electricity Distribution companies (DISCOMS) in India. Mention the steps taken by the government to resolve them and their outcome.

Ans. The Indian power sector has been under enormous financial stress over the decades. State-owned power distribution companies (DISCOMs), a crucial part of the power sector, have been at the centre of this problem. One of the key concerns has long been the inability of these companies to improve their operational and financial efficiencies.

➢ **Mounting losses and debt**

A major problem in the power sector are the heavy financial losses sustained by the State utilities which has led to them being in heavy debt. The cash losses of utilities, selling power directly to consumers, after accounting for subsidy from the State Governments, had been on the rise.

Discoms' problems have assumed alarming proportions with states struggling to pay for the electricity bought. The debt burden of Discoms is estimated to hit an all-time high of ₹ 4.5 trillion during 2020-21. The lockdown in 2020 due to the pandemic has added to the problems due to lower realisation of dues.

Discoms' outstanding dues to power generation firms (Gencos) rose steeply from ₹ 75,642 crore in April 2019 to ₹ 1.23 lakh crore in April 2020, a 63 per cent increase, reflecting stress in the sector.

Power producers give 60 days to Discoms for paying bills for the supply of electricity. After that, outstanding dues become 'overdues' and generators charge penal interest on that in most cases.

➢ **Losses in the power sector**

♦ **T&D loss:** The losses incurred in the power sector (that is, the difference between the units of power generated and distributed) are termed "Transmission & Distribution" (T&D) losses and are accounted as a percentage of output.

♦ **AT&C losses:** T&D losses together with loss in revenue collection (that is, commercial losses) give Aggregate Technical and Commercial (AT&C) losses.

- **A weak link:** Transmission and Distribution (T&D) are two of the weakest links in the power supply system in India leading to leakages and substantial revenue losses to the State distribution companies (Discoms).
- **Losses high:** T&D losses in India are one of the highest in the world and form an impediment in the development of the power sector. More than 75 to 80 per cent of the total technical loss and almost the entire commercial loss occurs at the distribution stage. The AT&C losses are due to following factors:
  - Energy dissipation in the transmission and distribution lines, transformers and other equipments used in the system.
  - Losses due to meter-reading errors, defective meters, unmetered supplies. and
  - Theft and pilferage of energy which is estimated to be about ₹ 20,000 crore annually.

Remedial measures

The government had targeted to bring down T&D losses in the power sector at All-India level from 22 per cent to 15 per cent by 2019 but it is still around 21 per cent, and it is much more in some states. Various remedial measures were taken by the government over the years as stated below but they are yet to deliver the expected results.

- **APDRP scheme:** The Accelerated Power Development and Reforms Programme (APDRP) was launched in March 2003 consisting of an investment financing component and an incentive component for improved performance.

  This scheme was later restructured to use technological and managerial tools such as smart metering and GIS mapping for real time monitoring and accountability at each distribution transformer with target set for the State Governments to bring down Aggregate Technical and Commercial (AT&C) losses.
- **IPDS scheme:** This scheme, launched in 2014, subsumed the Restructured APDRP. It aimed at:

  i. Reducing AT&C losses, establish IT-enabled energy accounting and auditing, and improve efficiency of collection.

  ii. Strengthening of sub-transmission and distribution networks in the urban areas.

  iii. Metering of distribution transformers / feeders / consumers in the urban areas.

  iv. Fixing roof top solar panels, and

  v. Adoption of IT in Distribution sector.

- **UDAY scheme:** The "Ujwala Discom Assurance Yojana" (UDAY) scheme was launched in 2015 to turn around the debt-ridden Discoms. UDAY was to bring down the cost of power, coal, and renewable energy by about ₹ 1.8 trillion every year by 2019. This would make Discoms financially sound without burdening the consumer with tariff increases.

  As the cost of power comes down, Discoms will be incentivized to buy more power and provide reliable services to consumers. The savings will also enable distributors to invest in smart meters and other infrastructure and upgrade the systems. It was, however, to be ensured that, in this process, the debt position of State governments was not adversely affected as the Discoms were allowed to convert their debt into State bonds.

  But as stated earlier, India's average AT&C losses are still at a high 21 per cent. Also, the gap between the cost of electricity bought (average cost of supply) and supplied (average revenue realized) for Discoms is still substantial in most states. At least ten states have electricity losses of more than 30 per cent that is posing a huge burden on their finances.

➢ **Other Reforms:** The government has taken other steps also to tackle the issues plaguing the sector, particularly the financial health of Discoms. These are:

- **Central Electricity Act 2003**

  The passing of a new Act known as the Central Electricity Act 2003, replacing the outdated legislation of 1948, was a major step towards reforming and revamping the power sector. It had the following objectives:

  - Promote competition to ensure healthy development of the sector.
  - Protect the interests of consumers.
  - Consolidate the laws relating to generation, transmission, distribution, trading, and use of electricity.
  - Take measures conducive for the development of electrical industry.
  - Supply of electricity to all areas.
  - Rationalization of electricity tariffs, ensuring transparent policies regarding subsidies.
  - Promotion of efficient and environmentally benign policies.

  The Act has provided a regulatory framework for the sector and prescribed the functions of the Central Electricity Authority and the Central Electricity Regulatory Commission. Setting up of State Electricity Regulatory Commission (SERC) in states was made mandatory.

■ **Amendments to Electricity Act, 2003**

The government has since proposed certain amendments to the 2003 Act to usher in much needed further reforms in the power sector. The main changes proposed are:

- **Cost reflective Tariff:** The Electricity Commissions shall determine tariffs that are reflective of cost so as to enable Discoms to recover their costs and make them viable.
- **Direct Benefit Transfer:** It is proposed that tariff be determined by Commissions without taking into account the subsidy, which will be credited directly by the government to the consumers.
- **Sanctity of contracts:** Once contracts are entered into, they should be honoured. To ensure this, a Central Enforcement Authority, headed by a retired Judge of the High Court, is to be set-up with powers of Civil Court to enforce performance of contracts related to purchase or sale or transmission of power between a generating, distribution or transmission companies.
- **Strengthening the regulatory regime: The strength of Appellate Tribunal (APTEL) to** be increased to seven Members, apart from the Chairperson, so that multiple benches can be formed to facilitate quick disposal of cases. APTEL will be empowered to enforce its decisions.
- **Renewable and Hydro Energy:** A **National Renewable Energy Policy is envisaged** for the development and promotion of generation of electricity from renewable sources of energy. Further, Commissions will specify that a minimum percentage of electricity is to be purchased from hydro sources of energy.
- **Penalties**: Non-fulfilment of obligation to buy electricity from renewable and/or hydro sources of energy will attract penalties.

  Many State governments have expressed reservations about the amendments stated above on the ground that they dilute the powers and authority of States, take away their powers and is violative of the federal principle. The Centre has agreed to take into account the views of State governments and modify the proposals.

■ **Relief package**

In May 2020, while announcing stimulus measures to revive the economy battered by the Covid-19 pandemic, the Union government granted a package of ₹ 90,000 crore for the power sector. This liquidity infusion was to help Discoms clear the dues owed by them to private and state-owned Generation companies (Gencos). This would subsume the extant schemes, IPDS and Uday referred to earlier. The amount in the relief package is expected to go up with more demands from the States.

This package was to improve their cash flows and credit rating and enable fresh funding. However, this bailout package would provide only a temporary relief to Discoms.

For a durable solution, the state-run entities were required to chart a pathway to bring down the losses. The release of funds under this scheme, in the form of loans and grants, is subject to effecting reforms and the pathway being adhered to.

State governments stand guarantee against the loans extended by Power Finance Corporation (PFC) and Rural Electricity Corporation (REC).

- **Conclusion:** The problems plaguing the power sector as a whole, and the Discoms in particular, can be overcome only if the reforms proposed are carried through by the Centre and the States working in tandem and close cooperation.

19. Employment generation is one of the biggest challenges Indian economy has been facing. In this context, discuss the role which infrastructure can play in generating employment and the steps to be taken by the government and industry in this regard.

Ans. One of the major challenges facing the Indian economy is the creation of adequate number of jobs, and that too of sufficiently good quality, to absorb the burgeoning labour force. It is estimated that a whopping 12 million people – about one million every month – are being added to the labour force every year and this trend is expected to continue for the next decade and more. This makes it a daunting task.

As already seen in **Chapter 7 (Qn. 4),** Indian economy faces many critical issues of labour and generating employment. These issues are summed up below.

Critical issues

- India's labour market faces a number of critical issues which need to be kept in mind while laying down policies to create more employment opportunities. These issues are:
- The pressure of population in the agriculture sector and the need to shift surplus labour to non-farm jobs.
- The paradoxical phenomenon of "jobless growth" observed in the last few years has also been a matter of concern. Even as the economy has been growing and expanding, it has not only not led to commensurate growth in employment but even shown decline from time to time.
- A related issue is the quality of jobs created and the share of employment in the Formal and Informal sectors. Nearly 90 per cent of India's workforce is employed in the Informal sector or in informal jobs in the Formal sector which are of low quality and the service conditions are less than ideal.

- There is mismatch between labour seeking jobs and the skills required for jobs on offer. Hence this necessitates imparting training to job seekers which involves considerable time and expenditure for the employers.
- Increasing trend towards automation of jobs in various sectors poses serious threat to potential for job creation.
- Lack of job opportunities locally where they reside forces workers to migrate to other states or cities or from rural areas to cities resulting in problems of urbanisation and pressure on infrastructure and civic services such as lack of proper housing, transportation, health and education issues.

Generating employment

A well-developed and modern infrastructure is an important pre-requisite for socio-economic development. While agriculture, industry and services are important and integral parts of an economy, infrastructure is another important cog in the wheels on which any economy moves. No other sector can develop and contribute to their fullest potential unless infrastructure is well developed. Physical infrastructure includes a whole gamut of facilities – roads, rail, air transport, shipping and ports and inland waterways, housing, etc. Investment in infrastructure has high potential for generating employment.

Infrastructure in India

A major drawback of Indian economy has been poor infrastructure which has been a drag on the economy. While highways, ports and airports have been lately developed to a great extent, other sectors like telecommunications and power are still not adequately developed to meet the growing needs of the economy. Unless all these facilities are upgraded further to international standards, India cannot aspire to attract foreign investment in manufacturing and industry which have high potential for creating jobs.

Thus, while infrastructure by itself could generate employment on a large scale, it will also have a multiplier effect on creation of jobs in many other sectors.

Lop-sided development

India's industries and manufacturing are mostly located in major cities and towns or in their periphery where infrastructural facilities are relatively better developed. These centres serve as magnet for industries and serve as 'engines of growth' drawing more and more development towards them. This has led to problems of excessive urbanisation in cities which are bursting at the seams for want of adequate housing, sanitation, water supply, etc.

On the contrary, many of the Tier-II and Tier-III towns grossly lack facilities like efficient rail connections, airports, hospitals, educational institutions, etc. For lack of these facilities, they are unable to attract investment for setting up industries and in services (tertiary) sector which would have provided much needed boost to employment opportunities in these towns. It would also have stemmed the migration to cities and given relief to major cities from overcrowding and consequent civic and other issues.

Regional imbalances

This raises the crucial issue of need for balanced development of all regions in the country. That India's industrial development over the years has been lop-sided is evident from the fact that despite the eastern and central regions of India being rich in mineral resources, much of the industrial growth has taken place in western and southern India.

Successive Five-Year Plans and Finance Commissions of India have focussed on the issue of regional imbalances in development and the need to devote attention to backward and less developed areas. As early as during the formulation of the Fourth Plan (1969–74), the Planning Commission had observed: "Measures are proposed to be taken for the development of industries in the backward areas. The normal economic forces governing the location of industries are at present so overwhelmingly in favour of the developed areas that the problem of dispersal of industries to backward regions would require co-ordinated action at the Central, State, and local levels. The problem is so widespread that during the Fourth Plan it would be possible to make only a beginning. It is through a continuing programme of economic development supported by measures to attract industries to backward regions that the present imbalance can be rectified over a period of time."

But despite concerted efforts, various studies have shown that most of India's industries and jobs are concentrated in the western and southern parts of the country. Five states, viz., Maharashtra, Tamil Nadu, Gujarat, Andhra Pradesh, Telangana and Karnataka account for over 50 per cent of factory jobs in the country. The share of the top five states has not changed much since the early 1970s.

Problem of migration

Lack of development in backward states such as Bihar, U.P., West Bengal, Orissa, Rajasthan and North-eastern states, some of which are states with large population, has led to large-scale migration of workers from these states to developed states in search of jobs. This has led to manifold problems in the recipient states where the workers, most of whom stay away from their families, do not have satisfactory living facilities. This vulnerability was starkly exposed in the wake of serious pandemic, Covid-19, which broke out in February – March 2020 and lasted for months disrupting Indian economy and caused untold hardship to migrant workers.

Potential for job creation

Developing proper infrastructure in the less developed states and smaller towns, as mentioned earlier, and encouraging industries to gravitate towards them could trigger exponential growth, create jobs locally and keep people aspiring for work nearer their homes and stem migration. These states could offer special incentives like land allotment, assured power and water supply and arrange industrial housing. The government has already planned housing for workers near industrial clusters but this should now be directed more towards the backward regions in a phased manner.

Construction and housing, improving health and education facilities in rural and semi-urban areas are potential areas for job creation. The 'Housing for All' scheme, promoting agro-based industries and building silos and cold storage chains and promoting small industries and artisans in rural areas will rejuvenate rural economy.

Conclusion

Infrastructure investment has a significant impact on economic growth, employment generation and quality of life. It is, therefore, imperative that governments get their investment priorities right and direct them to areas which deserve greater attention. Besides improving infrastructure, imparting necessary skills to workers required for industries to be set up in such areas will go a long way in attracting investment.

Of late, following the Covid-19 pandemic, many state governments have begun mapping the skills of workers, whose jobs were disrupted and had to return home, with a view to provide them jobs locally and stem migration to avert such hardships in future. This calls for sustained efforts and proper planning in the medium and long-term for their resettlement. The private sector also has to work in close coordination with the central and state governments to make this a success.

(For more on employment generation, see Question 4 in Chapter 7)

The World Bank Group helps developing countries build smart infrastructure that supports inclusive and sustainable growth, expands markets, creates job opportunities, promotes competition, and contributes to a cleaner future. We help countries address their unique infrastructure needs by working with the public and private sectors. Infrastructure improves lives by connecting people to opportunity.

Access to basic infrastructure services is critical for creating economic opportunities and bringing social services to the poor. Globally, 840 million people live more than 2 kilometres from all-weather roads, 1 billion people lack electricity, and 4 billion people lack Internet access. Achieving the Sustainable Development Goals will only be possible if we close these infrastructure gaps.

– The World Bank on the importance of Infrastructure

POPULATION ISSUES AND VITAL STATISTICS

One reason for a poverty trap is demographic trap, when impoverished families choose to have lots of children. These choices are understandable, yet the results can be disastrous. When impoverished families have large numbers of children, the families cannot afford to invest in the nutrition, health, and education of each child. They might only afford the education of one child, and may send only one son to school. High fertility rates in one generation, therefore, tend to lead to impoverishment of the children and to high fertility rates in the following generation as well. Rapid population growth also puts enormous stresses on farm sizes and environmental resources, thereby exacerbating the poverty.

- Jeffrey Sachs, economist, *The End of Poverty* (2005).

Topics Covered

- *Population trends in India*
- *Total Fertility Rate (TFR)*
- *Stages in demographic transition and the transition in India*
- *India's demographic dividend and its implications*
- *Social factors and Demographic changes*
- *Family planning in India.*

1. Examine the broad trends in India's population growth and mortality rates and see to what extent they have been brought under control. Also mention some of the States which have performed well, and those which have lagged behind, on these parameters.

Ans. The changes in population are influenced by complex inter-relationships between birth rate (fertility) and death rate (mortality) and the effectiveness of policies adopted to control these factors. Other factors like literacy and education levels, women's empowerment in society, public health facilities provided and the pace of economic development of the country also play a significant role in influencing population trends.

- **Pre-independence phase**

Prior to independence, between 1911 and 1940 India experienced low growth in population. In fact, between 1911 and 1921 there was even marginal decline due to epidemics and famine. But as these were controlled after 1921, there was moderate growth in population between 1921 and 1941 aided also by decline in death rate. Death rate kept declining because of more effective control of epidemics, better sanitation, and improvements in distribution system due to better transport facilities.

With modest growth in population between 1921 and 1951, India can be considered to have been in the second stage of demographic transition during this period.

- **Post-independence phase**

India's population which was 318 million in 1941 rose to 361 million by 1951. Since 1950s when economic planning was initiated, the size of population has been a basic issue as unrestrained increase in proportion to means of subsistence not only adversely affects the standard of living of people but tends to neutralise the benefits of social and ameliorative measures.

This was recognized as much by the planners when the First Plan (1951-56) document stated: "The recent increase in the population of India and the pressure exercised on the limited resources of the country have brought to the forefront the urgency of the problem of family planning and population control......It is, therefore, apparent that population control can be achieved only by the reduction of the birth-rate to the extent necessary to stabilize the population at a level consistent with the requirements of national economy. This can be secured only by the realisation of the need for family limitation on a wide scale by the people." (First Five-Year Plan).

- **Steady increase:** During the four decades from 1951 till 1991, there was steady and significant growth in population with the average annual growth rate ranging from 2.2 per cent to 2.5 per cent. This resulted in the population increasing from 361.1 million in 1951 to 846.3 million in 1991.

  Despite concerted and sustained efforts at family planning and birth control measures under the Five Year Plans starting with the very First Plan, with a slogan to restrict the number of children per family to two, the growth in population continued apace. This was because of persisting high fertility rates while the mortality rate came down as a result of improved living conditions and better healthcare facilities in urban and rural areas.

- **Decline in annual growth:** There has been a secular decline in the annual average growth in population since the 1971. It was 2.26 per cent in the period 1971-81, 2.13 percent in the period 1981-91, 1.95 percent in 1991-2001 and declined further to 1.62 percent in 2001-11 decade.

Though there is a visible reduction in the population growth rate, the population will grow in absolute terms and India will overtake China to become the most populated country sometime before 2030.

- **Decline in Fertility rates:** While fertility was rather high in India in the 1950-70 period, with the Crude Birth Rate (CBR) above 40 per 1,000 population, it has subsequently shown considerable decline from 37.2 per 1,000 in1971-80 to 21.4 per 1,000 in 2014.
- **Total Fertility Rate (TFR):** TFR, which indicates the average number of children that would be born to a woman during her entire child-bearing years in accordance with the prevailing age- specific fertility rates, is an important factor in population trends. A TFR level of 2.1 children per woman is 'Replacement level' fertility which ensures that each generation will exactly replace itself in the absence of migration.

  India's TFR which was as high as 5.2 in 1971 steadily declined to 4.5 in 1981, 3.6 in 1991 and to 2.2 in 2018. The TFR in rural areas has declined from 5.4 in 1971 to 2.4 in 2018 while in urban areas it has declined from 4.1 to 1.7 during the same period which is a positive sign.
- **Wide regional variations:** However, the performance of States in population control and reduction in fertility rates shows wide variations. Among the major States, 12 of them have not only attained replacement level of 2.1 by 2018 but have attained levels, even lower, ranging from 1.5 to 2.0 which is significant progress in containing fertility. And not only that, these States have achieved the target for both urban and rural areas.

  These 12 States are: Andhra Pradesh, Himachal Pradesh, Jammu & Kashmir, Karnataka, Kerala, Maharashtra, Odisha, Punjab, Tamil Nadu, Telangana, Uttarakhand and West Bengal.

  The States still lagging behind are: Bihar (3.2), Chhattisgarh (2.4), Gujarat (2.1), Haryana (2.2), Madhya Pradesh (2.7), Rajasthan (2.5) and U.P. (2.9). It is to be noted that Gujarat and Haryana, which are economically quite advanced, not having attained the TFR target of 2.1 seems incongruous and only points to the need for States to place adequate emphasis on social factors.
- **Mortality rates:** Mortality is one of the basic components of population change.
  - **Crude death rate:** India's crude death rate has steadily declined from 14.7 (per 1,000) in 1971 to 9.7 in 1990, 8.7 in 2001 and 6.2 in 2018. As per 2018 SRS data, male death rate exceeds female death rate in all bigger States/UTs except Bihar and Jharkhand.
  - **Infant mortality rate (IMR)**: IMR which denotes the probability of an infant dying between birth and exactly one year of age expressed per 1,000 live births, has declined from 129 in 1971 to 70 in 2001 and 32 in 2018, a significant progress.

Though early childhood mortality (IMR) has fallen, the level is still quite high, well above that in the developed world, and even higher than in many developing countries. Another matter of concern is that after 1991, the decline in IMR has not been as steep as during the 1970s and 80s.

As per SRS 2018, in these indices also, there are variations between the performances of States and there is need to improve the outcomes in the backward States which are lagging behind. IMR ranged from 7 in Kerala to as high as 48 in Madhya Pradesh in 2018. Besides Assam, Chhattisgarh, Odisha and U.P. all had IMR value above 40.

Further, IMR is higher in rural areas than in urban areas.

- **Life expectancy at birth:** Life expectancy at birth denotes the number of years a newborn infant would live, if prevailing patterns of age-specific mortality rates continue to be the same throughout the child's life.

  India's performance on this parameter has also shown steady progress. Life expectancy which was 49.7 years in 1970-75 period rose to 60.3 years by 1997 and to 67.4 years in 2011-15 period. It may be noted that in 2011-15 period, life expectancy of females was higher at 69.6 years as compared to males at 67.3 years.

  India's life expectancy figure for 2018 was 69 years which was less than the world average of life expectancy of 72.5 years for 2018.

Conclusion

Though India's population will continue to increase, the fall in fertility rate is a positive sign, with implications not just in terms of lowering population growth but also for the development and well-being of people, particularly women and children. India needs to show further progress in the following areas:

Bringing TFR to level 2.1 in the remaining States which are also more populous ones.

Reducing Infant and Under-5 mortality rates.

Improving life expectancy.

(For more on Total Fertility Rates, see Question 2).

2. Explain the term 'Total Fertility Rate' (TFR) used in population studies and its importance in population control. Assess the performance of various States in India on TFR and its implications for changes in India's population in the coming years.

Ans. Total Fertility Rate (TFR) denotes the average number of children that would be born to a woman during her entire child-bearing years in accordance with the prevailing age-specific fertility rates. A TFR level of 2.1 per woman is 'Replacement level fertility' and if this rate is sustained over a sufficiently long period, each generation will exactly replace itself, in the absence of migration.

Factors behind declining TFR

The decline in fertility at the national and state levels is in conformity with decline in fertility for females in the 20-30 age-group. Spread of higher education, rising female education, postponement of marriage, increased mobility, paid employment of women and their financial independence, overall prosperity, access to family planning methods, and continued decline in infant mortality have all contributed to this trend.

While family planning programs have played a major role in reducing fertility in India in the past decades, the above-mentioned socio-economic changes have manifested over the last 10-15 years.

Rising urbanization, improvements in health care, increase in female education, and other socio-economic factors are expected to drive the demographic change at the national and state levels up to 2041.

India's Total Fertility Rate

India's TFR has been steadily falling over the years – from nearly 6 births per woman in early 1950s to 4.9 in 1980, 3.3 in 2000 and to replacement rate of 2.2 by 2020. Though the decline in India's TFR has been more gradual when compared to the experience of other emerging economies, it significantly halved from 4.5 in 1984 to 2.3 as of 2016.

Not only that this is an impressive achievement, as many as 13 major states have TFR below 2.2 as of 2020. The large and more populous states of UP, Bihar, Rajasthan and MP still have TFR above 2.2 but they are also experiencing declining trend as a result of which the national TFR is expected to be below replacement level by 2021. This augurs well for stabilising India's population over time.

The TFRs for major States for the year 2018 worked out by Sample Registration System by Census Office are given below in Table 1.The total fertility rate has more than halved in both urban and rural areas.

All major states have witnessed a marked deceleration in population growth during this period. The slowdown in states with historically high population growth such as Bihar, Uttar Pradesh, Rajasthan and Haryana is particularly noteworthy. Population is now growing below 1 per cent in the southern states as well as West Bengal, Punjab, Maharashtra, Odisha, Assam and Himachal Pradesh. A key factor behind this trend has been the steady decline in India's total fertility rate (TFR) since the mid-1980s.

TheTFR may further decline by 2021and stabilize thereafter. Even Bihar, Uttar Pradesh, Madhya Pradesh and Rajasthan which are lagging behind in the fertility transition are expected to see TFR fall significantly below replacement level.

TFR at the national level will continue to decline rapidly and will lie below replacement level fertility at 1.8 as early as 2021 (Table 11.1). In line with the fertility patterns witnessed in other countries, TFR is expected to stabilize thereafter for some time around 1.7.

Table 11.1: Total Fertility Rate - India and Selected States, 2018

	Rural	Urban	Total		Rural	Urban	Total
Andhra Pr	1.7	1.5	1.6	Maharashtra	1.8	1.5	1.7
Odisha	2.0	1.3	1.9	Haryana	2.4	1.9	2.2
Punjab	1.7	1.5	1.6	Gujarat	2.4	1.8	2.1
Tamil Nadu	1.6	1.6	1.6	Rajasthan	2.7	2.2	2.5
Telangana	1.7	1.5	1.6	Madhya Pradesh	3.0	2.1	2.7
West Bengal	1.7	1.2	1.5	Uttar Pradesh	3.1	2.4	2.9
Karnataka	1.8	1.6	1.7	Bihar	3.3	2.5	3.2
Kerala	1.7	1.7	1.7	INDIA	2.4	1.7	2.2
				India	**2.2**	**2.4**	**1.7**

Note: Figures rounded off to one decimal point; Abbreviations used: Pr: Pradesh.

Source: Sample Registration System (SRS), Statistical Report, 2018: Census Commissioner & Registrar General of India.

However, notwithstanding the decline in TFR, India's population will continue to grow and is expected to overtake China before 2030. India's population is expected to peak by 2060 to an estimated 1.65 billion from 1.3 billion in 2020.

It is noteworthy that India has reached the current level of TFR of 2.2 at a relatively low per capita income when compared to the experience of major developed economies. But it is similar to the experience of some of the South-east Asian countries.

Implications of fall in TFR

With TFR reaching low levels and life longevity continuing to increase, India's population at the national level and in several states will begin ageing significantly in just a decade from now. The share of India's young population, i.e. 0-19 years, has already started to decline and is projected to drop further.

On the other hand, the share of elderly population, of 60 years and above, will continue to rise steadily, nearly doubling from 8.6 per cent in 2011 to 16 per cent by 2041.

All major states are projected to witness a decline in the share of young population and an increase in the share of elderly population over the next two decades. States ahead in the demographic transition, such as Himachal Pradesh, West Bengal, Maharashtra, Punjab and most of the southern states, would have less than one-fourth of the population under the age of 20 but about one-fifth or more population over the age of 59 by 2041.

These developments suggest that India has entered the next stage of demographic transition with population declining in some States, while it is set to grow, but slowly, in some States in the next two decades with increase in the share of working age population – the so-called "demographic dividend" phase.

Trends in Europe and Japan

The current demographic situation in the economies of Japan and Europe holds a lesson for the states in India which have attained TFR of 1.5 to 1.6, much below the replacement level of 2.1. Many of the European countries and Japan which have achieved such low TFRs are facing the problem of low fertility rate, population decline and ageing people with relatively small productive workforce.

According to the UN population data, Europe is home to the most aged populations in the world where one in four of all Europeans are aged 60 and over. It's an issue that is feared to have wide-ranging socio-economic consequences – such as lower economic growth, high public debt burdens, inter-generational tensions, higher health care and pension and social welfare costs. Europe will have to overcome the problem with immigration of suitable skilled labour force.

3. Explain what is meant by "Demographic transition". Outline the various stages in the changes in the population of a country. Examine at what stage of demographic transition is India now and what are its implications for its economy.

Ans. The term "Demographic transition" refers to a phenomenon that describes the changes or transitions occurring in the population of a country over time. The theory is based on studies by an early American demographer, Warren Thompson, begun in 1929, relating to past two hundred years of changes observed in the birth and death rates in industrialized societies. It showed transition of a country from high birth and death rates to low birth and death rates as it transforms from a pre-industrial, agrarian economy to an industrialized economy as a result of economic development.

Nations undergo demographic transition based on the progress they make in controlling fertility and mortality rates and health conditions as a result of socio-economic development.

➢ **Transition in stages**

Historically, it is seen that nations undergo changes in their demographic patterns, in four or five stages, depending on the pace of their socio-economic progress.

♦ **Stage I: Pre-industrial phase**

- In the initial stages, when an economy is traditional and agrarian in structure, it will have high levels of death rates and less longevity of life due to poor health and sanitation facilities, diseases, and epidemics.
- Birth rate will also be high because, due to the high mortality rate and the economic benefits of having a large family, people are inclined to have more children.

- Further, due to low levels of literacy and education and rigid modes of customs and beliefs, people tend to have more children. But the growth in population in this stage is somewhat balanced by the high death rates.
- In this phase, death rates and birth rates are high and are roughly in balance which is characteristic of a pre-industrial society.

♦ **Stage II: Development phase:** This is the condition of a country as it goes through the second stage when it is in development phase.

- As development takes place and living conditions improve, with more food intake and better health facilities, the "life expectancy" (longevity of life) improves and death rate tends to decline.
- But this trend is not accompanied by commensurate decline in fertility. Thus, in this stage, population will rise with increase in the average family size also.
- With death rates declining, without a corresponding fall in birth rates, countries in this stage experience substantial increase in population.
- India has been going through this phase for the last few decades when it has been on a growth trajectory.

♦ **Stage III: High growth and modernisation phase**

- In the third phase of industrial development and modernization of the economy, educational and public health facilities will be expanded.
- There will be improvement in the education and status of women, and their participation in economic activities outside the home will increase.
- Due to greater access to contraception, increases in wages and urbanization, birth rates tend to fall.
- As living conditions improve, there will be greater awareness of the benefits of small family size.
- With these social changes, the population "replacement rate" (2.1) is attained and the fertility rate will decline in this stage.
- With death rate already falling, the population will stabilize at a lower level.
- It can be said that some of the States in India have entered this phase but will take time to see its full and sustained impact.

♦ **Stage IV: Declining Birth and Death rates**

The fourth stage is one in which, with the reduction in the proportion of population in the reproductive age group and the birth rate falling below the replacement level, there will be negative growth in the population.

Many of the advanced economies in western Europe and Japan are presently going through this phase of declining and ageing population with the total fertility rates (TFR) less than the replacement level of 2.1.

- **A fifth stage:** Some theorists include a fifth stage in which fertility rates begin to transition again to either above or below that which is necessary to replace the percentage of the population that is lost to death. Some say fertility levels decrease during this stage while others hypothesize that they increase.

Demographic Transition in India

In India, the birth rate remained high up to the 1960s and began to fall thereafter while the death rate continued to decline. The gap between birth and death rates seems to have narrowed in the last decade resulting in a small decline in the population growth rate. India is passing through a phase of demographic transition of moving from the "middle transitional" stage (of decline in birth rates and continuing decline in death rates) to the "late transitional" stage (of continuing decline in birth rates and slowdown in the fall in death rates).

The current trends in vital rates in the country indicate that India is entering the third stage of transition with a death rate already at low level and a rapidly declining birth rate and would gradually find balance between mortality and fertility at lower levels. However, the pace at which India achieves this stage depends on the transition of vital rates in some of the major states like Bihar, UP, MP and Rajasthan which have larger population and are still in the initial phases of transition.

As the fertility and mortality rates differ considerably across states (and also within states), the transition, and the pace at which occurs, has not been uniform across the country. Fertility is expected to decline further, and India's population is expected to reach "replacement level" with low fertility and mortality in the foreseeable future. There is no consensus on when this will happen, but most projections expect it to occur well before the middle of the century.

A consequence of the demographic transition is that the age-structure of population would undergo a major shift, from young to old ages. By the middle of the century, the share of the young, of 0-14 years, would fall to nearly half of the level of 2001 and that of the old age group, of 60 years (or 65 years) and above, would more than double. Clearly, India's population would be ageing. The share of the working age group, of 15-59 years, would keep rising reaching a peak of 65 percent before beginning to decline.

4. What is meant by 'Demographic Dividend' in a country's population? India is now having the benefit of 'Demographic Dividend' in its population. Explain its implications and the benefits and challenges it poses for India.

Ans. "Demographic dividend" is when a country has a large labour force or working population which outgrows the number of people who are dependents – children and/or elderly people – who do not contribute to the country's productive activities and economic growth. In other words, a country is said to enjoy demographic dividend when the ratio of the working age population is high and the dependency ratio in terms of proportion of children and elderly people is low.

It occurs as a result of changes in the age-structure of a country's population brought on by a decline in fertility and mortality rates. It happens when nations go through different phases of "demographic transition" from a rural agrarian economy with high fertility and mortality rates to an urban industrial society characterized by low fertility and mortality rates.

Many Asian economies – Japan, China and South Korea – were able to use the 'demographic dividend' as 'growth potential' resulting from the shifts in their population's age-structure. This transition happened largely because of a decrease in the total fertility rate (TFR, which is the number of births per woman) after the increase in life expectancy got stabilised.

➢ **Benefits of Demographic dividend**

- The demographic dividend comes when there is significant increase in the proportion of working age people of 15 to 60 years in the population who contribute to economic growth and productivity.
- With greater productivity, it will stimulate the economy and lead to higher incomes and savings.
- This advantage can create the space needed to increase investments in enhancing human capabilities, which, in turn, can have a positive influence on growth and development.
- More workers will be added to the labour force and with falling fertility rates, there will be more participation of women in the workforce.
- In this phase, the proportion of the young population (0-14 years old) and that of the elderly (65 years and above) will be less, resulting in low "dependency ratio".
- With fewer births and smaller family size, parents are able to allocate more resources per child, leading to better educational and health outcomes and family welfare.

➢ **India's Demographic dividend**

The age-structure of India's population has undergone significant changes over the period 1961-2011 (See Table 11.2 below). The share of the working age (15-59 age group) in the total population increased from 53.32 per cent in 1961 to 60.52 per cent in 2011. It is estimated to have gone up further.

As of 2020, the share of working age population (of 15-65 years) is estimated to be 67.27 percent while that of 0-14 years is 26.16 percent and of those more than 60 years 6.57 percent. The share of the young (0-14 years old) and of the elderly (65 years and above) is thus much less.

India has entered the "demographic dividend" phase in which there will be marked increase in the share of working age population even as the growth of population will slow significantly in the next two decades.

According to a study by UN Population Fund (UNFPA), India has the window of opportunity of demographic dividend for five decades which started in 2005-06 and would last till 2055-56, longer than any other country in the world.

India's working-age population (i.e., people between 15 and 64 years of age) has grown more than the dependent population and this bulge in the working-age population is going to last till 2055.

Table 11.2: Demographic Profile of India Age-specific Population Data (1961–2011) (In Million and Percentage)

Age Group (years)	1961	1971	1981	1991	2001	2011
0 – 4	66.10 (15.07)	79.56 (14.52)	83.51 (12.56)	102.38 (12.28)	110.45 (10.77)	112.80 (9.35)
5 – 14	113.98 (25.98)	150.78 (27.51)	179.60 (27.01)	209.98 (25.18)	253.17 (24.68)	259.64 (21.52)
15 – 59	233.95 (53.32)	285.01 (52.01)	358.68 53.94)	464.81 (55.74)	585.63 (57.09)	730.07 (60.52)
60 and over	24.73 (5.64)	32.69 (5.96)	43.50 (6.54)	56.70 (6.80)	76.62 (7.47)	108.33 (8.98)
Total	**438.76 (100.0)**	**548.04 (100.0)**	**664.96 (100.0)**	**833.87 (100.0)**	**1025.87 (100.0)**	**1206.35 100.0)**

Note: Total excludes 'Age Not Stated' category.

Figures in brackets denote percentages to total population.

Source: Census of India, Registrar-General of India.

➢ **Divergence in Democratic Dividend**

However, an important feature of this trend is that this demographic dividend window will be available at different points of time in different states because of varying behaviour of the population dynamics. They fall into three categories:

- In Kerala, Tamil Nadu, Andhra Pradesh, Telangana, Gujarat, Punjab and West Bengal, this window of dividend opportunity may close in about five years.
- Then there are states which include Karnataka, Odisha, Himachal Pradesh, Maharashtra, Jammu and Kashmir, Assam, Uttarakhand and Haryana where the window will remain open for another 10-15 years.
- The window of dividend opportunity is yet to open in the high-fertility states in the hinterland which includes Chhattisgarh, Jharkhand, Madhya Pradesh, Rajasthan, Uttar Pradesh and Bihar. These states will have the window of opportunity even in the 2050s and 2060s.

- As India's fertility transition will be staggered, with the window of demographic advantage open in different regions during different time-periods, India will not draw a high dividend at any time but will have a moderate dividend over a longer time span.

➢ **Need for nuanced policies**

India will enjoy a longer span of demographic dividend because, as the window closes in some states, it will open in other states. This has important implications for planning socio-economic development policies based on the age and sex structures in states or a set of states. It calls for a differential and forward-looking approach in policymaking and programme planning to harness maximum potential of the demographic dividend.

For example, the focus in the states where the window is closing soon will have to be on ageing and migrant-friendly policies and programmes, while the focus in the states where the window is open and will close in the next 10-15 years will have to be on empowering girls and women, provisioning of health, education and skill development for young people, and employment generation.

The focus in the states where the window is yet to open will have to be threefold:

- Addressing harmful practices such as child marriage.
- Access to quality sexual and reproductive health services and family planning services to all, and
- Providing for health and education facilities, life and vocational skills to all the young people.

➢ **Challenges**

This varying population dynamics and the surge in the population of working age population also throws up challenges and opportunities for the economy as discussed below:

♦ Creation of jobs to absorb the burgeoning young population is a major challenge. This will require India to expand its manufacturing and industrial base. It is estimated that India need to sustain 8 to 8.5 per cent growth to gainfully employ 60 million new workers expected to join the labour force by 2030. The enormity of the task can be gauged from the fact that India is presently creating only about 4 million jobs per year against the 10 to 12 million persons joining the labour force each year.

♦ Construction and manufacturing sectors have the maximum potential to create jobs. The government has initiated steps to expand domestic manufacturing of defence, energy, telecom, and electronic items, pharmaceuticals and a range of other products, both for domestic consumption and exports.

♦ More speedy expansion of infrastructure projects and rural and urban housing, travel and tourism industry offer much scope for employment.

♦ Expansion of education and health sectors will be crucial not only from the point of view of job creation, for which they have great potential, but also to cater to the educational and skilling needs of the youth and health needs of an expanding and ageing population.

- Skilling the labour force to meet the increasing needs of industry, and continually upgrading skills to cope with the rapid technological changes is to be carefully planned. Suitable changes in educational curriculum have to be carried out, on a continuing basis, in consultation with domain experts and industry to ensure employability of labour.
- As there is bound to be increasing inter-state migration owing to shortage and surplus of labour in different states due to differing population trends, planning for jobs and housing and other infrastructure facilities have to be aligned with the demographic changes. Regional balance in development in line with changing demographic patterns is crucial. The lop-sided development India has had is evident from the fact that while Eastern and Central India are rich in minerals, much of the industrial development has taken place in Western and Southern India. This has led to large-scale migration of labour with consequent problems faced by the migrants as witnessed when the pandemic broke out in early 2020.

5. Socio-economic progress plays a vital role in bringing about demographic changes and enhancing the quality of life. Elucidate citing examples from the performance of Indian States.

Ans. Social factors such as literacy and education, gender bias and gender equity, women's role in decision-making, employment and empowerment of women all play a significant part in ensuring a just and equitable society and enhancing the 'quality of life'.

It must be borne in mind that female population in India constitute as much as 48 per cent of total population as against male population of 52 per cent.

A comparative study of the progress made by some of the developed and less developed states in India will reveal the important role that socio-economic factors, women's employment and gender equality play in improving the performance on various demographic indices which ultimately determine the standard of living of people. The study below covers aspects like sex ratio (female to male ratio), fertility rates, infant and maternal mortality rates, total fertility rate and life expectancy.

➢ **Literacy and Education**

Literacy and education both have significant impact in improving welfare of people, especially girls and women. In India, the opportunities for both these are weighted heavily against women as compared to men, especially in the case of those in the lower income brackets and those residing in rural areas as compared to those in urban areas.

Data in Table 11.3 (a) below show that literacy among women has all along lagged behind men though the gap has somewhat narrowed. So also, those living in rural areas have lagged behind those in urban areas in the matter of literacy and the gap is significant. (Table 11.3 (b).

Table 11.3 (a): Literacy Rate (Female-Male) in India (In Percentage)

	1951	1961	1971	1981	1991	2001	2011
Female	7.9	16.63	23.81	29.76	39.29	53.57	65.46
Male	25	43.78	49.75	56.38	64.13	75.26	82.14
Total	16.7	30.68	37.32	43.57	52.21	64.83	74.04

Note: For 1951, literacy rate relates to population aged 5 years and above. For data from 1961 to 2011, literacy rates relate to population aged 7 years and above.

Source: Census of India, Registrar General of India.

Table 11.3 (b): Literacy Rate (Rural-Urban) in India (In Percentage)

	1951	1961	1971	1981	1991	2001	2011
Rural	12.1	24.48	30.3	35.17	44.01	58.73	68.91
Urban	34.59	58.59	64.56	69.06	73.08	79.92	84.97
Total	16.7	30.68	37.32	43.57	52.21	64.83	74.04

Source: Census of India, Office of Registrar General, India.

Note: For 1951, literacy rate relates to population aged 5 years and above. For data from 1961 to 2011, literacy rates relate to population aged 7 years and above.

The literacy rate of males is much higher than that of females in all States, the exception being Kerala where it is nearly the same. The difference between female and male literacy rates is much more in Bihar, UP, Rajasthan and Madhya Pradesh where the female literacy rate is particularly low in the range of 52 to 60 percent. (See Table A on page 11.29 at the end of this chapter). This deficiency will have significant impact on various other social indicators in these four states as will be explained later below.

- **Education**

Educational attainment is an important pre-requisite for improving a person's quality of life. It enhances the person's capabilities, gives greater freedom of choice, helps improve productivity, widens access to more knowledge, and facilitate social mobility by helping one to move up the escalator in life. And deprived of a reasonably good education, the person is denied much of these. This has been the fate of large sections of our population in the disadvantaged sections both in urban and rural areas.

On the positive side, enrolment in education has been going up over the years, as will be seen from Table 11.4, and is quite high up to the Upper Primary stage (Classes VI to VIII). Also, in 2015-16, enrolment of girls is higher than that of boys in all the three stages. But at Secondary level (Classes IX-X), there is fall in enrolment which indicates drop-out from schools midstream. By 2015-16, the extent of drop-out of boys and girls is nearly the same. The drop-out may be due to various economic and social factors.

Table 11.4: Gross Enrolment Ratio in Primary, Upper Primary and Secondary Stages (In Percentage)

	Primary Stage			Upper Primary Stage			Secondary Education		
	(Classes I-V)			(Classes VI-VIII)			(Classes IX-X)		
	Boys	**Girls**	**Total**	**Boys**	**Girls**	**Total**	**Boys**	**Girls**	**Total**
1950-51	60.6	24.8	43.1	20.6	4.6	12.9	--	--	--
1980-81	95.8	64.1	80.5	54.3	28.6	41.9	--	--	--
2000-01	104.9	85.9	95.7	66.7	49.9	58.6	--	--	--
2005-06	112.8	105.8	109.4	75.2	66.4	71	57.6	46.2	52.2
2010-11	115.4	116.7	116	87.7	83.1	85.5	69	60.8	65
2015-16	97.9	100.7	99.2	88.7	97.6	92.8	79.2	81.0	80.0

Source: *Data for 1950-51 & 1980-81 from Ministry of Education cited in 'Selected Socio-Economic Statistics, India 2000' and for 2000-01 to 2010-11 from 'India: Education for All - Towards Quality with Equity', Ministry of Human Resources Development, 2014; Data for 2015-16 from Educational Statistics at A Glance, 2018, Ministry of Human Resource Development (Dept. of School Education & Literacy), Govt. of India.*

➢ Education and Social change

♦ **Fertility rates:** That education is a vital tool and catalyst for social advancement is a proven fact. There is a correlative relationship between literacy, education and social change. The spread of education creates greater awareness about the benefits of lower fertility, smaller family size and better living conditions. This is evident from the fact that states which have advanced the cause of education and health have performed better in attaining better female to male (sex) ratio, controlling birth rates and reducing infant and maternal mortality rates.

♦ **Female-Male (Sex) ratio:** The same holds good for improved female-male ratio (sex ratio) in the population of States. However, data as per 2011 census in Table A (given at the end of this chapter) shows some notable exceptions in the performance of major States.

While in 2011, Kerala was the only state with a ratio of over 1,000 – 1,084 females to 1,000 males, Tamil Nadu and Andhra Pradesh had a ratio of over 990. Odisha had a ratio of 979, higher than Gujarat (919), Maharashtra (929), West Bengal (950) and Karnataka (973).

The economically advanced states of Punjab (with 895) and Haryana (879) had much lower ratios than even the relatively less developed states of Madhya Pradesh (931), Rajasthan (928), Bihar (918) and Uttar Pradesh (912). It may also be noted that the ratio of Madhya Pradesh (931) is slightly higher than of even Maharashtra (929) and Gujarat (919).

- **Total Fertility Rate (TFR):** TFR measures the average number of children born to a woman during her entire reproductive period in accordance with prevailing age-specific fertility rates.

  By 2018, as many as 13 states have recorded TFR below the 'replacement level' of 2.1 which is a notable achievement. Table 11.5 shows some of these States which have achieved this. (If the 'replacement level' of 2.1 is sustained over a sufficiently long period, each generation will exactly replace itself in the absence of migration). Here again, it turns out that economic development and social sector attainments in education and health have played a significant role.

  The fertility level has been generally found to be higher at lower education levels of the parents. According to studies, it has been found that the TFR declines progressively with the rise in the level of education of women and mothers.

Table 11.5: Performance of Selected States on Literacy and Population Control

State	Literacy Rate			Birth Rate			TFR		
	1951	1971	2011	1960	1996	2018	1980-82	1990-92	2018
Kerala	40.7	60.4	93.9	22.6	17.8	13.9	2.9	1.8	1.7
Maharashtra	20.9	39.2	82.9	29.5	23.2	15.6	3.7	3.0	1.7
Tamil Nadu	20.8	39.5	80.3	28.0	19.2	14.8	3.4	2.2	1.6
Andhra Pradesh	13.1	24.6	67.6	21.2	22.7	16.0	3.9	3.0	1.6
West Bengal	24.0	33.2	77.1	19.2	22.8	11.5	4.1	3.2	1.5
Punjab	15.2	33.7	76.68	35.7	23.5	14.8	4.0	3.1	1.6
Karnataka	19.3	31.5	75.6	27.9	23.0	17.2	3.6	3.1	1.7
Odisha	15.8	26.2	73.45	24.6	26.8	18.2	4.2	3.3	1.9
Haryana	na	26.9	76.64	na	28.8	20.3	5.0	3.9	2.2
	1951	1971	2011	1960	1999	2018	1980-82	1990-92	2018
Uttar Pradesh	10.8	21.7	69.72	15.9	34.0	25.6	5.8	5.2	2.9
Bihar	12.2	19.9	63.82	11.4	32.1	26.2	5.6	4.6	3.2
Madhya Pradesh	9.8	22.1	70.63	18.1	32.4	24.6	5.2	4.7	2.7
Rajasthan	8.9	19.1	67.06	36.4	32.3	24.0	5.5	4.5	2.5

Source: *Literacy data from Statistical Abstract, India, CSO and Census of India; Birth Rate from Sample Registration System (SRS), Registrar General of India; TFR data from National Human Development Report, India200,1 and SRS, 2018, Registrar General of India.*

Note: Literacy data in percentage; Birth rate is number of live births per 1,000 population in a given year; TFR: Total Fertility Rate measures average number of children born to a woman during her entire productive period; na: not available.

TFR for India as a whole has also stabilised at 2.2 by 2018. Now, it is for the less developed states of Rajasthan with TFR at 2.5, Madhya Pradesh (2.7), Uttar Pradesh (2.9) and Bihar (3.2) to bring down the rate to 2.1 or below it.

Further, the factors influencing the decision-making process at household level, such as greater participation of women in decision making, empowerment of women by the spread of education and their income-earning capacity with paid employment have a decisive role in improving demographic indicators. These influences stand out in the success of demographic transition in the States of Kerala, Tamil Nadu and Maharashtra.

- **Mortality rates**
  - **Death Rate:** The death rate in India has been steadily coming down.As per crude death rate in 2018, the overall death rate was 6.2 per 1,000 population as against 9.7 in 1990. Death rate at 5.1 in urban area was lower than the rate of 6.7 in rural area. The female death rate is lower than male death rate both in rural and urban areas. The death rate for males is 6.6 per 1,000 population while it is 5.7 for females.

    Infant Mortality Rate (IMR) and Maternal Mortality Ratio (MMR) are two other important indicators of the state of health of the population.
  - **Infant Mortality Rate (IMR):** IMR refers to the probability of an infant dying between birth and exactly one year of age expressed per thousand live births. Similarly, under-5 mortality rate refers to the probability of child dying between birth and exactly five years of age, expressed per 1,000 live births.

    Table B given on page 11.30 at the end of this chapter shows IMR data for 1981 and 2018 for major states among male and female children. The mortality rate has come down significantly over these years among both male and female children and it is nearly at the same level for both. It is reflective of the health of the mothers and public health and life support systems available.
  - **Maternal Mortality ratio (MMR):** MMR refers to the annual number of female deaths from pregnancy-related causes per 100,000 live births and is considered a key health indicator. Maternal deaths are due to major complications during pregnancy and after childbirth. The causes are well known and are largely treatable and preventable if pregnant women receive timely healthcare when they need it. Pregnancy among adolescent girls, lack of proper medical care and delivery without the aid of skilled medical professionals are some of the major factors for higher level of maternal mortality in India.
  - **MMR in India:** The Government of India has been focusing on initiatives to improve maternal health indicators. Organisations like UNICEF and NGOs

are playing an important role in preventing maternal deaths. As will be seen from Table B at the end of this chapter on Page 11.26), MMR has come down perceptibly in the last two decades but the numbers are still high in the less developed (Group-II) states. For India as a whole, in 2014-16 period, the maternal mortality ratio was 130 per 100,000 live births.

According to the World Bank, recent research has shown that, for every 100,000 children born worldwide, 211 women still die due to pregnancy-related complications, most of which occur in developing regions.

- **Life expectancy:** Life expectancy at birth represents the number of years a newborn infant would live if prevailing patterns of age-specific mortality rates at the time of birth were to stay the same throughout the child's life.

  The Table C at the end of this chapter (on page 11.31)shows that during the period 2016-20, females in India have higher life expectancy than males, both at the national level and in the major states listed.

➤ **Conclusion**

The forgoing analysis of various demographic and human development indicators reinforces the argument that advancement in social fields such as education and health play a pivotal role in improving living standards and quality of life of people. In this endeavour, the role that women play cannot be over emphasized. Women's empowerment and their status in decision making is crucial.

Finally, though India may have successfully curbed its high fertility rate, it still has a long way to go in overcoming the population crisis. From India's demographic trend, it is estimated that the population will continue to rise at less than 1 per cent during 2021-31 and under 0.5 per cent during 2031-41 decades.

The population growth will pose challenges in the effort to eradicate poverty, achieve greater equality, combat hunger and malnutrition. India will have to further strengthen the coverage and quality of health and education systems to ensure that no one is left behind.

6. How does population growth affect economic development of a country? Can the age structure of population alter the pattern of development in a country? Examine in the light of the Indian experience.

Ans. Many social scientists and economists have viewed India's population as a major problem and hindrance to development. This was noted, as early as 1935, by a Committee of Indian National Congress, headed by Jawaharlal Nehru, which observed that unfettered increase in population neutralises the benefits of development and adversely affects the standards of living of people. This is in line with the Malthusian thesis, also dubbed Malthusian pessimism, propounded by Thomas Robert Malthus (1766-1834), an English Classical theorist of political economy, who argued that unchecked growth of population would outstrip food supply and the means of subsistence resulting in untold human suffering.

The changes in population and demographic pressures impact an economy and the development process in multiple ways. They impact the availability of land, labour and capital resources required for development. Besides, they impact on educational and health standards, infrastructural facilities, housing, sanitation, etc. These aspects are discussed below in the Indian context.

- **Demographic factors and Development**

  Demographic factors like fertility and mortality rates and changes in them and age-structure of the population play a significant role on socio-economic development. High birth and death rates, and high infant mortality rates affect the population structure.

  - **Age-structure and Dependency ratio:** Having a good percentage of the population in the working age group of 15-60 years is an advantage from the economy's point of view. On the contrary, with high proportion of population being infants and children (0-14 years) and aged people (of over 60-65 years), both of which are of non-working age, the economy will have a high "dependency ratio". In that case the working population have to support the young and the aged which would adversely affect productivity, level of savings, investment, etc.

    With higher proportion of people in the non-working age group, a share of investible resources has to be utilized for providing facilities and social security measures for the non-working segment. As long as society can produce basic consumption goods, mainly food, in adequate measure and can increase agricultural output using labour, the problem can be contained. But when a point is reached when agricultural output and productivity per worker can be further increased only by inputs involving capital expenditure such as irrigation, farm equipments, fertilizers, etc. which are expensive, the pressure on capital resources required to sustain the population will set in.

    The sheer magnitude of additions to the labour force will bring to the fore the constraints of capital required to absorb the labour force in non-farm occupations, skilling and equipping them and raise the productivity of labour. India is presently facing the situation of stagnation and saturation in agricultural sector and is faced with the challenge of expanding the industrial base and finding the capital required for it.

  - **India's demographic profile:** The age-structure in India's population has been undergoing change since 1951 (See Table E at the end of this chapter on page 11.32). India's working-age population (i.e., people between 15 and 59 years of age) has grown more than the dependent population especially between 1991 and 2011. The population in 15-59 age group rose from 464.81 million in 1991 to 730.07 million in 2011 and in percentage of total population from 55.74 to 60.52 during the same period. In 2011, the 0-14 age group constituted 30.87 per cent and 60 years and over 8.98 per cent. This has provided India with the window of opportunity of "demographic dividend" which is expected to last over a long time span as the window opens at different points of time in different states.

Having such a large proportion of population in working age group and much less in 0-14 years and over 60 years age groups means less "dependency ratio", i.e., less number of children and older people who do not contribute to productive activities and are to be supported by the working population. But in the Indian context, it poses the major challenge of creation of adequate jobs for the persons in working age group. This is an onerous task considering that about 10 to 12 million youth will be joining the labour force each year for the next decade and a half or more. This is in addition to the burden of shifting surplus labour from the farm sector to non-farm jobs. **(For more on these aspects, refer to Question 4 in this chapter)**.

➤ **Land and agriculture:** Availability of arable land for cultivation in proportion to the population and food requirements is an important aspect. The size of the workforce in agriculture is significant as it directly impinges on the most important asset in rural India, namely, land which is more or less fixed in physical terms.

This is even more pertinent in India where bulk of the population live in rural areas and depend on agriculture for sustenance. The percentage of rural population was as high as 82 per cent in 1961 and stood at about 69 per cent in 2011. And the percentage of rural population engaged in agriculture rose from 46.7 in 1951 to 49.8 in 1991 and 57.8 in 2011.

As the population grew, sub-division and fragmentation of land holdings has happened which has impacted farm productivity. About 68 per cent of farms are of less than one hectare in size which makes farming uneconomic in many cases.

♦ **Land fertility and Output:** The effective supply of land can be augmented through multiple cropping which is conditional on adequate water availability. Farm productivity can be raised by covering farms with irrigation which requires capital investment. In India where agriculture is heavily dependent on monsoon, which is quite unpredictable, only about 48 per cent of cultivated land is covered by irrigation.

Though India has been able to augment food production through the Green Revolution and has attained self-sufficiency in food, farmers continue to face many problems due to crop failures, rising input costs, unremunerative prices and financial burdens. All these point to the undue pressure of population in the agriculture sector.

- **Labour and Employment:** With a high proportion of people in rural areas, the pressure of population depending on agriculture is well documented. As stated above, the percentage of rural population engaged in agriculture has risen which shows the relentless pressure bearing on the farm sector. India has struggled over the last seven decades to reduce the pressure by shifting labour to non-farm jobs in rural and semi-urban areas but with only limited success.

  As a result, there is a high degree of disguised and under-employment, wastage of manpower and lower productivity in agriculture.

- **Industrialisation:** Historically, the economic development in the industrialized nations in Europe and America was accomplished with continuous transfer of economic activity and people from rural to urban areas, both within and between countries. As urban industries expanded, new employment opportunities were created, rural manpower requirements came down due to labour-saving technological progress in agriculture. Although urban slums and unemployment existed even in Europe in the 19th century, the combination of the above two phenomena enabled Western nations to undergo a major transformation through systematic rural-to-urban transfer of their human resources. The pace of industrialisation following Industrial Revolution enabled western nations to absorb the expanding labour force. Manufacturing became the 'engines of growth'.

  - **Challenge for India:** Today, these conditions no longer exist. Developing countries, including India, are beset by a historically unique combination of stagnant agriculture, large-scale shifts of population from rural to urban areas, and growing rural and urban unemployment and under-employment.

    Further, manufacturing has become highly skill-intensive and largely based on high level technology. With globalization, competition has also become more intense with many emerging countries vying for global markets. Therefore, much will depend on India's ability to procure advanced technology, rapidly upgrading the skills of labour and providing a competitive environment for corporations to invest and set up industries in India.

- **Migration:** The excessive population in rural India has forced a large percentage of them to migrate to urban areas in search of employment. It has also led to inter-state migration on large scale, a problem which came to the fore in recent times due to the widespread pandemic in 2020. As industries and other establishments closed down, the migrant labour had to revert back to their home states facing untold hardship.

- **Socio-economic factors:** India has controlled population to a great extent, improved fertility and mortality rates and health outcomes. But yet, large segments of population are still below poverty level and do not have access to proper housing, safe drinking water, sanitation facilities not to speak of satisfactory educational and health facilities. There are wide inequalities impeding the progress on these counts.

- **India's position:** Apart from the factors discussed above, India's position on demography and development has to be viewed against the background of two centuries of colonial rule which she had to endure. This has had a debilitating impact on India's economy and social fabric in manifold ways. While in the 17th century, India was relatively flourishing, the arrival of colonial rulers and the onset of Industrial Revolution in the west set the clock back for India and pushed the country onto the path of decline and degradation.

  During the colonial rule, many sectors were left to utter neglect and decay, and lakhs of people were thrown out of jobs. There was virtually no industrialization which meant the bulk of the population were left to toil in farms. Lack of improvements in health, prevalence of disease and pestilence and recurring famines took a heavy toll on the population.

  It was in this state of neglect that India gained independence and had to embark on an arduous journey of development. The ill-effects of all these impacted India for decades after independence when the population also grew at a steady pace. India has struggled over seven decades to bring the population under control with a sustained family planning programme and schemes to improve the health of the population.

  Despite these efforts and progress on human development indices, India is still way down in global ranking. In the 2019 Human Development Report of UNDP, India is placed in the Medium Human Development category at rank 129 out of 189 countries.

7. Examine the role 'Family Planning' programme played in controlling India's population growth since independence. Outline the challenges faced in its implementation and the results achieved from it.

Ans. Introduction

Though the rate of increase of population in pre-independence era was low, India's population steadily rose from 238 million in 1901 to 361 million by 1951, an increase of 123 million in a span of five decades. A Committee of Indian National Congress, headed by Jawaharlal Nehru, had recognized the population problem as early as 1935 and observed thus: "We agree with the view that the size of the Indian population is a basic issue in national economic planning, in so far as its unrestricted increase of proportion to means of subsistence, affects adversely the standards of living, and tends to defeat many social and ameliorative measures. The problem has been fundamentally caused by the lack of all-round co-ordinated economic development."

- **Family Planning in Five Year Plans**

  In 1950, India with no more than 2.5 per cent of global land, was the second most populous country in the world (after China which had 544 million in 1950) and was home to one-seventh of the world's population. Containing population growth was, therefore, one of the objectives of the Five-Year Plans and the government assigned, *inter alia*, priority to the Family Planning programme. In 1952, India became the first country in the world to formulate a National Family Planning Programme with the goal of lowering fertility and slowing the population growth rate.

The basic premises of the Family Planning programme from its very inception were:

- Population control can be achieved only by the reduction of the birth-rate to stabilise the population at a level consistent with the requirements of national economy.
- This can be secured only by the realisation of the need for family limitation on a wide scale by the people.
- Family limitation or spacing of the children is necessary and desirable in order to secure better health for the mother and better care and upbringing of children.
- Health care to women and children and provision of contraceptive services were key elements.
- The main appeal for family planning was based on considerations of health and welfare of the family.

  Measures to promote the above objectives formed part of the public health programme and there was steady expansion of family planning schemes in successive Plans.

➢ **Sustained campaign**

India launched a sustained campaign to reach out to people to educate them and create awareness on the benefits of having a small family. The programme over time expanded the range and reach of contraceptive options through rolling out new contraceptives and delivering a full range of family planning services at all levels. The strategy included:

- ♦ Increased focus on proper spacing of childbirth and healthcare of mother and child.
- ♦ Voluntary adoption of family planning based on felt need of the community.
- ♦ Focus on male participation.
- ♦ Rights-based approach to family planning.

Slogans such as "Small Family, Happy Family" and "Hum Do, Hamare Do" (meaning "We Two, Ours Two") were part of the campaign to urge married couples to restrict to having just two kids.

The programme adopted clinic-based approach to provide health care services in Family Planning centres set up by the government in urban and mofussil areas. In due course, the program was expanded to reach every nook and corner of the country and has penetrated into PHCs and SCs in rural areas. Couples were motivated to visit such centres for maternal and child health care and family planning services, were persuaded to use contraceptives and undergo sterilization of one partner in case their family was complete. States have shown increase in the use of modern contraceptives.

In 1979, the programme was renamed as "Family Welfare Programme" and enhanced integration of family planning services with those of Maternal and Child Health (MCH) and Nutrition for better outcomes.

Over the decades, the Family Planning programme was further refined in line with the objectives of various policies like National Population Policy 2000, National Health Policy 2002 and National Health Mission. Increasingly it became a medium of intervention for promoting reproductive and child health.

The programme also complimented India's commitments at International Forums such as International Conference on Population and Development (ICPD), UN Sustainable Development Goals (SDGs), FP2020, etc.

The government harnessed the expertise of various partners and organisations in the field of advocacy, capacity building and IEC for focused communications campaign, programme management, quality improvement, evaluation of outcomes.

➢ **Challenges and Constraints**

The programme faced many challenges in the course of implementation.

- In the 1950s, health care services in India were predominantly urban, hospital-based and general practitioners well versed in providing health care to women and children. But majority of the population belonging to the poorer sections and those residing in rural areas did not have access to health care due to which morbidity and mortality rates among them were quite high.
- Though the coverage of health and family welfare services in urban areas were much better than in rural areas, lack of safe drinking water and sanitation facilities, and the high population density in urban slums led to rapid spread of infections and had high incidence of vector-borne diseases.
- Poor housing conditions, exposure to heat and cold, air and water pollution, and occupational hazards added to the environmental risks for the poor. They were also vulnerable as they had no backup of savings, food stocks, or social support systems to tide over the crisis of illness.
- Public healthcare system in rural areas in many States and regions were in shambles. Extreme inequalities and disparities persisted both in terms of access to health care as well as health outcomes. This wide disparity across India placed the burden on the poor, especially women, scheduled castes, and tribes.
- Inequity was also reflected in the availability of public resources between the developed and less developed States.

➢ Critique of the Programme

There have been divergent views on India's implementation of the Family Planning programme. According to some social scientists, instead of obsessing about overpopulation and birth control from the 1950s, India should have paid greater attention to reduce infant and child mortality and provided social security for the elderly which would have led to decline in birth rates. According to them, population control was not necessary because economic development would have stabilised population.

But the planners in the early days were overwhelmed by a plethora of problems such as high level of illiteracy and poor educational and health standards, social inequities and economic backwardness that led them to conclude that there was need for affirmative action to check the growth of population. This also became necessary because as the birth rate continued to rise, death rates began to decline due to control of diseases like malaria and cholera and thus widening the gap between fertility and mortality rates.

Though the programme may have had certain deficiencies in planning and execution in the initial phase, it can be said that in the long run it did help to create awareness of the benefits of small family and birth control among a wide cross-section of the population. And the results are evident from the trends in various demographic indicators over the years. It is difficult to conceive what the situation would have been if India had not gone in for such a programme.

One major lapse in its implementation was that though the programme was voluntary, certain coercive steps taken for "compulsory sterilisation" in 1970s led to stiff resistance and backlash from the public. It was a lesson for the State to pursue the programme on a voluntary mode, if it was to receive acceptance by the public and be a success.

➢ Progress and Achievements

Notwithstanding the various constraints and problems faced, the family planning programme, aided by steady improvements in health facilities, made significant progress over the years and the results became visible with every successive Plan. The technological advances and improved quality and expanding health care coverage showed sustained progress in various demographic indicators. The last seven decades have seen significant improvements in the indicators as outlined below:

- **Birth rate:** Crude Birth Rate (CBRs) declined from 41.7 (per 1,000 population) in 1951-60 period to 32.5 in 1981-90 and 21.4 by 2014. It stood at 20.0 in 2018.

- **Total fertility rate** (TFR): TFR, i.e., the average number of children born to a woman, declined from 6 births per woman in early 1950s to 4.9 in 1980, 3.3 in 2000 and 2.2 by 2020 which is a major achievement. Apart from that, many states have attained TFR of 1.5 to 1.6, well below the replacement level of 2.1.
- **Couple Protection Rate (CPR):** CPR is the percentage of eligible couples effectively protected against childbirth by one or the other approved methods of family planning. The CPR percentage which was 10.6 in 1970-71 rose to 46.2 by 2000 but declined to 40.4 in 2011. Though CPR has come down, fertility rates are showing decline.
- **Death rate:** Crude Death Rate (CDR) fell from 22.8 (per 1,000 population) in 1951-60 period to 11.4 in 1981-90 and to 7.0 by 2014. It further came down to 6.2 in 2018.
- **Infant mortality rate (IMR):** IMR declined from 115 (per 1,000 live births) in 1961 to 71 by 2001 and to 32 in 2018.
- **Life expectancy at birth:** It rose from 49.1 years in 1970 to 60.3 years in 1991-95 and 67.4 years in 2011-15 period.

➢ **Comparative data**

The comparative data on relevant demographic indicators given below, based on data put out by UN Population Division, gives an idea of the relative performance and progress of India vis-à-vis the world averages and of the averages for Europe, Asia and Africa. India's data is also juxtaposed with data of Bangladesh which has outperformed India on some indicators.

The findings from Table 11.6 are summed up below:

(i) **Birth rate:** On birth rate, performance of India and Bangladesh has reached the same level of 20.4 per 1,000 population by 2010-15 period which is close to the world average of 19.6. The average for Asia as a whole is better at 17.8 while Europe's average of 10.8 is far better.

(ii) **TFR:** On TFR, both India (2.24 children per woman) and Bangladesh (2.05) have better figures than the world average of 2.47 by 2015-20 period. The progress has been significant considering that they started from a low base of 5.90 (India) and 6.36 (Bangladesh) in 1950-55.

It is noteworthy that Bangladesh has outperformed India on TFR both during 2000-05 period (2.94 against India's 3.14) and in 2015-20 (2.05 against India's 2.24). And in 2018, as per World Bank data, Bangladesh's TFR stands at 2.0 against India's 2.2.

On TFR, Africa with an average of 4.44 in 2015-20 is far behind Asia (2.15).

Europe's TFR during 2015-20 is low at 1.61, well below the replacement level of 2.1, a sign of declining population. But Europe has improved slightly from 2000-05 figure of 1.43.

Table 11.6: Demographic Indicators: Comparative data

1: Crude Birth Rate (Births per 1,000 population)

	1950-55	1980-85	2000-05	2010-15
World	36.9	27.8	20.8	19.6
Europe	21.5	14.3	10.1	10.8
Asia	41.8	29.0	19.5	17.8
Africa	48.1	44.6	37.8	35.8
India	43.6	35.5	25.3	20.4
Bangladesh	46.2	42.2	26.0	20.4

2: Total Fertility Rate (TFR - Births per woman)

	1950-55	1980-85	2000-05	2015-20
World	4.97	3.59	2.65	2.47
Europe	2.66	1.88	1.43	1.61
Asia	5.83	3.69	2.45	2.15
Africa	6.57	6.50	5.08	4.44
India	5.90	4.68	3.14	2.24
Bangladesh	6.36	5.98	2.94	2.05

3: Crude Death Rate (Deaths per 1,000 population)

	1950-55	1980-85	2000-05	2015-20
World	19.1	10.0	8.5	7.5
Europe	11.2	10.8	11.6	11.0
Asia	22.6	9.3	7.2	6.9
Africa	26.7	15.6	12.9	8.2
India	26.4	12.7	8.4	7.2
Bangladesh	24.8	13.7	9.3	5.5

4: Infant Mortality Rate (IMR - Infant deaths per 1,000 live births)

	1950-55	1980-85	2000-05	2015-20
World	140	75	49	29
Europe	72	18	8	4
Asia	155	78	46	25
Africa	183	111	81	47
India	181	106	60	32
Bangladesh	211	124	55	27

Source: United Nations, Department of Economic and Social Affairs, Population Division (2019), World Population Prospects 2015 Revision, DVD edn. and 2019, Online Edition. Rev. 1.

Fertility is generally high in Northern Europe and low in the South. France is an outlier with TFR stabilized and remaining at 1.84 children per woman in France in 2018.

One explanation given by demographers for low TFR in Europe is gender inequality. Women have lower status in the Southern Europe than in the North, and the gender division of tasks is more unequal. Also, fewer policies have been set in place to favour female employment and work–life balance in the South. Finally, societies in Southern Europe consider that mothers should not leave their children while having to go out to work, at least in their early years.

(iii) **Death rate:** On crude death rate, India's average (7.2 deaths per 1,000 population) is better than the world average (7.5) and that of African continent (8.2). But India lags behind Asia (6.9) and, more importantly, Bangladesh (5.5) which has better averages.

On death rate, in 2000-05 period, Bangladesh with 9.3 was behind India (8.4) but later improved upon India in 2015-20 period.

(iv) **IMR:** On Infant Mortality rate, the world average is 29 infant deaths per 1,000 live births. Europe with average of 4 is far ahead of Asia (25) and Africa (47). On IMR also, Bangladesh with 55 in 2000-05 and 27 in 2015-20 has outperformed India (60 in 2000-05 and 32 in 2015-20).

Thus, on TFR, Death rate and IMR, Bangladesh is ahead of India while on birth rate both are at the same level.

➢ **Conclusion**

Improvements in macro socio-economic variables such as literacy, education and health, industrialization and urbanisation, and rising status and empowerment of women and gender equity have contributed to a conducive environment in controlling population.

At the same time, the family planning programme has played a major role in this endeavour. Without such a focussed programme, India may not have been able to contain the surge of population growth as she has been able to do so far. Technological advances in family planning methods, improvement in quality and coverage of health care, implementation of disease control programmes and increasing awareness about the benefit of small family have also aided in the process. As a result, the family welfare programme can be regarded as having been beneficial and successful.

But there is no room for complacency as due to the phenomenon of "Population momentum", population would continue to grow even after India has achieved replacement level and till the stage of "Population stabilization" is reached. Because of the population momentum, there is a time lag between achieving replacement fertility and achieving population stabilization.

Hence India's population would continue to grow and is expected to overtake China before 2030. According to UN estimates, India's population, which stands at 1.35 billion in 2020, will reach its peak population by mid-century, touching 1.64 billion by 2050.

Table A: Sex Ratio & Literacy rates in Major States

Female-Male (Sex) Ratio			Literacy Percentage							
			Female				Male			
1	2	3	4	5	6	7	8	9	10	11
State	**2001**	**2011**	**State**	**1981**	**2011**	**2020**	**State**	**1981**	**2011**	**2020**
Kerala	1058	1084	Kerala	75.65	91.98	92.1	Kerala	87.73	96.02	96.1
Tamil Nadu	987	995	Tamil Nadu	40.43	73.86	73.4	Tamil Nadu	69.65	86.81	86.8
Andhra Pradesh	978	993	Andhra Pradesh	26.16	59.74	59.1	Andhra Pradesh	68.05	75.56	74.9
Maharashtra	922	929	Maharashtra	41.01	75.48	75.9	Maharashtra	65.14	89.82	88.4
Karnataka	965	973	Karnataka	33.17	68.13	68.1	Karnataka	59.93	82.85	82.5
West Bengal	934	950	West Bengal	36.07	71.16	70.5	West Bengal	58.51	86.27	81.7
Gujarat	920	919	Gujarat	38.46	70.73	69.7	Gujarat	58.73	87.23	85.8
Punjab	876	895	Punjab	39.7	71.34	70.7	Punjab	56.45	81.48	80.4
Haryana	861	879	Haryana	26.93	66.77	65.9	Haryana	55.56	85.38	84.1
Odisha	972	979	Odisha	25.14	64.36	64.0	Odisha	48.42	82.4	81.6
Rajasthan	921	928	Rajasthan	14.0	52.66	52.1	Rajasthan	44.77	80.51	79.2
Uttar Pradesh	898	912	Uttar Pradesh	17.19	59.26	57.2	Uttar Pradesh	47.45	79.24	77.3
Madhya Pradesh	919	931	Madhya Pradesh	23.97	60.02	59.2	Madhya Pradesh	46.83	80.53	78.7
Bihar	919	918	Bihar	16.52	53.33	51.5	Bihar	46.6	73.39	71.2

Source: Female-Male (Sex) Ratio from Census of India 2011, Registrar General of India; Literacy percentage, 1981, Census of India cited in National Human Development Report, India 2001, and for 2011 from Census of India 2011, Registrar General of India; Data for 2020 from Census of India 2021-Literacy rate of States.

Table B: Infant Mortality Rate (IMR) – Maternal Mortality Ratio (MMR) in Major States

State	Infant Mortality Rate (IMR)				Maternal Mortality Ratio (MMR)	
	1981		2018		1997	2014-16
	Female	Male	Female	Male		
Group I States						
Kerala	48	61	5	9	195	46
Tamil Nadu	93	114	14	16	76	66
Andhra Pradesh	82	100	29	30	154	74
Maharashtra	106	131	19	19	135	61
Karnataka	74	87	25	21	195	108
Telangana	-	-	26	27	-	-
West Bengal	57	103	22	22	267	101
Gujarat	110	120	27	29	-	91
Punjab	114	138	20	21	196	122
Haryana	119	132	29	31	105	101
Group II States						
Odisha	153	172	39	40	361	180
Rajasthan	135	146	38	37	677	199
Uttar Pradesh	128	131	44	43	707	201
Madhya Pradesh	140	158	46	51	498	173
Bihar	94	95	35	30	451	165

Source: IMR data for 1981 and MMR data for1997 from National Human Development Report, 2001, Planning Commission; IMR data for 2018 from SRS Report 2018, Registrar General of India; MMR data for 2014-16 from Central Bureau of Health Intelligence, Director General of Health Services, Govt. of India.

Table C: Expectation of Life at Birth in India & Major States

State	1981 – 85		1991 – 95		2016 – 20	
	Male	Female	Male	Female	Male	Female
Kerala	65.4	71.5	69.9	73.3	74.2	78.1
Tamil Nadu	56.5	57.4	62.3	64.4	69.6	73.0
Andhra Pradesh	57.2	59.8	60.3	62.8	68.4	72.1
Maharashtra	59.6	62.1	63.5	65.8	69.9	73.7
Karnataka	59.7	62.0	60.6	63.9	69.0	73.5
West Bengal	56.4	58.0	61.5	62.8	70.2	73.3
Gujarat	55.5	59.3	60.2	62.0	70.7	73.7
Punjab	62.6	63.6	66.1	68.4	70.7	73.8
Haryana	61.5	59.0	63.0	64.0	69.9	72.5
Odisha	53.1	53.0	56.6	56.2	66.3	69.6
Rajasthan	53.3	53.8	58.3	59.4	98.6	71.9
Uttar Pradesh	51.4	48.5	57.3	56.0	67.5	69.2
Madhya Pradesh	51.5	51.9	54.7	54.6	66.5	67.3
Bihar	54.2	51.5	60.1	58.0	69.6	70.2
India	**55.4**	**55.7**	**59.7**	**60.9**	**68.8**	**71.1**

Source: Sample Registration System, Registrar General of India; 2016 – 20: Report of the Technical Group on Population Projections May 2006; National Commission on Population, O/o Registrar General of India cited in National Health Profile 2018.

Table D: Per Capita Net State Domestic Product (NSDP)–Major States (In ₹ Crore)

Group I States				Group II States			
State	**1995- 96**	**2000-01**	**2016- 17**	**State**	**1995-96**	**2000-01**	**2016-17**
Haryana	11545	24423	143211	Rajasthan	7216	12840	72072
Maharashtra	13221	21892	133141	Odisha	5204	10208	63674
Gujarat	11649	17227	131853	Madhya Pradesh	6790	11150	53047
Kerala	8868	19809	128550	Uttar Pradesh	5256	9721	38934
Karnataka	8368	17352	124093	Bihar	2728	6554	25950
Tamil Nadu	10147	20319	117806				
Punjab	13008	25986	105386				
Andhra Pradesh	8071	16574	96374				
West Bengal	7492	16244	61245				

Source: Handbook of Statistics on Indian Economy, 2017 – 18, Reserve Bank of India.

Table E: Demographic Profile of India Age – Specific Population Data (1961 – 2011) (In Million and Percentage)

Age Group	1961	1971	1981	1991	2001	2011
0 – 4	66.10 (15.07)	79.56 (14.52)	83.51 (12.56)	102.38 (12.28)	110.45 (10.77)	112.80 (9.35)
5 – 14	113.98 (25.98)	150.78 (27.51)	179.60 (27.01)	209.98 (25.18)	253:17 (24.68)	259.64 (21.52)
15 – 59	233.95 (53.32)	285.01 (52.01)	358.68 53.94)	464.81 (55.74)	585.63 (57.09)	730.07 (60.52)
60 and over	24.73 (5.64)	32.69 (5.96)	43.50 (6.54)	56.70 (6.80)	76.62 (7.47)	108.33 (8.98)
Total	**438.76 (100.0)**	**548.04 (100.0)**	**664.96 (100.0)**	**833.87 (100.0)**	**1025.87 (100.0)**	**1206.35 100.0)**

Note: Total excludes 'Age Not Stated' category.

Figures in brackets denote percentages.

Source: Census of India, Registrar-General of India.

Our growing population

In 1950, five years after the founding of the United Nations, world population was estimated at around 2.6 billion people. It reached 5 billion in 1987and 6 billion in 1999. In October 2011, the global population was estimated to be 7 billion. A global movement "7 Billion Actions" was launched to mark this milestone. The world's population is expected to increase by 2 billion persons in the next 30 years, from 7.7 billion currently to 9.7 billion in 2050 and could peak at nearly 11 billion around 2100.

This dramatic growth has been driven largely by increasing numbers of people surviving to reproductive age, and has been accompanied by major changes in fertility rates, increasing urbanization and accelerating migration. These trends will have far-reaching implications for generations to come.

-- United Nations on World Population Growth

INTERNATIONAL ECONOMIC ISSUES

> Five years ago, at the start of the new millennium, the world's governments united to make a remarkable promise to the victims of global poverty...... they signed......a solemn pledge "to free our fellow men, women and children from the abject and dehumanizing conditions of extreme poverty". ....These targets .....include halving extreme poverty, cutting child deaths, providing all of the world's children with an education, rolling back infectious disease and forging a new global partnership to deliver results. .... the goals provide a crucial benchmark for measuring progress towards the creation of a new, more just, less impoverished and less insecure world order.
>
> – International Co-operation at Crossroads, *Human Development Report, 2005*, UNDP, New York.

Topics Covered

- *Globalization*
- *Is Globalization in retreat?*
- *Free Trade Agreements*
- *India's Free Trade Agreements*
- *RCEP and India*
- *CPTPP and TPP Free trade Agreements*
- *WTO and India's Food Subsidy regime*
- *Geopolitics and Development*
- *Climate Change and Global action*
- *Climate Change and India*
- *Transfer of Technology*

(On Tariffs and WTO, see also Chapter 6)

1. Discuss the different aspects of the process of 'globalization' and its pros and cons. Bring out the challenges and limitations to globalization.

Ans. Globalization implies integration of a nation's economy with the global economy. It results in much freer movement of goods, services, capital, technology and people between countries, across national boundaries.

The integration happens not only in the economic sphere but political, social, and cultural arenas too. International and regional political and economic groupings are indications of such integration. They help to speed up development by sharing one another's strengths, exchange of ideas, and expertise.

- **Not a new phenomenon:** Globalization has existed in different forms, and in varying degrees, through the centuries. Nations have been trading with one another for ages, people have been travelling form one country to another, and large scale economic and cultural migrations have been taking place. But as nations progressed, with industrialization and technological advances, particularly in transport and communications, the process gained momentum.

  Historically speaking, in the Age of Enlightenment in the 18th century Europe, thinkers like John Locke, David Hume and Immanuel Kant had envisioned harnessing science and technology for progress in social, political and economic life of humanity as a whole. Thomas Jefferson, one of the architects of American Constitution, spoke of the rights of "Life, Liberty and the Pursuit of Happiness" as a goal for mankind. The French Revolution, inspired by the writings of Voltaire and Rousseau, which gave the call for "Liberty, Equality and Fraternity" aroused the consciousness of people against gross inequalities in society which has found an echo in today's backlash against Globalization.

  The latest wave of globalisation, which began after the end of the Cold War and gathered pace throughout the 1990s and 2000s, has been a crucial factor in economic developments over the past thirty years. It has boosted economic growth, particularly in the emerging and developing countries and helped to bring down levels of poverty.

- **Benefits of Globalization**

  With cooperation among nations, sharing of knowledge, and optimizing the use of scarce world resources, globalization confers many benefits and provides immense opportunities for the international community in jointly promoting human welfare, solving problems like poverty, combating climate change challenges, and facing natural disasters.

  - Capital, which is surplus in one country, will tend to move to other countries which offer more attractive returns.
  - Skilled labour and manpower with highly professional expertise will also be in demand in other countries where such labour and manpower may be in short supply. Such movement is possible and becomes easier when economies are more open in a globalized and liberalized environment.
  - It further helps to build various global linkages such as:
    - Foreign exchange and capital markets get linked globally and work round-the-clock.
    - Communication links promoted through Internet and media networks.

- Trade links are promoted and overseen by the World Trade Organization (WTO).
- The multinational corporations (MNCs) which operate cutting across national borders share technology, capital and enterprise generating employment, especially in the developing countries.
- Interconnects global networks of non-governmental organizations (NGOs) and other civil society groups that transcend national boundaries and work for the common good of society.
- Fosters new rules – multilateral agreements on trade, services and intellectual property, backed by strong enforcement mechanisms and binding on national governments, reducing the scope for national policies at cross purposes.

➢ **Globalization trends: Trade, Growth and Inequality**

■ **Inequality:**One of the arguments in favour of globalization is that increased trade helps to narrow the income gap between rich and poor countries, with the developing world gaining from access to new technologies and new markets. But this is only partly true. While some countries are catching up and advancing, for many countries, globalization has resulted in marginalization.

While economic integration does help, trade is a driver of prosperity as well as global inequality.

■ **Human Development:** In UNDP's Human Development Report, 2019, out of 189 countries, 25 are considered as ***very highly developed***, 91 are categorized as ***highly developed***, 37 countries, mostly in Asia (including India) and Africa as with ***medium development***, and 36 countries, mostly in Africa, with ***low development***.

■ **Growth and Inequality in Asia:** According to Asian Development Bank (ADB)'s report, "*Inequality in Asia and the Pacific*" (2014), the Asia-Pacific region recorded remarkable achievements in growth and poverty reduction between 1990 and 2010. Developing Asia's outstanding growth performance played a critical role in pulling the global economy out of recession quickly following the 2007-08 global economic crisis.

However, this performance in growth and poverty reduction has been accompanied by rising inequality in a large part of the region. Of the 30 countries that have comparable data, 12 countries which account for about 82 per cent of developing Asia's population in 2010 experienced rising inequality of per capita expenditure or income, as measured by the Gini coefficient, during the period from early 1990s to the late 2000s.

These findings highlight the need for opportunities and benefits of globalization to be more inclusive and shared much more widely.

➤ Challenges and Limits to Globalization

Even as globalization confers many benefits, it also brings in its trail some major challenges as discussed below.

- **Sovereignty:** Globalization may involve making some compromises in a country's absolute sovereignty. To gain some advantage, a country may have to make some sacrifices in dealing with other nations. There is also often friction in such negotiations due to rigid and hard positions taken by some countries.
- **Conflicting interests:** As there could be conflicting national interests on matters of trade and market access, there would be hard bargaining between nations or groups of nations. This was witnessed in the various negotiations held under the aegis of the World Trade Organization (WTO). A glaring instance of this has been in the irony of developed countries, which extend farm subsidies or support to their farmers, demanding and insisting on developing countries to give up similar practice followed in their countries in support of farmers, such as the facility of Minimum Support Price (MSP) India provides for farmers or the subsidized Public Distribution Scheme (PDS) for sections of population.
- **Financial volatility and economic insecurity:** Due to integration, occurrences taking place in a country or a region could easily spread and impact other countries or regions. If the events are of adverse economic nature, they are bound to have cascading effect with adverse consequences for other countries. For instance, the southeast and east Asian financial crisis of 1997, which started in Thailand, spread to other countries in the region, viz., Indonesia and South Korea and, to some extent, Malaysia, Philippines, and Japan causing slump in those economies. Again, the subprime crisis that surfaced in the US around 2007 and the collapse of the Lehman Brothers in 2008 disrupted financial institutions there including the shadow banking system, leading to a crisis of confidence in the financial markets. This had a prolonged adverse impact on the economy of many countries.
- **Job and income insecurity.** In both poor and rich countries, dislocations from economic and corporate restructuring, and from dismantling the avenues of social protection, have meant greater insecurity in jobs and incomes. The pressures of global competition and need to attract foreign investment have led countries and employers to adopt more flexible labour policies with precarious work arrangements which jeopardize job security.
- **Illicit trade and Crime:** A new dimension which has emerged in the context of liberalised trade is the spawning of crime. Increasing trade ties has increased the possibility of criminal activities taking advantage of the relaxed custom controls. In the face of greater ASEAN integration, the UN Office on Drugs and Crime (UNODC) has cautioned about potential danger posed by criminal activities such as drug and human trafficking and maritime piracy in south-east Asia, if adequate security precautions are not taken. Illicit wealth flowing in the region due to trade in drugs, wildlife, and fake products could be used for funding crime syndicates.

➢ Conclusion

To sum up, certain events of the last few decades have put the spotlight on the fragilities and failings of globalization process.

- **Financial instability:** The volatility and shocks in the global financial system hurt many countries for a prolonged period.
- **Protectionism:** The protectionist policies and rising anti-free trade sentiments of many countries and their conflicting agendas have had an adverse impact on global trade which, in turn, hampered development, especially of the low and middle-income countries.
- **Brexit:** Britain's decision to exit from the European Union (EU), termed Brexit, was a clear vote against economic integration. This was triggered by a liberal immigration policy Britain followed which led to large-scale flow of immigrants from East European countries. This had adverse impact on job prospects for Britons themselves besides imposing social costs such as pressure on housing and living costs. Britain felt that by being a member of the Union, it was being held back by regulations imposed by the EU for which it did not get commensurate returns or benefits.
- **US-China trade conflict:** The prolonged US-China trade war has had a ripple effect on the economies of many countries.
- **Expansionism:** China's expansionist policies with neighbouring countries such as with some of the Asean nations in the South China sea, and with Japan in the East China sea, and its major threatening posture and aggression on borders with India have further dented the prospects of globalization. Further, China's attempts at strategic expansion to parts of Asia, Africa and Europe for trade and military purposes through the Belt Road Initiative (BRI) have aroused apprehensions among major powers like the US and the European Union. These actions of China to gain supremacy as a global power, which though China denies, have led to geopolitical tensions.
- **Pandemic:** The outbreak of the pandemic, Covid-19, which originated in China in early 2020, spread worldwide and has taken a toll of over a million lives in different countries. This has led to mistrust between China and many other nations and virtually thrown the global economy out of gear. China's efforts to thrust its advanced 5G telecom technology on other countries are being thwarted by other nations on the ground that it poses security threat as the system is feared to be controlled by China's State apparatus. This is an added reason for the prolongation of trade conflict between the US and China.

The above episodes point to the complexities of contemporary international relations. All nations need to adopt a pragmatic approach and manage an orderly and gradual process of reversing the "deglobalization" trend.

2. Is globalization in retreat and is there now a trend towards "deglobalization"? If so, examine the factors behind it and suggest remedial measures to counter the trend.

Ans. Globalization, a dominant force in the last decade of the 20th century has been shaping a new era of interaction among nations, economies and people. It has increased the contacts between people across national boundaries – in economy, technology, culture and governance. But it is also fragmenting production processes, labour markets, political entities and societies. So, while globalization has been a positive, innovative and dynamic force, it also has negative, disruptive and marginalizing aspects.

While global integration is proceeding at a fast pace and touching the lives of millions. the process has been unequal and unbalanced, with uneven participation of countries and people in the expanding opportunities.

A prevailing myth of globalization is that increased trade is narrowing the income gap between the rich and poor countries, with the developing world gaining from access to new technologies and new markets. While it is partly true, it has been more an exception than the rule. Trade is a driver of prosperity as well as global inequality. For the majority of countries, the globalization process has been one of divergence and marginalization.

➢ **Growth and Inequality**

- **Widening gap:** The widening gap between the developed and the developing countries has become the central problem of our times. Despite overall growth and reduction in poverty, global inequalities in income and living standards have been on the rise and have reached high proportions.
- **Uneven outcomes:** For instance, the Asia and Pacific region has recorded remarkable achievements in growth and poverty reduction in recent decades. This rapid growth has significantly improved living standards and lifted millions out of extreme poverty, especially in China and India. However, this performance in growth and poverty reduction has been accompanied by rising inequality in a large part of the region.
- **Lack of opportunities:** The inequality is not only in terms of income and wealth which, indeed, is significant but, more importantly, in opportunities available to large sections to improve living standards. Extreme adverse circumstances severely limit the opportunities for social advancement for a large segment of the population. These include the lack of, or unequal access to, good education, public health services, decent housing and quality jobs.

➢ **Globalization and the backlash**

Even as the rich and affluent, the corporate czars, domain experts and international agencies hold annual meets, like in Davos, and ostensibly debate about growth, poverty, climate change, etc., a rising tide of anti-globalization sentiment has been building up in different parts of the world. The opposition to globalization has been seen in strident protests by social activists and NGOs in Seattle, Davos, Prague, Washington, etc. during such global meets. Various factors, mentioned below, account for this divergence and widening gulf on globalization.

- The opposition is engendered primarily due to the asymmetry and inequality existing between the developed and less developed countries.
- Though the developed countries do their bit by extending financial and technical aid to the latter bilaterally or through multilateral aid agencies, the persisting differences in the levels of development and gross inequalities have led to erosion in mutual trust and confidence.
- The political and economic dominance of a small group of countries (read G8 nations) at world fora and in institutions like the UN, the IMF, and the World Bank, which may have been justified when they were created several decades ago, only exacerbates the hiatus.
- Though the world's balance of power has undergone significant change and many emerging nations have appeared on the world stage in their own right and there is strident clamour for rearranging the architecture of the international bodies, the few advanced nations are unwilling to concede it or let go of their vice grip on them for their own narrow, vested interests.
- The divergence has been aggravated by conflicts in global trade between the advanced and developing countries with many countries adopting increasingly protectionist measures. Also, the advanced nations demanding greater access to markets in developing countries while they themselves deny such access to developing countries has only exacerbated the situation. The stalemate witnessed in trade negotiations under the WTO, as in Doha Development Agenda and Agricultural Trade Rules on the issue of subsidies to farmers highlight these trends.
- The trade war between the US and China on various grounds such as high trade imbalance to the detriment of the US, transfer of technology and alleged theft of intellectual property rights (IPR) and technology by China have worsened the global trade position.

Need for Reconciliation

Unless the above issues are resolved by mutual consultations and consensus, and in a spirit of give and take, the irritants in international relations will continue hampering the cause of global cooperation and development process. Both the proponents of globalization and those opposing it have to meet halfway and strike a balance. Certain measures to achieve this are suggested below.

- **Equitable development:** There is some merit in the stand of anti-globalists that the fruits of progress are not shared in equitable manner between the developed and developing world. This calls for greater openness in market access on the part of the advanced nations without jeopardizing their economies.

At the same time, even developing countries need to be helped to open their markets in a gradual manner with greater flow of not only capital but technology to develop their industrial base, thereby skilling the workforce in those countries and enhancing employment opportunities.

- **Role of MNCs and SMEs:** The harsh and rigid stand and strident criticism by anti-globalists of the corporates and multi-nationals like Microsoft, Google, Walmart, Coke, Pepsi, Amazon, etc. is rather misplaced. After all, it is the corporates and large enterprises, who command large chunk of capital, create enterprises, generate jobs and bring about overall progress. But here again, these large enterprises must have, and strive to develop, linkages with small and medium enterprises (SMEs), especially those in developing economies, which would serve as their ancillaries for supply of components and intermediate goods. This would help the growth of SMEs to grow, create jobs and share the fruits of progress more equitably.

- **Global value chains:** This calls for SMEs in more and more countries being enabled to join global value chains (GVCs) in production processes. Such GVCs need to be spread evenly across the globe so that monopolistic tendencies are averted. It would ensure more equitable development among countries.

  This will avert concentration of supply chains in a few countries who become monopolies for certain products which could wholly disrupt the production processes as was seen during the Covid-19 pandemic in 2020 when for many items, countries had to depend on China which created lot of issues. Wider geographical spread of supply chains with production units for items in multiple countries would prevent such contingencies.

- **Role of CSR:** MNCs and big corporate houses have their industries located in the rural and semi-urban areas, besides in the periphery of large cities, in developing countries. Thus, they have a connect with the local populace living around their production units. Often, many of the workers in the factories are also drawn from the local population. Some of the large industries may have their own townships around the plant.

  Under a policy of Corporate Social Responsibility (CSR), they could do yeoman service by setting up schools, hospitals, and other facilities for the population in and around their units. The CSR widens the scope and responsibility of corporate houses to engage in a more profound way and bring about perceptible change in the lives of people and win their trust and co-operation. It is a unique opportunity to give back to society which, in many cases like FMCG units, may be part of their vast clientele. The local NGOs could co-ordinate with the enterprises and play a catalytic role in such noble ventures. Such an approach would take the wind out of the sail of the criticism of anti-globalists.

- **Philanthropy:** It must be noted in this context that quite a few of enlightened industry leaders and corporate houses in India and abroad have shown the way of giving back to society by setting up foundations and taking up noble social causes like campaigns against Aids, TB, polio, cancer, etc. or in the education field and science research by giving generous grants.

  The Giving Pledge: In this context, it would be relevant to look at some of the philanthropic initiatives across the world. "The Giving Pledge" was formed in 2010, by Bill and Melinda Gates and Warren Buffett, to encourage the wealthiest in the US to give a part of their wealth towards philanthropic activities. Later, they tried to widen the group's function outside the US to other countries.

  As of 2020, the initiative had garnered more than 200 of the world's wealthiest individuals, couples, and families, ranging in age from their 30s to their 90s, and globally representing 23 countries. They come from a wide range of fields – like finance, technology, healthcare and real estate development. Richard Branson of UK and Azim Premji from India are among those who have pledged funds.

  The Giving Pledge is a global, multi-generational commitment by the wealthiest to create a culture of giving in order to help tackle society's most pressing problems. The societal causes which the pledgers support include a wide a range such as climate change, education, healthcare and medical research, economic development, poverty alleviation and social justice.

  Besides, there are such initiatives in Africa, China, India and Brazil. Also, many corporates like the Tatas, M& M, Infosys and ITC and entrepreneurs like Shiv Nadar of HCL have foundations to support noble causes.

  Such initiatives could help to bring about a more egalitarian society and blunt the strident criticism of anti-globalists.

➤ Conclusion

Globalization is a double-edged sword. It helps big corporates from advanced nations to invest in developing countries, help them with capital and technology and thereby promote growth. At the same time, they enjoy several benefits such as cheap labour and land, low tax regime, and recourse to valuable natural resources like minerals, and in the process amass considerable profits which they may repatriate to other countries. It is this very kind of profiteering and exploitation of vulnerabilities of developing nations that invites the wrath of anti-globalist lobbies. A more humane approach on the part of corporate bodies is called for to dent such criticism.

For instance, even in Climate Action negotiations under the aegis of the UN, the industrialized nations are trying to pass on disproportionate burden and setting onerous targets on the poor and developing countries to contribute to reductions in global warming. Whereas it is the reckless action on the part of the advanced nations, during their initial and later stages of development, which they are loath to admit, that has led the world to the precipice of climate catastrophe that the world faces today.

The anti-globalist lobby is contesting the above-mentioned inequities and injustice in the development process which is acknowledged by international bodies like the UN, UNDP, The World Bank, Asian Development Bank, etc. and which are trying to reduce the disparities and create a level playing field.

3. What is meant by 'Free Trade Agreement (FTA)' and what are its advantages and drawbacks?

Ans. Free Trade Agreements (FTAs) are arrangements between two or more countries or trading blocs that primarily agree to mutually reduce or eliminate customs tariff and non-tariff barriers on substantial trade between them. FTAs normally cover trade in goods such as agricultural or industrial products, or trade in services such as banking, construction, trading etc. FTAs can also cover other areas such as intellectual property rights (IPRs), investment, government procurement, competition policy, etc.

➢ **Benefits of Free Trade Agreement (FTA)**

Countries entering into FTAs could derive many benefits from them as stated below.

- By eliminating tariffs and some non-tariff barriers, FTA partners get easier market access into one another's markets.
- FTA contributes to greater economic activity and job creation in the economy and deliver opportunities for big and small businesses to benefit from greater trade and investment.
- FTA don't just reduce and eliminate tariffs, but also helps address behind-the-border barriers that would otherwise impede the flow of goods and services.
- Encourages investment; and improve the rules affecting such issues as intellectual property, e-commerce and government procurement.
- Gives businesses and consumers improved access to a wider range of competitively priced goods and services, new technologies, and innovative practices.
- Helps to obtain more benefits from foreign investment.
- Promotes regional economic integration and builds shared approaches to trade and investment between the free trade partners.
- It can deliver enhanced trade and investment opportunities that contribute to the economic growth of less-developed economies.

- Supports stronger people-to-people and business-to-business links that enhance bilateral relationships with FTA partners.
- It can continue to provide additional benefits to the trading partners over time, including via in-built agendas that encourage ongoing domestic reform and trade liberalisation.
- Exporters prefer FTAs to multilateral trade liberalization because they get preferential treatment over non-FTA member country competitors.

➢ **Pitfalls in Free Trade Agreement (FTA)**

While FTA could provide various benefits mentioned above, it also has pitfalls and downsides to it if all aspects are not considered carefully while entering into the agreement as explained below.

- **Divergences:** If the parties entering into the pact are not at the same level of economic development and strength, it could turn out to be a lop-sided deal. While the trade deal is "free", it has also to be "fair" and the emphasis should be more on the latter. Often, while requiring a developing country to dismantle barriers, a developed country may raise significant tariff and non-tariff barriers as it negotiates on trade deals from a position of strength. Such a trend has been seen in many instances between developed and developing countries in multilateral and regional trade negotiations.
- **Unfair practices:** For instance, in the negotiations in agriculture and food under the aegis of the WTO, advanced countries like USA and those in European Union, have been adopting a hard stance wherein they object to subsidies given to farmers in developing countries like India and Brazil while they themselves provide subsidies on a much larger scale to farmers in their countries who are much better off. Such patently unfair negotiations and deals are inimical to the less developed countries.
- **Market access:** Further, developed countries are pressing developing nations to provide unfettered access to their markets for agricultural products while they themselves restrict entry for the products of developing nations. One of the sticking points in the negotiations under the Regional Comprehensive Economic Partnership (RCEP), one of the most ambitious trade pacts, was the fate of India's robust and growing dairy industry. India joining the pact under the terms being negotiated would have thrown open its dairy market to New Zealand, one of the largest exporter of milk and dairy products accounting for nearly 20 per cent of world exports worth $ 5.4 billion in 2018. Once RCEP came into force with India in it, New Zealand could dump its surplus milk and milk products in Indian market with severe consequences for India

which is the largest producer of milk globally. It would hurt the livelihood of millions of small and marginal dairy farmers. **(see Question 5 in this chapter for more on RCEP).**

- **Trade imbalances:** If a country which is a major industrial power is negotiating a deal with a country which is industrially less competitive, there is likelihood of the latter being flooded with industrial products resulting in trade imbalance and trade deficit issues. India has faced such a situation in free trade agreement with Japan and South Korea. Having free trade between a country with a per capita income of, say $4,000 per year, and one with $50,000 per year, has its own pitfalls. As stated earlier, free trade between trading partners pose a challenge if their level of development is vastly different.
- **Misuse of FTA:** A third country, outside the trade pact, could take advantage of tariff concessions provided in the FTA by routing its products through one of the partners in the pact. Such misuse of the concessions has been observed in India's FTA with Asean nations where products from China have been routed to India through some of the Asean countries thereby Chinese exporters getting the benefit of tariff concessions. It is not only a violation of the agreement but also places the domestic producers in India, whose products may be less competitive, at a disadvantage. It will also distort India's trade balance.

➢ **Conclusion**

Free trade agreements are useful for expanding a country's trade basket. But if it results in a surge in imports without corresponding expansion of exports, it would hurt domestic industry.

The success of an FTA is to be judged on the criterion of enhancing trade and fairness of the deal. If the proportion, and not just the absolute level, of both imports and exports between the countries concerned has grown, then the FTA is successful for both parties. It achieves the objective of moving trade in the direction of the FTA country relative to others. If only either imports or exports have grown, then the benefits would be one-sided.

At the same time, it is important that domestic producers should not take shelter behind protective tariff barriers. They must improve their production techniques, step up productivity and become competitive in global markets. It would be relevant to recall here India's inward-looking, import-substitution (IS) policy of the 1950s, in contrast to the forward-looking export-promotion (EP) strategy of East Asian economies, during the same period, which held back India's competitiveness and progress for the next three decades until she opened up and integrated with the global economy in the 1990s.

4. India propose to review Free Trade Agreements (FTAs) signed in the past as they have not achieved the desired objectives. Bring out the drawbacks found in the working of the FTAs and state how India could improve upon them.

➢ **India's Trade Agreements**

India has entered into Free Trade Agreements (FTAs) with many countries/groups of nations including Association of South-East Asian Nations (ASEAN), Japan and South Korea. Many other FTAs are under negotiation.

India has preferential access, economic cooperation and FTAs with about 54 individual countries. India has signed bilateral trade deals in the form of FTAs, Comprehensive Economic Partnership Agreement (CEPA), Comprehensive Economic Cooperation Agreement (CECA) and Preferential Trade Agreements (PTAs) with some 18 groups/countries. India is a late and cautious starter in concluding comprehensive and preferential tariff agreements covering substantially all trade with some of its trading partners.

CECA/CEPA are more comprehensive and ambitious that an FTA in terms of coverage of areas and the type of commitments. While a traditional FTA focuses mainly on goods; a CECA/CEPA is more ambitious in terms of a holistic coverage of many areas like services, investment, competition, government procurement, disputes etc.

➢ **Shortfall in outcomes**

India had signed a series of FTAs with Asian countries that came into force in the 2000s. Industry and policymakers have found that these FTAs have brought little tangible benefit to India while it has helped the partner countries. Further, they have adversely impacted India's manufacturing which the government has been trying to boost through 'Make in India' scheme.

- **India-ASEAN FTA:**

  A look at the pact India signed with Asean group and trends in trade would reveal how it has not been beneficial to India. This is a major trade pact being taken up for review.

  India signed the pact with the 10-member Asean group in 2010. The group includes Indonesia, Malaysia, Thailand, Philippines, Singapore, Vietnam, Myanmar, Laos, Cambodia and Brunei.

- **Widening trade deficit:** The data below shows the persisting trade deficit with imports from Asean nations outstripping India's exports to them.

(In $ billion)

	2014-15	**2015-16**	**2017-18**	**2018-19**	**2019-20**
Exports	31.81	25.13	34.20	37.40	31.54
Imports	44.71	39.90	47.13	59.32	55.36
Deficit	– 12.90	– 14.77	– 12.93	– 21.92	– 23.82
Total trade with bloc	76.52	65.03	81.33	96.72	86.90

Source: Dept. of Commerce, Govt. of India.

- **Factors behind trade imbalance:** The following factors have contributed to the imbalance in trade.
  - Imports have been higher in several product segments as domestic producers in India have been uncompetitive compared to foreign entities.
  - Products from 'third country' are found to be routed to India via India's FTA partners in the group. Particularly, products such as set-top boxes from China, which is outside the group, are sent to Asean countries where they are repackaged without value addition and exported to India. This benefits Chinese producers by enjoying the tariff concessions under the agreement.
  - Industries in India have also not been able to make full use of the lower duty benefits and step up exports to Asean nations.
  - **Anomalies in the pact:**There have been other anomalies too in the working of the pact as mentioned below.
    - Indian exporters have not been able to get a level playing field. Indonesia had lowered duties only on 50 per cent of the items while it was getting customs duty benefit on about 75 per cent of its products in India.
    - Against 35 per cent duty on rice for trade among Asean members, Indian rice faced a 50 per cent levy.
    - Japanese automobiles can be imported into Thailand and Indonesia at 5 per cent duty, while Indian cars faced 35 per cent tariff.
    - The services component in which India has advantage was signed only in 2019 and it is yet to be ratified.
  - **Impact on Electronic sector:** For instance, under the India-Asean FTA, for TV sets of screen sizes up to 105 cm., the basic customs duty is nil, as against 10 per cent duty levied when imported from elsewhere. When they can be imported at reduced or even zero duty, no one would want to manufacture the same product in India.

So also, the FTAs with Asean, South Korea, Japan and other countries hamper India's plans to emerge as a manufacturing powerhouse for electronic items. The problem has arisen because the agreements India has signed are with some of the economies who are major competitive producers of these items resulting in finished products being imported into India at a lower cost than could have been manufactured in India.

- **Digital India:** On the contrary, under the Digital India initiative, India has been able to step up production of mobile phones with major producers like Apple, Samsung, LG, Nokia, and Motorola setting up production facilities in India, apart from the presence of many domestic firms, which will boost the export of mobile phones from India. India is the world's second largest mobile phone manufacturer after China. There are over 100 firms engaged in mobile phone industry in India.

  It points to the need for India to create benign investment climate to attract major international forms to invest in India and set up manufacturing units and also for Indian industry to become improve productivity and become more competitive.

- **Automotive sector:** The performance of India in the automobile, two-wheeler and automotive components industry is a success story where there are many well established firms catering to not only domestic market but exporting on a substantial scale.

➢ **Review of Pact with ASEAN**

India propose to revamp FTA strategy to ensure that the treaties provide economic and strategic benefit. Asean has agreed to India's long-pending demand to review the pact. Earlier, Asean members were linking the review to India agreeing to join the Regional Comprehensive Economic Partnership (RCEP).

- **Rule of origin:** One of the main issues in FTA with Asean countries is the "Rule of Origin' clause. India has been demanding enforcing the rules of origin criterion as it apprehends that in its absence, third countries could circumvent the rules and dump goods into India through Asean countries thereby enjoying tariff concessions. As stated earlier, there have been instances of China routing goods into Indian market via India's FTA partner countries in ASEAN. India has since decided that the benefit of concessional customs duties, including zero duty, would be available to Indian importers only if they can prove that products have undergone "value addition" of at least 35 per cent in the country of origin. With this stipulation, a mere exporters' certificate for "country of origin" which was sufficient earlier will not be enough.

- **India and RCEP:** In this context, the protracted negotiations India has been having on joining the Regional Comprehensive Economic Partnership (RCEP) is pertinent.

  RCEP is a mega trade deal which was to include 10-member ASEAN group + 6 countries — Australia, China, India, Japan, South Korea and New Zealand. The grouping envisages regional economic integration, leading to the creation of the largest regional trading bloc in the world representing nearly 45 per cent of the world's population with a combined gross domestic product (GDP) of $21.3 trillion, 30 per cent of global trade and 26 per cent of FDI flows.

  Initiated in 2012, its conclusion was repeatedly delayed due to protracted negotiations. The pact which was finalized by 15 nations, excluding India, could provide the size and scale to unleash new growth potentials and write new rules of international trade order.

  India's concern in joining this bloc is India's trade deficit with Asean group and partner countries of RCEP. The deficit with the bloc rose from $9 billion in FY 2005 to $83 billion in FY 2017, of which China alone accounted for 60 per cent of the deficit. While India had offered complete liberalization on almost 75 per cent of tariff lines, the group demanded to liberalize over 90 per cent of total tariff lines.

  Apart from that, while India's strength lies in services trade, India was not getting a fair deal under the services pact. Greater market access in services and investment would have helped India to offset the loss in goods trade. Lack of reciprocity in the negotiations has been holding up India's decision.

  Due to these factors, India has not agreed to join RCEP though experts argue that joining RCEP will help to become more competitive and boost India's exports. The situation has further changed drastically with India's border tensions with China, with which India has a huge trade deficit, and China's aggressive military posture towards India which will have long-term consequences for the Indian economy. China's close political, economic and trade relations with Asean nations complicates the situation further for India.

  (For more on RCEP, see Questions 5 and 6 below).

5. Regional Comprehensive Economic Partnership (RCEP) is a major trading bloc formed in Asia Pacific region with much potential for economic co-operation and growth but India has been hesitant to join it. Examine the reasons for India's stand and the pros and cons of India joining it.

Ans. The proposal regarding Regional Comprehensive Economic Partnership (RCEP), an economic grouping of countries in Asia Pacific region, has been under negotiation since 2012 but could not be finalized for nearly eight years. The trade pact was finally signed by 15 nations, excluding India, in November 2020. That it has taken so long to be clinched and has involved protracted and intense negotiations is in itself an indication of the complexity of trade relations between the countries and the issues involved in the deal.

➢ **A Mega trade pact**

The RCEP is a group consisting of all major economies in Asia Pacific region and, by all accounts, would be the largest regional trading bloc in the world. It includes the 10-member ASEAN group consisting of Brunei, Cambodia, Indonesia, Laos, Malaysia, Myanmar, Philippines, Singapore, Thailand and Vietnam, plus five other countries – Australia, China, Japan, New Zealand and South Korea.

The pact envisages regional economic integration comprising countries with 2,1 billion people which accounts for about 27 per cent of the world's population, and 30 per cent of the global economy. The pact could provide the size and scale to unleash new growth potentials and write new rules of international trade order.

RCEP aims to create an integrated market spanning all the 15 countries, making it easier for products and services of each of these countries to be available across the region.

➢ **Protracted negotiations**

The finalisation of the deal was repeatedly delayed due to protracted negotiations, involving several sittings at the level of Trade Ministers from these countries. The negotiations involved many crucial areas mentioned below:

- Trade in goods and services
- Investment
- Intellectual property
- Small and medium enterprises
- E-commerce
- Economic co-operation, and
- Dispute resolution mechanism

All the RCEP participating countries, except for India, had concluded text-based negotiations for all 20 chapters of the proposed deal, as well as their market access issues and they finally signed the pact in November 2020. They have also said that as and when India decides and is ready to join the pact later, India would be welcomed into it.

➢ **India's stand and concerns on RCEP are explained below.**

♦ **Surge in imports:** India finds that the RCEP trade deal does not provide adequate protection against possible surges of imported goods from the region which comprises many major industrial production economies. In particular, India is concerned about cheap Chinese goods flooding the domestic market. Also, in the dairy sector, India is concerned that it would open a floodgate of cheaper dairy products from Australia or New Zealand which would impact the livelihood of millions of Indian dairy farmers and dairy industry.

- **Imports from China:** There is genuine concern that Indian industries would be unable to compete with Chinese goods. This is understandable given that China has massive overcapacity in manufacturing industries which receive substantial financial and trade support from the State which gives them an edge over competitors and trade partners.

  India had sought an auto-trigger mechanism that would allow it to raise tariffs on products when imports cross a certain threshold. India did not receive credible assurances on this or on its demand for more market access.

- **Non-tariff barriers:** India has concerns over non-tariff barriers raised by countries in RCEP like China which have resorted to non-tariff barriers (NTBs) to prevent India from increasing its exports to the country. Though China agreed to open over 90 per cent of its tariff lines expecting India to reciprocate the measure, India is concerned about NTBs like import licensing, customs clearance, pre-shipment inspection, labelling standards and product certification process which have hindered India's access to other markets.

- **Trade deficit:** India has combined trade deficit with FTA (Free Trade Agreement) partners like ASEAN, Japan and South Korea which has doubled in the last eight years. India's trade deficit with the RCEP countries of over $ 100 billion is almost 64 per cent of its total trade deficit, of which China alone accounts for over 60 per cent of the deficit.

- **Rules of origin:** India's proposal for strict "rules of origin" requirements was not being accepted by the partner countries. Rules of origin are critical as they determine the (national) source of a product for it to qualify for "preferential treatment". India has been suspecting that China was routing goods into Indian market via India's FTA partner countries in ASEAN to take advantage of preferential treatment on customs duties.

  India has since decided that the benefit of concessional customs duties, including zero duty, would be available to Indian importers only if they can prove that products have undergone "value addition" of at least 35 per cent in the country of origin. For instance, if a mobile is exported from Vietnam to India, it would qualify to be of Vietnam origin only if it is made significantly there and 35 per cent of its value is Vietnam's contribution.

  With this stipulation, a mere exporters' certificate for "country of origin" which was sufficient earlier will not be enough. Importers in India have to produce "certificate of origin" with all relevant details.

- **Trade in services, Lack of reciprocity:** India for long argued that other countries allow greater movement of labour and services like those of professionals, technocrats, engineers, nurses, etc. in return for opening up its own market. But India did not get greater market access to other RCEP countries in services, an area in which it is relatively strong. There was lack of reciprocity on this and other issues as brought out above.

- **Domestic opinion:** Concerns about India's widening trade deficits with RCEP countries and vociferous opposition to the agreement from industry bodies, political parties, trade unions and civil society organisations weighed in on the government in deciding not to sign the pact.

➢ **Counter views on India's stand**

Some economists and experts, however, are of the view that while India should bargain hard for a more balanced RCEP regime, India should, at the same time, strive to make its industrial and manufacturing sector more robust and competitive. In a globalized world into which India has been integrated since 1991, she cannot hope to have sustained industrial growth and become a manufacturing power without being internationally competitive.

- **Protection not the answer:** Increasing tariffs and continually protecting industries will not take India forward, especially when there is fierce competition from countries like Vietnam, Thailand, Malaysia, Indonesia and even Bangladesh to which many industries quitting China are moving. A benign investment climate with supporting tax, land and labour policies are essential for attracting foreign investors and major global industrial concerns into India.
- **Ease of Doing Business:** While India has taken several steps in this direction and on "Ease of Doing Business", still there are roadblocks, especially in regard to infrastructure and logistical facilities, predictability of tax policies and resolution of corporate disputes which deter potential investors. But the experience in the automobile sector in which India has been able to attract major foreign manufacturers and turn India into an export hub is indicative of what a friendly investment regime could achieve.
- **Incentive scheme:** Also, in the electronics and telecom sector, following the launch of Production Linked Incentive (PLI) scheme, India has been able to attract major players like Apple, Samsung and other companies to set up production units in India. There is considerable scope to extend such schemes in the hi-tech defence, aviation, railway and pharmaceutical sectors considering India's vast skilled technical and engineering manpower, and huge domestic requirements in these areas, apart from the potential for exports.
- **Regional Supply Chain:** A new opening has come up with India, Japan and Australia proposing to build "Resilient Supply Chain Initiative" (RSCI) in the Indo-Pacific that will be either independent or barely dependent on China. The effort follows a lesson learnt from Covid-19 pandemic which exposed the risks of over-dependence on a particular country (read China) for procurement of raw materials and intermediate goods. The Indian pharmaceutical industry faced much disruption due to non-supply of Active Pharmaceutical Ingredients (API) from China during the crisis. Various industries in many countries also faced problems in production due to disruptions in supplies from China.

This has led to calls to move many industries out of China and set up production units in different countries. Japan has already announced incentives to its firms to move out of China. India should take advantage of the situation, in collaboration with other friendly nations, and give a boost to the domestic industrial sector. RSCI, if and when implemented, would have significant impact on the RCEP countries.

Economists caution that India can no longer afford to revert to the old, failed policy of "protectionism" by creating tariff barriers which will only set the clock back.

6. Comprehensive and Progressive Agreement for Trans-Pacific Partnership (CPTPP) and Regional Comprehensive Economic Partnership (RCEP) are two major free trade pacts of which India is not a member. Critically examine why India has not joined them and its implications for Indian economy.

Ans. The environment for global trade policy has undergone a paradigm shift following the financial crisis that erupted in 2007-08, policies adopted by the US under Donald Trump since 2017, and in the aftermath of Brexit (Britain's exit from the EU). These have been further exacerbated by the US-China trade conflict and a weakening of the WTO regime.

As more and more countries have turned to trade protectionism in the last few years to safeguard their national economic interests and sovereignty, countries have been making strenuous efforts to form regional trade pacts to promote trade and development. These have involved conflicting interests and tortuous negotiations and hard bargaining between nations.

➢ **Regional trade pacts**

Two major free trade agreements have been concluded in the recent past, viz., Comprehensive and Progressive Agreement for Trans-Pacific Partnership (CPTPP) signed in 2018 and Regional Comprehensive Economic Partnership (RCEP) concluded in 2020. The CPTPP was formed after the Trans-Pacific Partnership (TPP) which was previously initiated by the US President Barack Obama could not be concluded as the US, under President Donald Trump decided to pull US out of it.

- **The CPTPP:** This free trade pact has been formed by 11 Asia-Pacific countries, viz., Australia, Brunei Darussalam, Canada, Chile, Japan, Malaysia, Mexico, New Zealand, Peru, Singapore, and Vietnam. Signed in March 2018, it came into force in December 2018, after a majority of signatories ratified the agreement. The group accounts for about 13.5 per cent of global merchandise trade, and the pact binds the members to freer trade and investment access.

- ♦ **The TPP:** This trade pact would have been a much bigger entity with the US, the world's largest economy being a part of it. It was to bring together 11 developed and emerging countries in the Pacific Rim region, including some of the Latin American countries, and was to include US, Canada, Japan, Australia, New Zealand, Mexico, Malaysia, Singapore, Vietnam, Peru, and Chile.

  The TPP aimed to advance economic growth, support high-paying jobs, and raise living standards across the region. It would have deepened economic ties between these nations, slashed tariffs and fostered trade to boost growth. Members also hoped to foster closer relationship on economic policies and regulation. The agreement was designed so that it could eventually create a new single market, somewhat akin to the European Union.

  The members in TPP accounted for 40 per cent of global trade spanning Asia and the Pacific Rim. Though a framework agreement was finalized, the deal fell through after former US President Donald Trump pulled US out of it on the ground that it favoured big business and other countries at the expense of American jobs and national sovereignty. It remains to be seen if US would reconsider its position under President Joe Biden's administration. If the US decides to join, the CPTPP regime would be strengthened and become a new entity. India should explore the possibilities of joining CPTPP or TPP if it is revived.

  China, the largest economy in Asia, was not part of the TPP negotiations, but it had welcomed the agreement and even put out feelers about joining it.

- ♦ **The RCEP:** This was to be a grouping of 10 members of ASEAN (Association of South-east Asian Nations) plus six other nations, viz., India, China, Japan, South Korea, Australia and New Zealand. It envisaged regional economic integration leading to the creation of the world's largest regional trading bloc, accounting for nearly 45% of the world's population with a combined gross domestic product (GDP) of $21.3 trillion.

  After protracted negotiations for eight years, the pact was finally signed by 15 nations, excluding India, in November 2020. China, which was pushing the deal, is the dominant partner in the group and stands to gain geo-political leverage over the ASEAN nations and Japan with which it has disputes on maritime and territorial issues.

➢ India and the Free Trade Agreements (FTAs)

■ India and RCEP

As regards RCEP, India envisions a trade deal that result in the realization of the potential of the three key pillars of RCEP – goods, services and investment. But India has reservations on many counts in joining it as explained below.

Lop-sided pact: While ASEAN members have been putting pressure on India to open up its market for more than 90 per cent of their traded goods, they remain reluctant to India's proposal to allow free movement of Indian skilled professionals in the RCEP region. The fact that most RCEP members are not ready to open up their services market, as proposed by India, makes the proposed deal more disadvantageous for India.

India has been insisting on concluding a balanced and collectively satisfactory RCEP agreement that includes a services pact.

The China factor: Besides, India has many issues with China which dominates the RCEP. India has over $50 billion (around ₹ 3.2 trillion) trade deficit with China. Tensions between the two countries have been high due to Chinese military intrusions. The China-Pakistan Economic Corridor is to pass through Pakistan-Occupied Kashmir to which India has strongly protested.

India has to take into account geostrategic issues while joining the RCEP as it will mean opening up the market to China.

India and ASEAN: Trade in services is growing faster than merchandise trade. Services are becoming a dominant driver of growth in both developed and developing countries. Services contribute almost two-thirds of India's GDP and surplus in services trade finances almost half of India's trade deficit.

India currently has around $10 billion trade deficit with the ASEAN grouping.

➢ **Potential for Exports and FTAs**

Need for bold approach

Economists and trade experts have been urging India to adopt a bolder and forward-looking approach on foreign trade. As one of the world's fastest-growing large economies and an important player in global economic governance, India cannot remain for long in a protected and secluded environment. India is an important trade and investment partner with major powers like the EU, US and Japan. Now that these major powers are also inclined to move away from, and reduce dependence on, China, it offers opportunities for India to take advantage of the situation.

As observed in *Economic Survey 2016-17*, "more FTAs, GST-induced tax rationalization, and labour law reform would add considerably to the job creation potential of the clothing and footwear sectors. All industrial policy aimed at promoting particular sectors are not without risks. But the externality generating attributes – employment, exports, social transformation – of the apparel and footwear sectors, India's potential comparative advantage in it, and the narrow window of opportunity available, make the risk worth taking. And, in any case, many of the proposed policy responses such as FTAs, tax rationalization, and labour law reform could have wider, economy-wide benefits." (*Economic Survey 2016-17*, Chapter 7, P. 137).

India has already initiated several steps like the GST, easing tax compliance, labour and agriculture marketing reforms, and various "Ease of Doing Business" measures. India has also launched Production Linked Incentive (PLI) scheme for selected sectors to incentivize domestic production and exports. These have already begun to show results in electronics and mobile manufacturing. Besides, India already has strong base in automobiles and auto components, defence and aero and space industries where India is catering to world markets.

Potential for other FTAs

- **India-EU FTA**

  Negotiations have been going on between the European Union and India since 2007 for a comprehensive Free Trade Agreement (FTA). This was suspended in 2013 due to a gap in the level of ambition expressed by the two sides. The EU has expressed that it still remains committed to working towards "an ambitious, comprehensive and balanced agreement FTA with India that responds to each side's key interests".

  At present, India is only the 10th largest trading partner of EU and accounts for just 1.9 per cent of EU's total trade in goods in 2019, well behind the USA (15.2%), China (13.8%) and the UK (12.6%). About 6,000 European companies are present in India, providing 1.7 million jobs directly and 5 million jobs indirectly in a range of sectors.

  Indian companies have invested over € 50 billion in Europe since 2000. The EU is one of the largest sources of foreign direct investment into India, with inflows of $90.7 billion between the periods April 2000 to June 2018, which was about 24% of the total FDI inflows during that period. An investment facilitation mechanism promotes and facilitates FDI inflows from the EU.

  An FTA with EU and UK will help in many ways. In the case of apparels and leather exports which have high employment potential, India stands at a disadvantage relative to competitors like Bangladesh, Vietnam and Ethiopia which already enjoy better and easier market access to Europe.

- **India-UK FTA**

  UK is now keen to have broader trade relations with India as she is exiting from the European Union and stands to lose trade benefits with EU countries. A bilateral meet at the highest levels between the Prime Ministers of both countries in April 2018 has presented an opportunity to re-invigorate the trade relations. The economic relationship between the two countries shows that while bilateral investment is strong and trade is growing the fact that UK can commence negotiating its own bilateral FTA during the transition period of Brexit gives room for further action between the Indian and UK governments. Lower tariffs and alignment of standards will accelerate the movement of goods and services and give bilateral trade a boost.

- **India-US Free trade pact**

  India and the US have also been holding talks towards a free trade agreement. Their leaders Indian PM and US President, decided to engage to move towards a free trade agreement between the two big economies. With this partnership with India, United States will also gain very significantly.

  India and the US will have strategic Energy Partnership in coming years as India is now the fourth largest export destination for US crude. India's LNG imports from the US are also increasing progressively since the imports started in March 2018. India is now the fifth largest destination of US exports of LNG.

  Though Indo-US trade has grown by over 50 per cent in the past 5 years, the current trade is only at $ 142 billion. To raise it to the shared goal of $500 billion, some more positive steps need to be taken and both countries must work out a trade deal that opens markets even more in both directions. India needs to simplify the single window clearances, institute a mechanism of automatic deemed approvals for no-objection certificates (NOCs), and further liberalise foreign direct investment (FDI) norms, among others.

➤ **Conclusion**

To sum up, domestic policies and reform measures need to be executed on continual basis for boosting manufacturing and services competitiveness and for better leveraging of Free Trade Agreements (FTAs). In fact, FTAs can be used to usher in such reforms.

7. Subsidy is a contentious issue and roadblock in the WTO negotiations. In the light of this, examine India's policies and stand in WTO for protecting the interests of farmers and consumers.

Ans. India provides various kinds of subsidies in services and facilities provided to the people. These include subsidies in food, fertilizers, electricity, and water, cooking gas, road and rail travel. etc. Besides the subsidies mentioned above, the government has been providing Minimum Support Price (MSP) to farmers and subsidised food to a target section of the population as explained below.

➤ **Price and Non-price support to Farmers**

Agriculture, employing 44 per cent of workforce (in 2018-19), being the most critical sector in the economy, successive governments have paid special attention to ensuring that farmers get remunerative prices for farm produce to insulate them from income losses and financial distress.

In 1965, a permanent body named Agricultural Prices Commission (APC) was formed and tasked with evolving a balanced price structure keeping in view the needs of the economy and with due regard to the interests of the producer and the consumer. It was only an advisory body with the final decision resting with the government. Later, the Commission was asked to take into account the "terms of trade between the agricultural and non-agricultural sectors" and examine the agricultural input costs in relation to output prices. In 1985, the Commission was renamed as Commission for Agricultural Costs and Prices (CACP).

The government has a 'procurement price policy' under which it sets prices based on the recommendations of the above Commission. The Commission provides expert advice to the government on price policy in the light of the prevailing cost of production, variations in supplies in relation to demand and overall price movements in the country as well as in world markets. Generally, the prices fixed by the government are higher than those recommended by the Commission. The policy of guaranteed Minimum Support Price (MSP) is confined to selected crops.

In India where the bulk of the farmers are small and marginal cultivators, non-price measures like investment in irrigation and power, support to farmers with supply of quality seeds and fertilizers, and providing farm implements, are as important as the price support to boost production.

Besides, India provides direct cash support under PM-KISAN scheme by way of direct benefit transfer (DBT) to farmers.

➢ **WTO and farm subsidies**

The subsidies provided to the farm sector have been a bone of contention between the developed and developing countries at WTO forums. The agricultural trade rules in the WTO's "Agreement on Agriculture" do not bar public procurement and stockholding for food security. However, if food for such programmes is acquired at administered prices and not market prices, then it is deemed to be support to farmers.

As per WTO rules negotiated in the Uruguay Round, all such support by developing countries has to be kept within a limit of 10 per cent of the value of production of the product in question based on 1986-88 prices and reported in dollar terms. In the case of developed countries, subsidies are to be within 5 per cent.

The above cap can constrain the procurement and food aid programmes in developing countries who contend that WTO has overlooked their interests and these conditions have been brought in keeping in view the interests of the developed countries.

These are issues of utmost concern to India which has a food procurement programme, minimum support price (MSP) policy in the interests of farmers, and an extensive Public Distribution System (PDS) to help especially the vulnerable sections of the population.

➢ **India's stand at WTO**

India has submitted comprehensive proposals to WTO on issues like Domestic Support, Market Access, Export Competition, and Food Security. India has urged the imperative need for protecting her food and livelihood security concerns by having freedom to take necessary domestic policy measures for poverty alleviation, rural development and rural employment, and also to create opportunities for expansion of agricultural exports by securing due access to markets in developed countries.

India and other developing countries, including China, Brazil and Indonesia, have been pressing for a permanent solution to the public stockholding and agricultural subsidy issues. There are two kinds of subsidies involved as stated below.

- India's total subsidy under its ongoing Public Distribution System (PDS), which has come under the ambit of the National Food Security Act (NFSA) from 2013.
- The general subsidy that India offers to the agriculture sector, including those for seeds and fertilizers.

Around 80 crore persons have been covered under the NFSA, for receiving foodgrains at highly subsidized rates. Rice, wheat and coarse grains are provided at rates of Rs. 3/2/1 per kg. respectively. Prices, not exceeding MSP, would be fixed, from time to time, by the Central Government.

➢ **The settlement: the "peace clause"**

- India secured an indefinite peace clause at the 2013 WTO Ministerial meet at Bali on the level of India's Food subsidy. The peace clause was arrived at after questions were raised at the meet on India's food subsidy.
- The truce, struck essentially between the US and India after the Bali meet, was that the latter's food subsidy would not be questioned before the WTO arrived at a permanent solution to the vexed issue. As per this agreement, the existing food subsidy programmes will not be challenged if they breach the 10 per cent limit. Despite this, India is needlessly questioned by the developed bloc whose farm subsidies, in fact, vastly violate WTO's Agreement on Agriculture (AoA) norms.
- However, the peace clause comes with an obligation under which countries need to notify their food subsidy levels to WTO till the previous year. Also, these countries are not allowed to start any new subsidized food programme beyond those that existed till 2013.
- India is nowhere near breaching the WTO limit of permissible subsidy being within 10 per cent of total agriculture output. The current figure of Rs. 3.26 lakh crore on subsidies includes permissible subsidies such as PM-KISAN and payments for relief for natural disasters (both in the form of cash support) which are not to be included in subsidy calculations.
- Yet, even as recent as 2018, the US has questioned the compatibility of India's agricultural subsidies with the relevant WTO norms, and targets the minimum support price (MSP) granted to wheat and rice, the two key food crops for India.

➢ **The Paradox**

- **Ironical stand:** The irony of the whole issue is that while objecting to farm support and food subsidies provided by India and other developing nations, the US and European countries themselves extend financial support to their farmers. It is patently unfair on the part of developed nations to extend support to their farming community which is relatively much better off while objecting to any support to the much poorer and indigent farmers in countries like India.

  African governments have long complained that the U.S. and European agricultural subsidies are undercutting African farmers. They say that western farm-support programs and cheap cotton dumped on the world market are impeding efforts to end Africa's cycle of poverty.

- **Market access:** The crux of the issue is that the developed nations want greater access for their farm products in the markets in developing countries like India, China, Brazil, Vietnam, etc.
- **Wide gap in subsidies:** The numbers reveal the wide gap that exists between the farm support offered by developed and developing economies. According to studies based on available data, when the level of support per farmer in the US was $7,253 (2016), it was $7,414 in Canada (2016), $222 in Australia (2017-18) and $1,068 in the EU (2016). On the contrary, India's was $49 (2018-19), while it was at $8 in Bangladesh and $7 in Indonesia (2018).
- **Total domestic support:** Further, if the "total domestic support" offered by the developed and developing countries to farmers is considered, it brings out the inequity even more starkly. According to latest reports from the respective countries, the per-farmer total domestic support (under various categories put together) was $61,286 in the US (2016), $13,010 in Canada, and $8,588 in the EU. As against this, the support for Indian farmers, in 2018-19 worked out to just $282.

8. In what way geopolitics and strategic interests affect economic development? Cite some instances where geopolitical factors in the emerging global order have impacted development of countries including India.

Ans. There is increasingly close linkage between geopolitics and economic development as seen from the emerging new world order. This linkage has become even stronger with the trend of globalization and increasing interdependence of nations in the economic sphere. Global trade, an important element in the development of nations, has been buffeted by political factors such as the long-drawn US - China trade conflict.

➢ **Interdependence and role of trade**

Trade is at the heart of the interdependence that binds countries together. Globalization and rapid expansion of world trade over the past two decades have played an important part in the progress of many developing nations, in reducing poverty, narrowing inequality and overcoming economic injustice.

But trade has not been an unmixed blessing. In many of the world's poorest countries, millions of poor people are still trapped in poverty and subhuman living conditions. The costs and benefits of trade have been unevenly distributed across and within countries, perpetuating a pattern of globalization that builds prosperity for some amid mass poverty and deepening inequality for others.

➢ **Geopolitics and development**

Despite opportunities for all-round development due to interaction between countries, trade and mutual assistance, many geopolitical factors and conflicting interests, discussed below, cause headwinds and tensions in international relations which harm socio-economic progress.

♦ **Conflicting interests:** Developed countries extol the virtues of open markets, level playing fields and free trade, in their dealings with developing and least developed countries (LDCs). Yet, the same governments maintain a formidable array of protectionist barriers against developing countries. For instance, the advanced nations also spend billions of dollars on agricultural subsidies to support their farmers but object to subsidies and support extended by developing nations to their farmers who are comparatively worse off.

  Developed nations demand free, open access for their agricultural products to markets in developing nations while they themselves deny access to their markets for developing nations.

  Such policies skew the benefits of globalization in favour of rich countries, while denying millions of people in developing countries a chance to share in the benefits of trade. Such double standards run counter to a rule-based multilateral system geared towards equitable development.

♦ **Emerging world order:** The political and economic dominance of a small group of countries (such as G8 nations) at world fora and in institutions like the UN, the IMF, and the World Bank may have been justified when these institutions were created several decades ago.

  The world's balance of power has since undergone significant change and many emerging nations have appeared on the world stage in their own right and there is strident clamour for rearranging the architecture of the international bodies. But the few advanced nations are unwilling to concede it or let go of their vice grip on them for their own narrow interests. Unless such issues are resolved by mutual consultations and consensus, the irritants in international relations will continue harming the cause of global co-operation and development.

- ♦ **Unethical practices:** Some countries resort to unethical practices in their economic and trading relationships with other countries to gain an edge which lead to friction between them. For instance, US accuses China of arm-twisting multinational corporations from the US investing in China to transfer high-end technology and even stealing technology, especially those in defence and strategic sectors, violating intellectual property rights (IPR).

  Again, China joined the WTO in 2001 committing to open its markets to foreign goods and investment in return for better access to foreign markets for its exports. While China benefited from the manufacturing boom and exports for the next two decades, it failed to keep the other side of the bargain, viz., to open up its markets in a similar way to other countries. Foreign investors and companies entering China face many barriers and conditions such as having to tie up with local partners and firms and transfer technology.

- ♦ **US – China trade dispute:** The mounting trade deficit of the US with China has become a contentious issue between the two countries. Though protracted negotiations have been held between the two countries, the issue is still unresolved. China's expansionist policies in the South and East China seas resulting in territorial disputes with some of the Asean countries and Japan respectively, and the controversial Belt Road Initiative (BRI) of China have added new dimensions to the trade dispute. (See sections further below for more on these).

  The belligerence and threatening postures of the isolationist regime of nuclear-armed North Korea, whose close ally and prop is China, has only compounded matters.

  These developments have had ramifications not only for trade between these two countries but impacted global trade itself. It has also impacted the development process in many other countries.

- ♦ **Hegemonic tendencies:** The tussle for political and economic supremacy and dominance between nations is a major factor in world politics affecting peace and development. Such a struggle was witnessed between the US and Soviet Union during the Cold War days between 1950 and 1990 until the latter disintegrated. A similar conflict has cropped up between China and the US with the rise of China as a major economic power, though it is still far behind the US in economic and technological prowess.

  Not only that China is flexing its muscles with all neighbouring countries, it has even annexed illegally the Exclusive Economic zones in the resource rich South China sea, which legitimately belong to Malaysia, Vietnam, Philippines, Taiwan and Brunei. China claims virtually the whole of the South China Sea and has built artificial islands, airstrip and oil rig in the disputed waters, and even constructed military facilities much to the chagrin of other claimant states. Due to this, the relationship between some of the ASEAN countries and China has been fraught with tension. The unilateral actions by China are in clear violation of international law and could affect vital trade routes through which about $5 trillion worth of goods pass a year. China also has dispute with Japan in East China sea over 'Senkaku' islands which the Chinese call 'Diaoyu' and which China claims to be its territory. These are all signs of China's growing economic clout and adding to regional tensions.

The US, Japan, Australia, etc. have raised objections over China's provocative actions and US carries out periodically freedom-of-navigation patrols in the area to which China has taken objection. These developments have a bearing on international peace and security and impact the economic progress of countries in the Asia Pacific region.

- **Political groupings:** The rivalry for global power and dominance by countries pose a threat to international peace and unity. It leads to factionalism and divisive tendencies among nations.

  Already certain countries are trying to form groups to counter the expansionist tendencies and policies of China. For instance, the US, Japan, India and Australia propose to form the "Quad", a political entity to protect the strategic interests of Indo-Pacific region. This grouping may also transform into an economic grouping to reduce dependence on China for supply of many products. They intend to diversify the global supply chains, over which now China has dominant control, by encouraging other countries to set up production units.

  The countries in the Quad group also carry out annual joint military exercises in Asia as a counter to China's military muscle flexing.

  In this scenario of rivalry between superpowers, many of the smaller nations are forced to take sides which could harm their economic interests in the long run.

- **China's Belt Road Initiative:** Another development initiated by China, under President Xi Jinping, is the Belt Road Initiative (BRI), launched in 2013. Under this, China has entered into agreements with some 70 odd countries stretching from East Asia to Africa and Europe to build infrastructure like roads, rail, ports, etc. and execute development projects in those countries. Besides, China is also setting up military bases at some strategic locations. China provides financial and material assistance and technical manpower for these projects. The initiative helps China to display its economic and military might and expand its political influence over these countries. The initiative has also faced opposition and criticism in some countries as the projects involving heavy outlays are pushing many of the less developed countries into debt and unsustainable financial burden.

- **Terrorism and Crime:** A new dimension which has emerged in the context of free trade and globalization is the spread of crime and terrorism. Increasing trade ties in south and south-east Asia have increased the possibility of criminal elements taking advantage of the relaxed custom controls.

  In the face of greater integration, the UN Office on Drugs and Crime (UNODC) has cautioned about potential danger posed by criminal activities such as drug and human trafficking and maritime piracy, if adequate security precautions are not taken in view of relaxed trade rules. Illicit wealth flowing in the region due to trade in drugs, wildlife, and fake products could be used for funding crime syndicates thus destabilizing the region. The loss in tax revenues reduces the benefits of trade liberalization and hurts law abiding businesses.

  Some countries throw open their borders to earn foreign exchange and are unprepared to do adequate surveillance of goods and people passing through their frontiers. There is a surge in tourist travel in the Asia-Pacific region and trade worth trillions of dollars pass through the south-east Asian waters which makes the task of enhanced security more imperative and challenging. The UNODC has called for countries to share real time intelligence using modern tools and technology.

  Apart from the dark side of crime, the world is also paying a heavy price on account of terrorism since the 9/11 attack in New York. According to the annual Global Terrorism Index, put out by the Institute for Economics and Peace (IEP), the acts of terror cost the world $52.9 billion in 2014 which compares with $51.5 billion cost in the aftermath of 9/11. The loss includes the value of properties damaged or destroyed, cost of death and injury including medical care costs, and lost earnings.

  The flow of migrants from terrorism ridden countries like Libya, Syria and Iraq to European countries have led to fresh problems and tensions in Europe.

➢ **Geopolitics and India:** Among the emerging economies, India plays an important role in global affairs. In view of its growing economic strength, the vast market that it commands and its strategic location in the Indian Ocean, many of the advanced and developing nations look to India on global issues. India also provides economic assistance to many developing and less developed countries (LDCs) in times of natural disasters and health emergencies like the pandemic, Covid-19, which has raised India's stature on the global scene. India is also a major source of supply of vital medicines for Aids, TB, etc. at economical prices to countries in Asia and Africa which has helped to forge friendly ties with many countries.

- **Regional Supply Chain:** India could take advantage of the "Resilient Supply Chain Initiative" (RSCI) which Japan and Australia have mooted to be formed with India in the Indo-Pacific region. This follows from the experience of Covid-19 pandemic which exposed the risks of overdependence on China for raw materials and intermediate goods. The Indian pharmaceutical industry faced much disruption due to non-supply of Active Pharmaceutical Ingredients (API) from China during the crisis. Various industries in many countries also faced problems in production due to disruptions in supplies from China.

This has led to calls to move many industries out of China and set up production units in different countries. India should take advantage of the situation, in collaboration with other friendly nations, and give a boost to the domestic industrial sector.

On the strategic front, as already mentioned, India has close defence relationship with the US, France, Japan, Singapore and Australia for strategic and logistical partnership and conducting periodic joint military exercises in the Indian Ocean. These countries also want India to play a critical role in the Indo-Pacific region which will act as a counterweight to China's overbearing dominance.

Furthermore, on Climate Change front, India has taken on a leadership role. India took the initiative, partnering with France, to form the International Solar Alliance (ISA) to promote solar energy across various countries. Since its launch, in five years 83 nations have joined the Alliance. ISA has set a target to install 1,000 GW of solar energy by 2030 across various sunshine-abundant countries and to mobilise US$ 1,000 billion to achieve the target.

➢ **Conclusion:**

Many countries are supporting the move to redraw the architecture of bodies like the World Bank and the IMF to give greater role to India. More importantly, there is strident demand to make few more countries, such as India and Germany, as permanent members of the UN Security Council to make it more representative and relevant to the contemporary global scene.

The above factors point to the impact geopolitics has in international affairs and on socio-economic development.

9. Environmental degradation and climate change are critical problems facing humanity. What are its causes and implications and what steps are proposed to be taken at global level to overcome them?

Ans. Environmental degradation and climate change are two of the most severe challenges facing humanity. Life on planet earth faces global warming catastrophe. Though the problem is the outcome of the actions of almost all countries, the problem got aggravated when the advanced nations embarked on large-scale industrialization and uncontrolled exploitation of natural resources, particularly the fossil fuels ever since the Industrial Revolution of the 18thand the 19th centuries.

➢ **A serious threat**

The problem came to the fore only some four decades back when the world started witnessing cataclysmic events causing untold misery in different parts of the world. The world has been witnessing heavy floods, hurricanes and typhoons, tsunami, erratic monsoon, monsoon failure and recurrent droughts, excessive heat, earthquakes, and above all mysterious and hitherto unseen changes in weather cycles. Much of these changes in nature has been attributed to greenhouse gas emissions, burning of coal, indiscriminate use of fossil fuels, deforestation, relentless urbanization, vehicular pollution, and so on.

➢ **Factors causing Climate change**

- **Dependence on fossil fuels:** Fossil fuels like coal, oil and natural gas which are used in power generation and transportation are major sources of emission and pollution causing global warming. Transportation accounts for the world's largest consumption of oil and is one of the fastest growing sources of carbon dioxide (CO2) emissions causing environmental pollution.
- **Agriculture:** Agricultural operations which are crucially dependent on climatic factors, water resources and energy have major environmental implications. The process of both production and consumption of food involve the use of energy and is estimated to account for about 30 per cent of the total energy consumption of the world. Food production, supply, and consumption chain also give rise to greenhouse gas emissions.

➢ **Impact on population**

The World Bank has warned that global warming could elevate levels of disease, ravage crops, and push 100 million people more into poverty by 2030. This is over and above the 900 million people expected to be living in extreme poverty, if development progresses slowly.

Global warming will have devastating effects on the poor who are more vulnerable to climate-related shocks than wealthier people because they are more exposed and lack the financial capacity and social safety nets that would allow them to better prepare and cope.

➢ **A universal emergency**

Climate change has now been universally recognized as a serious threat to the present and future generations and has been engaging the attention of international community since the First World Climate Conference, organized by the World Meteorological Organization (WMO) in 1979 in Geneva. Since then, several international meets have been held under the aegis of the United Nations as discussed later below.

Climate change is witnessed in different forms as explained below. These are being studied by experts of the Intergovernmental Panel on Climate Change (IPCC) set up under the UN Climate Conference.

- **Rise in temperature:** All over the world, mean temperatures have been rising by a few degrees each year. The majority of tropical areas are becoming inhospitable with populations migrating to different parts. Even temperate zones like Europe and North America are experiencing sweltering heat.
- **Melting of ice and glaciers:** The melting of Arctic sea ice and the Greenland ice sheet, at an unprecedented rate, are already visible. Melting of glaciers will have far-reaching effects on local ecology, and tipping points have already been reached in some places.
- **Monsoon patterns:** Changing weather patterns have a bearing on mountains as well. As the monsoon patterns change, it is expected that there will be incessant rain, leading to floods and landslides. Back-to back floods and massive landslides have occurred in Kerala and Coorg in Karnataka in recent years causing considerable loss of lives and property and throwing normal life out of gear for thousands of families. Studies by experts attribute the landslides to deforestation, mining, unscientific construction of roads and high-rise buildings in hilly areas. Data from ISRO's Remote Sensing Centre has shown that as much as 35 per cent of the fragile Western Ghat ranges have been destroyed in the course of the last century.
- **Ocean warming:** The world's oceans have since 1970, absorbed 90 per cent of the excess heat generated by greenhouse gas emissions. According to reports, between 1993 and 2017, the rate of ocean warming has doubled, as compared to 1969-93. Marine heat waves have doubled since 1982, and they have also become more long-lasting, more intense and more extensive. A warmer ocean means a rise in extreme weather events, like devastating storm surges in coastal areas and the increased likelihood of tropical cyclones of category 4 and 5 making landfall. Marine heat waves are the biggest threat to coral reefs, while increased ocean acidification could devastate fish stocks worldwide. While the world has been concerned about extreme events over land, such extremes could happen over the ocean, which would impact life over land.
- **Cyclones and hurricanes**: Cyclones and hurricanes have been occurring in different part of the world, including the eastern coast of India, with disastrous consequences for people living in the affected areas especially in Andhra Pradesh, Orissa and West Bengal. The west coast of India with six states bordering it – Tamil Nadu, Kerala, Karnataka, Goa, Maharashtra and Gujarat – is equally vulnerable and faces major ecological disturbances such as floods and cyclone.

  When cyclone "Fani" made landfall on the Odisha coast near Puri in May 2019, there were gusty winds of speed of 170-200 km per hour. It directly affected 16 million people and set back the state's economy by thousands of crores of rupees. But before making landfall, the cyclone had spent 11 days dilly-dallying over the

Bay of Bengal gathering strength for so long that the IMD had to revise its forecast multiple times. The uncertainty made it even more agonising for people in the area. It was only the second cyclone in 128 years to form in April, cross the mainland and make landfall in India in the pre-monsoon season. The last severe cyclone "Nargis" in 2008 devastated Myanmar.

According to an IPCC report, such once-in-a-century weather events are set to become more frequent in future emission scenarios. India has the seventh longest coastline in the Asian region, to a length of 7,500km. A warmer ocean feeds into the cyclone events. This will lead to a lot of devastation in future as it is predicted that the frequency and severity of the cyclones will also be more in the future.

Cyclones and hurricanes are recurring phenomena in the Caribbean and Pacific islands causing much devastation and suffering to the people in those parts.

- **Drought and Floods:** Rainfall is also affected by phenomena like El Niño and La Niña. El Niño occurs when sea surface temperatures rise to abnormal levels in the tropical Pacific Ocean causing acute drought conditions in the Asian region which adversely impacts agriculture and cause heat waves. While La Niña is caused by cooling of the central Pacific area, which could bring heavy rains to flood-prone regions of Asia and causing floods. According to experts, events such as El Niño and La Niña will occur with increasing frequency as the ocean temperatures keep changing.
- **Rise in sea levels:** According to IPCC studies, sea levels have been rising. Over the past 20 years, sea levels have risen by 6 to 8cm. This has implication for countries and island nations which are encircled by oceans. They would experience loss of land and coastal erosion, impacting the lives of the people living close to such areas. They would also face salt water contamination of fertile lands and freshwater reservoirs leading to food and water shortages.

➢ **Remedial measures: UN Climate meet**

Successive UN Conference of Parties (COP), consisting of member countries of the UN, have been deliberating on various measures to curb greenhouse gas emissions and adapt to climate change. At the 21st Conference of Parties (COP21) held in Paris in 2015, 195 nations reached a historic agreement which emphasized the following plan of action:

- To take steps to limit global temperature increase, during this century, to less than 2 degrees Celsius above pre-industrial levels, while pursuing efforts to limit the increase to even less – 1.5 degree Celsius.
- Towards this end, all countries are bound to communicate and maintain a "Nationally Determined Contribution" (NDC) and pursue domestic measures to achieve them.

- The accord encourages countries to conserve and enhance "carbon sinks" and reservoirs of greenhouse gases (GHG), including forests, and cut dependence on fossil fuels to reduce emissions responsible for global warming. ("Carbon sink" is any reservoir, natural or otherwise, that absorbs more carbon than it releases, and thereby lowers the CO2 in the atmosphere. Globally, the two most important carbon sinks are vegetation and the ocean.)
- Make provisions to enable the shift to clean energy sources such as solar and wind energy.
- Increase the ability to adapt to adverse impacts of climate change without jeopardizing food production.
- As all countries do not have the resources to undertake these efforts, the Conference acknowledged the disparities in the level of obligation and responsibility of rich industrialized countries and developing countries.
- Industrialized countries must take the lead with developing countries chipping in, thereby adopting the principle of "common but differentiated responsibilities" among countries.

➤ **Paris Agreement and after**

The Paris Agreement, the world's joint response to the problem of hotter temperatures, rising sea levels and other impacts of climate change, was a major breakthrough in UN climate negotiations after years of wrangling about the responsibilities of the advanced countries, on the one hand, and the developing and least developed countries (LDCs), on the other.

A major requirement is for the rich nations to keep up the commitment to provide \$100 billion a year by 2020 – from public and private sources alike – to help developing countries switch from fossil fuels to greener energy sources and adapt to the effects of climate change. French President Macron has urged wealthy nations and global companies to commit more funds to combating global warming and help poorer nations deal with the impact of climate change.

The ambitious climate pact, however, received a serious setback with President Trump deciding to pull the US, the second highest polluter after China, out of it. This has met with much criticism from other nations and experts. It remains to be seen if the US will reverse its decision at some point in the near future.

The Paris accord will not immediately solve the problem of climate change, but it commits about 200 nations to progressively bring down greenhouse gas emissions and stem the adverse impact.

10. Discuss the steps being taken by India on 'Climate Change', to fulfil the commitments made at 21st Conference of Parties (COP21), Paris. Examine in what way it would affect India's development prospects.

Ans. The UN Framework Convention on Climate Change (UNFCCC) and the eventual Paris Climate accord arrived at 21st Conference of Parties (COP21) by countries has brought the critical issue of threats posed by recurring changes in climate and weather patterns to the centre stage. The accord reached in Paris in 2015 and ratified by 125 nations by early 2017, set targets for countries to pursue to bring down carbon emissions and limit global warming by the end of this century.

➢ **India and Climate change**

India is the third highest emitter of greenhouse gases (GHG), behind China and the United States which have higher levels of absolute CO2 emissions. In absolute terms, China's CO2 emission (from fuel combustion) in 2018 was 10.06 GT (Metric gigatons), that of US 5.41 GT and of India 2.65 GT, according to the World Bank data.

However, due to their large population, India and China have low per capita emission. In 2016, India's per capita emission was 1.8 metric tons and China's 7.2 metric tons, while the world average was 4.8 metric tons, according to the World Bank.

➢ **India's commitment on Climate change**

While by per capita emission levels, India's contribution to global warming is very low, India is one of the leading nations when it comes to taking steps to address the issue. Ahead of COP 21, India submitted its Intended Nationally Determined Contribution (INDC) to UNFCC outlining the country's post-2020 climate actions.

Under the 2015 Paris Agreement, India has set ambitious goals and pledged to reduce the carbon intensity of its economy and promote renewable energy in a big way as mentioned below:

- To reduce India's GHG emissions intensity per unit GDP by 33 to 35 percent below 2005 levels by 2030.
- Create an additional carbon sink of 2.5 to 3 billion tonnes of carbon dioxide (CO2) through additional tree cover.
- Install 175 gigawatts (GW) of renewable power capacity by 2022 and increase the share of non-fossil-based energy in country's installed electric capacity to 40 percent by 2030.

➢ **Multi-pronged action**

India is taking multi-pronged approach to fulfilling the targets mentioned above. These include:

- Rolling out multiple initiatives, programs and incentives to accelerate the development of the renewable energy sector and reducing dependence on coal-based thermal power.

- Promoting electric vehicles in transport and mobility.
- Increasing forest cover.

Action initiated and progress on these fronts are discussed below.

- **Power sector**

- **Solar mission:** The National Solar Mission (NSM) was the first mission to be operationalized in 2010 under the National Action Plan on Climate Change (NAPCC).The initial target of installing 20 GW grid-connected "solar power" plants by 2022 was first enhanced to 100 GW. Solar power capacity has increased by more than 14 times in five years from 2.6 GW in 2014 to 37.5 GW in 2019. (1 Gigawatt = 1,000 Megawatt)
- **Higher renewable target:** Later in 2015, the Govt. of India revised the target to 175 GW of cumulative "renewable power" installed capacity by the year 2022. Against this, capacity of 85.90 GW of renewable power has been set up by December 2019, which constituted more than 23 percent of the total installed power generation capacity of 368.78 GW in the country.
- **Job potential:** Since 2013-14 till December 2019, the renewable power deployment has more than doubled and annually more than 10 million man-days of employment is being created in the sector.
- **Global ranking:** India is one of the leading generators of solar and wind power and holds the 5th and 4th global positions in solar and wind power deployment respectively.
- **Other sources:** India is also utilizing small hydro power and biomass for power generation as part of the renewable energy programme.
- **Thermal power – A major challenge:** A major challenge India faces in fulfilling the commitments made on Climate change and achieving the targets set is in regard to thermal power plants. Many of the state utilities have old and inefficient and polluting thermal plants which are to be closed or retrofitted to comply with emission standards. Presently, over 60 per cent of total installed capacity consists of thermal power and this has to be brought down considerably. About 170 such plants have been already closed.
- **Role of NTPC:** National Thermal Power Corporation (NTPC), which is the largest thermal power generating company in the country, has a major role to play in India living up to the target. It has total installed capacity of 62.9 GW, of which 45.4 GW is coal-based thermal power. NTPC is now adopting environmentally sustainable power generation.

  Adoption of clean coal technologies such as ultra-super critical thermal power technology could help reduce emissions. Experts are of the view that such technologies are available and techno-economically feasible to bring down emissions. NTPC has to adopt such technology in its thermal plants.

In a positive development, NTPC is adding renewable energy (RE) in its portfolio and, by 2032, it plans to have a 32 GW (32,000 MW) capacity through renewable sources which will be nearly 25 per cent of its overall power generation capacity. The initiative of NTPC, the major state-run thermal producing undertaking, to take up RE projects will be an added boost.

➢ **International Solar Alliance (ISA)**

India has also taken initiative at global level to promote solar energy by forming International Solar Alliance (ISA) in co-operation with France. ISA has set a target to install 1,000 GW of solar energy by 2030 across various sunshine-abundant countries and to mobilise US$ 1,000 billion to achieve the target.

Since its launch, in four years 83 nations have joined the alliance. The Alliance would help member countries, mostly developing economies, with solar power solutions and thus help reduce the global carbon footprint.

▸ **Transportation and mobility**

There is a growing realisation in India that hybrid and electric vehicles (EVs) are needed to counter the threat of environmental pollution which also poses serious health hazard. India unveiled in 2013 the 'National Electric Mobility Mission Plan 2020', an initiative by the Govt. of India to bring about a transformational shift in the transportation sector in the country.

Later in 2015, the government came up with the FAME scheme (Faster Adoption and Manufacturing of Electrical Vehicles). It aims to provide subsidy for EVs to boost its adoption in the country. Some of the automobile and bike manufacturers in India have already taken the initiative to produce electric vehicles and are planning to expand production facilities.

♦ **Benefits of Electric Vehicles:** Electric vehicles (EVs) have many advantages from environmental and users' points of view.

- **Energy efficient:** Electric Vehicles are more energy efficient as they do not consume electricity while stationary, unlike internal combustion engines which consume fuel while idling. With greater overall efficiency, the average amount of energy savings goes up to 40 per cent for an electric vehicle compared to a traditional fuel engine vehicle.
- **Cost-effective:** As electric engines are more energy efficient, they are inherently more cost-effective. The electricity cost to charge an EV averages to a third of the price of petrol per kilometre.
- **Less pollution:** Petrol-driven vehicles contribute to pollution right from the extraction of petrol to its burning and by release of harmful gases in the environment. EVs can use renewable energy.

- **Low maintenance:** EVs contain fewer components than a conventional petrol/diesel vehicle providing easier servicing and cheaper maintenance compared to their fossil fuel counterparts. EVs require much less maintenance over the course of their lifetime.
- **Saving on oil imports:** Adoption of EVs will help to reduce the dependency on crude oil imports which cost the country over $ 100 billion annually.

♦ **Progress:** Compared to other countries, the progress on adoption of EVs in India has been rather slow. There has been steady rise in the number of EVs on road with 5 million EV units across the globe in 2018, of which China, Europe and the United States account for the major shares. By 2025, more than 50 per cent of vehicle sales in Europe will be EVs.

- **India at nascent stage:** The Indian electric vehicles (EV) market is at a very nascent stage and is dominated by Two- and Three-wheelers. The EV market in India had about 25,000 units at the end of 2016-17.
- **EV sales:** In 2018-19, total EV sales in India stood at 1.3 lakh units of which 1.26 were two-wheelers, 3,600 cars and around 400 buses. Corresponding figures in 2019-20 were a total of 1.56 lakh units of which 1.52 lakh units were two-wheelers, 3,400 cars and 600 buses.
- **Improving facilities:** Electric cars are gradually becoming popular in India with energy stored in rechargeable batteries and with facility of plug-in electric charging stations. The government propose to set up EV charging kiosks at 69,000 petrol pumps across the country.
- **EV auto makers:** Automobile and bike companies like Tata Motors, M&M, Maruti, Toyota Kirloskar, Hero Motors, TVS Motors, etc. have evinced interest in manufacturing EV models and are entering this niche segment.The e-rickshaws or electric three-wheelers, with their greater affordability, fewer range-related issues due to their defined routes and short-distance commutes make their adoption easier.

♦ **Need to improve public transport:** A major step to be taken to make transport and mobility environment-friendly is to popularise mass public transport like public buses, both state and private, and Metro rail in cities. The financial viability of state bus transport needs to be improved as many of the State Transport units are running at losses due to a variety of reasons such as uneconomic tariffs, overstaffing and competition from private buses on overlapping routes. As a result, many of them are to be heavily subsidized. State transport bodies are also trying to switch to electric buses which is a positive step. Going forward, private buses also need to switch to EVs.

As for Metro rapid transit, there is considerable progress as Metro rail system has been introduced in many of the large cities and have good ridership. This has helped to reduce the load on city road transport.

Electrification of long-distance rail routes is another positive factor which reduces dependence on diesel with savings on foreign exchange and lessening environmental pollution.

- **Forest cover**

The third area of action on climate change and safeguarding environment is expanding forest and tree cover, important reservoirs of "carbon sink". ("Carbon sink" is any reservoir, natural or otherwise, that absorbs more carbon than it releases, and thereby lowers the CO2 in the atmosphere). India has agreed to enhance its forest cover which will absorb 2.5 to 3 billion tonnes of carbon dioxide (CO_2, the main gas responsible for global warming) by 2030.

Forest Survey of India (FSI), an organization under the Ministry of Environment, Forest and Climate Change, has been conducting nationwide survey of forest and tree cover and related biodiversity aspects keeping in view the above mentioned targets to be met by India.

- **ISFR Report, 2019:** According to the latest India State of Forest Report (ISFR) 2019 and earlier years' surveys, the data on forest and tree cover are as follows:

Table 12.1: India's Forest and Tree Cover

Year	Total Forest Cover	% of Total area of India	Total Tree Cover	% of Total area of India	Total Forest and Tree cover	% of Total area of India
1	2	3	4	5	6	7
2019	7,12,249	21.67	95,027	2.89	8,07,276	24.56
2017	7,08,273	21.54	93,815	2.85	8,02,088	24.40
2015	7,01,673	21.34	92,572	2.82	7,94,245	24.16
2013	6,97,898	21.23	91,266	2.78	7,89,164	24.01

Note: All Total figures are in sq. kms. Percentages shown are of total geographical area of India.

Source: India State of Forest Report, Forest Survey of India (FSI), Ministry of Environment, Forest and Climate Change.

The total forest and tree cover (FTC) of the country, as per the ISFR 2019 is 8,07,276 sq. km. which is 24.56 per cent of the total geographical area of the country. There is an increase of 5,188 sq. km. as compared to the FTC in ISFR-2017 and 13,031sq. km. as compared to FTC in ISFR, 2015.

For development and conservation of the forest cover in the country, Ministry has been taking several initiatives. These include ongoing Centrally Sponsored Schemes such as National Afforestation Programme, National Mission for a Green India and Development of Wildlife Habitats. Compensatory Afforestation Fund Rules, 2018 also contain provisions for taking up assisted natural regeneration, artificial regeneration and silvi-cultural operations in forests which contribute to increase in forest cover.

Table 12.2: Category of Forests

Forest type	2019	2017	2015	2013
Very dense forest	99,278 (3.02)	99,158 (2.99)	85.904 (2.61)	83,502 (2.54)
Moderately dense forest	3.08,472 (9.39)	3,08,318 (9.38)	3,15,374 (9.59)	3,18,745 (9.70)
Open forest	3,04,499 (9.26)	3,01,797 (9.18)	3,00,395 (9.14)	2,95,651 (8.99)
Total geographical area	32,87,469 (100)	32,87,469 (100)	32,87,263 (100)	32,87,263 (100)

Note: All figures are in sq. kms. Figures in brackets denote percentage to Total geographical area.

Source: India State of Forest Report, Forest Survey of India (FSI), Ministry of Environment, Forest and Climate Change.

- **The challenges:** There is concern over forest degradation that could mar India's prospect of creating an additional 2.5 to 3 billion tonnes of carbon sink through forestation by 2030.
  - Though as per data in Table 12.1, the forest cover has shown increase from 2013 to 2019, it still falls short of the required target. The total forest and tree cover percentage of 24.56 of geographical area reached, as per 2019 report, falls very much short of the target of 33 per cent to be reached to fulfil commitment under Climate change action.
  - As seen from Table 12.2, the area under "Very dense forest" has been increasing but the increase between 2017 and 2019 has been only marginal. So also, the increase under "Moderately dense forest" between 2017 and 2019 was almost negligible. Not only that the area under "Moderately dense forest" had shown decline from 2013 to 2017. It may be because part of the "Moderately dense forest" may have been converted to "Very dense forest" category. If that is so, it is a positive development.
  - The quality of forests has to be improved. Open forests, degraded forest and moderate forests should be converted to dense and very dense forests to reach the goals.

- While plantation is a key activity being carried out across the country through the Forest Department as well as government agencies, the "survival rate" of planted items is poor. This calls for concerted and sustained action to increase the forest area.
- Many species of plants and lower organisms are under threat and unsustainable removal of medicinal and aromatic plants is taking place on a large scale which denude tree cover.
- The shortage of firewood and fodder, the poverty among forest-dependent communities, the declining water table and the frequent occurrences of forest fire are also cause for concern as they would have adverse impact on the forestry sector.

➤ **Conclusion**

Even realizing the huge impact that climate change is exerting and the pressures it will have on different sectors of its economy and the country's development prospects, India has adopted ambitious targets to bring down carbon footprint. India is committed to enhance investments in vulnerable sectors like agriculture, water resources, coastal regions, health and disaster management to achieve the goals.

According to experts, while India's INDC is fair considering her low per capita emission levels and aspirations of large numbers of poor people, it is also quite ambitious, especially on renewable energy and forestry.

India has reiterated the need for international finance and technology support to meet its climate goals. In this regard, it has said it would require at least US $ 2.5 trillion (at 2014-15 prices) to meet its climate change actions between now and 2030.

India has to act on all the three fronts, viz., the power sector, switch to electric vehicles for mobility and increasing the forest cover if we are to adhere to the set targets. The Central and State governments have to work in close co-operation to ensure this.

(For more on Climate change and India's actions on Climate change, see Questions 15, 16 and 17 in Chapter 10).

11. Technology plays an important part in economic development. Examine the limitations and barriers in transfer of technology from the advanced nations to developing countries and the role played by international organizations in overcoming them.

Ans. Technological advances took place in countries in the Northern hemisphere, namely in Europe and North America, since the onset of Industrial Revolution in the 18th and 19th centuries. The application of science and technology to industrial production helped those countries in their quest for economic development and forge ahead.

Countries in Asia, Africa and Latin America, which are part of the Southern hemisphere and which were under the colonial rule of European countries were bypassed in this process of technological advancement and industrialization for well-nigh 200 years. This created a hiatus between the developed and developing countries in economic development and led to what is called the North-South divide.

- **Genesis of UNCTAD**

As the countries under colonial rule gained independence and embarked on the process of economic development in the 1950s, the need arose for them to harness the benefits of science and technology. On this these countries had to depend on the advanced nations in the western world and the issue of "transfer of technology" came to the fore by 1960s.

There were growing concerns in developing countries about their place in international trade and their ability to access to technology which was vital for their progress. This led many of those countries to call for a full-fledged conference specifically concerned with tackling these issues and taking appropriate action at international level. Thus was born the United Nations Conference on Trade and Development (UNCTAD) in 1964.

Given the magnitude of the problems at stake and the need to address them, the Conference was institutionalized to meet every four years, with inter-governmental bodies meeting between sessions. A permanent secretariat was also set up for providing the necessary substantive and logistical support on a continual basis.

- **Role of UNCTAD**

The main functions of UNCTAD are:

- To promote international trade between the developed and underdeveloped countries with a view to accelerating economic development.
- To formulate the principles and policies on International trade and negotiate multinational trade agreements.
- To promote research and support negotiations for commodity agreements and assist in the areas of trade and capital for developing countries.
- To generally review and coordinate the activities of other institutions within the fold of United Nations relating to international trade and economic development.

- **Transfer of technology**

The 1979 UNCTAD conference held at Vienna adopted a 'Programme of Action on Science and Technology (S & T) for Development'. It rested on two basic ideas:

- Strengthening of science and technology (S & T) capacities of the developing countries.
- Restructuring of the then existing pattern of international S & T relations which included transfer of technology.

Transfer of technology, especially advanced technology, helps developing countries to strengthen their creative and innovative capacities. Such transfers take place at the level of governments or through transnational corporations and involve complex issues such as:

- Choice of technology.
- Mode of acquiring it.
- Its absorption and indigenisation.
- Patent and intellectual property rights.
- Pricing and cost.

➢ **Concerns and Limitations**

The above-mentioned aspects involve tough negotiations and hard bargaining between the transferring and recipient countries and, in most cases, the under-developed countries are at a disadvantage vis-à-vis the developed country which possess the technology. The following are some of the major concerns and barriers in technology transfer.

- ♦ **Choice of technology:** Choosing the right technology in keeping with the recipient country's requirements is crucial. The technology transferred must be the one most appropriate and for which skilled manpower is locally available. Even for choosing the right system, the receiving country may not have the technical expertise and would have to depend on foreign experts. In such a scenario, organizations like UNCTAD could be of assistance.
- ♦ **Need for local adaptation:** The need for local adaptation of a technology transferred may arise due to the fact that the environment in which any technology operates is unique and the situation in which it is installed in the recipient country may differ radically from the environment for which the system or know-how was developed. Hence close examination of its suitability and need for any adaptation is imperative.
- ♦ **Benefits for transferring country:** This is particularly important because technology transfers are beneficial to the transferring country as it helps to create export market for their products such as machinery, and also for their services in the form of technical personnel provided.
- ♦ **Need to ensure up to date technology:** It has to be ensured that the technology being transferred is an up to date one. In many instances, the advanced countries may not provide the latest technology for fear of losing their exclusive control over it and transfer only an outdated, if not obsolete, one.
- ♦ **Niche areas:** Such issues crop up particularly in niche areas like advanced armaments required for defence and in frontier areas like nuclear plants, space technology, fighter aircrafts, etc. where advanced nations will be reticent to transfer sophisticated systems.
- ♦ **Expanding local base, skills:** The acquiring country will have to have to expand its capacity to generate, absorb, adapt and apply the S & T know-how to make full use of a technology. For this to happen, the condition that the transferring country would impart training and skill local manpower is to be built into the agreement.

- **Developing local expertise, R & D:** Undue dependence on foreign technology should not hamper development of technological competence or expertise in the recipient country. Even as it imports technology, it should develop S & T skills and R & D capabilities to become self-reliant going forward.
- **Pricing and costs:** The sale of technology is especially a complex transaction in which the basis of charging is not clearly spelt out. There may be implicit or hidden costs in the form of over pricing of imported equipments and intermediate products, over charging for services of technical experts provided or for the licence for use of patented technology. Often, the recipient country would not have the expertise to evaluate these costs. Here again, the role of organizations like UNCTAD could play a role in negotiating and final settlement.

➤ **Changing environment**

Over the years, there have been signs of change in the attitudes of advanced countries in transferring technology and providing aid. This has come about due to the active intervention of international organizations like the UNCTAD, The World Bank, Asian Development Bank, etc. which provide both technical assistance and financial aid for various projects and industries. They have played a catalytic role with the advanced nations and transnational corporations which undertake technology transfer in promoting international co-operation.

Other factors like increasing labour costs in developed countries and the need to expand markets for their products and innovations have compelled those countries to reach out to developing countries. This is evident from the willingness of countries like France, US, UK, Germany, Japan, etc. to start production of high-tech items in countries like China, India, Brazil, Mexico, etc.

The shifting of R & D units involving advanced technology and processes by some of the multinationals in the IT sector and starting of automotive manufacture and proposals to manufacture defence equipments, fighter aircraft and airplane components, etc. in India are examples of this. Such transfer of high-tech industries is beneficial to the developing countries which are able to absorb advanced technology and develop highly skilled manpower.

> Climate change is the defining human development issue of our generation....... The early warning signs are already visible.........Across developing countries, millions of the world's poorest people are already being forced to cope with the impacts of climate change......increased exposure to drought, to more intense storms, to floods and environmental stress is holding back the efforts of the world's poor to build a better life for themselves and their children...... Climate change will undermine international efforts to combat poverty .... Looking to the future, the danger is that it will stall and then reverse progress built-up over generations not just in cutting extreme poverty, but in health, nutrition, education and other areas.
>
> – Fighting climate change: human solidarity in a divided world, *Human Development Report, 2007/2008*, UNDP, New York.

PLANNING AND DEVELOPMENT

What greater or better gift can we offer the republic than to teach and instruct our youth?
– Marcus Tullius Cicero (106-43 B.C.), Roman statesman and orator.

Topics Covered

- *Pros and cons of 'Socialist pattern of society' policy*
- *Main features of Second Five Year Plan*
- *Vakil-Brahmananda model of development*
- *Dominant role of Public sector in the Plans*
- *Problem of migrant labour in India*
- *Impact of Covid-19 pandemic on Indian economy*
- *Role of education and health in socio-economic development*

1. In the initial stages of planning, India adopted 'Socialist pattern of society' as the objective of development. Do you think this was the correct approach? Give your views with arguments for and against it.

Ans. When India gained independence, the nascent nation-state had to grapple with a host of socio-economic problems such as the aftermath of World War II, the painful partition of the country and large influx of refugees. These developments placed a heavy strain on the scarce resources.

➢ **The Genesis of Planning**

Even during the pre-Independence days, the Indian National Congress was seized of the question of the path India should take for economic and social development once she attained freedom. As early as 1938, Congress had appointed a National Planning Committee headed by Pandit Nehru. The Committee explored several aspects of planned economic development and social transformation to be initiated and brought out its views in a 'Handbook of National Committee'.

- **The Bombay Plan:** Later, during the Second World War (1939-45) period, prominent industrialists including Sir Purushothamdas Thakurdas, J.R.D. Tata, G.D. Birla, and others studied the problems confronting the nation and came out with a detailed report titled '***A Plan for Economic Development of India***' which came to be known as the 'Bombay Plan'. Their report stressed the importance of developing basic industries, enlarging the role of the State as a facilitator and regulator, and taking steps to reduce inequalities in society.

- **The Planning Commission**

  Thus, by the time the country attained freedom, the stage was set for India to adopt 'planned development' as the primary goal to overcome the damages inflicted on the country by two centuries of economic exploitation. The Planning Commission was set up in 1950 with the objective of promoting rapid rise in the standard of living of the people by efficient exploitation of the resources of the country, increasing production, and providing opportunities for employment to all sections of people. The Prime Minister was Chairman of the Commission.

  The Commission was entrusted with the task of determining the priorities for development, assessing the resources available, and formulating plans for their effective and optimum utilization to achieve the set objectives. The mandate was to make optimum use of the vast untapped natural and human resources of the country and harnessing the benefits of modern science and technology for building a strong industrial base.

  After years of stagnation and stupor, the nation was reawakened to take the path of rapid progress and catch up with the industrialized nations.

➤ **Towards a Socialistic Model**

After the Great Depression of the 1930s and the ravages caused by an excruciating war the capitalist societies of the West were also in dire straits. Many of them were in shambles and struggling to recover and rebuild their economies.

- **The Soviet model:** Meanwhile, during this period – in the first half of the 20th century – Soviet Union was economically taking rapid strides following the Bolshevik Revolution in 1917. Vladimir Lenin had initiated a New Economic Policy (NEP), nationalized all landed properties and introduced 'Collectivization' of agriculture. Adopting the socialist path of Planning, she had built a large industrial network of basic and heavy industries, constructed large dams and power plants, and rebuilt the economy on an unprecedented scale while at the same time taking steps to reduce inequalities in the society under a Communist regime.

Thus, at a time when the world was facing grave economic crises brought about by capitalism, socialist ideals held out great appeal to many young nations which were under colonial rule and had gained independence. The so-called success of the Soviet Union through planning had shown a new way – planned socialist development as an alternative to crises-ridden capitalism to bring about rapid economic and social transformation.

The two concurrent developments – capitalism in crisis and the success of socialism – had a profound influence on the nascent, under-developed countries aiming to industrialize at a rapid pace, reduce inequalities and establish an egalitarian society.

The primary goal was to reduce inequalities in the distribution of income and wealth and prevent concentration of economic power. This system adopted by the Soviet Union held great appeal to many leaders in India, particularly Pandit Nehru, and under his leadership, the government decided to adopt planning as the mode of development. And soon after, India was to adopt formally the establishment of 'Socialist Pattern of Society' as its goal.

- **Five Year Plans:** The First Five-year Plan was launched in 1951 and ended in 1956. The next two Plans were from 1956-61 and 1961-66. Thereafter, there was a break because of the Indo-Pakistan conflict in 1965. Two successive years of drought in 1965 and 1966, devaluation of the Rupee in 1966, a general rise in prices, and erosion of resources also caused disruption in the planning process. Hence, there were three Annual Plans between 1966 and 1969, and then the Fourth Five-year plan was started in 1969.
- **Sectoral shares in GDP:** At the time of independence, the share of agriculture in national income was 49 per cent that of industry and mining only 17 per cent and of services and construction sector 34 per cent. As for employment, agriculture accounted for 71.8 per cent of the total workforce, industry for 9.5 per cent, and services for 18.7 per cent.

  Thus, India was then primarily an agrarian economy with bulk of the share in agriculture (the primary sector), little share for industry (the secondary sector) and only a moderate share for the services (the tertiary sector).
- **Early Plans (1951-66):** The main objective of the First Plan was to pull India out of the vicious cycle of poverty and promote growth with equity and social justice. Faced with a growing population and acute shortage of food, the Plan placed stress on agriculture, irrigation, power, and transport with the aim of averting food shortages while creating the base for more rapid industrial advance in the future. The Second and the Third Plans laid emphasis on industrial development.

➢ Role of the State

An important feature of the early Plans was the primacy accorded to the role of the State in development. This was considered necessary because India was facing basic problems of deficiency of capital and low level of savings. It was recognized that the State would be in a better position to mobilize resources, raise the level of domestic savings, put it to more productive use, and prevent concentration of wealth.

- **Socialist Pattern of Society:** In 1954, Parliament had adopted evolving a 'Socialist pattern of society' as the broad objective of economic development. And in 1955, at the Madras session of the Indian National Congress, a resolution was passed for attaining the goal of 'Socialist pattern of society'. This further reinforced the overarching role of the State in development.

  In such a polity, development not only aims at increasing national income and employment opportunities, but also ensuring equitable and fair distribution of wealth and incomes to bring down inequalities. Although India opted for a '**Mixed Econom**y' with roles for both the public and the private sectors, in the initial stages the private sector was given a relatively minor role.

- **Dominance of the State:** A large number of basic and heavy industries were set up in the public sector during the first three plans with the aim of industrializing and modernising the economy and creating the much needed employment opportunities. It was realized that with the heavy pressure of population on land, and a high degree of under-employment and disguised-unemployment in the agriculture sector, only the industry and services sectors could absorb the ever increasing labour force.

➢ Assessment of Early Plans

Much debate has since taken place among economists and others on as to whether the policies pursued by India in the early phase of planning, viz., the socialist stance adopted with a dominant role assigned to the State and the Public Sector in the development process, and relegation of private enterprise, hampered and slowed down the growth process and failed to realize the full potential of the country.

While India made much progress since the initiation of the planning process in 1951, the achievements fell short of the pressing needs and demands of an ever-increasing population. The population which stood at 361 million in 1951 rose to 439 million by 1961 and 548 million by 1971. Due to improvements in health standards, increasing birth rates, and falling death rates, population was rising at a steady annual rate of 2.1 per cent which partly neutralized the fruits of development.

♦ **An Inward-looking Approach:** The path India took in the early years of building a self-reliant economy, with inward-looking development strategy disassociated from global markets, has also been questioned by economists. India adopted an 'Import-substitution' policy instead of an 'Export-promotion' strategy, one which kept the Indian economy closed to external forces and influences. Lack of exposure to latest technologies also held back Indian industry.

India's growth story in 1960's and 1970's has been compared with the impressive growth registered during the same period by the South-east and East Asian economies. Emphasis placed by those Asian economies on literacy and education helped them to improve the productivity of the workforce and make quality products at competitive rates and capture world markets. While these countries too had a policy of state intervention to direct the course of the economy and protect larger social good, they encouraged the private sector to flourish and play a positive role in the development process.

- **Growth vs Poverty alleviation:** Some have argued that the early Plans neglected investment in areas more critical to the economy such as education and public health. The adverse impact of all this has been felt mostly by the poorer and lower strata of society. The poor cannot afford to send children to private institutions which are better run and better equipped, and have to depend on Government-run schools which are found wanting in many respects.
- **Neglect of School Education:** Another criticism of India's early planning is that while India did place considerable emphasis on higher education with its string of Universities, IIT's, IIM's, etc., the neglect of education at primary and secondary levels in the initial years has inhibited her developmental efforts. A strong literate and educated population with sufficient skills is considered to be an important prerequisite for development.

  The neglect of education at school level continued to be an issue for many years to come with lack of trained teachers affecting the quality of teaching, absence of teachers in schools, lack of infrastructure (labs, libraries, toilets, etc.), high drop-out of students at various stages, all of which compounded the problem.
- **Governance issues**: Considering the gross inequalities and mass poverty that prevailed when India gained independence, assigning a major role to the State, with a view to establish an egalitarian society, appeared quite justified and inevitable. But as things turned out, the system became highly centralized and interventionist with rigid bureaucratic control.

  The rigid policies of industrial licensing and state control, followed for over three decades – infamously dubbed as the "license-permit raj" –created vested interests, bred corruption and inefficiency in administration and stifled industrial growth. Private enterprise, which could have played a dynamic and complementary role, was virtually relegated to the background and not allowed to play its legitimate role.

  Further as time passed, there was a steady decline in the authority of the Central Government, the rise of regionalism and parochialism and friction between the Centre and the States leading to conflicting agendas. Deterioration and corruption in public services resulted in delays and cost overruns in projects. There was perceptible fall in the delivery standards of developmental and welfare schemes which impacted mostly the poor and the deprived sections of society. These deficiencies became more pronounced with each passing decade and the nation has had to pay a heavy price as evidenced by the persistence of poverty and deprivation amongst a still large segment of the population.

➢ **Conclusion**

It may be stated that within the various financial and other constraints, the nation made modest but insufficient progress in the first two decades of planned development. A major breakthrough came about in the 1970s and 1980s in the agriculture sector through the Green Revolution which was a significant achievement and helped India to become not only self-sufficient in food but also an exporter of food.

Though there were many dissenting voices against the socialist pattern adopted and the overarching role assigned to the State in the initial years, India continued on this path for nearly four decades. It was only when the nation faced a grave economic crisis in the early 1990s that she introduced major economic reforms, unshackled the economy and unleashed the power of private enterprise. These measures set her on a path of higher growth trajectory. **(For more on this, see also Question 2 below)**

2. Discuss the basic features of the Second Five Year Plan (1956-61) of India. Some of the policies adopted in the Plan came in for criticism. Examine the policies adopted and see how far the criticism is justified.

Ans. The primary objective of the early plans was to achieve growth with equity and social justice. The First Five-Year Plan (1951-56), drawn up when the nation was burdened with problems arising out of the Second World War and the Partition, was constrained by lack of financial resources. It aimed to pull India out of the vicious cycle of poverty into which it had lapsed under two centuries of colonial rule. The First Plan placed stress on agriculture, irrigation, power and transport with the aim of creating the base for more rapid economic and industrial advance. The First Plan thus laid the ground for more ambitious plans in future.

➢ **Stress on Industrialisation**

One of the greatest challenges before the Government on attaining freedom in 1947 was to provide a strong base in infrastructure and capital goods for economic and industrial development. The government, under the leadership of Prime Minister Jawaharlal Nehru, realized that India should develop a large manufacturing base, create employment opportunities and ensure the availability of adequate technically qualified personnel for sustained economic growth. This thinking provided the backdrop while preparing the Second Plan.

➢ **Second Five-Year Plan (1956–61): the Mahalanobis Model**

The Second Plan was conceptualized by Prof. P.C. Mahalanobis, a renowned statistician, and prepared, after wide consultations, by a group of planners under his guidance. The thrust of the strategy in this Plan was rapid industrialisation and sustaining an accelerated rate of growth in the long-term.

Mahanalobis presented a two-sector model in which the economy was divided into a basic capital goods sector, the K-sector, and a consumer goods sector, the C-sector. He also presented a four-sector model in which besides the capital sector, the C-sector was divided into three different sectors.

- **Rationale of Mahalanobis model:** The model adopted by Mahalanobis focussed on rapid development of the Capital-goods sector and enhancing the output of Consumption-goods sector at a subsequent stage. Current demand for consumption goods was to be met by utilizing labour-intensive means of production.

  The potential for employment in the medium term was to be balanced with the long-term objectives by encouraging small and village industries which are labour-intensive to produce mass consumption goods.

- **Role for the State:** It may be noted that while reiterating the idea of establishing a 'Socialist pattern of society', the Industrial Policy Resolution of 1956 had assigned an important role for the State to develop industries of basic and strategic nature in the public sector. Many key industries like steel, fertilizers, heavy engineering, chemicals, and machine building were set up to energize and modernize the economy. These large-scale industries were set up in the public sector as the private sector would not have ventured to invest in these areas which required heavy investment and had rather long gestation period.

  While the First Plan was about making a beginning and laying the foundation, the Second Plan sought to bring about structural transformation in the economy.

- **Plan outlay:** The total outlay envisaged in the Public sector under the Second Plan was ₹4,800 crore. Of this, about ₹3,800 crore represented investment, i.e. expenditure on building productive assets, and ₹1,000 crore for current expenditure for development. Besides, the investment in the private sector was estimated at ₹2400 crore.

  With a total investment of ₹7,200 crore, the Second Plan was ambitious and aimed to develop basic and capital goods industries which would provide a strong base for building a self-reliant economy.

The distribution of Public sector outlay under the first two Plans, by major heads of development, was as under:

Table 13.1: Plan provisions: First and Second Plans

Sector	First Plan (1951-56)		Second Plan (1956-61)	
	Outlay (₹ crore)	Per cent of total outlay	Outlay (₹ crore)	Per cent of total outlay
Agriculture & Community Development	357	15.1	568	11.8
Irrigation and Power	661	28.1	913	19.0
Industry and Mining	179	7.6	890	18.5
Transport & Communications	557	23.6	1,385	28.9
Social Services	533	22.6	945	
Miscellaneous	69	3.0	99	2.1
Total outlay	2,356	100.0	4,800	100.0

Source: Second Five Year Plan, Planning Commission

♦ **Shift in priorities:** The allocations under major heads of development show that there was a marked shift in priorities as between the First and the Second plan. Industries and mining claim about 19 per cent of the total public sector outlay in the Second plan as compared to 8 per cent in the First plan. In absolute terms, the increase of ₹711 crore in outlay on industries and mining in the Second Plan works out to nearly 400 per cent.

The share of Agriculture and Community Development which was 15 per cent in the First Plan came down to about 12 per cent though in absolute terms, the allocation increased from ₹357 crore in First Plan to ₹568 crore in the Second Plan. Further, the allocation for irrigation and power also increased from ₹661 crore to ₹913 crore in the Second Plan.

➤ **Criticism of the Second Plan**

The Second Plan came in for criticism and there were divergent views put forth by prominent economists from the academia and within the government even during the preparation of the Plan document as detailed below.

- **Change in priorities:** The Plan's over-emphasis on heavy industries to the relative neglect of agriculture was faulted. In fact, food shortages became a major problem and this forced India to depend on the US for import of food under the US government's PL 480 programme. Food shortages continued to be an issue until the Green Revolution turned the tide in 1970's.

- **Neglect of Social sector:** It was alleged that social sector which include domains like education and health did not receive adequate attention in the early Plans. The neglect of education at school level led to many problems such as lack of trained teachers, poor quality of teaching and standards in education, lack of infrastructure such as labs, libraries, toilets, etc. in schools and high drop-out of students at various stages. So also, public health facilities both in urban and rural areas have been very poor due to lack of adequate investment in them.

  Overburdened by the burgeoning population, both educational and health facilities suffered neglect and its impact has been mostly on the poorer sections who could not access private facilities which were more expensive and beyond their reach. These issues perpetuated poverty and widened the gulf between the 'haves' and the 'have-nots' in society.

- **Foreign exchange crisis:** A dissent note was submitted by B.R. Shenoy, a noted economist, who opposed the size of the Plan and resort to deficit financing as a means of raising resources, both of which had the potential to stoke inflation. In fact, the Plan faced serious foreign exchange crisis in 1956-58 by when India had exhausted the Sterling balances accumulated during Second World War.

  A policy of liberalization of imports and heavy import requirements of the Second Plan led to the exchange crisis. This necessitated the imposition of exchange controls which became endemic and developed vested interests.

- **Public versus Private sector:** The socialist policy of the government placed the State at 'commanding heights' of the economy and assigned a dominant role to the public sector. Over time, this stifled private enterprise. There were strident voices forgiving greater role to the private sector and market forces instead of leaving all decisions to bureaucracy. As it turned out, the lop-sided approach of the government led to excessive state intervention leading to red-tapism and spawning the notorious 'licence-permit-raj' which bred widespread corruption and stifled industrial development for over three decades. In the process, India lost precious time in opening up the economy and hastening the process of development.

- **Other issues:** It was argued by some that issues like inflation, availability of resources, and unemployment did not receive adequate attention in the Plan. The size of the Plan necessitating resort to deficit financing which was inflationary in nature was also criticized.

➢ **Vakil-Brahmananda Model:** A major criticism of the Plan came from two economists from the Bombay school – Professors C.N. Vakil and P.R. Brahmananda. They argued against all-out expansion of heavy industry and laid greater stress on agriculture and employment.

According to them, as the economy had surplus, under-employed labour in agriculture, and priority should be given to transfer such labour to more productive work in rural infrastructural schemes and small agro-industrial enterprises with focus on producing wage goods, i.e., food and industrial consumer goods. In the industrial sector, the need was to manufacture consumer goods both for domestic consumption and for exports. They argued against all-out expansion of heavy goods industry. This model, however, was not accepted. **(For more on Vakil-Brahmananda model, see Question 3 in this chapter).**

➢ **Counter arguments**

While there is merit in some of the critical views on policies adopted in the Second Plan, there is need to take into account the conditions prevailing then to arrive at a balanced conclusion.

♦ **Plan allocations**

Though percentage-wise, the allocations for agriculture and irrigation in the Second Plan were less than in the First Plan, in absolute terms it had increased as pointed out earlier (see "Shift in priorities" after Table 13.1 above). The increased emphasis on industry and mining in the Second Plan was a considered choice to promote large-scale basic industries to jump-start the economy which had suffered much neglect during the Colonial period.

It is pertinent to note that India, being endowed with vital mineral resources such as iron ore, coal, lignite, bauxite, manganese, etc., utilizing these to make India industrially self-reliant to a large extent was an imperative necessity. Economic strength and a degree of self-reliance was a *sine qua non* for a large country like India, then in the 1950s as it is now, to play its rightful role on the world stage. Thus, the approach adopted in those years made not only economic sense but had geopolitical implications.

The allocations made for various sectors need to be considered keeping in view the fact that the economy was then sorely constrained by lack of financial resources required to accomplish the mammoth tasks on hand.

➢ **Conclusion**

The Second Plan document had observed that "the acceptance of the goal of a socialist pattern of society reflects itself not only in the relative proportions of investment proposed in the public and private sectors but also in the approaches to institutional change both in the rural and in the urban sector. The fulfilment of the tasks outlined in the plan requires coordinated effort in both the public and private sectors, but the role of the public sector, as mentioned earlier, is the crucial one."

India could have provided more space to the private sector in the development of industries after the first three Plans (1951-66) by when the country had built a robust industrial base with many basic and heavy industries. But this realization was to come much later, after nearly two decades, despite the fact that planners and policy makers professed to adopt the policy of a "Mixed economy" in the early plan period with role for both the public and the private sectors.

The importance of the private sector has been highlighted in the Eleventh Plan (2007-12) document wherein it stated: "The private sector, which includes farming, micro, small and medium enterprises (MSMEs), and the larger private corporate sector, accounts for over 77% of the total investment in the economy and an even larger share in employment and output. Expansion in this sector will have to play a critical role in achieving the objective of faster and more inclusive growth."

3. Explain the salient features of the Wage-Goods model of development proposed by C.N. Vakil and P.R. Brahmananda. Do you think the wage-goods model would have been more appropriate for post-independence strategy of development? Justify your answer.

Ans. To appreciate the context in which Professors C.N. Vakil and P.R. Brahmananda of the Bombay School of Economics advocated the Wage-goods model of development, it is necessary to have a brief look at the first two Five Year Plans covering the period 1951-61.

- **First Plan (1951-56):** When India gained Independence in 1947, her socio-economic condition was dismal. The Second World War (1939-45), a painful partition of the country resulting in large influx of refugees and acute shortage of food and famines accentuated the problems.

  It was against this background that the First Five Year Plan was launched. The First Plan focussed primarily on revitalising the agriculture sector and expanding irrigation facility to boost food production and tackle the pressing problem of food shortage. Attention was also paid to set right the skewed land distribution and ownership, a legacy from the Colonial era, through land reform measures to incentivise farmers in the efforts to increase output.

  The Plan led to increase in foodgrains production from 50.83 million (mn.) tons in 1950-51 to 65.8 mn tons in 1955-56. Total irrigated area also rose from 51.5 mn acres to 57.76 mn. acres by 1956.

- **Second Plan (1956-61):** The Second Plan was conceptualized by Prof. P.C. Mahalanobis, a renowned statistician, and prepared, after wide consultations, by a group of planners under his guidance. The thrust of the strategy in this Plan was rapid industrialisation and sustaining an accelerated rate of growth in the long-term.

  Mahalananobis presented a two-sector and four-sector model focussing on rapid development of the Capital-goods sector and enhancing the output of consumption-goods sector at a subsequent stage. Current demand for consumption goods was to be met by utilizing labour-intensive means of production. in the medium term was to be promoted by encouraging small and village industries which are labour-intensive. These industries would produce wage-goods, which are mass consumption goods such as food, clothing, etc. demand for which would go up with the expansion of large industries and the tertiary sector under the Plan.

- **Criticism of the Second Plan**

The Second Plan was not without its critics and there were many divergent views put forth by prominent economists from the academia and within the government. It was argued by some that issues like inflation, availability of resources, and unemployment did not receive adequate attention in the Plan. The Plan's neglect of agriculture became a major problem leading to food shortages till the Green Revolution turned the tide in 1970's.

The Plan also faced serious foreign exchange crisis in 1956–58 when India had also exhausted the Sterling balances accumulated during Second World War. A policy of liberalization of imports and heavy import requirements of the Second Plan led to the exchange crisis. This necessitated the imposition of exchange controls which became endemic and stifled economic growth.

- **Vakil-Brahmananda Model**

It was against this background when the Second Plan was under preparation that Professors C.N. Vakil and P.R. Brahmananda came out with an alternate model of development. They had already published in 1952 a work "*Planning for a Shortage Economy: The Indian Experiment*". And in 1956, they came out with the alternate model in their book, "*Planning for an Expanding Economy: Accumulation, Employment and Technical Progress in Underdeveloped Countries*".

They argued against all-out expansion of heavy industry envisaged in the Mahalanobis model and batted for only industries needed for agriculture and making mass consumption goods or wage goods. They laid greater stress on agriculture and expanding the avenues of employment.

They held the view that with undue emphasis placed on heavy industries, agriculture and production of essential wage goods would suffer and it would also not help to promote employment to the extent required.

As the consumption levels were low, it would result in under-nourishment of labour and affect productivity. They urged the need to mechanize agriculture and augment food output by providing better implements and tools which consumer goods industries would produce.

The Indian economy was characterized by surplus labour and disguised unemployment in agriculture. According to Vakil and Brahmananda, the task was to transfer the disguised unemployed to more productive work in rural infrastructural schemes and small agro-industrial enterprises with focus on wage goods such as food and other consumer goods such as clothing.

In the industrial sector, the need was for manufacture of consumer goods both for domestic consumption and for exports. More production of consumer goods would have resulted in more employment and exports which would pay for import of capital goods needed by the consumer goods industries. Their model would have meant giving lower priority for heavy capital goods industry.

- **Deficiencies of Vakil-Brahmananda model**

But the Vakil-Brahmananda model was also somewhat flawed as neglecting capital goods sector at that stage of development would have held back India, which was already industrially weak and way behind other major countries, after having suffered centuries of neglect and deindustrialization during the Colonial era.

- **Case for industrial development:** For an economy like India with a large domestic market, abundant natural and mineral resources, and vast reserves of unskilled and skilled manpower, the building up of a strong and diversified capital-goods base was imperative even during the early stages of planning. Only with a strong industrial base could India hope to develop, fast enough, various other sectors like transport, communications, housing and construction which were vital both for economic growth and boosting employment.

- **Village and Small industries:** And it is not that the Second Plan did not recognize the importance of village and small industries. The Second Plan document observed thus highlighting the role of this sector:

  "Village and small industries in their different aspects are an integral and continuing element both in the economic structure and in the scheme of national planning. The primary object of developing small industries in rural areas is to extend work opportunities, raise incomes and standard of living and to bring about a more balanced and integrated rural economy.......

  "Village industries have a central place in rural development programmes. Diminishing opportunities for gainful employment account to some extent for the reduction in the standard of life of. some sections of the rural population. ....Development outside the rural sector has not been rapid enough to arrest the increasing pressure of population on the land. The development of village industries should, therefore, be as much a matter of State action as the increase of agricultural production. Indeed, one cannot be separated from the other, for, increase in agricultural production presupposes fuller utilisation of the available manpower and release of surplus workers for other occupations".

- **Plan allocations:** As for the allocations made, while expenditure on village and small industries in the First Plan amounted to ₹31.2 crore, the allocation in the Second Plan was ₹200 crore. Of this, the share of Centre was ₹25 crore and that of the States ₹175 crore. Thus, the bulk of the schemes were to be implemented by the State Governments. The total allocation for industry and mining in the Second Plan was ₹890 crore.

It may also be stated that the government appointed a Committee headed by D.G. Karve, a well-known economist, to study the issues connected with the implementation of programmes for "Village and Small Industries" during the Second Plan.The Committee made several recommendations for revitalizing the small industries sector including constantly upgrading the skills of workers and improving production techniques to avert technological unemployment and obsolescence, and for strengthening the decentralized nature of the sector. These were given effect to by the government in course of time.

- **Agriculture-Industry linkage:** It is also important to recognize the close linkage between industry and agriculture. Apart from the need for agro-based industries which support farm products like cotton, rubber, dairy products, etc., unless industrial development takes place on a substantial scale and incomes go up, the demand for foodgrains and other farm products – vegetables, fruits, spices, etc. – will remain sluggish which will impact the incomes of farmers themselves.

➢ **Conclusion**

The industrialization of India in the early stages helped India to modernize and energize the economy which was in a state of stupor and stagnation after centuries of colonial rule. It laid the foundations for expanding industrial growth in later years and developing scientific and technical skills of India's vast labour force. This may not have been possible if India had adopted a myopic view and chosen to delay building large, modern industries.

India's lapse was the delay in opening up the economy and following an import-substitution policy instead of striving for export promotion strategy. Due to this, India could not exploit the full potential from industrialization as the East Asian countries could achieve in 1970s and China since early 1980s. India introduced economic reforms and liberalisation only by early 1990s which set her on a high growth trajectory.

4. During post-independence era, India assigned the role of 'Commanding Heights' to the public sector undertakings. Was this policy right and should it be continued? Give reasons for your answer.

Ans. To appreciate the mode and path of industrialisation India adopted after independence and the implications it had for decades to come, it is necessary to have a brief look at the state of industries at the time of, and preceding, independence in 1947.

➢ **Colonial era**

After having been under the British rule for over 200 years and having suffered utter neglect in regard to industrial development, India, on attainment of freedom, could not brook any delay in embarking on industrialization. At the time of independence,

India virtually had no basic capital goods industries and could boast of only few steel and textile mills, apart from some cement plants and consumer goods industries. (See **Box 13.1**)

> **Box 13.1: Deindustrialization of India**
>
> "The relative backwardness of industrial development in India may be judged from the fact that in 1948-49 factory establishments accounted for only 6.6 per cent of total national income. The total labour force engaged in such establishments is about 2.4 million or 1.8 per cent of the working population in the country. While in the aggregate India's industrial output may look massive, per head of population it is very much lower than the industrial output in advanced countries..............
>
> "Prior to independence, there were virtually no capital goods industries and almost all the industries that came up were in the consumer goods sector. Without basic and capital goods sector, India could not have industrialized in any significant manner. No wonder that in 1950, India had to meet 90 per cent of its requirements of machinery and machine tools through imports." (First Five-Year Plan, Planning Commission, Govt. of India).

- **National Planning Committee:** Even prior to independence, India had planned and initiated steps for developing industries. As early as 1938, Indian National Congress had appointed a 'National Planning Committee' headed by Pandit Nehru to explore the path India should take for economic and social development once she attained independence. The Committee explored several aspects of planned economic development and social transformation to be initiated and brought out its views in a '*Handbook of National Committee*'.
- **The Bombay Plan:** It is also pertinent to note, in this context, that during the Second War (1939-45) period, prominent industrialists including Sir Purushothamdas Thakurdas, J.R.D. Tata, G.D. Birla, and others studied the problems confronting the nation and came out with a detailed report titled '***A Plan for Economic Development of India***' which came to be known as the '***Bombay Plan***'. Their report stressed the importance of developing basic industries, ***enlarging the role of the State as a facilitator and regulator***, and taking steps to reduce inequalities in society. Thus, even prominent industrialists had recognized that the Public Sector would have to shoulder greater responsibility in the process of industrialisation.
- **Industrial Policy, 1945:** The Statement of Industrial Policy issued in 1945 had stressed the need to set up basic and heavy industries such as iron and steel, heavy engineering, machine tools, and chemical industries. The idea of industrial licensing and establishing key industries under government control found mention in the statement.

➢ **Post-independence**

- **Industrial Policy, 1948:** After independence, further thrust was given when the Industrial Policy Resolution was issued in 1948 followed by the passing of the Industrial (Development and Regulation) Act of 1951. The 1948 Resolution emphasized the responsibility of Government in promoting, assisting, and regulating the development of industry in the national interest and it envisaged an increasingly active role for the public sector. It stressed the need for continuous increase in production and its equitable distribution and laid down a certain demarcation of fields for the public and private sectors in the industrial sphere.

  The broad-based industrialization which was initiated in the Second Plan was carried forward in subsequent Plans. While the First Plan was about making a beginning and laying the foundation, the Second Plan sought to bring about structural transformation in the economy.

- **Primary role for the State:** An important feature of the early Plans was the primacy accorded to the role of the State in development. This was considered necessary then because soon after independence, India was facing basic problems – deficiency of capital and low level of savings. It was recognized that the State would be in a better position to mobilise resources, raise the level of domestic savings, put it to more productive use and prevent concentration of wealth.

- **Socialist Pattern of Society:** In 1954, even as the First Plan was in progress, Parliament had adopted evolving a '**Socialist pattern of society**' as the broad objective of economic development. And in 1955, at the Madras session of the Indian National Congress, a resolution was passed for attaining the goal of 'Socialist pattern of society'.

  This further reinforced the overarching role of the State in development. In such a policy, development not only aims at increasing national income and employment opportunities, but also ensuring equitable and fair distribution of wealth and incomes to bring down inequalities. Although India opted for a 'Mixed Economy' with roles for both the public and the private sectors, in the initial stages the private sector was given a relatively minor role. It was against this background that the Second Plan was framed and implemented.

- **Dominance of Public Sector:** The Industrial Policy Resolution of 1956 reiterated the idea of establishing a 'Socialist pattern of society' and assigned an important role for the State to develop industries of basic and strategic nature in the public sector. Many key industries like iron and steel, fertilizers, heavy engineering and heavy electricals, chemicals, and machine building, locomotive, rail coach, aircraft and ship building, etc. were set up to invigorate and modernize the economy. (See **Box 13.2 at the end of this question).**

  These large-scale industries were set up in the Public Sector as private sector would not have ventured to invest in these areas as they required heavy investment and had rather long gestation period.

  Many more such units were set up in Public Sector in later years giving further prominence to the public sector.

It will also be seen that the government had made efforts to locate the industries not only in proximity to where raw materials were available but to ensure dispersal of plants in different locations to achieve balanced development of different regions.

The broad-based industrialization which was initiated in the Second Plan was carried forward in subsequent Plans. While the First Plan was about making a beginning and laying the foundation, the Second Plan sought to bring about structural transformation in the economy.

➢ **Dissenting Voices**

Even as India set herself firmly on path of Socialist mode of development, there was a chorus of dissenting voices from a section of the intelligentsia, political leaders and economists. They spoke vociferously against the socialist stance of the government and the policy which placed the State at 'commanding heights' of the economy and the dominant role assigned to the public sector thereby denying the private sector its due place in the scheme of things. They were for effecting economic reforms and for relying on market forces instead of leaving all decisions to bureaucracy. But the government paid no heed to these views and successive administrations continued on the socialist path.

♦ **Rationale of the policy:** The policy of assigning a major role to the State was considered imperative to establish an egalitarian society and was justified in view of the gross inequalities and mass poverty that prevailed when India gained independence. The prevailing view was that giving a larger role to the private sector would lead to concentration of wealth and resources in private hands. Also, as stated earlier, the private sector was in no position to make the huge investments required for the heavy industries set up in the early period.

♦ **Aftermath of the policy:** The policy led to excessive state intervention in various spheres leading to red-tapism and spawning the notorious 'licence-permit-raj' which bred widespread corruption and stifled industrial development for decades. Besides, as time passed, there was a decline in the authority of the Central Government, rise of regionalism and friction between the Centre and the States leading to conflicting agendas, deterioration and corruption in public services resulting in delays and cost overruns in projects.

The system became highly centralized and interventionist with rigid bureaucratic control, and for nearly the next two decades, free and private enterprise, which could have side-by-side played a dynamic and complementary role, was virtually relegated to the background and not allowed to play its legitimate role.

➢ **The shift in policy**

♦ **Public sector versus Private sector:** The share of the public sector continued to increase from the First Plan (1951-56) till the Fifth Plan (1974-79). There after, the gap was steadily bridged and from the Eighth Plan (1992-97), which is the post-1991 reforms period, investment in the private sector surpassed that in the public sector. **(See Tables 13.2 (a) and 13.2 (b) at the end of this question).**

This significance of this change in the policy and the importance of the role of private sector has been acknowledged by the Planning Commission in the

Eleventh Plan (2007-12) document when it observed thus, wherein it also cautioned against the trend of fall in public sector investment:

"An important structural change in the investment behaviour of the economy in the recent past is the change in relative shares of public and private investment........ Private sector investment continued to be buoyant throughout the Tenth Plan period so the share of public investment in total investment in the Tenth Plan fell to 22%.

"The rapid increase in private sector investment in the aggregate investment is in large part a reflection of the impact of the reforms initiated in the 1990s, which reduced restrictions on private investment and created a more favourable investment climate....... However, the declining trend in public investment as a percentage of GDP is a matter of concern. It reflects inadequate public investment in the Ninth Plan period in many critical areas such as agriculture and infrastructure. The reversal of the declining trend of public investment as a percentage of GDP in the Tenth Plan is a welcome development which needs to be continued in the Eleventh Plan.................

"The private sector, which includes farming, micro, small and medium enterprises (MSMEs), and the larger private corporate sector, accounts for over 77% of the total investment in the economy and an even larger share in employment and output. Expansion in this sector will have to play a critical role in achieving the objective of faster and more inclusive growth. The MSMEs, in particular, have a vital role to play in making the growth regionally balanced, and in generating widely dispersed off-farm employment, some of it in rural areas." (Eleventh Plan (2007-12), Vol I, Planning Commission).

- **Disinvestment of PSUs**

Public Sector Enterprises (PSEs) have played a notable role and made significant contribution to the economic development of the country. The large basic and heavy industries set up in the public sector have helped to create a vast and diversified industrial base, create a strong technical workforce, and save valuable foreign exchange.

But in quite a few cases, PSUs have incurred losses which have exceeded their net worth. Over the years, the government has been examining the viability of such enterprises and carried out disinvestment and privatization of selected PSE's.

The government has since come out with a "policy of strategic disinvestment pf public sector enterprises". As announced in the Union Budget for FY 2021-22, "the Government has approved the said policy. The policy provides a clear roadmap for disinvestment in all non-strategic sectors. We have kept four areas that are strategic where bare minimum CPSEs will be maintained and rest privatized. In the remaining sectors all CPSEs will be privatized." (Para 86 of Union Budget speech of Finance Minister delivered on February 1, 2021)

"To similarly incentivize States to take to disinvestment of their Public Sector Companies, we will work out an incentive package of Central Funds for States." (Para 88 of Union Budget speech of Finance Minister delivered on February 1, 2021

➤ Conclusion

It is thus evident that both the public and the private sector have a crucial role to play in the economy to ensure rapid growth and generate the much needed employment. The State alone cannot shoulder the burden of ensuring growth, and the two sectors are to be considered as complementary to each other. The delay of nearly two decades in enabling the private sector to play its legitimate part has cost the nation precious time in fast tracking economic growth.

The government has to be more of a facilitator in creating proper climate for investment and ensure that the growth is inclusive and equitable to all sections of society.

Box 13.2: Public Sector Undertakings (set up between 1947 and 1966)
(Years in which they were set up are shown in bracket).

Unit	Location	State
Hindustan Aircraft Limited (taken over by Govt. of India (in 1947), became Hindustan Aeronautics Limited (1964)	Bengaluru	Karnataka
Indian Telephone Industries (1948)	Bengaluru	Karnataka
Locomotives Factory (1950).	Chittaranjan in Asansol	West Bengal
Sindri Fertlizers (1951)	Sindri (near Dhanbad)	Jharkhand
Hindustan Cables (1952)	Rupnarayanpur	West Bengal
Hindustan Machine Tools (1953-62: 3 units in Bengaluru)	Bengaluru	Karnataka
Bharat Electronics Limited (1954)	Bengaluru	Karnataka
Integral Coach Factory (1955)	Perambur (near Chennai)	Tamil Nadu
Steel Plants (4 units)	Bhilai (1955)	Chattisgarh
Rourkela (1955)	Odisha	
Durgapur (1959)	West Bengal	
Bokaro (1964)	Jharkhand	
National Mineral Devt. Corpn. (1958)	Hyderabad	Telengana
Hindustan Photofilms (1960)	Ootacamund (Nilgris)	Tamil Nadu
Hindustan Shipyard (nationalised 1961)	Visakhapatnam	Andhra Pradesh
Heavy Engineering (1958)	Ranchi	Jharkhand
Nangal Fertilizers (1961)	Nangal	Punjab
Bharat Heavy Electricals	Bhopal	Madhya Pradesh
(3 plants in1964)	Tiruchirapalli	Tamil Nadu
	Hyderabad	Telengana
Bharat Earth Movers (1964)	Bengaluru	Karnataka
Hindustan Machine Tools (1965)	Kalamassery (near Kochi)	Kerala

Table 13.2 (a): Five Year Plan outlays: Public and Private sectors

	Public sector outlay	Private sector outlay (Figures in ₹ crore)	Total outlay
First Plan (1951-56)	1960	1800	3760
Second Plan (1956-61)	4670	3100	7770
Third Plan (1961-66)	6300	4100	10400
Fourth Plan (1969-74)	15902	8980	24882
Fifth Plan (1974-79)	37250	16160	53410
Sixth Plan (1980-85)	97500	74710	172210
Seventh Plan (1985-90)	218730	168150	386880
Eighth Plan (1992-97)	434100	437000	871000
Ninth Plan ((1997-2002)	814000	1357000	2171000

Source: Indian Public Finance Statistics, Dept. of Economic Affairs, Ministry of Finance and Plan documents, Planning Commission.

TABLE 13.2 (b): Total and Public and Private Investment in the 8th to 11th Five Year Plans

	Total Investment	Private Investment	Public Investment
	(As percentages of GDP at market price)		
Eighth Plan (1992-97)	24.4	15.9	8.5
Ninth Plan (1997-2002)	24.3	17.3	7.0
Tenth Plan (2002–07)	32.1	25.1	7.1
Eleventh Plan (2007-12)	36.7	28.7	8.0

Note: The figures are percentages of GDP at market price.

Source: Eleventh Plan (2007-12), Vol. I, Planning Commission

5. India has a sizeable section of migrant labour force, both within the country and outside. Examine the factors behind this phenomenon and the problems faced by migrant labour. Suggest remedies to overcome their problems.

Ans. Migration has emerged as a central issue in contemporary times. Each year, men and women in large numbers leave their homes and cross district and state borders in search of livelihood and financial security for themselves and their families. While many move after marriage, many others are motivated by desire to seek better work opportunities and earn higher incomes.

India has been witnessing high levels of work-related migration within the country (internal migration) and across the borders (international migration). While the phenomenon has been there since decades, it has accelerated following the spurt in economic growth after the 1980s.

➢ **Migrant worker:** According to Census, a migrant within India is one who is enumerated in census at a place other than his or her place of birth. External migrants are those who go out of India and work and live in a foreign country but remain to be citizens of India.

- **Inter-State migrant worker:** The Code on Social Security, 2020 enacted by the Parliament in September 2020, as part of the labour reforms, defines an "inter-State migrant worker" as a person who is employed in an establishment and
  (i) has been recruited directly by the employer or indirectly through contractor in one State for employment in an establishment in another State, or
  (ii) has come on his own from one State and obtained employment in an establishment of another State (called destination State), and
  (iii) drawing wages not exceeding ₹18,000 per month or a higher amount notified by the Central Government from time to time.

➢ **Internal migration**

To understand the magnitude of the problem, it is necessary to have an idea of the scale of migration taking place within India and from India to other countries. Despite wide divergences and heterogeneity among the peoples in different states in the country, language, social or cultural diversities have not been a barrier in inter-state migration. The same holds good for international migration out of India.

➢ **Level of Internal Migration**

■ **Census estimates**

- According to 2011 Census estimates, during the decade 2001-11, the annual rate of growth of labour migrants nearly doubled compared to the previous decade, increasing from 2.4 per cent in 1991-2001 to 4.5 per cent per annum in 2001-11.
- Successive Censuses have estimated annual average number of migrants to be about 3.3 million.
- **Intra-state migration:** Between 2001 and 2011, there was an increase in the growth rate of migrants moving to places within their own states (intra-state) as compared to those leaving for other states (inter-state).
- **Inter-district migration:** Not only are people moving within states, they are also moving within districts. As per census, the rate of growth of inter-district migrants (within the same state) increased from 30 per cent between the 1991 and 2001 to 58 per cent between 2001 and 2011.

■ **Other estimates**

However, other studies have found that migration within India is at a much higher level than estimated in the Census. Ministry of Finance's *Economic Survey of 2016-17* has confirmed this and observes as follows.

- Annually, inter-state labour mobility averaged 5-6 million people between 2001 and 2011, yielding an inter-state migrant population of about 60 million and inter-district migration as high as 80 million during the decade.
- The first-ever estimates of internal work-related migration using railways' passenger data for the period 2011-2016 indicate an annual average flow of close to 9 million people between the states.
- In 2007-08, the NSSO estimated the size of India's migrant labour to be seven crore which was 29 per cent of the total workforce of the survey year.
- The above estimates are significantly higher than the Census estimates.

➢ **Pattern of Internal migration**

The pattern of movement of people is broadly in line with popular conception, i.e., more people migrating out of less affluent states, while the most affluent states are the largest recipients of migrants. The cost of moving for people is about twice as much as it is for goods.

♦ **Skewed pattern:** India's migration patterns are skewed on more than one count. Uttar Pradesh and Bihar have a disproportionately high number of out-migrants, while migrants constitute more than one-third of the population in metros like Delhi and Mumbai.

♦ **Bihar and UP top in Outward migration:** According to the 2011 Census, 20.9 million people migrated outside the state from the two states. This is 37 per cent of the total number of inter-state migrants according to that enumeration.

♦ **UP has both Outward and Inward migrants:** Paradoxically, Uttar Pradesh has both outward and inward migrants. While people leave UP in search of livelihoods, there are also people who head to UP in search of livelihoods.

♦ **Hindi belt, the main source:** The Hindi belt is the main source of migrants. According to the census, four states of Uttar Pradesh, Bihar, Rajasthan and Madhya Pradesh accounted for 50 per cent of India's total inter-state migrants.

♦ **Major recipient states:** On the other hand, Maharashtra, Delhi, Gujarat, Uttar Pradesh and Haryana are recipient states for 50 per cent of the country's inter-state migrants.

➢ **Factors behind Internal Migration**

- One of the major reasons for migration is the lop-sided industrial development. Paradoxically, it is some of the states in eastern and central India, which are richly endowed with mineral resources and have much potential for industria development, that witness large scale migration. Lack of educated and skilled labour in those states has also been a contributory factor for this. In fact, the Planning Commission had emphasized the need for balanced regional development from as early as 1950s in the Second Plan (1956-61) and even in the Third (1961-66) and Fourth (1969-74) Plans. **(See Box 13.3 at the end of this Question for more on this).**

- In the initial stages of development, when a country transforms itself from an agrarian economy to more an industrialized economy, there will be more migration from rural areas to urban centres. Such movement of people paves the way for the release of "surplus labour" from relatively low-productive agricultural activities (primary sector) to higher productivity sectors, viz., industry (secondary) and service (tertiary) sectors.
- Migration of people for work and education has been a phenomenon that happens with structural transformation of economies.
- A primary reason for migration within a country and across the national borders is livelihood and in search of jobs with better prospects and higher emoluments.
- Marriage and moving with households are also major factors for migration. An important feature is the growing share of female migrants. Until the 2000s, migration was largely a male dominated phenomenon.

➢ **Problems faced by migrants**

It is well known that migrants face a host of problems which are deep-rooted and existing for long. Only that this was exposed, in a stark and visible manner, before the whole nation during the stringent lockdown impose in March-April 2020 due to the widespread Covid-19 pandemic.

- **Housing:** A major issue migrant workers face is proper housing and accommodation. Living away from one's family and mostly living in unsatisfactory and unhygienic conditions, lacking in basic amenities, this has a deep impact on the psyche and productivity of the workers.
- **Lack of access to PDS:** Lack of access to benefits like food under the public distribution system (PDS) at the place of work where they reside (away from home) as their entitlement for this will be where their family resides. This is due to the Family Ration Card being not portable across states.
- **Lack of welfare benefits:** Migrant workers are not covered under the Employees State Insurance (ESI) and Employees Provident Fund (EPF) benefits due to non-fulfilment of criteria on certain minimum number of employees and wages prescribed for extending these benefits.
- **Lack of job security:** Majority of the migrant workers are employed in informal jobs and in the informal sector which does not ensure job security. Due to this, they could be retrenched anytime causing undue hardship to them.

- **Worker safety:** A sizeable section of migrant labour is engaged in construction and other work which are of hazardous nature prone to accidents and they are not covered by medical benefits or insurance.

➢ **Remedial measures**

♦ **Housing:** Solving the housing issue faced by migrant workers should be a priority as the problem got magnified during the Covid-19 pandemic which broke out in March 2020. For lack of proper housing and unable to pay rental following the outbreak, crores of migrant workers had to flee the cities and towns where they worked and return to their home towns and villages. And for lack of proper transport facility due to sudden imposition of total country-wide lockdown as an emergency health measure, these hapless migrants had to trudge hundreds of miles bracing the summer heat with even some fatalities occurring en route.

The Central government has since announced a scheme for building "**Affordable Rental Housing Complexes (ARHCs) for Migrant Workers/ Urban Poor"** which is being pursued by the Ministry of Housing. It aims to ensure ease of living to urban migrants in Industrial Sector as well as in non-formal urban economy to get decent, affordable rental housing close to their workplace. The ARHC scheme will be implemented through two models:

- Utilizing existing Government funded vacant houses to convert into ARHCs through Public Private Partnership or by Public Agencies.
- Construction, Operation and Maintenance of ARHCs by Public/ Private Entities on their own vacant land.

Considering the magnitude of the task involved, this scheme calls for close co-operation between the Central and State governments, Industry bodies and Building and Construction agencies. A medium-term plan has to be drawn up to achieve set targets.

♦ **Welfare provisions:** While the following welfare provisions have been made in the Occupational Safety, Health and Working Conditions Code, 2020, a condition is put that it would apply to establishments in which ten or more inter-State migrant workers are employed. This may leave out many small units where less than ten workers are engaged.

- **ESI and EPF benefits:** Under the above Code, inter-State migrant workers are to be provided the benefits of Employees' State Insurance (ESI), Employees' Provident Fund (EPF), facility of medical check and other benefits which are available to workers in the establishment.
- **Portability of PDS facility:** The new labour code approved has laid down that the concerned Government shall provide the option to inter-State migrant workers to avail the benefits of public distribution system (PDS) either in his native State or the destination State where he is employed. For

this purpose, technology is being developed to have "One Nation one Ration Card" which will to enable migrant workers to access ration under PDS from any Fair Price Shop, either at their native place or their place of work.

- **Travel fare:** The employer will pay every inter-State migrant worker in his establishment an annual lump sum to cover the fare for to-and-fro journey from the place of his employment to his native place.
- **Registration:** The Act provides for registration of inter-state migrant workers on a portal that the Central government and the state governments are required to set up which is a positive step as it will help in data collection, access to, and provision, of welfare benefits, etc.
- **Contract workers:** In the case of contract workers, the welfare provisions in the Safety and Health code apply to establishments with fifty or more contract labour. This condition again may leave out many units where less number of labour is employed.

♦ **Database of workers:** One lacuna observed when Covid-19 pandemic broke out was that there was no proper data of migrant labour working in various cities and towns and the State to which they belonged. This caused much confusion and untold hardship when, following the lockdown imposed overnight in March 2020, several lakhs of migrants desired to go back to their homes.

The government is creating a national database of the unorganized workforce, including migrant labourers, and will seed their profiles with the 12-digit Aadhaar number to provide them social security coverage, the labour ministry had announced in the Parliament. As part of this exercise, the skills of the workers could also be mapped which will help to provide them suitable employment nearer home to the extent feasible.

In this task, the next Census as well as NSS surveys could also be utilized to collect reliable data of both inter-state and intra-state migrant workers.

➢ **Deficiencies in the new laws**

While the new labour laws do address many of the issues faced by the working class, experts point out some deficiencies in them particularly in regard to migrant workers.

■ **No separate law for Migrants:** By subsuming the Inter-State Migrant Workmen Act, 1979 into the Occupational Safety Code 2020, the new Code gloss over certain special needs of migrant labour. Having a separate legislation addressing the complex issues faced by the vulnerable migrant workers would have been ideal.

- **Intra-state migrants:** While Part I of the Code deals with Contract workers, Part II relates to Inter-state migrant workers. Thus, the Code makes no mention of intra-state migrants, i.e., those who migrate *within* a state and so do not cover intra-state migrants.

  However, under the Social Security Code passed by the Parliament, it is laid down that "The State Government shall frame and notify, from time to time, suitable welfare schemes for unorganised workers, including schemes relating to (i) provident fund; (ii) employment injury benefit; (iii) housing; (iv) educational schemes for children; (v) skill upgradation of workers; (vi) funeral assistance; and (vii) old age homes."

  It is to be seen if all States will enact laws to protect the interests of migrants within their borders also, apart from inter-state migrants, with measures such as housing, PDS portability, medical assistance, etc. as per the above provision.

  As per the 2011 Census, out of a total of 45 crore migrants, 39.57 crore people (i.e., 88 per cent) moved only within the state borders while inter-state migrants constituted just 5.43 crore (12 per cent). Hence the importance of intra-state migrants.

- **Threshold limitations:** Certain thresholds of number of workers employed have been prescribed to be covered under the new Codes.
  - ♦ In the case of Contract labour, the establishment in which fifty or more contract labour are employed or were employed on any day of the preceding twelve months.
  - ♦ Under the Code on Social Security 2020 approved by the Parliament, its stated: A "factory" is defined as:
    - Premises where ten or more employees are working and where manufacturing process is carried on using power.
    - Premises where twenty or more employees are working and where manufacturing process is carried without the aid of power.

  Such conditions would mean that a large number of very small units, with lesser number of workers (which form a large percentage), would get excluded from the social security benefits which will be a major setback in achieving the laudable objectives of the labour codes.

> **International migration**

India is a major country for workers migrating across national borders and is also a destination for emigrants from other countries. As per official data, there are over 30 million Indians overseas, with about nine million of the Indian diaspora concentrated in the GCC (Gulf Cooperation Council for the Arab states) region. Over 90 per cent of Indian migrant workers, most of whom are low- and semi-skilled workers; work in the Gulf region and South-East Asia.

Migration has both positive and negative aspects. It helps those migrating to earn better salaries, support families better and improve their lives. In fact, huge remittances from migrants to India has helped the economies of some of the states like Kerala, UP, Tamil Nadu and Andhra Pradesh. But migration throws up various problems also, both for the migrants and families back home in the case of those who go abroad for leaving family behind.

■ **Migrants' issues**

♦ International migrants also face problems similar to what migrants within India confront.

Besides – both white and blue collar migrants – face other problems like culture shock, living and working in a totally alien environment and getting assimilated into, and accepted by, the local society, all of which take time.

♦ While their salaries are usually better than what they earn in their home countries, those who take up less skilled jobs abroad, in particular, face problems pertaining to proper living accommodation, long working hours, job security, etc. despite the standards laid down by ILO.

♦ There have also been many instances of exploitation due to improper and unauthorized job contracts and dubious sponsors, at home and abroad, taking innocent job seekers for a ride. Those who go as domestic help may face various other forms of exploitation if their employers are not compassionate and are unscrupulous.

♦ In the case of white collar migrants who are skilled and take up certain professional jobs at higher levels, they could face some resistance from the local community abroad as they may be depriving the native people of their job prospects. Sometimes this leads to tensions and even racial feelings disturbing social harmony, though such cases may be isolated.

■ **Mandatory checks**

- To prevent exploitation and abuse of migrant workers and protect them, the government has taken various measures over the years. Under the Ministry of External Affairs, there is the Protector General of Emigrants who is responsible for protecting the interest of Indian workers going abroad.
- Besides, the International Labour Organization (ILO) has also laid down various standards on working conditions and humane treatment of migrants, especially the labour class. ILO also works closely with all governments to ensure compliance of the standards.
- From 2016, recruitment of Indian nurses and domestic workers to be done only through authorized state-run recruitment agencies was made mandatory. There are such agencies in Kerala, UP, Andhra Pradesh, Telangana and Tamil Nadu.

- Also, a minimum age criterion of 30 years was prescribed for all women (except nurses) emigrating on ECR (Emigration Check Required) passports to ECR countries, irrespective of the nature of employment.

■ **Reverse trends**

Since the last few years, Indian migrants, particularly semi-skilled and unskilled workers, have lost jobs and have had to return home in large numbers. This has been due to a variety of reasons such as global recession, slowdown in many economies, "localisation" policy by which native workers are given preference in jobs, etc. This has been compounded by the pandemic, Covid-19, which has caused serious health issues placing undue burdens on economies the world over. This has raised the issue of rehabilitating returning migrants for many states.

Box 13.3: Regional imbalance in Development

One of the major reasons for migration is the lack of development in the states from where the exodus of workers takes place in search of jobs. Paradoxically, it is some of the states in eastern and central India, which are richly endowed with mineral resources and have much potential for industrial development, that witness large scale migration. In fact, as early as 1950s, the Planning Commission had observed in the Second Plan (1956-61) document thus:

"This brings us to the question of regional disparities. In any comprehensive plan of development, it is axiomatic that the special needs of the less developed areas should receive due attention. The pattern of investment must be so devised as to lead to balanced regional development..............

"The question was discussed recently by the National Development Council and it has been agreed in principle that within the resources available, every effort must be made to provide for balanced development in different parts of the country. The problem has to be approached in a variety of ways. In the first place, the National Development Council has recommended programmes for setting up decentralised industrial production. Secondly, it has been suggested that in the location of new enterprises, whether public or private, consideration should be given to the need for developing a balanced economy for different parts of the country."

The Commission even recognized that "Some industries have to be located in particular areas in view of the availability of the necessary raw materials or other natural resources." (Second Plan, Chapter 2, Approach to Second Five Year Plan).).

This was emphasized in subsequent Plans too. The Third Plan (1961-66) stated: "......Such a plan should be conceived not merely in broad national terms but should take into account the possibilities of development of resources in different regions of the country so as to spread the benefits of development as widely as possible without slowing down growth itself." (Third Plan, Chapter 2, Long-term Economic Development).

And the Fourth Plan (1969-74) observed: "In terms of regional development, there has been a natural tendency for new enterprises and investments to gravitate towards the already overcrowded metropolitan areas because they are better endowed with economic and social infrastructure. Not enough has been done to restrain this process. While a certain measure of dispersal has been achieved, a much larger effort is necessary to bring about greater dispersal of industrial activity." (Fourth Plan, Chapter 1, Approach and Policy).

Again, the Fourth Plan emphasized: "Second important consideration in industrial planning is the desirability of dispersed industrial development. The requirement of non-farm employment is so large and so widely spread throughout the country that a greater dispersal of industrial development is a matter of necessity." (Fourth Plan, Chapter 14, Industry and Minerals).

6. Discuss the impact which the pandemic, Covid-19, that broke out in 2020, had on the Indian economy and its consequences in the short and medium term. Critically analyse also the steps the government took to tackle them and for the recovery of the economy.

Ans. The pandemic, Covid-19, which broke out in China in early 2020 and spread all over the world has turned out to be a humanitarian crisis, something like which has not been seen in a century. A comparable episode is the Spanish flu which occurred in 1918, affected an estimated 500 million people the world over and took a heavy toll of some 50 million deaths.

Though India has had a history of epidemics of cholera, malaria, etc., they were more localised in nature and could be brought under control in shorter spells. Whereas Covid-19 has infected about 40 million people globally, took a toll of over one million people between February and October 2020 and was still raging. India itself recorded about 7.5 million people infected and with over one lakh deaths due to it. The pandemic not only showed no signs of abatement, but by March-April 2021, it came back with even more virulence and ferocityas a second wave. The incidence of cases multiplied and took even much higher toll of lives than before. A sense of complacency over having contained the first wave of the pandemic, and a lack of adequate preparedness to counter a possible resurgence,led to a situation of shortage of medical supplies, vital oxygen support and inadequate supply of vaccines all of which combined to exacerbatethe position. It caused the already strained health infrastructure and healthcare personnel to be overstretched and overburdened. Even the large-scale flow of medical aid from other countries, though much valuable, could only help in the later stages of countering the effects of the revived pandemic,by when many precious lives were lost.

➢ **Impact on Economy**

Covid-19 has struck a devastating blow to global and Indian economy. As a sudden, stringent and nationwide lockdown had to be imposed in the initial phase to contain its spread and further lockdowns had to be imposed in phases, the impact was severe, both on lives and livelihood of people. No sector was spared and due to virtual cessation of all economic activity, millions of people sustained not only loss of incomes but even their jobs. The surge in the pandemic with a second wave further impacted the economy adversely and was bound to prolong the prospects of economic recovery.

- **Economy on downward trend:** The impact was compounded by the fact that even prior to the outbreak of Covid-19, Indian economy was already on a downward trend since 2015-16 and the annual GDP growth had declined to 4.2 per cent in 2019-20. Due to this, the impact of Covid-19 may be somewhat prolonged and the process of complete revival would also take time.

➢ **Sectoral position**

♦ **Industry and Services:** The industry and services sectors suffered the most. And among them, the segments which were virtually devastated were the self-employed (shops, small businesses, etc.), building and construction, hotels, hospitality and tourism, the entire transport spectrum (road, rail, shipping and air) and MSMEs to name only a few. This apart, all large industrial establishments and factories had to be shut for about five months bringing production processes to a grinding halt.

♦ **Agriculture:** Relatively speaking, rural areas were less impacted, compared to urban areas, and so farm activities could be carried on and India is predicted to have a good harvest during the year 2020-21. In a way, the performance of agriculture being critical to rural demand, this helped to lessen the overall impact of the pandemic on the economy.

➢ **Problems of Migrant labour**

One of the most disastrous outcomes of the pandemic was the untold hardship which the vast numbers of migrant labour had to go through. There are about 50 million "seasonal" migrant workers in India (though the total number of migrants as per Census is much more). The migrant labour, who hail from distant rural areas, is engaged in the construction of buildings, and roads, civic works, factories and in diverse service activities, mostly in large cities and towns.

♦ **Reverse migration:** Deprived of jobs and income and unable to sustain themselves at their places of work when the total lockdown was imposed without notice, hundreds of thousands of migrant workers had to trudge back to their villages on foot covering several hundred miles to get back to their respective villages. When train services resumed, huge crowds of migrant labour gathered at railway stations to travel back to their home. Due to the sheer number of people involved and lack of preparation, the arrangements were chaotic.

- **Temporary relief:** Back in the villages, the Central and State governments had activated the MNREG scheme on a wide scale to provide temporary work and source of income to these distressed labour force. By September, part of these labourers started returning to cities to resume work as economic activity had gradually begun to pick up. However, it will take time for the economy to bounce back to pre-Covid-19 levels and absorb all the displaced labour.

➢ **Loss of Jobs**

Out of the total workforce of about 465 million, over 80 per cent of the workers are in informal employment. And with loss of jobs and an uncertain future, they are at risk of falling into poverty.

There have been varying estimates of jobs lost during the first five months from April when the economy came to a virtual halt. It was a fluid situation since even after opening up, there have been periodic localised lockdowns due to spread of Covid-19 in some parts of the country. This again disrupted supply chains affecting the functioning of industries. About 122 million jobs are reported to have been lost in April, the first month of complete lockdown and nearly half of them were blue collar jobs. In the next few months more jobs were lost.

➢ **Relief measures: their potential and limitations**

Given the dire state in which the economy was when the pandemic broke out, and especially the state of the financial institutions, the policy options available to the government to deal with the economic crisis were limited. Unlike the advanced economies, India did not have the financial heft and social support systems to dole out huge sums in cash to counter the onslaught of the pandemic.

After the Prime Minister announced the broad vision of "Atmanirbhar Bharat" (a Self-reliant India) to be built, the Finance Minister announced a slew of measures ranging from structural reforms and easing of rules to inject more liquidity into the economy. These included support in cash to women and farmers, loans at concessional rates and debt relief to businesses and MSMEs, moratorium on loans and additional funds for rural jobs programme to help displaced migrant workers.

Within the limited fiscal space available, the government and the RBI took steps and provided stimulus to the economy in phases in different ways as mentioned below. (**These measures are detailed in Box 13.4 at the end of this question).**

- **Support in cash and kind:** Free food and income support to workers, farmers and the poor for a limited period estimated to cost ₹32,700 crore, deposit of ₹500 per month for 3 months into over 20 crore women's Jan Dhan accounts which worked out to ₹30,600 crore, ₹1,000 ex-gratia payment for 3 crore poor senior citizens, poor widows, and poor Divyangs, ₹2,000 paid under existing PM-KISAN scheme to 8.7 crore farmers and free LPG gas cylinders for 8 crore poor families for 3 months.

- **Funds for MNREG job scheme:** Increase in allocation for the Mahatma Gandhi National Rural Employment Guarantee Scheme (MNREGS) from ₹61,500 crore to about ₹1.01 trillion to provide work for the migrant labourers who lost their jobs and had returned to the villages. MNREGA wages raised from ₹182 to ₹202 a day which was to benefit 13.62 crore families.
- **Loans and subsidies:** Credit-linked subsidy scheme (CLSS) for the middle-income group which was expected to give a boost of ₹ 70,000 crore to the housing sector, a tranche of ₹3 trillion provided for giving collateral-free loans, backed by government guarantee, for businesses, including MSMEs and collateral free lending increased from ₹10 to ₹20 lakh for Women Self-Help Groups which was to benefit 6.85 crore households.
- **Help for workers:** Other measures included portion of monthly wages to be credited into the PF accounts of wage-earners of certain categories, non-refundable advance from Employee Provident Fund to benefit five crore workers, use of welfare funds for relief to Building and Construction Workers.
- **Steps by RBI:** RBI undertook various steps to ease and enhance liquidity in the economy. These included raising the "Ways and Means advance" limits of States and Overdraft duration, reduction Cash Reserve Ratio (CRR) resulting in liquidity increase of ₹1,37,000 crore, increasing banks' borrowing limits which enabled banking system to avail additional ₹1,37,000 crore, investing bonds, commercial paper, and non-convertible debentures of NBFCs, and MFIs to the tune of ₹1,00,050 crore, special refinance facilities to NABARD, SIDBI and the NHB for a total amount of ₹50,000 crore, three months 'moratorium on payment of instalments and interest on Working Capital
- **Measures for Businesses, MSMEs and Discoms:** Various other measures were taken to help businesses and MSMEs. These included: Collateral-free loans for businesses and MSMEs, liquidity infusion for MSMEs, EPF support for businesses and workers, liquidity facility and Credit Guarantee Scheme for NBFCs and MFIs and liquidity Infusion for DISCOMs.

➢ **Reactions to relief measures**

There have been diverse views and opinions expressed by economists and experts on the measures taken by the Government to provide relief to businesses, workers, farmers, the poor and vulnerable sections and the public at large. The devastation caused to the entire economy was so widespread, and distress caused to the people so severe, that the general expectation was the government would give liberal hand-outs in cash and provide fiscal stimulus to the economy in a substantial way.

While it did provide free food and income support to workers, farmers and the poor, these were for a limited period unless further extended. The purpose behind boosting liquidity in the economy is that people and businesses would borrow more and then spend. With this, consumer demand will be revived, and businesses and the overall economy will benefit. But unlike a fiscal stimulus which puts money in the hands of people, loans will have to be repaid.

A fiscal stimulus is essentially a case where the government gives cash hand-outs, cuts taxes or increases spending to revive the economy. The objective is to put more money and disposable income in the hands of people, so that they can spend it. In the process, consumer demand and economic growth would get a fillip.

The overall reaction to the measures announced was that it fell far too short of the needs to counter the enormous damage sustained by the economy in the aftermath of the pandemic and experts kept urging the government to provide more stimuli to the badly mauled economy. The government, on its part, took a step-by-step approach of announcing different measures intermittently keeping in view also the fiscal position.

- **India's fiscal deficit:** Apart from the fact that the economy was in dire straits even during the pre-Covid period, India's fiscal deficit was one of the limiting factors which stood in the way of the government extending direct cash support on a substantial scale following the pandemic. The combined fiscal deficit of the Centre and the States for 2020- 21 could go up to 14 per cent against the mandated level of 6 per cent. While the banks should not be too shy of lending, they need to be cautious also lest the loans given out do not turn non-performing assets (NPAs).

  India's fiscal stimuli in the form of direct income support to low-income households, migrant workers who lost jobs, farmers, small and medium enterprises, etc. added up to barely 2 per cent of GDP. As against this, the fiscal stimulus provided by Japan was about 21 per cent and that by the US about 13 per cent of GDP and they were contemplating further stimulus measures.

  According to the IMF, advanced economies have provided, on an average, stimulus of 9 per cent of GDP. IMF has also urged India to step up stimulus to limit the damage from the pandemic.

Recovery path

The issue confronting all economies and the global economy, battered by the pandemic, is how to revive and restore them to the pre-Covid levels and how soon this could be accomplished. There are no easy answers to this as it is subject to many imponderables. Experts and international bodies like the World Bank and the IMF are predicting different scenarios. The pace and level of recovery would also vary from country to country.

The pandemic, having thrown out of gear not only the economy, but sectors like health and education, travel and tourism, it could be a long haul before full normalcy is restored.

Remedy for the pandemic: The single most critical factor for restoration of economies is the development and distribution of effective vaccine(s) for cure and prevention of Covid-19. This itself being in different development stages in various countries, there is no certainty about when they would be available. In the meanwhile, various other steps, mentioned below, could be taken to ensure recovery to the extent feasible.

Opening up the economy: Even while exercising caution to prevent the spread of the pandemic, economic activity needs to be stepped to allow various sectors to function in tandem so that supply chains to ensure production are in place. This would allow industries to function near normalcy, increase employment and ensure incomes and consumer demand.

Financial support: For a considerable time, industries, especially the MSMEs, and sectors like construction, infrastructure, travel, hospitality, health and education, all of which have high potential for employment, will need financial support in different forms – tax reliefs, loans on easy terms, interest subvention, subsidies, etc.

Structural reforms: Two major reforms initiated are in regard to agriculture marketing and labour reforms. The former affords farmers greater freedom to market their produce anywhere and are assured of Minimum Support Price (MSP) for the produce. The labour reforms have simplified the labour laws into three labour Codes which incentivises industry and employers while also protecting the interests of employees. The reactions to these reform measures have been mixed but the government has assured that the interests of all concerned sections will be protected as they are implemented. **(For details on Agricultural marketing reforms, see Question 3 in Chapter 8 and on Labour reforms, see Question 5 in Chapter 7).**

Boost to Industry: The pandemic has come in the midst of the raging US – China trade dispute and with US and many other countries blaming China for causing global spread of Covid-19 due to its inaction and alleged cover-up in the early stages of its outbreak. China's dominance in the supply of a host of intermediate products required by a large number of industries in other countries resulted in severe disruption to supply chains, following the outbreak, and this adversely impacted production in other economies. Realizing the pitfalls of excessive dependence on China for various products, many industries have started moving out of China to avert similar disruptions in the supply chain in future.

This has opened opportunities for India to invite large conglomerates to set up production units in India which offers both a large domestic market and skilled manpower. While India has initiated many steps on this and some positive outcome has been seen in the electronics, telecom and defence sectors, she faces severe competition from Vietnam, Thailand, Bangladesh, etc. India will have to provide attractive tax regime and other sops to bring in more industries.

➢ **Conclusion**

While the economy has started showing signs of revival, economists and various specialised bodies have predicted sharp reduction of Indian economy during 2020-21. The gross domestic product (GDP) contracted 23.9 percent in April-June quarter of 2020 that saw a stringent lockdown. The RBI has said that India's GDP growth will be negative, estimated at minus (-) 4.5 percent, in 2020-21.

The World Bank has stated that India's gross domestic product (GDP) is expected to contract by 9.6 per cent in during 2020 - 21 whereas the IMF has predicted growth for the year 2020-21 to be minus 10.3 per cent. India could register 8.8 per cent growth in 2021-22 with concerted efforts and support to various sectors but full recovery to 2019 levels may happen only by 2022.

The fiscal support will have to be more in the form of direct spending and tax relief than just liquidity enhancing measures.

Box 13.4: Relief Packages announced by the Government due to Covid-19

♦ **Pradhan Mantri Garib Kalyan Package (1)**

A ₹20-lakh-crore economic package provided in May 2020 focussed on measures to help migrants and farmers. This included:

- Free ration of wheat or rice and pulses for 3 months for 80 crore poor people.
- ₹500 per month for 3 months for 20 crore women Jan Dhan account holders.
- Free LPG gas cylinders for 8 crore poor families for 3 months.
- ₹1,000 ex-gratia for 3 crore poor senior citizens, poor widows and poor Divyangs.
- Insurance cover of ₹50 lakh per health worker.
- MNREGA wage raised from ₹182 to ₹ 202 a day which was to benefit 13.62 crore families.

♦ **Pradhan Mantri Garib Kalyan Package (2)**

- Front-loaded ₹2,000 paid under existing PM-KISAN to benefit 8.7 crore farmers.
- 24 per cent of monthly wages to be credited into the PF accounts of wage-earners earning below ₹15,000 p.m. in businesses having less than 100 workers for three months.
- Five crore workers registered under Employee Provident Fund (EPF) to

get non-refundable advance of 75 per cent of the amount or three months of the wages, whichever is lower, from their accounts.

- Building and Construction Workers Welfare Fund allowed to be used to provide relief to workers.
- Limit of collateral free lending increased from ₹10 to ₹20 lakh for Women Self-Help Groups supporting 6.85 crore households.
- District Mineral Fund (DMF) to be used for supplementing and augmenting facilities of medical testing, screening etc.

♦ **Other Measures by the Government**

- All the pending income-tax refunds up to ₹5 lakh were issued benefiting around 14 lakh taxpayers. All pending refund and drawback claims under Special Refund and Drawback Disposal Drive issued. These measures amounted to refund of ₹18,000 crore.
- Sanctioned ₹15,000 crore for Emergency Health Response Package
- At the instance of the government, RBI raised the Ways and Means advance limits of States by 60 per cent and enhanced the Overdraft duration limits.
- Due dates for filing income tax and GST returns were extended to give relief.

♦ **Measures by the Reserve Bank of India**

The Reserve Bank of India (RBI) also took various steps to ease liquidity position and help banks, NBFCs and Mutual Fund institutions (MFIs).

- Reduction of Cash Reserve Ratio (CRR) resulted in liquidity increase of ₹1, 37,000 crore.
- Long Term Repo Operations (TLTROs) of ₹1, 00,050 crore taken up for fresh deployment in investment grade corporate bonds, commercial paper, and non-convertible debentures.
- TLTRO of ₹50, 000 crore taken up for investing in investment grade bonds, commercial paper, and non-convertible debentures of NBFCs, and MFIs.
- Increased the banks' limit for borrowing overnight under the marginal standing facility (MSF), enabling banking system to avail additional ₹1, 37,000 crore of liquidity at the reduced MSF rate.
- Announced special refinance facilities to NABARD, SIDBI and the NHB for a total amount of ₹50,000 crore at the policy repo rate.
- Announced the opening of a special liquidity facility (SLF) of ₹50,000 crore for mutual funds to ease intensified liquidity pressures.
- Moratorium of three months on payment of instalments and payment of

interest on Working Capital Facilities for all Term Loans.

- For loans by NBFCs to commercial real estate sector, additional time of one year has been given for the date for commencement for commercial operations (DCCO).

♦ **Measures for Businesses, MSMEs and Discoms**

- ₹3 lakh crore for Collateral-free Automatic Loans for Businesses, including MSMEs.
- ₹20,000 crore Subordinate Debt for MSMEs.
- ₹50,000 crore equity infusion through MSME Fund of Funds.
- ₹2500 crore EPF support for Businesses and Workers for 3 more months.
- EPF contribution reduced for Business & Workers for 3 months amounting to ₹6750 crore.
- ₹30,000 crore Liquidity Facility for NBFC/HCs/MFIs.
- ₹45,000 crore Partial Credit Guarantee Scheme 2.0 for NBFC.
- Extension of Registration and Completion Date of Real Estate Projects under RERA.
- ₹90,000 crore Liquidity Injection for DISCOMs
- ₹50,000 crore liquidity through TDS/TCS reductions.
- ₹90,000 crore Liquidity Infusion for DISCOMs.

7. While many states in India have performed well on socio-economic indicators like education, health and gender equality, some other states have lagged behind. Examine the factors behind such divergences in performance citing also some examples.

Ans. While India has made considerable socio-economic progress since attaining Independence, the performance of States and Union territories (UTs) has varied widely and shows a mixed picture. While some states have forged ahead and made substantial progress – some states like Kerala being even comparable, on social indicators, to middle-income group countries among the Emerging economies – some other states have lagged behind. A number of factors account for the divergences in development among the states. These include affirmative action by the states on literacy and education, health, women's participation in workforce, girls' and women's empowerment and gender equality. All these factors these have a deep and enduring impact on various social indicators like birth, death and infant mortality rates, life expectancy, sex ratio, status of girls and women in society, gender bias, etc.

This will be evident from a comparative study of the data on these indicators of some of the states which have performed well and those who have lagged behind. Table 13.3 shows data on some of the health indicators.

➢ **Population stabilisation**

From the very First Plan (1951-56), India has been making concerted efforts to control birth rates and bring down population growth through intensive "family planning" programmes.

- **Total Fertility Rate:** Bringing down the Total Fertility Rate (TFR) to the Replacement level of 2.1 has been an important goal. At Replacement level of 2.1, the population of a country will remain stable if there is no migration.

  While the performance of States on this has been varied until recently, by 2019, many states have been able to bring TFR well below 2.1 as will be seen from Table 13.3. This is a significant achievement in India's demographic transition. But Bihar (3.2), UP (2.9), MP (2.7) and Rajasthan (2.5) still have higher rates which act as a drag on India's overall performance.

- **Birth rate:** Over the years, the birth rate has come down and is below 20 (per 1,000 population) in all the states in Table 13.3 except Bihar, UP, MP, Rajasthan and Haryana.

- **Death rate:** All the states covered in Table 13.3 have brought down death rate (per 1,000 population) significantly.

- **Sex ratio and Gender inequality:** Gender inequality is a crucial disparity prevalent in society. A low sex ratio, which is adverse to females, where the number of females is less than 1,000 to 1,000 males, is an indicator of gender inequality. It may be due to prevalence of pre-natal sex determination and sex selection practices, female infanticide or perverse social and cultural factors related to marriage and dowry. Disparities in literacy and education are also important factors engendering inequality between women and men.

  These factors undermine the role of women not only in society at large but within the households. They would have less decision-making powers on vital issues such as managing household affairs, handling finances, spacing of pregnancy, nutrition and ensuring their and children's health and overall well-being.

  On sex ratio data for 2013-15 periods, Table 13.3 shows a mixed picture. Among the weaker states, only Odisha has a high sex ratio of 950 while Bihar and MP have ratio above 900, even better than Maharashtra, Gujarat, Punjab and Haryana, all of which have ratio less than 900. More surprisingly, Tamil Nadu's ratio is even less than that of Bihar and MP.

Table 13.3: Social Indicators of Selected States

Indicator	Bihar	UP	MP	Raj	Odis	Ker	TN	Mah	Karn	Guj	Punj	Hary
Density	1102	828	236	201	269	859	555	365	319	308	550	573
Literacy	61.80	67.68	69.32	66.11	72.87	94.0	80.09	82.34	75.36	78.03	75.84	75.55
Sex ratio	916	879	919	861	950	967	911	878	939	854	889	831
B/R	26.2	25.6	24.6	24.0	18.2	13.9	14.7	15.6	17.2	19.7	14.8	20.3
D/R	5.8	6.6	6.7	5.9	7.3	6.9	6.5	5.5	6.3	5.9	6.6	5.9
TFR	3.2	2.9	2.7	2.5	1.9	1.7	1.6	1.7	1.7	2.1	1.6	2.2
IMR	32	43	48	37	40	7	15	19	23	28	20	30
Life Exp	69.1	65.3	66.5	68.7	69.3	75.3	72.1	72.5	69.4	69.9	72.7	69.8

Notes:

1. **Abbreviations used for states:** UP: Uttar Pradesh; MP: Madhya Pradesh; Raj: Rajasthan; TN: Tamil Nadu; Mah: Maharashtra; Karn: Karnataka; Guj: Gujarat; Punj: Punjab; Hary: Haryana.
2. **B/R (Birth rate):** B/R is the number of live births per thousand population in a given year, also referred to as Crude birth rate; **D/R (Death rate):** D/R is the number of deaths per thousand population in a given year, also referred to as Crude death rate; **TFR (Total fertility rate):** TFR is defined as number of live births a woman would expect to deliver, if she were to live through her reproductive years (age 15 to 49 years) and to bear children at each age in accordance with the prevailing age-specific fertility rates. At a TFR value of 2.1, the population of a country will remain stable if there is no migration; **IMR (Infant mortality rate):** IMR is the probability of dying between birth and exactly one year of age, expressed per 1,000 live births.

   Life Exp (Life expectancy at birth): It denotes the number of years a new-born infant would live if prevailing patterns of age-specific mortality rates continue to be the same throughout the child's life.

   Source: Density and Literacy (2011 Census data), **Sex Ratio** (2013-15), SRS data from Registrar General of India cited by NITI Aayog; **Birth rate, Death rate, IMR and TFR**, SRS 2018, Registrar General of India.

   Expectation of Life at Birth, Statement 3, SRS-based Abridged Life Tables, 2014-18, Registrar General of India.

➤ **Literacy and Education**

As already mentioned earlier, literacy and education play an important part in empowering people. Education is perhaps the single most important means for individuals to improve personal endowments, build capability levels, overcome constraints and, in the process, enlarge their opportunities and choices to improve their well-being. It not only helps to enhance human capital and productivity, but is equally important for acquisition and communication of information and knowledge, which enhances a person's quality of life.

- **Literacy: Table 13.4** presents literacy levels, gender-wise and for Rural and Urban areas, for the selected states from Sample survey done by NSSO for period July 2017 to June 2018.
  * It will be seen that barring Kerala, which also has the highest percentage of literates, in all the other states, female literacy is much less than male literacy.
  * Further, literacy rate of females in rural areas is far less than that of females in urban areas, again in all states barring Kerala, which places women in rural areas at a much greater disadvantage.
  * These point to the weaker position in which women are placed vis-à-vis men placing them at a disadvantage in intra-family matters and in society.
- **Role of education:** Concomitant to literacy is education. Mere literacy does not take a person far in life. It is a proven fact that education plays a significant role in the performance of states on parameters such as fertility rate, infant mortality rate (IMR), maternal mortality rate (MMR) and nutritional levels, all of

Table 13.4: Literacy Rate for selected States (in Percentage)

State	Rural			Urban			Rural + Urban		
	Male	Female	Person	Male	Female	Person	Male	Female	Person
(1)	(2)	(3)	(4)	(5)	(6)	(7)	(8)	(9)	(10)
Bihar	78.6	58.7	69.5	89.3	75.9	83.1	79.7	60.5	70.9
Uttar Pradesh	80.5	60.4	70.8	86.8	74.9	81.2	81.8	63.4	73.0
Madhya Pradesh	77.9	61.0	69.8	91.4	79.5	85.8	81.2	65.5	73.7
Rajasthan	77.6	52.6	65.5	91.1	74.6	83.5	80.8	57.6	69.7
Odisha	82.0	67.3	74.9	94.4	85.9	90.2	84.0	70.3	77.3

State	Rural			Urban			Rural + Urban		
	Male	Female	Person	Male	Female	Person	Male	Female	Person
(1)	(2)	(3)	(4)	(5)	(6)	(7)	(8)	(9)	(10)
Kerala	96.7	94.1	95.4	98.2	96.4	97.3	97.4	95.2	96.2
Tamil Nadu	84.2	70.8	77.5	92.3	85.9	89.0	87.9	77.9	82.9
Maharashtra	87.0	71.4	79.4	95.3	87.6	91.7	90.7	78.4	84.8
Karnataka	78.2	63.1	71.0	92.5	83.7	88.3	83.4	70.5	77.2
Gujarat	85.7	68.0	77.0	95.2	86.3	91.1	89.5	74.8	82.4

Note: Data is for persons of age 7 years and above in percentage.

Source: Table A-6 Table (2.1): Household Social Consumption: Education in India as part of 75th round of of National Sample Survey, from July 2017 to June 2018.

Which affect the health of families, especially women and children. States which have forged ahead in the field of education have generally shown a good record of socio-economic development.

The level of fertility has been, generally, found to be higher at lower education levels of the parents.

- **Women's empowerment:** Spread of education empowers women and results in their effective participation in decision-making process at household level with overall benefit to the family. It helps to strengthen gender equality and bring down gender bias in intra-family matters.

  Data presented in Tables 13.5 (a) and 13.5 (b) shows the comparative position of enrolment at the Primary, Upper Primary and Secondary levels in the two groups of states and how girls have fared as compared to boys. Education at the primary stage is crucial because it lays the foundation for future advancement in life.

- **Good performance by weaker states:** It is heartening to note that the enrolment rate of girls in 2015-16 has been very good in comparison to boys in all the states. What is more, some of the states considered weak such as Bihar, UP and Rajasthan have even higher enrolment rate for girls at the primary level than Kerala and Maharashtra. And at the upper primary level, Bihar and MP have much higher enrolment rate for girls than boys, while Rajasthan and Odisha have nearly the same rate for boys and girls.

  It is also noteworthy that barring UP at the upper primary level, the performance of all the weaker states at both primary and upper primary levels compares reasonably well with that of the developed states in Table 13.5 (b).

Table 13.5 (a): Education: Gross Enrolment Rate (GER): 2015-16

	Primary			Upper Primary			Secondary		
State	Boys	Girls	Total	Boys	Girls	Total	Boys	Girls	Total
Bihar	104.35	111.30	101.67	98.21	119.39	107.89	72.42	85.43	78.37
Uttar Pradesh	88.63	96.16	92.15	68.24	83.49	75.08	67.65	67.86	67.75
Madhya Pradesh	95.35	93.52	94.47	90.49	98.13	94.02	81.54	79.30	80.49
Rajasthan	101.27	99.48	100.43	91.46	91.21	91.34	81.15	70.12	76.06
Odisha	104.91	102.50	103.73	94.86	93.63	94.26	79.40	79.83	79.61

Table 13.5 (b): Education: Gross Enrolment Rate (GER): 2015-16

	Primary (I-V)			Upper Primary (VI-VIII)			Secondary (IX-X)		
State	Boys	Girls	Total	Boys	Girls	Total	Boys	Girls	Total
Kerala	95.45	95.44	95.44	94.55	96.28	95.39	102.31	102.58	102.44
T Nadu	103.39	104.43	103.89	92.55	95.65	94.03	91.86	96.18	93.92
Maharashtra	97.86	9760	97.74	97.44	101.38	99.24	91.97	87.62	89.95
Karnataka	102.93	103.04	102.98	92.43	94.39	93.37	82.35	84.19	83.22
Gujarat	95.64	99.11	97.24	94.70	96.99	95.73	80.26	66.82	74.13

Source: Educational Statistics at a Glance, 2018, Table 40: Dept. of Schoo Education & Literacy

Statistics Division, Ministry of Human Resource Development, Govt. of India

However, at the Secondary level, the five states in Table 13.5 (a) and Karnatak and Gujarat in Table 13.5 (b) have much lower rates than that of the develope states. This is also an indication of the extent of dropouts from the Upper Primar to the Secondary stage in the weaker states.

- **Pupil - Teacher Ratio:** Pupil Teacher Ratio is an important indicator of th standard and quality of teaching in schools. As per the "Right of Children t Free and Compulsory Education (RTE) Act, 2009", the Pupil Teacher Ratio (PTR for Primary schools (I -V) should be 30:1 and for Upper Primary school (VI-VIII) should be 35:1. The "Rashtriya Madhyamik Shiksha Abhiyan (RMSA) stipulates that the PTR at Secondary level (IX-X) should be 30:1.
- Going by these norms, as per data in Table 13.6, all the states, barring Bihar an UP at the Primary level have fulfilled the norms at both the Primary (30:1) an Upper Primary (35:1) levels. However, Bihar, UP, MP and Gujarat have a muc lower ratio than the normof 30:1at the Secondary level. In fact, most of thes states have a healthy ratio which is a positive sign.

A low teacher-student ratio results in overburdening teachers and adversely affect the quality of teaching which in turn adversely affects students' learning outcomes

- **Toilet facility in Schools:** Infrastructure in schools — libraries, labs, toilets, etc – is an important aspect of school education which is a formative period i children's lives. Toilet facility is a critical factor impacting children's educatio especially of girls, and is one of the factors for drop out of girls in schools. Fo want of separate toilet for girls, many drop out of education midstream as the go up to higher standards.

The data in Table 13.6 shows that most states have achieved a high percentage o coverage, ranging from 95 to 99 per cent. But a related critical issue, importan from the health point of view, is maintenance of toilets in hygienic conditio availability of adequate water supply and cleanliness, factors which are ofte neglected. This needs to be closely watched by the school management, educatio authorities and even parent-teacher groups so that children do not suffer.

Table 13.6: Pupil Teacher Ratio and Schools with Girls' Toilet

State	Pupil Teacher Ratio			Schools with Girls' Toilet (Percentage)		
State/ Schools	Primary	Upper Primary	Secondary	Primary	Upper Primary	Secondary
Bihar	36	24	66	89.85	96.43	94.98
Uttar Pr.	39	31	56	99.80	99.84	99.66
MP	20	18	39	96.90	97.55	97.49
Rajasthan	17	10	21	99.69	99.86	99.79
Odisha	17	14	20	97.82	96.79	95.49
State/ Schools	Primary	Upper Primary	Secondary	Primary	Upper Primary	Secondary
Kerala	18	14	17	99.06	99.77	99.74
T Nadu	18	15	21	99.88	99.99	100
Maharashtra	24	17	23	99.31	99.76	99.84
Karnataka	19	13	16	99.78	99.97	99.96
Gujarat	19	13	34	99.97	99.97	99.93

Source: Pupil Teacher Ratio, 2015-16, Table 47 &Schools with Girls' Toilet (in Percentage), Table 49:

Educational Statistics at a Glance, 2018, Table 40: Dept. of Scholl Education & Literacy Statistics Division, Ministry of Human Resource Development, Govt. of India.

- **Thrust on Education:** The improvements seen in the education sector are the result of years of concerted drive to enhance the outcomes, both quantitative and qualitative, including steps like "Sarva Shiksha Abhiyan" and the "Right to Education" to ensure no child is out of school.

  Better infrastructure, increasing number of classrooms and teachers and better training of teachers have also paid dividends.

  Still there are many areas like improving government and municipal schools, ensuring regular attendance of teachers, ensuring the quality of midday meals and more facilities like libraries and labs for giving better exposure to children to be implemented, especially in the weaker states.

➢ **Health**

Healthcare is a vital issue in the quest for attaining high level of socio-economic growth. In a developing country like India, the problem is not only availability of adequate health infrastructure but also its accessibility and affordability for all sections of society.

♦ **Expenditure on Health:** India's combined expenditure of Centre and States on health in 2018-19 (including expenditure on Public Health, Family Welfare and

Water Supply and Sanitation) worked out to 1.5 per cent of GDP. This increased from 1.2 per cent in 2014-15 to 1.5 per cent 2018-19.

The National Health Policy, 2017 had stated that health spend by government should be 2.5 per cent of GDP by 2025.

Out of pocket expenditure on health is one of the biggest reasons for people falling into poverty in India.

- **Facilities in rural areas:** The Sub Centre (SC) is the most peripheral and first contact point between the primary health care system and the community in rural areas. And Primary Health Centre (PHC) is the first contact point between village community and the medical officer. The PHCs are envisaged to provide an integrated curative and preventive health care to the rural population.
- **Disparities in Facilities**: As regards healthcare facilities available, there is also considerable disparity between urban and rural areas. Table 13.7 (a) and 13.7 (b) shows the facilities available in rural areas in selected states. Some states like Kerala, Tamil Nadu, Karnataka and Gujarat

Table 13.7 (a): Health Facilities in Rural Areas (as on July 1, 2019):

Selected States: Comparative study

1.Sub Centres & HWC-SCs	**Bihar**	**Uttar Pradesh**	**Madhya Pradesh**	**Rajasthan**	**Odisha**
Required	21337	34726	13935	12761	8382
In position	9949	20782	10226	13512	6688
Shortfall	11388	13944	3709	**	1694
Shortfall (%)	53	40	27	**	20
2. PHCs and HWC-PHCs					
Required	3548	5781	2233	2073	1345
In position	1899	2936	1199	2082	1288
Shortfall	1649	2845	1034	**	57
Shortfall (%)	46	49	46	**	4
3. CHCs					
Required	887	1445	558	518	336
In position	150	679	309	571	377
Shortfall	737	766	249	**	**
Shortfall (%)	83	53	45	**	**

Table 13.7 (b): Health Facilities in Rural Areas (as on July 1, 2019): Selected States: Comparative study

1. Sub Centres & HWC-SCs	Kerala	Tamil Nadu	Maharashtra	Karnataka	Gujarat
Required	2340	7355	14112	8028	8055
In position	5380	8713	10668	9758	9166
Shortfall	**	**	3444	**	**
Shortfall (%)	**	**	24	**	**
2. PHCs and HWC-PHCs					
Required	388	1222	2299	1318	1308
In position	848	1422	1828	2127	1476
Shortfall	**	**	471	**	**
Shortfall (%)	**	**	20	**	**
3. CHCs					
Required	97	305	574	329	327
In position	227	385	364	198	362
Shortfall	**	**	210	131	**
Shortfall (%)	**	**	37	40	**

Abbreviations used: SC:Sub Centre; and HWC: Health & Wellness Centre; PHC:Primary Health Centre; CHC: Community Health Centre.

Notes: 1. The requirement is calculated using the prescribed norms and on the basis of rural population estimation for mid-year for 2019.

The symbol** indicates there is no shortfall.

Source: Table 8, Rural Health Statistics, 2018-19, Ministry of Health and Family Welfare, Statistics Division, Government of India.

have facilities well in excess of the norms. It is noteworthy that among the weaker states, Rajasthan has exceeded the norms in all the three categories while Odisha has only marginal shortfall in SC and PHC.

- **Deficient states:** Whereas other weaker states like Bihar, UP and MP have heavy shortfall in all the three categories – SCs & HWSCs, PHCs & HWPHCs and Community Health Centres. This would mean that people in rural areas in these states grossly suffer from inadequacy of health facilities. It is a sign of poor governance despite funds being available.

  It is also worth recollecting that both Bihar and UP had instances of serial deaths of newborn infants for lack of proper medical facilities and attention. Apart from this, the overcrowding and the unhygienic and filthy state of many of the government hospitals is well documented, crying for drastic improvements.

- ♦ **Ayushman Bharat:** This scheme aims at Universal Health Coverage and has two components:
  - Health & Wellness Centres to provide comprehensive primary health care, and
  - Pradhan Mantri Jan Arogya Yojana (PMJAY) to provide health cover upto ₹ 5 lakh per family per year to 10.74 crore poor and vulnerable families for secondary & tertiary hospitalization.

➢ **Women in Labour force& Empowerment**

Besides women's education, the other most important factor in empowering women and reducing fertility rates is women's employment. Both these factors, education and employment, help in women's emancipation, raising their self-confidence and esteem in society.

- ■ **Gender issues in Labour and Wages:** In labour participation rate and employment, women lag behind men. Early marriages and multiple child-bearing in working age are major handicaps for women in India which result in lower female participation rate in the labour force.
- ■ **Decline in FLPR:** As observed in *Economic Survey, 2019-20*, female labour force participation rate (FLPR) declined by 7.8 percentage points from 33.1 per cent in 2011-12 to 25.3 per cent in 2017-18. Though female LFPR is higher in rural areas as compared to urban areas, the rate of decline was also sharper in rural areas compared to urban areas
  - More women in rural areas now pursuing higher education has delayed their entry into the labour market.
  - It could also be because household incomes have risen in rural areas on account of higher wage levels which is dragging women out of the labour market.
  - In most households, both in urban and rural areas, women are constrained to tend to domestic chores and are unable to take up employment. The services rendered by women at home are invisible, not given due credit and is not reckoned at all or not reckoned properly in the National accounts.
- ■ **Wage disparities:** Though it is mandated that women are to be paid wages equal to men for comparable work, they are paid less than men for similar work in many sectors and especially in jobs in the informal sector. This is widely prevalent in jobs on farms which is a major source of employment of women in rural areas, though a 2011-12 NSSO survey has shown some decline in gender wage gap due to MG National Rural Employment Guarantee Scheme (MNREGS).
- ■ **Worker Population Ratio:** As per the Annual Employment-Unemployment (EUS) Surveys conducted by Labour Bureau in the year 2012-13and2015-16, the Worker Population Ratios (WPR) for females aged 15 years and above, on "Usual Status" basis at All India level, were 25.0 per cent and 25.8 per cent respectively. The data on this for selected states is given below.

Table 13.8: Female (aged 15 years and more) Worker Population Ratio (In Percentage)

	2012-13	2015-16		2012-13	2015-16
Bihar	10.4	17.8	**Kerala**	20.3	23.7
Uttar Pradesh	11.4	12.0	**Tamil Nadu**	35.0	39.3
Madhya Pradesh	32.1	17.2	**Maharashtra**	32.8	32.8
Rajasthan	27.4	31.9	**Karnataka**	32.2	33.3
Odisha	25.3	23.7	**Gujarat**	16.4	19.9

Source: Employment and Unemployment (E&U) Surveys, Labour Bureau, Ministry of Labour, Govt. of India.

The data above shows that WPR for females has gone up in Bihar, Rajasthan, Kerala, Tamil Nadu and Gujarat during this period while it has declined considerably in Madhya Pradesh and marginally in Odisha.

However, the rates are much lower than the national average in Bihar, UP, MP and Gujarat and they need to take steps to increase them.

- **Employment schemes:** The Government has taken various steps for increasing employment including female employment. These include:
  - PM's Employment Generation Programme (PMEGP) run by Ministry of MSMEs.
  - Rural employment under MGNREGS.
  - Grameen Kaushalya Yojana (GKY) schemes of Ministry of Rural Development, and
  - National Urban Livelihoods Mission (NULM) run by Ministry of Housing & Urban Poverty Alleviation.
- **Female labour participation:** Besides, certain specific measures have been taken to increase participation of women in labour force. These are:
  - ♦ **Maternity benefit:**The Maternity Benefit (Amendment) Act, 2017 has provided for:
    - Enhanced paid maternity leave from 12 weeks to 26 weeks.
    - Mandatory crèche facility in the establishments having 50 or more employees.
  - ♦ **Factories Act, 1948:** Under this, advisory issued to States for permitting women workers in the night shifts with adequate safety measures.
  - ♦ **Equal Remuneration Act, 1976**: This provides for payment of equal remuneration to men and women workers for same work or work of similar nature without any discrimination.

- **Minimum Wages Act, 1948**: As per this Act, the wages fixed by the concerned Governments are equally applicable to both male and female workers and the Act prohibits discriminate on the basis of gender.

- **Governance**

The foregoing comparative study of the performance of some selected states, highlight the importance of governance in ensuring speedy and seamless socio-economic progress. That some states have been able to forge ahead on various parameters while some other states have lagged behind clearly points to the need for the lagging states to strengthen governance and improve implementation of various schemes and projects.

Corruption is another scourge afflicting public administration in various states. India, with a score of 41 points, has been ranked78 among 180 countries in Transparency International's global "Corruption Perceptions Index" for 2018.

- **Lack of transparency:** Lack of transparency in awarding contracts, time and cost overruns in projects and political interference have impeded smooth implementation of well-intentioned schemes. Leakages in schemes like Public Distribution System (PDS), Integrated Child Development Scheme (ICDS), Mid-day Meals in schools and other welfare measures adversely affect the beneficiaries of such schemes, especially the poor and vulnerable sections.
- **People's awareness:** Social and political awareness of people, which comes with education, will go a long way in putting pressure on government agencies and people's representatives in ensuring improved delivery of public services. Governance reforms like making services online and adopting direct benefit transfer (DBT) of welfare benefits to beneficiaries' bank accounts have also helped to streamline and enhance efficiency of administration.
- **Role of Corporates & NGO's:** The Corporates under the "Corporate Social Responsibility" (CSR) mandated under the Companies Act, 2013 and NGOs could play a pivotal role in the Social sector to improve education and health schemes. It is noteworthy that already the foundations many of the large Corporates like the Tatas, Mahindra & Mahindra, Infosys, Azim Premji, HCL and ITC are rendering yeoman service in these fields.

> Development can be seen, it is argued here, as a process of expanding the real freedoms that people enjoy......Development requires the removal of major sources of unfreedoms: poverty as well as tyranny, poor economic opportunities as well as systematic social deprivation, neglect of public facilities as well as intolerance or overactivity of repressive states. Despite unprecedented increases in overall opulence, the contemporary world denies elementary freedoms to vast numbers - perhaps even the vast majority - of people.
>
> – Amartya Sen, economist, *Development as Freedom* (1999).

THE COLONIAL LEGACY

> Injustice in the end produces independence.
>
> - Voltaire, (pen-name of François-Marie Arouet) (1694-1778), French philosopher and writer.

Topics Covered

- *Agriculture during the pre-independence era*
- *Land tenure system in British India*
- *De-industrialization of India*
- *Tariff policy in Colonial period in India*
- *Role of Railways in Colonial period*
- *Progress on social indicators before and after Independence*

1. Critically examine the condition of agriculture and rural economy of India during the pre-independence era.

Ans. The colonial era which lasted over 200 years became a drag on India's agricultural and industrial development and led to stagnation in many respects. Agriculture was the only occupation in the villages and three-fourths of the country's population depended on farming.

The main reasons for the backwardness of agriculture in the pre-independence period were the feudal system of control of land by the zamindars and big landowners, who did not invest capital for improvements, sub-tenancy of lands with no security of tenure, extortionist rents extracted from tillers, high indebtedness and harassment of farmers by usurious moneylenders.

Agricultural performance in the colonial era was dismal and the annual growth rate of agricultural output was negligible. Most parts of the country being dependent on monsoon, which was uncertain and unpredictable even in those days, agriculture was beset with many problems. In times of drought and famines caused mainly by the failure of monsoon, the rural community suffered the most.

- **Agricultural Growth**

  Any absolute increase in production was mainly due to increase in acreage under cultivation and not due to increase of crop yield. Also, farmers holding more fertile and irrigated lands shifted from food crops to non-food, commercial crops which yielded better returns, thus adversely affecting food production.

  - **Agricultural output:** One of the systematic studies on agricultural productivity in the colonial era is George Blyn's *Agricultural Trends in India, 1891-1947: Output, Availability, and Productivity*. Blyn's study showed that yearly production growth in food crops from 1891 to 1947 was no more than 0.11 percent. Per capita agricultural production declined at the rate of 0.72 per cent per year during 1911-41 period.
  - **Foodgrains output**
    - Per capita foodgrains output declined even more by 29 per cent between 1911 and 1941.
    - Between 1911 and 1941, the rate of increase of crop yield per acre was almost nil. There were also inter-regional differences in yields.
    - Between 1921 and 1941, while the population increased from 251.2 million to 318.5 million, food output failed to keep pace resulting in acute food shortages and declining availability of food per head.
    - Production and yield of non-food crops rose while that of food crops declined. The increase in the yield and output of non-food crops was at the cost of foodgrains as cultivators shifted better and irrigated land and capital resources to commercial crops which fetched more income.

- **Irrigation**

  All through India's history, rivers have played an important part in national and local life. Successful agriculture would not have been possible in most parts of the country without utilizing the river waters.

  - **In Ancient India:** The Grand Anicut was an ancient dam built on the Kaveri river in Tamil Nadu by a Chola king in the 2nd century A.D. to irrigate fertile delta region via canals. The large numbers of tanks, found in the Deccan, have been in existence for centuries. The Yamuna canals were originally constructed around the 14th century.
  - **During British rule:** One redeeming feature of British policy on the agriculture front was in regard to irrigation.

- According to Planning Commission document on the First Five-Year Plan (1951–56), by around 1850, about two million acres of land were irrigated by several indigenous irrigation works in the form of small tanks in southern India, inundation canals in northern India, and reconditioned canals. About five million acres were under well irrigation at that time, mostly in northern India.
- The first major irrigation work constructed in India was the Ganga Canal in Uttar Pradesh, opened for irrigation in 1854. This was followed by the Upper Bari Doab canal in the Punjab and the Godavari and Krishna delta systems in Madras Presidency.
- A number of other large irrigation works were constructed towards the end of the 19th and the beginning of the 20th century. Sir Arthur Cotton was the engineer behind some of the major irrigation projects in British India, who built a dam on Kaveri and the massive dams on Godavari and Krishna rivers in Andhra Pradesh in the middle of the 19th century for which he is still revered by people in those regions.
- Another great personality, Sir M. Visvesaraya, built the Krishnaraja Sagar dam across Kaveri river in the then Mysore (now Karnataka) state.

➢ **Commercialisation of Agriculture**

This was another factor which adversely impacted food production during the colonial era.

- **Commercial crops:** The administration promoted cultivation of a variety of crops of commercial importance and value such as tea, coffee, tobacco, indigo, opium, cotton, jute, and sugarcane. These crops were introduced with different motives such as higher revenue and export.
  - **Cotton:**The area under cotton cultivation, including the native states, increased from 14.5 million acres in 1900 to 25 million acres in 1913.
  - **Opium:**Indian opium was exported mainly to China but by 1913, this export was discontinued at the behest of China. Thereafter, opium produced was used for internal consumption and for export to some other countries for medicinal purposes.
  - **Indigo:** Indigo was sent to England and used as a dyeing agent for cloth produced in Britain. Unfortunately, cultivation of indigo sapped the fertility of land for some years which acted as a disincentive for the farmers to cultivate it.
  - **Plantations:** The plantations of tea and coffee were mostly controlled by British firms who invested capital and their ownership often changed hands. The workers on the plantations worked under severe hardships.

➢ **Lack of Investment and Research**

Multiple factors, as explained below, held back progress in agriculture during the colonial period.

- Holders of large tracts of farmland, the zamindars and jagirdars, did not invest in land to bring about improvements. These landlords took no interest in agriculture beyond collecting rent. They utilized savings to acquire more land or to become moneylenders which was a lucrative avenue to amass wealth.
- Tenancy and sharecropping dominated the zamindari areas. And the vast masses of tenants and small farmers, who were already subject to exorbitant rents by the landowners, had no resources to make any investments either. As a result, over time there was deterioration in the quality of land, productivity and yields.
- Though the government made efforts to improve farming practices such as use of hybrid seeds, providing irrigation facilities, etc., these efforts were directed primarily to enhance the production of non-food cash crops which would serve as raw material for the mills and factories in Britain.
- There was barely any investment in flood control and drainage schemes or measures to improve the fertility of soil.
- There was no investment in technology to improve production techniques. The farm implements such as ploughs which were in use were outmoded. Modern machinery was conspicuous by its absence.
- The government hardly promoted education in agriculture. For a country in which 70 per cent of the population was engaged in farming, there were very few agricultural institutions to train people. Even on the eve of independence, there were just nine agricultural colleges with a little over 3,000 students.
- It was not until the early part of the 20th century that any organized research in agriculture was initiated with the setting up of the Imperial Agriculture Research Institute at Pusa in Bihar in 1905 (which was later shifted to Delhi where it functions now).

  To sum up, due to such neglect, farm productivity and yields remained low and stagnant for long. As the farming was mostly at subsistence level and for self-consumption, there was little scope for ploughing back any capital for investment to improve the systems and increase production.

➢ **Occurrence of Famines and Epidemics**

There were several occurrences of famine in different parts of the country all through the British rule between the 18th and the 20th centuries. Due to shortage and maldistribution of food, poverty and lack of purchasing power leading to starvation, unhygienic conditions of living and want of proper medical facilities, famines and epidemics, such as cholera, plague, smallpox and malaria took a heavy of human lives.

Between 1770 and 1900, 25 million people are estimated to have died due to famines in India. The Famine Inquiry Commission reporting on the Great Bengal famine of 1943 (which was a period in the midst of Second World war) put the death toll officially at about 1.5 million though going by the Commission's own method of calculation, the toll was much higher to be around three million.

Conclusion

The lack of progress and stagnation in agriculture during the colonial era can be gauged from the fact that even at the time of independence in 1947, India, with over 80 per cent of the population living in rural areas, had about 70 per cent of the workforce still engaged in agriculture with low productivity and very poor yields. With the acute pressure of population on land, there was high degree of under-employment and disguised unemployment in the agrarian sector.

This points not only to the neglect of agriculture but to the lack of industrialization which could have pulled the surplus labour from farming to industries and services sectors, increased employment and raised living standards. But this did not happen due to the gross indifference shown by the colonial administration for over two centuries.

2. Land tenure system during the British period was responsible for sustained poverty in India and stagnant growth of Indian economy. Discuss.

Ans. While examining the "land revenue or land tenure systems" that prevailed during the British colonial rule, it would be relevant to have a brief look at the historical background.

- **Historical background:** During the Mughal era, under the "mansabdari" system introduced by Emperor Akbar, land revenue was being collected in the 16th and 17th centuries by non-hereditary, transferable state officials. After the collapse of Mughal rule in the early 18th century, these local officials gained power in several areas, and often became de facto hereditary landlords and petty chiefs in their local areas.

- **From Trading to Empire-building:** The British who came to India initially started as traders and the East India Company received its first permit to build a factory at Surat from the Mughal emperor, Jahangir in 1613. Following their victories in the battle of Plassey in 1757 and the battle of Buxar in 1764, the British began building the empire and obtained political control of the state of Bengal which then included the present states of Bihar and Orissa.

  The Company consolidated its hold over large parts of India in the 18th and 19th centuries by fighting against the Sikhs, the Marathas, and the Mysore kings. They also did outright annexation or control of princely states by asserting their power through treaties and alliances. The Indian rulers acknowledged the Company's hegemony in return for limited internal autonomy and on being assured of their defence and protection by the Company.

- **Revenue collection:** Land revenue or land tax was the major source of revenue for the Mughals as well as the British. The British formally gained revenue-collection rights in Bengal in 1765. By 1841, land revenue constituted 60 per cent of the total British administration's income. This proportion gradually declined as resources began to be raised through additional sources.

  The British administration collected land revenue from the cultivators of the land and laid down as to who was liable to pay the land tax and who had "property rights" on the land.

  - **Three systems:** The colonial government adopted three systems of land revenue collection in different parts of India. These were the Zamindari, the Mahalwari and the Ryotwari systems. The implications and consequences of these systems are discussed below.

    - **Zamindari system:** The East India Company tried to set aside the Zamindari system prevalent during the Mughal period and collect land taxes either directly through company officials, or through revenue-farmers, who collected the rent from peasants and paid a lumpsum to the government. The new system led to widespread corruption and repression at the hands of officials and the peasants suffered much hardship.

      - **Permanent Settlement:** To reform the system, Lord Cornwallis, Governor-General, decided to restore the old system and introduced the 'Permanent Settlement Act' in 1793 in Bengal Presidency, Central Provinces and parts of Madras Presidency

        Under this system, proprietary and hereditary rights over the land were granted to the zamindars (landlords) in the villages. The colonial administration fixed the revenue the landlords had to pay the government which they collected from the tenant-farmers. In many places, lower class families were usually sub-tenants of intermediary owners of land, rather than direct tenants of the zamindars. Often there were multiple layers of tenancy between the zamindars and landlords and the actual tiller. Sub-tenants had no security of tenure and were in many instances exploited by the intermediaries and moneylenders who levied exorbitant rents.

    - **Mahalwari system:** This village-based system was adopted in North-West Provinces and Panjab under which village bodies that jointly owned the village were responsible for collecting and paying the land revenue. Village bodies could be in charge of varying areas, from part of a village to several villages.

In some areas, it was a single person or family on the pattern of the zamindari landlord system, while in other areas, where the village bodies were larger, each person was responsible for a fixed share of the revenue. This share was either determined by ancestry or based on actual land possessed.

- **Ryotwari system:** This was cultivator-based system prevalent in most areas of Madras and Bombay Presidencies and also in Assam. Under this, the revenue settlement was made directly with the individual ryot or cultivator. In these areas, extensive survey of the land was done and a detailed record-of-rights was prepared, which served as the legal title to the land for the cultivator.

  Revenue rates were calculated as the money value of a share of the estimated average annual output. This share typically varied from place to place, was different for different soil types and was also adjusted in response to changes in the productivity of the land.

Choice of Land Revenue System

The British chose different systems in different areas with a view to ensure a steady and sizeable source of revenue for the Government based also on certain political considerations. To begin with, the administration was handicapped by lack of information on the conditions in different areas. Hence, they had to go by the existing land records and the views of individual administrators or local village bodies in fixing rates.

Consequences of the Revenue system

- **Multiple layers:** Often there were multiple layers of tenancy between the zamindars and landlords and the actual tiller. This led to more exploitation and harassment of tenants by the intermediaries.
- **Lack of security and high rents:** Sub-tenants had no security of tenure of land and were in many instances exploited by extortionist rates of rent by the intermediaries and moneylenders.
- **Inequalities:** Under the landlord system, landlords were given the authority to extract as much as they could from the tenants, and, as a result, they were in a position to appropriate most of the gains in productivity and output. They could even exercise judicial and other administrative powers that were vested in them by the colonial government as a part of the settlement. This gave room for them to coerce the poor peasants and extract maximum rents. As the 19th century was a period of significant growth in productivity, the landlord class grew rich over a period leading to widening inequality among the rural population.

In contrast, in the individual cultivator areas, rents were raised by the British evenly though the view was to extract as much as possible from the tenant. In this system, there was less scope for treating tenants differently and hence inequalities were less.

- **Lack of incentives:** There were differences in motivations to improve between those who cultivated their own land and those who cultivated other people's land. As is well-known, in cultivating other people's land, there will be less incentive to augment investment, productivity and yields. And with insecurity of the farmer over the land tenure and the power exercised by the landlords the farmer had even less inclination to invest more with the risk of extra gains being expropriated by the landlord. These factors added to the problems of poor tillers.
- **Vested interests:** These systems of land tenure created vested interests with a class of landed gentry – zamindars, jagirdars, and other dominant groups – with large landholdings who were loyal to the colonial masters. This led to widening disparities in wealth and status between different sections of society. Such differences, which persisted over time, adversely impacted the people in the lower rungs most and accentuated their backwardness in education, health and access to various other social opportunities.

➢ Conclusion

The land tenure system adopted by the colonial government was exploitative in nature and did little good to Indian agriculture. Land ownership was concentrated in the hands of few while the number of landless labour increased with increasing population, majority of whom had to depend on agriculture. While incomes in villages increased, the disparities in income also widened. The role of usurious moneylenders became more dominant. A majority of farmers, and labour who worked for them did not possess the know-how to adopt improved farming methods.

Thus at the time of independence, India inherited a semi-feudal agrarian structure with complex tenure arrangements over large parts of India. This was as a result of highly iniquitous land tenure system perpetuated by the colonial administration. And after independence, the government had the onerous task of implementing land reforms which faced considerable resistance from the big landowners and other vested interests.

The concentration of economic and political power in the hands of an elite, resulting from the landlord-based land tenure system, continues to be a burden even now. The glaring disparities have led to class conflicts and insurgency in some parts of the country affecting social harmony.

3. Discuss the industrial policy followed by the British during the colonial period. Would it be correct to say that their policy led to de-industrialisation of India?

Ans. To understand the extent to which the colonial rule impacted Indian economy and industry, in particular, it is necessary to know the condition in which India was when colonialism took roots in the country.

- **The setting**

  In the seventeenth century, before the colonial powers, viz., the Portuguese, the Dutch, the British and the French arrived, India was a relatively urbanised and commercialised nation with a buoyant export trade, consisting largely of cotton textiles, silk, spices and rice. India was the world's main producer of cotton textiles and had a substantial export trade to Britain, as well as many other European countries.

  India had a thriving handloom and handicrafts sector and was renowned for cotton and cloth from Surat and Masulipatnam. The art of spinning and weaving had attained perfection and Indian handloom catered to world market. India was rich in minerals and manufacture of wrought iron had attained excellence.

- **Share in World trade and Output**

  According to the historian, Angus Maddison, until the early 18th century, China and India were the two largest economies by output. And India's share in the world economy was as high as 24.4 per cent in 1700 but it steadily declined thereafter.

  India's share of global industrial output also declined from 25 per cent in 1750 to 2 per cent in 1900. At the same time, Britain's share in the world economy rose from 2.9 per cent in 1700 to 9 per cent in 1870, and Britain replaced India as the world's largest textile manufacturer in the 19th century.

- **Industrial Revolution**

  A major turning point was the series of inventions which took place in Britain, between 1740 and 1860 that brought about a major transformation in industrial production, especially in the textile industry. Inventions like spinning jenny, water frame and spinning mule revolutionised the textile industry in Britain. It made production much faster and more organised.

  Many other sectors like metallurgy, machine tools, chemicals, paper, and glass too underwent change and were modernised in their processes. This was followed by a second wave of Industrial Revolution with the invention of steam engine by James Watt and steam locomotive by George Stephenson which ushered in the modern means of transportation by railways.

♦ The Factory System

These transformational developments paved the way for the new factory system where production methods underwent a sea change leading to much higher productivity and lower costs of production. It transformed the industrial conditions not only in Europe but also in other parts of the world.

The series of inventions revolutionized the industrial methods of the great powers and brought about perceptible progress and changes in trade and commerce. In the face of these changes and mass production, India, with her traditional manufacturing methods, could not withstand the intense competition from Britain. England's shipping opened up new markets and products manufactured in the factories in Britain were dumped on markets in India and other countries in Asia.

England's enormous profits, industrial and commercial, made her a financial and economic powerhouse, which further strengthened her position as an imperial power.

♦ Reversal of Trade and Industrial decline

While hitherto, India exported many products to the West, the trend was drastically reversed. India became the exporter of raw materials to feed the factories in Britain and importer of finished goods.

The textile industry of India faced stiff competition from items manufactured in Britain. Raw cotton was exported from India and cloth made in British mills were dumped on India crippling the local mills. The Indian handloom industry which had flourished earlier suffered decline as the factory-manufactured textile products imported from Britain were of superior quality and cheaper.

Industries in India were crippled and workers devoid of skill and expertise, and handicapped for want of capital and modern machinery, were thrown out of jobs. Many of these workers had to fall back upon agriculture which was already under much stress. India which was once famous for the manufacture of the most delicate fabrics in the world, became a purely agricultural country exporting raw materials and food items.

♦ Shipping: A case of discrimination

Before the British arrived, India had seafaring prowess and a thriving shipping and ship-building sector. Till the mid-18th century, Indian ships plied the Arabian sea and the Bay of Bengal carrying sizeable goods and products.

After 1757, the East India Company took control over much of these and gave rights to British ships. Duties were imposed on Indian merchant vessels which crippled them and Indian vessels were confined to coastal shipping carrying low-value native products.

A glaring example of discrimination against Indian initiatives is the shipping company pioneered before World War I by V.O. Chidambaram Pillai, a staunch nationalist, in South India which was not allowed to succeed. Pillai was jailed for his nationalist activities and the shipping company was eventually liquidated.

➢ **Industrial policy: De-industrialisation of India**

With a view to promoting their industries in Britain, the colonial government adopted a deliberate policy of discouraging development of industries in India. This process got intensified after the Industrial Revolution when British industries needed raw materials for their industries like textiles, iron and steel and metallurgy.

Apart from trying to secure a monopolistic trading position, Britain sought to source raw materials from India and turn India into a free market for her manufactured products. The introduction of railways in India by the 1850's facilitated easy movement of goods over long distances from the hinterland to the ports in India for transporting to Britain. The net result was the draining away of the natural resources of India and impeding the growth of Indian industries.

Though India had ample iron ore and coal deposits and Britain possessed the know-how of steel manufacture, no step was taken to build an iron and steel plant in India. Though a steel-making plant, the Bengal Iron Works, was started in 1870, it could not withstand the competition from imported steel and the plant did not survive.

♦ **Textile and Jute industry:** It was not until 1850's that textile mills could be set up in India with financial, technical and managerial help from the British. From the 1860s onwards India became a significant manufacturer of machine-made cotton yarn, and cloth. The Bombay cotton industry pushed Lancashire out of the yarn market in China and Japan during the 1880s, and also catered to a significant proportion of the domestic market for machine-made yarn. But due to famine, plague, domestic recession and the rise of Japanese competition, India lost its Asian markets in the 1890s, and to compensate for this, the Indian mills began to manufacture cloth for the domestic market. It was around the same time that few jute mills came up in Calcutta.

Whatever little industrialization had taken place in India during this period was due to the initiative and enterprise of Indians.The Iron and Steel plant pioneered by Jamshedji Tata opened in 1907 at Jamshedpur and the few cotton and jute mills in the country were prime examples of this.

➢ **Trade policy**

The trade policy adopted by the British administration was also directed against Indian interests. The import of Indian goods to Europe was repressed by prohibitive duties to prevent them from gaining competitive advantage, while the export of

British goods into India was supported by nominal duties. England herself had followed a policy of 'Protection' until her nascent industries had reached a stage when they no longer needed protection.

After the First World War (1914-18), under nationalist pressure, the colonial government started to favour Indian enterprise in its purchase of stores and it agreed to create a Tariff Commission in 1921 which started raising tariffs for protective reasons. (For more on Trade policy, see next question).

➢ **Dominance of British interests: Drain of wealth**

Before independence, the services and industrial sectors were dominated and controlled by the British who brought in capital and invested in them. Most of the ventures in which they invested virtually enjoyed monopoly and catered to British interests and foreign markets.

Petroleum and mining companies, tea and coffee plantations, banking, insurance and mercantile firms, and shipping companies were all run by the British, with the top management consisting of Englishmen.

A good portion of the profits of these companies were repatriated to Britain. Remittances made by the foreign personnel in these companies and by those in the military and civil administration in India and their pensionary liabilities also caused a heavy drain on the wealth of India.

♦ **Nationalist backlash**

The deliberate neglect of Indian interests and exploitation of the country perpetrated by the colonial rulers began to draw sharp reaction from nationalist leaders towards the late 18th and early 19th century.

Prominent leaders like Dadabhai Naoroji, Mahadev Govind Ranade, Bal Gangadhar Tilak and Gopal Krishna Gokhale raised their voice against the exploitation and misrule of the colonial regime which sapped the nation's energy and impoverished her. Some of them wrote copiously on India's poor socio-economic condition during that time.

Naoroji published his work titled "***Poverty and Un-British Rule in India***" in 1901 and termed the rampant exploitation of the country by the foreign ruler as 'Drain theory' as they drained away the country's resources to feed the factories in Britain to the utter neglect of India's development. Ranade and Romesh Chandra Dutt wrote extensively on India's economic condition under the British rule.

♦ **The First Steps of Industrialisation**

It was only in the first half of the 20th century that some semblance of industrialization took place. This was due to the growing resentment among the nationalist leaders and the intense pressure brought to bear upon the government by them.

A significant structural change took place in the 1930s, as consumer goods came to be increasingly manufactured in India. Demand among the urban middle class supported this trend. And local production of tea, processed foods, cloth and clothing, bicycles, and other consumer and intermediate goods expanded to meet this demand. There was also significant expansion in domestic production of cement, rubber goods, simple machinery and metal castings and electricity supply plant. In this decade a number of major Indian industrial groups expanded rapidly to become major suppliers of the domestic market.

The Great Depression of 1930's which impacted the western nations adversely, and the two World Wars also gave a fillip to these industries due to growing demand and the necessity to look for alternative sources of supply. British and American multinational corporations set up manufacturing units in India in the 1930s, largely to tide over tariff walls and to develop local domestic marketing and sales networks. During the Second World War (1939-45), India became a major source of supply of munitions, clothing and simple equipment to the Allied armies in Asia.

But as pointed out by the Planning Commission, "prior to independence, there were virtually no capital goods industries and almost all the industries that came up were in the consumer goods sector. Without basic and capital goods sector, India could not have industrialized in any significant manner. No wonder that in 1950 (on the eve of launching the First Plan), India had to meet 90 per cent of its requirements of machinery and machine tools through imports."

♦ **Indian entrepreneurship**

One positive outcome of these industrial ventures, however limited they were, was that it helped to nurture a breed of promising Indian industrialists and entrepreneurs who laid the foundations upon which India could build further after independence. This positive trend also helped to develop a pool of managerial and technical talent among Indians and also build a base of technically skilled labour force.

➢ **Conclusion**

In the final analysis, Indian economy suffered neglect at the hands of British colonial regime. The trade and industrial policies were clearly designed to favour British interests and British industry and suppress India's industrialisation and hold back development. Even the introduction of railways and communication facilities was done more to serve the interests of the colonial administration.

However, some British historians have argued that the colonial rule did benefit India in many ways. While the colonial rule did confer some benefits, the fact remains that the widespread poverty and backwardness India has had to suffer is the legacy and baggage of two centuries that the colonialists left behind. Had India not been colonised and subjected to the various repressive measures detailed above, an independent India would have taken advantage of the Industrial Revolution and scientific progress much earlier and brought about greater socio-economic progress for her people.

4. The trade policy adopted by the British in India was mainly to serve the British interests. Do you agree? Justify your views.

Ans. The British colonial regime had no consistent trade policy until the mid-nineteenth century. The three Presidencies of Bengal, Bombay and Madras operated largely independently. By the time the East India Company's administration consolidated its hold over Indian territory, an all-India trade policy emerged.

- **Tariff policy:** The trade policy of the British administration did not promote the interests of most Indian producers or consumers. The British followed a discriminatory tariff policy under which the import of Indian goods to Europe was repressed by prohibitive duties to prevent them from gaining competitive advantage, while the export of British goods to India was supported by nominal duties. This is in contrast to the policy of 'Protection' England herself had followed in the initial stages of industrialization when her nascent industries needed protection.

  The colonial regime imposed heavy tariffs (export duties) on India's export of handicraft products and free import of British products to India.This made Indian exports costlier and its international demand fell drastically. At the same time, the policy allowed free export of India's raw materials to Britain to feed the factories in Britain.

  - **Indian Textiles and Britain's Protectionism**

    The policy Britain adopted towards Indian textile industry exemplifies her protectionist trade policy towards India. From the late 17th century Indian cotton textile items like calicoes, muslins, printed and cotton goods flooded European markets in ever larger volumes. Local English manufacturers could not compete with the Indian imports in terms of price or quality. India was the centre of the world's cotton textile production in the 18th century but by the mid-19th century, it had shifted to Europe.

In 1685, Britain imposed 10 per cent import duty on Indian goods and in 1690 doubled it to 20 per cent. In 1701, the Calico Act was passed banning imports of dyed, painted or printed fabric. While these early tariff measures were imposed to protect the woollen, silk and linen textile producers of Britain, they also helped to protect the cotton manufacturers.

With such a protected home market, British manufacturers were able to develop and apply the technologies developed following the Industrial Revolution during the second half of the 18th century. Britain's cotton textile industry became dominant by the mid-19th century.

It was only from 1850 that India could set up textile mills on modern lines with financial, technical and managerial help from the British.

- **Exports from India:** Till the 18th century, India was the world's main producer of cotton textiles and had a substantial export trade to Britain as well as many other European countries, But following the industrial revolution, India's export basket comprised mainly of primary products like sugar, jute, silk, etc. Opium, indigo, sugar, and raw cotton were the major commodities exported by India in 1849. By 1920, exports remained overwhelmingly basic, unfinished commodities: raw cotton, jute manufactures (mainly gunny sacks), raw jute, raw skins and hides, and tea. Between 1865 and 1920, Britain's share of Indian exports fell from 67 per cent to 22 per cent.

- **Imports into India:** While till the mid-18th century, India had been exporting many finished products to Britain and Europe, the trend was drastically reversed after the industrial revolution.

  As the British cotton industry underwent a technological revolution during the late 18th to early 19th centuries, the Indian industry stagnated. India became the exporter of raw materials to feed the factories in Britain and importer of finished goods from that country.

  Between 1840 and 1865, the principal commodities of import included cotton twist and yarn, cotton goods, machinery, raw metals (particularly copper and iron), metal manufactures, and railway materials. Between 1870 and 1895, India was the biggest customer of Britain's Lancashire cotton industry. By 1920, imports included cotton manufactures, sugar, iron and steel, machinery and millwork, and mineral oils.

  India's imports were technologically more advanced and had greater value-addition than her exports. For basic industrial inputs – machinery, metals, and chemicals – India depended upon overseas production. Further, 90 percent of all India's imports in 1919-20 originated from Britain.

- **India's recovery:** Indian entrepreneurs began to set up their own modern textile mills after 1850 and very slowly began to recapture the domestic market. In 1896, Indian mills supplied 8 per cent of the total cloth consumed in India, which increased to 20 per cent by 1913 and 62 per cent by 1936.

  Although India did not participate in global trade expansion between 1870 and 1913, Indian businessmen made substantial profits during the First World War (1914-18), which they reinvested after the war. Thus, India's manufacturing output grew at 5.6 percent per year between 1913 and 1938, well above the world average of 3.3 percent.

  The British government finally provided tariff protection from the 1920s, which helped industrialists to expand and diversify.

- **India, a prized asset for British Empire:** In the 19th century, as colonial rule began to take its modern form, India became an asset of growing value to Britain, commercially, financially and militarily. India, being a large country with high population and rich natural resources, made all the difference to Britain among all her colonies.

  In1913, India was Britain's largest market, taking 16 per cent of all British exports, particularly textiles, Britain's most important industry. Britain was also the largest supplier of industrial goods to India and controlled virtually the entire invisible trade of India.

  Despite professions of *laissez-faire*, Britain used her dominion over India to intervene actively in the economy to ensure the free flow of her goods, ostensibly to promote development of India as a producer of raw materials required by British industry and to make India a safe haven for British investments.

- **First World War and after:** During the First World War, imports from Britain declined and this helped to strengthen the hold of Indian firms on the domestic market for textiles and steel. After the war, under nationalist pressure, the colonial government started to favour Indian enterprise in its purchase of stores and it agreed to create a tariff commission in 1921 which started raising tariffs for protective reasons.

➢ **Indian Fiscal Commission:** The Indian Fiscal Commission, 1921-22 was tasked to study all aspects of the Tariff policy of the Government of India. While five Members of the Commission gave a dissenting note arguing for a policy of 'unqualified protection', the Commission finally recommended the adoption of a policy "protection with discrimination in the best interests of India".

By 1925, the average tariff level was 14 per cent compared with 5 per cent during the pre-war period. The procedure for fixing tariffs was lengthy and tariff protection was granted more readily to foreign-owned companies than to Indian firms. British imports were accorded a margin of preference.

- **Britain's decline:** The trade policy adopted by Britain in India was also influenced by Britain's own status in the then global economy. While in 1850, Britain had 40 per cent share in world trade, by 1900, its share declined to 28 per cent. Britain's share in world manufacturing, which was two-thirds of the combined share of Germany, France and US in 1870, declined to less than a quarter in 1913. In the second half of the 19th century, Europe and US were also advancing industrially and this affected the dominant position Britain had acquired following the Industrial Revolution between 1740 and 1860.
- **India's financial position:** In spite of its constant favourable balance of trade, India acquired substantial debts. By 1939 foreign assets in India amounted to $2.8 billion, in the form of government debt and foreign direct investment mainly in tea, other plantations and the jute industry. The 'drain' of funds to England continued during the interwar period (1920-40) because of home charges and profit remittances. But during the Second World War, India's financial position was transformed due to India's contributions during the war.
    - **Sterling Balances:** A significant aspect of Indian economy at the time of Independence was that India was not a debtor country. By the end of the World War II (1939–45), India had liquidated its foreign public debt of ₹ 450 crore and accumulated Sterling balances of over ₹ 1,700 crore. This foreign exchange asset was on account of purchases made by Britain in India for her requirements for the war. This asset came quite handy after independence to pay for imports and developmental purposes.
- **Conclusion:** In conclusion, it may be said that the trade and economic policy adopted by the colonial administration in India was tilted in favour of Britain and her interests. This led to suppression of Indian industries and India's overall socio-economic progress. This will be evident from the progress recorded over two centuries from 1757 and that achieved by India in seven decades since independence. **(On this, see Box 14.1 at the end of this chapter).**

5. How did railways contribute to India's economic development in the pre-independence era?

Ans. Railways were the most important infrastructure development in India from 1850 to 1947 and it impacted all facets of Indian society. In the context of the economy and India's development, railways played a major role. It helped in linking peoples and different parts of the country, integrating markets and increasing trade and commerce.

Domestic and international economic trends shaped the pace of railway construction and the demand for traffic flow to the Indian ports. Railways helped the finances of the colonial government and native states. At the same time, Indian political institutions influenced railway ownership and policy, which in turn, influenced the railway's performance.

- **Pre-railway era - Infra limitations and costs**

  Before the advent of railways, the Indian transportation network was in a poor state. Roadway system was inadequate and poorly constructed and maintained, and many of them were inaccessible and unusable during the monsoons.

  Water transportation was limited to the coastal areas, barring the Indus and Ganga river systems which connected parts of the north to the western and eastern coasts respectively. Outside of the river systems or the Grand Trunk Road connecting Calcutta to Peshawar, costs of transportation were generally high. Due to transport bottlenecks, markets for most bulky goods were limited and confined to nearby areas. Only high value luxury goods like printed cotton textiles and jewellery items could reach national or international markets.

- **Genesis of Railways**

  The first railroad built using steam locomotives was opened in 1825 in Great Britain. A line opened in 1830 was the first modern railroad. It was a public carrier of both passengers and freight. By 1870, Britain had about 21,700 km of railroad.

  The history of Indian Railways dates back to1850s. In 1853, the first passenger train operated between Bombay and Thane, a distance of 34 km.

  - **Need and Push for Railways**

    The initial push for developing railways in India came from the mercantile interests in London and Manchester. It was expected that railways would lower transport costs and allow English merchants easier access to raw cotton from India. Simultaneously, railways would open Indian markets to British manufactured products such as cotton textiles.

    Neither the promoters of railways nor the East India Company envisioned much of a demand for passenger traffic to begin with. But this proved to be a short-sighted view because passenger traffic was to eventually become a major source of revenue.

  - **Rapid growth**

    The initial development of the network was slow under the East India Company, but it picked up pace once the British crown took control in 1858.

The first railway lines were laid to hinterland parts from major ports as those were the landing points for the British in the country. Later, as lines extended further inland, they were interconnected to form trunk-routes linking major cities and towns.

In due course, railway lines spread across all over India rapidly and by 1900, undivided India had 24,000 km of railway track and more than 50 scheduled services. The British Government and princely states pitched in with their own networks.

By the early 1900s, India had the fourth largest rail network in the world. However, the scale of the network relative to India's population was not as impressive.

Freight and passenger traffic grew at roughly the same rate until the 1930s when freight traffic far outstripped passenger traffic.

At independence in 1947, the railways had a total of 54,693 km. in terms of route kilometre. And, in seventy years since 1947, the total route kilometre had touched 67,368 km by March 2017.

➢ **Objectives and Role of Railways**

The British introduced railways in India with varied objectives as mentioned below.

- **Governance:** To govern a huge country of sub-continental size like India, comprising diverse groups efficiently, the British realized the imperative need of having a vast and speedy transport network like the railways.
- **Economic and Commercial:** It served an important economic purpose of moving raw materials to the Indian ports from where they were shipped to Britain to feed the home industries. It also helped to transport the imports from Britain from the ports to various parts of India. It thus served the commercial interests of Britain in taking advantage of the vast Indian market for the manufactures of British industries. The launch of the railways followed the industrial revolution and was thus timely to capture Indian markets.
- **Military and Strategic interests:** The importance of the railway system in India for military purposes was recognized at the very outset, and great stress was laid on this in Lord Dalhousie's minute of 1853. But it was only at the outbreak of the Second Afghan War in 1878, that a comprehensive view was taken of the criticality of frontier areas and a program for railway construction for mainly military purpose was taken up. Military and strategic concerns also influenced which cities received priority for railway stations.

- **Wartime service:** Railways played a crucial role during wars and served many strategic functions during the First World War (1914-18). The most important was for troop movement and to carry war supplies. During this war, the railways were used to meet the needs of the British forces outside India. During the Second World War (1939-45), trains from Indian railways were diverted to the Middle East, and railway workshops were converted into munitions workshops. Both these wars severely crippled the railways from the organisational and financial angles.
- **Railways and Famines:** Railways played a useful role during famines in moving food supplies to critically affected areas. Following the famine of 1877, the First Famine Commission, set up in 1878, recommended state intervention in food trade during famine. The colonial government drew up an agenda of protective works including certain famine-specific railway lines such as the Southern Mahratta system in south India and the Bengal Nagpur rail in central India.

  The rail network grew rapidly in the 1880s and 1890s following the recommendations of the Famine Commission.

➢ **Finances**

The revenue position of the railway services indicates the value it had for Indian economy. In1901, railway revenues were approximately 2.6 per cent of national income. By 1919, it rose to 3.2 per cent and by 1939 to 4.9 per cent. Thus, the importance of railways in the economy grew with time.

➢ **Shortcomings and Limitations**

While introducing and expanding railways was a signal contribution of the colonial administration, there were shortcomings in its execution.

- The expansion of railways before independence was stunted and tardy when compared to its expansion after independence and gauge conversion done from meter and narrow gauges to broad gauge.
- There is also a criticism that passenger services were not given adequate attention.
- Fares prevalent were quite high considering the income levels in India.
- Improvements in quality were also ignored at times. For example, there was a long debate about whether toilets were necessary in third-class carriages.
- Greater attention to comfort and lower fares would have certainly increased travel.

- ♦ There was near total absence of adoption of modern technology, safety standards were not given due importance and investments on renewal of tracks, coaches, etc. were inadequate. Hence the task of modernization of railways cast a heavy burden after independence.

➢ **Conclusion**

India being a vast sub-continent, railways, despite its various shortcomings, have played an important role in the pre-independence era. It continues to play an important role in the development and integration of the nation. Criss-crossing the length and breadth of the country, it brought together, then as now, people from different parts and helped in fostering a sense of oneness and social harmony.

6. Social indicators of Pre-independent and Post-independent India show that India suffered much neglect during the colonial rule. Critically analyse this statement with relevant supporting data.

(See also Question 3 in Chapter 2 for more on this).

Ans. The brief study and statistical presentation below on various social indicators will amply show the extent to which the British colonial administration neglected the basic and genuine needs of Indian population during the rule spanning 200 years (1757-1947). Needless to say, it held back India's progress in the fields of literacy, education, health and social awareness and upliftment of people resulting in mass illiteracy, ill-health and widespread poverty. It was a deliberate policy to keep the native population in check and deprive them of meaningful progress.

Whatever little improvements that may have been achieved during this period of darkness was marred by the gross neglect and indifference shown by the colonial rulers. The contrast in progress before and after independence, as seen from the data below, proves that an independent India would have recorded much more progress during these "lost years".

Box 14.1 State of India on Social indicators in Pre-independent and Post-independent India

Data presented below will show comparative progress of India on various social indicators during the two centuries of colonial rule and about 70 years (1947-2020) of post-independence era.

On many crucial indicators, some of which are shown below, the performance during the colonial period was far from satisfactory. Apart from these data, it must be kept in mind that India faced several famines and epidemics prior to independence. It points to the state of neglect and indifference shown by the colonial administration in regard to the availability of food and its proper distribution to the masses, and in providing public health facilities (see Section VI below).

These and other aspects are analysed with relevant data below.

I : Literacy rates

Literacy rates were appallingly low in the case of both males and females prior to independence. Also, the rates were much worse in the case of females which would have affected their status

Table 14.1: Literacy rates

Year	Male	Female	Total	Year	Male	Female	Total
1901	9.8	0.7	5.4	1951	25.00	7.900	16.7
1911	10.6	1.0	5.9	1961	34.40	13.00	24.0
1921	12.2	1.8	7.2	1971	39.40	18.70	29.5
1931	15.6	2.9	9.5	1981	56.38	29.76	43.57
				1991	64.13	39.29	52.21
				2001	75.26	53.67	64.80
				2011	82.14	65.46	74.04

both within home and outside. This is also a reflection on the importance attached to "literacy and education" by the colonial government in the scheme of things. After independence, India took sustained effort to improve the literacy rates. And there have been significant gaps between males and females even since 1981 (Sixth Plan period) though the gap is being reduced. (**For more on literacy rates, see Section 4 of Appendix - Part II**).

II : Birth rate and Death rates

Before independence, both the birth and death rates were more or less at the same level though death rate had shown decline after 1911-20 period. Birth rate declined after 1931-40.

Table 14.2: Birth rate and Death rate (per 1,000 population)

Year	Birth Rate	Death Rate	Year	Birth Rate	Death Rate
1901-10	49.2	42.6	1951-60	41.7	22.8
1911-20	48.1	47.6	1961-70	41.2	19.0
1921-30	46.4	36.3	1971-80	37.2	15.0
1931-40	45.2	31.2	1981-86	33.2	12.2
1941-50	39.9	27.4	1990-91	30.2	9.7
			2010-15	20.4	7.4

From 1951, death rate steadily came down indicating better health and medical facilities. While the birth rate held stable till 1970, it started declining after that due to intensive family planning programmes implemented.

And total fertility rate (TFR) has also come down significantly and for the country as a whole it stood at 2.2 in 2018, as against the Replacement rate of 2.1 which is the target. It is also noteworthy that many states have attained TFR below even 2.2, with rates around 1.5 to 1.7. This again is the result of sustained family planning programmes implemented from the First Plan (1951-56) to restrict family size.

III : Life expectancy

Life expectancy was very low for both males and females prior to independence, again a reflection of the state of health condition and facilities. Since independence, it has shown steady improvement though it is still low compared to the rates in the advanced countries where it ranges between 75 and 80 years.

Table 14.3: Life Expectancy at Birth (In years)

Year	Male	Female	Total	Year	Male	Female	Total
1901-10	22.6	23.3	23.0	1951-60	41.9	40.6	41.3
1911-20	19.4	20.9	20.2	1961-70	46.4	44.7	45.6
1921-30	26.9	26.6	26.8	1971-80	50.9	50.0	50.5
1931-40	32.1	31.4	31.8	1981-86	55.6	56.4	56.1
1941-50	32.4	31.7	32.1	1992-96	60.1	61.4	60.7

IV : Percentage of Rural & Urban Population

Urbanisation is a sign of economic progress. Historically, the economic development of western Europe and north America was accomplished with continuous transfer of economic activity and people from rural to urban areas, both within and between countries. As urban industries expanded, new employment opportunities were created and, over the same period, rural manpower requirements were reduced due to labour-saving technological progress in agriculture. Although urban slums and unemployment existed in the 19th century Europe, the combination of the above two phenomena - industrialization and increased employment opportunities - enabled Western nations to undergo a major transformation through systematic rural-to-urban transfer of their human resources.

In India that did not happen during the colonial period as there wasn't industrialisation to the extent required to withdraw the surplus labour from agriculture to industries and services. It will be seen from data below that the percentage of rural population continued to be well over 80 per cent till independence. In fact, even after independence, the percentage of rural population continued to be above 80 per cent till the middle of the Fourth Plan (1969-73).

Table 14.4: Percentage of Rural & Urban Population

Year	Rural	Urban	Total	Year	Rural	Urban	Total
1901	89.2	10.8	100.0	1951	82.7	17.3	100.0
1911	89.7	10.3	100.0	1961	82.0	18.0	100.0
1921	88.8	11.2	100.0	1971	80.1	19.9	100.0
1931	88.0	12.0	100.0	1981	76.7	23.3	100.0
1941	86.1	13.9	100.0	1991	74.3	25.7	100.0
				2001	72.2	27.8	100.0
				2011	68.2	31.8	100.0

It was only after the impact of large-scale industrialisation implemented from the Second (1956-61) and Third (1961-66) Plans that the urban population started showing increase and rural population has been declining.

As for the percentage of people employed in the agriculture sector, it was 69.1 per cent in 1951 and even by 1983, it came down to only 65.42 per cent apparently due to the steady increase in population. But during the next three decades, it has shown substantial decline to 50.2 per cent in 2006-07 and 48.9 per cent in 2011-12. With this, the percentage of urban population has been going up though at a rather moderate pace. There is need to withdraw more workers from agriculture and employ them in industries and service sectors in a more productive way.

At the same time, India has to tackle the problem of migrant labour due to regional imbalances in development. It is ironic that the migration of labour is taking place from the mineral-rich states in eastern and central Indian states to the western and southern states. It points to lack of industrial growth in states from where there is out-migration of people on large scale in search of employment and better job opportunities. This issue came to the fore during the Covid-19 pandemic in 2020. **(For more on problems of migrant labour and regional imbalances in development see Question 5 and Box 13.3 on Page 13.28 in Chapter 13.**

V : Female-Male (Sex) Ratio (No. of Females per 1,000 Males)

The number of females per 1,000 males in the population, termed as "**Female-Male (Sex) ratio**" is one of the indicators of the status of women and the extent of gender equality prevailing. Advanced countries in Europe, the US, etc. have healthy sex ratio in which females outnumber males. However, the Third World and developing countries in Asia and Africa have skewed sex ratio with males outnumbering females.

Sex ratio in India as per data shown below has been in favour of males both in pre- and post-independence era. In fact, the sex ratio was comparatively better before independence.

Table 14.5: Female-Male (Sex) Ratio (No. of Females per 1,000 Males)

Year	No. of Females to 1,000 Males	Year	No. of Females to 1,000 Males	Year	No. of Females to 1,000 Males
1901	972	1951	946	1991	927
1911	963	1961	941	2001	933
1921	955	1971	930	2011	940
1931	950	1981	934		
1941	945				

There have been very few exceptions among states with females being more than males. Kerala and Pondicherry (now called Puducherry) both had more females than males as per 2001 and 2011 census. Kerala had 1,058 females in 2001 census and 1,084 females in 2011 census to 1,000 males. And Puducherry had 1,001 females in 2001 census and 1,037 females in 2011 census to 1,000 males. Other states have all had more males than females. **(See Table A on page 11.29 of Chapter 11)**.

The main cause for the decline in sex ratio in India is low level of literacy and education and an overtly biased attitude towards women in society including cases like female infanticide.

VI : Famines and Epidemics

Another stark contrast between the period before and after independence has been the periodic occurrence of severe famines in the pre-independence era which caused untold hardship to, and took a toll of, millions of lives. That such famines have not been seen since independence can be attributed to the political consciousness of the people and political parties in a democratic setup, and the presence of an alert free press all of which makes the government more accountable. There was hardly any such accountability during the colonial rule with the ruling dispensation riding rough shod over the natives. A list of horrific and grisly famines which occurred at regular intervals and devastated the lives of people in different parts of colonial India is given below.

Great Bengal Famine (1770)

Madras famine (1782-83)

Chalisa famine (1783-84) in Delhi and adjoining areas

Dojibara famine (1791-92) around Hyderabad

Agra famine (1837-38)

Upper Doab famine of 1860-61 in Agra, Delhi region

Orissa famine (1866-67)

Rajaputana (Rajasthan) Famine of 1869-70

Bihar famine (1873-74)

Southern India famine (1876-78)

India famine (1896-1900)

Bombay famine (1905-06).

And the most notorious **Great Bengal famine** occurred in 1943-44 in the midst of the Second World War (1939-45) which took the lives of an estimated 1.5 million though, going by the state appointed Famine Commission's own method of calculation, the death toll was close to three million.

Famines and starvation are not always or only caused by shortages of food. Even when enough food supply is available, many may go without it due to sheer poverty and lack of income, earnings and purchasing power. Or else, why should India still have people even now without getting food despite overflowing granaries with excess buffer stocks of foodgrains, and an extensive public food distribution system (PDS) and the "right to food" guaranteed under the National Food Security Act.

Many are deprived of their entitlement of ration just due to not having the Family (Ration) card or due to exclusion and maldistribution of rations or sheer lack of wherewithal to buy food. That apart, merely the items supplied through PDS may not be sufficient to provide adequate nutrition which is why malnourishment continues to be a chronic problem in India. Food and nutrition are complex issues and grinding poverty lies at the root of these problems.

Successive famines which occurred in pre-independent India culminating in the Great Bengal Famine of 1943-44 vouch for the above assertions. That even after independence and sustained efforts of successive governments, it has not been possible to completely eradicate hunger and malnutrition reinforces such conclusions.

It is pertinent to note that the colonial regime did not introduce a public distribution system (PDS) for food as was done after independence, except the rationing introduced during the Second World War. Had it been done during the early days of colonisation or even later, much of the misery and hardship which the poor had to endure, not only in times of famine but even in normal times, could have been averted to a great extent. This is yet another instance of the callousness and indifference shown by the British administration in India towards the people. **(For more on poverty in India and its alleviation, see Chapter 3: Inequality and Poverty).**

Epidemics: Apart from all these, several instances of epidemics such as plague, cholera, smallpox, malaria, etc. struck different parts of India during the colonial era. The lack of sanitation and proper public health facilities and consequent unhygienic conditions of living aggravated the problems for the people. Though health facilities fall short of the needs of the people even after independence, situation has vastly improved.

It is, of course, to be conceded that medical science has also advanced considerably since the colonial era which has made much difference to health conditions.

> Many politicians are in the habit of laying it down as a self-evident proposition that no people ought to be free till they are fit to use their freedom. The maxim is worthy of the fool in the old story who resolved not to go into the water till he had learned to swim.
>
> \- Thomas B. Macaulay (1800-1859), English historian and politician.

CONTENTS

Part 2: Comparative Performance of Selected Indian States and UTs on Socio-Economic Indicators – A Study

Explanatory Note

This appendix contains, as the title itself suggests, a brief study of the "Comparative Performance of Selected Indian States and Union Territories UTs" on select Socio-Economic Indicators. It is a reflection of the efficiency of the political dispensation and governance in these states and UTs over the years but is also conditioned and influenced by a range of factors such as population growth and its density, resource endowments, literacy and education levels, gender equality and gender bias and social and political awareness of the citizenry.

The data given in all the Tables are for select years to show the extent of progress and improvement achieved by the states/UTs on the various parameters.

For rendering the comparison realistic, **in all Tables**, the selected States are grouped into three categories: In Group I are major states that are relatively less developed, while in Group II are major states which are more developed on social and/or economic indicators. In Group III are some of the smaller States and Union Territories (UTs).

As is generally known, the states in Group II are, in many respects, more advanced both on social and economic indicators while those in Group I are lagging behind. Though the states and UTs in Group III are small, on many counts they have performed well and score high, and even outperform some of the states in the other two Groups; on some of the indicators like literacy, fertility and mortality rates, health and hospital facilities, per capita NSDP, etc.

Those interested in a wider comparative study could gather State/UT-wise data for more years and for various other indicators, some of which are listed below.

Rate of growth of population and Total fertility rate.

Infant Mortality Rate (IMR) - Under 5 years.

Education: Gross Enrolment ratio of Girls and Boys in Primary, Elementary and Secondary standards.

Public expenditure on Education.

Labour Force Participation Rate (LFPR)

Female Labour force Participation Rate (FLPR)

Public debt levels and Debt to GDP ratio.

Poverty levels – Population below Poverty line.

There are many sources from which data can be gathered for these studies. These include:

Reserve Bank of India's Handbook of Statistics on Indian Economy.

Reserve Bank of India's Handbook of Statistics on Indian States.

Census of India publications.

Selected Socio-Economic Statistics, Central Statistical Organisation.

Statistics put out by NITI Aayog, various Ministries of Govt. of India and State governments.

Annual Reports of Ministries of Govt. of India.

Economic Surveys of Ministry of Finance.

Indian Public Finance Statistics, Dept. of Economic Affairs, Ministry of Finance

All India Educational Surveys.

National Health Profile by Central Bureau of Health Intelligence, DGHS, Ministry of Health & Family Welfare, Govt. of India.

National Family Health Surveys.

Rural Health Statistics.

For international data:

World Bank Data.

UNDP's Human Development Reports.

UN Population Division Statistics.

Asian Development Bank statistics.

STATISTICAL TABLES

PART I: INDIA data

TABLE 1: INDIA: DEMOGRAPHIC DATA AT A GLANCE

Table 1.1: Population (In Millions)

Pre-independence		Post-independence			
Year	Population	Year	Population	Year	Population
1901	238.3	1951	361.0	1991	846.3
1911	252.0	1961	439.1	2001	1028.7
1921	251.2	1971	548.2	2011	1210.6
1931	278.9	1981	685.2	2018*	1349.8
1941	318.5				

* 2018 Population: Estimated

Table 1.2: Decadal Growth of Population (Increase in Million & percentage)

Decade	In million	Percentage	Decade	In million	Percentage
1951–61	78.14	21.64	1981–91	162.97	23.85
1961–71	108.93	24.80	1991–2001	180.71	21.35
1971–81	135.17	24.66	2001–11	181.83	17.68

Table 1.3: Density of Population

(population per sq. km.)

Year	Density	Year	Density
1951	117	1991	267
1961	142	2001	325
1971	177	2011	382
1981	216		

Table 1.4: Rural & Urban Population (In percentage)

Year	Rural	Urban	Year	Rural	Urban
1961	82.03	17.97	1991	74.29	25.71
1971	80.09	19.91	2001	72.19	27.81
1981	76.62	23.38	2011	68.84	31.16

Table 1.5: Female & Male Population (In millions)

Year	Female	Male	Year	Female	Male
1951	175.56	185.53	1991	407.07	439.2
1961	212.94	226.29	2001	495.74	531.2
1971	264.11	284.05	2011	586.47	623.7
1981	329.96	353.37			

Table 1.6: Sex Ratio (Number of females per 1,000 males)

Year	Sex Ratio	Year	Sex Ratio
1951	946	1991	927
1961	941	2001	933
1971	930	2011	943
1981	934		

Source: Tables 1.1 to 1.6: Census of India reports, Registrar General of India.

TABLE 2: VITAL STATISTICS

(The source for Vital statistics data is Census of India - Sample Registration System (SRS)

Table 2.1: Birth Rate

(Number of live births per 1,000 of the population per year)

Year	Birth Rate	Year	Birth Rate
1971	36.9	2000	25.8
1976	34.4	2010	22.1
1986	32.6	2015	20.8
1990	30.2	2018	20.0

Table 2.2: Death Rate

(Number of deaths per 1,000 of the population per year)

Year	Death Rate	Year	Death Rate
1971	14.9	2000	8.5
1976	15.0	2005	7.6
1986	11.1	2010	7.2
1990	9.7	2018	6.2

Table 2.3: Infant Mortality Rate (IMR)

(The probability of dying between birth and exactly one year of age per 1,000)

Year	IMR	Year	IMR
1971	129	2000	68
1986	96	2010	47
1990	80	2018	32

Table 2.4 Life Expectancy at Birth

(The number of years a newborn infant would live if prevailing patterns of mortality at the time of birth were to stay the same throughout the child's life.)

Year	Life Expectancy	Year	Life Expectancy
1970-75	49.7	2002	63.7
1976-80	52.3	2010-	67.9
1990-94	60.0	2018	69.4

Table 2.5: Total Fertility Rate (TFR)

(Total fertility rate is the average number of children that would be born alive to a woman during her lifetime if she were to bear children at each age in accordance with prevailing age-specific fertility rates.)

Year	Total Fertility Rate (TFR)
1980-82	4.5 (Rural & Urban combined)
1985	4.3
1990-92	3.7 (Rural & Urban combined)
1995-97	3.4
2005	2.9
2018	2.2

Source: Tables 2.1 to 2.5: SRS Bulletins, Registrar General of India.

Table 2.6: Family Planning: Couple Protection Rate (CPR) (Percentage of couples effectively protected by all methods of family planning)

Year	CPR (In percentage)	Year	CPR (In percentage)
1971	12.7	1990	43.3
1980	22.3	1993	43.5
1985	32.1	1999	48.6

Table 3: Growth Performance in the Five Year Plans

Plan Period	Target	Achieved	Plan Period	Target	Achieved
1. First Plan (1951–55)	2.1	3.5	7. Sixth Plan (1980–84)	5.2	5.5
2. Second Plan (1956–60)	4.5	4.2	8. Seventh Plan (1985–89)	5.0	5.6
3. Third Plan (1960–65)	5.6	2.8	9. Annual Plan (1990–91)	–	3.4
4. Annual Plans (1966–68)	–	3.9	10. Eighth Plan (1992–96)	5.6	6.5
5. Fourth Plan (1969–73)	5.7	3.2	11. Ninth Plan (1997–2001)	6.5	5.5
6. Fifth Plan (1974–78)	4.4	4.7	12. Tenth Plan (2002–2006)	7.9	7.7

Source: Eleventh Five Year Plan (2007-12), Vol I, Planning Commission.

Note: The growth targets for the first three Plans were set with respect to National Income. In the Fourth Plan, it was Net Domestic Product. The actual growth rates are in terms of GDP at factor cost. Average growth rates over a short period can be misleading because of fluctuations in agricultural output due to variable monsoon.

Table 4 India's Poverty Ratio Data

Population Below Poverty Line (in percentage)

S. No.	States	Lakdawala Methodology		Tendulkar Methodology	
		1993-94	2004-05	1993-94	2004-05
1	Andhra Pradesh	22.2	15.8	44.6	29.9
2.	Assam	40.9	19.7	51.8	34.4
3.	Bihar	55.0	41.4	60.5	54.4
4.	Gujarat	24.2	16.8	37.8	31.8
5.	Haryana	25.1	14.0	35.9	24.1
6.	Himachal Pradesh	28.4	10.0	34.6	22.9
7.	Jammu & Kashmir	25.2	5.4	26.3	13.2
8.	Karnataka	33.2	25.0	49.5	33.4
9.	Kerala	25.4	15.0	31.3	19.7
10.	Madhya Pradesh	42.5	38.3	44.6	48.6
11.	Maharashtra	36.9	30.7	47.9	38.1
12.	Orissa	48.6	46.4	59.1	57.2
13.	Punjab	11.8	8.4	22.4	20.9
14.	Rajasthan	27.4	22.1	38.3	34.4
15.	Tamil Nadu	35.0	22.5	44.6	28.9
16.	Uttar Pradesh	40.9	32.8	48.4	40.9
17.	West Bengal	35.7	24.7	39.4	34.3
18.	**All India**	36	27.5	45.3	37.2

Source: Databook December 2014, Planning Commission.

Table 5: India's rank in UNDP's Human Development Reports (for select years)

Year	Rank	HDI	Year	Rank	HDI
2019	131	0.645	2005	128	0.619
2014	130	0.609	2003	127	0.602
2013	135	0.586	2002	127	0.595
2010	119	0.519	2000	124	0.577
2006	134	0.427	1998	128	0.563

Source: UNDP's Human Development Reports for various years.

APPENDIX

COMPARATIVE PERFORMANCE OF SELECTED INDIAN STATES AND UTs ON SOCIO-ECONOMIC INDICATORS - A STUDY

I. Demographic data

1. Area, Population and Density

The data on the area and population of select major and smaller States, Union Territories and India is given in Table 1.

Area of States/UTs

Among the 28 States in India, the largest in area is Rajasthan with 342,239 sq. kms and the smallest in area is Goa with 3,702 sq. kms. Among the 8 Union Territories (UTs), the largest in area is Jammu & Kashmir with 125,535 sq, kms. followed by Ladakh with 96,701 sq. kms. The smallest UT in area is Lakshadweep with 32.62 sq. kms.

Table 1: Area, Population and Density of Population

Table 1 (a): Group I States

State	Area*	Population #	Density
Bihar	94,163	104.10	1102
Madhya Pr	308,252	72.60	236
Odisha	155,707	41.95	269
Rajasthan	342,239	68.62	201
Uttar Pr	240,928	199.58	828
Chh'tisgarh	135,191	25.54	189
Jharkhand	79,714	32.97	414
Uttarakhand	53,483	10.12	189
Himach Pr	55,673	6.86	123
Assam	78,438	31.17	397
J & K	222,236	12.55	124

Table 1 (b): Group II States & India

State	Area*	Population #	Density
Maharashtra	307,713	112.37	365
Gujarat	196,024	60.38	308
Tamil Nadu	130,058	72.14	555
Karnataka	191,791	61.13	319
Haryana	44,212	25.35	573
Telangana	112,077	35.00	312
West Bengal	88,752	91.35	1,029
Andhra Pr	160,205	49.67	308
Punjab	50,362	27.70	550
Kerala	38,863	33.39	859
INDIA **	3,287,240	1210.19	382

Table 1 (c): Group III States/UTs

State	Area*	Population#	Density	State	Area*	Population#	Density
Meghalaya	22,429	2.96	132	Arun Pr	83,743	1.38	17
Tripura	10,486	3.67	350	Puducherry	492	1.24	2,598
Manipur	22,327	2.72	122	Goa	3,702	1.46	394
Mizoram	21,081	1.09	52	Delhi (NCT)	1,483	16.75	11,297
Nagaland	16,579	1.98	119	Chandigarh	114	1.05	9,252

Note:

1. In both Tables: *Area in sq. kms; ** The area of India shown includes 120,849 sq. km. of area under the illegal occupation of Pakistan and China. Area of J & K shown as 222,236 sq km in Table 1 (a) includes area of Ladakh.
2. # Population in 2011 in million.
3. Density: No. of persons per sq. km., as per 2011 Census.

Abbreviations used: Pr: Pradesh. Himach Pr: Himachal Pradesh; Arun Pr: Arunachal Pradesh.

NCT: National Capital Territory.

Source: Area: Area of India from Census 2001. Area of states/UTs: Selected Socio-Economic Statistics, India, 2017, CSO, Ministry of Statistics and Programme Implementation; Population and density as per 2011 census, Registrar General of India.

Population of States/UTs

The state with the largest population, as per 2011 census, is Uttar Pradesh with 199.58 million (or 19.96 crore) as per 2011 census. And the state with the least population is Sikkim with 6,10,577 (or 6.10 lakh).

Among the UTs, the UT with largest population is Delhi with 16.79 million, followed by Ladakh with 60.4 million and Jammu & Kashmir with 12.55 million. And the UT with the least population is Lakshadweep with 64,429 as per 2011 census.

Density

Density of population, which is the number of persons per sq. km., reflects the pressure of population on land. As per 2011 population data given in Table 1 (a), Bihar has the highest density of 1,102 per sq. km. followed by West Bengal (1029), Kerala (859) and Uttar Pradesh (828).

Among those shown in Table 1(c), National Capital Territory (NCT) of Delhi, which consists of metropolitan area of Delhi along with census town and villages, has the highest density.

Physical features and Socio-economic progress

The area, climate, resource endowments and the attainments of the population have implications for socio-economic progress. A state too vast and unwieldy for administration may find that certain parts of it get neglected on various counts such as education, health, industrial development, etc.

This happened with the former undivided states of Bihar, Madhya Pradesh and Uttar Pradesh which were bifurcated and led to the formation of Jharkhand, Chhattisgarh and Uttarakhand respectively in 2000. Though Jharkhand and Chhattisgarh were endowed with rich mineral resources, they did not make much headway in development before the separation.

In 2014, the former Andhra Pradesh state was bifurcated to form the new state of Telangana.

The bifurcation of J & K state into two separate territories as J & K and Ladakh was also done on similar grounds. Ladakh is a vast mountainous area with distinct geographical features and problems which needed special attention and which only an administration centred there and vested with independent administrative and financial powers could effectively address.

2. Urbanisation in Indian States and UTs

As per Census 2011, about 31 per cent of India's population, live in urban areas. This proportion is small compared to other large developing countries such as China with 45 per cent, Indonesia (54 per cent), Mexico (78 per cent) and Brazil (87 per cent).

Before independence, India (which was undivided) had just 25 million urban population, which was 10.8 per cent of total population of 238.40 million. It rose to 44 million (13.9 per cent) by 1941 and 63 million (17.3 per cent) by 1951. By 1981, the urban population stood at 160 million (23.3 per cent) and 285 million (27.8 per cent) in 2001.

Table 2: Urban Population

Table 2 (a): Group I States

State	1971	1991	2011
Bihar	10.0	13.14	11.30
Madhya Pr	16.29	23.18	27.63
Odisha	8.41	13.38	16.68
Rajasthan	17.63	22.88	24.89
Uttar Pr	14.02	19.84	22.28
Chhattisgarh	-	-	23.24
Jharkhand	-	-	24.05
Uttarakhand	-	-	30.55
Himach Pr	6.99	8.69	10.04
Assam	8.82	11.10	14.08
J & K	18.59	23.83	27.21

Table 2 (b): Group II States and India

(in Percentage)

State	1971	1991	2011
Maharashtra	31.17	38.69	45.23
Gujarat	28.08	34.49	42.58
Tamil Nadu	30.26	34.15	48.45
Karnataka	24.31	30.92	38.57
Haryana	17.67	24.63	34.79
Telangana #	-	-	-
West Bengal	24.75	27.48	31.89
Andhra Pr #	19.31	26.89	33.49
Punjab	23.73	29.55	37.49
Kerala	16.24	26.39	47.72
INDIA	**19.9**	**25.7**	**31.16**

Table 2 (c): Group III States/UTs

(In Percentage)

State	1971	1991	2011
Meghalaya	14.55	18.60	20.08
Tripura	10.43	15.30	26.18
Manipur	13.19	27.52	30.21
Nagaland	9.95	17.21	28.97
Arunachal Pr	3.70	12.80	22.67
Puducherry	42.04	64.00	68.31
Goa	25.56	41.01	62.17
Delhi	89.70	89.93	97.50
Chandigarh	90.55	89.69	97.25

Note: Abbreviations: Pr: Pradesh; Himach Pr: Himachal Pradesh.

Data for Andhra Pradesh is for the former undivided state. Telangana was formed in 2014.

Source: Data for 1971 and 1991: Table 7 (b): Percentage of Urban Population to Total Population, Selected Socio-Economic Statistics, India, 2000, CSO, Ministry of Statistics and Programme Implementation.

Data for 2011: Census of India, 2011, Registrar General of India.

Economic growth and Urbanisation

With more rapid growth of the Indian economy, the rate of urbanisation is bound to increase. Urban centres are engines of growth and they open more avenues for entrepreneurship and employment than what dispersed rural areas could provide.

There is a concentration of the urban population in large cities and existing urban agglomerations. As per 2011 census, there were 53 million plus cities accounting for about 43 per cent of India's urban population.

Urban-Rural links

At the same time, the close inter-relationship of the urban and rural sector cannot be over-emphasized.

The prosperity of the urban sector ensures steady demand for the produce of farm sector as much as the vitality of agriculture is essential to create demand for the products of industry. Any setback to agriculture due to drought, poor rainfall, etc. causing rural distress, adversely impacts the industrial sector and the overall performance of the economy.

Besides, in the Indian context, there is need to withdraw the vast surplus and largely under-employed labour from the rural agrarian sector and redploy them in the industrial and services sectors, which would be centred in and around urban areas.

Challenges in Urbanisation

The exodus of rural Indians into the cities over the coming decades will pose tremendous challenges for government, particularly the municipalities who will be primarily responsible for providing the services that the new migrants – and established residents – will need.

Urban expansion calls for careful planning and provision of essential services like housing, water and power supply, transport facilities and sanitation arrangements to cater to the needs of increasing population. It is well known that these facilities are grossly deficient even for the existing population and expanding them for the additional population will be a mammoth task.

The urban planning would, therefore, involve diligent land-use planning and developing peripheral areas away from existing cities and towns and creating new townships with all such basic services. Schemes like Jawaharlal Nehru National Urban Renewal Mission (JNNURM) launched in December 2005, building Metro rail system in major cities and improving housing and public transport were steps in the right direction.

Role of Local Bodies

In Indian polity, the Local governments – Municipalities in towns and Panchayats in villages occupy an important place. The 73rd and 74th Amendment Acts of 1992 under the Constitution have given primacy to these local bodies in governance.

Local governments are significant as they are grassroot organizations working at the local level and are closest to the people they serve. Their governance and activities touch upon the day-to-day lives of the people and their efficient functioning and accountability is, therefore, of critical importance.

The local bodies manage functions like building and upkeep of roads, public transport, supply of water and power, maintaining drainage and sewerage, etc. all of which are critical from the viewpoint of the citizenry. And experience has been that most of these entities have been deficient in their performance. These are partly due to structural issues like non-devolution of power and finances by the State governments to the urban local bodies and due to poor governance by local authorities. The budget and utilization of finances by the local bodies are mostly opaque and there is hardly any accountability to the people they serve.

Remedial measures

The government has been trying to strengthen urban governance by setting up Services Regulators, adoption of Information Technology for ensuring transparency, introducing Citizens' Charter and giving greater role for Ward Committees for wider participation of people in local governance.

Conclusion

Urbanisation should be guided towards inclusive, equitable and sustainable growth of towns and cities with proper civic amenities. Good urbanisation would ensure that towns and cities are free from slums and provide adequate opportunities for productive employment and a decent quality of life to all their inhabitants, especially the poor and vulnerable sections.

3. Decadal Growth in Population and TFR

India's population grew at a steady pace since independence. From 238.3 million (23.83 crore) in 1951, it increased to 1210.19 million (121.2 crore) in 2011. During these years, India carried out intensive family planning programmes to contain the population growth. It is significant that these programmes have borne fruit and the pace of growth in India's population has started decelerating.

It is commendable that several Indian states, such as Kerala, Goa and Andhra Pradesh had much lower decadal growth rate in population than other states between 2001 and 2011. (See Table 3 below). Further, Himachal Pradesh, Punjab, West Bengal, Odisha, Tamil Nadu, Karnataka and Maharashtra also had relatively lower growth rates.

Table 3: Decadal Growth in Population: 1981 to 2011: States/UT (in percentage)

Table 3 (a): Group I States				Table 3 (b): Group II States & India			
State	**1981-1991**	**1991-2001**	**2001-2011**	**State**	**1981-1991**	**1991-2001**	**2001-2011**
Bihar	23.38	28.43	25.07	**Maharashtra**	25.73	22.57	15.99
Madhya Pr	27.24	24.34	20.30	**Gujarat**	21.19	22.48	19.17
Odisha	20.06	15.94	13.97	**Tamil Nadu**	15.39	11.19	15.60
Rajasthan	28.44	28.33	21.44	**Karnataka**	21.12	17.25	15.67
Uttar Pr	25.55	25.80	20.09	**Haryana**	27.41	28.06	19.90
Chhattisgarh	25.73	18.06	22.59	**Telangana**	-	-	-
Jharkhand	24.03	23.19	22.34	**West Bengal**	24.73	17.84	13.93
Uttarakhand	24.23	19.20	19.17	**Andhra Pr***	24.20	13.86	11.10
Himach Pr*	20.79	17.53	12.81	**Punjab**	20.81	19.76	13.73
Assam	24.24	18.85	16.93	**Kerala**	14.32	9.42	4.86
J & K	30.34	29.04	23.71	**INDIA**	**23.86**	**21.34**	**17.64**

Table 3 (c): Decadal Growth in Population: 1981 to 2011: States/UTs

Group III States/UTs

State/UT	1981-1991	1991-2001	2001-2011	State/UT	1981-1991	1991-2001	2001-2011
Meghalaya	32.86	29.94	27.82	**Arun Pr**	36.83	26.21	25.92
Tripura	34.30	15.74	14.75	**Puducherry**	33.64	20.56	27.72
Manipur	29.29	30.02	18.65	**Goa**	16.08	14.89	8.17
Mizoram	39.70	29.18	22.78	**Delhi (NCT)**	51.45	46.31	20.96
Nagaland	56.08	64.41	– 0.47	**Chandigarh**	42.16	40.33	17.10

Note: * Andhra Pradesh data is for the former undivided state. Telangana was carved out of it in 2014.

Abbreviations: Pr: Pradesh; Aruna Pr.: Arunachal Pradesh. Himach Pr: Himachal Pradesh.

Source: Data from Census of India, Registrar General of India.

Declining fertility rates

Census data shows a declining trend as decadal growth rate during 2001-2011 was 17.64 per cent as against 21.34 per cent during 1991-2001, 23.86 per cent in 1981-91 and 24.7 per cent in 1971-81.

There has also been declining fertility trend in the country. Total Fertility Rate (TFR) indicates the average number of children that would be born to a woman during her entire child-bearing years in accordance with the prevailing age-specific fertility rates.

According to the National Family Health Survey (NFHS), the TFR has declined from 3.4 in 1992-93 to 2.2 in 2015-16. The Sample Registration System Survey (SRS), 2017, also reported the TFR of 2.2 for the country. This figure is close to the replacement level fertility of 2.1 per woman, which implies that the country is on course to achieving population stabilization. NFHS 4 reports that 24 states and Union Territories have already achieved at par or below replacement level fertility. The TFR of 1.8 for urban areas in the country is already below replacement level of 2.1 which is the target.

(For more on TFR, see section 6 in this Appendix).

II: Social Indicators

4. Literacy rates

That literacy and education play an important role in the progress of a society goes without saying. Educational attainment is an important prerequisite for improving a person's quality of life. It enhances the person's capabilities, gives greater freedom of choice, helps improve productivity, widens access to, and acquire, more knowledge, and helps to move up further in life. And deprived of a reasonably good education, the person is denied much of these.

It is also seen that states which have higher attainments in literacy and education have performed better on social indicators like birth control, fertility rates, gender equality and empowerment of women than states which have lagged behind. The progress of Kerala, Tamil Nadu, Maharashtra, Karnataka, Goa, etc. attest to this.

The level of literacy attained among males and females by the various States and UTs in the last two decades can be seen in tables presented here.

However, progress on social indicators alone does not, by itself, translate into economic progress. That Kerala, despite its impressive credentials on social parameters, has not made much headway points to the need for having, and creating, proper enabling environment for economic progress. Apart from the fact that Kerala has limited land area and a high density of population and is not endowed with much mineral resources required for industrialisation, the state is also hobbled by issues like labour problems which deter the entry of industries.

Table 4: Literacy rates (in percentage)

Table 4 (a): Group I States

	2001			2011		
STATE	**Total**	**Female**	**Male**	**Total**	**Female**	**Male**
Bihar	47.00	33.12	59.68	63.82	53.33	73.39
Madhya Pr	63.74	50.29	76.06	70.63	60.02	80.53
Odisha	63.08	50.51	75.35	73.45	64.36	82.40
Rajasthan	60.41	43.85	75.70	67.06	52.66	80.51
Uttar Pr	56.27	42.22	68.82	69.72	59.26	79.24
Chhattisgarh	64.66	51.85	77.38	71.04	60.59	81.45
Jharkhand	53.56	38.87	67.30	67.63	56.21	78.45
Uttarakhand	71.62	59.63	83.28	79.63	70.70	88.33
Himachal Pr	76.48	67.42	85.35	83.78	76.60	90.83
Assam	63.25	54.61	71.28	73.18	67.27	78.81
J & K	55.52	43.00	66.60	68.74	58.01	78.26

Table 4 (b): Group II States

STATE	2001 Total	2001 Female	2001 Male	2011 Total	2011 Female	2011 Male
Maharashtra	76.88	67.03	85.97	82.91	75.48	89.82
Gujarat	69.14	57.80	79.66	79.31	70.73	87.23
T Nadu	73,45	64.43	82.42	80.33	73.86	86.81
Karnataka	66.64	56.87	76.10	75.60	68.13	82.85
Haryana	67.91	55.73	78.49	76.64	66.77	85.38
Telangana	-	-	-	-	-	-
W Bengal	68.64	59.61	77.02	77.08	71.16	82.67
Andhra Pr*	60.47	50.43	70.32	67.66	59.74	75.56
Punjab	69.65	63.36	75.23	76.68	71.34	81.48
Kerala	90.86	87.72	94.24	93.91	91.98	96.02

Table 4 (c): Group III States/UTs & India

	2001 Total	2001 Female	2001 Male	2011 Total	2011 Female	2011 Male
Meghalaya	62.56	59.61	65.43	75.48	73.78	77.17
Tripura	73.19	64.91	81.02	87.75	83.15	92.18
Manipur	69.93	60.10	79.54	79.85	73.17	86.49
Mizoram	88.80	86.75	90.72	91.58	89.40	93.72
Nagaland	66.59	61.46	71.16	80.11	76.69	83.29
Aruna Pr	54.34	43.53	63.83	66.95	59.57	73.69
Puducherry	81.24	73.90	88.62	86.55	81.22	92.12
Goa	82.01	75.37	88.42	87.40	81.84	92.81
INDIA	**64.83**	**53.67**	**75.26**	**74.04**	**65,46**	**82.14**

Note: * Andhra Pradesh data is for the former undivided state. Telangana was carved out of it in 2014.

Abbreviations: Pr: Pradesh; Aruna Pr.: Arunachal Pradesh.

Source: Census 2011, Registrar General of India.

At the other end of the spectrum are states in eastern and central India which, though blessed with plentiful mineral resources like coal, iron ore, manganese, bauxite, etc., have not been able to benefit from them to the fullest potential and remain relatively backward. This is also partly explained by their backwardness on social indicators.

- Kerala's high literacy rate, all through, is attributed to the vision and foresight shown by the Royals of Travancore and (the then) Cochin states in promoting Primary and Elementary education in the 19th century. Equally significant were the pioneering efforts of Christian Missionaries who were given all support by the enlightened rulers of the two states to promote education.

- Mizoram's literacy rate is the highest among the NE states/UTs and almost matches Kerala's high rate which is creditable.
- Among the hill states in the North-east, Tripura and Nagaland also have very good literacy rate above 80 per cent.
- Among the hill states, Himachal Pradesh (HP) has a high rate, male literacy at 90.83 and overall rate in 2011 at 83.78.
- And among Group – I states, HP and Uttarakhand stand out while Odisha, MP, Rajasthan, Chhattisgarh have rates above 80 per cent for male literacy in 2011.
- In all the states and UTs, though the female literacy rate has gone up, significantly in some cases between 2001 and 2011, females still lag behind males in literacy which points to the need for stepping up efforts to promote literacy among females and bring them on par with males.

5. Female – Male (Sex) Ratio

Female – Male or Sex ratio indicates the number of females for every 1,000 males in the population and is an important indicator of the status and empowerment of women in society. Presented below are data from census over three decades from 1981 to 2011.

Table 5: Female – Male (Sex) Ratio

State	1981	2001	2011	State	1981	2001	2011
Bihar	946	919	916	Maharashtra	937	922	925
Madhya Pr	941	919	930	Gujarat	942	920	918
Odisha	981	972	978	Tamil Nadu	977	987	995
Rajasthan	919	921	926	Karnataka	963	965	968
Uttar Pr	885	898	908	Haryana	870	861	877
Chhattisgarh	-	989	991	Telangana	-	-	-
Jharkhand	-	941	947	W Bengal	911	934	947
Uttarakhand	-	962	963	Andhra Pr*	975	978	992
Himach Pr*	973	968	974	Punjab	879	876	893
Assam	na	935	954	Kerala	1032	1058	1084
J & K	892	892	883	INDIA	**934**	**933**	**940**

Table 5 (c): Group III States/UTs

State/UT	1981	2001	2011	State/UT	1981	2001	2011
Meghalaya	954	972	986	**Arun Pr**	862	893	920
Tripura	946	948	961	**Puducherry**	985	1001	1038
Manipur	971	974	987	**Goa**	981	961	968
Mizoram	919	935	975	**Delhi (NCT)**	808	821	866
Nagaland	863	900	931	**Chandigarh**	769	777	818

Note: ** Andhra Pradesh data is for the former undivided state. Telangana was carved out of it in 2014.*
Abbreviations: Pr: Pradesh; Aruna Pr.: Arunachal Pradesh. Himach Pr: Himachal Pradesh.

Source: Data for 1981 from Census of India, A Handbook of Population Statistics issued for First Data Users' Conference for 1991 Census, New Delhi, April 1988. Data for 2001 and 2011 from Census of India 2011, Registrar General of India.

- Kerala has consistently had a sex ratio of well over 1,000 which is a remarkable achievement attributable mainly due to the matriarchal system in which women have a pivotal role and voice. It had a ratio of 1022 in 1961, 1016 in 1971, 1032 in 1981 and 1036 in 1991.
- Emphasis on education with high literacy levels has also played a significant role in female-male ratio in states. This clearly points to the need for all states lagging on social parameters to step up on education if they are to improve the status of girls and women.
- It is noteworthy that Puducherry also had sex ratio over 1,000 in the census of 2001 and 2011.
- States such as Bihar, Rajasthan, MP, Odisha and UP, which lag behind on many other indicators, have all outperformed the progressive states of Punjab and Haryana with sex ratio of over 900. The sex ratio of Punjab and Haryana is below 900.
- Chhattisgarh, Jharkhand, Uttarakhand and Himachal Pradesh all have good sex ratios as per 2011 data. The ratios of all these states as well as of Odisha, MP and Rajasthan exceed the ratio of Maharashtra and Gujarat. in 2011.
- Bihar and UP also have a ratio over 900.
- Tamil Nadu and Andhra Pradesh have a ratio close to 1,000.
- It is also significant that all the north-eastern states included here have high ratios over 900.

6. Total Fertility Rate (TFR)

Total Fertility Rate (TFR) indicates the average number of children that would be born to a woman during her entire child-bearing years in accordance with the prevailing age-specific fertility rates. TFR is an important factor in population trends. A TFR level of 2.1 children per woman is 'Replacement level' fertility which ensures that each generation will exactly replace itself in the absence of migration.

TFR for the country as a whole was 2.3 in 2016, whereas it was 2.5 in rural areas and 1.8 in urban areas. By 2018, it declined to 2.2 for country and 2.4 in rural and 1.7 in urban areas.

Table 6: Total Fertility Rates: 1998 & 2016

State	1998	2016	State	1998	2016
Bihar	4.3	3.3	Maharashtra	2.7	1.8
Madhya Pradesh	3.9	2.8	Gujarat	3.0	2.2
Odisha	2.9	2.0	Tamil Nadu	2.0	1.6
Rajasthan	4.1	2.7	Karnataka	2.4	1.8
Uttar Pradesh	4.6	3.1	Haryana	3.3	2.3
Chhattisgarh	-	2.5	Telangana	-	1.7
Jharkhand	-	2.6	W Bengal	2.4	1.6
Uttarakhand	-	1.9	Andhra Pradesh	2.4	1.7
Himachal Pradesh	2.1	1.7	Punjab	2.6	1.7
Assam	3.2	2.3	Kerala	1.8	1.8
J & K	2.7	1.7	INDIA	3.2	2.3

Table 6 (c): Group III States/UTs

State	1998	2013
Meghalaya	4.57	2.7
Tripura	-	1.3
Manipur	3.04	1.5
Mizoram	2.89	1.5
Nagaland	3.77	1.6
Arunachal Pradesh	2.52	na
Puducherry	-	1.7
Goa	1.77	1.4

Note: na: Not available.

Source: 1. 1998 data for States, UTs and India: Draft Tenth Five Year Plan (2002-07), Vol. III, State Plans, Trends Concerns and Strategies, p.46, Planning Commission, Govt. of India.

2. 2016 data for Group I & II States: SRS Statistical Report, Registrar General of India cited in Table 1.2.12, Total Fertility Rate (TFR) of Major States, National Health Profile 2018, Central Bureau of Health Intelligence DGHS, Ministry of Health & Family Welfare, Government of India

3. Data for Group III states/UTs is for 2013 from Sample Registration System cited by NITI Aayog on its website: https://niti.gov.in/content/total-fertility-rate-tfr-birth-woman

As discussed in detail in Chapter 11 (Question 2) and as will be seen from 2016 data for Group I and II states in Table 6 (a & b) and 2013 data for Group III states/UTs in Table 6 (c), the Total Fertility Rate (TFR) has been steadily declining in many states and is even below the Replacement rate of 2.1 in many states and UTs.

This is a positive trend towards containing population growth in the country. However, it has other implications for the age-structure of India's population in the years to come. The share of elderly population, of 60 years and above, will continue to rise steadily, nearly doubling from 8.6 per cent in 2011 to 16 per cent by 2041.

All major states are projected to witness a decline in the share of young population and an increase in the share of elderly population over the next two decades.

A consequence of this demographic transition is that the age-structure of population would undergo a major shift, from young to old ages. By the middle of the century, the share of the young, of 0-14 years, would fall to nearly half of the level of 2001 and that of the old age group, of 60 years (or 65 years) and above, would more than double. Clearly, India's population would be ageing. The share of the working age group, of 15-59 years, would keep rising reaching a peak of 65 percent before beginning to decline.

India is going through varying stages of "demographic dividend" in different states. While the phase will come to a close earlier in some of the states, it will be prolonged in many other states.

These trends will also call for nuanced socio-economic policies to cater to the changes in population structure. For example, the focus in the states where the window will close sooner will have to be on ageing and migrant-friendly policies and programmes, while the focus in the states where the window is open and will close in the next 10-15 years will have to be on empowering girls and women, provisioning of health, education and skill development for young people, and employment generation.

(For more on TFR and changing age-structure, see Chapter 11, Questions 2 and 3).

7. Infant Mortality Rates

The Infant Mortality Rate (IMR), which is widely accepted as a crude indicator of the overall health scenario of a country or a region, is defined as the deaths of infants, aged less than one year, per 1,000 live births in a given time period and for a given region.

The present all-India (total) level of IMR of 31 (36 in Rural and 23 in Urban) infant deaths per thousand live births, for the year 2018, is about one-fourth as compared to 1971 (129 infant deaths per 1,000 live births). In the last ten years, IMR has witnessed a decline of about 35% in rural areas and about 32% in urban areas.

Table 7: Infant Mortality Rates

Table 7 (a): Group I States

	1999			2018		
STATE	**Rural**	**Urban**	**Total**	**Rural**	**Urban**	**Total**
Bihar	64	55	63	32	30	30
Madhya Pr	96	55	90	52	36	48
Odisha	100	65	97	41	31	40
Rajasthan	85	59	81	41	26	37
Uttar Pr	88	66	84	46	35	43
Chhattisgarh	95	47	78	42	35	41
Jharkhand	76	48	71	31	26	30
Uttarakhand	75	27	52	31	29	31
Himachal Pr	63	38	62	20	14	19
Assam	79	36	76	44	20	41
J & K	na	na	na	23	20	22

Table 7 (b): Group II States

	1999			2018		
STATE	**Rural**	**Urban**	**Total**	**Rural**	**Urban**	**Total**
Maharashtra	58	31	48	24	14	19
Gujarat	70	45	63	33	20	28
T Nadu	58	39	52	18	12	15
Karnataka	69	24	58	25	20	23
Haryana	70	58	68	33	25	30
Telangana	-	-	-	30	21	27
W Bengal	55	40	52	22	20	22
Andhra Pr*	75	37	66	33	21	29
Punjab	57	39	53	21	19	20
Kerala	14	16	14	9	5	7

Despite the decline in IMR over the last decades, one in every 31 infants die within first year of their life at the National level (irrespective of rural/urban); one in every 28 infants in rural areas and one in every 43 infants in urban areas still die within one year of life. Among the States/ Union Territories, the IMR ranges from 4 in Nagaland to 48 in Madhya Pradesh for 2018.

Table 7 (c): Group III States & India

	1999			**2018**		
STATE	**Rural**	**Urban**	**Total**	**Rural**	**Urban**	**Total**
Meghalaya	59	33	56	35	17	33
Tripura	43	33	42	26	31	27
Manipur	22	24	25	12	9	11
Mizoram	22	14	19	7	2	5
Nagaland	na	16	na	5	3	4
Aruna Pr	45	10	43	38	28	37
Puducherry	32	15	22	9	12	11
Goa	23	17	21	8	7	7
INDIA	**75**	**44**	**70**	**36**	**23**	**32**

Note: *IMR is the probability of an infant dying between birth and exactly one year of age, expressed per 1,000 live births.*

Source: Data for 1999, Registrar General of India cited in Selected Socio-Economic Statistics, India 2000, CSO, Ministry of Statistics and Programme Implementation. Data for 2018 from Sample Registration System, SRS Bulletin May 2020, Vol. 53, No. 1, Table 1, Registrar General of India.

- Nagaland tops the list with least IMR (4 per 1,000) outdoing even Mizoram (5), Kerala and Goa (both with 7), all of which have very low rates which is a commendable achievement.
- The infant mortality rates (IMR) have come down significantly in most states/UTs in the last twenty years.
- But the rates are still relatively high in states in Group I except Himachal Pradesh, Assam and J & K. and even in some of the progressive states such as Haryana, Andhra Pradesh, Gujarat and Telangana.
- Among the Major states in Group II, Kerala stands out with very low figures of infant mortality rates (IMR).
- It is remarkable that even in 1999, some of the North-eastern states – Manipur and Mizoram – have much lower IMR than many of the progressive states.

8. Maternal Mortality Ratio

Maternal Mortality Ratio (MMR) is number of Maternal Deaths in the age group 15-49 years per 1,00,000 live births.

Maternal deaths due to complications in pregnancy and childbirth are among the leading causes of death among women in a number of States in India. As per WHO, maternal death refers to a woman, who while pregnant or within 42 days of termination of pregnancy irrespective of the duration and the site of pregnancy dies from any causes related to or aggravated by pregnancy or its management but not from accidental or incidental causes.

Table 8: Maternal Mortality Ratio in India: Major States

State	1998	2007-09	2014-16	State	1998	2007-09	2014-16
Bihar	452	261	165	Maharashtra	135	104	61
Madhya Pr	498	269	173	Gujarat	28	148	91
Odisha	367	258	180	Tamil Nadu	79	97	66
Rajasthan	670	318	199	Karnataka	195	178	108
Uttar Pr	707	359	201	Haryana	103	153	101
Chhattisgarh	-	-	**	Telangana#	-	-	81
Jharkhand	-	-	**	W Bengal	266	145	101
Uttarakhand	-	-	**	Andhra Pr^	159	134	74
Himach Pr*	na	na	na	Punjab	199	172	122
Assam	409	390	237	Kerala	198	81	46
J & K	na	na	na	**INDIA**	**407**	**212**	**130**

Note: *** Figures for Jharkhand, Uttarakhand and Chhattisgarh are included in figures of Bihar, UP and MP respectively. na means 'not available'.*

- *Andhra Pradesh data for 1998 and 2007-09 is for the former undivided state. Telangana was carved out of it in 2014.*

*Abbreviations: Pr: Pradesh. *Himach Pr: Himachal Pradesh.*

Source: Data for 1998 from National Human Development Report 2001. Data for 2007-09 from Special bulletin on maternal mortality in India, 2011-13, Registrar General of India cited, in National Health Profile 2018, Central Bureau of Health Intelligence, DGHS, Ministry of Health & Family Welfare. Data for 2014-16 from Special Bulletin on Maternal Mortality in India 2014-16, SRS, Registrar General of India.

Factors behind Maternal Mortality

The causes for maternal mortality include haemorrhage, sepsis, puerperal complications, obstructed or prolonged labour, unsafe abortion, toxaemia, anaemia, etc. In addition, the chances of dying increase if complications arise in deliveries that do not take place in health institutions or if they cannot be quickly transported to a referral unit in case the need arises. A large number of these deaths are preventable, if attention is paid to some of the conditions prevailing in India from which women often suffer.

These include poor health care, often, on account of lack of awareness of good health practices; poor nutrition; early marriage of women, particularly in Northern and Central parts of the country; high and closely spaced fertility that often stretches from adolescence to menopause; and the low status of women that marginalises them in decision making process at all levels.

The prevalence of under-nutrition – a condition resulting from inadequate intake of food or essential nutrients resulting in deterioration of health – is widespread. Protein/energy malnutrition is a common form of malnutrition. Iron deficiency anaemia which is quite common in children, is also found among women, particularly pregnant women.

Rural-Urban disparity: Lack of medical care

Field studies have shown that there exist considerable inter-regional and rural-urban disparities in MMR in India. It points to the imperative need for adequate medical attention during pregnancy and institutional delivery in a medical centre under the care of skilled medical personnel.

A field investigation of deaths among women of reproductive ages, conducted in Anantapur district of Andhra Pradesh during 1984-85, estimated maternal mortality ratio of 830 in rural areas, and 545 in urban areas, per hundred thousand live births. The maternal mortality rate was 142 and 42 per hundred thousand women aged 15-49 for rural and urban areas respectively. The maternal mortality ratio in a 'poorly developed' village was nearly 4 times higher than in a 'highly developed' village.

Over 80 per cent of maternal deaths in rural areas of Anantapur were of those women who had not made even a single visit for antenatal check-up. In contrast, none of the women who had made 5 or more visits for ante-natal check-up died. According to this Study, 41 per cent of deaths were definitely preventable, 37 per cent possibly preventable and remaining unavoidable.

Control of infection and early transfer of patients to hospitals for skilled care could have prevented most of these deaths.

Maternal Mortality Ratio in India

The maternal mortality ratio, defined as the number of maternal deaths per 100,000 live births, was 408 at the national level in 1998 as per the estimates of Registrar General of India. The ratio at State level varied from 707 in Uttar Pradesh to 28 in Gujarat as shown in Table 8 (a) & 8(b). Over the years, the ratio has come down significantly in Kerala, Maharashtra, Tamil Nadu, Andhra Pradesh and Telangana. Whereas it is still quite high in Assam, UP, Rajasthan, Odisha, MP and UP.

As per the data available for 2014-16, Maternal Mortality Ratio is highest in Assam (237) and lowest in Kerala (46). (See Table 8 (a) & 8 (b)).

9. Rural Health Infrastructure – Sub Centres, PHCs & CHCs

Health infrastructure and health personnel available are important indicators of the efficacy of health care delivery. It is also indicative of the priority accorded to investments made in the sector. Investments in health care and education signify, to a large extent, the state of welfare system prevalent in a country.

India's public health care system faces many challenges. Despite considerable expansion of health facilities since independence, the growth has been lop-sided as the expansion has been more in private health care facilities which is beyond the reach of bulk of the population due to exorbitant costs involved. There are also wide disparities in facilities available in rural and urban areas.

Apart from the shortfalls in health infrastructure provided in rural areas, there is also the issue of shortfalls in manpower – qualified doctors and nurses – in rural health centres. (For shortfalls in rural health infrastructure, see Tables 13.5 (a) and 13.5 (b) under Question 7 in Chapter 13).

➢ **Rural Health Infrastructure**

- **Sub Centre:** The Sub-Centre is the most peripheral and first contact point between the primary health care system and the community. It is manned by at least one Auxiliary Nurse Midwife (ANM)/Female Health Worker and one Male Health Worker.
- **Primary Health Centre (PHC):** PHC is the first contact point between village community and the Medical Officer. The PHCs are to provide integrated curative and preventive healthcare to the rural population. It is a referral unit for 6 Sub-centres, with 4–6 beds, with a Medical Officer supported by 14 paramedical staff.
- **Community Health Centre (CHC):** CHCs are being established and maintained by the State Government. As per minimum norms, a CHC is required to be manned by four Medical Specialists, i.e., Surgeon, Physician, Gynaecologist, and Pediatrician, supported by 21 paramedical and other staff. It has 30 indoor beds with one OT, X-ray, Labour Room, and Laboratory facilities.
- **Health and Wellness Centres:** To ensure delivery of Comprehensive Primary Health Care (CPHC) services, the government decided that under the Ayushman Bharat scheme, the existing Sub Centres would be converted to Health and Wellness Centres (HWCs). PHCs in rural would also be converted to HWCs.

➢ **Norms for Rural health facilities**

The population norms laid down for setting up SC, PHC and CHC are as shown below.

Table 9.1: Three Tier System of Rural Healthcare Infrastructure

	Centre	Population norms	
		Plain Area	**Hilly/Tribal/Difficult Area**
1.	**Sub-Centre**	**5,000**	**3,000**
2.	**Primary Health Centre**	**30,000**	**20,000**
3.	**Community Health Centre**	**1,20,000**	**80,000**

➢ **Rural Health Centres**

Public health and hospitals being a State subject, the primary responsibility for provision of public healthcare and strengthening it and address the shortage of hospitals and doctors lies with the respective State/UT Governments. However, under National Health Mission (NHM), technical and financial support is provided to States/UTs for strengthening their healthcare systems on the basis of proposals received from States/ UTs in their Programme Implementation Plans (PIPs).

NRHM: The National Rural Health Mission (2005-12) sought to provide effective healthcare to rural population throughout the country with special focus on 18 states, which had weak public health indicators and/or weak infrastructure.

These 18 States were Arunachal Pradesh, Assam, Bihar, Chhattisgarh, Himachal Pradesh, Jharkhand, Jammu & Kashmir, Manipur, Mizoram, Meghalaya, Madhya Pradesh, Nagaland, Orissa, Rajasthan, Sikkim, Tripura, Uttarakhand and Uttar Pradesh.

The Mission was an articulation of the commitment of the Government to raise public spending on health from 0.9% of GDP to 2 to 3 percent of GDP. It will be seen from Tables 11.1 (a, b, c) in Section 11 in this Appendix that the position has improved in many of the above-mentioned states and UTs.

With significant expansion, some States and UTs have rural health centres in excess of the norms prescribed, while some other states still have shortfalls as will be seen from Tables 13.5 (a) and 13.5 (b) under Question 7 in Chapter 13). Thus, there is considerable inter-state disparity in the health facilities in rural areas.

➢ **Increase in Outlays on Health systems**

Following the major pandemic which occurred in 2020-21 period, the provision for health systems has been substantially increased in the Union Budget for 2021-22 as mentioned below. The Fifteenth Finance Commission has also recommended to enhance expenditure of health.

➢ A new centrally sponsored scheme, **PM AtmaNirbhar Swasth Bharat Yojana**, will be launched with an outlay of about ₹ 64,180 crore over 6 years. This will develop capacities of primary, secondary, and tertiary care Health Systems, strengthen existing national institutions, and create new institutions, to cater to detection and cure of new and emerging diseases. This will be in addition to the **National Health Mission**. The main interventions under the scheme are:

a. Support for 17,788 rural and 11,024 urban Health and Wellness Centres;

b. Setting up integrated public health labs in all districts and 3382 block public health units in 11 states;

c. Establishing critical care hospital blocks in 602 districts and 12 central institutions;

d. Strengthening of the National Centre for Disease Control (NCDC), its 5 regional branches and 20 metropolitan health surveillance units;

e. Expansion of the Integrated Health Information Portal to all States/UTs to connect all public health labs;

f. Operationalisation of 17 new Public Health Units and strengthening of 33 existing Public Health Units at Points of Entry, that is at 32 Airports, 11 Seaports and 7 land crossings;

g. Setting up of 15 Health Emergency Operation Centers and 2 mobile hospitals; and

h. Setting up of a national institution for One Health, a Regional Research Platform for WHO South East Asia Region, 9 Bio-Safety Level III laboratories and 4 regional National Institutes for Virology.

(Source: Para 30 of Union Budget 2021-22)

Besides, the following schemes are also underway to improve overall health of the population:

- Nutrition Programme is being intensified and steps being taken to improve nutritional outcomes across 112 Aspirational Districts.
- The World Health Organisation (WHO) has repeatedly stressed the importance of clean water, sanitation, and clean environment, as pre-requisites to achieving universal health.
    - Nearly half of the country's households do not have access to piped water. Under Universal Coverage of Water Supply scheme - the **Jal Jeevan Mission** launched in 2019 - the Government is providing tap connections for providing potable water to each household. The programme includes intensive water harvesting and water conservation schemes.
    - The "Swachch Bharat, Swasth Bharat" mission will focus on waste management and waste water treatment, reduction in single-use plastic and reduction in air pollution.

10. Health Personnel and Hospitals

India has shortfall of both Doctors and Nurses going by the norms laid down by the World Health Organisation (WHO). India had 1.2 million allopathic doctors registered as of September 2019. Assuming 80 per cent availability, 9,61,000 may be available for service, giving a doctor-population ratio of 1:1,404 which is below the WHO prescribed ratio of 1:1,000 (taking India's population to be 1349.80 million in 2018).

Allopathic Doctors: Data on Allopathic Doctors registered (up to 2018) with State Medical Councils/Medical Council of India, and Government hospitals and Hospital beds for selected States/UTs is given in Tables 10.1 (a, b, c).

Table 10.1: Doctors, Govt. Hospitals & Hospital Beds

Table 10.1 (a): Group I States

State	Population # 2018- (Mn)	No. of Doctors*	Doctors per 10,000 population	Govt. Hospitals (Total No.)	No. of Hospital Beds	Beds per 10,000 population
Bihar	121.74	40649	3.3	1147	11664	1.0
MP	82.96	38180	4.6	465	31106	3.7
Odisha	46.17	22521	4.9	1806	18519	4.0
Raj'than	77.12	43388	5.2	2850	47054	6.1
Uttar Pr	223.90	77549	3.5	4635	76260	3.4
Chat'garh	27.13	8771	3.2	214	9412	3.5
Jh'khand	34.15	5764	1.7	555	10784	3.2
U'khand	11.45	8309	7.3	460	8512	7.4
Him Pr	7.23	3054	4.2	801	12399	17.1
Assam	32.65	23804	7.3	1226	17142	na
J & K	14.59	15038	10.3	143	7291	5.0

Table 10.1 (b): Group II States

State	Population # 2018- (Million)	No. of Doctors*	Doctors Per 10,000 population	Govt. Hospitals (Total No.)	No. of Hospital Beds	Beds per 10,000 population
Maharashtra	124.95	173384	13.9	711	51446	4.1
Gujarat	68.93	66944	9.7	438	20172	2.9
Tamil Nadu	80.29	133918	16.7	1217	77532	9.7
Karnataka	68.16	120261	17.6	2842	69721	10.2
Haryana	28.24	5717	2.0	668	11240	4.0
Telangana	35.00	4942	1.4	863	20983	6.0
W Bengal	98.79	72016	7.3	1566	78566	8.0
Andhra Pr	53.60	100587	11.5	258	23138	
Punjab	30.47	48351	15.9	682	17933	5.9
Kerala	34.73	59353	17.1	1280	38004	10.9

Skewed distribution

Apart from shortage, the skewed and uneven distribution of both doctors and hospitals is a major issue. There are wide disparities in their distribution between various States as well as

Table 10.1 (c): Group III States

State	Population # 2018-(Mn)	No. of Doctors*	Doctors Per 10,000 population	Govt. Hospitals (Total No.)	No. of Hospital Beds	Beds per 10,000 population
Meghalaya	3.26	na	na	157	4457	
Tripura	3.91	1718	0.44	156	4429	
Manipur	2.93	na	na	30	1427	
Nagaland	2.06	116	0.05	36	1880	
Aruna Pr	1.51	973	0.6	218	2404	
Puducherr y	1.24	na	na	14	3569	
Goa	1.56	3840	2.46	43	3012	
Delhi	16.75 (2011)	21394	12.7	109	24383	

Note: 1. na: Not available. # Population in 2018, estimated except for Delhi which is of 2011.

2. * Doctors Possessing Recognised Medical Qualifications (Under I.M.C Act) Registered with State Medical Councils/Medical Council of India (MCI) as of

December 2018. Besides, there are 52,666 Doctors mentioned under MCI for which no State-wise breakup is shown. Total number of Doctors work out to 1154686 (i.e., 11.55 lakh).

Source: 1. Number of Doctors Possessing Recognised Medical Qualifications sourced from Medical Council of India.

2. Number of Govt. Hospitals and Beds in Rural and Urban India from NHP 2019.

between urban and rural areas. It is found that 52 per cent of these doctors are practising in just five States – Maharashtra (15%), Tamil Nadu (12%), Karnataka (10%), Andhra Pradesh (8%) and Uttar Pradesh (7%).

Delhi, Assam and Odisha have 2 per cent of the total Allopathic doctors while Haryana, Chhattisgarh, Uttarakhand, Telangana and Jharkhand have 1 per cent.

Other Systems of Medicine

Apart from allopathic doctors, there are around 7.88 lakh Ayurveda, Homeopathy and Unani doctors in the country. If they are also taken into account, India's doctor-patient ratio works out to 1:848 which fulfils the prescribed WHO norm of 1:1000.

State-wise position (as per Table 10.1)

Among Group I states, J & K has the best doctor-population ratio. Among Group II states, Karnataka leads followed by Kerala, Tamil Nadu, Punjab and Maharashtra. Among Group III states/UTs, Delhi leads while others have low ratio.

Remedial measures

To augment the strength of allopathic doctors, the government has been taking various steps. These include:

- Increasing undergraduate seats in medical colleges and enhancing maximum intake capacity at MBBS level from 150 to 250.
- The existing state and central government medical colleges were upgraded by increasing the MBBS seats.
- New medical colleges attached with district/referral hospitals were set up preferably in under-served districts of the country.
- The government has also increased postgraduate seats.
- The ratio of teachers to students has been revised from 1:1 to 1:2 for all MD/MS disciplines and from 1:1 to 1:3 in certain disciplines in all medical colleges across the

country. Further, teacher-student ratio in public funded government medical colleges for Professor has been increased from 1:2 to 1:3 in all clinical subjects.

- Relaxation in the norms of setting up medical college in terms of requirement for land, faculty, staff, bed/bed strength and other infrastructure.

11. Public Expenditure on Health

Investment in health infrastructure – hospitals, primary and community health centres in rural areas, municipal dispensaries, etc. – and public spending on health are important indicators of priorities accorded by States and UTs to this vital segment of social services sector.

The increase in expenditure on social services, particularly health and education, affirms the commitment of the government towards the well-being of society.

Role of Centre and States in Health Sector

In India, while both the Centre and States spend on health, the primary responsibility for delivery of healthcare services is that of state governments. Under the Constitution, public health and sanitation, hospitals and dispensaries fall under the purview of State governments while population control and family planning, medical profession and medical education are in the Concurrent list for which both the Centre and the States have a role.

Public expenditure on health is incurred by three tiers of the Government: the Central Government, the State Governments and the local bodies. The Central Government spends directly on health and also provides grants-in-aid to State Governments for incurring health expenditure. The State Governments, in addition to spending out of the grants-in-aid received from the Centre, incur health expenditure directly out of the resources available with them. Their health expenditure also includes transfers to rural and urban local bodies for health spending.

Expenditure on Health

The expenditure on social services as a whole (education, health and others) by the Centre and States as a proportion of Gross Domestic Product (GDP) increased by 1.5 percentage points from 6.2 to 7.7 per cent, during the period 2014-15 to 2019-20 (Budget Estimates).

The increase was witnessed across all social sectors during this period. For health, it increased from 1.2 per cent to 1.6 per cent of GDP.

Table 11.1 (a, b & c) shows the expenditure on health incurred by States and UTs as percentage of total State/UT expenditure and Gross State Domestic Product (GSDP) and per capita expenditure.

Table 11.1: Public Expenditure on Health: 2015-16

Table 11.1 (a): Group I States

State	Health Expenditure as % of Total State expenditure	Per capita Health Expenditure (in ₹)	Health Expen-diture as % of GSDP
Bihar	3.94	491	1.33
Madhya Pr	4.17	716	1.04
Odisha	4.80	927	1.19
Rajasthan	5.61	1360	1.44
Uttar Pr	5.07	733	1.42
Chhattisgarh	5.28	1354	1.33
Jharkhand	4.82	866	1.25
Uttarakhand	6.07	1765	1.06
Himachal Pr	6.67	2667	1.68
Assam	7.09	1546	2.21
J & K	5.93	2359	2.46

Table 11.1 (b): Group II States

State	Health Expenditure as % of Total State expenditure	Per capita Health Expenditure (in ₹)	Health Expen-diture as % of GSDP
Maharashtra	5.08	1011	0.60
Gujarat	5.86	1189	0.72
Tamil Nadu	4.99	1235	0.74
Karnataka	5.03	1124	0.69
Haryana	3.59	1119	0.63
Telangana	4.80	1322	0.82
W Bengal	5.33	778	na
Andhra Pr	4.70	1013	0.82
Punjab	5.87	1173	0.87
Kerala	5.85	1463	0.93

Among Group I states, Assam, Himachal Pradesh, Uttarakhand and Jammu & Kashmir incur higher percentage of expenditure on health than other states in both Group I & II.

Table 11.1 (c): Group III States/UTs

State	Health Expenditure as % of Total State/UT expenditure	Per capita Health Expenditure (in ₹)	Health Expenditure as % of GSDP
Meghalaya	6.73	2223	2.40
Tripura	6.62	2183	2.41
Manipur	5.45	2061	2.79
Mizoram	8.34	5862	4.20
Nagaland	5.79	2450	2.97
Aruna Pr	5.73	5177	3.29
Puducherry	8.82	3340	2.13
Goa	6.07	3643	1.34

Note: Abbreviations used: Pr: Pradesh; Aruna Pr: Arunachal Pradesh.

Source: 1. National Health Profile, 2018: Table 4.1.5: Public expenditure on health by components across States, 2015-16; Health Sector Financing by Centre and States/

UTs in India 2015-16 to 2017-18, National Health Accounts Cell, Ministry of Health & Family Welfare.

2. State Finances: A Study of Budgets, Reserve Bank of India
3. "Report of the Technical Group on Population Projections, May 2006", National Commission on Population, Registrar General of India.

Also, states/UTs in Group III have higher percentages of expenditure on health than most of the states in Group I & II. Similar is the position in respect of per capita health expenditure as seen from Tables 11.1 (a) & 11.1 (b).

Trends in India's public expenditure on health in the last few years are given in Table 11.2.

Table 11.2: Trends in India's Public Expenditure on Health

Year	Public expenditure on Health (in ₹ crore)	Per capita Public expenditure on Health (in ₹)	Public expenditure as % of GDP
2009-10	72536	621	1.12
2013-14	112270	913	1.00
2014-15	121600.23	973	0.98
2016-17 (RE)	178875.63	1397	1.17
2017-18 (BE)	213719.58	1657	1.28

Source: Public expenditure on Health from "Health Sector Financing by Centre and States/ UTs in India 2015-16 to 2017-18", National Health Accounts Cell, Ministry of Health & Family Welfare.

While India's public expenditure and per capita public expenditure on health has increased over time, it still remains very low compared to other countries (See Table 11.3).

15th Finance Commission on Health Sector

Presently 35 per cent of the public health expenditure is borne by the Centre and 65 per cent by the state governments. In the presentation before the 15th Finance Commission, the Union Health Ministry, in the context of the pandemic Covid-19, stressed the importance of the need to strengthen the public health sector, surveillance and public health management, preventive and promotive health care with special focus on urban health.

The National Health Policy (NHP) 2017 targets include increasing public health expenditure to 2.5 per cent of the GDP, in a progressive manner, by 2025, Primary Health Expenditure to be 2/3rd of the total health expenditure and increase state sector health spending to more than 8 per cent of their budget by 2020.

The Commission agreed that there was a need to increase public sector health outlay and also to develop a professional cadre of health workers.

How India compares with other Countries

Table 11.3 shows how India compares with other select countries on health expenditure as percentage of GDP and per capita expenditure on health. Though India's health expenditure has gone up over the years, it still remains low compared to many other countries, including emerging countries like Brazil, Thailand, Sri Lanka and Malaysia. It will be seen that all the advanced countries in Group II have a high percentage of health expenditure and per capita expenditure.

Among Group I countries, Brazil and South Africa have a percentage comparable to that of advanced countries in Group II. Among BRICS (Brazil, Russia, India, China, South Africa) countries, apart from Brazil and South Africa, Russia and China have high percentage of over 5.

Table 11.3: Health Expenditure (as % of GDP) and Per capita expenditure on Health - 2017

International comparison

Group I Countries			**Group II Countries**		
Country	**Health expenditure (% of GDP)**	**Per capita Expenditure (inter-national $)**	**Country**	**Health expenditure (% of GDP)**	**Per capita Expenditure (inter-national $)**
India	**3.53**	**253.32**	USA	17.06	10246.14
Bangladesh	2.27	94.30	Canada	10.57	4928.63
Bhutan	3.19	290.42	UK	9.63	4338.37
Sri Lanka	3.81	503.56	France	11.31	5011.20
Indonesia	2.99	367.94	Germany	11.25	5922.64
Thailand	3.75	670.88	Japan	10.94	4563.46
Malaysia	3.86	1138.96	South Korea	7.60	2980.16
China	5.15	841.11	Australia	9.21	4816.15
Brazil	9.47	1472.23	New Zealand	9.17	3767.51
South Africa	8.11	1097.82			
Russia	5.34	1404.22	**World (average)**	**9.88**	**1408.75**

Source: World Bank data: Current Health Expenditure as Percentage of GDP (2017)

World Health Organization - Global Health Expenditure database.

12. Factories and Employment

This section provides data on the spread of factories and workers employed in them in select states and UTs.

Factories and Employment

Among Group I states, Uttar Pradesh has the highest number of factories with 15,830 followed by Rajasthan with 9,212 factories. All other states in Group I have much less number of factories ranging from 1,019 in J & K to 4,538 in Assam. On the number of workers employed also, the position is more or less the same.

Tamil Nadu, which, with 37,787, has the highest number of factories among all the States presented here, is followed by Gujarat, Maharashtra, Andhra Pradesh and Telangana,

Tamil Nadu also has the highest number of workers and persons employed. It is followed by Maharashtra, Gujarat, Karnataka and Uttar Pradesh.

Table 12: Number of Factories, Workers and Persons Employed

Table 12 (a): Group I States

States	Factories	Workers	Total Persons Employed
Bihar	3,461	1,04,057	1,21,772
Madhya Pr	4,533	2,81,063	3,78,022
Odisha	3,066	2,29,036	2,79,496
Rajasthan	9,212	4,32,434	5,56,103
Uttar Pr	15,830	8,39,121	10,70,841
Chhattisgarh	3,352	1,47,310	1,85,805
Jharkhand	2,866	1,53,026	1,92,282
Uttarakhand	2,998	3,39,694	4,26,587
Him Pr	2,671	1,46,633	2,05,781
Assam	4,538	1,80,489	2,17,155
J & K	1,019	58,005	73,498

Table 12 (b): Group II States

States	Factories	Workers	Total Persons Employed
Maharashtra	26,393	14,14,565	20,07,794
Gujarat	26,586	14,03,204	18,26,748
Tamil Nadu	37,787	20,95,223	25,23,483
Karnataka	13,518	8,28,689	10,65,346
Haryana	8,891	6,74,373	8,58,313
Telangana	15,263	6,69,220	7,94,520
W Bengal	9,534	5,16,740	6,63,751
Andhra Pr	16,296	4,86,846	5,97,292
Punjab	12,726	5,69,266	7,08,232
Kerala	7,649	2,41,789	3,10,326

Table 12 (c): Number of Factories, Workers and Persons Employed

Group III States/UTs

States	Factories	Workers	Total Persons Employed
Meghalaya	133	10,758	12,689
Tripura	607	23,393	26,632
Manipur	191	7,334	8,532
Nagaland	186	5,227	6,004
Arunachal Pradesh	117	2,671	3,298
Puducherry	681	39,738	51,816
Goa	715	51,377	76,214
Delhi	3,432	68,630	1,02,248

Note: Abbreviation Pr. Stands for Pradesh.

Source: Table 3: Principal Characteristics by Major States in ASI 2017-2018, Annual Survey of Industries, 2017-18, Ministry of Statistics & Programme Implementation. http://mospi.nic.in/asi-summary-results/844

Both on number of factories and workers and persons employed, most of the other States among Group I in the Table above lag behind. Most of them have far less number of factories with much fewer number of workers and persons employed in them.

Industrial Development and Migration

The lack of development in the industrial and services sectors is what causes migration of people from the less developed states. Though the government has been trying to ensure regional balance in industrial development through the Five Year Plans, yet the states in eastern and central India which are rich in mineral resources have lagged behind. And it is from these states that out-migration to the west, north and south that takes place. **(For more on this, see Questions 5 and 6 in Chapter 13.)**

Economic Survey 2016-17 (hereafter referred to as ES study), which had done a detailed study of inter-state and inter-district (within a state) migration, has highlighted the pattern of migration and factors behind such phenomenon. The ES study conforms to many known patterns of migration as well as some exceptions too.

There has been an increasing rate of growth of migrants over the years. The numbers show that internal migration has been rising over time, nearly doubling in the 2000s relative to the 1990s. One plausible hypothesis for this acceleration is that the rewards (in the form of prospective income and employment opportunities) have become greater than the costs and risks that migration entails. Higher growth and a multitude of economic opportunities could therefore have been the catalyst for such an acceleration of migration.

- **In-migration-Recipient states**

In the fivers between 2011-12 and 2015-16, the state receiving the largest number of migrants was Delhi region, which accounted for more than half of migration in 2015-16 while Maharashtra, Goa and Tamil Nadu had major net in-migration.

Relatively more developed states, viz., Goa, Delhi, Maharashtra, Gujarat, Tamil Nadu, Kerala and Karnataka have net in-migration.

States like Delhi, Maharashtra, Tamil Nadu, and Gujarat attract large swathes of migrants from the Hindi heartland of Uttar Pradesh, Bihar, and Madhya Pradesh.

And districts with high net in-migration tend to be city-districts such as Gurugram, Delhi and Mumbai.

Kolkata in West Bengal attracts migrants from nearby states of Jharkhand, Uttar Pradesh, and Odisha.

- **Out-migration:**

Relatively less developed states such as Bihar and Uttar Pradesh have high net out-migration.

Uttar Pradesh and Bihar taken together account for half of total out-migrants., while Jharkhand and Madhya Pradesh had major net out-migration.

Districts with high net out-migration are located in the major sending states such as Uttar Pradesh and Bihar.

For example, flows from Gujarat to Tamil Nadu are about 7 lakhs annually.

13. Micro, Small and Medium Enterprises (MSMEs)

The Micro, Small and Medium Enterprises (MSMEs) in India are playing a crucial role by providing large employment opportunities at comparatively lower capital cost than large industries. They also help in a substantial way industrialization of rural & backward areas, inter alia, reducing regional imbalances in development, and ensuring more equitable distribution of national income and wealth.

As per the National Sample Survey (NSS) 73rd round, conducted by National Sample Survey Office, Ministry of Statistics & Programme Implementation during 2015-16, there were 633.88 lakh unincorporated, non-agriculture MSMEs in the country engaged in different economic activities.

Of the above number of total units, 196.65 lakh were in Manufacturing, 0.03 lakh in Non-captive Electricity Generation and Transmission, 230.35 lakh in Trade and 206.85 lakh in Other Services excluding those MSMEs registered under the Factories Act, 1948, Companies Act, 1956 and certain entities in construction activities.

The MSME units provided total employment to 1112.71 lakh (11.12 crore) persons.

Number of Units and Employment

State of Uttar Pradesh had the largest number of estimated MSMEs with a share of 14.20% of MSMEs in the country. The following top 10 States accounted for a share of 74.05% of the total estimated number of MSMEs in the country.

1. Uttar Pradesh
2. West Bengal
3. Tamil Nadu
4. Maharashtra
5. Karnataka
6. Bihar
7. Andhra Pradesh
8. Gujarat
9. Rajasthan
10. Madhya Pradesh

Data on the number of MSME units and employment provided is given in Table 13.1 (a, b, c) for selected States and UTs.

Table 13.1: Number of MSME Units & Total Employment

Table 13.1 (a): Group I States

STATE	Number of MSME Units (lakh)	Total Employment (lakh)
Bihar	34.36 (5)	53.07
Madhya Pr	26.74 (4)	49.25
Odisha	19.84 (3.1)	33.26
Rajasthan	26.87 (4)	46.52
Uttar Pr	90.00 (14.2)	165.38
Chhattisgarh	8.48 (1.3)	8.48
Jharkhand	15.88 (2.5)	25.03
Uttarakhand	4.17 (0.65)	6.60
Himachal Pr	3.92 (0.61)	6.48
Assam	12.14 (1.9)	18.16
J & K	7.09 (1.1)	10.89
All India	**633.92**	**1112.71**

Table 13.1 (b): Group II States

STATE	Number of MSME Units (lakh)	Total Employment (lakh)
Maharashtra	47.78 (8)	91.23
Gujarat	33.16 (5)	61.18
Tamil Nadu	49.48 (8)	96.82
Karnataka	38.34 (6)	71.45
Haryana	9.70 (1.5)	19.12
Telangana	26.05 (4.1)	40.26
West Bengal	88.67 (14)	135.34
Andhra Pr	33.87 (5)	56.19
Punjab	14.65 (2.3)	24.80
Kerala	23.79 (3.7)	44.92

Table 13.1 (c): Group III States & India

STATE	Number of MSME Units (lakh)	Total Employment (lakh)
Meghalaya	1:12 (0.17)	1.91
Tripura	2.11 (0.3)	
Manipur	1.80 (0.28)	2.92
Mizoram	0.35 (0.05)	
Nagaland	0.91 (0.14)	1.77
Aruna Pr	0.23 (0.04)	
Puducherry	0.96 (0.15)	1.84
Goa	0.70 (0.01)	1.60
All India	**633.92**	**1112.71**

Note: Figures in bracket are percentage to total number of MSME units. Abbreviations: Pr: Pradesh; Aruna Pr.: Arunachal Pradesh.

Source: NSS 73rd round (2015-16), RBI Handbook of Statistics on Indian States, 2019-20 and Development Commissioner, Ministry of Micro, Small and Medium Enterprises (MSME), Govt. of India.

Position of Weak Major States

It is significant as seen from Table 13.1 (a) that UP, which is generally considered a laggard, tops in both the number of MSME units and employment provided followed by West Bengal. Next comes Tamil Nadu and Maharashtra.

That UP, Bihar, Madhya Pradesh and Rajasthan, from where much of migration of labour to other states take place, have sizeable number of units and provide fairly high level of employment only shows that these states which lag behind other major states could promote more industries and generate jobs and help to arrest migration of labour.

Achievements of MSME sector

The following facts for the year 2019-20 (as of December 2019) further highlight the critical role the MSME sector plays in the economy.

- The National Small Industries Corporation (NSIC) achieved total business of more than ₹ 321.09 crore and earned net profit before tax ₹ 85.79 crore during the year.
- Khadi and Village Industries Commission (KVIC) sold Khadi products worth ₹ 2833.71 crore and village industries products worth ₹ 60,343.69 crore.
- During the year, Coir Board achieved coir production of 5,67,000 MT and the value of Coir exports amounted to ₹ 2100 crore.

Scope and Need for Upgradation

The number of persons employed in different categories of enterprises in rural and urban areas is given in Table 13.2. It shows that Micro enterprises are somewhat evenly distributed in rural and urban areas whereas Small enterprises are predominantly in urban areas. This has implications for regional balance in industrial development and for migration of people from rural to urban areas.

Table 13.2: Distribution of employment by type of Enterprises in Rural and Urban Areas (Numbers in lakh)

Sector	Micro	Small	Medium	Total	Share (%)
Rural	489.30	7.88	0.60	497.78	45
Urban	586.88	24.06	1.16	612.10	55
All	1076.19	31.95	1.75	1109.89	100

Source: Annual Report 2019-20, Ministry of Micro, Small and Medium Enterprises, Govt of India.

There is need to increase the number of Small and Medium units in rural areas and also for Micro units to grow to become Small and Medium units to achieve scale, technological upgradation and greater efficiency and competitiveness. This has great relevance as India is trying to enhance domestic production in defence, electronics, aviation and space sectors and assign greater role to the private sector. The MSME units could play an important role in this process as ancillaries to major industrial units.

(For more on MSME sector, see Question 5 in Chapter 9).

14. NET STATE DOMESTIC PRODUCT (NSDP) and NSDP Per capita

GDP and NDP

Gross Domestic Product (GDP): GDP is the sum total of the value of final goods and services produced within the domestic territory of a country in a particular year. To put it differently, GDP measures the aggregate production of final goods and services taking place within the domestic economy during a year. It includes "depreciation" or the replacement investment of the depreciation of "capital stock".

Net Domestic Product (NDP): NDP is the aggregate value of goods and services produced within the domestic territory of a country in a particular year. It does not include the depreciation of capital stock.

Net State Domestic Product (NSDP): NSDP is the aggregate value of goods and services produced in a state which does not include consumption of capital stock.

Table 14.1 (a, b, c) gives the NSDP of select States and Union territories (UTs) at constant prices for certain years between 2004-05 and 2018-19. (Computing it at "constant prices" of one particular **base year** provides a more realistic measure of the growth of the economy than when computed at "current prices" which keep changing year to year).

TABLE 14.1: NET STATE DOMESTIC PRODUCT

(At Constant Prices)

Table 14.1 (a): Group I States **(₹ crore)**

Indicator	Bihar	Uttar Pradesh	Madhya Pradesh	Rajasthan	Odisha
2004-05	70,167	2,31,029	99,940	1,12,636	67,987
2011-12	2,23,052	6,02,976	2,70,498	3,77,478	1,93,471
2018-19	3,28,672	9,29,281	4,22,498	5,59,408	2,97,447

Table 14.1 (b): Group II States **(₹ crore)**

Indicator	Kerala	Tamil Nadu	Mahara-shtra	Karna-taka	Gujarat	Punjab	Haryana
2004-05	1,04,776	1,93,645	3,70,023	1,48,729	1,72,265	86,108	86,222
2011-12	3,00,266	6,16,015	9,90,644	5,01,156	4,69,124	2,26,373	2,47,689
2018-19	4,53,991	9,54,231	15,56,760	8,79,413	8,69,157	3,20,756	4,13,837

Table 14.1 (c): Group III States/UTs (₹crore)

Indicator	Meghalaya	Tripura	Manipur	Mizoram	Nagaland	Arun Pradesh	Puducherry	Goa
2004-05	5,846	8,170	4,603	2,400	5,421	3,188	5,033	10,999
2011-12	17,032	17,006	11,316	6,576	10,444	10,021	13,154	35,048
2018-19	20,158	31,558	16,509	12,279	14,969	14,090	18,315	48,911

Among Group I states, in 2018-19, Uttar Pradesh, which is the largest by population, has the highest Net SDP in all the years presented here, followed by Rajasthan and Madhya Pradesh.

Among Group II states, Maharashtra leads followed by Tamil Nadu, Karnataka and Gujarat.

And among Group III states/UTs, Goa has the highest NSDP followed by Tripura and Meghalaya.

However, the data in Table 14.2, shows a different picture as some other states have higher per capita (p.c.) NSDP. For instance, in 2018-19 among Group I states, Rajasthan has the highest p.c. NSDP followed by Odisha as per capita depends also on the population of the state.

Among Group II states, in 2018-19, Haryana has the highest p.c. NSDP followed by Gujarat and Karnataka. Kerala has higher p.c. NSDP than both Maharashtra and Tamil Nadu.

Among Group III states/UTs, in 2018-19, Goa retains its lead in p.c. NSDP also followed by Puducherry and Mizoram. It will also be seen that most of the states/UTs in Group III have higher p.c. NSDP than the states in Group I.

Table 14.2: Per Capita Net State Domestic Product

State-wise (At Constant Prices)

Table 14.2 (a): Group I States (in ₹)

Indicator	Bihar	Uttar Pradesh	Madhya Pradesh	Rajasthan	Odisha
2004-05	7,914	12,950	15,442	18,565	17,650
2011-12	21,750	32,002	38,497	57,192	48,499
2018-19	28,668	44,421	56,498	78,570	76,417

Table 14.2 (b): Table 14 (b): Group II States (in ₹)

Indicator	Kerala	Tamil Nadu	Mahara-shtra	Karna-taka	Gujarat	Punjab	Haryana
2004-05	32,351	30,062	36,077	26,882	32,021	33,103	37,972
2011-12	97,912	93,112	99,597	90,263	87,481	85,577	1,06,085
2018-19	1,48,078	1,42,941	1,47,450	1,53,276	1,53,495	1,15,882	1,69,409

Table 14 (c): Group III States/UTs (in ₹)

Indicator	Meghalaya	Tripura	Manipur	Mizoram	Nagaland	Arunachal Pradesh	Puducherry	Goa
2004-05	23,079	24,394	18,547	24,662	30,441	**26,721**	48,302	76,968
2011-12	60,013	47,155	39,762	57,654	53,010	73,068	1,19,649	2,59,444
2018-19	62,458	82,632	51,180	1,07,853	73,276	93,191	1,42,583	3,68,685

Note: Abbreviation used: Arun Pradesh: Arunachal Pradesh.

Source: Table 10: Per capita Net State Domestic Product (at Constant Prices), Handbook of Statistics on Indian Economy, 2019-20, Reserve Bank of India

15. The Production Linked Incentive (PLI) Scheme

Salient Features and its Implications

Could the scheme make India a Manufacturing hub for the world?

The Production Linked Incentive (PLI) Scheme was notified by the Govt. of India in April 2020 to provide financial incentives to boost domestic mobile and electronics manufacturing and attract large scale investments.

Later, in subsequent months, the scheme was expanded and it now covers diverse sectors such as pharma for bulk drugs and Active Pharmaceutical Ingredients (API) and medical devices, automotive and auto components, textiles, air conditioners, batteries, LED lights, solar PV modules, battery storage, food processing and specialty steel.

➢ **The scheme**

- Companies registered in India and involved in manufacturing of goods covered under the target segments are eligible under the PLI scheme.
- The government will pay a certain percentage of the value of additional production that companies make after fulfilling incremental investment and production criteria.
- The companies could earn as direct payments, on an average, 4 to 6 per cent more than what they would otherwise get.

- The scheme is not location-specific and companies can operate existing or new manufacturing unit(s) at one or more locations in the country.
- The scheme, though supported by incentives provided by the State, is compliant with WTO regulations.

➤ **Rationale for the scheme**

- The scheme would significantly boost investment, production and creation of jobs. For instance, the electronics sector could create 2 lakh direct and 6 lakh indirect jobs over five years.
- It would offset higher costs incurred by industry due to high taxes, power tariffs, logistics costs, land prices, etc. and thus help manufacturing sector achieve scale and become globally competitive.
- This is especially opportune when MNCs are planning to relocate from China to other countries due to cost considerations and many geopolitical factors and security issues.
- To promote exports and reduce dependence on imports for many critical items. Of an estimated production of ₹10.5 lakh crore, around 60 per cent would be exported.

➤ **Implications of the scheme**

Mobiles and Electronics

The scheme has given an initial fillip especially for the manufacture of mobiles and the electronics sector. Major foreign companies like Apple and Samsung and domestic companies are setting up additional production capacities with potential investment of ₹11,000 crore over five years. This could result in foreign firms producing ₹ 9 lakh crore worth of mobile phones (of unit price of ₹ 15,000 or more) and the domestic firms making additional ₹ 1.24 lakh crore worth of feature and smart phones. It would fetch the government about ₹ 36,000 crore in tax revenue against payment of about ₹ 40,000 crore worth of payments as incentives.

IT Hardware

Next to mobiles, IT hardware would see much expansion. The thrust is on desktops, laptops, tablets and servers which are currently mostly or wholly imported. The proposed incentive outlay is about ₹ 7,000 crore and with this the domestic value addition in IT hardware will go up by about 25 per cent by 2025. The incentive of ₹12,000 crore for telecom equipment would cover 4G/5G network, switches, routers and transmission systems.

Pharma sector

The scheme relating to the pharma sector would cover 41 critical, mostly imported, drug ingredients or intermediaries. It may be recalled that when the Covid-19 struck in 2020, India and much of the world struggled to get Active Pharma Ingredients (API) from China which was the major source for them and it led to serious disruption in the production of many drugs in many countries. This exposed the weakness of over-dependence for such vital inputs on one country. The scheme would also help in developing high-tech items used in emerging therapies and medical devices currently not made in India. The sector has already received in the initial phase committed investment of over ₹ 5,000 crore.

Automotive sector

The Indian automobile industry, employing 35 million people, is the fifth largest producer of cars and seventh largest producer of commercial vehicles in the world. India, now the world's fourth largest vehicles market, is expected to become the third largest market by volume by 2026. The sector, including auto components manufacturing, is expected to be valued [1] 16 to 18 trillion (about US$ 250 to 280 billion) by 2026. The electric vehicle (EV) segment itself, driven by two- and three-wheelers, is estimated to be valued ₹ 50,000 crore by 2025. Recognizing the potential of this sector, a major PLI scheme with an incentive of over ₹ 57,000 crore is proposed for it, spread over the period 2022-23 to 2026-27. Besides, ₹18,000 crore is envisaged for promoting batteries for E-mobility which would also help electronics and renewable energy sectors.

Textiles

India is the sixth largest exporter of textiles and apparels but has only 5 per cent of global market share. The PLI scheme of ₹10,600 crore is timely as the sector, which is one of the most labour-intensive, has been adversely hit by the Covid-19 pandemic. The scheme aims to develop the man-made fibre segment with fabric, design and product development and setting up mega textile parks.

Other sectors

Other important sectors covered under the scheme include food processing industry and speciality steel. The food processing industry will have an outlay of ₹10,900 crore to promote cooked items, processed fruits and vegetables and marine products. This is a vital sector, not only from the viewpoint of employment generation potential, but also to reduce spoilage of fruits and vegetables as their wastage is as high as 30 to 40 per cent. With reduced wastage, it will also help farmers and growers of fruits and vegetables to realize better prices for their produce. Promoting marine products would go a long way to help fisheries sector and improve the lot of fishermen who face many problems due to seasonal factors, diminishing potential of marine produce due to excessive exploitation and pollution of seas, etc.

Production of speciality and high-end steel has assumed importance with metro and high-speed rail systems under construction and increase in demand both domestically and for exports.

➢ **Challenges**

- While the PLI scheme has come none too soon considering the opportunities thrown up by problems faced by China which has hitherto dominated manufacturing and has been factory to the world. Many industries located in China are trying to relocate due to rising costs there, technology theft and IPR issues and objections by the US and European Union in dealing with China's State-supported enterprises with security concerns involved.

- But India faces challenges posed by competition from other emerging countries like Viet Nam, Indonesia, Malaysia, Brazil, Mexico, South Africa and even Bangladesh vying to attract investment and MNCs to those countries.
- Many of the manufacturing schemes which India is trying to promote through this scheme are high-tech and highly competitive at the global level and may not in every case bring in returns in the short-term. It will require sustained efforts in skilling the required technical workforce as they involve advanced and rapidly changing technology like robotics, artificial intelligence, machine learning, internet of things, etc.
- Hence to keep abreast of the cutting-edge technologies, India will have to invest in R & D on a substantial scale and the industry and the academia have to work in close collaboration.
- Above all, the Covid-19 pandemic which has disrupted the entire global economy has changed the global market conditions and demand. As this has occurred just when India has launched the PLI scheme, it has made its implementation even more challenging. Much will depend on how soon and how well India and other countries emerge from this unprecedented crisis and return to normalcy.

(See also Question 3 in chapter 9 on page 9.7 on 'Make in India' initiative).

GLOSSARY

Agricultural seasons: There are two main cropping seasons, in northern India, viz., 'Kharif' and 'Rabi'. The 'kharif' season coincides with the June- September south-west monsoon when rice, bajra, jowar, tur, cotton and jute are grown. The 'rabi' season is during winter, beginning in October-November and ending in March-April, when the temperatures are low when wheat and gram are grown. In southern India, where temperatures are high, tropical crops can be grown during any part of the year when there is soil moisture.

Balance of Payments: It covers all aspects of a country's transactions with the rest of the world such as exports, imports, remittances, interest payments, aid receipts and foreign loans from IMF and other international aid agencies.

Balance of payments consists of '*Current account*' and '*Capital account*'.

The '**current account**' refers to trade in goods (also called merchandise or visible trade) and services plus profits and interest earned from overseas assets, net of those paid abroad. Items in the current account which are not visible goods are called '**invisibles**'. Invisibles are mainly services like financial services such as banking and insurance, tourism, shipping and air transport services. Gifts sent abroad and received from abroad, interests, profit and dividends and private transfer of funds also form part of invisibles.

The '**capital account** 'is made up of inward and outward flow of money for investment and international loans and grants.

Birth rate: Is the number of live births per thousand populations in a given year. It is also referred to as Crude birth rate.

Capital account: See under 'Balance of Payments'.

Capital expenditure: It refers to expenditure incurred by the government which leads to creation of physical or financial assets or reduction of financial liabilities. Expenditure on acquiring land, buildings, machinery, etc. fall in this category.

Capital formation: Additions to fixed assets or capital stock, i.e., capital goods, in the economy is known as capital formation or investment in economic parlance. Fixed assets or capital goods consist of machinery, buildings, infrastructure like roads, bridges, rail, ports, airports, etc. Investment or capital formation is categorized as 'gross' or 'net' as explained below.

Gross fixed capital formation (GCFC) or gross investment consists of value of capital goods added to during a year. It includes 'depreciation', i.e., capital goods which have worn out and need to be replaced. Net investment excludes depreciation; in other words, it is the net addition to the capital stock.

Capital goods: These are goods of a durable character like tools, equipments and machinery which are used for the production of other commodities. They are not final goods to be ultimately consumed and they are not transformed in the process of production.

Capital-output ratio (COR): COR is the ratio of capital required to produce a unit of output over a period of time. Incremental capital-output ratio (ICOR) refers to the additional capital required to generate additional output.

Capital receipts: Capital receipts include loans raised by the government from the public which are called market borrowings, borrowings from the Reserve Bank of India, commercial banks and other financial institutions through sale of Treasury bills, loans from foreign governments and aid agencies, recoveries of loans granted by the Central government to States, funds raised from small savings through post offices and proceeds from disinvestment of government shares in public enterprises.

Carbon credits: These are credits earned by enterprises which shift to cleaner technologies in their operations and productive activities, thus saving on energy consumption and thereby reducing greenhouse gas (GHG) emissions. For a certain quantum of carbon dioxide (the major GHG) emissions avoided, the entity can get a carbon emission certificate which they can sell either immediately or through a futures market, just like any other commodity. The credits can be exchanged between businesses or bought and sold in the international markets at the prevailing market price. Credits can be used to finance carbon reduction schemes between trading partners. The scheme is aimed at mitigating global warming and issues arising out of climate change.

Carbon sink: A forest, ocean or other natural environment which has the ability to absorb carbon dioxide (CO_2) from the atmosphere. Vegetation and the ocean are the most important carbon sinks. It is any reservoir, natural or otherwise, that absorbs more carbon than it releases and thus lowers the concentration of CO_2 from the atmosphere. In climate negotiations, this temporary reduction of CO_2 in the atmosphere is known as "negative emissions".

Carbon tax: It is a tax imposed on firms and units that cause emissions or pollution and is based on the polluter-pay principle. The tax will be based on the extent of damage or suffering caused by the pollution and the revenue earned from it can be used to compensate those who were adversely affected by it.

Cash Reserve Ratio (CRR): CRR is the proportion of the deposits which the commercial banks are required to keep with the Central Bank, in India, the Reserve Bank of India.

Closed economy: Closed economy is one that does not interact with other countries. It does not indulge in imports or exports of goods or services or any economic or trade transactions with the rest of the world.

Consumer goods: These are goods which are consumed when purchased by the ultimate consumers. Food, clothing and services like recreation are consumer goods.

Current account: See under 'Balance of Payments'.

Death rate: Is the number of deaths per thousand population in a given year. It is also referred to as Crude death rate.

Deficit financing: This is resorted to by the government to cover the excess of government's expenditure over the revenue from taxes, earnings from state enterprises, borrowing from public and other sources. Fiscal deficits are covered by borrowing from the central bank (the RBI in India) which is as good as printing money, or by borrowing from other domestic and foreign sources. These measures, if carried on beyond a limit, increases the financial burden of the government. It leads to a debt trap and would also lead to inflationary pressures in the economy.

Deflation: Deflation refers to a sustained reduction in the general price level. Deflation is often, though not necessarily, accompanied by decline in output and employment.

Deflation is to be distinguished from '**disinflation**' which refers to a reduction in the rate of inflation. In other words, prices are still rising but the rate of increase has come down.

Demography: It is the study of the characteristics of human populations, such as size, rate of growth, density, gender ratio, distribution between urban and rural areas and vital statistics. (See under Vital statistics).

Depreciation: Depreciation refers to the reduction in the value of an asset through wear and tear. In other words, it is the result of consumption of fixed assets. Depreciation is taken into account and allowance made for it while calculating the profit of an enterprise.

Devaluation: It means decreasing or lowering the exchange value of domestic currency against other (foreign) currencies under pegged exchange rate through official action. A pegged or fixed exchange rate implies a regime where the exchange rate is set or maintained by government decisions or actions.

Devaluation helps to promote the exports of a country as foreigners importing the items will have to pay less in their currency due to devaluation of the currency of the exporting country. Conversely, the imports into the country which has devalued its currency will become more expensive as now the importers will have to pay more of their currency per a unit of the foreign currency.

Disguised unemployment: (see under Unemployment).

Ecosystem: Eco system, in the strict sense, refers to an ecological community together with its physical environment, considered as a unit. The term when applied to any sector or activity encompasses all aspects, internal and external, which influence it, and the complex set of relationships and inter-action between them, and the likely future trajectories and behaviour of the activity.

Exchange control: It implies controls that a government may impose to ban or restrict the amount of foreign currency or local currency that is allowed to be traded or purchased. Common exchange controls include banning the use of foreign currency and restricting the amount of domestic currency that can be exchanged within the country. Article XIV of the Articles of Agreement of the IMF provides for a country to impose exchange controls. It is economies in transition or the weaker economies that resort to exchange controls. With globalization, free trade and the trend towards economic liberalization, the tendency or need to impose such controls has come down.

Externalities: Externalities mean the benefits or harm accruing to a person or any entity resulting from the actions of another person or entity in the course of an economic activity. No payment is made for the benefit received nor is any compensation given for the harm caused to the other party. For example, an industry causing pollution to the water source used by the population in the neighbourhood is causing harm which is an externality. Other examples are smoke emanating from thermal plants, the untreated effluents discharged by industries into nearby rivers or lakes, pollution caused by vehicles on roads, all of which cause harm to others. (See **'Carbon tax'**).

Fiscal deficit: Fiscal deficit is the difference between the government's total expenditure and its total receipts excluding borrowing. Total receipt include revenue receipts and capital receipts which are not borrowings and are not debt – e.g., it includes recovery of loans and proceeds from sale of public sector undertakings. Fiscal deficit is financed through borrowing.

Fiscal policy: The planned actions of a government to mobilise financial resources such as taxes for meeting its expenditure and regulating the economic activities of a country.

Foreign exchange: Refers to foreign currency and all currencies other than the domestic currency of a country.

Foreign exchange (also briefly known as Forex) reserves: It means the foreign assets mainly foreign currencies, foreign treasury bills and foreign government securities, held by the Central Bank of a country. In a broad sense, it also includes gold reserves and Special Drawing Rights (SDRs) held by the Central Bank with the International Monetary Fund (IMF). See under Special Drawing Rights (SDRs)

Free trade (Agreements-FTAs): Free trade is the condition which ensures free flow of goods and services through foreign trade without being restricted or encouraged by direct government intervention. It involves removal of import and export barriers. Economists view international free trade policy as helping to optimise world output and income levels in the long run. FTAs may be bilateral between two nations, or multilateral involving many nations, like the Regional Comprehensive Economic Partnership (RCEP) negotiated between Asia-Pacific nations.

Gig economy: In a gig economy, workers take freelance work or short-term contracts for the gigs (informal jobs) they do. There is no formal contract signed with the employee. The main companies driving this economy are food delivery companies, fast service food joints, logistics and e-commerce firms and transportation network companies. These employees get few benefits that regular employees get such as graded wages with increments, bonus, health and insurance benefits. There is no security of job though they may earn reasonably good salaries when they work.

Gini coefficient: This concept was developed by an Italian statistician, Corrado Gini (1884-1965). It shows the inequality in a Frequency Distribution, say distribution of personal income. Its value ranges from 0 to 1, Gini coefficient of zero indicating complete equality while the maximum value 1 represents complete inequality. As in the Lorenz curve in a graph, a 45 degree line represents complete equality while the curvature below it will show the degree of inequality. (See under Lorenz curve).

Globalization: Globalization implies integration of a nation's economy with the global economy and it results in much freer movement of goods, services, capital, technology and people between countries, across national boundaries. It involves geographic dispersion of industrial and service activities across national borders.

Glocalisation: While countries, especially the developing nations, are integrating with the world economy, they are also devolving more power to local governments and communities. This combination of globalisation and localisation is called 'glocalisation'. In this process, the centralised nation state is giving space to both supra-national and sub-national institutions.

Gross Domestic Product (GDP): GDP is the sum total of the value of final goods and services created within the geographical boundary of a country in a particular year. To put it differently, GDP measures the aggregate production of final goods and services taking place within the domestic economy during a year.

GDP includes incomes earned by foreigners within the domestic economy and excludes incomes earned by the citizens in a foreign country.

GDP growth rate is one of the important indicators of the economic performance of a country.

Nominal and Real GDP: GDP can be assessed in two ways. The value of GDP at the current prevailing prices is known as **Nominal GDP**. Whereas GDP evaluated at some constant prices or constant set of prices is called **Real GDP**. If the real GDP goes up or down, it indicates that the volume of production has changed since in this case the prices remain fixed or constant.

Gross National Product (GNP): GNP = GDP + Factor income earned ***abroad*** by the domestic factors of production – Factor income earned by the factors of production ***of the rest of the world*** in the domestic economy.

In other words, GNP = GDP + Net factor income from abroad (NFIA).

Net factor Income from Abroad (NFIA): Factor income earned by domestic factors of production employed abroad – Factor income earned by factors of production of other countries employed in the domestic economy.

GNP includes depreciation on fixed assets whereas Net National Product (NNP) excludes it. In other words, NNP = GNP –Depreciation.

Gross value added: See under 'Value added'.

Human Development: It is a process of improving people's choices and standard of living with better access to education and health, better housing, means of livelihood and higher per capita income. It implies higher longevity of life, higher literacy and education, food security and nutrition. In short, it should lead to a person's well-being and better quality of life.

While earlier, when the GDP or the per capita income of a country increased, it was considered to be a sign of development. But later, economists argued that mere increase in incomes alone does not signify human development but that there should be improvement in the various attributes, referred to above, reflecting in better '*quality of life*' for the people. One of the reasons for adopting this approach is that even if incomes rise, it may not be distributed fairly, resulting in wide disparities in the living conditions of people. Hence the need for a better measure.

UNDP's HDR: United Nations Development Programme (UNDP), has been studying human development (HD) across countries since 1990, using various socio-economic parameters such as longevity of life, education as per school enrolment ratio, mean years of schooling, adult literacy, and per capita GDP and per capita Gross National Income (GNI) to assess the progress made by each country. Based on these, UNDP assigns a HD Index and ranks the countries according to it. It also collects and publishes in the Human Development Report (HDR) updated statistical data on a wide range of issues like literacy and education, health conditions, availability of, and people's access to, water and sanitation, gender inequality and bias, empowerment of women, income inequality, political freedom, etc. Each year, the HDR issued by the UNDP focusses on a specific socio-economic theme which is of international concern and will impact future generations and relate to sustainable development.

Infant mortality rate (IMR): The probability of dying between birth and exactly one year of age, expressed per 1,000 live births.

Under-five mortality rate: The probability of dying between birth and exactly five years of age, expressed per 1,000 live births.

Inflation: Inflation is a sustained increase in the general price level of goods and services in an economy over a period of time. As the price level rises, each unit of currency will buy fewer goods and services. In other words, inflation results in a reduction in the purchasing power of money.

Informal economy: The underground, parallel economy which carries on economic activity in an unauthorised manner, avoiding payment of taxes and operates outside government regulations. It operates on, and generates, black money or illicit wealth. This causes much harm to, and distorts, the normal functioning of an economy.

Invisibles: See under 'balance of payments'.

Intellectual property right (IPR): Intellectual property (IP) is a monopoly conferred by the government under law on an inventor for an innovation of a product or process. Inventors could hold the right for an assigned period exclusively or could license its use to others for a consideration or royalty payment.

Investment: See under 'Capital formation'.

Kharif season: See under 'Agricultural seasons'.

Labour force: All persons who are working and those not working but seeking and/or are available for work are deemed to constitute the labour force. As a corollary, all those who are not working or are neither seeking nor available for work are considered to be outside the labour force.

Work force: A distinction is made between labour force and work force. Work force refers to the number of persons actually working and does not account for those who are willing or are offering themselves to work.

Liberalization: Liberalization implies relaxation or removal of government restrictions and controls, especially in economic and social spheres. Under this policy, trade barriers are lifted, free enterprise is allowed with greater role assigned to private entities and private sector and there is labour market flexibility.

Life expectancy at birth: It denotes the number of years a new-born infant would live if prevailing patterns of age-specific mortality rates continue to be the same throughout the child's life.

Liquidity: In economic parlance, liquidity denotes the degree to which an asset can be quickly and cheaply turned into money.

Liquidity preference: It refers to the desire to hold money rather than other forms of wealth, e.g. stocks and bonds. This preference can arise from transaction motive, speculative motive or precautionary motive.

Literacy rate: Percentage of literates to the population of a country, usually in the age group 7 years and above. Literacy rate can be assessed for different age-groups also like 'adult literacy rate' of those of 15 years of age and above.

Lorenz curve: This is a concept developed by Marx O. Lorenz (1880- 1962), an American economist. Lorenz curve is a graphical representation which shows the degree of inequality in a Frequency Distribution in which the cumulative percentages of a population are plotted against the cumulative percentages of a variable, say, the percentage of population having certain levels of income, or paying income tax.

A straight line at an angle of 45 degrees from the start of the graph indicates perfect equality – say, top 10% of population account for 10% of total income, top 30% of population account for 30% of income and so on. Where a small number of people earn bulk of the income and large number of people account for much less of the income, the distribution will be unequal and highly skewed. When this is plotted on a graph, a curve will be formed below the 45 degree line and the degree of the curvature will be greater the greater the inequality.

A related concept is Gini coefficient. (See Gini co-efficient)

Maternal mortality ratio (MMR): The annual number of female deaths from pregnancy-related causes per 100,000 live births.

Mixed economy: An economy in which both the capitalist and the socialist system operates. It is also one where the public sector and the private sector operate. They compete for the same limited resources in development but the government, as the sovereign authority, regulates the functioning of the economy.

Monetary policy: It is a government's policy, managed by the Central Bank of a country, on regulating the quantity of money in the economy, the rate of interest and the exchange rate of the currency. It has a predominant role in the control of aggregate demand, price levels and inflation.

Monopoly: A market in which there is only one supplier. In a monopoly market, the firm is motivated by profits, stands alone and prevent new firms from entering the industry. The monopolist, by its own actions, is able to affect the market price of its output. It will make profits in excess of those necessary to just stay in business, and no pressure exists for the price to fall. According to theory, under monopoly, prices are higher and output lower than they would be under "perfect competition". Given these characteristics, most nations choose to control monopolies. (See 'Oligopoly').

Creative destruction: But a distinction is made between a monopoly that has achieved dominance, and one that has not. According to Joseph Schumpeter, the American economist, it is possible that, in the long run, consumers benefit from monopoly if the profits generated act as a spur to innovation. He stressed the evolutionary nature of the capitalist system and argued that under monopoly capitalism, firms would place less emphasis on price competition but would engage in technological and organisational innovation, thus causing "gales of creative destruction" through the economic system.

Monopolistic and imperfect competition: A state of competition in industry in which there are many firms each producing products which are similar but not perfect substitutes. The products are slightly differentiated, say by packaging, labelling, etc., and consumers are attracted and exhibit "brand loyalty" to the extent that they remain loyal to the brand even with increase in the price. Under monopolistic competition, other firms are able to enter the market if the profits are attractive.

This concept which lies between monopoly and perfect competition was developed by economists Edward Chamberlin in the US and Mrs. Joan Robinson in Cambridge in the UK. (See "Perfect competition").

Monopsony: A market in which there is only one buyer for the item sold. In this condition, being the sole buyer and because of his unique position, he is able to wield a lot of power and control the market. A monopsonist buyer, which is a large firm, could use its size to its advantage and bargain to obtain low prices because rival sellers would vie for its business. The single buyer has greater leverage to negotiate prices and terms with their suppliers and is in a controlling position to drive price levels down. For example, a winery which is the sole producer of a particular and popular brand of wine could negotiate with grape growers from a position of strength and obtain the best terms of price and sale.

Most favoured nation (MFN) policy: Under this policy in international trade, one country grants to another country favourable trading terms and specific trade benefits, such as reduced tariffs on imported goods, in foreign exchange allocations, facility for setting up enterprises of the other country's nationals in its territory, etc. MFN status is critically important for smaller and developing countries as it gives them access to the larger market. It lowers the cost of their exports in view of reduced trade barriers which makes their products more competitive.

National Income: National income (also known as Net National Product at Factor cost or NNP at FC) is Gross National Product (GNP) minus the value of depreciation on fixed assets.

GNP includes depreciation on fixed assets whereas NNP excludes it. NNP at FC (National Income) = GNP – Depreciation. (See also under Gross Domestic Product).

Net value added: See under 'Value added'.

Oligopoly: Oligopoly is a market structure in which there are a few firms none of which can prevent the others from having significant influence. These small number of firms collude, either explicitly or tacitly and act like a cartel to restrict output and/or fix prices, in order to achieve above normal market returns. Firms in oligopolistic markets recognize their inter-dependence and that they are affected by the actions and behaviour of their rivals. One among them may be a leader setting the price that others follow. All firms benefit from the stability and predictability of the industry. There is no precise upper limit to the number of firms in an oligopoly, but the number must be low enough that the actions of one firm significantly influence the others.

The firms resort to product differentiation through advertising and other marketing strategies like gifts and free offers to win over customers. The economic and legal concern is that an oligopolistic industry can block new entrants, slow innovation, and increase prices, all of which harm consumers.

Open economy: An open economy is one that trades with other nations in goods and services and also in financial assets. It involves imports and exports with other countries. Total foreign trade (imports + exports) as a proportion of the GDP is a measure of the degree of openness of an economy.

Open Market Operations: Open market operations is a mechanism of credit control employed by the Central Bank (RBI in India) under which it sells or purchases securities. The sale of securities results in contraction of credit which helps to contain inflation, while the purchase of securities leads to expansion of credit which helps to stimulate the economy.

Perfect competition: Perfect competition signifies a perfectly competitive industry in which there are many buyers and sellers. All firms sell an identical, homogenous product or commodity, and none of them can influence the market price of their product which is determined by supply and demand. The large population of both buyers and sellers ensures that forces of supply and demand remain constant in the market. As such, buyers can easily substitute products made by one firm for another. Buyers have complete or "perfect" information about the product being sold and the prices charged by each firm. Firms can enter or exit the market freely and there is perfect mobility of labour. Firms earn just enough profit to stay in business and no more. If they were to earn excess profits, other companies would enter the market and drive profits down.

A market where perfect competition exists is a theoretical construct and it does not exist in real world scenario.

Primary sector: Agriculture and allied activities such as fisheries, forestry, horticulture constitute the primary sector.

Private sector: It refers to all establishments, industries, etc. which are owned and operated by individuals or group of individuals.

Public debt: Public debt, also known as National debt, is the total outstanding borrowings of the government. The public debt of India includes the internal and external debt of the Government of India. A more comprehensive definition of Indian public debt would include the debt of all the three levels of government – Centre, States and Local – and all public enterprises, to the domestic private sector and the external sector.

Public good: These are goods and services which are consumed collectively and which do not exclude any one from enjoying its benefits. They are non-rivalrous in nature and non-excludable, and consumption by one does not deprive others from using or consuming them.

Public sector: It refers to all establishments and enterprises which are owned and operated by the government. They include those run by the Central, State or Local governments independently or jointly.

Purchasing power parity (PPP): PPP denotes the number of units of a country's currency required to buy in the domestic market the same basket of goods or services as one US dollar would fetch in the US. For example, if for the same basket of items, it costs $1 in the US and ₹ 20 in India, then the exchange rate between the Indian Rupee and the US dollar as per the PPP concept will be $1 = ₹20. The PPP concept helps to determine the purchasing power of each currency and also compare the cost of living vis-à-vis the income levels in different countries.

Quantitative easing: It is a monetary policy stance under which the Central bank of a country buys government securities or bonds from commercial banks or other financial institutions to increase money supply (liquidity) in the economy. This method is adopted when an economy is going through a low growth phase when investor confidence is low and there is little incentive to spend and to prevent the economy going into a deeper depression. This has been resorted to on a large scale by the Central bank of UK, USA (the Federal Reserve System), Japan, etc. following the financial and banking crisis of 2007-08 to stimulate the economy.

But when the economy shows signs of recovery or inflationary trends show up and concerns arise out of too much money feeding into the system, the Central Bank may start winding down the purchase of assets and selling the assets it purchased. This gradual withdrawal or reversal of 'quantitative easing' is called '**Tapering**' in economic parlance.

Rabi season: See under 'Agricultural seasons'.

Repo (Repurchase) rate: It is the rate at which the Reserve Bank of India lends shot-term money to commercial banks against securities. When the repo rate increases, borrowing from RBI becomes more expensive for banks. Similarly, when the RBI reduces the repo rate, it becomes cheaper for banks to borrow money. (See Reverse Repo rate).

Revenue deficit: Revenue deficit is the excess of government's revenue expenditure over revenue receipts. Revenue deficit results in government using up the savings or resources meant for capital or welfare expenditure to finance part of its consumption expenditure. It not only adds up to debt and interest liabilities, but will also adversely affect the development and welfare programmes of government.

Revenue expenditure: It is the expenditure incurred by the government for purposes other than the creation of physical or financial assets. It includes expenditure incurred for normal functioning of the government, interest to be paid on debt incurred by the government and grants given to State governments for purposes other than creation of assets.

Reverse Repo rate: It is the rate which the Reserve Bank of India (RBI) pays banks when they park their short-term excess liquidity with the RBI. Reverse repo rate signifies the rate at which the Central Bank absorbs surplus liquidity from the banks. (See also Repo rate).

Scalability: Scalability is the capability of a system, network, or process to handle a growing amount of work, or its potential to be enlarged in order to accommodate that growth. For example, it can refer to the capability of a system to increase its total output under an increased load when resources (typically hardware) are added. In the context of a company or business model, it implies the potential for growth of the business.

Secondary sector: Mining and quarrying, industry and manufacturing, electricity, water, etc. and construction constitute the secondary sector in an economy.

Sectors in an economy: See under terms Primary, Secondary and Tertiary.

Share-cropping: Also known as 'tithe' cultivation. A system under which a tenant cultivator keeps a portion of the farm produce while the landowner gets the rest. This system is quite common in many of the developing countries.

Social overhead capital: Also known as infrastructure, social overhead capital consists of public utilities such as roads, railways, airports, telecommunications, water supply and sewage systems. Development of infrastructure is *sine qua non* for the progress of any economy.

Special Drawing Rights (SDR's): SDR's is an international reserve asset, created by the International Monetary Fund (IMF) to supplement the existing official reserves of member countries. SDR is neither a currency but a potential claim on the freely usable currencies of IMF members. Member countries of IMF holding SDRs can obtain these currencies in exchange for their SDRs in two ways: either through the arrangement of voluntary exchanges between members or by the IMF designating members with strong external positions to purchase SDRs from members with weak external positions. Besides its role as a supplementary reserve asset, the SDR also serves as the unit of account of the IMF and some other international organizations.

Until recently there were four freely usable reserve currencies that constituted the SDR. They were the US dollar, the euro, UK's pound sterling and the Japanese yen. From October 1, 2016, China's 'yuan' gained a new status as a member of the IMF's SDR basket. That makes it a part of one of the global economy's exclusive clubs.

Stagflation: A condition in an economy of slow economic growth and relatively high unemployment and inflation. It is a state of economic stagnation accompanied by rising inflation rates.

Statutory Liquidity Ratio (SLR): SLR is the fraction of the total demand and time deposits, with the commercial banks, which they are required by the Reserve Bank of India to invest in specified liquid assets – gold, cash or other approved securities.

Sterling balances: Sterling balances was the foreign exchange asset India had accumulated by the end of the World War II (1939-45). This was on account of purchases made by Britain in India for her requirements for the war. This asset came quite handy after independence to pay for imports and for developmental purposes.

Swiss challenge method: It is a new process of giving contracts. Any person with credentials can submit a proposal to the government for a notified project. That proposal will be thrown open and other persons can give suggestions to improve and better that proposal. The best proposal will be selected, and the original proposer will get a chance to accept it if it is an improvement on his proposal. In case the original proposer is not able to match the more attractive and competing counter proposal, the project will be awarded to the counter-proposal. This is a transparent method of approving and granting contract.

Tapering: See under 'Quantitative easing'.

Terms of Trade: Terms of trade is the value of a country's exports relative to that of its imports or the ratio of the index of export prices to the index of import prices. There will be improvement in terms of trade if export prices rise more quickly than import prices or fall more slowly than import prices. The concept could also apply to the relationship between the prices of the products of one sector and the prices of products of another sector, say, between the products of agriculture and those of industry in an economy.

Tertiary sector: Trade, hotels and restaurants, transport and communication, storage and ware housing, and other services like banking and insurance, IT sector, etc. constitute the Tertiary sector. It is also referred to as the Services sector.

Total Fertility Rate (TFR): Total Fertility Rate indicates the average number of children that would be born to a woman during her entire child-bearing years in accordance with the prevailing age-specific fertility rates. TFR is an important factor in population trends. A TFR level of 2.1 children per woman is 'Replacement level' fertility which ensures that each generation will exactly replace itself in the absence of migration.

UNDP's HDR: See under Human development.

Unemployment: Unemployment refers to those who are not working but are willing and seeking to work but cannot find employment. It also includes those who are not seeking work but when asked whether they are available for work reply in the affirmative.

Voluntary and Involuntary unemployment: Economists make a distinction between these two types of unemployment. Voluntary unemployment occurs when a person in the labour force choose not to take up a job for reasons such as not willing to work at the going wage rate or for any other reason of his own volition.

Whereas involuntary unemployment occurs when a person is willing to work at the prevailing wage rate, yet he cannot find a job and remain unemployed. In an economy with involuntary unemployment, there is a surplus of labour at the current wage rates.

Disguised unemployment: Disguised unemployment exists where part of the labour force is either left without work or is working in a redundant manner where worker productivity is virtually zero. An economy or a sector demonstrates disguised unemployment when productivity is low, and where too many workers are there when the need is for a much lesser number of persons. In such a situation, the total output will not be affected even if the surplus labour is withdrawn.

Disguised unemployment exists in the agricultural sector in India which has surplus labour due to the pressure of population on the limited land available and dearth of non-farm jobs in rural areas.

Value added: Value added is the net contribution made by firms in an economy. It is the value of the production of the firm minus the value of intermediate goods (like raw materials or other inputs) used by the firm in production. In this method of calculating the aggregate value of goods and services, there will be no double counting of items used in production.

Gross value added (GVA) will include depreciation or consumption of fixed capital, i.e., wear and tear of machinery, etc.

Net value added (NVA) will not include depreciation.

Vital statistics: Refers to data that record significant events and changes in human life, such as the rate of births, deaths, fertility and longevity of life (life expectancy at birth).

Wage goods: Wage goods include food items, clothing and other basic items of daily personal consumption.

Work force: See under Labour force.